THE NEW OXFORD HISTORY OF MUSIC

VOLUME III

PART ONE

THE VOLUMES OF THE
NEW OXFORD HISTORY OF MUSIC

MUSIC AS
CONCEPT AND PRACTICE
IN THE LATE
MIDDLE AGES

EDITED BY
REINHARD STROHM
AND
BONNIE J. BLACKBURN

OXFORD
UNIVERSITY PRESS

This book has been printed digitally and produced in a standard specification
in order to ensure its continuing availability

OXFORD
UNIVERSITY PRESS

Great Clarendon Street, Oxford OX2 6DP

Oxford University Press is a department of the University of Oxford.
It furthers the University's objective of excellence in research, scholarship,
and education by publishing worldwide in

Oxford New York

Auckland Cape Town Dar es Salaam Hong Kong Karachi
Kuala Lumpur Madrid Melbourne Mexico City Nairobi
New Delhi Shanghai Taipei Toronto
With offices in
Argentina Austria Brazil Chile Czech Republic France Greece
Guatemala Hungary Italy Japan South Korea Poland Portugal
Singapore Switzerland Thailand Turkey Ukraine Vietnam

Oxford is a registered trade mark of Oxford University Press
in the UK and in certain other countries

Published in the United States
by Oxford University Press Inc., New York

© Oxford University Press 2001

ISBN 978-0-19-816205-6

Cover illustration: Fiddler and female dancer, early 14th century.
University Library, Graz, Cod.32, fo.106ᵛ. Used by permission.
For the proportional arrangement of the figures, see Rudolf Flotzinger,
Musik in der Steiermark, Landesausstellung 1980 (Graz, 1980), no 1.31.

CONTENTS

LIST OF ILLUSTRATIONS

MAPS

LIST OF MUSICAL EXAMPLES

ABBREVIATIONS

AH; *AH Register*	Guido Maria Dreves and Clemens Blume (eds.), *Analecta hymnica medii aevi*, 52 vols. (Leipzig, 1886–1922); *Register*, ed. Max Lütolf, 2 vols. (Berne, 1978)
CAO	René-Jean Hesbert (ed.), *Corpus antiphonalium officii*, i: *Manuscripti 'Cursus romanus'*; ii: *Manuscripti 'Cursus monasticus'*; iii: *Invitatoria et Antiphonae*; iv: *Responsoria, Versus, Hymni et Varia*, v: *Fontes earumque prima ordinatio* (Rerum ecclesiasticarum documenta ser. major, Fontes 7, 8, 9, 10, 11; Rome 1963–75)
Census-Catalogue	*Census-Catalogue of Manuscript Sources of Polyphonic Music, 1400–1550*, Compiled by the University of Illinois Musicological Archives for Renaissance Manuscript Studies, 5 vols. (Neuhausen-Stuttgart: American Institute of Musicology–Hänssler Verlag, 1979–88)
CS	Edmond de Coussemaker (ed.), *Scriptorum de musica medii aevi nova series*, 4 vols. (Paris, 1864–76; repr. Hildesheim, 1963)
CSM	Corpus scriptorum de musica
DMA	*Dictionary of the Middle Ages*, ed. Joseph R. Strayer, 13 vols. (New York, 1982–9)
EM	*Early Music*
EMH	*Early Music History*
Fenlon, *Music*	Iain Fenlon (ed.), *Music in Medieval and Early Modern Europe* (Cambridge, 1981)
GS	Martin Gerbert (ed.), *Scriptores ecclesiastici de musica sacra potissimum*, 3 vols. (St. Blasien, 1784; repr. Hildesheim, 1963)
JAMS	*Journal of the American Musicological Society*
La Fage	La Fage, Adrien de (ed.), *Essais de diphthérographie musicale* (Paris, 1864; repr. Amsterdam, 1964)
Lowinsky, *Culture*	Edward E. Lowinsky, *Music in the Culture of the Renaissance and Other Essays*, ed. Bonnie J. Blackburn, 2 vols. (Chicago and London, 1989)
LU	*Liber usualis* (various editions)

MGG	*Die Musik in Geschichte und Gegenwart*, ed. Friedrich Blume, 16 vols. (Kassel, 1949–79)
MGG²	*Die Musik in Geschichte und Gegenwart*, 2nd edn., ed. Ludwig Finscher (Kassel, 1994–)
MQ	*Musical Quarterly*
MSD	Musicological Studies and Documents
New Grove	*The New Grove Dictionary of Music and Musicians*, ed. Stanley Sadie, 20 vols. (London, 1980)
NOHM ii	Dom Anselm Hughes (ed.), *Early Medieval Music up to 1300* (The New Oxford History of Music, ii; Oxford, 1954)
NOHM ii²	Richard Crocker and David Hiley (eds.), *The Early Middle Ages to 1300* (The New Oxford History of Music, ii, new edn.; Oxford, 1990)
NOHM iii	Dom Anselm Hughes and Gerald Abraham (eds.), *Ars Nova and the Renaissance (1300–1540)* (The New Oxford History of Music, iii; Oxford, 1960)
NOHM iv	Gerald Abraham (ed.), *The Age of Humanism (1540–1630)* (The New Oxford History of Music, iv; Oxford and New York, 1968)
Palisca, *Humanism*	Claude V. Palisca, *Humanism in Italian Renaissance Musical Thought* (New Haven and London, 1985)
RISM B/iii.1–6	*The Theory of Music* (Répertoire International des Sources Musicales, B/iii), 1: *From the Carolingian Era up to 1400*, ed. Joseph Smits van Waesberghe with the collaboration of Pieter Fischer and Christian Maas (Munich, 1961); 2: *From the Carolingian Era up to 1400*, ed. Pieter Fischer (Munich, 1968); 3: *Manuscripts from the Carolingian Era up to c. 1500 in the Federal Republic of Germany*, ed. Michel Huglo and Christian Meyer (Munich, 1986); 4: *Manuscripts from the Carolingian Era up to c. 1500 in Great Britain and in the United States of America*, ed. Christian Meyer, Michel Huglo, and Nancy C. Phillips (Munich, 1992); 5: *Manuscripts from the Carolingian Era up to c. 1500 in the Czech Republic, Poland, Portugal and Spain*, ed. Christian Meyer, Elżbieta Witkowska-Saremba, and Karl-Werner Gümpel (Munich, 1997)
RISM B/iv.3–4	Kurt von Fischer, *Handschriften mit mehrstimmiger Musik des 14., 15. und 16. Jahrhunderts*, 2 vols.

	(Répertoire International des Sources Musicales, B/iv.3–4; Munich, 1972)
RISM B/iv.5	Nanie Bridgman, *Manuscrits de musique poly-phonique, XVe et XVIe siècles: Italie* (Répertoire International des Sources Musicales, B/iv.5; Munich, 1991)
RISM B/ix.2	Israel Adler, *Hebrew Writings Concerning Music* (Répertoire International des Sources Musicales, B/ix.2; Munich, 1975)
RISM B/x	Amnon Shiloah, *The Theory of Music in Arabic Writings* (Répertoire International des Sources Musicales, B/x; Munich, 1979)
Sachs, *Contrapunctus*	Klaus-Jürgen Sachs, *Der Contrapunctus im 14. und 15. Jahrhundert* (Beihefte zum Archiv für Musikwissenschaft, 13; Wiesbaden, 1974)
Strohm, *Rise*	Reinhard Strohm, *The Rise of European Music, 1380–1500* (Cambridge, 1993)
Strunk	Oliver Strunk, *Source Readings in Music History* (New York, 1950)
Strunk²	Oliver Strunk, *Source Readings in Music History*, rev. edn., ed. Leo Treitler (New York, 1998)
Tinctoris, *Opera*	Johannes Tinctoris, *Opera theoretica*, ed. Albert Seay, 3 vols. (CSM 22; Rome, 1975–8)
Tinctoris, *De inventione*	Karl Weinmann, *Johannes Tinctoris, 1445–1511, und sein unbekannter Traktat 'De inventione et usu musicae'*, ed. W. Fischer (Tutzing, 1961)
TVNM	*Tijdschrift van de (Koninklijke) Nederlandse Vereniging voor Muziekgeschiedenis*
Zaminer	Frieder Zaminer (ed.), *Geschichte der Musiktheorie*, 8 vols. to date (Darmstadt, 1984–), iii: Michael Bernhard *et al.*, *Rezeption des antiken Fachs im Mittelalter* (1990); v: Hans Heinrich Eggebrecht *et al.*, *Die mittelalterliche Lehre von der Mehrstimmigkeit* (1984)

LIST OF CONTRIBUTORS

BONNIE J. BLACKBURN is a member of the Faculty of Music, Oxford University, and General Editor of the Monuments of Renaissance Music. Her research has focused on fifteenth- and sixteenth-century music, music theory, and publishing.

HOWARD MAYER BROWN, at the time of his death in 1993, was Ferdinand Schevill Distinguished Service Professor in the Department of Music, University of Chicago. His extensive knowledge of instruments and instrumental music, both as scholar and performer, was but one aspect of his wide-ranging interests, which bore fruit in monographs, editions, and his still indispensable *Instrumental Music Printed before 1600: A Bibliography* (1965).

JAN HERLINGER is Derryl and Helen Haymon Professor of Music at Louisiana State University. He has edited and translated treatises by Marchetto da Padova and Prosdocimo de' Beldomandi, and has written on various aspects of medieval music theory.

ANDREW HUGHES is President of the Medieval Academy of America and Distinguished University Professor in the Centre for Medieval Studies and Faculty of Music at the University of Toronto. His current research focuses on late medieval liturgy and the transmission of plainchant, concentrating on the offices for Thomas Becket.

KEITH POLK is Professor Emeritus at the University of New Hampshire. He has published extensively on instrumental music of the Middle Ages and Renaissance. At the same time he has enjoyed a career as a performer of both the modern valved horn and the natural horn.

WALTER SALMEN is Emeritus Professor of Musicology at Innsbruck University. He has published widely on the social status of musicians, the iconography of music, and particularly on the history of dance.

AMNON SHILOAH is Emeritus Professor of the Department of Musicology, Hebrew University. His numerous publications, especially on Arab music theory, have laid the foundations for the history of music in the Middle East and medieval Spain.

REINHARD STROHM is Heather Professor of Music at Oxford University. His research has focused on late-medieval music (*Music in Late Medieval Bruges*, 1985; *The Rise of European Music, 1380–1500*, 1993), on eighteenth-century music, and on the history of opera.

TOM R. WARD is Professor of Music at the University of Illinois at Urbana-Champaign. His research has been concerned with fifteenth-century sacred music, musicians, and institutions in central Europe.

MAP 1. The Umayyad Caliphate

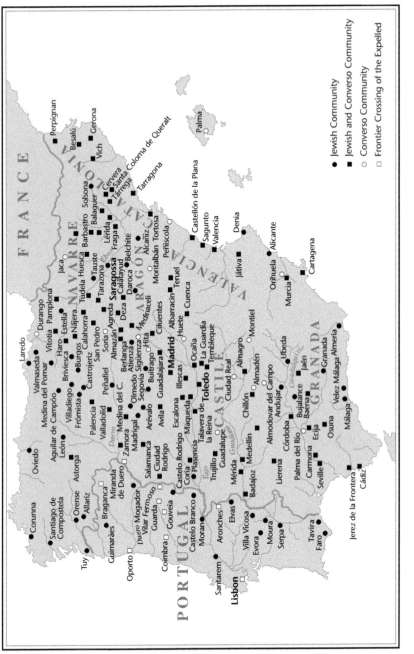

MAP 2. The expulsion of the Jews from Spain and Portugal

Jewish Community
Jewish and Converso Community
Converso Community
Frontier Crossing of the Expelled

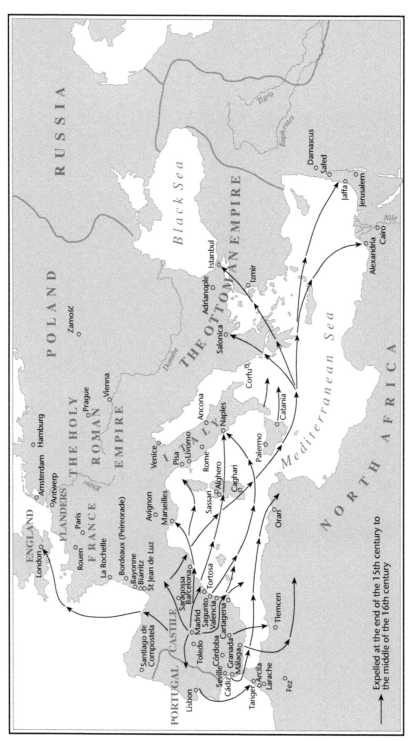

MAP 3. Emigration waves of the Jews expelled from Spain

Expelled at the end of the 15th century to
the middle of the 16th century

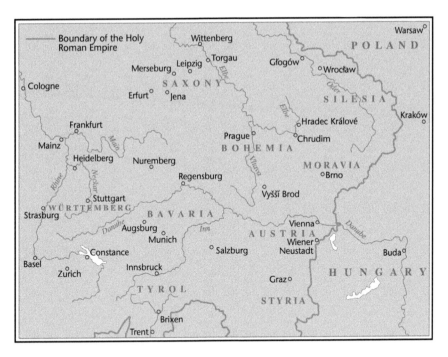

MAP 4. South Central Europe

INTRODUCTION

THIS volume of the new edition of the *New Oxford History of Music* appears at a time when we can no longer rely on a consistent body of knowledge about medieval music. Consistency is an achievement of the earlier efforts in this multi-volume project, from H. E. Wooldridge's two volumes in the *Oxford History of Music* (1901–5)[1] on music before 1600—seen as the development of polyphony—to Dom Anselm Hughes's Volumes II and III in *The New Oxford History of Music* (1954 and 1960, respectively; the latter co-edited by Gerald Abraham).[2] Those were magisterial statements, based on shared beliefs of the Western musicological community at large. The editors and contributing musical scholars identified the Middle Ages with Latin Christendom, as was usual in medieval studies more generally. Dom Anselm Hughes's introduction to Volume II speaks of 'that medieval Christendom which, with all its shades and distinctions, was an undivided, all-embracing whole, ordered and (at least in theory) systematic'.[3]

The subject matter of NOHM ii and iii comprised the two art-forms of Christian liturgical chant and of written polyphonic music; the discussion extended to vernacular song of the twelfth and thirteenth centuries. In the chapters on music other than chant, the musical repertories described belonged to only three nations: France, England, and Italy—notwithstanding a few excursions into 'peripheral' repertories. Other subjects such as music theory, the study of instruments, or the social history of music received only secondary or marginal recognition. Chant was understood as a system of repertories; its discussion was guided by the well-known notational and regional classifications, and by genetic approaches. In the treatment of the non-chant material, the ruling criteria were those of 'style' and 'language': the former a verifiable ingredient of written artefacts, subject to historical change in such a way as to allow the tracing of an evolution; the latter an inborn characteristic of artistic practices tying them to certain geographic and ethnic locations. The two criteria inescapably

---

[1] Harry E. Wooldridge, *The Polyphonic Period*, 2 vols. (The Oxford History of Music, i and ii; Oxford University Press, 1901–5); 2nd edn. 1929–32.

[2] Dom Anselm Hughes (ed.), *Early Medieval Music up to 1300* (The New Oxford History of Music, ii; London: Oxford University Press, 1954) (NOHM ii); and Dom Anselm Hughes and Gerald Abraham (eds.), *Ars Nova and the Renaissance (1300–1540)* (The New Oxford History of Music, iii; Oxford: Oxford University Press, 1960) (NOHM iii).

[3] NOHM ii, p. xvi.

coalesced to form the notion of national styles, particularly in the later periods. Overall, the music of the Middle Ages was viewed as a series of origins (or originations): a successive build-up of ever-new genres, styles, repertories, techniques, and aesthetic functions which eventually became the multi-layered organism Western music is for us today.

Insofar as these observations imply criticism of the music historians who wrote these volumes, let it be said at once that obvious alternatives to their decisions were neither available to them nor are they to us. It is not by a superior verdict of history but by our own taste that we may judge their omissions as crucial, their perspective as distorted. We do not really know better than they did what medieval music is (where it begins and ends, what it embraces) or how to describe it (as a beginning, an end, or a middle). The very same questions have remained unanswered in the study of the 'Middle Ages' in general. Furthermore, musicology is a young discipline: in the twentieth century it has still been exploring unfamiliar sounds and signs for much of the time. It is also a hybrid discipline, depending on interactions with contemporary artistic production such as few scholars of medieval literature, history, or art will ever have to consider. Our musicological forebears conceived medieval music as music, not as paper science, and for that reason their interest was attracted by those of its parameters which had survived into the musical and cultural practice of their own time—the institutional and the national, the stylistic and the linguistic. Continuing the same exploratory and empathetic attitude, our generation tries to revalue the (cross-)cultural, the technological, the performative, and the spiritual aspects of medieval music. I am often surprised to learn how much even of this matter has already been researched and understood by earlier musicologists.

The exploratory attitude of medieval musical scholarship, the desire to learn unfamiliar sounds and signs, is one of the reasons why it has become progressively more difficult to conceive of the subject as a single history. The relative success or failure of one-volume histories of medieval music (or of even longer time-spans) may reflect this development. And, for reasons which had only partly to do with the quantity of data, a chasm appeared between the older and the younger medieval volumes of *The New Oxford History of Music*. The contents of *The Early Middle Ages to 1300* (NOHM ii) form a more coherent narrative chain than those of the volume entitled *Ars Nova and the Renaissance (1300–1540)* (NOHM iii), which no longer purports to tell a single story. The relatively unrelated chapters assembled there, some of them magnificent scholarly explorations, demonstrate that this period harbours much more than the straightforward stylistic evolution which seems to be promised in the title. A chapter entitled 'The Transition on the Continent' begs the question whether it describes the transition from the Ars Nova to the Renaissance, and instead implies that there are perhaps no more continents of knowledge, no more safe transitions between them.

In our second edition of the series, both the contrast between the volumes and their individual disunity has increased. This is a matter of chronological divisions as well as of large-scale emphasis. Volume II, still entitled *The Early Middle Ages to 1300* (NOHM ii[2]),[4] has been available since 1990; nobody should be surprised that its procedures proved inapplicable to the present Volume III. Like its predecessor, NOHM ii[2] is still orientated towards the traditional dichotomy of 'Chant and non-Chant'. The contents form two large slabs of up-to-date repertorial analysis which, particularly for the monophonic repertories, successfully deepens and widens former results, for example with more elaboration of the structures of Roman chant as a ritual practice. Little of the subject matter is thematically unprecedented (except for a broad-minded chapter on musical instruments)—but awareness of the wider cultural world of early Christianity tempts the senior editor (Richard Crocker) into considering a split of the material in two:

Once past the Gregorian repertory, . . . this book will deal exclusively with medieval music of Western Europe. This, beginning with the discussion of 'New Frankish forms', would be a logical place to start a book, once the preceding material had been placed in a volume of its own, as 'Music under the Roman Empire'. Yet even that solution would not be completely adequate . . .'.[5]

Thus Crocker senses a foreclosing of the panorama of musical historiography at the point where Latin chant begins to be written and confined to the 'West'. We then settle on the three countries mentioned above. Perhaps as a result, the narrative of the remaining chapters betrays confidence in the framework of this tradition, suggesting that a representative picture of a consistent body of phenomena may yet be attainable. A sense of evolution of musical styles is also conveyed, if at the expense of a recognition of late or 'peripheral'

---

[4] Richard Crocker and David Hiley (eds.), *The Early Middle Ages to 1300* (The New Oxford History of Music, ii, new edn.; Oxford: Oxford University Press, 1990).
[5] Ibid., p. xix.

forms and repertories. The volume, to be sure, maintains a sort of exploratory dynamic. The editors and authors themselves appear to have widened their own previous ranges of expertise to fulfil this challenging task.

The present volume (NOHM iii², pt. 1), which was planned since 1988, aimed at greater novelty. Like dwarves standing on the shoulders of giants, the editors saw that the hitherto coherent land route through the history of Western music now seemed to give way to an archipelago of cultures. This, they presumed, was the reason that *Ars Nova and the Renaissance* had already lost its intended way from 'A' to 'R', exploring flowery islands instead. For the new volume, the editors decided to embrace the inevitable. A total of seventeen entirely new chapters on contrasted fields of music were commissioned from specialists, without regard to a common theme. Coverage was sacrificed to a speculative sort of balance: some of the topics requested were far-flung and novel, others central and traditional; some long, others wide. The volume was to form a system with holes, an admission of defeat vis-à-vis the late medieval cultural world—but a signal of its breadth and variety.

Several of the commissioned chapters were expected to present and update the traditional study of institutional and national repertories, genres, and composers, concentrating on the stylistic evaluation of written music. These were to be matched by more exploratory chapters and more remote types of repertory and methodology. But even among the 'mainstream' chapters the borderlines between genres, regions, and sub-periods were newly drawn. The outer borderlines of the 'late Middle Ages' were left undecided and the evolutionary perspective of 'Ars Nova and Renaissance' was spurned.[6]

The apparently superior wisdom of scholarly practice then defeated this editorial concept. Only eight of the seventeen chapters were ultimately submitted—none of them belonging to the 'mainstream' lot. In this form, the volume has now been published: a torso of a book planned for the 1990s, but perhaps a satisfactory whole for the 2000s? It will be for the reader to judge. Of course, the editorial concept has prevailed in one respect: we would not be able to publish a book at all if only 'mainstream' chapters had been planned.

---

[6] The two volumes covering the period 1300–1630 in *The New Oxford History of Music* have in common that the historiographical concepts forming their titles remain unexplained within the volumes themselves. The latter volume is Gerald Abraham (ed.), *The Age of Humanism (1540–1630)* (The New Oxford History of Music, iv; Oxford and New York: Oxford University Press, 1968) (NOHM iv).

Ironically, the relationships between theory—or 'concept'—and practice have retained their relevance for the book. This brings us to the description of its contents.

The theory of music is given some prominence in this volume, as it is considered an integral part of musical history. 'Theory' may include the contemplation and the reflection of music in the minds of its practitioners; it may be complementary, not opposed to, practice. Jan Herlinger and Bonnie Blackburn explain internal structures of the Western theoretical tradition, the former systematically, the latter in historical order. The concepts they describe served musicians in the daily practice of performing, teaching, and composing music. This conceptual tradition had certain organizational features of its own: for example, a hierarchical distinction between commonly known 'fundamentals' and more specialized subjects which was at the same time of practical (didactic) relevance. Historically, the tradition underwent important shifts in coverage and structure as well as in emphases and norms: for example, when a dialogue between music and other arts began to open up. By the same token, theory maintained its own diachronic continuities and dialogues between the generations. There was a relative autonomy of the theoretical discourse after all.

In the cultural traditions described in Amnon Shiloah's chapter, by comparison, musical 'concept' (or science) and 'practice' (or history) seem more intertwined. Many of the testimonies of theorists, poets, and philosophers adduced here refer to living musical practice; science and contemplation are cultural pursuits at the centre of society. But generalizations are dangerous in this field of historical knowledge. We are looking at vast areas of time and space which have only been punctuated by a few writers; there certainly is a literary tradition of writing about music although not *of music*.

The 'concept' of music takes on yet another flavour when music begins to be viewed not as a cultural practice but as an artefact. The revival of humanist learning, discussed in the last chapter, achieved a reinterpretation of music which may seem paradoxical. For the Renaissance humanists, music was not only a pleasurable practice guided by science and contemplation—a status which it had indeed possessed in antiquity—but also a literature of self-contained and transmittable musical works. This analogy to verbal literature had not been accorded to ancient music: it probably was an idea based on the experiences of written medieval music, even if humanists were inclined to deny such ancestry.

In fact, where the volume now falls short of the familiar treatments of the late medieval period is in discussing musical works, written genres, composers, and styles. As explained, this shortfall came about fortuitously, and not in the light of an alternative historiography. It may, however, stimulate alternative considerations in the future.

First, the consideration of music as cultural practice should include, not exclude, that of music as a literature where there is an established written tradition. Creating, writing, and transmitting music are musical practice, too. The oral tradition enwraps the written tradition. Andrew Hughes chronicles the development of a 'literature' of liturgical Office chants, paying tribute to individual works, composers, genres, and styles. He hints at notions of originality, innovation, and decline. The structures of chant as a ritual practice are briefly outlined as a background for the developing repertories. It would have been a step backward if this music had been presented in a de-historicized fashion as an age-old performance practice, spontaneously creating its forms to serve purely ritual needs. Not surprisingly, the tendency to de-historicize chant in this way has usually led to the neglect of its late medieval literature as well as practice.

The contribution by Andrew Hughes, in fact, has in common with the seemingly unrelated chapter by Tom R. Ward that they both historicize repertories which earlier historians had considered as peripheral—and therefore ignored. Ward's reappraisal of central Europe as a musical region is not concerned with a particular type of narrative. It describes repertories, practices, and institutions in their historical circumstances, demonstrating that these changed in Austria, Bohemia, and Poland, too. The compensatory value of this contribution would have been lost if it had overemphasized difference.

As regards difference, each of the foregoing chapters leaves open—or opens up—the question what other areas would have to be covered to complete these particular pictures. A book on medieval music in which the chants of the liturgical Office are discussed but not those of the Mass, in which central Europe receives a reappraisal but not Scandinavia, Eastern Europe, the Celtic region, or the Iberian peninsula, is obviously lopsided. Similarly, the contribution on Arabic and Jewish musical traditions in the Mediterranean area highlights our omission of non-Christian traditions in other regions. Our defence must be that such lopsidedness has come about by a process not of exclusion but of exploration; other books on this period have excluded all of these repertories, and by design.

Nothing in medieval music seems so challenging to the modern aesthetic experience as the technicalities of its production.[7] Although this is probably an illusion—the minds and ears of medieval people may have resembled ours even less than their fiddles resemble our violins—the study of pre-modern instruments and their uses has become a paradigm for the exploration of difference. (The study of defunct notations was its predecessor in that respect.) Musical instruments are discussed in NOHM iii; to that volume, Yvonne Rokseth also contributed a valuable chapter on instrumental repertories. For the new edition, Howard M. Brown picked up these and other threads—new research on the written repertories, on performance and social structure—to prepare an integrated study of instrumental music in terms of cultural practice, embracing the technical, social, aesthetic, and performative aspects. This was written in collaboration with Keith Polk, who also revised the whole chapter after Brown died. Finally, the editors made a few further revisions. The reason that this chapter has become one of the longest in the book is not only the exploratory dynamic of this particular sub-field, but also its underlying methodology: documentary research.

Archival documents are quickly becoming a main hunting-ground for medieval studies in general, and thus for music research, where this resource is typically available only for the period after 1300. But there is also a growing appreciation for narrative and iconographic sources, which survive from much earlier periods. Together, these centrifugal types of documentation strengthen the view of music as cultural practice and as a discursive, performative rather than authorial art.[8] Moreover today's interest in music manuscripts—not at all absent from the present volume—converges with the study of cultural practice and performance, for example when they are viewed by Tom R. Ward in their relationship with living repertories. In other areas, the import of 'life' on music can be observed even more vividly. Walter Salmen has chosen to demonstrate this with a chapter on dance music (translated by Cyril Edwards), which illustrates practices and musical genres from the evidence of archival, narrative, and iconographic documentation. Salmen's central argument, however, focuses on 'meaning': for him, dance 'possessed a heavenly, cosmic, indeed universal meaning' and '. . . is thus an essential signifier of the world-view of late medieval and

---

[7] It may be precisely this difference from modern 'instrumental music' which has made us isolate the 'instrumental' element also in medieval music; musical classifications of the Middle Ages did not privilege the criterion of sound production in the same way.

[8] In medieval music studies, much of the impetus towards documentary research is owed to André Pirro and his school (Yvonne Rokseth, Jeanne Marix, Nanie Bridgman, and others).

Renaissance society'. The word 'essential' may be read as revisionist: while the potential of medieval music to signify has never been seriously doubted, 'meaning' has not usually been ascribed to dance, perhaps because in the Western tradition, dance has remained a non-authorial art much longer than music.

It is at this point that the present volume may have something real to offer to future historical studies. It considers circumstances where the meaning of the tradition resides not only in the document emanating from an authorial source but may variously be spread over collective memories—aural, visual, and verbal. Liturgical chant, as we perceive it, is endowed with meaning in just this way—although it also harbours authorial intentions and literary traditions. Dance, instrumental music, theory, and liturgy are all collective surfaces of music (theory at least in its application to didactic practice—although it also has work character and is a literature), where cultural signification happens through diversity and participation. This discursive process excludes neither individuality and authorship nor written creation and transmission, and it includes the receiving centuries, groups, and individuals.

The 'Middle Ages' is a concept—some might say a misconception—of our modern age, based on humanist discourses of the fifteenth century, and legitimately ensconced in our tradition. Since the concept functions in our minds not as a bridge to antiquity but as a demarcation between the present as a better-known 'inside' and the past as a lesser-known 'outside', it is not equally suitable for the articulation of that outside area. The sense of self-contradiction in the term 'late Middle Ages' is compounded when we ask about its beginning. At least from the perspective of the subject matter considered here, there is no beginning of a 'lateness' in culture but only a gradual diversification or completion. Accordingly, the musical traditions of the Mediterranean area, and of liturgical Office chant, are discussed here as they grow up within a much longer time-span, and the other subjects are picked up as they found themselves in the fourteenth and fifteenth centuries, not implying a break with traditions. The volume continues and completes the previous volume on 'early medieval music' not only chronologically but also thematically. By the same token, it is incomplete when judged from the hindsight perspective of the modern age, which would also seek to identify in this period the growing up of the Western composer, the consolidation of the polyphonic musical art-work, of national styles, and other such matters. But again, these themes, as well as that of the 'Renaissance', are of modern coinage; short of their elaboration and description, the book only arrives at the point of their early conceptualization.

Having attempted to make a virtue of the insufficiencies of the book, and having almost praised the contribution of those who did not contribute, the editors feel an even greater desire to thank those who did. The courtesy and immense patience of the contributing authors over ten years of collaboration deserves first mention. Bonnie Blackburn, in her role as co-author, co-editor, and copy-editor, has played the most significant role in creating this book. Bruce Phillips, as the commissioning editor, Helen Peres da Costa, Music Books Editor, and Dorothy McLean, who oversaw the final stages of production, have our warm thanks for helping the book to take the hurdle into the new millennium. We do hope it has arrived in it.

R.S.

Oxford
April 2000

I

MUSLIM AND JEWISH MUSICAL TRADITIONS OF THE MIDDLE AGES

By AMNON SHILOAH

PART I: Musical Cultures of Muslims in Spain

INTRODUCTION

IN 1492, with the fall of the last Arab stronghold—the Nasarite Kingdom of Granada—eight centuries of Muslim domination over the Iberian Peninsula, as well as over Sicily and southern Italy, came to an end. After the conquest in 711, particularly with the inception of the emirate of ʿAbd al-Raḥmān II, who succeeded his father al-Ḥakam in 206/822, the Iberian Peninsula became the scene of one of the most fascinating examples of intercultural contacts. ʿAbd al-Raḥmān's reign represented a pivotal point in the process leading to the creation of an Andalusian culture that culminated under his successor ʿAbd al-Raḥmān III. The latter proclaimed himself Caliph in 929 and envisaged the transformation of Córdoba, his capital, into a cultural centre capable of rivalling Baghdad, seat of the only legal, recognized caliph.

Members of a highly diversified society encompassing Arabs, Berbers, Hispano-Christian converts to Islam, Jews, Mozarabs, Negroes, and freed slaves from Eastern and Western Europe all took part in crystallizing a social and cultural symbiosis, wherein music occupied a prominent place. Arabs of pure extraction constituted only a minority, but they were a substantial part of the aristocratic elite who were determined to assert their hegemony and achieve the sought-after homogeneity. Arabization was their most positive way of achieving this goal and of counteracting the growing effect of acculturation. Although this drive to integrate the heterogeneous components of Andalusian society was similar in principle to procedures followed in the East after the advent of Islam, the particular circumstances prevailing in Spain were conducive to a different kind of symbiosis.

One of the major differences stemmed from the large number of neo-Muslims, Berbers, freed slaves of European extraction, and Jews; their respective cultural situations and participation in political life were also contributory factors. On the other hand, the rulers of Spain encouraged exploration of the philosophic sciences—a cultural area common to Muslim and non-Muslim Arabic-speakers—and the Christian and Jewish elite used this intellectual sphere as a stepping-stone to integration into Arab society. Finally, the great distance separating Andalusia from Near Eastern cultural centres, along with an eagerness to compete with them in the effort to create a superior cultural model, were factors conducive to the emergence of a new cultural style. As far as music is concerned, the protagonists of the new style never aspired completely to abandon the basic principles and values of the Great Musical Tradition (GMT) as elaborated under the Umayyad and ʿAbbasid caliphates (8th to 10th centuries) and subsequently adopted in all major centres. Borrowed from the work of Redfield and Singer,[1] the term GMT designates in our context the 'high' and sophisticated musical art style elaborated in Near Eastern music after the advent of Islam and widely adopted by the cultures under Islamic influence. In this sense the GMT seems to have continued to inspire the local art in its formative stages.

On the other hand, there can be no doubt that the determined quest for innovations was a decisive factor in establishing the specific nature of the Andalusian style. Innovation is indeed the key concept involved in today's polemics, called forth by a famous report which for years has been at the core of all discussions revolving around the emergence of the Andalusian style under the reign of ʿAbd al-Raḥmān II. For the sake of clarification, it should be noted here that, hampered by the lack of documents, one has to glean information about the nature, development, and sound of the music itself from various literary, historical, philosophical, and other written sources which must be interpreted with considerable caution.

THE EMERGENCE OF AN ANDALUSIAN STYLE IN MUSIC

We are told that a significant change occurred in musical life and in the history of Andalusian music under ʿAbd al-Raḥmān II due to the great Bagdadi musician ʿAlī ibn Nāfiʿ, known as Ziryāb. He arrived at the Córdoban court in 822 and his story was recounted in highly

---

[1] R. Redfield and M. Singer, 'The Cultural Role of Cities', in R. Sennet (ed.), *Classical Essays in the Culture of Cities* (New York, 1954), 206–33. See also Amnon Shiloah, *Music in the World of Islam* (London and Detroit, 1995), 19–23.

colourful detail by a later Maghreban littérateur and biographer, al-Maqqarī (1577–1632), whose source is the historian ibn Ḥayyān (987/8–1076). According to this story, Ziryāb was a pupil of the great musician Isḥāq al-Mawṣilī; his personality and remarkable musical talent impressed caliph Hārūn al-Rashīd but roused the jealousy of his master, who insisted that Ziryāb leave Baghdad. The young musician moved to North Africa and was eventually invited to the court of Córdoba. Al-Maqqarī described Ziryāb as a highly gifted, inspired innovator who soon after arriving at the court of ʿAbd al-Raḥmān II became chief court musician and was charged with enhancing the level of all musical activities. He was credited with improving the strings of the ʿūd, increasing their number from four to five, and replacing the plectrum with an eagle's feather. He was considered the inventor of a three-part form or performance sequence: *nashīd–basīṭ–ahzāj* (vocal improvisation, metrical slow movement, and rapid rhythmic finale respectively); the invention of the sophisticated compound form, the *nūba*, is also attributed to him, along with the related modal concept and arrangement. Ziryāb also distinguished himself as an educator and is reputed to have conceived a unique educational method. He pioneered institutionalization of musical education, his school having been widely known and respected.[2]

This summary of al-Maqqarī's report inevitably elicits wonder; indeed, it has stirred the imagination of all those who have written about Andalusian music in our own epoch.[3] The recent discovery of a new source has shed new light on the subject. It is an extensive treatise on music by the Tunisian lexicographer and literary man Aḥmad al-Tīfāshī (1184–1253), entitled *The Ear's Pleasure in the Science of Music.* The part devoted to Andalusian music in this work is one of the best sources found on this subject. This treatise constitutes volume 41 of al-Tīfāshī's vast encyclopedia entitled *An Oration for Wise Men Concerning the Perceptions of the Five Senses.* Most of this encyclopedia has been lost, but a manuscript of vol. 41 is preserved in a Tunisian private library. The latter was first mentioned in 1959 in a study in Arabic by the Tunisian historian Ḥasan Ḥusnī ʿAbd al-Wahhāb.[4] It was subsequently discussed by the Spanish scholar Emilio García

[2] Aḥmad ibn Muḥammad al-Maqqarī, *Nafḥ al-ṭīb,* ed. Iḥsān ʿAbbās (Beirut, 1968), iii. 122–33; see also Amnon Shiloah, *The Theory of Music in Arabic Writings (c. 900–1900)* (RISM B x; Munich, 1979), 271–2.

[3] See e.g. Rafael Mitjana, 'L'Orientalisme musicale et la musique arabe', in *Monde oriental* (Uppsala, 1906), 207–21; Henry George Farmer, *A History of Arabian Music to the XIIIth Century* (London, 1929), 128–30.

[4] Ḥasan Ḥusnī ʿAbd al-Wahhāb, 'al-Tīfāshī', *al-Fikr,* 4/9 (1959), 818–22.

Gómez,[5] and in 1968 the Moroccan author Bin Tawit al-Tanji provided an edition of chapters 10 and 11 of the treatise on music with
an introduction including valuable details about the whole work.[6] An
English translation was published in 1989.[7] In 1992 Christian Poché
devoted an extensive study to the text under the significant title 'Un
nouveau regard sur la musique d'al-Andalus: le manuscript d'Al-
Tīfāshī'.[8] He questions some of the achievements attributed to Ziryāb,
wondering whether the traditional story does not reflect an attempt to
depict him as a 'civilizing hero'. In his argumentation Poché refers to
the great Spanish polygraph ibn ʿAbd Rabbih (860–940); although ibn
ʿAbd Rabbih was born only years after Ziryāb's death, his famous
encyclopedia al-ʿIqd al-farīd (The unique necklace) does not particularly extol the musician's achievements.[9] Furthermore, he states that
al-Iṣfahānī (d. 950), the author of the monumental work *The Book of
Songs*, dedicated to all great poets and musicians up to his own time,
does not mention Ziryāb. Finally, Poché wonders if al-Maqqarī, who,
as noted, essentially based his information on the work of his illustrious predecessor ibn Ḥayyān (987–1076), had focused all the weight of
musical civilization on the inventor.[10]

It is clear that the new views offered by al-Tīfāshī in the section on
Andalusian music inform the major part of Poché's study. Poché
rightly observes at the outset that the overall picture offered by al-
Tīfāshī's work is one of a dynamic process abetted by several
renowned musicians working in at least three major centres. In his
study on 'Music in Muslim Spain', Owen Wright devotes a considerable section to Ziryāb and al-Tīfāshī.[11] After presenting a summary
of Ziryāb's biography as related by al-Maqqarī, based on the historian ibn Ḥayyān, Wright concludes:

On the surface there is nothing controversial or incoherent about ibn
Ḥayyān's narrative, and we may add that the historical importance of Ziryāb

[5] E. García Gómez, 'Una extraordinaria página de Tīfāshī y una hipótesis sobre el
inventor del zajal', in *Études d'orientalisme dediées à la mémoire de Levi-Provençal* (Paris, 1962),
ii. 517–29.

[6] Muḥammad bin Tawit, 'al-ṭarāʾiq wal-alḥān al-mūsīqiyya fī Ifriqiyya wa'l-Andalus', *al-
Abḥāth*, 21 (1968), 93–113.

[7] In Benjamin Liu and James Monroe, *Ten Hispano-Arabic Songs in the Modern Oral
Traditions: Music and Poetry* (University of California Publications in Modern Philology, 25;
Berkeley and Los Angeles, 1989).

[8] International Conference of the International Musicological Society, Madrid, 1992, Round
Table IV, in *Revista de musicología*, 16/1 (1993), 367–79; see also id., *La Musique arabo-andalouse*
(Paris, 1995), 34–48.

[9] Ibn ʿAbd Rabbih, *al-ʿIqd al-farīd*; see Shiloah, *The Theory of Music*, 138–9.

[10] 'n'a pas agi en focalisant sur le créateur, tout le poids d'une civilisation musicale';
'Un nouveau regard', 369.

[11] In *The Legacy of Muslim Spain*, ed. Salma Khadra Jayyushi (Leiden, 1992), 555–79.

was still recognised in the 7th/13th century by al-Tīfāshī, according to whom he introduced a style that was to dominate until the 5th/11th century. Nevertheless, on closer scrutiny a number of the statements made about him appear less than convincing.[12]

Wright goes on to analyse some of the details, showing that they do not accord with other reports, such as the short description in the aforementioned *al-ʿIqd al-farīd*, and the fact that Ziryāb's name does not appear at all in *Kitāb al-ʾAghānī* (Book of songs).

Based on more obvious elements, one can argue that according to the widely accepted technique used in Muslim historiography and anecdotal literary works, it would be difficult to give absolute preference to one version or another that circulated partly in manuscript, and was in part transmitted orally through individuals who had extraordinary memories. This is a technique that affords a well-rounded description of a single event without implying any fixed point in time, nor is it ever restricted to mean an organically connected series of events. Its formulation gives preference to dramatic situation and colour.[13] In this sense one may express doubt even with respect to al-Tīfāshī's work, which was conceived in the same spirit and employs the same techniques. Furthermore, al-Tīfāshī, who lived in Tunisia, did not directly witness the events he described. Bearing this in mind, we should add that the Spanish historian ibn Ḥayyān, from whose lost work al-Maqqarī gleaned his story, lived much closer to Ziryāb's time than al-Tīfāshī, and he is described in the *Encyclopedia of Islam* as 'the greatest historian of the Middle Ages in all Spain both Muslim and Christian . . . he has set standards for subsequent chroniclers'.[14] As to al-Maqqarī, the same encyclopedia describes him as essentially a compiler who fortunately preserved a host of texts that otherwise would have been lost; about his work in which Ziryāb's story appears, the text reads: 'an immense compilation . . . of inestimable value which put it in the first rank of our sources of Muslim Spain from the conquest to the last days of the Reconquista'.[15]

I am not making a brief in defence of Ziryāb's honour or achievements, and I certainly do not seek to minimize in any way the new and highly valuable information provided by al-Tīfāshī. Nevertheless, Ziryāb should not be viewed merely as the 'civilizing hero' Poché refers to. I fully agree with Wright's statement that 'the importance of Ziryāb himself, it might be argued, is also primarily

[12] Ibid. 556–7.
[13] See F. Rosenthal, *The History of Muslim Historiography* (Leiden, 1968), 66.
[14] *The Encyclopedia of Islam*, new edn., vi (Leiden and London, 1971), 789.
[15] Ibid. 787.

symbolic'. I also accept Wright's explanation of the concept 'symbolic': 'According to this view he embodies the introduction, establishment, and diffusion of certain traditions in a way that confirmed the nascent cultural equality between Córdoba and Baghdad and the increasing self-confidence that went with it.'[16] At that time it was highly important for the assertion of Arab hegemony that the desired release from the bonds of Oriental models would appear not in the form of divorce but rather as clever improvements and innovations to be grafted on to the principles of the Great Musical Tradition of the East. This is the tenor of the al-Maqqarī–ibn Ḥayyān version. Al-Tīfāshī's later description of those events, although admitting Ziryāb's role as innovator, refers to more practical reality: the common effort of different segments of Andalusian society to create a new, typically Andalusian, art. His revealing text, written after al-Maqqarī's work based on ibn Ḥayyān, represents a different approach from that of his two predecessors.

LANDMARKS IN AL-TĪFĀSHĪ'S ACCOUNT

After the fall of the Córdoban Caliphate in 912, al-Andalus was split into a number of petty kingdoms. This coincided with the initial efforts of the Reconquista. Nevertheless, despite the rivalries, wars, and political upheavals, the arts and sciences continued to flourish under the patronage of the rulers of these kingdoms. A new dimension was added to the local musical style and the foundations of the Great Musical Tradition intermingled with elements inspired by other sources. In this context al-Tīfāshī's work affords us significant testimony. Following a pattern used in other branches of knowledge, al-Tīfāshī introduces his source, the scribe and littérateur Abu 'l-Ḥasan ʿAlī (ibn Saʿīd al-Andalusī),[17] guaranteeing authenticity by supplying a series of witnesses. First he refers to the period preceding the Umayyad dynasty, during which 'the songs of the people of Andalus were either in the style of the Christians, or in the style of the Arab camel drivers',[18] meaning that at that time music was mainly at an ethnic and folkloristic stage. Under the Umayyads a more sophisticated kind of Arabian music emerged; it reached its zenith with the arrival of 'the foremost expert in this art, Ziryāb', who

[16] Wright, 'Music in Muslim Spain', 558.
[17] The historian and geographer ibn Saʿīd al-Andalusī or al-Maghribī was born near Granada in 1213 and died in Tunis in 1286. Al-Tīfāshī, who was his contemporary but of an older age, used as his source al-Maghribī's already famous work, *Kitāb al-mughrib fī ḥula al-Maghrib*. See below, n. 66.
[18] See Liu and Monroe, *Ten Hispano-Arabic Songs*, 42.

introduced previously unheard of [innovations], and his style was systematically adopted, while all others were forgotten, until Ibn Bajja, the most illustrious expert, appeared and secluded himself for several years with skilled singing girls, whereupon he improved the *istihlāl* and the *'amal* and combined the songs of the Christians with those of the East, thereby inventing a style found only in Andalus, toward which the temperament of its people inclined, so that they rejected all others.[19]

This delightful tale about the creation of a new style suggests a procedure resembling an alchemist's experimental method. I have quoted it in full here because it constitutes a rare testimony of this nature, particularly as it emanates from an Arabic source. It corroborates the assumed or anticipated consequences of the fascinating intercultural contacts that occurred in the Iberian Peninsula.

Before commenting on this passage, I should like to refer to the outstanding figure of Abū Bakr ibn Bājja. This great Spanish philosopher, known in Europe as Avempace, a physician and vizier, was also skilled in the art and science of music. Al-Tīfāshī's major source, ibn Sa'īd al-Andalusī [al-Maghribī], mentions a book on music written by Avempace that had the same reputation in the West as al-Fārābī's *Kitāb al-mūsīqī* had in the East. Unfortunately, this book has not come down to us. We do, however, possess a short passage, a two-page manuscript, entitled 'Tract on melodies'. It deals with the correspondence between the proportions of celestial and earthly music: the natural elements, humours, etc., which are supposedly associated with the strings of the lute.[20]

As to the *istihlāl* and *'amal* said to have been improved by ibn Bājja, they should be considered part of the endeavour to combine contrasting forms in a single sequence that culminates in the establishment of the sophisticated Andalusian compound suite—the *nawba* or *nūba*. In an eleventh-century treatise, al-Ḥasan al-Kātib mentions a sequence of *nashīd* and *basīṭ*, the first a free, and the second a metric form.[21] Al-Maqqarī writes that 'It was constant in al-Andalus that whoever presented a musical session used to begin with a *nashīd* followed immediately by a *basīṭ* and concluding with the *muḥarrakāt* and *ahzāj* in accordance with the method established by Ziryāb.'[22]

While the *istihlāl* corresponds to the *nashīd*, as stated by al-Tīfāshī himself when referring to the *Khusrawānī* mode,[23] the *'amal* (lit. work,

[19] Ibid. 42.
[20] See Shiloah, *The Theory of Music*, 156–7.
[21] *La Perfection des connaissances musicales*, trans. Amnon Shiloah (Paris, 1972), 56 n. 1.
[22] Al-Maqqarī, *Nafḥ al-ṭīb*, 128.
[23] Liu and Monroe, *Ten Hispano-Arabic Songs*, 38.

action) presents us with a new term. Incidentally, a Jewish contemporary of ibn Bājja, the famous poet and philosopher Judah ha-Levi (1075–1141), used the same term in plural form in his philosophical work *hak-Kuzari*. Ha-Levi uses the term as follows: *al-alḥān dhawāt al-aʿmāl*, which can be roughly translated as 'worked out or elaborated melodies'.[24] In this sense *ʿamal* is fairly close to *ṣanʿa* (craftsmanship), which is still used in the Moroccan *nawba*. It also implies the consummate skill involved in the development of songs and reaches its highest point in the *ṣanʿa mashkūla*—ornate artistry expressed by making frequent use of nonsense syllables for embellishment.[25] This characteristic is anticipated by al-Tīfāshī, who said, when comparing Andalusian singing with that of the East: 'the style of the Andalusians is slower and has more notes',[26] meaning that it is melismatic. This can be inferred from another statement of his to the effect that in one Andalusi singer's performance of a single line he had counted no fewer than seventy-four *hazzāt* (vibrations),[27] probably indicating vocalises and a heavily melismatic line. At another outstanding event al-Tīfāshī attended, a singing-girl spent no fewer than two hours on one line. One is tempted to draw a parallel between these attestations and the improvised Moroccan vocal piece called *bitain* (two verses), which is part of the *nawba* form. These are not the only signs leading us to assume that this period probably saw the burgeoning or crystallization of the typical and most prestigious future achievement of Andalusian music—the *nawba*, simultaneously marking its incipient deviation from the previous Eastern model.

THE *NAWBA* TRADITION

It is difficult to determine exactly when the sophisticated system of twenty-four *nawba*s (suite form) was established. In referring to what has been known as Ziryāb's innovation, Josef Pacholczyk suggested the earlier existence of a hypothetical source-suite in the Eastern tradition, thus inferring that Ziryāb was only a transmitter and modifier rather than a creator.[28] One should, however, note Wright's contention that 'As

---

[24] Amnon Shiloah, 'Melody and Meter in Juda's ha-Levi ha-Kuzari', *Tazlil*, 5 (1965), 5–8 (in Hebrew).

[25] The *nawba* is a compound form governed not only by modal unity but also by rhythmic acceleration that reaches its peak towards the end of the *nawba*. It comprises measured and freely measured instrumental and vocal pieces that represent an autonomous phase. For further information see Shiloah, *Music in the World of Islam*, 132–4.

[26] Liu and Monroe, *Ten Hispano-Arabic Songs*, 37.

[27] Ibid.

[28] Josef Pacholczyk, 'Early Arab Suite in Spain: An Investigation of the Past through the Contemporary Living Traditions', International Conference of the International Musicological Society, Madrid, 1992, Round Table IV, in *Revista de musicología*, 16/1 (1993), 358–66.

ibn Ḥayyān does not use the word in this context it would be more precise to speak in relation to Ziryāb of a proto-nawba.'[29] Poché goes so far as to express doubt about the credit given to Andalusians for the establishment of the fully elaborated system, stating that in al-Tīfāshī's work he found evidence only of a micro-, not a macro-suite: this leads him to assume that the *nawba* as a macro form might have been a later North African creation.[30] This interesting hypothesis, however, is contradicted by what we find when consulting available sources.

Manuscript 5307 in the Biblioteca Nacional of Madrid contains a collection of five treatises dealing with Andalusian and North African music. Unfortunately, the manuscript, written by different hands, is defective. The third text is a poem dealing with the natures (temperaments), elements, and modes, attributed to al-Salmānī ibn al-Khaṭīb (fl. 1294). The name of ibn al-Khaṭīb, which appears in the opening line, is almost erased and there is an interlineal addition reading 'Rather by the shaykh Sīdī 'Abd al-Wāḥid al-Wansharīsī' (d. 955/1540).[31] In his introduction to the translation of this text, Henry George Farmer, who published all the texts of the Madrid manuscript with an English translation, argued in favour of ibn al-Khaṭīb's authorship,[32] but he later changed his mind.[33] The poem classifies Andalusian and Maghreban modes into four principals and their branches and also distinguishes their respective relationships to humours, elements, and natures. Another anonymous poem in the same collection lists the twenty-four *ṭubūʿ* and their respective inventors. The use of the term *ṭubūʿ* (pl. of *ṭabʿ*), which means nature or character, as equivalent to musical mode, indicates the network of cosmic relations to music.[34] The concept of *ṭubūʿ* is the object of another poem by the Moroccan polygraph 'Abd al-Raḥmān al-Fāsī (1631–85). Appearing in a manuscript of the Staatsbibliothek of Berlin under the title *al-djumūʿ fi 'ilm al-mūsīqī wa'l-ṭubūʿ* (Gatherings in the theory of music and the musical modes), the poem deals briefly with twenty-three subjects, underlined in red ink. Here also the number of modes listed with their cosmological affiliations is

[29] Wright, 'Music in Muslim Spain', 559.

[30] Poché, 'Un nouveau regard', 377–8.

[31] Shiloah, *The Theory of Music*, 317–18.

[32] Henry G. Farmer, *An Old Moorish Lute Tutor. Being four Arabic Texts from Unique Manuscripts in the Biblioteca Nacional, Madrid, No. 334 and Staatsbibliothek Berlin, Lbg 516, edited with translations, commentary and Appendix* (Collection of Oriental Writers on Music, 1; Glasgow, 1933).

[33] In his new edition of *The Sources of Arabian Music* (Leiden, 1965), under entry 326 (p. 64) the same work is attributed to the Moroccan jurist and literary man al-Wansharīsī (1475–1548).

[34] Shiloah, *The Theory of Music*, 424.

twenty-four.[35] Farmer comments that this work, written in 1650, 'appears to be a versified reproduction by the above author of theories contained in one or more older treatises on music'.[36]

In all three examples we move back and forth between Spain and Morocco within a time-span extending from the beginning of the fourteenth century to the middle of the seventeenth; during this period the *nawba* tradition seems to have been well established. My assumption is that the final shaping of the *nawba* as perpetuated in the North African centres occurred in Spain itself, probably starting with the fourteenth century.

SLAVE SINGING-GIRLS

Based on al-Tīfāshī's account of ibn Bājja's establishment of a new Andalusian style with the collaboration of singing-girls, as well as the two-hour performance of a single line by a singing slave girl, we can infer that those songstresses occupied a prominent place in all walks of Andalusian musical life and in the propagation of a local style. Seville, known for the manufacture of excellent instruments, also seems to have been the major centre for training singing-girls. Al-Tīfāshī reports that in Seville:

Expert old women teaching singing to slave girls they own, as well as to salaried half-Arabs, that is to say, (girls) born of an Arab father and a non-Arab mother. The slave girls are sold from Seville to all the kings of the Maghrib and Ifriqiyya, and each of those slave girls is sold for one thousand Maghribi dinars . . . She is never sold without an accompanying register containing all the songs she has memorized . . . Among them (her talents), a singing girl is required to have an elegant handwriting, and to display what she has memorized to one who can certify to her mastery of the Arabic language . . . Sometimes she is an expert in all instruments and all kinds of dance, and in *khayal* (possibly shadow play or theatre), and she comes with her instrument, along with [an entourage of] slave girls to beat the drum and play the reed for her. She is then called a 'consummate' artist, and is sold for many thousands of Maghribi dinars.[37]

Among those girls were white Christians who had been taken as slaves. They were called *rumiyya* and in poetry were often likened to doves in the treetops. Frequent reference to them can be found in the literature describing the *zambra*s and *leila*s,[38] the nocturnal music and dance sessions that were held in palaces and private homes.

[35] Shiloah, *The Theory of Music*, 108–9.
[36] Farmer, *Old Moorish*, 14.
[37] Liu and Monroe, *Ten Hispano-Arabic Songs*, 37–8.
[38] The terms derive from the Arabic *samra* and *layla*.

In his *Ḥadīqat al-afrāḥ*, the author al-Shirwānī tells the story of a
writer who visited Málaga in 1016 and could not sleep at night because
of the noise emanating from a *zambra* being held in a neighbouring
house. At a certain point, fascinated by a musical piece, he goes outside, and observes the event, which he describes as follows:

In the middle of a vast dwelling there was a big garden in the centre of which
twenty guests were seated in a row, wine goblets and fruit within reach. Young
girls holding *ʿūd* and *ṭunbūr* [short and long-necked lutes respectively], *miʿzaf*
(cithar), *mizmār* (an oboe-like instrument), and timbrels, stood aside without
playing. A female musician was seated alongside them, her lute in her lap:
the eyes of the entire audience were on her, their ears attuned to her songs
that she accompanied with her instrument.[39]

The female ensemble described by this eyewitness was called *sitāra*;[40]
they played with the soloist and also accompanied the female dancer.
Male musicians also participated in such typical Iberian entertainment
sessions.

One of the favourite dances, the *kurraj*, is frequently included in this
type of entertainment or *zambra*, and is one of the games described
by ibn Khaldūn (1332–1406), who may have been the greatest historian and sociologist of the Middle Ages. 'Ibn Khaldūn', writes George
Sarton, 'came too late not only to be translated into Latin and thus
to fall in the stream of Western learning; he came too late even to be
appreciated by his own people.'[41] In the chapter on music of his Pro-
legomena ibn Khaldūn describes the *kurraj* as follows:

Other dancing equipment, called *kurraj*, was also used. The *kurraj* is a wooden
figure (resembling) a saddled horse and is attached to robes such as women
wear. (The dancers) thus give the appearance of having mounted horses. They
attack and withdraw and compete in skill (with weapons). There were other
such games intended for banquets . . .[42]

MUSICAL INSTRUMENTS

The instruments mentioned in the previous section are but a few of
the many that were known in Spain. One of the longest lists extant
includes thirty instruments, some with names that are found nowhere
else. This list appears in one of the most important works dealing with

---

[39] Aḥmad ibn Muḥammad al-Shirwānī, *Ḥadīqat al-afrāḥ* (Bulaq, 1865).
[40] In the East, the term is used to designate the curtain that separated the monarch from the
performing musician.
[41] George Sarton, 'Arabic Scientific Literature', in *Ignace Goldziher Memorial Volumes*, ed.
S. Löwinger and J. Somogyi (Budapest, 1948), i. 66.
[42] Ibn Khaldūn, *al-Muqaddima*, trans. F. Rosenthal, 3 vols. (Princeton, 1967), in the chapter
on the Craft of Music, V, §31, ii. 404–5.

the question of the propriety of listening to music (*samā*): *Kitāb al-imtāʿ wa'l-intifāʿ fi masʾalat samāʿ al-samāʿ* (The book of joy and profit in listening to music). Referring to a question usually debated from a religious standpoint, this work was written for the Almoravid Sultan Yaʿqūb ibn Abī ʿAbd al-Ḥaqq, who reigned from 1286 to 1307. At the end of the text the name of Muḥammad al-Shalaḥī is appended as the copyist, but he may well have been the author. The commentary on the thirty instruments fills six folios of the manuscript Madrid, Biblioteca Nacional, Res. 246, dated 1301. The instruments to which the author refers in his commentary belong to three classes: membranophones, cordophones, and aerophones.[43] By comparison with this list, the one provided by al-Tīfāshī is very small, containing only seven instruments, two of which do not appear in al-Shalaḥī: the *ruṭa* (crowd, rote) and the *shiz* (castanets). Another important source on instruments is that of abu'l-Walid al-Shaqundi (d. 1231). In his tract *On the Merits and Superiority of al-Andalus over the Lands Overseas* [North Africa], the author extols the excellence of Seville in all instruments and accoutrements of pleasure. He provides a list of nineteen terms thought by many scholars as corresponding to musical instruments. However, some of the most intricate terms refer to entertainment with singing and instrumental accompaniment in which dance, mimics, comic representations, shadow theatre (*al-khayal*), and the saddle-horse dance (*al-kurraj*) are involved.

Among the fifteen or so instruments listed by al-Shaqundi are the *zulami* (double-reed instrument), also mentioned by ibn Khaldūn, two types of oboe-like instruments (*mizmar*), and the *būq*, which is described by ibn Khaldūn as 'One of the best wind instruments at this time',[44] and by al-Tīfāshī: 'The noblest instrument among them, and the one producing the greatest pleasure in dancing and singing is the *būq*, in which the people of al-Andalus specialize.'[45] Indeed, there are many references to the various roles the *būq* played. It is said about one of the famous composers of *zajal* (see below), 'He composed *zajal*s in the vein of those usually sung to the accompaniment of the *būq*', which is often extolled in poetic texts. This instrument was widely used for both art and folk music. In a passage by ibn Ḥayyān one reads that emir Muhammad the First had a number of *būq* virtuosi in his service, and he himself excelled in playing his golden ebony *būq*, set with precious stones.[46]

---

[43] For the list see Shiloah, *The Theory of Music*, 323–4. Odeimi Bachir identified the author as Ibn al-Darraj in his article published in *Arabica*, 38 (1991), 40–56.

[44] Ibn Khaldūn, *al-Muqaddima*, trans. Rosenthal, ii. 396.

[45] Liu and Monroe, *Ten Hispano-Arabic Songs*, 43–4.

[46] See E. Levi-Provençal, *Histoire de l'Espagne musulmane* (Paris, 1950–3), i. 186.

A close examination of the details in both ibn Khaldūn and al-Tīfāshī leaves no doubt that the upper part of the *būq* corresponds to a double-reed instrument—a shawm. Why, therefore, has it not been identified simply as a shawm? Obviously because we are dealing here with a special type of instrument that may be a combination of shawm and horn. Examining the miniatures that illustrate the Cantigas de Santa Maria manuscripts, I have found a solution and hope that my suggestion will prove plausible. I refer to the *albogon* in the miniature of Cantiga 300 of the Alphonsine Codex E1. The miniature shows an instrument with a name that might have been derived from *al-būq*; it has a bell made of a large horn, a conical wooden tube with pierced fingerholes, and a double reed surrounded by a circular disk on which the player's lips rest.[47] In addition to providing important information about the instruments in vogue at that time, the celebrated thirteenth-century miniatures demonstrate that Christians, Jews, and Muslims played together at the court of Alfonso el Sabio, king of León and Castile (1252–84), but unfortunately only few illustrations of the rich instrumentarium have survived.

THE ADVENT OF NEW POETIC GENRES

A common denominator of sorts seems to have been reached when the different groups could take advantage of the remarkable local invention of new strophic genres: the *muwashshaḥ*, which used classical Arabic, and the *zajal* in the vernacular dialect. The eminent Spanish scholar E. García Gómez writes: 'The *muwashshaḥ* is undoubtedly the most original product of the Umayyad culture, rising far above the provincial level of its other achievements.'[48]

The inventor of the *muwashshaḥ* is said to have been the blind poet Muqaddam ibn Muʿāfa (end of the ninth or beginning of the tenth century). We do not know when or by whom the *zajal* was created, but the form reached its peak with the outstanding poet Muḥammad ibn Quzmān, who died in Córdoba in 1160. In both genres the fundamental unit is the strophe with rhymes that vary from strophe to strophe; the most characteristic feature is the recurrence, at the end of each strophe, of a refrain that maintains the same rhyme consistently. A striking feature of the *muwashshaḥ* is the use of concluding verses in Romance called *kharja* (clausula, exit). Some writers

---

[47] R. Álvarez, 'Los instrumentos musicales en los códices Alfonsinos: su tipología, su uso y su origen, algunos problemas iconográficos', *Revista de musicología*, 10/1 (1987), 83–4; Z. Falvy, *Mediterranean Culture and Troubadour Music* (Budapest, 1986), 46–7. Both sources include good illustrations.

[48] 'La Poésie hispano-arabe et l'apparition de la lyrique romane', *Arabica*, 5 (1958), 113–30.

believe that some of these verses may have been borrowed from popular lyrics, while others were composed by the poet for incorporation into the *muwashshaḥ*. In 1948 Samuel M. Stern discovered this surprising unit at the end of Hebrew poems and later at the end of Arabic poems, a discovery of tremendous literary importance. It also provoked a heated argument between Romanists and Arabists about the origin of the two genres under discussion, as well as the meaning of the *kharja*.[49]

In 1912 the eminent Spanish scholar J. Ribera y Tarrago (1858–1934) had launched this debate in the course of a lecture on the outstanding composer of *zajal*, the poet ibn Quzmān. He contended that the two genres, born in Muslim Spain in imitation of already existing Romance-language lyrics, had exerted considerable influence on the lyrics of the troubadours in Provence as well as in the rest of Europe. His conclusions elicited furious polemics.[50] Ribera's disciple, E. García Gómez, offered further support for his master's thesis. A similar debate was initiated by Ribera y Tarrago in connection with the Cantigas de Santa Maria. In a ceremonial lecture delivered in 1921 in celebration of seven hundredth anniversary of the birth of King Alfonso, Ribera suggested that the king had naturally addressed himself to the best and most flourishing music of his time, that is, to the music of the Arabs. He also argued not only that the rhyme scheme of most of these cantigas corresponds to that of the *zajal* but also that the whole work in its original form was performed by famous professional musicians of the three faiths. He was refuted by another noted Spanish musicologist, Higinio Anglés, who produced a monumental study of Alfonso's Cantigas.[51]

Since then many scholars have tackled this question, which is difficult to resolve. We all agree, of course, that the *muwashshaḥ* and *zajal* were normally sung and that the formal structure of the song coincided with that of the verse, but while both music and texts of the Cantigas de Santa Maria are available, only the texts of the *muwashshaḥāt* have been preserved for posterity. Leo Plenckers compared the Cantigas and the *muwashshaḥ* based on the present-day Algerian *ṣanʿa*, assuming that 'the Algerian *ṣanʿa* which is considered a direct offshoot of the Andalusian *muwashshaḥ* still has the same

[49] Samuel M. Stern, *Hispano-Arabic Strophic Poetry*, ed. L. P. Harvey (Oxford, 1974). See also below, n. 63.

[50] J. Ribera y Tarrago, *La música de las cantigas: estudio sobre su origen y naturaleza*, 3 vols. (Madrid, 1922; repr. 1990).

[51] Higinio Anglés, *La música de las cantigas de Santa Maria del Rey Alfonso el Sabio*, 3 vols. (Barcelona and Madrid, 1943–58).

musical form as its predecessor'.[52] Ismael Fernández de la Cuesta, historian of Spanish medieval music, took up the debate that followed the publication of Ribera's theory about Arabian influence. He offered a re-evaluation of that theory, reviewing its different premises in the light of Higinio Anglés's refutation. He argued that Ribera's approach provided elements that contribute to a better understanding of the Cantigas de Santa Maria and other medieval monodic musical traditions.[53]

One of the strong supporters of Ribera's thesis was the celebrated expert on Arabian music Henry George Farmer, who placed particular stress on the entire question of Arab influence. In 1925 he published a pamphlet called 'Clues for the Arabian Influence on Musical Theory'[54] where he drew attention to the instruments that were adopted by the West, namely the lute (al-'ūd), the rebec (rabāb), the guitar (qītār), adufe (al-daff), and pandor (al-bandair). Some of Farmer's far-reaching arguments about innovative compositional procedures such as organum, the notational system, and the rhythmic modes, etc. were harshly refuted by Kathleen Schlesinger. Her views engendered counter-attacks by Farmer, who was finally led to write his book *Historical Facts for the Arabian Musical Influence*.[55] All in all, however, one must concede that unlike the obvious Arab influence on medicine, mathematics, astronomy, philosophy, etc., the influence on musical theory was rather meagre. The popularity enjoyed by al-Fārābī's book *Ihsā' al-'ulūm* (Classification of sciences) as a result of its many Latin translations does not prove the contrary (see below), since it includes only definitions concerning music and its components and contains nothing specifically Muslim or Arab. Al-Fārābī's masterpiece, *The Great Book of Music*, was not among the many Arabic works that were translated into Latin.

It seems likely that the question of the influence naturally accruing from contact beween two different cultures can best be considered from the standpoint of the nature and degree of impact on the music. Nevertheless, borrowing certain musical elements from another culture does not necessarily imply adopting the other culture's music:

[52] Leo J. Plenckers, 'The Cantigas de Santa Maria and the Moorish *muwashshah*: Another Way of Comparing their Musical Structure', International Conference of the International Musicological Society, Madrid, 1992, Round Table IV, in *Revista de musicología*, 16/1 (1993), 354–7 at 355–6.

[53] Ismael Fernández de la Cuesta, 'Reflectura de la teoría de Julian Ribera sobre la influencia de la música arábico andaluza en las Cantigas de Santa Maria y en las canciones de los trovadores, troveros y minensingers', International Conference of the International Musicological Society, Madrid, 1992, Round Table IV, in *Revista de musicología*, 16/1 (1993), 385–95.

[54] *Journal of the Royal Asiatic Society* (1925), 61–80.

[55] London, 1930 (repr. Hildesheim, 1970). See also Shiloah, *Music in the World of Islam*, 78–83.

general and philosophical ideas cross cultural boundaries much more easily than do stylistic, creative, and sentient components. This is particularly true in the case of music, which is an emotional language laden with culturally bound symbolic codes; hence it is understood, felt, and appreciated only by those who are entirely integrated within a given culture.

PART II: Jewish Musical Traditions in Spain, Provence, and Southern Italy

INTRODUCTION

Jewish settlement in the Iberian Peninsula dates back to ancient times; traces of it can be found as early as AD 70, when the Second Temple in Jerusalem was destroyed by the Romans. Additional waves of Jews came later from North Africa and Provence. After the conquest of the Peninsula by the Visigoths, who by the end of the sixth century had converted to Christianity, the Jews suffered various forms of persecution. This oppression culminated under the reign of King Sisebut, who in 613 confronted them with the choice of becoming Christians or leaving the territories under his rule. Many who ostensibly converted to the new faith formed the first communities of Marranos on Iberian soil. In view of their difficult circumstances, it is not surprising that the Jews considered the Arab conquest as a sign of redemption; they put their knowledge of the terrain and of the vernacular language at the disposal of the conquerors who crossed the Straits of Gibraltar in 711. Consequently, the Jews were accorded freedom of worship and participated actively in the process of establishing the new Andalusian culture.

As the Jews were an important component of the diverse Iberian society engaged in crystallizing a new social and cultural symbiosis, within which music occupied a prominent place, the question arises as to what kind of music the Jews had at that time and the extent to which some, if any, of its elements were eventually incorporated into the new Andalusian style. In one of the few attempts to describe Jewish music in Spain before the expulsion of 1492, Higinio Anglés wrote about the period prior to the Arab conquest: 'And because the Jews lived in the Iberian Peninsula for so many centuries, it is not difficult to imagine that the traditional song of Iberian Jews absorbed and elaborated, with the passage of time, many elements of native Spanish art.'[56]

---

[56] Higinio Anglés, 'La Musique juive dans l'Espagne médiévale', *Yuval*, 1 (1968), 48–64 at 48.

While acknowledging the existence of Jewish traditional song, Anglés refers to a well-known process experienced by every musical tradition that has undergone long exposure to another culture. But the thorny question is: what are the Jewish fundamentals Anglés obviously recognized? Do they involve remnants of the music of ancient Israel brought to Spain by the first Jewish settlers? Some eighty years ago, linking loyalty to ancient ancestral tradition with loyalty to the tradition created by Sephardi Jews on Iberian soil, A. Z. Idelsohn stated: 'They had remained faithful to the nation's ancestral tradition as well as to that which they created in Spain during the thousand years they lived there.'[57] With respect to the period prior to the Arab conquest, one can assume that neither thesis is devoid of logic, but they cannot be proven convincingly. Indeed, in another passage, Anglés himself argues that the lack of comprehensive studies of Jewish peninsular music in the remote past is due to the paucity of 'artistic monuments capable of reflecting a faithful image of what such Jewish music in Spain was'.[58] For this reason, the bulk of his article refers to the period after the ninth century, and all eighteen known Jewish musicians mentioned by him were indeed active in lands under Muslim or Christian dominion.

In view of what has been said, one should note that a scholar wishing to study Jewish music of that period—in any land—is hampered at the outset by the lack of notated documents. A search for melodies actually heard during the period under discussion would be much like groping through the darkness of time. Therefore, in his attempt to shed light on the music presumably perpetuated through oral transmission, the scholar has to rely on various types of textual sources. There is one exception which, despite its enormous value, in our case does not radically change the situation described above. Some time in the 1920s a fragment of a Hebrew hymn together with its notated tune was discovered in the Cairo Genizah.[59] Scholars have identified its scribe as Obadiah the Norman proselyte, who lived in the twelfth century. Together with the discovery in 1965 of two more Genizah fragments notated in neumatic script by the same hand, these unique

[57] A. Z. Idelsohn, *Ozar Neginot Israel* (Thesaurus of Hebrew Oriental Melody), iv (Jerusalem, Berlin, and Vienna, 1922), 1.

[58] 'La Musique juive', 50.

[59] Israel Adler, 'Les Chants synagogaux notés au XIIᵉ siècle (ca 1103–1150) par Abdias, le prosélyte normand', *Revue de musicologie*, 51 (1965), 19–51; H. Avenary, 'Genizah Fragments of Hebrew Hymns and Prayers Set to Music', *Journal of Jewish Studies*, 16 (1966), 87–104; id., 'The Interpretation of the Music Notation of Ovadia the Proselyte', in *Encounters of East and West in Music* (Tel-Aviv, 1979), 136–8; Norman Golb, 'Obadiah the Proselyte, Scribe of a Unique Twelfth-Century Hebrew Manuscript Containing Lombardic Neumes', *Journal of Religion*, 45/2 (1965), 19–51.

documents aroused great and justified interest among specialists, although these experts held divergent views about Obadiah's dates, his geographic provenance, and the musical modes of his notated examples. Following his conversion in the first half of the twelfth century, it seems that Obadiah left Italy and went to live as a Jew in the Orient. There he received full instruction in Judaism and Hebrew.[60]

THE GOLDEN AGE OF JEWISH CULTURE

The Umayyad 'Abd al-Raḥmān III, who in 929 assumed the title caliph, conceived the idea of reconciling the followers of the different religions and ethnic groups and of fusing them into one nation. He erected a new capital near Córdoba designed to symbolize the splendour of his Umayyad kingdom, and endeavoured to base his reign on the collaboration of the various national groups under his aegis. It was in these favourable circumstances that the first Jewish courtier, Hasdai ibn Shaprut, rose to eminence when the caliph appointed him director of customs in the 940s. He was a man of wide culture, a distinguished physician who knew Hebrew, Arabic, Latin, and Romance —the vernacular spoken by the indigenous Christians. Moreover, ibn Shaprut proved himself a skilful diplomat in the execution of various official missions assigned to him by the caliph, who also made him the leader of the Jewish settlement in the kingdom. In this last capacity, it is commonly acknowledged that ibn Shaprut's influence was felt in all spheres of Jewish life. Ibn Shaprut's eagerness to help develop Jewish culture on Spanish soil motivated him to patronize a galaxy of Jewish scholars and poets.

An Arab intellectual of those days was moulded by ideals that traced the source of Muslim power to the vitality of the Arabic language, scripture, and poetry. Pursuant to this approach, the hallmark of a cultured Jew became his polished command of Arabic style and the ability to display the beauty of his own heritage through a philological mastery of the text of the Hebrew Bible, as well as through the writing of new Hebrew verse. Hence the active support of the viziers of Granada—Hasdai and then ibn Nagrelas—and the patronage of ibn Ezra, ibn Megash, and ibn Albalias, who were high officials in Granada and Seville, as well as of many others, were definitive for the efflorescence of Jewish culture, including secular and religious poetry and music.

---

[60] Adler, 'Les Chants', 24–6; Avenary, 'The Interpretation', 133.

An innovation introduced by the poet and synagogue cantor Donash ibn Labrat, who came to Córdoba from Baghdad in 950 and became a protégé of Hasdai, was a turning point in the development of Hebrew poetry and music. Donash, who was also a talented musician, is credited with introducing Arabic quantitative metre and prosodic principles to Hebrew verse. This innovation was indeed of great importance and led to a reorientation whereby sacred Hebrew poetry and the entirely new secular Hebrew poetry became more fluent and polished. According to Eliyahu Ashtor, 'People of that era saw no contradiction in the composition of gay, secular verse and the writing of sacred poetry condemning mundane vanities.'[61] The new metric rules had far-reaching implications for the art of singing, as they resulted in increased use of various defined rhythmic types of organization, an outstanding characteristic of Arabic quantitative metre. Like the prescribed combinations of short and long syllables in poetic metre, defined rhythmic organization too functions in accordance with the principle of organized duration along the time axis. This does not mean that the two are necessarily congruent, but in the latter case the reference is to inspiration deriving from the basic structural patterns. The intimate affinity with music of well-defined metric rhythmic organization was propounded by the great Jewish poet and philosopher Mosheh ibn Ezra (1055–1135) in his Arabic-language book *Kitāb al-muḥāḍara wa'l-mudhākara* (Book of conversations and memories), the first Jewish poetic treatise.[62] It should be noted that in addition to adopting quantitative metres, Hebrew poets also took full advantage of the newly invented strophic forms described earlier in this chapter: the *muwashshaḥ* and the *zajal*.[63] They even rapidly penetrated liturgical and para-liturgical singing due to their inherent musical potential: the short lines evoked light rhythms and increased the worshippers' participation in the singing of responses and refrains.

THE JEWISH MUSICAL TRADITION

Crystallization of the Jewish musical tradition in Spain is directly associated with social and cultural transformations that occurred in the lives of the Jewish communities in the mid-tenth century. In part, it represents some of the new cultural patterns that sprang from the

---

[61] E. Ashtor, *The Jews of Moslem Spain*, 3 vols. (Philadelphia, 1973–84), i. 261.

[62] Mosheh ibn Ezra, *Kitāb al-muḥāḍara wa'l-mudhākara*, ed. and trans. A. Sh. Halkin (Jerusalem, 1975).

[63] I. Benabu, 'Rivers of Oil Inundated the Valley of Stones: Towards a Methodology for Reading the Hispano-Romance Kharjas Characters', in A. Jones and R. Hitchcock (eds.), *Studies in the Muwashshaḥ and the Kharja* (Oxford, 1991), 16–28.

intellectual merging of Jewish and Arabic culture, and it accords well with the new 'aristocratic' social organization wherein the courtier acquired a leading position in spheres of intellectual and artistic creativity, making his mark on its development and quality. The secular music heard in the Jewish milieu was much like the music heard in the courts of Arab rulers. At literary gatherings and banquets, male and female soloists, as well as choirs, sang to instrumental accompaniment. The Hebrew songs celebrated feasts, gardens, landscapes, fountains, and songbirds.

In his history of Jews in Muslim Spain, Ashtor somewhat fancifully depicts scenes of Jewish banquets, including details that might well have been authentic. One of his descriptions is of a festive gathering organized by a rich Jew who had been appointed to a high post in Granada. The banquet took place in the enclosed courtyard of his sumptuous home. In the midst of flower beds, with a fountain in the background, the guests were regaled by a singer who accompanied herself on a lute and was followed by another girl playing the flute to the accompaniment of a drummer. The evening culminated in the solemn recitation of a new poem by a renowned Jewish poet.[64]

It may be assumed that the most talented Jewish and non-Jewish performers of Andalusian art music heard at these festive occasions were active in various courts where on the whole religious differences were not an issue. It is only natural that of the many fine musicians, only the names of the most outstanding would be mentioned in the sources. The earliest one referred to is al-Manṣūr al-Yahūdī, whose name appears in the detailed account about Ziryāb reported by the seventeenth-century Maghriban historian al-Maqqarī. Al-Maqqarī's source is the historian ibn Ḥayyān (987–1076),[65] who says that al-Ḥakam, the monarch of Córdoba, sent his favourite Jewish musician, al-Manṣūr al-Yahūdī, to Kairawan (in today's Tunisia) to meet the famous Ziryāb and try to bring him to Córdoba. Just before leaving Kairawan, Ziryāb heard the sad news of al-Ḥakam's death, and changed his mind. It was only after al-Manṣūr's invitation had been renewed by the new ruler that Ziryāb consented to go to Córdoba. Despite doubts expressed earlier in this chapter about the credibility of some details in al-Maqqarī's report, one is inclined to believe this particular anecdote, as an Arab source would have been unlikely to extol the prestige of a Jewish musician without good reason. It may

---

[64] Ashtor, *The Jews of Moslem Spain*, i. 400–2.
[65] See above, nn. 2 and 14.

therefore be assumed that this court musician really existed and must
have been held in high esteem.

In the first half of the twelfth century the name of another Jewish
musician, Isaac ben Shimeon al-Yahudi, is listed by the Arab historian and littérateur ibn Saʿid al-Maghribī among the most illustrious and learned Córdoban music masters. He describes al-Yahudi
as 'one of the wonders of his time in his outstanding musical master-
ship both as singer and instrumentalist'.[66] Al-Maghribī adds the
important information that Isaac ben Shimeon was a follower
(perhaps a disciple) of the famous philosopher and musician ibn
Bājja, known in the West as Avempace (d. 1139), who, as we have
seen, was considered a moving force in the establishment of the
Andalusian style.[67]

At about the same time the Arab author ibn Bassām (d. 1147), in
his work *al-Dhakhīra*, mentions the musician Dānī al-Isrāʾīlī (the
Israelite), writing: 'His musical talent surpassed that of Ibrāhīm al-
Mawṣilī';[68] the latter was the most outstanding musician at the brilliant court of caliph Hārūn al-Rashīd in Baghdad. Dānī is also included among the eighteen known Jewish musicians listed by Anglés,
who refers to the French scholar Henry Peres; he tells us that on a
festive occasion organized by al-Maʾmun in Toledo an Israelite named
Dani directed the ensemble and made an overwhelming impression on
all the guests.[69]

All the other names listed by Anglés from a variety of sources refer
to Jewish musicians and entertainers who served at the courts of
Christian kings and nobles. In addition, Anglés mentions Jewish musicians from the schools of Toledo, Seville, and Murcia; they collabo-
rated with endeavours to realize the cultural policy of the enlightened
King Alfonso el Sabio and participated in performing the repertory of
the Cantigas de Santa Maria.[70]

The growing activity of Jewish musicians in the territories
under Christian dominion was due to the expansion of the Reconquista and the flight of Jews from Muslim lands. The increasing
number of Jewish communities living thereafter in those territories,
combined with intensified contact with the trans-Pyrenean Jews
of Provence, led to important cultural transformations that will be
dealt with below.

[66] In Saʿid al-Maghribī, *al-Mughrib fī ḥula al-Maghrib*, ed. Shawqi Dayf (Cairo, 1953), i. 128–9.
[67] See above at n. 20.
[68] Ibn Bassām, *al-Dhakhīra* (Cairo, 1945), iv/1, p. 105.
[69] Anglés, 'La Musique juive', 53–4.
[70] Ibid. 59–60.

SYNAGOGUE AND FOLK MUSIC

All instances we have cited so far have referred to what might be called sophisticated secular music practised by aristocratic circles in both Muslim and Christian areas. While it seems logical for the Jews totally to have adopted art music in the secular realm, it is appropriate here— in view of their propensity to support new cultural patterns and the resultant socio-cultural changes wrought in the Jewish milieu—to ask whether their synagogue and folk music had a distinctive nature. Although our knowledge is very meagre in this respect, we may assume that during their long presence in Spain prior to the Arab conquest, the Jews must have had some synagogal and folk music of their own, representing a fusion of old Jewish elements with borrowings from indigenous songs. It seems unlikely that, with the advent of new Andalusian art music, an old cherished musical patrimony would have been abandoned immediately. It is more reasonable to assume that the old forms continued to coexist with the new ones. On the other hand, however important the Andalusian art music may have been, it probably underwent a gradual decline as a result of new and different cultural contacts in the territories reconquered by the Christians.

In his attempt to 'prove' the existence of typically Jewish music, Anglés refers to a fifteenth-century chronicler who described the participation of Jews in mourning ceremonies held after the death of their benefactor Alfonso, king of Aragon and Naples. According to this testimony, at an assembly of Jews held in the town square of Cervera (Catalonia) in the afternoon hours, six rabbis intoned Hebrew lamentations around the coffin and weeping Jewish women chanted special dirges.[71] Better proof may perhaps be found in the repertory of hymns and songs the exiles took with them to their new places of refuge after 1492. In the post-exilic period they faithfully perpetuated their musical heritage, comprised essentially of Hebrew hymns and a rich repertory of Judaeo-Spanish folk songs, including ballad-romances, popular genres such as *canticas de parida*, *cantos de boda*, *coplas*, and *endechas*-lamentations. Throughout the centuries the overall textual and musical components of this repertory continued to demonstrate a profoundly vital attachment to strong Judaeo-Spanish roots—an attachment which, generally speaking, does not exist in relation to sophisticated Arabic art music.[72]

---

[71] Anglés, 'La Musique Juive', 53.

[72] See Israel J. Katz, *Judeo-Spanish Traditional Ballads from Jerusalem: An Ethnomusicological Study*, 2 vols. (Brooklyn, 1971–5); Samuel G. Armistead and Joseph Silverman, with musical

THE MYSTICAL DIMENSION

As a result of an important development in Spain with respect to mysticism and kabbalah, the sphere of sacred and religious music underwent one of the most fruitful developments in Jewish history. The roots of the kabbalistic doctrine lay in the esoteric and theosophical schools of thought subscribed to by Jews in Palestine and Egypt during the time of the Second Temple. However, as a historical phenomenon, the kabbalah begins only in the twelfth century, when the earliest kabbalistic text, the *Bahir Book*, appeared in Provence. It was from there that the doctrine of the kabbalah spread to Spain, where it reached its peak in the thirteenth century in the city of Gerona. Gerona offered fertile soil for the germination and growth of the ideas of the early kabbalists, whose work culminated in the *Sefer ha-Zohar* (Book of splendour) written by Mosheh de León between 1280 and 1286. The *Zohar*, which marks a lengthy process of development that affected the kabbalistic tenets, is not a single book, but a large literary treasure-trove embracing many and varied parts. Rather than expounding its ideas in the systematic, orderly fashion of the kabbalah, it expresses them by means of homiletics and commentaries on the Pentateuch. Hence concepts relating to the importance and virtues of macrocosmic and microcosmic music that developed in the mystical doctrine are so interwoven with the symbols comprising the world of the kabbalah that it is often difficult to treat them separately. However, by interpreting those symbols and concepts, it emerges that prayer with mystical intention (*Kavvanah*) and the singing of hymns were perceived as elevating the soul to celestial realms where it could bask in the supreme glory. This ecstatic state can be described as profound meditation through which the mysteries of the Divine Name reveal themselves to the enlightened. Further elaboration occurs in thirteenth-century Spain with the advent of the school of 'Prophetic Kabbalism', the outstanding proponent of which was Abraham Abulafia (b. Saragossa, 1240). In his search for a practical method of acquiring the spirit of prophecy and of freeing the soul from the bonds of ordinary perception, Abulafia developed a theory of the mystical combination of Hebrew letters in which the alphabet takes the place of musical notes. Maintaining that its influence on the soul was the same as that of music, he compared such intellectual exercise based on pure thought with composing music.

transcription and studies by Israel J. Katz, *Judeo-Spanish Ballads from Oral Tradition* (Berkeley and Los Angeles, 1986); S. Weich-Shahaq and J. Etzion, 'The Spanish and Sephardic Romances: Musical Links', *Ethnomusicology*, 32 (1988), 173–209; J. Etzion, 'The Music of the Judeo-Spanish Romancero: Stylistic Features', *Anuario musical*, 43 (1988), 221–56.

With the decline of Spanish Jewry, the mystical teachings of the kabbalah and the messianic apocalyptic ideas it embraced became an expression of yearning for redemption and seemed to offer a spiritual lifeline to salvation. By the mid-sixteenth century, a major centre of kabbalistic activities was established in the small Palestinian town of Safed. A circle of mystics, including exiles from Spain, was formed under the outstanding leadership and gifted teaching of Rabbi Isaac Luria, known as ha-Ari (the Lion). In conformity with the Lurian doctrine, singing was made a major component of their rituals and worship. Their belief in the power and function of song was immediately transferred from the theoretical to the practical, concrete level. From the Safed period onwards, *Sefer ha-Zohar* became the major source of esoteric studies. The nation sanctified it as a canonical text and used it to help guide Jewry through the labyrinthine byways of life.[73]

WRITINGS ON MUSIC

Following in the footsteps of their Arab neighbours, the Jews of Spain, Provence, and Sicily regarded the science and philosophy of music as a basic component of secular learning and education. Initially, Jewish authors wrote their philosophical and scientific works in Arabic, the lingua franca of all educated people at that time, but they used Hebrew letters. Most of their contributions on music and the science of music are incorporated in philosophical, ethical, historical, or philological writings. Ordinarily these works contain little original speculative or theoretical materials, although their authors were well acquainted with the masterworks of earlier generations of Eastern theorists. Nevertheless, from a cultural viewpoint, the texts on music written by Jewish authors emphasize specifics; above all they extol the music of ancient Israel and the universality of its achievements in practice and theory.

The superb status of music in biblical times was already dealt with in an early (unpublished) work, *The Book of the Garden: On Metaphor and Reality*, by the poet and philosopher Mosheh ibn Ezra (1055–1135), mentioned earlier. This work, in Arabic but written in Hebrew characters, discusses the question of Hebrew metaphor. It includes a passage dealing with the production and qualities of sounds and the link between speech and music. Paying tribute to the moral power of singing and playing instruments, acclaiming Arab and Greek

---

[73] For further information see Amnon Shiloah, *Jewish Musical Traditions* (Detroit, 1992), ch. 6.

theorists—the most illustrious of whom he mentions are Plato, Aristotle, al-Kindī, Thabit ibn Qurra, and al-Fārābī—ibn Ezra quotes numerous biblical verses related to music. The quotations, starting with the ante-diluvian story of Jubal, the inventor of music, are designed to support the author's theory that all intellectual human achievement, including the science and practice of music, originated in the Bible.[74]

Ibn Ezra was well versed in music and musical theory and offers further interesting thoughts on the subject in his other book, the only treatise on poetry written by a Jew: *Book of Conversations and Memories*.[75] In this book, also in Arabic but written in Hebrew characters, the author refers to music from two standpoints. It first appears in his discussion on the nature of the science of poetry, which he considers part of the trivium, and then he includes music as part of the 'logical and universal sciences', that is to say, of the quadrivium. Ibn Ezra then argues that 'metre' used in the science of poetry should be affiliated with the universal sciences 'because it draws upon musical principles and harmonic relations'. Such a linkage of poetry and music and the connection between knowledge of the Hebrew language and music in the education system of those days leads the author to recommend: 'It is advantageous for [one] to learn the science of music after studying grammar as it [music] shares with grammar in the creation of song.'[76] It should be noted in this respect that in medieval Europe it was common to link grammar, metre, and music.

Returning to the ancient music of Israel, another famous poet and philosopher of that generation, Judah ha-Levi (1072–1144), makes an interesting comment in his book *The Kuzari: An Argument for the Faith of Israel*.[77] In a dialogue between the Jewish Sage and the king of Khazars, the Sage maintains that like all other realms of knowledge, the science of music achieved its highest perfection in biblical times when the art of music was reserved for the elite (the professional class of musicians, the Levites), and had a special place in the Temple of Jerusalem, where its chief role was to enhance ritual worship. Ha-Levi, in the person of the Sage, further maintains that due to its ability to rouse elevating spiritual reactions, 'music was a respectable art and not

---

[74] See Amnon Shiloah, 'The Musical Passage in ibn Ezra's Book of Garden', *Yuval*, 4 (1974), 211–24.

[75] See above, n. 62.

[76] Ibid. 136.

[77] This book about the king of the Khazars deals with the uniqueness of the religious history of the people of Israel and their special connection with God. It was translated into Hebrew by the well-known translator from Arabic to Hebrew, Yehuda ben Shaul ibn Tibbon (b. Granada 1120, d. Marseilles 1190).

to be deplored. Many representatives of the Persians and Greeks used to come to King Solomon for instruction.'[78] The Sage concludes that the current decline of music was due to the oppressive conditions under which the Jews lived in the diaspora.

In another paragraph of the same book, the king wonders how the Sage can attribute superiority to Hebrew over other languages— implying Arabic, with its refined poetry and sophisticated metric organization that make it perfect for singing. The Sage argues in response that the Jews have a special method of chanting suitable for the sacred texts so that even when the rendition is adorned with melismatic embellishment, it remains subordinate to the textual content, structure, and punctuation. This method helps transmit information implicit in the written word by dint of the musical component, and facilitates the incorporation of highly variegated rhetorical and intonational nuances into the melodic sheath. Finally, the Sage discloses to the king of the Khazars the special 'invention' of Hebrew culture: the establishment of graphic symbols to translate the various elements that shape melodious speech (cantillation). These are the biblical accents (ta'amei ha-miqra).[79]

As the years passed, the perception of chanting as a hallmark of Jewish music had further ramifications. It is sufficient to cite examples taken from the works of two grammarians. Profiat Duran from southern France (d. c.1414) deals with the purpose of biblical cantillation in his book Ma'aseh Efod and quotes the Kuzari to prove the superiority of free chanting over metric singing.[80] More than a century later, the Italian grammarian and poet Samuel ben Elhanan Archivolti (1515–1611) devotes most of chapter 31 of his book 'Arugat hab-bosem (The garden of spices) to an interesting expatiation of the theory enunciated by Judah ha-Levi.[81]

The unpublished commentary on Gen. 4: 21 about Jubal, 'the father of them that play upon the harp and the organ', by the Italian poet and biblical exegete Immanuel ben Shelomo ha-Romi (the Roman) (1261–after 1330) belongs to this quest for the biblical roots of Jewish music as a model of universal achievement. Written in a transitional period during which the Jewish centre of cultural activity was in the process of moving from Spain to Provence and Italy, Immanuel's commentary offers us a broader ideological

---

[78] See Sefer ha-Kuzari, ed. and trans. Yehudah Shmuel even Shmuel (Tel-Aviv, 1973), paragraphs II, 64 and II, 65.
[79] Ibid., paragraphs II, 69–77.
[80] See Israel Adler, Hebrew Writings Concerning Music (RISM B ix/2; Munich, 1975), 126–30.
[81] Ibid. 96–103.

view; it forms a bridge between earlier developments in Spain
and Provence and the eventual advent of a flourishing Jewish
culture in Italy, wherein music and its related science held a prominent
place.[82]

In the realm of music, the name of Immanuel is associated with
a well-known distich included in his sixth *mahberet* (section). It is
a polemical debate regarding the merits of Spanish Provençal
and Italian Hebrew poetry. A 'fool', a pretentious Provençal poet
who claims the supremacy of Provençal poetry, is challenged by
Immanuel, who agrees to submit himself to a huge quiz in verse that
touches on various areas of knowledge. One of the questions is: 'What
says the science of music (*ḥokhmat ha-niggūn*) to the Christians?'
The answer is: 'It was stolen from the land of the Hebrews.'[83] This
statement, made by one of the pioneers of the growing Hebrew Italian
literature on music, offers views that conform to those of his Jewish
predecessors and those of Italian Jews who wrote about music in
the centuries that followed. As stated, Immanuel submits that Jubal
was the inventor of *ḥokhmat ha-niggūn*—meaning music and the
science of music. As a matter of fact, medieval Christian treatises
dealing with the question of the origin of music frequently discuss
Jubal's position as its inventor.[84] In the same spirit, Immanuel states
that art music reached its zenith as practised by the Levites in the
Temple. The deterioration of this magnificent art and its corrup-
tion by the Christians is due to the misuse of music in taverns and
as a vehicle for songs of sensuous passion. This opinion concords
with the harsh attack led by the Jewish Provençal scholar Ya'aqov
ben Abba-Meri on the music of the troubadours.[85] At the same
time Immanuel complains bitterly about the total absence of this
art among his contemporary co-religionists. A similar statement
was made by Immanuel's famous cousin, the rationalist philosopher Yehuda Romano, who was the Hebrew teacher of King Robert
II of Anjou (Naples and Avignon, 1309–43). Romano said that he
had to leave the Synagogue for some time because the worshippers
could not sing properly and would scream; as a result he was unable
to grasp the words of the prayers. He reports that he resumed
reciting the two important prayers *kaddish* and *kedushah* in public

[82] Amnon Shiloah, 'A Passage by Immanuel ha-Romi on the Science of Music', in *Italia* (Jerusalem, 1993), 9–18.

[83] Ibid. 9–10.

[84] See Judith Cohen, 'Jubal in the Middle Ages', *Yuval*, 3 (1974), 83–99.

[85] Cited by Hanoch Avenary, in 'Science of Music and the Jews of the 13th and 14th Centuries', in *Proceedings of the World Congress of Jewish Studies* (Jerusalem, 1973), iv. 5 (in Hebrew).
This commentary, which achieved great popularity, was published in 1487.

only after he had succeeded in imbuing them with philosophical content.[86]

An elaboration of this highly intellectual approach is found in a work by a later Jewish author—Ḥayyim ben Abraham ha-Cohen, a native of Jativa who was about 25 years old when exiled with his fellow Jews in 1492. In the section on music included in his essay on poetics, *Ez Ḥayyim*, the author claims that music is the tool that hones an individual's mind and helps him attain the highest goals. Thus the singing and playing of the Levites in the Temple was intended to prepare their minds for speculation, as befits those who fulfil sacred tasks, thereby proving that the objective of music is indeed to spur the listener to intellectual activity.[87]

The major portion of Immanuel's commentary consists of a passage borrowed textually from Falaquera's book *Reshit ḥokhmah* (The beginning of wisdom), which in itself is a Hebrew translation of *Iḥṣāʾ al-ʿulūm* (Enumeration of sciences) by the great Arab philosopher and music theorist al-Fārābī.

THE ROLE OF THE JEWS IN THE TRANSMISSION OF KNOWLEDGE

Immanuel's use of translated material should be viewed as part of the larger picture of intensive translation activity that began during the thirteenth century in Spain, Provence, Sicily, southern France, and Italy. The turning point is marked by the linguistic changeover of musical literature from Arabic to Hebrew, which corresponds to the increasing number of Jews in Christian Spain and the advent of a new approach favouring Hebrew as the language of studies. Advocated by the Spanish author Shem Tov ibn Falaquera (1225–95) in his two encyclopedic works, *Reshit ḥokhmah* and *ha-Mevaqqesh* (The seeker),[88] the Jews of Provence followed the same approach when they appointed Andalusian authors to translate scientific books into Hebrew. In this major centre of Jewish learning and literature, as well as among the Sicilian Jews under the Normans, Jews benefited from the rise of humanism in Europe and from endeavours to create a spiritual European culture independent of ecclesiastic dogma. Under these circumstances Jewish intellectuals who had a share in Latin, Italian, and

---

[86] Yehuda Romano, 'Introduction to Commentary on *Kaddish* and *Kedusha*', Cod. Vat. Hebr. no. 91, fos. 1ʳ–2ᵛ (quoted in G. Sermoneta, 'Prophecy in the Writings of R. Yehuda Romano', in *Studies in Medieval Jewish History and Literature*, ii (Cambridge, Mass., 1984), 351–2).

[87] Amnon Shiloah, 'La Musique entre le divin et le terrestre', *Anuario musical*, 38 (1983), 3–14.

[88] See Shiloah, *Jewish Musical Traditions*, 56–8.

Arabic culture became instrumental in bringing Arabic scientific works, including music, to Europe.

The two encyclopedic works, written in Hebrew by ibn Falaquera for educational purposes, present music in the framework of the quadrivium, and in both books he borrows the section on music from al-Fārābī's *Enumeration of Sciences*.[89] In its day, al-Fārābī's book, which lists and defines the nature of all then-known sciences, elicited the greatest respect. In addition to ibn Falaquera and Immanuel ha-Romi, the Jewish philosopher ibn ʿAqnin (*c*.1150–*c*.1220) incorporated a section on music in his ethical work *Ṭibb al-nufūs* (Hygiene of the soul).[90] Immanuel's friend the Provençal philosopher Kalonimos ben Kalonimos (1286–after 1328), who served King Robert II of Anjou as translator of scientific works, translated the *Iḥsaʾ* into Hebrew;[91] a poetic adaptation of it is included in the didactic poem *Miqdash meʿaṭ* (A little sanctuary) by Moses ben Isaac Rieti (1388–after 1460).[92] This work became known in medieval Europe through several Latin translations.[93]

The Canon on medicine of ibn Sina (Avicenna), which includes a paragraph on the relationship between pulse and music, was the object of three Hebrew translations and thirty commentaries: two of the latter concern the paragraph on music. One is by the physician Isaiah ben Isaac (fl. second half of the fourteenth century),[94] the second by Shem Tov ibn Shaprut (born some time in the middle of the fourteenth century).[95]

Two musical works that were translated from Arabic into Hebrew for the Jews of Provence are of particular interest: the first is still in manuscript and became known through its Hebrew version, while the Arabic original of the second has been lost. *Ādāb al-Falāsifa* (The sayings of philosophers) by Ḥunain ibn Isḥāq (808–73), the greatest translator from Greek and Syriac into Arabic, contains three chapters of aphorisms about music uttered at banquets dealing with music's ethical, cosmologic, and thera-

[89] Al-Fārābī, *Kitāb Iḥṣāʾ al-ʿulūm* (Classification or Enumeration of Sciences), ed. M. A. ʿUthmān (3rd printing, Cairo, 1968).

[90] See Adler, *Hebrew Writings*, 155–7.

[91] A. Shiloah, 'Qalonimos ben Qalonimos, Maʾamar be mis-par ha-hokhmot, tr. annotée du chapitre sur la musique', *Yuval*, 2 (1971), 25–38.

[92] See Adler, *Hebrew Writings*, 284–5.

[93] Henry George Farmer, *Al-Fārābī's Arabic–Latin Writings on Music* (Glasgow, 1934; repr. London, 1965).

[94] A. Shiloah, 'Two Commentaries on Avicenna's Section in the Canon Dealing with the Pulse', in *Proceedings of the Fifth World Congress of Jewish Studies* (Jerusalem, 1973), iv. 117–24 (in Hebrew).

[95] Id., '"Ên kol"—commentaire hébraïque par Šem Tov ibn Šaprût sur le Canon d'Avicenne', *Yuval*, 3 (1974), 267–87.

peutic power.[96] The Hebrew version, *Muserei ha-Filosofim*, was rendered by the Spanish poet Yehuda al-Ḥarizi (1170–1235).[97] The second work is an extensive Arabic treatise on music theory by the Andalusian philosopher and physician Umayya ibn abi 'l-Ṣalt, which essentially is no more than a skilful compilation based on al-Fārābī's Great Book on Music. This treatise, which has survived only in its Hebrew translation, was used by two aforementioned Jewish authors, Profiat Duran and Isaiah ben Isaac in his commentary on Avicenna's Canon. In an annotated publication of the text from a manuscript, Hanoch Avenary suggests ascribing the Hebrew version to a translator who worked for the Jews of Provence during the fourteenth century.[98] This manuscript constitutes the first part of a collection of texts on music contained in Paris, Bibliothèque Nationale de France, fonds hébreu 1037, dated in the second half of the fifteenth century or the beginning of the sixteenth. It is followed by an anonymous Latin treatise translated into Hebrew by Judah ben Isaac and an anonymous Hebrew translation of a fragment of an Italian treatise attributed to Marchetto of Padua. Both texts involve elementary treatises of *musica plana* and deal with the Guidonian hand, hexachords, mutations, and modes; the first also presents measurements of organ pipes.[99]

These texts, with the addition of an unknown music student's Hebrew notebook that refers to teachings of J. Vaillant (*c.*1400), and Levi ben Gershom's Latin treatise *De numeris harmonicis*, commissioned by Philippe de Vitry in 1343, belong to a new wave of Hebrew-language musical writings.[100] They mark the beginning of the exploitation of European sources and the increasing adoption of European music in practice, endeavours apparently connected with the proto-Renaissance movement fostered by King Robert d'Anjou.

---

[96] The musical aphorisms are included in chs. 18–20; see Shiloah, *The Theory of Music*, 134–5.

[97] English translation and commentary in E. Werner and I. Sonne, 'The Philosophy and Theory of Music in Judeo-Arabic Literature', *Hebrew Union College Annual*, 16–17 (Cincinnati, 1941–3), 225–32.

[98] H. Avenary, 'The Hebrew Version of abu'l-Ṣalt's Treatise on Music', *Yuval*, 3 (1974), 7–82.

[99] Israel Adler, 'Le Traité anonyme du manuscrit hébreu 1037 de la Bibliothèque Nationale de Paris', *Yuval*, 1 (1968), 1–47; id., 'Fragment hébraïque d'un traité attribué à Marchetto de Padoue', *Yuval*, 2 (1971), 1–10.

[100] See E. Werner, 'The Mathematical Foundation of Philippe de Vitry's Ars Nova', *JAMS* 9 (1956), 128–32 at 130.

II

LATE MEDIEVAL PLAINCHANT FOR THE DIVINE OFFICE

By Andrew Hughes

INTRODUCTION

FOR seven hundred years, from the ninth to the sixteenth century, church musicians all over Europe were composing and adapting plainsong for the services of the Roman Catholic Church. This chapter deals only with the offices. The following paragraphs review the services and the genres within them, summarizing, with a few additional details, the excellent account of the standard repertory and its liturgical setting to be found in the second volume of the revised *New Oxford History of Music*.[1] Rather than referring to, say, the third responsory of Matins, I shall use abbreviations established elsewhere.[2] Within the liturgical day, the relevant services are: First Vespers, Matins, Lauds, Prime, Terce, Sext, None, Second Vespers, and Compline.[3]

Services		*Genres*	
V	First Vespers	A	antiphon
M	Matins	R	responsory and V its verse
L	Lauds	I	invitatory antiphon
W	Second Vespers	E	Gospel antiphons (*ad Evangelium*) and the monastic canticle antiphon at Matins

I acknowledge the help, over the years, of Martha Parrott, Marcy Epstein, Diane Droste, and Peter Binkley.

Examples are set out thus. Small incises on the two lowest spaces of the stave mark textual divisions of the poetry, not always coinciding with convincing musical phrases. The latter, and sometimes other musical and textual motifs or phrases, are occasionally marked with brackets. Except where the significance is obvious, an explanation is provided. Translations are given with the example or in the subsequent text.

In the text, can. stands for canonized, tr. for translated.

[1] By Richard Crocker; NOHM ii[2], 118–33.

[2] Andrew Hughes, *Medieval Manuscripts for Mass and Office: A Guide to their Organization and Terminology* (Toronto, 1982; rev. paperback edn., 1995). The abbreviations listed on the inside covers have been modified slightly.

[3] Ibid., chs. 2 and 4, esp. pp. 117–20.

Gospel antiphons are those for the Magnificat, Benedictus, and Nunc dimittis.

Hymns, lessons, prayers, and dialogues also occur in the offices. Frequently, the hymns are not newly composed but are standard texts appropriate to the feast. But a huge repertory of hymns with new texts and chants originated in this period, and many must have been composed for the new offices, probably by the same musician-poets, and at the same time as the office. Although occasionally a new antiphon text is identical with a stanza of a hymn, various features make it clear that hymns were not regarded as a part of the office proper. Indeed, they were not accepted into Roman and secular use generally until the twelfth century. The account of hymns in the previous volume is adequate.[4] Proper hymns would have to be investigated in any specialized study. So would the lessons and prayers, which are often the source for the texts of the new chants. Only in rare cases are the dialogues of any musical importance, but the *Benedicamus Domino* versicle that concludes each service sometimes uses elaborate music related to a responsory melisma.[5]

Compline rarely has proper texts and chants, and the Little Hours (Prime, Terce, Sext, None) usually repeat antiphons 2–5 of Lauds; where necessary these services are abbreviated to their first letter, and the Little Hours to H. Two-letter abbreviations, sometimes with a numeral, represent service and genre, thus: LA3 signifies the third antiphon at Lauds, WE the Magnificat antiphon at Second Vespers. With considerable variation possible, secular and monastic offices are structured as in Table 2.1. Thus the former have some twenty-eight antiphons and about ten responsories, and the latter some thirty-two antiphons and more than a dozen responsories. Alternatives for ferias after the feast may be provided. Offices therefore have some fifty or sixty items sung to chant.

The elaborate nocturnal service of Matins is the heart of the feast. Betraying its origin in the historical and biographical lessons of Matins, the common term for offices, especially when newly composed, is *historia*.[6]

---

    [4] NOHM ii[2], 232–43.

    [5] Frank Ll. Harrison, *Music in Medieval Britain* (London, 1958), 7. See also Anne Walters Robertson, '*Benedicamus Domino*: The Unwritten Tradition', *JAMS* 41 (1988), 1–62.

    [6] See the references in Peter Wagner, *Einführung in die gregorianischen Melodien*, 3 vols. (Leipzig, 1911–21; repr. Hildesheim, 1962), 129–30 n. 2. The first volume, in which rhymed offices are discussed, is translated into English: *Introduction to the Gregorian Melodies*, i (2nd edn., 1907), trans. A. Orme and E. G. P. Wyatt, repr. with a new introduction by Richard Crocker (New York, 1985), 115.

TABLE 2.1 The structure of secular and monastic offices

Secular	
VA1(–5) VR VE	or V = AnRE[a]
MI MA1–3 MR1–3 MA4–6 MR4–6 MA7–9 MR7–9	or M = IA3R3.A3R3.
	A3R3 (or M = secular)
LA1–5 LE	or L = A5E
WA1(–5) WR WE	or W = AnRE

Monastic	
VA1(–4) VR VE	
MI MA1–6 MR1–4 MA7–12 MR5–8 ME MR9–12	or M = IA4R4.A4R4.
	ER4 (or M = monastic)
LA1–5 LE	
WA1(–4) WR WE	

A concise method similar to that on the right of this table will be used for purposes such as indicating the modal order.

[a] Where n is a numeral, or omitted.

THE CHURCH INSTITUTIONS

For new offices, the services and genres were conventional. So were the institutions in which they were performed and the choirs that sang them. But the increasing importance of grammar schools, collegiate churches, private chapels, and universities brought changes in the composition of choirs and the musical skills of their members. Schoolboys with higher ranges, for example, may have sung certain parts of the chants.

Confined to their cloisters, monks sang the monastic night offices, Matins and Lauds. Clerics not truly cloistered but living according to a rule (and thus called regular clergy) and clergy in aristocratic chapels followed a different—the secular—form of the office; they perhaps also performed the full round of services communally. But for the most part secular clergy probably sang only the day offices, reciting the nocturnal services privately. Itinerant friars living a life of poverty perhaps recited all services alone and entirely without music. But even the earliest Franciscan rule states that friars shall have the books necessary to perform the services:[7] Franciscan records tell us that offices were sung solemnly *cum nota* even if only three brothers were present.[8]

[7] *DMA*, under 'Franciscan rite'.

[8] The chronicler Eccleston, speaking of Cambridge in 1225, refers to three brothers, all named, one of whom was a lame novice who had to be carried around on a stretcher. Hilarin Felder, OP, *Histoire d'études dans l'ordre de saint François*, trans. Eusèbe de Bar-le-Duc (Paris, 1908), 447.

Furthermore, conventual divisions of itinerant Orders soon arose and by the end of the thirteenth century had become predominant.

THE NATURE OF THE INNOVATIONS

Few surprises occur in the services, the musical genres, or the performance methods. What ingredients then caused many generations of scholars to refer to late medieval chant as decadent or degenerate?[9]

Other than in genres such as tropes and sequences, the offices were the principal outlet for personal expression. In contrast to the sobriety, restraint, and generally unobtrusive nature of standard chant, technical artifice played a large part in the new compositions, often making them aurally (or visually) striking and thus disrupting.

Prose, the normal vehicle for standard plainchant, was rejected. From the literary point of view, conceits abound in the texts in the form of regular accent, rhyme, alliteration, acrostics, and puns. Occasionally the musical setting involved little more than trivial adaptation of stereotyped melodies of the conventional repertory. But generally these too were rejected. Continuity of the musical style lies in the motif or the modal formula. Normally there was real creative activity, a process of real composition, or 'placing together' of new words with both old and new plainsong motifs to create a chant distinctly new in style yet whose ancestry is easily recognizable. The most obvious musical innovations in the chant, then, concern the amount and kind of ornamentation of chant formulas, the manner in which they are linked together, and the range.

Musically and poetically, the new repertory fully displays this common kind of medieval creative activity. For most of the era of written music before the Counter-Reformation, musicians all over Europe were continuously active in composing chant. It was thus, as Crocker says, 'the normal musical expression of the time'.[10] Composers and poets gave their most continuous and sustained creative effort throughout the later Middle Ages to the composition of plainsong.

GENERAL OVERVIEW

The seven centuries from c.850 to c.1550 correspond to 'the Frankish-Roman' era outlined by Richard Crocker in Volume II of this history,

---

[9] Fr Dominique Delalande, OP, *Le Graduel des Prêcheurs: vers la version authentique du Graduel grégorien* (Bibliothèque d'histoire dominicaine, 2; Paris, 1949), 121, etc. See also Robert B. Haller, 'Early Dominican Mass Chants: A Witness to Thirteenth-Century Chant Style' (Ph.D. diss., Catholic University of America, 1986).

[10] NOHM ii², 283.

'lasting until the reforms of the Counter-Reformation at the end of the sixteenth century'.[11] Unfortunately, this categorization suggests a static musical culture of little interest except as a background to and source of tenors or texts for part-music. And we can still read: 'The choirbooks . . . were relatively uniform in their contents and readings, the culmination of the efforts of leading churchmen from Pope Gregory the Great on to realize conformity in the liturgy and its musical setting.'[12] This statement refers to books of about 1100: a treatise of about 1148, on the other hand, says:

Granted that [antiphonaries] are almost all alike in having defects; yet in the areas in which they could reasonably agree, they are so inconsistent with each other that not even two provinces sing the same antiphonary. It must, therefore, seem remarkable just why the false versions and the defective ones have greater authority and more widespread acceptance than the true and sound ones. Just to mention a group of churches in the same province: take the antiphonary of Rheims and compare it with that of Beauvais or Amiens or Soissons, which [Rheims] has almost at its door; if you find any similarity, thank God.[13]

The period is one of extraordinarily diverse activity. It is also one of almost continuous reform. But neither the earlier reforms of Gregory, or those of Charlemagne, the Cistercians, Dominicans, or Franciscans, brought about complete conformity in the liturgy and its musical setting.[14] Although more successful than earlier attempts, even

---

[11] Ibid., ch. 4, 'Liturgical Materials of Roman Chant', 115.

[12] *Hucbald, Guido, and John on Music: Three Medieval Treatises*, trans. Warren Babb, ed. Claude V. Palisca (Music Theory Translation Series, 3; New Haven, 1978), 87.

[13] *Epistola S. Bernardi: De revisione cantus Cisterciensis* and *Tractatus scriptus ab auctore incerto Cisterciense: Cantum quem Cisterciensis ordinis ecclesiae cantare*, ed. Francis J. Guentner, SJ (CSM 24; American Institute of Musicology, 1974), 59 (trans. emended, R.S.). This passage relates to the Cistercian reforms to be described below. The Latin is on p. 40: 'Licet enim in vitiis omnia fere conveniant, in quibus tamen rationabiliter convenire possent adeo disconveniunt, ut idem antiphonarium nec duae canant provinciae. Mirum proinde videri potest quare maioris fuerint auctoritatis atque communioris notitiae, falsa quam vera, vitiosa quam sana. Ut enim de comprovincialibus loquar ecclesiis, sume Remense antiphonarium, et confer illud Belvacensi vel Ambianensi, seu Suessionensi antiphonario, quod quasi ad ianuam habet; si identitatem inveneris, age Deo gratias.' See pp. 14–19 with respect to the word *habet*.

[14] Ralph of Tongres says that by the time of Nicholas III (1277–80) all antiphonals, graduals, missals, etc., that were not Franciscan had been suppressed at Rome. Franciscan chant and its notation had been introduced in all churches and it was said that the only chant sung was in the manner of the Franciscans. The statement is cited in Felder, *Histoire*, 450 n. 3: 'Nicolaus III . . . fecit in ecclesiis urbis amoveri antiphonarios, gradualia, missalia et alios libros officii antiquos quinquaginta, et mandavit, ut de caetero ecclesiae urbis uterentur libris et breviariis Fratrum Minorum . . . , unde hodie in Roma omnes libri sunt novi et Franciscani et forma notularum in cantu antiqua, qua tam Ambrosiani quam Alemaniae nationes utuntur . . . , ab urbe relegata.' Ralph of Tongres, *De canonum observantia liber*, propositio 22, in *Maxima bibliotheca patrum*, xxvi (Lyon, 1677), 314.

the reforms of the Council of Trent, aided by the widespread use of printing, were not fully able to achieve uniformity.

In fact, although we are only beginning to examine details, we can observe quite different styles of poetry and chant emerging over time and by geography. Tentatively, we may identify these sub-periods: (i) Carolingian or Roman-Frankish, 850–950, (ii) post-Carolingian or Romanesque, 950–1150, overlapping with (iii) the era of poetry, 1100–1580. Within the last, we need to distinguish an era of new Orders and Uses, 1100–1250. Eventually, we may be able to isolate a period in the fifteenth century when there are signs of a revival of classical metres and possibly new musical styles.

But unlike part-music and secular monophony, where newer styles displaced older ones and can to some extent be analysed independently, the plainsong repertory must be regarded as a whole. The oldest style, the Carolingian, remained in daily use. Some of the oldest offices of the newer styles remained in use until the Counter-Reformation. Some were still in use in the eighteenth century. A few still survive. Presumably many more, for which the evidence has disappeared, were similarly long-lived. Their chants were sometimes, many centuries later, adapted to texts in a style different from that of the original composition. It is therefore essential thoroughly to review the whole period, including centuries before those with which this volume is concerned.

CAROLINGIAN AND ROMANESQUE OFFICES, 850–1150

For the first two sub-periods, the repertory consists of the texts and chants transmitted by manuscripts collated in the *Corpus Antiphonalium Officii* (*CAO*), confirmed and refined by the earliest tonaries. In these sources are 'the texts and repertory of antiphons and responsories as they were actually used in the period 850–1100'.[15] *CAO* gives only the texts.[16] Since it gives no chants, and many of its sources transmit them in a notation that is not specific as to pitch, few scholars know much of this repertory. We can see, however, that it contains two layers. The characteristics of the earlier layer—essentially the Roman-Frankish archetype—will emerge in contrast to the later layer.

Continuing the Carolingian activities of editing, classifying, and organizing, the later layer shows signs of more systematic organiza-

---

[15] Crocker, in NOHM ii², 117.

[16] The word chant is often used, loosely, to refer to the text of items that are sung. I think it mandatory to reserve the original significance of *cantus* for the musical setting, with or without its text.

tion: on the basis of a small sample, nearly a third of the texts in *CAO* have some sort of literary structure other than prose. Because the chants are still unspecific as to pitch, we can only suppose that the musical formulas are similarly more structured,[17] but, as Crocker has shown,[18] we can ascertain that the modes are often in numerical order. Although Ritva Jonsson discussed the origins and styles of many offices of this period in her book *Historia*,[19] the repertory has still to be analysed thoroughly, taking into account the characteristics of both texts and chants.

The Carolingian and post-Carolingian period, transmitting both the archetype and the layer of more structured additions, ends about 1100. The texts and chants, especially those of the archetype, survive in active performance through the next eras, which take us to the Counter-Reformation. But most of our knowledge of plainsong, if it does not stem from nineteenth-century editions quite far removed from medieval realities and aesthetics, depends on sources heavily reformed and edited in the twelfth and early thirteenth centuries. This period of reform follows, and no doubt was the result of, the establishment of pitch-specific notation on the stave.

TWELFTH- AND THIRTEENTH-CENTURY REFORMS:
THE ERA OF NEW ORDERS AND USES: 1100–1250

We know little of the changes that took place in the twelfth and thirteenth centuries. Part of the difficulty is our lack of detailed knowledge of the earlier corpus: comparisons are hard and we cannot precisely describe the differences.

In England, for example, little survives of the Anglo-Saxon liturgy and chant, said to represent an ancient layer of Roman use brought by St Augustine of Canterbury. After the Norman Conquest of 1066, partly through the efforts of Osmund, the Norman bishop of Salisbury in the late eleventh century, a new Use evolved in the twelfth. Although Continental influence is obvious, its origins are unclear. But by the thirteenth century this Sarum Use (of Salisbury) was established as the main rite of England. One senses that the Use was carefully organized. What kinds of musical activity were involved cannot yet be stated.

---

[17] An initial attempt to present some literary and musical features in more detail is in my 'Literary Transformation in Post-Carolingian Saints' Offices: Using all the Evidence', in Sandro Sticca (ed.), *Saints: Studies in Hagiography* (Medieval and Renaissance Texts and Studies, 141; Binghamton, 1996), 23–50.

[18] 'Matins Antiphons at St Denis', *JAMS* 39 (1986), 441–90.

[19] *Historia: Études sur la genèse des offices versifiés* (Acta Universitatis Stockholmiensis, Studia Latina Stockholmiensis, 15; Stockholm, 1968).

Soon after the foundation of the Cistercian Order about 1098, a reform of plainsong for the Order was undertaken. Examination of contemporary material, especially a treatise beginning *Cantum quem*, indicates that by about 1148 supposed barbarisms of chant were removed.[20] Confusion between plagal and authentic modes was eliminated, excesses of range were condemned and corrected, and unnecessary accidentals were avoided by transposition, so that modal prescriptions were more closely obeyed. Elaborate melismas, motivic repetitions, and notational sophistications were excised. The reformers recognized the anti-traditional nature of the result: 'we have been compelled in contrast to the use of all the churches to correct this antiphonary . . . If we are criticized for making the work unique and different from all other antiphonaries, we have this consolation—that reason made ours different . . .'.[21]

The reformers largely eliminated features that make later chant distinctive. In fact, although *Cantum quem* was surely concerned, at least primarily, with the texts and chants of the standard repertory, it could just as easily refer to newly composed chants. We may perhaps infer that the 'new' chant of the later twelfth century, and from the thirteenth to sixteenth, rather than being innovative, merely continued styles already well established. Without the reforms undertaken in the twelfth century and, as we shall see, in the thirteenth, most chant that survived as the 'standard' repertory might have been in the style so often dismissed as decadent and debased.

The Cistercians desired uniformity and authenticity. Similarly, after the establishment in the early thirteenth century of the Dominican Order, intended at first for itinerant preachers, new chant-books for the Order were compiled. A study of the early Dominican gradual reveals that its music was heavily influenced by the Cistercian prac-

---

[20] The Cistercian reforms are also described in detail in Delalande, *Le Graduel des Prêcheurs*, 29 ff. and elsewhere. St Bernard's letter describing the need for the reforms and how they were brought about, and the treatise *Cantum quem* itself, are published in Latin and translation, edited by Guentner (see above, n. 13). Modern scholars, presumably on the basis of medieval evidence now lost, attribute this treatise to Gui, abbot of Cherlieu. Another contemporary treatise dealing with the same issue ends with the words *Regulae domni Guidonis abbatis de arte musica*. Surviving medieval evidence points to Gui d'Eu as its author. It now seems likely that the two are identical (the latter name being the author's place of origin, used prior to his elevation). The reform and the resulting antiphonal are therefore nowadays attributed to Gui, abbot of Cherlieu.

[21] *Epistola S. Bernardi*, ed. Guentner, 59. The Latin is on p. 40: 'contra usum omnium ecclesiarum antiphonarium hoc corrigere coacti sumus . . . Si ergo opus singulare et ab omnibus antiphonariis diversum fecisse reprehendimur, id nobis restat solatii quod nostrum ab aliis ratio fecit diversum . . .'.

tices just described, but that these were applied in a less doctrinaire fashion and with much concern for returning to the traditional chant.[22] As with Sarum chant, an examination of the complete Dominican office-chant repertory results in an impression of tidiness, and of conformity and regularity that suggests a thorough editing process. 'Compilation', in fact, is a word associated with the beginnings of the Dominican liturgy.[23] Conformity—certainly sought by the Order—was eventually to a new mid-thirteenth-century prototype known as Humbert's Codex (see Pl. I), prepared accurately and carefully so that texts and chants, checked against it, would be uniform in every Dominican house.[24] Instructions to Dominican scribes were quite explicit.[25] Uniformity of ceremonial, ritual, text, and chant, although mandated to some extent by doctrine, was equally a practical matter: itinerant friars could expect to be able to participate in services in Dominican houses anywhere.

The chants of the Franciscan Order, also founded in the early thirteenth century and at first intended for itinerant friars, were similarly uniform,[26] and the close relationship between the Order and the papal curia brought about reforms of the liturgy of the latter so that Franciscan and Roman Use were henceforth almost indistinguishable.[27]

Despite these important moves towards a universal rite and ceremony, including chant, in other Orders and institutions an immense variety of practice and text and chant remained normal. The later importance of the Roman rite, made authoritative and widespread by printing in the late fifteenth century, has overshadowed this extraordinary variety. Even though the Use of Sarum was widespread, for example, in England and on the Continent,[28] even within England other

---

[22] Delalande, *Le Graduel des Prêcheurs*, studies only the Temporale of the Gradual. It is only an assumption that the same features apply to the Sanctorale and to the Antiphonal.

[23] Ibid. 3, 10.

[24] For Humbert's Codex see Leonard E. Boyle, 'Dominican Lectionaries and Leo of Ostia's *Translatio S. Clementis*', *Archivum Fratrum Praedicatorum*, 28 (1958), 362–94, and *MGG* under 'Dominikaner'. Recent research on the book as a result of the conference *Liturgie, musique et culture au milieu du XIIIᵉ siècle: Autour du Ms. Rome Santa Sabina XIV.L1, prototype de la liturgie dominicaine* (Rome, March 1995) is to be published. My own extensive work on chants of the Antiphonal of the Codex is unpublished.

[25] Michel Huglo, 'Règlement du XIIIᵉ siècle pour la transcription des livres notés', in Martin Ruhnke (ed.), *Festschrift Bruno Stäblein zum 70. Geburtstag* (Kassel, 1967), 121–33.

[26] *MGG* under 'Franziskaner'.

[27] Stephen J. P. Van Dijk (with Joan Hazelden Walker), *The Origins of the Modern Roman Liturgy* (London, 1960) and *Sources of the Modern Roman Liturgy* (Leiden, 1963).

[28] Terence Bailey, *The Processions of Sarum and the Western Church* (Studies and Texts, 21; Toronto, 1971), pp. ix–x.

secular Uses, those of York, and Hereford, and monastic and other regular Uses, were different in ways that have yet to be described.

Cistercian, Sarum, Dominican, Franciscan, and other Uses of the thirteenth century consist fundamentally of the archetypal, or Carolingian, repertory. To at least the Dominican and Franciscan Uses substantial additions were made from the thirteenth century up to the Counter-Reformation. Even while the reforms or clarifications were being carried out, new offices, texts, and chants were being composed, increasingly often in the newer styles.

THE ERA OF POETRY: 1100 TO 1580

Poets and composers continued writing prose offices, and texts with other kinds of structure like those of the Carolingian repertory. An accounting of these has yet to be made. But predominantly from the twelfth century, composition is characterized by new texts in strictly classical or accentual metres, with regular rhyme involving two syllables, and by new chants that are phrased to conform closely with modal requirements. Flourishing from 1100 to the 1580s, the rhymed repertory is the main focus here. The date 1300, a convenient turning point in polyphony from *ars antiqua* to *ars nova*, is of no significance for this body of texts and chants, which develops clearly and steadily from roots laid down well before the twelfth century.

Words such as metre, accent, and rhythm are horrendously difficult to define and must be used carefully. Ambiguities can lead to misleading interpretations, especially for musicians unfamiliar with poetic terminology.[29] The poetry of the new kind is either qualitative (i.e. in classical metres) or accentual. Foreign words meaning metrical or accentual, *ritmico, rhythmische, rythmique*, carry no implications of rhythm in the generally accepted musical sense.

These poetic types recur: (a) iambic dimeters—lines of eight syllables, more or less regularly accented; (b) Victorine sequence stanzas with lines of eight and seven syllables in arrangements such as 887 887 (typically rhymed aab ccb) or 8787; (c) goliardic stanzas with lines of seven and six syllables, similarly arranged.

Texts of the rhymed repertory, to the extent that it was known in the late nineteenth century, were published in some ten volumes of the monumental *Analecta hymnica*.[30] A comprehensive index

---

[29] The terminological habits of numerous scholars, literary and musical, past and present, must be carefully assessed: in the literary and musical worlds, for example, rhythmic and metrical are sometimes used with almost completely exchanged meanings. See Hughes, 'Literary Transformation'.

[30] Henceforth identified by volume and the number of the office or page, thus *AH* 5, no. 25 or *AH* 13, p. 97.

of incipits has recently been published.[31] A complete electronic word concordance of the repertory known at the time of writing is available.[32]

Despite the availability of these tools, few scholars are investigating this repertory of poetic chant. A few hundred chants have been studied of the scores of thousands still extant in thousands of manuscripts. As a consequence, generalizations are risky. The examples used here, often chosen arbitrarily because they were available and transcribable, may not be typical. Caution is necessary with any study claiming typical or atypical qualities for its data. We simply do not yet know.[33] This chapter is based on knowledge of some 4–5,000 chants, a mere tenth of the estimated extant repertory. What remains must be a mere fraction of what existed. The geographical and chronological scope dwarfs that of other repertories, of whatever period.

Most offices were for local feasts and saints, probably authorized at first by the local bishop. Although the forms themselves had not been changed drastically, the additions became so numerous that they tended to overwhelm and to obscure the principal purpose of Christian worship, the veneration of God and his Son. Eventually, especially in response to the Reformation, papal authority was asserted and a more or less universal Kalendar of feasts established. As with earlier reforms of liturgy and chant, the ostensible aim was to make ritual, ceremony, and music universal for the whole of the Christian world and to remove excesses of text and music. About 1582, along with other monophonic sacred repertories of the period, such as tropes and sequences, the Council of Trent removed most traces of this vibrant, varied, and flourishing style of composition. Only for a few institutions and Uses were exceptions made, such as the Ambrosian rite in Milan, and some of the regular Orders: the Benedictines, Franciscans, and Dominicans were allowed to keep some special texts, chants, and feasts, especially those of their founders.

RELICS AND CANONIZATION

Two factors of the later Middle Ages caused the profusion of new feasts: the protection of existing relics, and the creation of new ones. The first factor was the frequency of invasions, when relics and shrines

---

[31] *AH Register.*

[32] Andrew Hughes, *Late Medieval Liturgical Offices: Texts* (Subsidia mediaevalia, 23; Toronto, 1993). (Hereafter *LMLO.*)

[33] A good deal of what follows, unless it is otherwise documented, is based on personal research, much as yet unpublished.

were robbed and destroyed. Apart from their religious significance, these were often a valuable source of income, especially from pilgrims seeking miracles. To protect their spiritual and economic investments, then, local communities, when forewarned of danger, hid or moved their treasures. In the former case, the recovering or rediscovery of relics required a new feast, the Invention. In the latter case, or when relics were moved for rebuilding or repair of the church, a ceremony known as a Translation was required.

The second factor, the creation of new relics, was important all over Europe. New saints were honoured or old ones promoted, with new texts and chants, and a day of the church year was set aside for their veneration. This day was the main feast-day. Probably in an attempt to authorize the additions and to keep track of the church Kalendar, the process of canonization was instituted in the twelfth century. This was a long and complicated affair that could last many years and required documented proof of the saint's life and miracles in a form that was akin to that of a historical biography. Such *Vitae* are sometimes our only source of information. In order to bolster the case for canonization, and perhaps to create pressure by demonstrating that a cult was already being practised, the new texts (and perhaps also chants) for the services might have been included in the documentation. Certainly, in many cases local churches celebrated new feasts before they were authorized by Rome.

Many relics and local saints were invented in the modern sense of the word, creating for us the difficulty of distinguishing real from fictional inspiration for a new feast. That is a problem for the church historian: for the musician there seems to be no difference in the kinds of text and chant.

THE NEW FEASTS

Not all new translations, inventions, and feast-days were concerned with saints, however. Some were to venerate relics other than people or body parts. Nicholas of Clairvaux, in the twelfth century, wrote a complete office for the Holy Cross.[34] A shroud in the Cistercian monastery of Cadouin, alleged to be that of Jesus (but not the Turin shroud), was the object of an office found in manuscripts of that abbey and preserved in a printed edition of the early sixteenth century.[35] In

---

[34] I thank Calvin Bower for drawing my attention to this office and others by Nicholas: they are in the British Library, MS Harley 3073.

[35] Solange Corbin, 'Le Fonds manuscrit de Cadouin', *Bulletin de la Société historique et archéologique du Périgord*, supplément, 81 (1954), 1–7.

the thirteenth century Louis IX of France, himself later canonized and the object of an office, had the Holy Crown of Thorns brought—translated—from the Holy Land by the Dominicans, and built the Sainte-Chapelle to house it. An appropriate office resulted.[36]

Other feasts were to honour various occasions connected with the Blessed Virgin, and several important new Marian feasts were established in this period. A few feasts were of the Temporale—new offices for Trinity Sunday and Corpus Christi, for example, and a feast for the Transfiguration.

Slightly fewer than a hundred feasts formed the Sanctorale of the Carolingian repertory.[37] By the sixteenth century, there is scarcely a single day of the year, other than the major feasts of the Temporale, that does not have one and sometimes several saints' celebrations. Indiscriminately putting together all the different saints for whom offices are known, some 800 feasts result, about 100 in October alone. It would not be possible to compile a full list. Some 1,300 fully rhymed offices, including different ones for the same saint, have been identified.

Many of the rubrics or reports that mention offices imply and sometimes state that both text and chant were composed by the churchman mentioned, who is often named as the author of such other documents as the saint's *Vita*. Usually it seems safe to assume that poet and composer are the same.[38] The processes of composition seem little different from those used by many later musicians, and that term will be used. But perhaps implying some lessening of interest in this compositional style as the Middle Ages wane, later offices of the rhymed repertory are sometimes substantially modelled on earlier ones, using identical poetic metres, and thus perhaps also the same chants almost without modification.

MODELS AND EVOLUTION OF THE GENRE

The use of models goes to the heart of the musical vocabulary and creativity of the later chant style. We will be able to understand the nature of chant composition better after a great deal more analysis has been carried out, particularly of earlier offices in which the new styles may have had their genesis. In the fully rhymed repertory, composition is occasionally reduced to minor adaptation.

---

[36] Douglas Karl Kirk, '*Translatione corona spinea*: A Musical and Textual Analysis of a Thirteenth-Century Rhymed Office' (Ph.D. diss., University of Texas, 1980).

[37] NOHM ii², 119.

[38] It is not possible here to cite and argue complex evidence: on the basis of the facts available, the judgements below seem secure.

Numerous records of the process are to be found in chronicles and in other medieval documents. The word *composuit* is used frequently, perhaps meaning simply that text and chant, or individual words and motifs, were placed together. In the absence of common and standard metres, a good deal of adaptation might well be necessary. This could have taken place, most likely, in one of two ways.

On the one hand, whole melodies might retain their general configuration. Several melody-types for both antiphons and responsories were in common use in the standard repertory. Although using such models is clearly one conventional way of producing new items, how far these tunes are used for new offices in general is really not known. They seem to be little used in rhymed offices proper.

On the other hand, a new item might be compiled from individual chant motifs adjusted in very minor ways to suit new words, reused in varying orders, and mixed with linking motifs that may be more or less original. This process seems to underlie most composition in this genre. It is akin to centonization. In the most interesting and innovative offices, the linking motifs are the most characteristic part of the music, occasionally overwhelming the conventional motifs so that the aesthetic nature of standard chant often seems far removed. It is possibly these processes of adjusting and modifying formulas and recombining them with original and up-to-date musical idioms to which writers refer when they use terms such as *edidit*.

Occasionally, a specific musical term such as *neumatizavit* is used. As with all medieval terminology, we probably cannot expect consistency of meaning to attach to particular terms, nor to be able to ascertain exactly what was meant in individual cases.

The melody-types and conventional formulas of the common chants of the Roman-Frankish archetype, together with some influence of Gallican chant, were the most likely models for the new chants of the Carolingian era. In the same way, they and the new chants were probably the models for the chants of the earliest structured offices, and perhaps even for new offices much later in the era. In any case, in order fully to understand late office chant we must try to seek its origins.

Although Martin Gerbert (d. 1793) made some comments about the later repertory and listed prominent examples,[39] Abbé Lebeuf, about the same time, was the first writer in modern times to attempt some historical perspective.[40] Peter Wagner, early in the last century,

---

[39] *De cantu et musica sacra* (St Blasien, 1774).
[40] *Traité historique et pratique sur le chant ecclésiastique* (Paris, 1741; repr. Geneva, 1972), 15–54 and elsewhere.

included a substantial chapter on rhymed offices, with some stylistic observations, in his book on plainsong.[41] More recently David Hiley, in his splendidly compendious survey of Western plainsong, briefly revisited the repertory,[42] with a further section on metre, accent, and rhyme in late medieval chant.[43]

Numerous other scholars in the past decade have edited and researched individual offices. But until the extent and significance of late chant in general is better known, we shall remain ignorant of (to repeat) 'the normal musical expression of the time'. Here, then, reminding the reader of many compositions already recognized by Lebeuf, Wagner, and Hiley, it will be useful to give a brief account of a few early offices that are possibly of considerable importance. It is not yet possible to link these into coherent schools or to trace patterns of influence or development. Two factors are involved: the importance for liturgy and plainsong of the composer or of the location where the office was composed; or the longevity and wide distribution of the new office. For most of those mentioned, the chant is extant, although not necessarily from a source contemporary with the origin.

NEW COMPOSITIONS: 850–1150

Many of the texts of the compositions referred to in the next paragraphs are to be found in the manuscripts inventoried in *CAO*.

Lower Lorraine

The best-known offices in this category are the three by Stephen of Liège, d. *c*.920. His offices for St Lambert and for St Stephen remained local but were in use probably at least until the thirteenth century. In the former, some responsories have terminal melismas of the 'detachable, formularized' kind referred to by the Carolingian liturgist Amalarius (*c*.830), and representing 'a late stage of development'.[44]

Such extensions do not occur in Stephen's most important office. The texts and chants of his office for Trinity Sunday found a permanent place in the church books, although in a few places they were replaced for a time by newer compositions. Its full title should be *Gloria tibi*

---

[41] Wagner, *Einführung* or *Introduction*, i, ch. 15: a good deal of the account consists of lists of composers and offices, repeating those of Lebeuf and Gerbert.

[42] David Hiley, *Western Plainchant: A Handbook* (Oxford, 1993), 273–9.

[43] Ibid. 280–6. See also Margot Fassler, 'Accent, Meter, and Rhythm in Medieval Treatises "De rithmis"', *Journal of Musicology*, 5 (1987), 164–90.

[44] NOHM ii², 245; the Latin citations are in Wagner, i. 134–5; Eng. trans. 119–20.

Trinitas / *Benedicat nos Deus* / *O beata et benedicta.*[45] Without further comment, Gerbert acknowledged the different quality of this office.[46] Many subtle instances of threefold emphasis in both texts and chants occur,[47] features of a kind not to be expected in traditional chant settings. Its opening text and chant are full of potential for the later, completely accentual and regular repertory (see Ex. 2.1).

Ex. 2.1. Office for Trinity Sunday: VA (First Vespers antiphon) *Gloria tibi trinitas* (Glory to you, o Trinity and one equal God)

Divorced from its text and considered as a normal plainsong phrase, this melody rises to the reciting-note ornamented with the minor third above and extended by a cadential formula: this analysis, shown below the stave, involves a phrase articulated, if at all, in unequal parts. It might be a phrase from the standard repertory. The text, however, involves two lines: accentual iambic dimeters, not yet completely regular, but exactly balanced in length, and rhymed. The text, then, and the musical rhyme that corresponds to the textual rhyme, and the nature of the second part of the tune as a modified transposition of the first, force a completely balanced structure onto an otherwise prose-like melody. This analysis is shown above the stave. But was the composer conscious of the poetic structure, not found widely elsewhere in this office? Was a prose text intended, and the balanced and rhymed couplet merely an accident? Was the

---

[45] Offices should be referred to by three incipits: of the first item, MR1, and LA1. Despite contrary assertions, it is not a medieval custom to name offices by their first item: it is simply too variable. Because of its variability, it may be better to omit it altogether and retain only the incipit of MR1 (which medieval writers usually use) and LA1, items that are extremely stable. To omit it, however, would be to omit the name by which many offices have become known. To indicate the poetic metre, I try to give the whole of the first poetic line, but this sometimes results in cumbersome length. I have nevertheless tried always to give an incipit sufficiently long for adaptations of it in later descendants to be recognizable.

[46] *De cantu*, ii. 40: 'In officio Sanctae Trinitatis Stephani Leodiensis magis apparet, quam in ullo alio, mutatio gustus.' But in his edition and discussion, Antoine Auda thinks the melodies are close to a traditional style: *L'École musicale liégeoise au Xe siècle: Étienne de Liége* (Brussels, 1923), 111. See Hiley, *Western Plainchant*, 274.

[47] I thank Jennifer Griesbach for this observation. See also the recent article by Gunilla Björkvall and Andreas Haug, 'Text und Musik im Trinitätsoffizium Stephans von Lüttich', in Walter Berschin and David Hiley (eds.), *Die Offizien des Mittelalters: Dichtung und Musik* (Regensburger Studien zur Musikgeschichte, 1; Tutzing, 1999), 1–24.

ambiguity perhaps deliberate? Was the musical influence more important than the textual? In any case, perhaps because the implications for musical rhyme and balance were recognized, phrase x itself
becomes a formulaic motif. In various guises, it will recur in subsequent examples.

Stephen's offices deserve a thorough literary, liturgical, and musical
study. Recently, such a study has been accomplished for the works of
Hucbald of Saint-Amand.[48] A twelfth-century writer tells us that this
music theorist and hagiographer, c.850–930, among other things
wrote the melody of antiphons for St Andrew, 'composuit de sancto
Andrea modulamen antiphonarum'[49] and the offices for saints Cilinia,
Theodoric, and Peter. The last was widely distributed in northern
France and northern Italy and forms a part of the Sarum and Dominican liturgies. Citing publications of the 1890s, the editor of *AH* assigns
to Hucbald the composition of an office for St Rictrude, and suggests
that he might also have been responsible for offices to Maurontus and
Eusebia:[50] all were venerated at the Abbey of Marchiennes, near Saint-
Amand, and their offices survive in manuscripts for Marchiennes into
at least the late sixteenth century.

Difficulties and uncertainties surround almost every aspect of the
repertory: as with Hucbald, surviving reports and manuscripts with
the offices may have originated several centuries after the author's
death; evidence collected and cited in the late nineteenth century is
hard and sometimes impossible to confirm, many sources having been
destroyed in the World Wars.

France

Fulbert of Chartres, d. 1028, wrote hymns and offices for the Nativity of the Blessed Virgin, and for local saints Lubin, Eman, Cheron,
Giles, Laumer, and Piat.[51] Some are prose. Some are in classical metres,
including the important Marian compositions, two of which (*Solem
iusticie* and *Stirps Iesse*) survived to this century with other texts
(*Calix benedictionis* and *Comedetis carnes*) in the modern office for
Corpus Christi. The responsory *Stirps Iesse* was also the source of an
important tenor in thirteenth-century motets, *flos filius eius*.

---

[48] Yves Chartier, *DMA*, s.v. 'Hucbald', and *L'Œuvre musicale d'Hucbald de Saint-Amand: les
compositions et le traité de musique* (Cahiers d'études médiévales: Cahiers spécial, 5; Montreal,
1995).
[49] Rembert Weakland, OSB, 'The Compositions of Hucbald', *Études grégoriennes*, 3 (1959),
155–63 at 156.
[50] *AH* 13, pp. 135 and 227.
[51] Yves Delaporte, 'Fulbert de Chartres et l'école chartraine de chant liturgique au XIe siècle',
Etudes grégoriennes, 2 (1957), 51–81. All of this activity is dismissed in three words by the author
of the article in *DMA*.

Upper Lorraine

At about the same time in Alsace-Lorraine, Bruno of Toul (1002–54), later Pope Leo IX, was associated with numerous offices.[52] Madeleine Bernard attempts to draw Stephen of Liège's and Fulbert's work into comparison with other offices of the period, trying to show their possible influence on Bruno.[53] Unfortunately, her musical and textual analysis relies on assumptions and speculations, and is implicitly pejorative.

With respect to Bruno's authorship, there are some difficulties. Bernard alludes to the possibility that in order to bring greater prestige, authors occasionally falsely attributed their work to more famous men: who would confer more authority than a pope? In this case, however, there seems little doubt that Bruno, before he became pope in 1049, was responsible for at least the musical parts of offices for Hidulphus (1039), Ciriacus (1049), Odilia, patron of Alsace, and Gregory (1042–52), and according to later writers also for offices for Gorgonius (1049), Columbanus, and Deodatus, and perhaps also for Nicholas. Humbert, a man of letters and a poet, may have been responsible for the texts. But Bruno was later praised as *musicus insignis*. The issue, then, is whether (a) Humbert wrote only the *vita* and the lessons, not sung, and Bruno composed the texts and chants of the antiphons and responsories, or (b) Humbert wrote all the texts, in which case Bruno was responsible only for the chants of the sung items. The saints are mostly associated with local abbeys, as abbots or founders. Nevertheless, the surviving offices (if they are indeed copies of Bruno's compositions) are predominantly secular in form. For several a possible date of composition (given in parentheses above) can be suggested from our knowledge of dedications and translations. The office to Hidulph, abbot of the monastery of Moyenmoutier, was still used in the eighteenth century.[54]

Bruno's office for Gregory, *Gloriosa sanctissimi / Fulgebat in venerando / Gregorius vigiliis*, was extremely important and widespread. An early version in twelfth-century Aquitanian heighted neumes appears in many later sources.[55] The extremely complex net-

---

[52] Because of difficulties in attribution, in many cases it may be appropriately cautious to use the phrase 'associated with' rather than 'composed or written by'. Madeleine Bernard puts the issues with respect to Bruno very well; 'Les Offices versifiés attribués à Léon IX (1002–1054)', *Etudes grégoriennes*, 19 (1980), 89–164.

[53] Ibid.

[54] Ibid. 91.

[55] Ibid. 99 and in Bernard, 'Un recueil inédit du xiie siècle et la copie aquitaine de l'office de saint Grégoire', *Etudes grégoriennes*, 16 (1977), 145–59.

work of relationships and borrowings in many of the important sources of the Romanesque period and later, involving a special version with different chants for England,[56] has yet to be investigated. But the version attributed to Bruno was the nucleus (essentially the responsories of Matins) used in most parts of Europe. Stylistically, the chants seem much like those of the standard repertory. This unobtrusive quality may be the reason for its survival and wide use.

Its texts are in accentual iambic dimeters, except for the invitatory, which is a classical hexameter. This arrangement is frequent in Bruno's offices. Musically, too, its chants are unexceptional. Antiphons are relatively simple, rarely exceeding two or three notes per syllable, or the conventional modal range. Responsories are much more elaborate, with noteworthy melismas: these long melodic extensions are all terminal and involve sequential motifs (see below, Ex. 2.4). The chants are essentially in modal order, Lauds beginning with mode 2.[57] Some follow a predictable melodic shape, using formulas that are quickly recognizable. Other than the presence of melismas, a few other hints of later compositional practices can be observed. Three antiphons and the first responsory have points of interest.

The openings of VE, MA1, and MA9, in mode 1, are similar, rising from the final to the reciting-note, followed by a higher phrase (see Ex. 2.2). This opening is so common as to be a 'melody-type'.[58] Yet VE and MA9, alike in both phrases, are different from MA1. They are perhaps distinct sub-types. The responsory, MR1, is constructed, phrase by phrase, from formulas already identified. But in a manner typical of late offices (and even more typical later in the Middle Ages), to this process the composer adds a subtle alignment of formula and emphasis of the text (see Ex. 2.3). First, each simple formula as seen in the antiphons is elaborated with ornaments; second, a wider vocabulary of formulas is used, phrases x and y from both 'melody-types' of the antiphons being concatenated; third, once the reciting-note is reached, the formula x, which in Ex. 2.2(b) seemed like an excursion

[56] Andrew Hughes, 'British Rhymed Offices: A Catalogue and Commentary', in Susan Rankin and David Hiley (eds.), *Music in the Medieval English Liturgy: Plainsong and Medieval Music Society Centenary Essays* (Oxford, 1993), 239–84. David Hiley has recently discussed this version in 'The English Benedictine Version of the Historia Sancti Gregorii and the Date of the "Winchester Troper" (Cambridge, Corpus Christi College, 473)', *International Musicological Society Study Group Cantus Planus: Papers Read at the Seventh Meeting, Sopron, 1995*, ed. László Dobszay (Budapest, 1998), 287–303. He discusses the main office and transcribes a responsory and antiphon in *Western Plainchant*, 275–6.

[57] Andrew Hughes, 'Modal Order and Disorder in the Rhymed Office', *Musica disciplina*, 37 (1983), 29–52.

[58] Cf. Crocker, NOHM ii², Exs. 50 and 51.

Ex. 2.2. Office for St Gregory: (*a*) VE (First Vespers, Magnificat antiphon) *Gloriosa sanctissimi* (The glorious solemnities of most holy Gregory); (*b*) MA1 (Matins, first antiphon) *Gregorius ortus Rome* (Gregory, born of Rome and the blood of senators); (*c*) MA9 (Matins, ninth antiphon) *Qui solebat in sericis* (He who was accustomed to walk in silks . . . in divine things)

Ex. 2.3. Office for St Gregory: MR (Matins responsory) *Fulgebat in venerando* and verse 'Beatus vir'

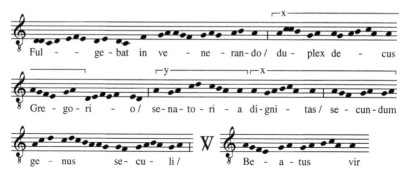

into the higher range, here seems more like merely an ornamental extension of the reciting-note, as in Ex. 2.1. Furthermore, this motif, *x*, sets only part of a line rather than a complete line of text, as in the antiphons, and is continued by a descending line. Only then does the higher tetrachord appear, with the two formulas, *y* and *x*, setting one line of text and part of the next. The distribution of formula with respect to text is always worth noting carefully. On hearing the reciting-note, emphasized with an ornamental extension, we anticipate the upper tetrachord, an expectation set up in the antiphons and of course in the general melodic type. Why does Bruno choose to descend again?

Judging by the more frequent occurrence of this feature in the later repertory (and its appearance in the standard repertory much more frequently than is generally admitted), the reason has to do with the text. Here, there is a reinforcement of both the general syntax and a particular word. In the first two lines, the constituents are split up, so that the subject is separated from its verb, and the noun from its adjective: 'a twofold nature shines in the venerable Gregory'.[59] Sometimes, as here, the word order is used in conjunction with the chant to lend emphasis. The phrase *Fulgebat in venerando* rises a fifth and is balanced by and linked to *Gregorio* by the descending fifth. The unexpected return to the final also emphasizes the saint's name; another link is provided between the name and the word *Beatus* which begins the verse.

The 'word-painting' or 'emphasis' is subtle, but typical. In the Gregory office only one other example seems significant: the word *clarus*, in MA7, is set to the highest pitch in the office. One of the most elaborate melismas sets the word *glorie* (see Ex. 2.4). Such enhancing and linking of important words by musical means characterizes much of the later repertory.

Ex. 2.4. Office for St Gregory: MR7 (Matins, seventh reponsory) *Sanctus papa Gregorius*

England

In England, too, a number of early offices were important enough to survive the Norman Conquest and the resulting purge of Anglo-Saxon saints unfamiliar to the invaders.[60] A substantial part of an apparently elaborate office to Birinus, bishop of Dorchester-on-

---

[59] Gregory's twofold nature is his character as a patrician and as a voluntary pauper. Such allusions as this, common in hagiographical and other medieval literature, are often very obscure.

[60] For all English offices in this chapter, see Hughes, 'British Rhymed Offices'.

Thames, survives with its music, but no post-Conquest source is known.[61] More important for the later Middle Ages are the offices to Cuthbert and Alban.

The former composition was written by a clerk of the Low Countries for King Athelstan in the 930s and its obvious poetic structure makes it one of the very earliest rhymed offices known. By adding several items distinct in poetic and musical style, the Normans transformed it from a secular into a monastic office, perhaps for the translation of the saint to the Norman monastic cathedral of Durham in 1104. The chant survives only in post-Conquest manuscripts, so we cannot be certain whether the music for the texts that were in the tenth-century version is Anglo-Saxon in origin.

The very important office for Alban, the protomartyr of England, was written by an abbot of St Albans, either Leofric (after 995) or (perhaps less likely) Aelfric (early eleventh century). It exists in a manuscript with Anglo-Saxon neumes *in campo aperto* and thus virtually untranscribable,[62] but five chants can be recovered from later books and two others may be in common with the Cuthbert office just described. Its use as a model for several later saints, especially in Scandinavia, may eventually enable us to reconstruct more chants. The loss of the music in this case is particularly unfortunate since the tenors of several polyphonic pieces of the later Middle Ages—Dunstaple's fifteenth-century *Albanus roseo rutilat* for example—are drawn from the office.

The office to Edmund, king and martyr, also provides texts and chants for later offices, and for fourteenth-century English isorhythmic motets.[63] The immediate source of the texts dates from before 987, but the office itself, including a complete monastic Vigil preceding the main feast, was probably associated with the foundation of Bury St Edmund's Abbey in 1020. Its largely structured but irregular texts, extremely long and elaborate, were complemented by a Norman abbot with regularly accentual antiphons.

Probably in 1091, Goscelin, the renowned precentor of St Augustine's Abbey, Canterbury, wrote the texts and chants for the monastic office to Mildred, a local saint. Only the VE is written in fully accentual verse: other texts are rhymed and structured but irregular. This

---

[61] Drew K. Hartzell, 'A St. Alban's Miscellany in New York', *Mittellateinisches Jahrbuch*, 10 (1975), 20–61.

[62] Ibid.

[63] Rodney M. Thomson, 'The Music for the Office of St Edmund King and Martyr', *Music and Letters*, 65 (1984), 189–93; Manfred Bukofzer, 'Two Fourteenth-Century Motets on St Edmund', in *Studies in Medieval and Renaissance Music* (New York, 1950), 17–33.

office is important because it is the earliest known insular source with such clear notation on what is really a true stave.[64]

No account of late office chant would be complete without some allusion to the four offices by Radulphus Niger (d. *c*.1217).[65] They are secular offices for the four major feasts of the Blessed Virgin. The texts and chants are by Ralph, and are prose: they thus offer us a good opportunity to compare new chants for prose with those written for poetry at about the same time.

Swabia

Similar activity was taking place in other areas of Europe well known for the cultivation of music theory and the production of musical books. As we know from Berthold's almost contemporary life of Hermannus Contractus of Reichenau (d. 1054), that musician, well known as a theorist, *neumatizavit et composuit* several offices, of which five are named. One of them, his office to St Afra, remained in use at Augsburg (and surely the region) at least until the fifteenth century and still exists in numerous sources.[66] Although similar documentary evidence is lacking, there seems no reason to doubt that Hermann's contemporary at Reichenau, Berno (d. 1048), wrote at least an office to Ulrich, and another to Meinrad, translated in 1039 to Reichenau (and later to Einsiedeln). The former was copied, if not in use, in the eighteenth century,[67] and the latter is found in a manuscript known to have been written in the early fourteenth century.[68]

Summary

Perhaps a score of other composers, mostly of single offices and associated with the north of France, were active in the tenth and early eleventh century. Only one need be cited, because of the following interesting statement: with respect to the office for Julian of Le Mans,

---

[64] Andrew Hughes, 'Word Painting in a 12th-Century Office', in Bryan Gillingham and Paul Merkley (eds.), *Beyond the Moon: Festschrift Luther Dittmer* (Musicological Studies, 53; Ottawa, 1990), 16–27. See also Richard Sharpe, 'Words and Music by Goscelin of Canterbury', *EM* 19 (1991), 93–7, and 'Goscelin's St. Augustine and St. Mildreth', *Journal of Theological Studies*, NS 41 (1990), 502–16.

[65] G. B. Flahiff, 'Ralph Niger', *Mediaeval Studies*, 2 (1940), 104–26.

[66] Hans Oesch, *Berno und Hermann von Reichenau als Musiktheoretiker* (Publikationen der Schweizerischen Musikforschenden Gesellschaft, ser. 2, 9; Berne, 1961), 153–5. See also *MGG*, s.v. 'Hermannus', and Ruth Steiner, 'Gruppen von Antiphonen zur Matutin des Afra-Offiziums', in Walter Berschin and David Hiley (eds.), *Die Offizien des Mittelalters: Dichtung und Musik* (Regensburger Studien zur Musikgeschichte, 1; Tutzing, 1999).

[67] Oesch, *Berno und Hermann von Reichenau*, 81, maintains that it was copied from an 11th-c. book, St Gallen MS 898. This copy could of course have been made by one of the historians, such as Martin Gerbert, who had begun to interest themselves in medieval theory and chant.

[68] Einsiedeln MS 111, written under the abbacy of John of Schwanden at Einsiedeln. Oesch, ibid. 82.

composed by Letaldus of Micy at the end of the tenth century, another writer says:

and in composing the office for St Julian he did not want to abandon the likeness of old chant, lest he fabricate barbarous and inexpert melody; for, he said, I am not pleased by the novelty of certain musicians, who use such strangeness that they fail in every way to follow the old authors.[69]

Much work has to be done in order to understand comments of this kind, to confirm the nature of the activity of these writers, and to find out whether similar activity was taking place in areas of Europe less well documented. Most noticeably absent from the geography of early offices is Italy. The apparent lack of interest in the genre continues into the later Middle Ages and was observed by Ralph, Dean of Tongres, as late as the second half of the fourteenth century:

All nations have *historiae* of the Temporale that conform to the Roman antiphonal. And *historiae* of the Sanctorale, or saints' days, in Italian churches conform to Rome because [the Italians] admit few proper saints. But Gallican, English, and especially German churches allow many more proper saints' offices. But as for the Roman antiphonal, it is normal that in different nations and churches there occur differences in the order of responsories and verses. For they have neither similar verses in common, nor does the same order of responsories and antiphons serve everywhere.[70]

Some features common to most of these offices are obvious. First, the authors are often known (although many early English examples are anonymous). Naming the compilers of offices will continue to be a common feature. Secondly, nearly all offices, except those by Stephen of Liège, Fulbert of Chartres, and Bruno of Toul, are monastic.

---

[69] Cited from Lebeuf in Wagner, i. 314 n. 4, and in the recent translation, 272, n. 4: 'Porro in componendo S. Juliani officio excedere noluit a similitudine veteris cantus, ne barbaram aut inexpertem melodiam fingeret; non enim mihi placet, ait ille, quorundam musicorum novitas qui tanta dissimilitudine utuntur, ut veteres sequi omnino dedignentur auctores.' See also David Hiley, 'The *Historia* of St. Julian of Le Mans by Létald of Micy: Some Comments and Questions about a North French Office of the Early Eleventh Century', in Margot E. Fassler and Rebecca A. Baltzer (eds.), *The Divine Office in the Latin Middle Ages: Methodology and Source Studies, Regional Developments, Hagiography* (New York, 2000), 444–62.

[70] Cited in Wagner, i. 301 n. 1 (cf. 78, where Ralph's century is mentioned) but not in the recent translation: 'Omnes nationes satis uniformiter habent historias temporales sive de tempore, Antiphonario romano concordantes. Sed de sanctis sive de diebus sanctorum Italianae ecclesiae romano magis se conformant, quia proprias historias sanctorum minime admittunt. Deinde ecclesiae gallicanae, deinde anglicanae, postremo alemannicae ecclesiae ad historias sanctorum proprias magis se dilataverunt. Sed quoad Antiphonarium romanum, hoc sustinendum est, quod in ordine Responsoriorum et in versibus eorundem occurrunt saepe ad diversas nationes et ecclesias varietates. Nam nec similes versus communiter habentur, nec idem ordo responsoriorum et antiphonarum ubique servatur.' Ralph of Tongres, *De canonum observantia liber*, propositio 12, in *Maxima bibliotheca patrum*, xxvi, 299 ff.

Emphasizing the nature of Matins and Lauds as the essential monastic services, items other than the Gospel antiphons are rarely provided for the other services. Thirdly, a great many involve texts that consist predominantly of iambic dimeters. The rhyme schemes are frequently quite irregular, using primarily assonance or monosyllabic rhymes with only a single consonant in common. Invitatories often use classical hexameters. Several offices, especially those of the twelfth century, use rhyming hexameters (leonines) throughout.

Musically, it is often clear from various clues that the chants were in modal order.[71] Otherwise, the chants generally seem more like those of the so-called standard prose repertory, less structured than those setting regularly poetic texts. This prose-like character may be more apparent than real:[72] we need to evolve methods of careful analysis, designed to suit the repertory and concerned to show both obvious and obscure relationships between the text and chant.

Geographically, the repertory is cultivated over most of northern Europe, by dozens of composers. But most offices are local. A few persisted for centuries in the establishment or region that inspired them: these may have influenced late composers of the area. But longevity and wide distribution are probably of more significance for the genre as a whole. The offices for Trinity and Gregory clearly qualify as the most important.

THE TWELFTH AND THIRTEENTH CENTURIES

By the twelfth century, regularly accentual poetry is the norm, and several offices with such texts occur in manuscripts assigned to this time.[73] By the thirteenth century, fully rhymed offices, often stereotyped in poetic form, are common. Undoubtedly, the foundation of the new Orders encouraged the new popularity and regularity of the genre, and the frequency with which later offices are contrafacts of earlier ones.

In a contrafact, the music most securely establishes the relationship of an adaptation to its model. In most cases, without having comprehensive analyses available, scholars have predicated the use of models on identity of poetic form, together with other pointers such as the ecclesiastical Order of the saint, making no attempt to consider the chant. Although a poetic analysis of all known surviving offices has

---

[71] See e.g. Weakland's article on Hucbald, 158–9.
[72] See Hughes, 'Literary Transformation'.
[73] See ibid.

now been completed,[74] making it possible to trace every literary echo, judging by the texts alone is not adequate. So few poetic schemes were in use that identity of the poetic forms alone is not a reliable indication that offices are related. Furthermore, poetic schemes sometimes differ in offices whose relationship is established definitely by other means (see the discussion of David, below). Only a substantial identity in the chants, with or without identity of the poetic scheme, can settle the issue.

Transcription and comparison of the chants has not progressed to a stage where comprehensive lists of models and dependants can be constructed. Eventually, analysis of the relationship of one office to another will perhaps allow us to trace the descent and dissemination of offices, and it will become possible to write a stylistic or evolutionary history.

Prior to the thirteenth century it seemed appropriate to deal primarily with composers, since a number of them composed many offices. Secondarily this led to geography as an important issue, and to major centres of cultivation well known in other musical respects.

Henceforth, composers seem mostly to be responsible for only one or two offices. But regional geography is still quite important. A brief examination of manuscripts of the later repertory corroborates Ralph of Tongres' statement: German (and Austrian) books are full of rhymed offices; French and English books a little less so; Italian (and Spanish) books often have only one or two, perhaps a really important universal office, plus an office to the local patron saint.[75] Local geography is also important: poets and composers worked in the principal centres of learning such as cathedral cities and monasteries, and were in communication with other centres. Interestingly, in Paris, a centre noteworthy in many musical respects, rhymed liturgical material was uncommon, although composition of other kinds of offices continued.[76] Discriminating later offices on the basis of geography, chronology, and style may be possible, once a sufficient number of reliable transcriptions is available. More than a thousand offices are available for analysis.

But whatever the importance of individual composers, geography,

---

[74] It is included with the electronic word-concordance in *LMLO*.

[75] The appearances, however, may be misleading: unlike elsewhere in Europe, where antiphonals and breviaries abound, Italian and Spanish books are primarily the huge *corali*, almost none of which has been properly inventoried, and many of which are difficult even to investigate. Although some may date from the 13th c., *corali* are often from quite late in the period, being a product essentially of the early Renaissance.

[76] Craig Wright, *Music and Ceremony at Notre Dame of Paris, 500–1550* (Cambridge Studies in Music; New York, 1989), 123, 358.

chronology, or style, the grouping of offices primarily by ecclesiastical order or use must now have priority. Marian offices form an independent group.

Later Franciscan and Dominican feasts often use the chants and sometimes the poetic schemes of the offices to their founder saints. The efforts of those Orders to establish uniformity and a centralized authority make it necessary to ask in these cases why many later offices did not use the model. Benedictine houses were more independent. An office to St Benedict was widespread in Germanic countries, but at the moment it is known to have served as a model for only a few later Benedictine saints. It also appears in a few Cistercian books. But the Cistercians in general, as might be expected from their preference for austerity, generally shunned these elaborate forms of celebration. Carthusians used none. The Carmelite liturgy included several rhymed offices, some of them unique. Like Benedictine houses, Carmelite priories were to some extent independent,[77] sometimes using different settings for the same office. For other Orders, in particular Augustinians, numerous offices are known, but we cannot yet state whether later compositions are modelled on earlier ones. To complicate the issue, the Dominicans largely adopted Augustinian practice, and the Carmelites largely took over Dominican Use.

Within these Orders, the importance or validity of a composition could be enhanced by referring it to the authority of an established model, following the common medieval reverence for *auctoritas*. Most later offices were important to the Order wherever it existed, or were of universal importance within the Church. Conversely, other than within the local diocese, secular uses had no wider network within which this system of homage or memorial could operate. Saints and feasts celebrated universally had their own traditional texts that were replaced with new ones only for very special reasons: with the exception of Marian feasts, new celebrations not associated with a monastery or an Order were likely to be performed only within the church or diocese of their origin. In these cases, it will undoubtedly be difficult to find models and lines of influence. Nevertheless, a few local saints were so important that their celebrations were adopted more or less universally and their offices often served as models: of these, Thomas of Canterbury is the most prominent.

Important, then, are these offices:

---

[77] James Boyce, O.Carm., 'Cantica Carmelitana: The Chants of the Carmelite Office' (Ph.D. diss., New York University, 1984), 33. Boyce transcribes the Carmelite offices.

Monastic:

1. For the Conception of the Blessed Virgin Mary, *Gaude mater ecclesia / Fulget die hodierna / Conceptus hodierna Marie*;
2. for St Benedict, *Preclarum late / Florem mundi / Armis precinctus*;
3. for Thomas of Canterbury, *Pastor cesus in gregis medio / Studens livor / Granum cadit*.

Secular:

The office for Thomas of Canterbury, adapted for Sarum use. The identification of other important secular offices must await further research.

Regular:

4. For St Francis of Assisi, *Franciscus vir catholicus / Franciscus ut in publicum / Sanctus Franciscus*;
5. for St Dominic, *Gaude felix parens Hispania / Mundum vocans / Adest dies*.

These offices may serve to establish the styles and compositional techniques likely to occur, and what criteria must inform analysis of the chants. Details of doctrinal, liturgical, allegorical, and symbolic matters in the text and its sources must be glossed over. Unfortunately, apart from a brief allusion by Solange Corbin with respect to 1 and 5,[78] the sources of these and similar germinal offices in earlier ones or in standard chant have yet to be explored, and none of the musical settings has been published in a complete and reliable edition. Musical examples derive, therefore, mostly from offices for which no published material exists.

Office for the Conception of the Blessed Virgin

Gaude mater ecclesia / Fulget die hodierna / Conceptus hodierna Marie is first known in an early twelfth-century source, now fragmentary, from the Lyon area. Anselm of Canterbury, a passionate devotee of the Conception and until recently thought to be the author of a tract on it, was exiled near Lyon around 1100: in 1106 Pope Pascal II, while dedicating a local abbey, consecrated an altar to the Virgin and gave relics.[79]

The texts are mostly regular as to poetry, predominantly using accentual dimeters, with some classical lines and a few Victorine sequence stanzas. The chants are moderately elaborate, antiphons using many puncta, and responsories few melismas. Conventional chant formulas are obvious. Nothing very distinctive can be identified. This feature may

---

[78] Solange Corbin, 'L'Office en vers *Gaude mater ecclesia* pour la conception de la vierge', in *Congresso internazionale di musica sacra, Roma 1950*, ed. Iginio Anglès (Tournai, 1952), 284–6.

[79] *AH* 5, no. 12; see Corbin, 'L'Office en vers', and Bernard, 'Un recueil', 151–2 and 160.

have made the style sufficiently like that of standard chant for the office to have been widely acceptable. It is distributed throughout the later Middle Ages. Some items were used as polyphonic tenors.

Although no direct descendants can yet be identified, its great popularity demands its inclusion. Veneration for the Virgin was an important feature of the twelfth century: furthermore, from its foundation in the early thirteenth century, the Carmelite Order was greatly devoted to the Virgin and several important Marian feasts have rhymed offices unique to the order.[80]

About a dozen other offices for the Conception seem to date from the fourteenth and fifteenth centuries and have yet to be investigated.

Office for St Benedict

Preclarum late / Florem mundi / Armis precinctus has its earliest source in a manuscript said to date from 1180.[81] According to the editors of *AH*, several manuscripts describe the office as *historia nova*: it presumably therefore replaced an earlier office.[82] A source said to be of the fifteenth century directs the user to 'seek the new office . . . at the end of the book',[83] indicating that another (the earlier?) office was still in use in that century. The 'new' one is known in numerous manuscripts from southern Germany, Austria, and Switzerland till the sixteenth century, and was used (textually, at least) as the model for several later Benedictine saints.[84] A few secular adaptations are preserved. Most versions, including some in Cistercian books, are monastic in form.

The poetry presents intriguing questions that cannot be addressed here, and uses a surprising variety of classical metres. We need to ask whether the chant is similarly varied to suit the texts. Modally, the chants are in numerical order, and even the monastic items beyond the eighth are largely so:[85]

$$V = 1234.1$$
$$MA = 4.123456.781456.1 \quad MR = 1264.5678.1236$$
$$L = 23456.7$$
$$W = .1$$

---

[80] Boyce, 'Cantica Carmelitana', describes these offices and identifies borrowings.

[81] *AH* 25, no. 52. In the absence of explicit evidence within the book, dating liturgical manuscripts by paleographical means is likely to be quite inaccurate (see my *LMLO: Sources and Chants*, §§310–19).

[82] Where and why older offices were replaced is one of the intriguing questions that remain to be addressed.

[83] 'novam historiam de sancto benedicto quere post cantica in fine libri', *AH* 25, no. 52.

[84] For the office to Benedict's sister Scholastica, however, only the sixth MR and MV are common.

[85] In this scheme, antiphons and responsories of Matins are kept separate, and sections of services, e.g. Gospel antiphons, invitatory, and nocturns, are separated by a dot. The

Interestingly, Lauds begins with mode 2, which seems more suitable for a secular format.[86] Why the third responsory of Matins is modally incorrect is not clear. Observing the order of the modes (in the manuscripts from which the transcription was made) shows that, in *AH*, VA3 and VA4 are reversed: examination of the texts alone would not reveal such an error.[87]

Musically, the office is quite interesting. In the antiphons the underlying motifs of conventional plainsong are often evident. At the very beginning, however, VA1 displays characteristics typical of many rhymed office chants (see Ex. 2.5).

The literary characteristics of this poem are typically sophisticated. The syntax is contorted by the demands of metre and rhyme, but the parallelism of the lines, which helps to ascertain the meaning, is extraordinarily clever:

Preclarum	late	tibi vir	sine fine	beate
nomen	non ficte	fidei	manet	o Benedicte

The two leonines, broken at the caesura, are set as four musical phrases. The first phrase begins with an incipit standard for antiphons in mode 1,[88] and its failure to rise above the F brings a hint of the plagal mode. The authentic range is strongly asserted in the following phrase, with its opening leap of a fifth, rising to the seventh.

Ex. 2.5. Office for St Benedict: VA1 (First Vespers, first antiphon) *Preclarum late* (For you, o man of faith, o blessed Benedict, your distinguished name endures without end, far and wide, unfeigned)

transcription is from Würzburg, University Library MS M.p.th.f.130, fos. 182ʳ–189ʳ and Munich, Bayerische Staatsbibliothek MS 7381, fos. 155ʳ–162ᵛ.

[86] Andrew Hughes 'Modal Order'.

[87] Another common error in *AH* is the confusion of repetendum with verse: the former is never marked explicitly, as it should be. In this office, the repetendum of MR9 is transcribed as the verse, and the latter omitted. Using a source with the chant would enable editors to avoid this kind of elementary error.

[88] Antiphon incipits are called *variationes*. See the Sarum tonary edited by Walter Howard Frere in *The Use of Sarum*, 2 vols. (Cambridge 1898–1901; repr. 1969), ii, App., pp. i–lxxiv: this intonation is the sixteenth *variatio* of mode 1, p. viii.

Musically, this phrase could end with the word *fine*, with its standard cadence to the reciting-note, and where the phrase would tend to balance the first. Because of the uneven parts of the hexameter, and emphasizing the textual and musical rhyme with *late* and the word *beate* itself, phrase 2 is extended with a somewhat abrupt drop to the range of the final. This looks like two standard phrases of an antiphon in mode 1 artificially extended to fit a hexameter. Phrase 3, in the upper tetrachord, also uses a standard formula, and again with a dislocation: the formula ends at *fidei*, on the reciting-note, whereas the textual caesura is after *ficte*. Phrase 4 incorporates a rapid descent, rather more dramatic than is normal in conventional chant, from the B♭ to the C below the final. This resting place, common at this point in a chant, in this case sets off the invocation to the saint. Is this chant an instance of a conventional chant, with more or less balanced phrases, adapted for the unbalanced hexameter?

The antiphons of Lauds seem more elaborate than those of Matins, with conventional motifs still perceptible beneath the ornaments (see Ex. 2.6). The pun on the saint's name and the word 'blessed' for the antiphon to the Benedictus is of course deliberate.

In the responsories, on the other hand, it is hard to see the skeletal structures, and there seem fewer conventional gestures. Most responsories have a short terminal melisma, sometimes with sequential motifs. Particularly in these chants, the range is extended, and the amount of decoration considerable (cf. Ex. 2.7). Were it not for the contemporaneous extravagantly soaring liturgical compositions by the Benedictine abbess Hildegard of Bingen (1098–1179), very

Ex. 2.6. Office for St Benedict: LE (Lauds, Benedictus antiphon) *Benedictus es Domine* (Blessed are you, o Lord, who, while you confer the joys of heaven on the soul of Benedict, glorify his limbs on earth: since through you the virtue of Benedict shone forth from the cave in which he was hidden)

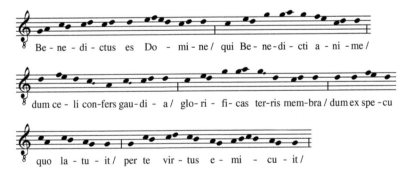

Ex. 2.7. Office for St Benedict: MR7 (Matins, seventh responsory) *O Isra-
helita* (A true Israelite, having extended his heart into God, who saw every
creature circumscribed within himself, (V) seeing the holy soul of the brother
to have been carried to heaven)

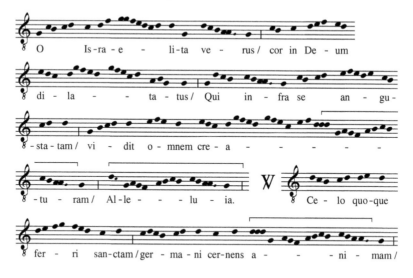

similar in style, the earliest date suggested (1180) might be difficult
to accept.[89]

Many items have a terminal *alleluia* because the celebration may fall
within Eastertime. Sometimes the chant for this (optional) word is
bound to the responsory and its terminal melisma, and occasionally
to the responsory verse as well, creating a formal structure of motivic
repeats unlike anything normally seen in conventional chant (see Ex.
2.7). With this and the next example, in order fully to understand what
the text means, no doubt we shall have to examine the life of the saint,
and commentaries on his works. As in this case, the verse usually has
no resemblance to the responsory tone.

The Vespers antiphons all have the refrain *o Benedicte*, set differently each time (compare the setting of the name Apollonia, below).
In MR5, the repetendum begins in the middle of a poetic line, requiring the chant at that point to make a musically satisfactory link with

---

[89] In view of Hildegard's stature as probably the most prolific composer in the Middle Ages
and the earliest well-known composer of superb music in Europe, and as a woman, she deserves
more than the two paragraphs devoted to her in NOHM ii[2]. Her compositions are mainly concerned with texts for new saints, principally setting the genres of the offices. Whether her works
were intended for use in the liturgy is perhaps open to question. The musical relationship with
contemporary office composition needs much further exploration.

the end of the verse. As in many offices, the name of the saint is often set to a motif incorporating the highest note of the chant, as in the VE and LE. Hints of musical emphasis of other words could be ignored as the wishful thinking of one too steeped in ideas of word-painting, if it were not for the appearance of this feature, more or less obviously, once or twice in most offices. Plenty of turbulent musical descents occur in this office, especially in melismas: one descent of a somewhat different kind surely cannot be ignored. The musical setting of LA5, with its short five-syllable Adonic lines, is predominantly one note to a syllable, steady within the line, halting at the intrusive cadence with repeated notes that terminates each musical phrase. Towards the end of this context is the smoothly melismatic, directed, and flowing setting of the word *flumina*, 'rivers' (see Pl. II and Ex. 2.8):

Huic iubilate   quo pater iste   par fit Elie
par quoque Moysi   dum lapis illi
flumina fundit   corvus obaudit.

This item, like so many others, informs us about matters of pronunciation and text-setting: for the metre, *huic* and *Moysi* must have one syllable and two syllables respectively, yet in the musical setting two and three neumes are provided. Musical setting often does not respect the metrical demands of the poetry.

Ex. 2.8. Office for St Benedict: LA2 (= PA) (Lauds, second antiphon = Prime, antiphon) *Huic iubilate* (Rejoice in him, by whom this father is made the equal of Elijah and Moses: while the stone yields him rivers, the raven obeys him)

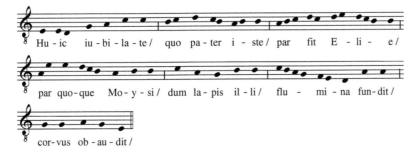

Main Office to Thomas of Canterbury

Pastor cesus / Studens livor / Granum cadit and its chants were written by the Benedictine Abbot Benedict of Peterborough, probably about 1173;[90] although monastic in origin, the same office was very quickly adapted for secular (Sarum) use, perhaps as early as 1174. It was vastly popular largely because of the importance of the saint himself and the widespread nature and fervour of his cult, and served as a model for dozens of other saints, both monastic and secular. Even the offices to Francis and Dominic, to be described, seem to borrow a few of its textual motifs.[91] The use of both texts and chants in part-music from the thirteenth to sixteenth century has been described elsewhere,[92] and the several publications that deal substantially with this office make it necessary only to summarize its important characteristics.

Its chants seem somewhat more neutral to the meaning of the words than in some other offices. Only the melismatic setting of the words *aer*, 'air', in the upper (authentic) tetrachord of a plagal chant, and of *maria*, 'sea', in the same responsory seem noteworthy.[93] But the relation between word and chant in other respects is quite distinctive. Especially in the more elaborate chants—responsories, for example—there is a distinct correlation between the accented syllable of a word and the number of pitches in its musical setting. As Stäblein observed, stressed syllables tend to receive several pitches, unstressed syllables only one.[94]

The phrase structure is clear, in both text and music, and dislocations between standard motifs and poetic lines, such as those observed in the Benedict office, do not occur. This is partly, perhaps, because longer phrase-length motifs are replaced by formulas setting individual words. As Stäblein also observed, important words are set predominantly to motifs that are neatly modal, beginning and ending on important pitches, usually the final or reciting-note. Taking this observation a stage further, I coined the concept of the *chantword*, that is, the concatenation of a particular word of text with (codes representing) the musical pitches to which it is set: *dominus.1.5.3*, for example,

---

[90] Andrew Hughes, 'Chants in the Rhymed Office of St Thomas of Canterbury', *EM* 16 (1988), 185–202; see also Bruno Stäblein, *Schriftbild der einstimmigen Musik* (Musikgeschichte in Bildern, 3/iv; Leipzig, 1975), 162 ff.; John Stevens, *Words and Music in the Middle Ages: Song, Narrative, Dance and Drama, 1050–1350* (Cambridge Studies in Music; Cambridge, 1986), 252; and *Matins, Lauds, and Vespers for St David's Day*, ed. Owain T. Edwards (Cambridge, 1990), 160–1.

[91] Andrew Hughes, 'Echoes and Allusions: Sources of the Office for St Dominic', paper delivered at the Conference on *Liturgie, musique et culture au milieu du XIIIᵉ siècle. Autour du Ms. Rome Santa Sabina XIV.L.1, prototype de la liturgie dominicaine*, Rome, March 1995 (to be published).

[92] Denis Stevens, 'Music in Honor of St. Thomas of Canterbury', *MQ* 56 (1970), 311–48, and Heinrich Husmann, 'Zur Überlieferung der Thomas-Offizien', in *Organicae Voces: Festschrift Joseph Smits van Waesberghe* (Amsterdam, 1963), 87–8.

[93] Hughes, 'Chants in the Rhymed Office', Ex. 7.

[94] See *Schriftbild*, 53, 58–9, 65, 72, 103, 162–5. See the antiphon and responsory transcribed and discussed by Hiley in *Western Plainchant*, pp. 278–9.

signifies this word sung to the final, fifth, and third of the mode in question. Applying this concept to standard chant as well as to later material has facilitated a great many interesting discoveries with respect to the relation between chant and text, and makes more feasible the comparison of chants as a whole.[95]

In the case of this office, since chantwords are modally defined within themselves, the chants as a whole are easy to adapt: the melodies can be broken into phrases of different lengths with a reasonable assurance that each will end appropriately within the mode. The use of chantwords (or discrete phrases) seems a more promising method of establishing relationships between offices than does the comparison of whole melodies.

We are familiar with the concept of melody-types in standard chant, and the adaptation of melodies to create new ones. But based on a small amount of data, provided by the Thomas office, and on unsystematic recollection of many other offices, I would assert that, except for the short responsories of Vespers and Lauds, not often included as Proper items, the usual melody-types are infrequently the basis for new chants.

In his monograph on the rhymed office for St David, Owain Edwards found the source of many antiphons and responsories of that office in the Thomas office and in the standard liturgy, and dealt at some length with the problems of adaptation.[96] In place of the goliardic metre or lines of 4 + 6 syllables that characterize the Thomas office, for example, the poet of the David office uses a variety of metres. Only ten correspond to the metre in Thomas. As in the Thomas poems, the distinctive feature whereby stressed syllables tend to receive several pitches, and unstressed syllables only one, is preserved: where the number of syllables differs, then, it is necessary for single-syllable pitches to be regrouped into short melismas, or vice versa.

The date of composition of the David office is not known and hard evidence is lacking: a possible date within the twelfth century is rejected by Edwards, who suggests about 1224 or 1285, using various hints. The earliest extant source may originate from anywhere between 1320 and 1390,[97] and nothing in the style of the office would be inconsistent even with the latest of those dates. Many similar adaptations of the Thomas office originated in the fourteenth or even fifteenth century. Thus, like standard plainsong, later chant endures for centuries as the 'normal musical expression of the time'.

---

[95] Andrew Hughes, 'Chantword Indexes: A Tool for Plainsong Research', in *Words and Music*, ed. Paul Laird (Acta, 17; Binghamton, 1993), 31–49.

[96] *Matins, Lauds, and Vespers*, ed. Edwards. For a list of metres and how they are adapted, see pp. 136 and 138–41.

[97] Ibid. 35.

The David office is very substantially dependent on the Thomas office, mostly for the chants rather than the texts. Edwards's monograph is a model for an edition of an office, including: (a) a description of the manuscript in which the office is found (not necessarily a part of editing an office); (b) a complete facsimile; (c) an inventory of the office; (d) a complete transcription in modern notation; (e) a thorough musical and liturgical analysis, identifying models in various liturgical sources; (f) a detailed discussion of the musical styles and modes; (g) a complete edition of the literary text with a translation and commentary similar to that for the chants, seeking biblical and other sources and identifying literary and etymological sophistications; (h) a discussion of matters such as poetic metres and accentuation, and pronunciation (e.g. *David* clearly rhymes with words ending in *-avit*); (i) a general historical perspective. Since all or most of these elements must be investigated and described, an article in a periodical, although welcome as a partial presentation, is hardly adequate as a method for bringing even a single such major composition properly to notice.

Office of St Francis of Assisi

Franciscus vir catholicus / Franciscus ut in publicum / Sanctus Franciscus was written about 1232 by Julian of Speyer.[98] Compared with the extravagant roulades of the Benedict office and the sophistication of the Thomas office, the chants are simple and unassuming. Lauds antiphons, in particular, mostly use only one note for each syllable. The metre is predominantly that of the Victorine sequence. The modes are strictly in order, Lauds beginning with mode 2. If there is a terminal melisma in a responsory, it lacks sequential motifs. Some antiphons are so conventional that they could serve as skeletal models for elaboration. Using the letters **fpah** for **f**inal, **p**lagal and **a**uthentic reciting-note, and the **h**igh tetrachord, for example, four-phrase antiphons in authentic modes often follow one of these patterns:

fa, aha, misc. (ending on the pitch below the final, or on **p** in modes 5 and 6), **(p)af**

---

[98] The biographical and chronological details are extremely complex. See P. Ottone Tonetti, OFM, 'L'Uffizio ritmico di san Francesco d'Assisi di fra Giuliano da Spira', *Rivista internazionale di musica sacra*, 3 (1982), 370–89; Julian of Speyer, *Vita e uffizio ritmico di San Francesco d'Assisi*, ed. Eliodoro Mariani (Vicenza, 1980); and Fr E. Bruning, OFM, *Giuliano da Spira e l'officio ritmico di s. Francesco* (Edizioni 'Psalterium', Rome), extr. from *Note d'Archivio*, 1–4 (1927), 129–202; and *Die liturgischen Reimoffizien auf den heiligen Franciscus und Antonius. Gedichtet und componiert durch Julian von Speier*, ed. Hilarin Felder (Freiburg i.d. Schweiz, 1901). There is no up-to-date discussion or edition of the chant. I am preparing my own monograph on the office.

fa, misc., **aha**, beginning on the pitch below the final (or on **p** in modes 5 and 6), then **pf**.

In plagal modes the plagal reciting-note would take the position of the authentic pitch and the authentic pitch that of the high tetrachord:

fp, **pap**, . . . , **pf**, for example.

The frequent appearance of the sub-final pitch near the end of a chant, often with the triad above it (e.g. CEG in mode 1), is a well-known gesture. Slight modifications of these patterns occur according to the mode (see Ex. 2.9). This rather hymn-like structure may have resulted in the unfortunate tendency, from the sixteenth century, to regard all plainsongs as 'hymns'.

The next example demonstrates a similar kind of shape, adapted for six lines, in a plagal mode (see Ex. 2.10). As in these examples, the phrases are often strongly directional, and thus unlike standard chant.

Nevertheless, scholars have described some items in this office as 'essentially Gregorian'.[99] If by this is meant 'standard plainsong', then that is a reminder that what most scholars know as standard plain-song is in fact a product of the twelfth and thirteenth centuries, clearly edited and often articulated in some way. The Francis chants are naturally typical of thirteenth-century composition. In fact, VA1, the antiphon explicitly referred to, has several passages where the melody moves doggedly in one direction rather than circling back and forth in the manner of typical plainsong settings of prose texts (see Ex. 2.11). Consider, for example, the setting of *-e teneri* and *presbyteros* and *pre cunctis*. Moreover, the exact repetition in adjacent phrases for these last two words is unlike typical plainsong behaviour. And phrase 2, not directional at all, is too static, suggesting, like the repetition, that the composer did not quite know what to do next, or how to compose a six-line chant.

This example is certainly not extreme, and one could easily find similar passages in the standard repertory. It is rather the frequency with which such passages occur that counts, and their exaggeration or prolongation. In the Francis office, for example, are phrases moving an octave downwards (in the LE), or a seventh upwards (in MA8).

Unlike many offices of this general period, this one seems to make less use of the newer kind of cadence, the cadence rising a step to two repeated pitches, used in many of the preceding examples. This avoid-ance of a striking cadential formula makes the phrases less strongly

---

[99] Tonetti, 'L'Uffizio ritmico', 383–7, citing Bruning's comment with regard to VA1. We may ignore, with Tonetti, Bruning's belief that Julian's chants were 'strongly affected by the popular and fresh music of 13th-century Paris'.

Ex. 2.9. Office for St Francis: MA5 (Matins, fifth antiphon) *Iam liber patris furie* (Now free of the fury of his father, he does not yield to the unruly, claiming himself to be suffering evils for the sake of Christ)

Ex. 2.10. Office for St Francis: VA4 (First Vespers, fourth antiphon) *Franciscus evangelicum* (Francis transgressed the Gospel not one jot, not one tittle: nothing [is] more sweet than the yoke of Christ, nothing more light than this burden in the round of this life)

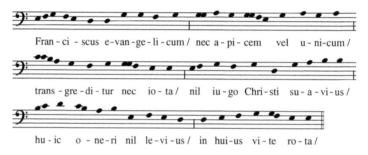

Ex. 2.11. Office for St Francis: VA1 (First Vespers, first antiphon) *Franciscus vir catholicus* (Francis, catholic and most apostolic man, taught the faith of the Roman church to be maintained, and admonished that priests be revered before all things)

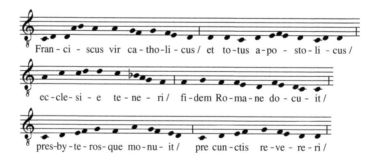

articulated than would otherwise be the case, and makes the chants suitable for adaptation to poems with different metres. The office of St Anthony of Padua, also by Julian of Speyer, uses the same chants, but is quite different poetically.

Ex. 2.12. Office for St Francis: MR (alternative Matins responsory) *Regressis quos emiserat*

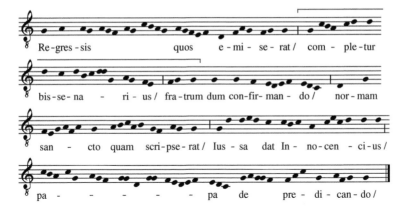

Re-gres-sis   quos   e - mi - se - rat /   com - ple-tur

bis-se-na   -   ri - us /   fra-trum dum con-fir- man - do /   nor - mam

san   -   cto   quam   scri-pse-rat /   Ius - sa   dat In - no-cen - ci - us /

pa -   -   -   -   - pa   de   pre - di - can - do /

Julian occasionally has a sense of coordinating the textual sense with the new cadence form. Consider one of the responsories (see Ex. 2.12). The poem is here laid out in sections illustrating the sense rather than the poetic form, with the rhymes in italics:

regressis quos em*iserat*,   8
completur bissenar*ius* fratrum.   10
dum con*firmando* normam sancto quam scr*ipserat*   13
iussa dat Innocent*ius* papa de pr*edicando*.   15

'When those whom he had sent out [to preach] had returned': the first word group is a complete clause that could be removed without making nonsense of the poem: it ends with the strong cadence. So does the second word group, flowing over into the third poetic line to complete the sense: 'There was a twelvefold complement of brothers.' The object *normam* of *confirmando* also flows over into the fourth poetic line, and the musical gesture on the rhyme of *confirmando* is very unstable: 'while by confirming the rule to the saint . . .'. Before the relative clause '. . . that he had written', at *quam*, is a weak pause on the final, and a somewhat stronger one ends the relative clause. At the next rhyme, on *ius*, where the sense is again complete, the chant rises to a repeated note with the cadential formula: in this case, however, the pitch of arrival is the high D, quite unstable in mode 8, so that the musical flow continues, as does the textual flow, into the last line, 'Pope Innocentius gave orders about preaching'.

If these musico-textual points were deliberately contrived, the relationship between text and music is rather subtle. Unfortunately, we have no means of assessing whether this is conscious artifice, or merely accident. Finding other examples in this office is not easy and only infrequently is there real evidence of a close relation between the textual form and the chant.

But let us also analyse the Magnificat antiphon of First Vespers, VE. This is a long antiphon, consisting of sixteen lines divided into what amounts to four stanzas (see Ex. 2.13):

1, 2	O stupor et gaudium	o iudex homo mencium
3, 4	tu nostre milicie	currus et auriga
5, 6	ignea presentibus	transfiguratum fratribus
7, 8	in solari specie	vexit te quadriga
9, 10	in te signis radians	in te ventura nuncians
11, 12	requievit spiritus	duplex prophetarum
13, 14	Tuis asta posteris	pater Francisce miseris
15, 16	nam increscunt gemitus	ovium tuarum

The first four lines consist of two vocative invocations to Francis, and the subject, *tu* (that is, Francis), of the verb that appears in line 13.

Ex. 2.13. Office for St Francis: VE (First Vespers, Magnificat antiphon) *O stupor et gaudium*

Lines 5–8 are self-contained, treating Francis now as the object of the action of the verb: 'in the presence of the brothers, a chariot of fire carried you, transfigured, in the likeness of a sun'. Similarly, the next four lines are self-contained, the first two being parallel adjectival phrases: 'radiating with signs, announcing the future, the twofold spirit of the prophets rested in you'. Setting these two sets of four lines aside, we can see the main action of the antiphon: (lines 1–4) 'O wonder and joy, o human judge of thoughts, chariot and driver of our soldiers' (and lines 13–16) 'assist o father Francis thy miserable followers, for the groans of thy sheep increase'.

Does the chant help to strengthen these divisions? Ending lines 4 and 8 are cadences rising a semitone to the final: these are quite strong tonal arrival points. The same cannot be said at the end of line 12, where that line rises to the reciting-note in preparation for the high F with which the last four lines begin. This highest point of the chant, occurring in lines 13 and 14, however, is a striking musical gesture: to have placed a strong cadence immediately before it, presumably to the low F, would have entailed an octave leap between these phrases. That leap is certainly not impossible, however, as it appears in MR11 between phrases whose sense is continuous.

The sense of a fourfold tune is almost as strong as is the sense of a four-stanza poem. The relationship between the first and last sections, which belong together textually, is strong, too: lines 15 and 16 are a condensed version of lines 1–4. Lines 13 and 14, where the main action is centred, are musically parallel, almost matching the rhymed words *posteris* and *miseris* that belong together: the linking of words by explicitly giving them the same melodic and notational phrase would not be very likely in standard plainchant. Line 14, ending on a very unstable pitch, leads directly to the condensed recapitulation. That the last lines are intended to recall the opening is surely demonstrated by the F GA F F setting *nam incre-*. This matches exactly the opening notes, set melismatically to *O*, and repeated at a higher pitch for the second *O* (line 2, A BCA A).

Not all features of the tune can be explained nicely, and although the ones described are striking, some similar gestures make no particular sense with respect to the shape of the text or the significance of the words. The little opening melisma also appears at its highest pitch on the word *in* (line 10, C DEC). No reason for linking this word or line with the other places is apparent. The striking leaps of fifths in lines 9, 11, and 12, and the seven-note melisma on the first syllable of *ovium* seem inexplicable.

Perhaps the most we ought to conclude is that this chant has a generally fourfold shape corresponding to the stanza-like construction of the text. The motivic integration that it demonstrates can be found in other chants in the office, in particular MR5, and to some extent indeed in the whole office itself: several chants, for example, are linked by a strictly syllabic motif rising a fourth. A stepwise movement ascending a fourth in single unligated pitches occurs in about twenty locations, reasonably prominently, especially at the beginning of phrases. It may begin on almost any pitch (I have not found one beginning on G), most often beginning on D. I list the item and text:

(VA2) *cursumque sub*	(VA3) *ecclesie*
(VE) *pater Fran-*	(MI) *Christo confi-*
(MA2) *mirifice*	(MA3) *qui captis ar- . . . ad plenum mu-*
(MR2) *pauperibus . . . pecuniam*	
(MV3) *et spiritu*	(MV4) *in nivis fri-*
(MA6) *sua patri*	(MA9) *his nova tra-*
(LA1) *oratio-*	
(LA2) *et quem non ho- . . . novumque no-*	
(LA5) *laus illi sem-*	

and for the octave

(VE) *sacer Francis*	(VE) *tanti patris*

Until we know how common such practices are, the relative frequency and distribution of the motif, and its frequent association with important words, should not necessarily be given too much weight.

The other motif is even shorter, but it appears more often, and I think it is a little more significant. It consists of a downward third, nearly always by leap but occasionally filled in, and usually followed by another similar melodic cell. That the filled-in version is a simple variant is demonstrated by comparing different manuscripts, where the alternative nature of the two versions is apparent. When filled in it is often notationally in the form of currentes; otherwise it is usually a two-note ligature. Its normal notation in ligature and its semi-sequential character inevitably associate it with melismas and thus the more elaborate items of the Office. All these features make its appearance reasonably distinctive. Several instances of it are in the melismas in Ex. 2.12.

One aim of detailed analysis of this kind would be to ascertain whether identifiable compositional features can be distinguished, and to separate one composer's work from that of another. In the present case, it would be ideal to see distinct features in those items known to have been by other composers. This seems not to be possible at any reliable level. It is possible, of course, that a later composer might match his compositional style to that of preceding work. Much more likely is that the styles are in general quite anonymous. One could point to the tiny melismatic motif CBAB or FEDE or BAGA used a few times in the antiphon composed for the office by Cardinal Raineri, *Celorum candor*, and not used in the rest of the office. But this evidence is far too slender to constitute reliable evidence.

Another more significant use of detailed analysis in the present case, but subject to the same frustrations, would be to compare Julian's style in this office with that of the office for St Dominic, to try to ascertain whether any of that office can be identified as the items Julian is said (by self-serving propagandists for the Franciscans) to have written.

For the moment, however, we must continue simply to gather evidence and to compile lists and tables of motifs and compositional procedures. It is difficult, given the present state of our knowledge about the style of later medieval chant, to isolate individual fingerprints that might identify or distinguish composers. The art of composing chant, in any case, even at this later period, was still probably quite impersonal and the stylistic features probably fairly universal. In this office, there do seem to be some rather vague unifying characteristics, we cannot say whether they are conscious attempts on Julian's part, or whether they are merely part of common practice.

As is true of most later offices, responsory verses are set to newly composed music, rather than adopting a standard tone. In general, however, the new tunes tend to keep to the same bipartite division into parallel halves that typify the psalmodic nature of the standard texts. In Julian's office, the verses all have three lines of text. It is interesting to observe, however, that these are sometimes structured to allow a division, textually and musically, into halves. In MV1, the poetic division into three lines is clear, making a Victorine sequence stanza, but the musical division into halves clarifies well the syntax of the poetry (see Ex. 2.14):

> Deum quid agat un*icum* consultans,
> audit cel*icum* insigne sibi dari.

In MV3, the three lines are divided after line 2, again making sense textually and musically in parallel halves. Since this verse has to provide music for the bipartite psalmodic Doxology, the division is confirmed. On the other hand, the three lines of MV2 do not allow such a neat division into halves.

Assessing an office depends on the point of view and the knowledge

Ex. 2.14. Office for St Francis: MV1 (Matins, first responsory verse) *Deum quid agat unicum* (Consulting the one Lord about what he might do, he hears a heavenly sign to be given to him)

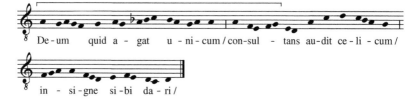

De - um   quid a - gat   u - ni - cum / con - sul - tans au-dit ce - li - cum /

in - si -gne si -bi da - ri /

of the context. Franciscans writing about this office and its position in the worship of their order are naturally full of wonder and praise, because for them it is an inspirational matter of faith. The chant scholar Peter Wagner, writing in the early twentieth century and marvellously expert in the standard repertory, says that the office is organically constructed and of such a firm character that further development of the genre is hardly possible.[100] Seeming recently to echo this opinion, Agostino Ziino says that Julian's work (the Francis office and the one for St Antony of Padua) represents 'l'ultimo stadio, il più evoluto' in the artistic development of the rhymed office.[101] Since these offices, along with the others described in this section, stand at the beginning of at least 250 years of development, these statements seem a little odd. My own conclusion is that the Francis office is rather undistinguished and adopts the new styles somewhat tentatively.

Office of St Dominic

Gaude felix Hispania / Mundum vocans / Adest dies was probably written by Petrus Ferrandi (d. 1254).[102] Plate I shows the office as it appears in Humbert's Codex. From the literary point of view the office

---

[100] Wagner, i. 312; Eng. trans. 270.

[101] Agostino Ziino, echoing Giulio Cattin's judgement (*Music of the Middle Ages*, i (Cambridge, 1979), 117), in 'Liturgia e musica francescana nei secoli XIII–XIV', 131, in *Francesco d'Assisi*, ed. Carlo Pirovano, i. 127–58. Ziino mentions only the Francis offices and those for St Antony and St Clare.

[102] The authorship of the office is very hard to establish definitively, and what evidence we have does not appear explicitly to refer to the chant. Some portions of the office, attributed to Peter, are known to have existed in 1239, and these items appear later in the standard office. In one report Constantin of Orvieto is said to have written an office, which seems not to have been the one now known: in another, much later, report Julian of Speyer is said to have written some items, leaving the office incomplete at his death. The two items for ferial use are known to be by Pope Clement IV, probably before his accession. The most recent serious work on the problem seems to be that of H.-Chr. Scheeben, 'Petrus Ferrandi', *Archivum Fratrum Praedicatorum*, 2 (1932), 329–47. My critical judgement about the chants, in the following paragraphs, may indicate that a number of hands were responsible for the composition.

is untidy: several different metres are used, even within the same service, and the verse may use a metre different from that of its responsory. An unusual metre, with lines of 4 + 6, 4 + 6, 4 + 6 followed by a line with 6 syllables, is common for the responsories. This and the distinctive variety of metres makes it easy to identify textual descendants. From the aesthetic point of view, the office is somewhat nondescript: liturgically such a quality might be valued if the desire was to emulate standard, unobtrusive chant. We remember that one of the aims of the Dominican reforms was to return to tradition. Compared with those of many later offices and those of the Benedict and Thomas offices, the chants are relatively simple, and often quite conventional. In this respect and others, such as the virtual absence of terminal melismas, the Francis and Dominic offices are alike. Modal order is followed, but (unlike Franciscan practice) Lauds begins the series again with mode 1. Responsory verses do not use the tones.

Two antiphons are shown in Ex. 2.15.[103] The general shape of these tunes should be compared with those of Exs. 2.9 and 2.10. Gospel antiphons aside, the second chant in Ex. 2.15 is one of the more elaborate antiphons. For comparison with Ex. 2.9, see Ex. 2.16. From the musical point of view, the repetitive twofold nature of this tune, generally aba'b', is somewhat uninspired. Does it echo the structure of the poem and the word 'twin'?

Several features call to mind the Thomas office: a distinctive textual motif;[104] goliardic and ten-syllable lines; in a few responsories, accented syllables with more pitches than unaccented ones. Whether these are adequate to demonstrate influence (rather than adaptation of a model) must await further research.

Summary

Varied styles characterize these models. Poetically, the nature of the text has little bearing on the overall complexity of the office in performance: no matter how intricate its metres, rhyme schemes, or literary conceits, such details will be obscured—and indeed, are often ignored—in the musical setting. The setting may even destroy the metre by requiring more or fewer syllables for certain words. Only when there is a real coordination of textual phrase (with its rhyme) and musical phrase (with a prominent cadential gesture) is there an effect on the musical performance, creating a hymn-like composition with four (or more) balanced phrases.

---

[103] These and three others are transcribed and discussed in Hiley, *Western Plainchant*, 276–8.
[104] Hughes, 'Echoes and Allusions'.

Ex. 2.15. Office for St Dominic: (*a*) MA9 (Matins, ninth antiphon) *Liber carnis vinculo* (Free from the bond of flesh, he entered heaven where he tastes from a full cup what he thirsted for); (*b*) LA1 (Lauds, first antiphon) *Adest dies leticie* (This is the day of joy on which Dominic, noble citizen, enters the vestibule of the heavenly court)

Ex. 2.16. Office for St Dominic: LA5 (Lauds, fifth antiphon) *Fulget in choro virginum* (The teacher of truth shines in the chorus of virgins, carrying with the blessed the related twin of honour)

Modally, chants are arranged in a strict sequence. An office changed from secular to monastic, or vice versa, may show disruptions of this order. In other cases, a dislocation of the modal order is generally an indication of some later adaption, modified in this respect for some reason as yet unknown. Responsory tones and melody-types of the standard repertory are normally avoided.

Musically, the Benedict office has the most highly elaborate chants, with terminal melismas and sequential motifs, but it has yet to be established that the chants were used as models. The Thomas office is similarly elaborate, but seems more disciplined, more sophisticated, and thus has the restraint we have come to associate with traditional chant. The two offices for the mendicant Orders seem comparatively skeletal, allowing three-, four-, and the occasional five-note melismas in the more important Gospel antiphons and in the responsories, but mostly two- and the occasional three-note melismas in the ordinary antiphons. Even so, tunes that are essentially the same in overall melodic contour can still be remarkably different in detail. This circumstance makes a considerable degree of unanimity necessary, both in shape and in detail, before borrowings can be established. Where and when similar tunes become different is one of the most difficult analytical decisions to face any scholar of late medieval liturgical monophony.

THE LATER RHYMED OFFICE

For the later repertory, catalogues for specific categories exist only for British rhymed offices and for monarchs,[105] where information fuller than that supplied in the general catalogue published in *LMLO* may be found. The remainder of this chapter presents a repertory list with some balance of country, Use, century, and ecclesiastical Order. A few important offices are described in detail. From such a survey few firm conclusions can result.

Mostly, the list consists of offices known to have been written near the date under which they are described.[106] In a few cases, the only direct evidence for the date is that of the earliest known source. For a few others, I give the barest information[107] or a reference to a modern edition that includes some description. Favoured are publications in which the complete chant is edited. For each category, hundreds of others could be described: most would probably be much more local than those identified in this preliminary history.

The following typical features will be assumed: (a) regular poetry

---

[105] Hughes, 'British Rhymed Offices' and 'The Monarch as the Object of Liturgical Veneration', in Anne J. Duggan (ed.), *Kings and Kingship in Medieval Europe* (King's College London Medieval Studies, 10; London, 1993), 375–424.

[106] We know the dates of some of these offices from various pieces of evidence: the date of canonization or promulgation; independent evidence from a reliable chronicle; information about the poet or composer; evidence from local civil or ecclesiastical history. Sometimes all we have is an earliest date: we may assume (not always entirely safely) that an office was written after the saint's death. It seems clear, for instance, that no office for St John of Bridlington could date from before his death in 1379. But an office may certainly date from and indeed have been used before official canonization.

Sometimes the only evidence for dating is that of the manuscripts (see above, n. 81). And the earliest known source may be well after the date of composition, earlier books having been lost. But when the number of sources is large and they are geographically widely distributed, some indication of the date and place of origin can be gained. Judging by the style is the least reliable method of ascertaining date, especially for a repertory whose analysis is in its infancy. Some examples of problems with dating will be cited in the text.

[107] The source in *AH* is not given for these. Either I have not examined the chant or it does not exist, or else it has not been identified.

or metre, with rhymes; (b) verses occasionally prose, or different poetically from the responsory; (c) the presence of occasional other prose
items; (d) no responsory tones; (e) modal order of some kind; (f) nondescript praise in the texts; (g) the frequent use of recognizable chant
formulas, often highly ornamented.

Characteristics making an office individual and interesting are: (h)
sophisticated literary imagery; (i) aphoristic literary expression; (j)
literary conceits such as alliteration, acrostics, and puns; (k) specific,
biographical narrative; (l) distinctive and striking melodic or other
musical gestures, especially the use of larger intervals; (m) word-
painting or word-emphasis.

Many offices of national importance in Eastern Europe have been
edited and described. Most sources date from the fourteenth century,
although there are apparently (late) thirteenth-century manuscripts.

Poland

Adalbert (Wojciech). Many of the compositions of the office *Benedic
regem / Gloriosum in beato / Sanctus lugens Adalbertus* 'have passed
into present-day Polish patronal usage'.[108] The chants are moderately
elaborate, with some astonishing alleluia melismas ending responsories already quite melismatic.

Hedwig, can. 1267. The elaborate monastic office *Gaude solum Silesie
/ Gaude prole / Hedwigis Dei* 'holds an exceptional position in the
history of Polish music . . . poetry . . . and fine arts'.[109] Two other
offices, possibly abbreviations for secular use, are closely related. This
office is interesting because it is probably Cistercian, originating from
the monastery in which Hedwig was buried.

Stanislaus (patron of Kraków). The texts and chants of Stanislaus'
office were written about 1250 by the Dominican Vincent of Kielce.
An archbishop like Thomas of Canterbury, Stanislaus was also mar-
tyred protecting the church. There are clear textual borrowings from
the Thomas office but no musical relationships.[110]

---

[108] See the editions by Jerzy Morawski, *Historia rymowana o św. Jadwidze* (Kraków,
1977), and *Historia rymowana o św. Wojciechu* (Kraków, 1979) [*The Rhymed History of St
Hedwig . . . St Adalbert*]: lacks musical and literary analysis. See also Jerzy Pikulik, 'Les Offices
polonais de saint Adalbert', in id. (ed.), *État des recherches sur la musique religieuse dans la
culture polonaise* (Warsaw, 1973), 306–72. For St Adalbert, see also Zijlstra, 'The Office of St
Adalbert: Carte de Visite of a Late Medieval Dutch Abbey', *Plainsong and Medieval Music*, 3
(1994), 169–83.

[109] Morawski, *Historia . . . św. Jadwidze.*

[110] Andrew Hughes, 'Chants in the Offices of Thomas of Canterbury and Stanislaus of
Poland', *Musica antiqua*, 6 (Bydgoszcz, 1982), 267–77.

Bohemia

Ludmilla (patron saint of Bohemia). The monastic office of Ludmilla, *Ecce iubar* / *Gaude celum primo* / *Beata martyr*, probably originated from the convent of St George in Prague.[111]

Procopius, can. 1204. This saint's cult was greatly expanded in Bohemia in the fourteenth century. The office, *Letare Bohemia* / *Quasi vitis fructifera* / *Laudes iubar*, is the object of one of the most thorough studies undertaken within an article: texts borrowed from Proper offices of earlier saints and from the Common of Saints are identified; a dozen Benedictine and two Cistercian manuscripts are collated and compared with a group of secular sources; and—in one of the most taxing tasks associated with this repertory—lists show comprehensively how the order of the texts varies from source to source.[112]

Hungary

The offices for St Emmerich, for Stephen, king of Hungary, and for Ladislaus have been published.[113]

General

1298. In July and August 1298, Magister Petrus de Cruce (of Amiens), surely the theorist and composer Pierre de la Croix, was paid for the expenses of compiling an office to the blessed Louis, but it is unclear to which of the known offices this might refer.[114]

1301–6. An office for St Louis IX, king of France, d. 1270, can. 1297, was written by the Dominican Arnaut of Prat, known to have composed other kinds of songs. A monastic version and several other offices for the king, including one for his translation, were fairly widespread in

[111] Dominique Patier, 'L'Office rythmique de sainte Ludmila', *Études grégoriennes*, 21 (1986), 51–96. Poetry and chants are thoroughly discussed.

[112] Dominique Patier, 'Un Office rhythmique tchèque du XIVème siècle: étude comparative avec quelques offices hongrois', *Studia musicologica*, 12 (1970), 41–131.

[113] Zoltan Falvy, 'Drei Reimoffizien aus Ungarn und ihre Musik', *Musicologia hungarica*, NS 2 (Budapest, 1968); the material on the office for Stephen is revised from Falvy's 'Die Weisen des König Stephan-Reimoffiziums', *Studia musicologica*, 6 (1964), 207–69.

[114] *Les Journaux du Trésor de Philippe IV, le Bel*, ed. Jules Viard (Paris, 1940), entries 799, 902, and 1008:

3 July 1298: 'Magister Petrus de Cruce de Ambianensis, pro expensa facienda ad compilanda hystoriam beati Ludovici, 10.l.p.'

15 July 1298: 'Magister Petrus de Cruce, pro expensis compilando hystoriam beati Ludovici, 20 l.p.'

2 August 1298: 'Magister Petrus de Cruce de Ambianensis, pro expensis suis et sociorum suorum compilando hystoriam beati Ludovici, 30 l.p.'

Philippe le Bel's association with King Louis makes it almost certain that these entries refer to the king rather than to the contemporary archbishop Louis of Toulouse, whose office is described under 1317. See Hughes, 'The Monarch'.

Ex. 2.17. Comparison of passages from (*a*) Office for St Louis, king: VA1 (First Vespers, first antiphon) 'transit felix ad celi solium'; (*b*) Office for the Holy Crown of Thorns: VA1 (First Vespers, first antiphon) 'felix mater ecclesia'; (*c*) Office for St Dominic: VA1 (First Vespers, first antiphon) 'felix parens Hispania'

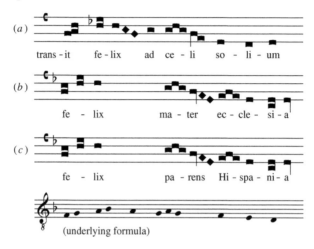

France. They share many items with Arnaut's office. Marcy Epstein explores the relationships, discussing the role of memory in the process of adaptation, and pointing to numerous textual similarities, none reflected in the chants: even some identical texts are set differently.[115]

Louis was closely associated with the Dominican order. The author of the office was a Dominican. After Louis had bought the Holy Crown of Thorns in Constantinople, Dominicans transported it to Louis's newly built shrine, the Sainte-Chapelle. Are there affinities between Arnaut's office and the office for St Dominic, whose chants were reused wholesale for the Holy Crown of Thorns?[116] Seeking to demonstrate a musical relationship, Epstein cites passages from VA1 of all three offices, raising important issues about how close a musical similarity must be (see Ex. 2.17).[117]

In Arnaut's office, the antiphon texts are carefully shaped to fit the psalms, which are themselves chosen for their references to kingship. Most items have only four lines (six for responsories). Many are quite elaborate ornaments of recognizable chant formulas: in MR7, for

---

[115] *AH* 13, no. 71. Marcy J. Epstein, '*Ludovicus decus regnantium*: Perspectives on the Rhymed Office', *Speculum*, 53 (1978), 283–333.

[116] This is the office in *AH* 45, no. 2, rather than the one edited and described by Kirk, '"Translatione . . ."', which is *AH* 5, no. 9.

[117] Epstein, '*Ludovicus decus regnantium*', app. II.

example, four syllables receive what in other offices would be a full musical phrase. Most responsories have no terminal melismas. The antiphons of Lauds make it quite clear that the author was well aware of the connection between *Ludo*vicus and *Laud*ate.

1312. The Carmelites adopted the feast of the Transfiguration, borrowing most of the chants of Matins from the office of Trinity Sunday, and some from the twelfth-century office composed by Peter the Venerable.[118]

can. 1317. Louis, Franciscan archbishop of Toulouse, d. 1297. Five offices exist, one only in a printed source of 1530. The single one studied[119] bears only a remote musical relationship with the office for Francis, using (once) a four-note opening motif that plays a striking role in some items of the earlier office (see above, Ex. 2.13).

can. 1320. Thomas of Hereford, bishop and doctor, d. 1282, tr. 1349.[120] His office is still in the printed breviary of 1505. Only a few items survive with the chant; none seems musically related to the office of Thomas of Canterbury.

can. 1323. Thomas Aquinas, Dominican doctor, d. 1274, tr. 1369. Both the main office, *Felix Thomas / Sancti viri / Adest dies*, and that for his translation[121] almost exclusively borrow much of the poetic form, some textual motifs, and most of the chants from the office for St Dominic.

1264–1323. In 1264 Urban IV promulgated a bull decreeing the universal celebration of Corpus Christi, together with the office he wished to serve in place of an earlier office. The complexities of the relationship among these two offices and Urban's bull, and with later offices for the feast, are considerable.

The office beginning *Sacerdos in eternum*, issued with Urban's bull, became the standard text and remained so until recently. It exists in an interesting manuscript, perhaps emanating from the papal curia in Urban's reign, between 1264 and 1295: in the margins of this book, the source of the chants is given. The feast of Corpus Christi having some affinity with that of All Saints, the chants are drawn from a pantheon of earlier saints' and Temporal offices, including: Trinity, Ascension, Dedication, All Saints, the Blessed Virgin, Thomas of Canterbury,

---

[118] Boyce, 'Cantica Carmelitana', i. 184–94.

[119] *AH* 26, no. 93.

[120] *AH* 13, no. 95. See Brian L. Trowell and Andrew Wathey, 'John Benet's "Lux fulget ex Anglia—O pater pietatis—Salve Thoma"', in Meryl Jancey (ed.), *St Thomas Cantilupe, Bishop of Hereford: Essays in his Honour* (Hereford, 1982), 159–80.

[121] *AH* 5, nos. 84 and 85.

Nicholas, Bernard, and several from Dominic.[122] All the texts of *Sacerdos in eternum* are prose. In several cases, then, a chant originally setting a rhymed text has been transformed for use with prose, an interesting reversal of procedure that would make a thorough analysis welcome.

Thomas Aquinas is traditionally regarded as the author, but much evidence weakens this attribution. First, in 1317, fifty years after Thomas's death, his confessor wrote that Aquinas had composed the office, mass, and all the chants: although evidence from one so close to Thomas would seem unassailable, its reliability has been questioned. Furthermore, a catalogue of Thomas's works by his scribe does not mention it. Secondly, textual and doctrinal motifs derive from Thomas's thought and writings: but any Dominican author commissioned to write such an office would surely have known and cited many of Thomas's words.

Confusing the matter further, but really providing the strongest contrary argument is that the Dominican Order, to which Thomas belonged, did not adopt the feast until 1317, and seemed not to know then of Thomas's authorship. Consequently, in 1318 another Dominican, the Master-General Hervé de Nédellec, was commissioned to provide a liturgy, which was approved by the Order in 1321/2. Nevertheless, in 1323 the Order adopted *Sacerdos in eternum* because, as the document says, 'it was asserted' that Thomas was its author.

Although lacking the authority of a theologian such as Aquinas, Hervé de Nédellec's office, *Gaude felix mater ecclesia / Mundos vocans / Vere digna hostia*, is appropriate for Dominicans: as its opening words indicate, it is extraordinarily closely modelled on that of St Dominic in poetic metre, which we have seen is rather distinctive, in textual allusions, and almost exactly and completely as to chant:[123] an unusual statement confirms this dependence, stating that Master Hervé made the Corpus Christi office conform in chant (*in nota*) with the historia of St Dominic.[124] An interesting monastic version of this office complements Hervé's secular items with several from *Sacerdos*.[125] Two of the very few instances in which the Dominic model has been modified may be cited (see Ex. 2.18). Examples 12.18(*a*) and (*b*) differ minimally in the final melisma; (*c*) and (*d*) also differ minimally, but the poetry

[122] The complete list is in Thomas J. Mathiesen, 'The Office of the New Feast of Corpus Christi in the *Regimen Animarum* at Brigham Young University', *Journal of Musicology*, 2 (1983), 13–44 at 24. This article is one of the very few to address the musical issues.

[123] Hervé's office is published in *AH* 24, no. 6. It is not, as previous scholars have thought, the one in *AH* 5, no. 5.

[124] Cited in Pierre-Marie Gy, 'L'Office du Corpus Christi et S. Thomas d'Aquin', *Revue des sciences, philosophie, et théologie*, 64 (1980), 491–507 at 491 n. 2.

[125] Kassel, Landesbibliothek MS Licht 15, fos. 73ʳ–79ᵛ.

Ex. 2.18. Comparison of passages from (*a*) Office for St Dominic: MR5 (Matins, fifth responsory) 'matris pellit tristiciam' (he dispels the mother's sadness); (*b*) Office for Corpus Christi: MR5 (Matins, fifth responsory) 'dat graciarum copiam' (he gives copious thanks); (*c*) Office for St Dominic: MR9 (Matins, ninth responsory) 'ascendenti de valle lubrici' ([Angelic choirs applaud] the one rising from the slippery valley of the earth); (*d*) Office for Corpus Christi: MR12 (Matins, twelfth responsory) 'ascendentem Christum de hac miseria' (We follow Christ rising from this misery)

of the latter (the later office) accommodates itself better to the proper phrasing of the chant.

1334. In 1334 Trinity Sunday was made a universal feast, no doubt strengthening and widening the use of Stephen of Liège's office. But an important new office had been written by John Pecham, Franciscan archbishop of Canterbury, d. 1292.[126] This office is *Sedente super solium / Confirmat hoc mysterium / Quam clara testimonium.* Borrow-

---

[126] *AH* 5, no. 1; a short biography of Pecham is in *AH* 50, pp. 592–4.

ing the poetic form and chants of the Francis office, this continued to be used within the Franciscan Order and, according to *AH*, in at least one monastic institution. Accepted by Pope Sixtus IV, 1471–84, it found its way into the printed Roman breviary, but was finally removed at the time of the Council of Trent, under Pius V, 1566–72.

1342. Feast of the Three Marys (sisters of Mary). These rhymed offices are found principally in Carmelite sources. For *Ecce dies gloriosa / Sollemnitas beatarum / Cum Maria Magdalene*, the Carmelites in Mainz and Florence used different chants: conflicts between musical

Ex. 2.19. Mainz Carmelite Office for the Three Marys: (*a*) melody-type and MR2 (Matins, second responsory) *Ante regis solium* (Charming and noble Esther stands before the king's throne, strengthened through the ministry of the two women); (*b*) responsory tone and MV7 (Matins, seventh responsory verse) *Felices matertere* (The happy sisters of the aunt of the Christ-bearing woman are devoting themselves to us with the gift of their virtues)

(*a*)

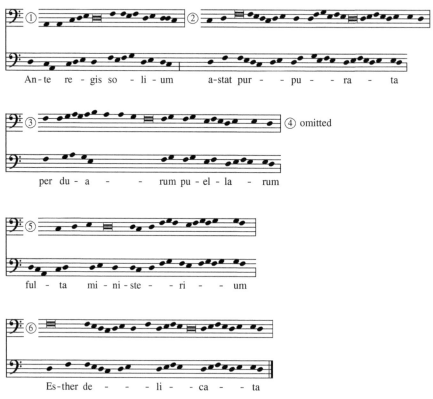

(b)
Fe - li - ces ma - ter - te-re / so - ro - res
Chri-sti - fe - re / cum vir - tu - tum mu - ne - re /
ad nos ap - pli - can - tur

phrases and textual sense suggest that the melodic phrases were predetermined.[127]

In the Mainz setting standard models certainly seem to be used. Most items are quite nondescript, with a small range and undeveloped formulas. Antiphons resemble the simple ferial chants of the standard repertory, but with four rather than two phrases. Most of the responsories probably use melody-types from the standard repertory; most verses certainly use the standard tones. Ex. 2.19 shows MR2 set against the Gregorian melody-type,[128] and one of the few verses (MV7) that differs from the tone. The bipartite responsory tone is used partly as a model for a four-line verse: line 1 and the first word of line 2 follow the tone closely; the end of line 2 and the beginning of 3 are freely composed; the end of line 3 picks up the end of the first half of the tone; line 4 is essentially free.

In the Florence setting, the chants are more elaborate: tones are not so routinely used, and a few responsories have small terminal melismas, occasionally with sequences.

[127] *AH* 5, no. 25. Boyce, 'Carmina Carmelitana', i. 210–14, transcription in ii. 267–341; and 'Die Mainzer Karmeliterchorbücher und die liturgische Tradition des Karmeliterordens', *Archiv für mittelrheinische Kirchengeschichte*, 39 (1987), 267–303. See also his article 'The Carmelite Feast of the Presentation of the Virgin: A Study in Musical Adaptation', in Fassler and Baltzer (eds.), *The Divine Office*, 485–518.

[128] As analysed by Ruth Steiner in *New Grove* under 'Responsory', xv. 761.

can. 1347. Ivo, priest confessor, one patron of Brittany, d. 1303. Four offices are known.[129]

? 1368. Mary of the Snows. Four full offices are known, one by Johannes of Jenstein, archbishop of Prague, d. 1400.[130]

can. 1369. The Franciscan Elzearius, and his wife, d. 1323, were associated with Avignon and Apt. The office is based on that of St Francis.[131]

1372. The feast of the Presentation of the Blessed Virgin was established in the West by Gregory XI after a campaign by Philippe de Mézières, who brought the office to Avignon. Other than that office, nine others are edited in *AH*, each from a few mostly fifteenth- and sixteenth-century German or Bohemian sources. Another French office exists only in a printed source of 1595. According to the printed Roman breviary, the feast was celebrated principally in France, England, and Spain.[132]

The main office, associated with Philippe, is widely distributed in many sources: *Fons hortorum redundans / Mente sancta fuit et / Lauda felix ecclesia* was recently re-edited by William Coleman, but without the chants.[133] Two manuscripts, owned by Philippe himself, are the prototypes of the copies that were first distributed.

Acrostics appear in both the accompanying mass and the office itself. That in the mass yields *Ave Maria benedico te. Amen.* The acrostic in the office raises interesting problems of liturgy, text, biography, and music. It requires the initial letters of each stanza of the hymn at both Vespers and Matins, thus involving the hymns integrally in the office in a way unusual for the repertory. They must therefore be proper to the office.[134] Also required is the responsory and its verse at First Vespers. No reference to the responsory is in the prototype manuscripts mentioned above, leading to the claim that the acrostic is 'spoilt'.[135] But such omissions are common and medieval cantors would know where to find the item. In this case, it must be taken from

---

[129] *AH* 13, nos. 66–9.
[130] *AH* 48, no. 400.
[131] *AH* 18, no. 19, and *AH* 13, no. 44, are essentially the same.
[132] Cited in *AH* 25, p. 79 'in presentatione Virginis Marie quod festum primo fuit celebratum in Francia ad instantiam christianissimi regis Francorum nec non et in ceteris eiusdem regni provinciis; dehinc in Anglia, Hispania atque aliis partibus mundi; nunc noviter sanctissimus papa Sixtus quartus [1471–84] ipsum publicavit, ut per totum mundum fieri debeat, ac indulgentias concessit celebrantibus hoc festum et sancti Josephi sub maiori duplici in eadem bulla.' See also my 'Fons hortorum—the Office of the Presentation: Origins and Authorship', in Berschin and Hiley (eds.), *Die Offizien des Mittelalters*, 153–77.
[133] *AH* 24, no. 25. *Philippe de Mézière's Campaign for the Feast of Mary's Presentation. Edited from Bibliothèque Nationale Mss latin 17330 and 14454,* ed. William E. Coleman (Toronto Medieval Latin Texts, 11; Toronto, 1981). A new edition is being prepared by Coleman and James Boyce.
[134] *AH* 52, p. 44.
[135] *Philippe de Mézière's Campaign,* ed. Coleman, 12.

one of the extra responsories listed at the end of Matins.[136] A variant in the third stanza of the Vespers hymn in the two prototype sources does make the reading incorrect.

With the hymn stanzas (noted by dots) and responsory verses added to the schema for services the correct acrostic is produced thus:

Vespers   Matins

A A A A A R V H . . . . E I H . . . . A A A R V R V R V A A A R   V R V R V A A A R V

F r a t e r   R ostag nu s virg i n e m t o t o c o r d e m a g n i f i c a t.

The musical problem is with the seventh Matins responsory and verse yielding the final -at: as chants in mode 1, they are out of place in the sequence. An extra responsory is in the correct mode but does not have the required letters.

The identification in *AH* of Frater Rostagnus with Philippe himself was rejected by Coleman because of the 'spoilt' acrostic in Philippe's own manuscripts. New evidence confirms the latter conclusion: Frater Rostagnus, a Dominican friar from Provence, was in Avignon in 1350.[137] What he has to do with the office remains to be discovered. Coleman suggests that we should trust Philippe's own account of the history of the office and its mass. The feast had long been celebrated in the Greek church. Philippe came across it in Cyprus, whither it had probably come from Jerusalem, took it with him first to Venice, then to Avignon, and eventually to Paris.

In Cyprus, the complete Propers with chant were sung according to the Roman Curia.[138] The office in the so-called prototype is therefore unlikely to be the one celebrated in Cyprus. First, Rome did not encourage rhymed offices. Secondly, many of the chants are drawn from the Dominic office. They include almost all the responsories and one antiphon for Matins, the ordinary antiphons of Lauds, and the invitatory. One Vespers antiphon comes from the office for the Dominican Thomas Aquinas. Others have not yet yielded to identification. This extensive adoption of an earlier office raises curious problems. Why, for example, was the seventh responsory (the one not in modal order in the Presentation office) not borrowed along with all the others? Why was the first responsory of Dominic drastically shortened for the first of the Presentation, yet kept intact as one of its extra responsories? Why were the antiphons in general not used as models?

---

[136] Hughes, *Medieval Manuscripts*, 63–4, and '*Fons hortorum*'.

[137] Heinrich Denifle, 'Quellen zur Gelehrtengeschichte des Predigerordens', *Archiv für Literatur- und Kirchengeschichte des Mittelalters*, 2 (Berlin, 1886), 165–302 at 233.

[138] *Philippe de Mézière's Campaign*, ed. Coleman, 12 (and fully on p. 43) cites Philippe's original letter.

Other fascinating problems are raised by a German version.[139] Its texts are almost identical. All its responsories and verses use different chants. Only two of its antiphon chants are more or less identical, and a few use completely different chants. In the remainder, some phrases are borrowed identically, others are completely different, and many phrases have variants more or less remote from the French model. I have not encountered this apparently haphazard borrowing elsewhere in the parts of the repertory studied. The relationship seems quite certain, even though the variants are sometimes considerable. It is as though the compiler had only echoes, or distant memories, of the models. MA7 and LA1 are given in Ex. 2.20. Note the alliteration of *c*s and *s*s in Ex. 2.20(*a*), a literary conceit appearing also in the *fl*s of Ex. 2.20(*b*), and how the *sic* and *fl* of the adaptation are echoes of the model. This kind of relationship allows an extremely good test to ascertain how far an apparently new text depends on an earlier one, and, musically, how the use of the same mode generates the same motif for the same text.

In 1393 the Carmelites adopted the feast and, as so often in the Order, instituted unique texts.[140] Antiphons for Vespers and Lauds appear in Florentine sources. A complete office in manuscripts from Mainz, using the same texts, however, is based almost entirely on chants drawn from the office of Thomas of Canterbury. Modal order in the responsories is not followed. Comparing the opening words of the VE—*Pastor dives in celi solio*—with those of the Thomas office (*Pastor cesus in gregis medio*) indicates the textual relationships.

1378–1389. The feast of the Visitation of the Blessed Virgin was instituted by Urban VI in 1378, and promulgated by Boniface IX in 1389. A dozen different offices are known, some in only a single later source. There is a complex web of relationships and borrowings, especially from earlier offices for the feast.

Urban VI was prevented by his death in 1389 from making universal the office by Johannes Jenstein, cardinal and archbishop of Prague (d. 1400). The poetic parts of this office are in a manuscript corrected by Johannes himself.[141] Complemented by several items in prose, the full office is *Exurgens autem Maria / O preclara stella / In Marie virginis.* Known in Carmelite books (where it borrows a few chants from the Carmelite office for the Three Marys), it was also used for the celebration when it was instituted in Cambrai cathedral by

---

[139] Cologne, Erzdiözesanbibliothek MS 299.
[140] Boyce, 'Carmina Carmelitana', i. 155–62, ii. 222–66.
[141] *AH* 48, no. 399. See also 48, p. 421.

Ex. 2.20. (*a*) Office for St Dominic: MA7 (Matins, seventh antiphon) *Siciebat servus Christi* (The servant was thirsting for the martyrdom of Christ as the hart thirsts for the river of water); (*b*) Office for the Presentation of the Virgin: MA7 (Matins, seventh antiphon) *Flos in floris tempore* (The flower in the time of the flower is sent to the place of the flower, as he is conceived gloriously from the body of the flower); (*c*) Office for the Presentation of the Virgin: LA1 (Lauds, first antiphon) *Lauda felix ecclesia* (Praise, o happy church, the infancy of the bountiful mother, whose immense grace prepared glory for you; (*d*) (cfr. Ex. 2.15(*b*))

canon Michel de Beringhen in 1455. It appears in the printed Cambrai antiphonal.[142]

The use of this office in such important sources and places is puzzling, since Boniface IX authorized a different office (the Carmelite Chapter of Frankfurt that mandated the observance, in fact, specifically refers to the one ordained by Boniface).[143] Adam Easton, cardinal and Benedictine (d. 1397), wrote the office *Accedunt laudes / Surgens*

[142] Cambrai, Médiathèque municipale MS XVI C 4. See Barbara H. Haggh, 'The Celebration of the *Recollectio Festorum Beatae Mariae Virginis*, 1457–1987', *Studia musicologica*, 30 (1988), 361–74.

[143] Boyce, 'Carmina Carmelitana', i. 154 for the citation. I cannot explain this discrepancy.

Maria gravida / Sacra dedit eloquia.[144] Numerous contemporary references confirm that this is the version authorized by Boniface. But clearly
this office had problems: a breviary of Speyer, printed in 1509, refers to
its barbarisms and ineptness, on account of which Philip, bishop of
Speyer, allowed the office of Johannes of Jenstein to be printed and
read. Do we see here hints that the rhymed repertory and the style of
late chant are beginning to lose their fascination (important parts of
Jenstein's office are prose)?

If so, it is unlikely to be the fault of the chant: as one report tells
us, Adam's office was 'cantatur juxta cantum beati Francisci'. The
chants of the Francis office are borrowed wholesale. Moreover, if this
office went out of favour, it had earlier had wider distribution and use
than most offices: two complete pages of *AH* are taken up listing the
sources in which Dreves observed the text, surely a small percentage
of those that still exist. Only in England was the office apparently not
widely used.

Instead, another office seems to have been preferred. This is
Eterni patris filius / Elisabeth ut virgini / Scandit montes,[145] allegedly by
John Horneby.[146] It is in fifteenth-century Sarum antiphonals and
the sixteenth-century printed breviaries of Sarum, Aberdeen, and
York. The first item, VA1, makes a gesture to Francis, borrowing its
chant from MA1 of his office. Several other items, however, use chants
from the office for Thomas of Canterbury, often varied to some extent.
Raising interesting questions about transmission and relationship
between rites, a good many texts of this office are shared with one that
seems to be associated primarily with monastic uses in northern
Italy.[147]

Yet another office, also very widespread, especially in Austria, Italy,
and Spain, is *Candida plebs / Pium mentis viaticum / Circa matris
viaticum*.[148] Appearing in Roman–Franciscan books, and in some
printed breviaries of the late fifteenth century, it depends heavily on
chants from the Francis office. An Italian version was recently published, with several facsimiles and a transcription in rhythmic notation
that most scholars would nowadays agree is inappropriate.[149]

Not to be outdone, the Dominicans had their own office, written by
Raymond of Capua, and widely distributed in manuscripts of the

---

[144] *AH* 24, no. 29. See also 24, pp. 92–4, for documentation in this paragraph.

[145] *AH* 24, no. 37.

[146] Karlheinz Schlager, 'Reimoffizien' in *Geschichte der katholischen Kirchenmusik*, ed. Karl
Gustav Fellerer (Kassel, 1972), i. 293–7 at 296; Schlager cites no source for this information.

[147] *AH* 24, no. 32.

[148] *AH* 24, no. 31.

[149] Piero Damilano, 'Un antico "ufficio ritmico" della Visitazione nella biblioteca capitolare
di Fossano', *Rivista internazionale di musica sacra*, 5 (1984), 133–63.

Order. The incipit of MR1 indicates its dependence on the office for Dominic: *Colletentur corda fidelium* / *Mundum vocans* / *Cum Deus ex virgine*.[150]

late 14th and 15th century. Although there is a Milanese office by Origo Scaccabarozzi, d. 1293, and a Cistercian one by Christian von Lilienfeld, d. before 1332 (both unique to their locality), the cult of Anna was widespread only from the late fourteenth century. More than twenty offices are edited in *AH*. All of Europe had the cult, especially the Dominicans and Carmelites. Even the Cistercians had an office. A popular and widespread English version was written about *1381*, probably by the Dominican Thomas Stubbs, and using the chants of the Dominic office. It was printed in early sixteenth-century breviaries.

can. 1391. Birgitta (Bridget) of Sweden, d. 1373. Three offices for this founder of the Bridgettine Order are extant, two of them by prominent Swedish bishops.[151]

1393. Carmelite Marian offices for the Presentation and Visitation, referred to above.

can. 1401. John of Bridlington, Augustinian prior and confessor, d. 1379, tr. 1404. John was credited with the English victory at Agincourt, and was a favourite saint of the Plantagenet kings. An early fifteenth-century mass is based on a plainsong from this office.[152]

1417–20. Edmund Lacy, bishop of Hereford cathedral, wrote an office for the archangel Raphael.[153]

can. 1456/7. Osmund, bishop of Salisbury, was the last British saint of the Middle Ages to be canonized. An office with chant survives in one manuscript. The poetry is partly in goliardic stanzas and partly in leonine hexameters; two responsories are in elegiac couplets. This resurgence of classical metres, coordinated with the chant in sophisticated ways, is a sign of the incipient Renaissance. A brief use of blatant word-painting illustrating a ladder is published elsewhere in

---

[150] *AH* 24, no. 30.
[151] *AH* 25, no. 57 (by Neils Hermansson, bishop of Linköping, d. 1391); *AH* 25, no. 58 (by Birger Gregorius, archbishop of Uppsala, 1366–83); and another office in *AH* 25, no. 56. For *AH* 25, no. 57 see '*Rosa rorans*': *Ett Birgittaofficium af Nicolaus Hermanni*, ed. Hermann Schück (Meddelanden från det literaturhistoriska seminariet i Lund, 2; *Lunds universitets årsskrift*, 28 (1893). For *AH* 25, no. 58 see *Birger Gregerssons 'Birgitta-officium'*, ed. Carl-Gustav Undhagen (Svenska fornskriftsällskapet, ser. 2; Latinska skrifter, 6; Stockholm, 1960).
[152] Margaret Bent (ed.), *Fifteenth-Century Liturgical Music II: Four Anonymous Masses* (Early English Church Music, 22; London, 1979).
[153] *AH* 13, no. 86. See Philip A. Barrett, 'A Saint in the Calendar: The Effect of the Canonization of St Thomas Cantilupe on the Liturgy', in Jancey (ed.), *St Thomas Cantilupe*, 153–7 at 155.

photographic reproduction.[154] Some unusual modal transpositions and other features make the chant of more than common interest.

1457. In the cathedral of Cambrai, canon Michel de Beringhen founded a new veneration of the Virgin, the *Recollectio*,[155] commemorating the other feasts of the Virgin. Gilles Carlier wrote the rather conventional texts in poetry. Dufay wrote its rather conventional chants. Dufay is the only significant composer of part-music known to have written chants for a new office: since most composers of liturgical polyphony were clerics, however, no doubt others did contribute to the repertory. Uniquely, as far as I know, for MA9, following those in the normal modal order 1–8, Dufay uses a chant in the *tonus peregrinus*. The office was used until the Council of Trent in Cambrai, the Netherlands, and Aosta, and it has connections with polyphonic works of composers of the late fifteenth century. The Council allowed the original texts and Dufay's chants to be sung only at Cambrai: elsewhere new texts and chants were substituted.

can. 1461. The Dominican Catharine of Siena, d. 1380, was instrumental in returning the papacy to Rome after its exile in Avignon. Raymond of Capua wrote her office.[156]

Attempt at canonization, *1484*. Catharine of Sweden, d. 1381, tr. 1488. Catharine was the daughter of Birgitta of Sweden and final founder of the Bridgettines. One office dates from before 1461; another from a single source of 1690, where it has been 'accommodated' to the Roman breviary.[157]

can. 1450. Bernardinus of Siena, a Franciscan, d. 1444. Three full offices are known.

1450–68. Simpertus, Benedictine abbot of Murbach, bishop of Augsburg, d. 807, can. 1468. *Eia presul alme Dei / Stirps regalis linee / Vere Dominus regnavit*. One of the puzzling features of this office is that, although monastic in form, it appears to have originally been secular: MR4 and MR8 show modal, musical, and textual evidence of having been added later.[158]

---

[154] Hughes, 'British Rhymed Offices', 244.

[155] Haggh, 'The Celebration of the *Recollectio*'. I thank Professor Haggh for sending me photocopies of this office. See also A. P. Frutaz, 'La *Recollectio Festorum s. Mariae Virginis*: testi liturgici in uso nella diocesi di Aosta dal sec. XV al sec. XIX', *Ephemerides liturgicae*, 70 (1956), 20–40.

[156] *AH* 24, p. 98: the office is in 45, no. 53. See n. 158.

[157] *AH* 26, no. 75 and *AH* 45, no. 54 respectively.

[158] *AH* 5, no. 80. I owe the translations and much of this summary to unpublished work by Terry David Brown, 'Songs for the Saints of the Schism: Liturgy for Vincent Ferrer and Catherine of Siena' (Ph.D. diss., University of Toronto, 1995).

First mentioned in 1450, when the cult was authorized, the office appears in some sources of this date, although it was not used until his canonization in 1468. Demonstrating its prior existence—perhaps in fact by more than two hundred years—a chronicle of Simpert's abbey tells us that the canonization was obtained 'so that we might . . . sing the *historia* and readings . . . , which were held in our library in very ancient writing'.[159] It is thus possible that the office, in some form, perhaps only as poetry, may date from the first half of the thirteenth century, when Adilbert, abbot of SS Ulrich and Afra 1230–47, wrote the *vita* of the saint and, according to one account, also a *historia*.[160] But lacking any known source from Adilbert's time, we can only speculate that this is the same composition.

The obvious priority of musical sound over textual sense in a few striking cases may suggest fifteenth- rather than thirteenth-century aesthetics. The chant follows the rhyme scheme rather than the syntactical structure, for instance, twice in one brief antiphon (see Ex. 2.21). Noteworthy features are shown in Ex. 2.22. The vigorous conjunction of tetra- and pentachord, in (*a*) setting the word *vivens*, 'living', occurs in other chants, as in (*d*). In (*b*), both the notational form and the melodic motif (for a single word) are unusual. If any (obscure) depiction of a flower is intended, it is purely in the notation, and perhaps uniquely in the manuscript consulted. In (*c*) the striking concatenation of three perfect fifths certainly attracts attention, aurally and visually. In another form, in the seventeenth century, the quadratum accidental was occasionally used near the word 'cross'. In (*d*) the extravagant sequential passage occurs not as a terminal melisma but at the repetendum, where the end of the verse rejoins the responsory, and, set syllabically and without the motivic repetition, in the verse itself.

can. 1455/58. The Dominican Vincent Ferrer, d. 1419.[161]

1471–84. The Visitation (see above).

can. 1482. The Franciscan bishop and doctor Bonaventure, d. 1274. Two offices are known, one based on the office for Francis.[162] This office seems known only in Italy.

---

[159] 'canonizationem impetravit . . . ut infra monasterium nostrum . . . possimus . . . cantare eius historiam et eadem legendam, quae habetur in libraria nostra in antiquissima litera . . .'; cited in *AH* 5, p. 223. The singular verb *habetur*, of course, invites the possibility that the relative clause refers only to the legend. On the other hand, a *historia* and its readings go together as a unit.

[160] *Acta Sanctorum* October, vi. 251.   [161] See n. 158.

[162] *AH* 25, no. 59, and 26, no. 60.

Ex. 2.21. Office for St Simpertus: LA4 (Lauds, fourth antiphon) *Benedictus rex celorum* (Blessed king of heaven, with whom reigning, the voice of the mute returns; the blind brow is graced with light; Satan is weakened)

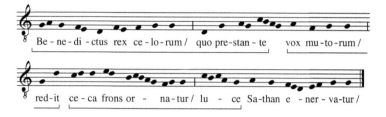

Ex. 2.22. Office for St Simpertus: (*a*) LE (Lauds, Benedictus antiphon) 'vivens sine'; (*b*) MA1 (Matins, first antiphon) 'flos'; (*c*) MA4 (Matins, fourth antiphon) 'crucis'; (*d*) MR8 (Matins, eighth responsory) 'Emendata'

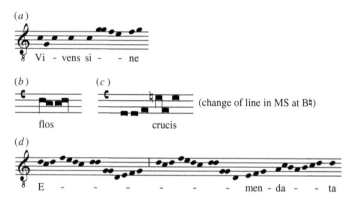

late 15th century. Judging by the sources that remain, two offices for Apollonia are from the latest layer of the repertory.[163] One displays the characteristics that will transform the fluid and soaring qualities of true plainsong into the banal symmetry of the hymn. It is perhaps noteworthy that the plica for the diphthong is still maintained (see Ex. 2.23). Many of the other items are considerably more elaborate. The other office has an interesting emphasis for the saint's name, setting it to the same melodic motif, regardless of the genre or mode of the chant in which it occurs (VA1 and VR in mode 1; VA5 and WE2 in mode 5; WA in mode 7); see Ex. 2.24. This kind of compositional procedure smacks more

---

[163] *AH* 5, no. 43; Prague, University Library MS XII A 9 for Ex. 2.23. *AH* 25, no. 37; Brussels, Bibliothèque Royale MS 6434 for Ex. 2.24.

Ex. 2.23. Office for St Apollonia: MA8 (Matins, eighth antiphon) *Rem audite inauditam* (Hear the strange thing: that friendly person [*equus* interpreted as classical *aequus*] was speaking to the chaste pearl, while blessing the girl)

Rem au - di - te in - au - di - tam / ad hanc ca-stam mar-ga - ri - tam /

lo -que -ba -tur e -quus il - le / be -ne - di -cen- do pu-sil - le /

Ex. 2.24. Office for St Apollonia: (*a*) VA1, VR, VA5, and WE2 'Apollonia'; (*b*) WA 'Apollonia'

A - pol - lo - ni - a /   A - pol - lo - ni - a

of artistic creativity than of liturgical sobriety. We have reached the Renaissance.

But the genre is not yet quite dead—

can. 1594. Hyacinth, a Dominican, the 'apostle' and patron of Poland, d. 1257. The office is in a missal printed in 1545, decades before the official canonization: it may have been excised, as a result of the Council of Trent, before the feast was properly authorized.[164]

CONCLUSION

This chapter has concentrated on offices for feasts of more or less universal importance to the medieval world. Of more than local interest, they have received much attention, making this complementary study possible. The fourteenth century seems to have been dominated by Francis, Dominic, and Thomas of Canterbury. Fifteenth-century offices borrow less from the first two of these, perhaps reflecting what the church thought it necessary to make universal. But many paths still need to be explored. In particular, it would be useful to identify a monastic, specifically Benedictine, group of offices: because of the lack of centralization, this group may contain many more local saints. In the later fifteenth century there seems to be a greater concern for word-painting or word-emphasis, and for settings that approximate the syllabic hymn with balanced phrases.

---

[164] *AH* 45, no. 45.

Chants of one office are often said to be related to those of another because the melodic shape of the tunes is similar. In this matter lies some of the great fascination with the repertory. The same shape is used repeatedly for chants in the same mode. Yet those same shapes are moulded in an infinite variety of ways, each of which is individual and was perhaps recognized as distinct. The criteria for asserting that a chant is borrowed from elsewhere are much more rigorous than might be thought from a casual appraisal, involving not only melodic shape, but also notation, the division into ligatures, and the underlay of words and syllables.

The chants of this repertory represent the normal musical expression of the period. Discovering how the principles and aesthetics of chant composition and adaptation influenced other repertories is a task for the next generation of musicologists.

III

INSTRUMENTAL MUSIC,
c.1300–*c*.1520

By Howard Mayer Brown† *and* Keith Polk

Part I: Instrumentalists

A NOTE ON SOURCES

SOURCES of information concerning medieval instrumentalists and their music are profoundly inconsistent. Most musicians did not belong to the elite layers of society and therefore did not attract much description or comment in the writings of the time. We must glean our information on their social contexts from scattered and disparate sources. Written collections of music can rarely tell us anything about the players or instruments; sources made for specific purposes such as keyboard performance are concentrated in a relatively narrow region and time-span (see also below). As regards archival records, very few documents give any details concerning freelance musicians, except perhaps when mentioning the instruments which were played. Members of court retinues or civic ensembles, on the other hand, are far better documented, as thousands of payroll records have survived (civic records, however, are more consistently preserved than those of the courts). Church records, preserved in great numbers, also occasionally mention the participation of instrumentalists.[1] Most of the

---

[1] Archival documents mentioning secular musicians are surveyed or excerpted in Madeleine B. Bernhard, 'Recherches sur l'histoire de la corporation des ménétriers ou joueurs d'instruments de la ville de Paris', *Bibliothèque de l'École des Chartes*, 3 (1841–2), 377–404; 4 (1842–3), 525–48; 5 (1843–4), 254–84, 339–72; Frank A. D'Accone, *The Civic Muse: Music and Musicians in Siena during the Middle Ages and the Renaissance* (Chicago, 1997); Louis Gilliodts-Van Severen, *Les Ménestrels de Bruges* (Bruges, 1912); Lewis Lockwood, *Music in Renaissance Ferrara, 1400–1505* (Cambridge, Mass., 1984); Jeanne Marix, *Histoire de la musique et des musiciens de la cour de Bourgogne sous le règne de Philippe le Bon (1420–1467)* (Strasburg, 1939; repr. Baden-Baden, 1974); Timothy J. McGee, 'In the Service of the Commune: The Changing Role of Florentine Civic Musicians, 1450–1532', *Sixteenth-Century Journal*, 30 (1999), 727–43; Hans Joachim Moser, *Die Musikergenossenschaften im deutschen Mittelalter* (Rostock, 1910); Gerhard Pietzsch, *Fürsten und fürstliche Musiker im mittelalterlichen Köln* (Cologne, 1966); Keith Polk, *German*

many narrative sources, such as chronicles and *romans*, are usually too general in their sporadic references to instrumental music to be very informative. On occasion, however, they can make comments of astonishing specificity. A chronicle from Bruges, for example, names the specific piece performed by the city's ensemble on a given occasion.[2] Guild records are generally confined to statutes, which are valuable in conveying a sense of the general procedures of the profession, but we lack the day-to-day documents that would tell us how the procedures actually worked. Tax listings, available only for a few centres, tell us that some musicians were quite comfortable—but other sources also indicate that many players faced poverty in old age. Legal records suggest that most late medieval players were probably reasonably well-behaved. There were, of course, a few spectacular exceptions. A wind player in Augsburg, for example, was banned from the city for the attempted murder of his landlady—in a rage following an argument he picked her up and threw her in the river Lech.[3] That the documentation concerning our subject is so erratic in so many ways constrains a cautious approach.

STATUS AND EDUCATION

During the Middle Ages and the Renaissance, musicians received professional training in two very different ways: either through schools attached to cathedrals and collegiate churches, intended to educate choirboys; or through apprenticeship to a master player, intended to prepare young men (and some young women) for careers as minstrels (*ménéstrels, menestrelli, giullari, juglares, spellieden, Spielleute, igric, histriones, joculatores*, etc.). Most minstrels played instruments, although some also sang. Minstrels constituted the largest group of instrumentalists in the fourteenth and fifteenth centuries, even though other classes of people also cultivated the art of playing instruments.

Instrumental Music of the Late Middle Ages (Cambridge, 1992); Walter Salmen, *Der Spielmann im Mittelalter* (Innsbruck, 1983); Heinrich W. Schwab, *Die Anfänge des weltlichen Berufsmusikertums in der mittelalterlichen Stadt* (Kieler Schriften zur Musikwissenschaft, 24; Kassel, 1982); Reinhard Strohm, *Music in Late Medieval Bruges* (Oxford, 1985; rev. edn., 1990); Edmond Vander Straeten, *Les Ménestrels au Pays-Bas* (Brussels, 1878); Craig Wright, *Music at the Court of Burgundy: A Documentary History* (Brooklyn, 1979); Sabine Žak, *Musik als 'Ehr und Zier' im mittelalterlichen Reich* (Neuss, 1979); Giuseppe Zippel, *I suonatori della Signoria di Firenze* (Trento, 1892); and many other smaller publications. Of particular value for the study of a specific region is Anna Maria Corbo, *San Ginesio e la tradizione musicale maceratese tra la fine del '300 e l'inizio del '500: giullari, suonatori e strumenti musicali* (Comune di San Ginesio, 1992), which combines archival and pictorial documentation on minstrels and their instruments in the Italian province of Macerata; a valuable localized study is Kenneth Kreitner, 'Music in the Corpus Christi Procession of Fifteenth-Century Barcelona', *EMH* 15 (1995), 153–204.

[2] Strohm, *Music in Late Medieval Bruges*, 86–7.

[3] The incident is recorded in Augsburg, Stadtarchiv, *Achtbuch*, 1374 (Register 34), fo. 107a.

Some choirboys, for example, had the opportunity to learn to play the organ or other instruments, and ability to play certain kinds of instruments was regarded as a desirable social accomplishment by members of the upper classes. Workers and peasants cultivated a repertory of music that is now almost completely lost since it was hardly ever written down, and some of them also played instruments.

Most minstrels came from the artisan classes. Once their education was complete, however, they had open to them a variety of jobs that could change their inherited social position. Some worked at princely courts, for example, as members of wind bands or as chamber musicians, and a select few of these even became intimates of kings and princes (see below). They could serve as members of a town band, combining a regular schedule of civic performances with occasional service at civic or courtly celebrations. Members of town bands could also be required to perform the duties of watchmen.[4] Still other minstrels worked as freelance musicians in towns and cities. Some performed alone, singing and playing the fiddle, for example, for anyone who would pay them. Others banded together with several other musicians to earn their living by playing for weddings, banquets, and other occasions when music was appropriate. There was also a class of itinerant ne'er-do-wells who eked out a bare subsistence wandering from town to town, and who sometimes combined other sorts of entertainment—acrobatics, story-telling, and the management of trained animals, for example —with their musical performances. Women were seldom recorded as professional players, although some are known to have taken part in professional engagements. Many minstrels appear to have thought of themselves primarily as instrumentalists, although on occasion guild records and other documents identify them as singers.[5]

At the beginning of the fourteenth century, most minstrels, not yet included within urban social organizations such as guilds and confraternities, were regarded with suspicion by respectable citizens.[6] Often itinerant, they were held to be of such questionable morals that the Church regarded many of them unworthy of the sacraments. Even at that time, however, a few minstrels served as private entertainers and

---

[4] In some areas such as northern France and Flanders, civic wind ensembles seem to have originally been tied to watchmen ensembles. In other regions (Germany and eastern sections of the modern Netherlands, for example) town ensembles seem to have been from the beginning more exclusively musical in character. See Mariëlla Beukers, '"For the Honour of the City": Utrecht City Minstrels between 1377 and 1528', *TVNM* 41 (1991), 3–25 at 11–12.

[5] On women as professional performers and on 'vocal' minstrels, see e.g. Wright, *Music at the Court of Burgundy*, 27–9.

[6] The social status of minstrels has been discussed extensively in Salmen, *Spielmann*, 31–46 and Schwab, *Anfänge*; see also Žak, *Musik als 'Ehr und Zier'*; Lawrence Gushee, 'Minstrel' in *New Grove*.

confidants to kings and princes. Men like the thirteenth-century minstrel Gausbert de Poicibot, for example, clearly enjoyed special rank in courtly society. Gausbert was born to a privileged family, but became impoverished and turned to minstrelsy, travelling from court to court, performing and composing songs (accompanying himself, apparently, on the fiddle). He was so successful at his chosen trade that he was eventually rewarded with lands and a knighthood.[7] One further example of a musician successful in the courtly world was Elias Cairel, who had been of common birth (he was a goldsmith at one time) and who became a professional minstrel—a composer of songs and poems, and specifically a fiddle-player.[8]

Throughout the later Middle Ages the prospect for extraordinary status remained open for a privileged few musicians. Discerning courtly patrons sometimes offered a distinguished instrumentalist an honoured place. In French-speaking centres such musicians as Baude Cordier would be designated as 'valet de chambre', and Paul Hofhaimer, organist at the Habsburg court at the turn of the sixteenth century, was made a knight. Particularly striking was the situation in Italy, where a class of poet-improvisers flourished in aristocratic circles. Figures like Pietrobono of Ferrara, singer, improviser, and player of the gittern and lute, became central to the splendour of court life—and it is an open question whether such men with their distinctly elite status should be equated with minstrels of more ordinary rank.[9] The achievements of these courtly musicians, however, are related to the same basic conditions that affected a broader range of musicians within late medieval society. It is clearly unwise to generalize about the abilities of professional instrumentalists in the fourteenth and fifteenth centuries, not only because of the lack of solid evidence, but also because there obviously were vast differences in ability and repertory between the best- and the worst-educated minstrels; and furthermore their character, working conditions, and duties changed radically between 1300 and 1520.

At least two groups of professional instrumentalists should be considered apart from the others. The players of trumpets and drums, to

---

[7] Christopher Page, 'Court and City in France, 1100–1300', in James McKinnon (ed.), *Antiquity and the Middle Ages* (London, 1990), 197–217 at 208–9. Gausbert was not specifically mentioned as a player of the fiddle, but when a youth, an early patron furnished him with 'a minstrel's equipment, clothes and a horse', ibid. 209; the equipment would most likely have included some form of fiddle.

[8] Christopher Page, *Voices and Instruments of the Middle Ages* (London, 1987), 175–6; Page, 'Court and City', 199.

[9] On courtly *valets de chambre* see Strohm, *Rise*, 301–2; Marix, *Histoire de la musique*; Wright, *Burgundy*. On Pietrobono and Italian *improvvisatori*, see below.

name the first group, were responsible for ceremonial music and military signals, were trained separately from other instrumentalists, and apparently kept their own identity within ensembles throughout the fourteenth, fifteenth, and later centuries. The second group were the organists who began to be regularly attached to cathedrals and princely chapels during the fourteenth century. They were usually trained as choirboys in cathedral schools; their education and professional duties allied them with singers and other members of the musical elite, and distinguished them from minstrels.

So far as we now know, patrons expected general competence of minstrels, rather than specialization on any one instrument. Thus the group of musicians in Verona who had been responsible for most of the city's music in the years around 1484 claimed, when they applied to become the official musicians of the city, that they could sing as well as play shawms, trumpets, flutes, harps, lutes, and organ.[10] Virtuosi seem to have grown up in the course of the fifteenth century, and not even all of those specialized in a particular instrument. Conrad Paumann, the blind organist, also played the lute (and, indeed, seems to have been responsible for devising German lute tablature); the Burgundian court minstrels Jean Fernandez and Jean Cordoval are identified in court records both as lutenists and as fiddle players; and Pietrobono, court musician of Ferrara, played both gittern and lute.[11] Many minstrels seem to have specialized instead on playing a variety of instruments of the same range.[12] Both the versatility of instrumentalists and their specialization on instruments of particular ranges have wide implications for our knowledge of performance practice, the former because it seems possible to apply what is known about one instrument to others, and the latter because each particular player can be more reliably identified in the sources as soon as we know his preferred range.

---

[10] Enrico Paganuzzi, *La musica a Verona* (Verona, 1976), 80.

[11] On Paumann and the invention of tablature see Sebastian Virdung, *Musica getutscht: A Treatise on Musical Instruments*, ed. Beth Bullard (Cambridge, 1993), 6 and 156. Concerning doubling by Paumann and at the Burgundian court see Polk, *German Instrumental Music*, 13–15; for Pietrobono see Lockwood, *Music in Renaissance Ferrara*, 98–108.

[12] Concerning the naming of players by ranges see Lockwood, *Music in Renaissance Ferrara*, 100 and 142, and William F. Prizer, 'Bernardino Piffaro e i pifferi e tromboni di Mantova: strumenti a fiato in una corte italiana', *Rivista italiana di musicologia*, 16 (1981), 151–84 at 180. For a survey of documents referring to players by voice ranges see Polk, *German Instrumental Music*, 53, 165. The specialization by ranges is noted first in documents early in the 15th c., and appears to have been more general by mid-century. A concern for range may have influenced the development of families of instruments, which appears to have taken place in the later 15th c. On this development see Gerhard Stradner, 'Zur Ausbildung verschiedener Instrumentengrössen', in Walter Salmen (ed.), *Musik und Tanz zur Zeit Kaiser Maximilians I.* (Innsbruck, 1992), 177–82.

A good deal more is known about the training and repertory of singers—who have traditionally constituted the central strand in writing about medieval and Renaissance music and in conceptualizing its history—than about the education or the repertory of instrumentalists. We lack information about the training of minstrels partly because it was private and secretive in order that professionals could maintain their monopoly on the services they provided (see also below on guild regulations). Moreover, the art of professional instrumentalists was largely unwritten and much of their music may well have been improvised.

We can assume, though without much evidence, that apart from learning the techniques of various instruments, minstrels memorized a lot of music, learned how to improvise a new part against a cantus firmus, and also developed other techniques for elaborating a composition from some initial musical idea, perhaps by applying to a basic ground plan a set of melodic formulas. Only a sparse handful of medieval documents give any detail at all concerning the kinds of pieces that young players would learn, and repertory is rarely specified. It is clear, however, that not only dance tunes and popular melodies were mastered, but that well-known polyphonic pieces also formed a part of the core of the medieval musical curriculum.[13] In certain places, performers mastered sacred as well as secular polyphony, for professional contracts would specify that motets and antiphon settings were to be performed.[14] Technical matters, of course, would be conveyed to the young musician. Accurate intonation, for example, must have been as much a concern for medieval musicians as it is for players of our time. We know, at any rate, that a player could lose his job if he played out of tune.[15]

The degree or extent to which minstrels in the fourteenth and fifteenth centuries could read music remains an open question. On the one hand, much of their repertory, especially early in the period, may well have been monophonic: a collection of tunes and formulas that could be memorized and elaborated in performance, and an arsenal of improvisatory techniques that obviated the necessity of written music. On the other hand, there is some evidence, discussed below, that minstrels played polyphony even in the fourteenth century—they

---

[13] Strohm, *Rise*, 347–8.

[14] See Strohm, *Bruges*, 86, and Polk, *German Instrumental Music*, 135–6.

[15] A court player in Milan was dismissed because he could not play in tune with other members of the ensemble ('intonare con loro'), and thus his playing was discordant ('per essere lo aere soe dissonante et discorde'); see Guglielmo Barblan, 'Vita musicale alla corte sforzesca', *Storia di Milano*, ix (Milan, 1961), 787–852 at 800.

certainly did by the mid-fifteenth century—for which an ability to read notation may well have been necessary.

Among the various opportunities for minstrels to refine their art and compete with other professionals, the secular and sacred festivities of larger cities—such as trade-fairs, civic holidays, and religious feast-days—were most important. The seasonal fairs around Christmas, Easter, and Ascension were often used by visiting minstrels from distant places in search of employment or education. In some regions, the confluence of musicians on a certain local feast was in itself a long-standing tradition and was sometimes recorded in civic documents year after year.[16]

So-called 'minstrels' schools' flourished in the fourteenth century.[17] They were gatherings usually held in the Lenten season when employment opportunities for minstrels were reduced, and appear to have been less formal educational enterprises than arenas for the free exchange of instruments, new tunes, manners of ornamentation, and ideas about music, a late medieval equivalent of modern scholarly conferences. The 'schools' thrived primarily in northern France, the Low Countries, and in eastern Germany (sources from other important areas such as southern Germany, Italy, and southern France do apparently not mention them). The large annual gatherings would attract musicians from hundreds of miles away, as both courts and cities would provide travel subsidy for their players. The minstrels' schools appear to have died out early in the fifteenth century as musicians' guilds and other more local networks became established and performed the same functions more efficiently.

GUILDS AND PATRONAGE

By the middle of the fourteenth century, musicians in the cities were adapting more and more to the patterns of urban society. They formed guilds, for example, and joined in the activities of confraternities. Since the earlier Middle Ages, guilds (associations of those engaged in a particular trade or profession) had provided a fundamental vehicle for town residents to achieve a measure of power.[18] The dominant guilds

---

[16] As is the case of the minstrels of the Macerata province, documented in Corbo, *San Ginesio*. For some early examples, see Schwab, *Anfänge*, 24–8.

[17] They are discussed by Wright, *Burgundy*, 32–3; Salmen, *Spielmann*, 110–13; Schwab, *Anfänge*, 48–9; Gordon Greene, 'The Schools of Minstrelsy', *Studies in Music*, 2 (1977), 31–40; Strohm, *Bruges*, 78; Maricarmen Gómez, 'Minstrel Schools in the Late Middle Ages', *EM* 18 (1990), 213–15.

[18] The literature on guilds is vast, as almost every writer on medieval economic, political, or social history discusses them. A brief general survey may be found in Fritz Rörig, *The Medieval Town* (Berkeley, 1967), 9–10, 90–3, 149–60. For a sample of a more detailed analysis, concerning the political struggles of the guilds in Italy, see Lauro Martines, *Power*

were the larger ones most involved in the central economic activities of the town. The social pattern of each city was unique: in some the traditional oligarchies retained control, sometimes managing to eliminate guilds altogether. In others the guilds gained the upper hand.[19] By about 1400—after some two centuries of often ferocious internal struggles—many cities had achieved some balance of power between elite elements and guilds. For tradesmen and artisans the guild specified conditions within their professions. The guild also served to define the place of their members within urban society, providing some voice in government, acting as a focus for social activities, and offering aid to sick and elderly members.

Musicians' guilds were initiated much later than the more powerful merchants' guilds, and, in fact, only in the largest cities was guild membership large enough for the organization to be effective. In Paris, Antwerp, and Bruges, for example, musicians' guilds appear to have exercised a formidable role, establishing basic rules for the profession, setting contract conditions and general pay scales, and instituting educational standards. They also provided significant social services.[20] In most towns, however, the number of musicians was too small to make a separate guild either effective or worthwhile. Some towns of middling size did have organizations of musicians, but these were too small to have much power within the larger political network of the community. More critically, they were hobbled in attempts to regulate the most gifted and prominent musicians.

Outstanding players were difficult to control for several reasons. A central thrust of guild regulation was to protect members by reducing competition. They strictly limited the number of apprentices a master

and Imagination: City-States in Renaissance Italy (New York, 1979), 38–41, 46–53, 77–8, 133–7.

[19] Nuremberg was a city in which guilds were forbidden: see Gerald Strauss, *Nuremberg in the Sixteenth Century* (Bloomington, Ind., 1976), 97–101. The situation of the guilds was different in every city and region. Harry Miskimin, *The Economy of Early Renaissance Europe, 1300–1460* (Cambridge, 1975), 106–11, discusses the control of the guilds by the monarchy in France, while J. A. van Houtte, *An Economic History of the Low Countries, 800–1800* (London, 1977), 77–80, surveys the situation in the Low Countries. Colin Platt, *The English Mediæval Town* (London, 1979), 137–42, provides a very readable description of the guilds in England. A colourful survey, with a more Marxist slant, is available in Catharina Lis and Hugo Soly, *Poverty and Capitalism in Pre-Industrial Europe* (Atlantic Highlands, NJ, 1979) 33–9.

[20] See, respectively, Bernhard, 'Recherches'; Léon de Burbure, *Aperçu sur l'ancienne corporation des musiciens instrumentalistes d'Anvers* (Brussels, 1862); and D. Van de Casteele, 'Préludes historiques sur la ghilde des ménestrels à Bruges', *Annales de la Société d'Émulation de Bruges*, 23 (1870), 105–74. See also Moser, *Die Musikergenossenschaften*. For recent discussions of the Paris guild, see Christopher Page, *The Owl and the Nightingale* (London, 1989), 61–9, and Kay Brainerd Slocum, '*Confrérie, Bruderschaft* and Guild: The Formation of Musicians' Fraternal Organisations in Thirteenth- and Fourteenth-Century Europe', *EMH* 14 (1995), 257–74.

player could train, for example, as a way of controlling the number of professional instrumentalists available in any one locality.[21] All members were required to be citizens of the town, and the guild leadership would usually obtain the concession from the city council that only guild members could practise the profession within the walls. They would also try to establish uniform pay and quality standards. The most successful musicians, however, those hired by courts and under contract as official city musicians, were largely untouched by the rule concerning citizenship. In fact, positions in urban ensembles were often filled by outside players. In 1453/4, when a new civic ensemble was engaged in Bruges, where the guild would appear to have exercised considerable authority, the new players were all from outside the city (and even from outside Flanders).[22] Such outsiders were awarded special resident status or granted citizenship outright. Contracted players could also be exempted from local taxation; their incomes would continue in economically hard times, a benefit not enjoyed by local independent musicians. Furthermore, contracted players could obtain a monopoly of certain services within the city walls, despite any efforts of the guilds to regulate such competition. Court musicians similarly flouted restrictive efforts and they, too, performed within the city confines, frequently compensated by the city council itself. When the city councils (or individual members of the ruling elites) hired such brilliant outsiders as Conrad Paumann or Augustein Schubinger to perform, the musicians' guild could not bar this diversion of local resources to 'foreign' musicians.[23] Attempts at quality control and uniform conditions might work reasonably efficiently in some trades. They did not work well in music, however, where individual qualities

[21] On such guild regulations see e.g. Edmond Vander Straeten, *La Musique aux Pays-Bas avant le XIXe siècle*, 8 vols. (Brussels, 1867–88; repr. New York, 1969), ii. 22–36, and iv. 94, 150, and 208.

[22] Gilliodts-Van Severen, *Les Ménestrels de Bruges*, 43. The musicians were all from Valenciennes. In 1479/80, when a new minstrel was needed, the city paid one of its minstrels to journey to Namur, Maastricht, and Cologne to audition potential replacements; see ibid. 49.

[23] Paumann, though blind, travelled and performed widely as an organist and lutenist throughout Bavaria (with visits and payments for performances recorded in such cities as Augsburg, Nördlingen, and Regensburg) and he even made a journey to Italy. On the Italian journey see William F. Prizer, 'The Frottola and the Unwritten Tradition', *Studi musicali*, 15 (1986), 3–37 at 13–16; for biographical details see Franz Krautwurst, 'Konrad Paumann', in G. Pfeiffer and A. Wendenburg (eds.), *Fränkische Lebensbilder* (Veröffentlichungen der Gesellschaft für fränkische Geschichte, ser. VII A, vol. 7, 1977), 33–48. Augustein Schubinger, player of cornetto, lute, and trombone, in his younger days served in civic ensembles in Augsburg and Florence, and was associated with the Habsburg courts under Maximilian and Philip the Fair. He performed often in the Low Countries, with appearances recorded in Brussels and Mechelen, and probably in Bruges as well (where payments for Habsburg musicians were entered as lump sums, without giving names). See Keith Polk, 'Patronage, Imperial Image, and the Emperor's Musical Retinue: On the Road with

are often highly prized. No guild regulation could protect the lacklustre local lutenist, for example, from the effects of the greater popularity of a Paumann or Schubinger. This is not to say that guild membership was without benefits, especially for local freelance players. Despite its relative political weakness and its difficulties in providing effective protection, the guild remained the essential focus for collective activity of many medieval instrumentalists.

Cities and towns provided the most obvious focus for the activities of guilds. Some trades also organized themselves within larger geographical boundaries.[24] Musicians, too, formed regional 'brotherhoods' (*Musikergenossenschaften*) in some areas. This is revealed by the recurring designation of a prominent player as the 'king of the minstrels'. Jean Facien carried the title of 'roy des menestrels', first at the French court under King Charles VI, then after Charles's death in 1422 at the court of the Duke of Burgundy. Facien's authority evidently held sway in all regions which recognized the king of France as overlord.[25] In the late fourteenth century a trumpeter of the Duke of Austria was appointed 'king' of the minstrels, who 'ruled' within the territory controlled by the Bishop of Basle.[26] The names of the 'kings' of the Alsatian Brotherhood of Musicians (perhaps the most famous of the *Musikergenossenschaften*), are preserved through the entire fifteenth century and beyond.[27] The practical effect of these figures remains quite obscure, however, as there is too little evidence concerning their authority or the operation of these regional confederations.

Another positive force leading to a broader acceptance of musicians within medieval society was their activity in religious confraternities. Such confraternities could be relatively large-scale organizations which embraced a wide spectrum of citizens (i.e. they were not necessarily restricted to one profession or to one narrow stratum of society).[28] Their religious activities often required musical perfor-

Maximilian I.', in Walter Salmen (ed.), *Musik und Tanz zur Zeit Kaiser Maximilian I.* (Innsbruck, 1992), 79–88.

[24] In the Rhine area, for example, the Count Palatine claimed regional authority over metalworkers (*Kessler*), potters, ropemakers, tinsmiths, and makers of wooden shoes. See Henry J. Cohn, *The Government of the Rhine Palatinate in the Fifteenth Century* (Oxford, 1965), 129–31.

[25] Marix, *Histoire*, 20, 265–9.

[26] Martin Vogeleis, *Quellen und Bausteine zu einer Geschichte der Musik und des Theaters im Elsass 500–1800* (Strasburg, 1911; repr. 1979), 73–4.

[27] Moser, *Musikergenossenschaften*, 68–9.

[28] On the nature of confraternities, see Ronald F. E. Weissman, 'Cults and Contexts: In Search of the Renaissance Confraternity', in Konrad Eisenbichler (ed.), *Crossing the Boundaries: Christian Piety and the Arts in Italian Medieval and Renaissance Confraternities* (Early Drama, Art, and Music Monograph Series, 15; Kalamazoo, 1991), 201–20.

mances not only for liturgical services such as Masses for patron saints, but also for the frequent related processions. In short, music clearly played a prominent role in the activities of these groups. In 's-Hertogenbosch, for example, the Confraternity of Our Lady hired the organist Jan van Rijswijc to teach its members how to sing or play an instrument.[29] The confraternities thus opened up not only possibilities for income, but also access for musicians to influential, deeply rooted networks of patronage. These networks were an essential feature of medieval urban governance; without such contacts, musicians would have been doomed to remain outsiders.[30]

The most profound changes working on musicians were those which affected the basic nature of patronage. The fourteenth and fifteenth centuries were characterized by intense conflict. All elements of society, the Church, the nobility, and the cities, were rent by dissension and bloody struggles for power. After the first decades of the fifteenth century currents ran in favour of centralization. Larger cities swallowed up smaller ones, and monarchs brought rebelling elements under control. Power and wealth consolidated in fewer hands. These developments benefited musicians, for not only were the rich and powerful able to maintain larger stables of retainers, it became perceived as a kind of imperative to do so.

The idea took root that it was essential to present an image of power, majesty, and 'magnificence'.[31] Music became bound up with this image. Musical groups had been rather small in the fourteenth century. Around 1300 even the higher nobility usually supported no more than a handful of players, and only few of the larger cities subsidized musical ensembles. By the late fifteenth century, in contrast, a king or the emperor would support a dozen or so

---

[29] A. Smijers, *De Illustre Lieve Vrouwe Broederschap te 's-Hertogenbosch* (Amsterdam, 1932), 32.

[30] Emphasis on networks of patronage within urban struggles has been cultivated in much recent scholarship. In the recent set of essays *Patronage, Art, and Society in Renaissance Italy*, ed. F. W. Kent and Patricia Simons (Canberra and Oxford, 1987), see esp. Ronald F. E. Weissman, 'Taking Patronage Seriously: Mediterranean Values and Renaissance Society', 25–45. See also Werner Gundersheimer, 'Patronage in the Renaissance: An Exploratory Approach', in Guy F. Lytle and Stephen Orgel (eds.), *Patronage in the Renaissance* (Princeton, 1981), 3–23.

[31] On this point see A. D. Fraser Jenkins, 'Cosimo de' Medici's Patronage of Art and the Theory of Magnificence', *Journal of the Warburg and Courtauld Institutes*, 33 (1970), 162–70. That the impulse to present a façade of magnificence motivated an outburst of building of private palaces in Florence in the late 15th c. is an underlying theme of Richard Goldthwaite, *The Building of Renaissance Florence* (Baltimore, 1980). Similar attitudes stimulated patronage elsewhere; see e.g. Gordon Kipling, 'Henry VII and the Origins of Tudor Patronage', in Guy F. Lytle and Stephen Orgel (eds.), *Patronage in the Renaissance* (Princeton, 1981), 117–64. Concerning musical patronage, Žak, *Musik als 'Ehr und Zier'*, is a fundamental survey. See also Strohm, *Rise*, 300–19.

trumpets, a wind band of six, and a contingent of players of soft instruments—and all cities of any pretension supported their own ensembles.[32] Social entertainments such as banquets and dances became settings for competitive displays of splendour, and bidding wars for outstanding talent became the order of the day. Not only were more musicians able to find employment, but their material conditions, too, seem to have improved. Tax records from Augsburg, for example, reveal that the declared wealth of contracted city players there placed them in the upper 15 per cent of the city's population. Such factors as titles of 'master', ownership of property, and a sharp decline in the involvement in violent crime suggest that musicians were fully integrated into society. What must have made the trade of music even more attractive to talented young instrumentalists is that while musicians appear to have been better paid as the century progressed, the salaries of artisans and tradesmen in general seem to have declined.[33]

In sum, by about 1500, minstrels, and especially those who worked at princely courts or for a civic corporation, could hope to become quite prosperous. A gifted instrumentalist in the late fifteenth century could expect to have a substantial income, reasonable job security, and a respectable status within his community.

EUROPEAN CIRCULATION AND DEVELOPMENT OF THE ART

The expanding waves of patronage which rippled throughout Europe engendered more than just prosperity. The trade of minstrelsy, as John Stevens once remarked, was international, and the cosmopolitan quality of instrumental music became more emphatic.[34] Some performers travelled as musical representatives of their patrons—and such travel was especially demanded of courtly players. Others, as documents reveal in increasing numbers from the late fourteenth

---

[32] For some comparative tables showing changes in the levels of patronage see Keith Polk, 'Patronage and Innovation in Instrumental Music in the 15th Century', *Historic Brass Society Journal*, 3 (1991), 151–78 at 163–5.

[33] For a discussion of the general economic climate of the 15th c. see Robert Lopez and Harry Miskimin, 'The Economic Depression of the Renaissance', *Economic History Review*, 2nd ser., 14 (1962), 408–26, and Robert Lopez, Harry Miskimin, and Carlo Cipolla, 'The Economic Depression of the Renaissance: Rejoinder and Reply', *Economic History Review*, 2nd ser., 16 (1964), 509–29. For a classic statement of the effects of the economy on the arts see Robert Lopez, 'Hard Times and the Investment in Culture', in *The Renaissance: A Symposium* (New York, 1953, repr. Boston, 1958), 50–63. A more recent survey is Richard A. Goldthwaite, *Wealth and the Demand for Art in Italy, 1300–1600* (Baltimore and London, 1993), 14–16 and 20–9. See also John Munro, 'Economic Depression and the Arts in the Fifteenth-Century Low Countries', *Renaissance and Reformation*, 19 (1983), 235–50.

[34] John Stevens, *Music and Poetry in the Early Tudor Court* (London, 1961), 308.

century onwards, accepted appointments in regions often quite removed from their home territories.

Concerning the former, as musical ensembles developed into icons of prestige, wide-ranging travel was demanded. The groups most often in the public eye were those of the great princes. Ensembles associated with the court of Burgundy, for example, appeared throughout France, the Low Countries, in Germany, and in northern Italy in the mid-fifteenth century. A few decades later those associated with the Habsburg retinues of Maximilian and Philip the Fair spread over an even wider geographic range. This travelling activity was fired by the necessities of politics, for the upper aristocracy was both extremely international and intensely competitive. Princes and princesses from what we might be tempted to think of as the most isolated and far-flung corners of Europe—Portugal, Scotland, and Cyprus, for example—could appear with their musicians, assuming influential roles at the very centres of power.[35] Often the linking mechanism was marriage alliances, as England could be linked to Burgundy, Bavaria to France, or Brandenburg to Mantua. Such alliances produced in turn regular, continuing contacts between players of the regions concerned.

Many courts (and a few cities as well) hired highly prestigious foreign players on long-term contracts which formed the other major conduit for international contact and exchange. Sometimes national specialities seem to have been the issue. English harpists seem to have been in vogue in Italy.[36] The hiring of foreign players occurred in many regions, but Italy appears to have been especially hospitable to outside players. Furthermore, while many regions contributed to the musical traffic, German instrumentalists were the pre-eminent players, and distinctly the ones most in demand.

The prominence of the Germans was long obscured because the musical manuscripts which have formed the basis of much of our evaluation of medieval artistic life do not tell us much about the performers. German players began to appear in foreign lands in the fourteenth century, and soon were scattered to all corners of Europe. The courts of northern Spain vigorously sought them, hiring both wind and string players. French aristocratic centres in the south, too, such as Foix and Savoy, provided handsome rewards to German players.[37]

[35] See Strohm, *Rise*, 307–13, 522.

[36] A Giovanni dall'arpa Inglese was at the court of Ferrara in 1450, for example; see Lockwood, *Music in Renaissance Ferrara*, 317.

[37] See Salmen, *Der Spielmann*, 104–13. See also Keith Polk, 'Innovation in Instrumental Music 1450–1510: The Role of German Performers within European Culture', in John Kmetz (ed.), *Music in the German Renaissance* (Cambridge, 1994), 202–14 at 204–8.

Political realities, of course, played a significant role in the traffic in players. Isabel, Queen of France (1385–1422) was a Wittelsbach of Bavaria, and the French court served to introduce her country-men into the musical scene in Paris. Holland, Hainaut, and Zee-land were ruled from 1328 to 1429 by the Wittelsbach dynasty, whose members intermarried with princes of France and the Low Countries.

That Germans were favoured in Italy seems, on the other hand, to have been a matter more of musical taste than of politics. The favour enjoyed by the northerners is attested by a variety of contemporary documents. The poet Folgore da San Gimignano calls fair maidens to his side, citing the following attractions:

> An ambling palfrey, a Spanish steed,
> and people accustomed to sing like the French,
> to dance like the Provençaux
> with new instruments from Germany.[38]

At a more mundane level, the minutes of deliberations of the town council of Florence show that German skills were so highly regarded that the council ruled in 1445 that henceforth all members of the civic ensemble would not be local but foreign (which meant in effect German).[39] Pay records, too, second their pre-eminence. The highest salary for a musician in the court of Ferrara between 1456 and 1476 went not to one of the fine singers there, nor to Pietrobono, but to Corrado d'Alemagna, a German wind player.[40] The development of the civic ensembles of Siena—city trumpeters as well as wind band (*pifferi*)—has been amply documented by Frank A. D'Accone, showing many changes of conditions until a decline of both groups in the late sixteenth century.[41]

More important than pre-eminence of any one national group, however, were the effects on music of the European connections, both of musicians and of patronage. The finer musicians moved freely in a very fluid world, taking with them not only playing techniques, instru-ments, and ensemble concepts, but the best pieces as well. The very latest French repertory could appear in a manuscript from Silesia, an Italian trombonist could write out pieces by an English composer, and

---

[38] 'Ambiante palfrens, destrier di Spagna / e gente costumata a la francesca / cantar danzar a la provenzalesca / con instrumenti novi d'Alemagna', *Scrittori d'Italia*, i: *Secoli XIII–XV*, ed. Natalino Sapegno (Florence, 1973), 100.

[39] See McGee, 'The Changing Role', 732.

[40] Lockwood, *Music in Renaissance Ferrara*, 177–81.

[41] D'Accone, *The Civic Muse*.

a German tune could pop up in the most recent Italian song book, manuscript or printed.

Awareness of these connections may shed some light on some of the obscure questions relating to instrumental music, for example within the dance repertory. Dancing was enormously popular in Germany in the fifteenth century. Nördlingen, a relatively small town, built a dance house of astonishing size.[42] Oddly, however, no German collections of dance tunes appear to have survived from this period, to match those which contain Franco-Burgundian and Italian repertories.[43] On the other hand, settings of a surprising number of French and Italian dance tunes do turn up in German manuscripts. The details of the German repertory remain murky, but when we realize that the German aristocracy frequently interacted with the nobility in Italy, France, and the Low Countries, and that German musicians resident in all those areas communicated with their homelands, it will appear perfectly natural that German dancers demanded a Continental repertory which could be provided by resident musicians with connections abroad. Italian dance tunes such as *Colinetto*, or French/Burgundian ones such as *Une fois avant que morir*, could appear in the Buxheim Organ Book; Hartmann Schedel could copy two French melodies into his music book (Munich, Bayerische Staatsbibliothek, Cgm 810), and sophisticated as he was, he could identify them as 'Italian tunes for dancing'.[44] His mistake is understandable as he almost certainly learned them during his student days in Padua—quite possibly from German performers.

Not all musicians or localities were so well connected; some regions seem to have resisted international currents. The court of Naples during the mid-fifteenth century, for example, seems not to have been so accessible to northern players as other Italian courts.[45] Even in southern Germany, which was strongly disposed to international exchange, some players would be trained in a town and remain there for their entire professional careers, sometimes playing with the same players for two decades and more.[46]

---

[42] See the contribution of Walter Salmen in this volume.

[43] Concerning the Franco-Burgundian tunes see Frederick Crane, *Materials for the Study of the Fifteenth-Century Basse Danse* (Brooklyn, 1968). For the Italian repertory see Otto Kinkeldey, 'Dance Tunes of the Fifteenth Century', in David Hughes (ed.), *Instrumental Music* (Cambridge, Mass., 1959), 3–30, 89–152. Concerning dance music in Germany, see Walter Salmen and Walter Wiora, 'Die Tanzmusik im deutschen Mittelalter', *Zeitschrift für Volkskunde*, 3/4 (1953), 164–87.

[44] Daniel Heartz, 'Hoftanz and Basse Dance', *JAMS* 19 (1966), 13–36 at 19–20. On Schedel's songbook, see Strohm, *Rise*, 495–9.

[45] See Allan Atlas, *Music at the Aragonese Court of Naples* (Cambridge, 1985), 98–113.

[46] In Augsburg, for example, the shawmist Claus von Sulgen was appointed to the civic ensemble in 1440 (Augsburg, Stadtarchiv, *Baumeisterbuch*, 1440, fo. 62ᵛ) and served until at least 1473

As power and wealth become more centralized in the fifteenth century, the patrons themselves are increasingly found to be amateur performers. This kind of diversion, too, intertwined with the desire to present a flattering self-image. Refined leisure activities such as dancing, playing an instrument, or singing became status symbols. International figures as diverse as Charles the Bold of Burgundy, Isabella d'Este, and Rudolph Agricola were more than basically competent musicians, and their active participation was imitated by others. Amateurs, while second to professionals in matters of musical techniques and practices, played determining roles in such areas as repertory. If the French and Burgundian aristocracy took a fancy to Spanish or Moorish dance tunes, for example, elites in Italy, Germany, and England would soon be demanding the same pieces. Another notable impact of amateurs was that they would have required written sources. Professional instrumentalists, as observed above, usually performed from memory or improvised; the less experienced but affluent amateur not only needed manuscripts, but could afford to pay for them. Amateurs also influenced the development of instruments. The rapid acceptance of the viol at the turn of the sixteenth century appears to have hinged on the popularity of the instrument in courtly circles in Italy just before 1500, and in humanist circles in southern Germany shortly thereafter. In short, the vogue for the instrument was tied to amateur rather than professional activity.[47]

PART II: Musical Sources and Performance

In order to understand late medieval instrumentalists, including minstrels, we need to know what music they played, on which instruments, and how they played it. Such questions are not easy to answer, because the details of a minstrel's education were shielded by the apprenticeship system from being public knowledge, and because so much of the music they played was either improvised or memorized and thus never

(*Baumeisterbuch*, fo. 65ᵛ; accounts for the next three years are missing, and Claus is not included from 1477 onwards). He remained in the city, however, paying extraordinarily high taxes, 14 florins in 1477, for example, which placed him in the top 4 per cent of the income levels of the city (Augsburg, Stadtarchiv, *Steurbuch*, 1477, fo. 6d). Ulrich Schubinger the Elder was his colleague there for the last twenty years or so of his career (Ulrich was appointed in 1457, BB, fo. 112ᵛ). See also Polk, 'Instrumental Music in the Urban Centres of Renaissance Germany', *EMH* 7 (1987), 159–86 at 179.

[47] Ian Woodfield, *The Early History of the Viol* (Cambridge, 1984), chs. 4 and 5, traces the history of the instrument in Italy and southern Germany. Polk, *German Instrumental Music*, 33–8, adds further details to the chronology of developments in Germany.

written down. To a much greater extent than with singers' music and with vocal performance practice, for instrumental repertories and practices we must rely on a wide variety of sources, and not just written music. Some theoretical treatises provide valuable information about the musical practices of instrumentalists; archival documents record who the instrumentalists were and how they were organized, as well as occasionally telling us the names of their instruments; some paintings, manuscript illuminations, and sculptures show instrumentalists in action; and literary works—lyric poetry, romances, and other fiction as well as chronicles and other historical works—give a more three-dimensional view of the life and character of the men and women who played instruments in the late Middle Ages. Nevertheless, the proper starting point for a consideration of instrumental music is with the relatively few collections of written music from the fourteenth and fifteenth centuries that can be associated with minstrels and other instrumentalists.

EARLY AND MONOPHONIC SOURCES OF INSTRUMENTAL MUSIC

Notated music destined for instrumental usage appears in manuscripts only sporadically before the fifteenth century. It is therefore almost impossible to construct a continuous history of instrumental music, or to know how one repertory relates to another. The history of written instrumental music properly begins with a handful of compositions found in several English and French manuscripts of the thirteenth century.[48] Most of them are based on the formal principle of the double versicle: a series of immediately repeated sections, with refrains finishing with *ouvert* and *clos* endings. These extant compositions seem to represent the three instrumental forms, all with double versicles, described in enigmatic terms by Johannes de Grocheio, a French theorist active in the years around 1300: the estampie, the ductia, and the nota.[49]

The composition without text or title added to MS Douce 139, Bodleian Library, Oxford (a late thirteenth-century collection of statutes from Coventry, where the manuscript almost certainly originated) is clearly divided into sections, although it is not so certain

---

[48] Survey and introduction: Leo Schrade, *Die handschriftliche Überlieferung der ältesten Instrumentalmusik* (Lahr, 1931), 27–31, 39–60; Christopher Page, 'Instruments and Instrumental Music before 1300', in NOHM ii², 445–84.

[49] For a discussion of Grocheio's use of these terms, see *Medieval Instrumental Dances*, ed. Timothy McGee (Bloomington, Ind., 1989), 8–13; Christopher Page, 'Johannes de Grocheio on Secular Music: A Corrected Text and a New Translation', *Plainsong and Medieval Music*, 2 (1993), 17–41.

whether all or only some should be repeated.[50] Although the composition is mostly monophonic, it ends with a polyphonic refrain for three voices. The three untitled compositions added to another late thirteenth-century English manuscript, MS Harley 978 of the British Library, are also polyphonic.[51] The lower of the two voices has a repetition structure of the sort described by Grocheio—but the repetitions do not follow Grocheio's specifications precisely and there are no refrains—while the upper voice changes with each repetition. These four compositions, quite possibly all dances, are evidence of an instrumental tradition of some sort in the late thirteenth century, which included polyphonic music. The status of the copies is that of casual additions to manuscripts containing French motets. It seems probable that they were intended for instruments, although it is not clear just how, when, where, or by whom they were meant to be performed.

The double-versicle form is prominent in the largest single collection of late thirteenth-century instrumental music: the pieces included in MS fonds fr. 844 of the Bibliothèque Nationale de France, Paris, the so-called 'Chansonnier du Roi', which dates from the beginning of the fourteenth century and contains mostly trouvère songs.[52] There are eight estampies and three dances (in the manuscript, one is called *danse*, a second *danse real*, while the third has no title although it appears to be a dance); all of them have repeated sections ending with refrains. Scholars have sometimes regarded the estampies as dances. Those in the 'Chansonnier du Roi' certainly have dance-like characteristics, with their jaunty modal rhythms and symmetrical phrases. Nevertheless, there is little evidence to support such an idea about their function. They may be instrumental fantasias, or related in some way to the poetic form called estampie. The trouvère song *Kalenda maya*, a poetic estampie, was said to have originated as an instrumental piece to which words were later added—a legend implying a close relationship between medieval instrumental and vocal music. Since all the estampies and one of the dances in the 'Chansonnier du Roi' are described as royal, the music may have been intended for the royal court, and perhaps for performance by courtly minstrels. The only other written music from this period that can be related to minstrels are four motet tenors in the Montpellier Codex, three of them labelled 'Chose Tassin' and one 'Chose Loyset'—perhaps names of

---

[50] For a recent edition see *Medieval Instrumental Dances*, ed. McGee, 54–6.

[51] See ibid. 126–9; Wulf Arlt, 'Instrumentalmusik im Mittelalter: Fragen der Rekonstruktion einer schriftlosen Praxis', *Basler Jahrbuch für historische Musikpraxis*, 7 (1983), 32–64.

[52] See *Medieval Instrumental Dances*, ed. McGee, 57–70.

courtly minstrels with whom the melodies were associated. There is also the tenor 'In seculum viellatoris' ('The fiddler's *In seculum*') and several related pieces in the Bamberg motet manuscript.[53]

Our knowledge of the musical practices of English or French minstrels in the fourteenth century largely depends on passing remarks in literature or in treatises. Jerome of Moravia gives tunings for various instruments, and Johannes de Grocheio, as mentioned, comments on instrumental form, but since both authors were writing for an upper-class Parisian audience, they may not refer to the practices of minstrels.[54] It is similarly difficult to evaluate (and even to understand) the enigmatic passing comment of Guillaume de Machaut (in *Le Livre du voir dit*) that a particular chanson is especially apt for the bagpipe.

Monophonic instrumental music from the fourteenth century appears in the Italian manuscript London, British Library, Add. MS 29987, from the period around 1400.[55] It contains eight *istanpitte* (i.e. estampies), four saltarelli, a trotto, two dances in two contrasting sections, and four *chançonete tedesche* ('German songs') that may have been used as tenors for bassadanze.[56]

Much more than the French estampies, the Italian istanpitte seem to have been used as instrumental fantasias, with their long, sprawling phrases of irregular length and their changes of mensuration. They are traditionally described as having been constructed in double versicles, but in fact the refrains at the ends of each section are so long in these pieces that it is almost more accurate to describe them as strophic, with each strophe preceded by a brief new introduction. Moreover, some have more complicated patterns of repetition than those outlined by Grocheio. They may exemplify the way instrumentalists constructed relatively long pieces by stringing together melodic formulae and ornamenting them. As with the earlier English and French instrumental music, we have little idea about who played these pieces or where or when. Their ranges are so large that the fiddle or perhaps the harp would be the only instruments then in common use which were capable of playing all the notes. Perhaps they belong to the category of pieces 'outside the hand' (that is, with ranges larger

---

[53] See ibid. 121–3.

[54] For a discussion of these and other Parisian theorists, see Page, *Voices and Instruments of the Middle Ages: Instrumental Practice and Songs in France 1100–1300* (Berkeley and London, 1987), 50–76.

[55] See *The Manuscript London, B. M. Add. 29987*, facs. edn., ed. Gilbert Reaney (Rome, 1965); Giuliano Di Bacco, 'Alcune nuove osservazioni sul codice di Londra', *Studi musicali*, 20 (1991), 181–234.

[56] See *Medieval Instrumental Dances*, ed. McGee, 71–118, 124–5.

than those encompassed by the Guidonian hand) mentioned by
Jerome of Moravia. Their fanciful names have not yet been satisfac-
torily explained. *Istanpitta Ghaetta* may refer to the port city south of
Rome; *Tre fontane* was a Cistercian monastery in Rome; *Isabella* is a
common aristocratic name in the fourteenth century; *Parlamentio* suggests a piece descriptive of many people coming together; and the
others refer to emotions or states of mind: joy (*Chominciamento di
gioia*), aggression (if *Bellicha* does in fact mean 'war-like'), impetuous
courage (if *In pro* does in fact refer to the Provençal word with that
meaning), and virtue (*Principio di virtù*).

The single dances in London 29987 have the same kind of quasi-
strophic double-versicle structure as the istanpitte, with progressively
longer introductions for each strophe. We can guess, although without
any solid evidence, that the saltarelli and the single trotto were upper-
class couple dances rather than the more popular circle or line dances
(which may normally have been danced while the performers sang).[57]
The two two-section dances—with a first section in duple metre and
a second (called *rotta*) in triple metre based on the same melodic material—were probably solo or couple dances as well, whether or not that
is connected with the subject matter of their titles. The first is called
Il lamento di Tristano after the harp-playing hero of the Arthurian
legend who had more than one occasion to lament, and the second *La
Manfredina* after the thirteenth-century king of Sicily who was such
an important patron of the arts. Another two-section dance, called
dança amorosa and followed by a *troto*, survives among the papers of
a late fourteenth-century Florentine notary.[58]

The four monophonic *chançonete tedesche* of MS London 29987
may have served as cantus firmi around which minstrels improvised
their counterpoint.[59] Their form resembles that of *Bel fiore dança* in
the Faenza Codex (see below), with a highly florid melodic line over
a slow-moving tenor of just the same sort as here. The four melodies
may have been called 'German' simply because they arrived in Italy
along with the baggage of the many German wind players employed
in Italian courts.

This handful of instrumental pieces found in only a few manuscripts
gives us tantalizing glimpses of what may have been a lively practice
of instrumental playing in the thirteenth and fourteenth centuries. The
surviving sources contain some polyphonic music for ensemble and

---

[57] On dancing practices, see the chapter by Walter Salmen in this volume.
[58] For the first two dances see *Medieval Instrumental Dances*, ed. McGee, 115–17. The source
for the third is Florence, Archivio di Stato, Antecosimiano No. 17879; see ibid. 119.
[59] Ibid. 124–5.

some monophonic pieces of great formal and rhythmic complexity; it may be assumed, however, that a large amount of simpler music existed which has not survived because its transmission depended much less on writing.

Music for instruments appears in much larger quantities in fifteenth-century sources, either in written forms that appear to be arrangements for particular instruments, or notated in parts in the manner normally used for vocal music. In the latter case, the instrumental destination or use of the music must be deduced from other types of evidence. Many of these sources are devoted entirely to polyphonic music (see below). Although we can assume that monophonic music remained an important part of what instrumentalists played in the fifteenth century, little direct evidence of that repertory is available.

A starting point for the recognition of secular monophony used by instrumentalists might be found in those song manuscripts where the collaboration of an instrument seems at least an implied possibility. These include sources of art-song such as the manuscripts containing the works of the Monk of Salzburg and Oswald von Wolkenstein, the Lochamer Liederbuch (southern Germany, c.1450), the Flemish Gruuthuse Manuscript of c.1390, or the early fifteenth-century Italian polyphonic songbook Paris, Bibliothèque Nationale de France, n.a.f. 4379 (part III). Also various textless fragments survive, often in simple forms of notation, which might conceivably have been used by minstrels. In several of these sources, apparently single lines—often the 'tenor'—of a polyphonic song, or the introductory melisma of a monophonic one, is separately notated as if played on an instrument. To these cases may further be added the collections and identifiable fragmentary sources of dance tunes (for example of the basse danse), which would reflect the activities of individual minstrels who played for dancing.[60] There are various other sources containing a few melodies whose instrumental use is only a matter of guesswork.

The anthology of music used by an Italian ship's trumpeter, Zorzi Trombetta, deserves separate mention.[61] His personal commonplace book containing a shipbuilding treatise and various financial, medical, and musical matters (British Library, MS Cotton Titus A.XXVI) is an

---

[60] On these repertories, see Strohm, *Rise*, 344–60; Daniel Heartz, 'The Basse Dance, its Evolution circa 1450 to 1550', *Annales musicologiques*, 6 (1958–63), 287–340; Crane, *Materials*, and the contribution of Walter Salmen to this volume.

[61] See Daniel Leech-Wilkinson, 'Un libro di appunti di un suonatore di tromba del quindicesimo secolo', *Rivista italiana di musicologia*, 16 (1981), 16–39, and Lorenz Welker, ' "Alta Capella": Zur Ensemblepraxis der Blasinstrumente im 15. Jahrhundert', *Basler Jahrbuch für historische Musikpraxis*, 7 (1983), 150–61.

especially precious witness to the practice of a kind of musician whose skills are not usually accessible to us. It appears from the diary entries in the book that Zorzi used to play music for dancing and entertainment in various ports during his sea travels. The book includes incompletely notated polyphonic chansons as well as three tenors which, however, are less apt to have been used as single-line tunes than as starting points for polyphonic improvisation. Zorzi, who also apparently played the shawm, has now been identified as the Giorgio de Modon who later achieved considerable prominence as head of the civic instrumental ensemble of Venice.[62]

A number of manuals instructing courtiers how to dance also survive from fifteenth-century Italy, and some of them include single-line melodies. Like other fifteenth-century melodies that can be associated with instrumentalists, these Italian dance tunes either served as scaffolding for polyphonic improvisation or they were elaborated as tunes.[63] The repertory of French monophonic dance tunes, on the other hand, served chiefly as cantus firmi for basse dances. The elegant basse dance manuscript in Brussels (Bibliothèque Royale, MS 9085), evidently intended not for practical use but merely as a luxurious artefact, as well as various other fragments of melodies and schemes for dance steps, all reflected a common upper-class practice of courtly dancing.[64] The melodies, mostly in long notes, served as scaffolding for improvised polyphony by the standard professional dance band of the fifteenth century, two shawms and a trombone, or a shawm, a bombard (that is, a tenor shawm), and a sackbut (trombone). If Johannes Tinctoris is to be believed, the bombard played the structural notes as given in the written sources, notes that controlled the choreography as well as the polyphony, while the smaller shawm and sackbut added florid contrapuntal lines.[65] Some late fifteenth-century manuscripts include written-out versions of such music—for example of the basse dance tune *La Spagna*—which give us a sample of the sound of such improvised polyphony. To sum up, notated fifteenth-century melodies that can in one way or another be associated with instrumental playing often functioned as a framework

---

[62] Concerning Zorzi see Rodolfo Baroncini, 'Voci e strumenti tra Quattro e Cinquecento', *Rivista italiana di musicologia*, 32 (1997), 327–65 at 348 and 360–1.

[63] For editions and surveys of the Italian repertory, see Kinkeldey, 'Dance Tunes'; W. Thomas Marrocco, 'Fifteenth-Century *ballo* and *bassadanza*: A Survey', *Studi musicali*, 10 (1981), 31–41.

[64] French dances are discussed in Heartz, 'The Basse Dance'.

[65] See Anthony Baines, 'Fifteenth-Century Instruments in Tinctoris's "De Inventione et Usu Musicae"', *Galpin Society Journal*, 3 (1950), 19–27, and Polk, *German Instrumental Music*, 80–3.

for polyphonic playing, not just as a transmission of the tune alone. The monophonic repertory of the minstrels, for which there is much less evidence, might have been a combination of popular tunes and specifically instrumental melodies of a sort entirely lost, with perhaps an occasional cantus part or other particularly melodious voice from a polyphonic song.

TABLATURES

One large musical repertory remains of which there is little doubt that it was arranged specially for instruments. Some of the written sources in question are notated in early forms of what was later called 'tablature'. Even within this category, however, questions arise about which instruments were intended. The repertory has traditionally been considered keyboard music, and especially music for the organ, presumably the positive organ, since much of it is secular and thus not appropriate for large church organs, and smaller portative organs seem to have been used almost exclusively to play single lines. The strongest argument in favour of considering these manuscripts keyboard music stems from the fact that the music is polyphonic and notated in score. Performers on instruments best suited for playing a single line, such as lute, gittern, or fiddle, could read from the same music as singers (if they read from written notation at all). They did not need to make separate parts for themselves. On the other hand, players of "chordal" instruments, like the organ and harp (which regularly played more than one voice at a time), needed to prepare for themselves special versions of the music they wished to perform, putting into score what was normally set out in parts.[66]

In any case, such collections are unquestionably instrumental, and offer a conspectus of the nature of a player's repertory in the fifteenth century. They reveal that instrumentalists played at least three kinds of pieces: dances, abstract instrumental music, and arrangements of vocal music. Arrangements of polyphonic secular song made up by far the largest part of their repertory. Some of these manuscripts include a handful of other pieces of a sort particularly apt for organ, that is, polyphonic settings of plainchant cantus firmi, presumably to be used in alternatim performances during sacred services.

The earliest of these 'keyboard' manuscripts is the fourteenth-century English anthology known as the Robertsbridge Codex

---

[66] Timothy McGee, 'Instruments and the Faenza Codex', *EM* 14 (1986), 480–90, argues that 'most' of this repertory notated in score may alternatively have been intended for such instruments as lutes and gitterns, each playing a single line; this is refuted in Strohm, *Rise*, 92.

(London, British Library, Add. MS 28550). Consisting of two folios added at the end of a register from Robertsbridge Abbey, the manuscript was perhaps intended for an organ in church (though quite possibly a positive organ), and hence it contains no dances. But several other genres are represented: estampies (if these pieces were not, in fact, dances: see above), intabulations of vocal music (two motets and, apparently, a ballade setting), and what is probably the polyphonic elaboration of a plainsong cantus firmus. One other English fragment, now in Oxford and datable *c*.1400, contains a second plainchant setting, over *Felix namque*.[67]

The Faenza Codex, dating from the early fifteenth century, confirms the heterogeneous nature of the instrumentalist's repertory.[68] Its largest group of pieces—twenty-three out of forty-eight—consists of arrangements of polyphonic secular songs: ballades, virelais, and rondeaux by Machaut and other French composers, as well as ballate and madrigals by Jacopo da Bologna, Francesco Landini, Bartolino da Padova, and Antonio Zacara da Teramo. (Yet another Landini ballata appears in the early fifteenth-century Reina Codex notated in score, and it, too, is thought to be an intabulation for a keyboard instrument.) In all these arrangements, the anonymous intabulator has added even more florid ornamentation to the already highly decorated top voice of his model. The lower line in music *a 2*, by contrast, is stated simply, whereas in music *a 3*, the two bottom lines of the vocal model are condensed into one, which sounds the structurally more important notes, usually those from the original tenor. In eight pieces in the Faenza Codex, an anonymous composer has added a highly ornamented top voice to a sacred cantus firmus; in addition, one piece is explicitly labelled as a dance (*Bel fiore dança*), and one other piece (*Biance flour*) is based on the dance tune *Collinetto*.[69] These two pieces are highly important, for they are the only surviving polyphonic realizations of dance melodies that can be associated with the fourteenth or early fifteenth centuries. A number of pieces in the Faenza Codex remain unidentified, although it is clear that among them are some arrangements of as yet unidentified vocal pieces, some sacred

---

[67] The pieces from the Robertsbridge Codex and the Oxford fragment have been edited in *Keyboard Music of the Fourteenth and Fifteenth Centuries*, ed. Willi Apel (Corpus of Early Keyboard Music, 1; Rome: American Institute of Musicology, 1963), 1–10.

[68] See *Keyboard Music of the Late Middle Ages in Codex Faenza 117*, ed. Dragan Plamenac (Rome, 1973). There is a facs. edn., *The Codex Faenza, Biblioteca Comunale, 117 (Fa)*, ed. Armen Carapetyan (Rome, 1961). See also Michael Kugler, *Die Tastenmusik im Codex Faenza* (Tutzing, 1972); Yvonne Rokseth, 'The Instrumental Music of the Middle Ages and the Early Sixteenth Century', in NOHM iii. 406–65; McGee, 'Instruments and the Faenza Codex'; Strohm, *Rise*, 90–2, 367–70.

[69] For *Bel fiore* see *Keyboard Music*, ed. Plamenac, 102, for *Biance flour*, p. 60.

cantus-firmus settings, some dances, and some pieces that were originally conceived for instruments, as abstract instrumental music.[70]

As said above, scholars do not agree about the instrument or instruments for which the Faenza Codex was intended. It might be for a
chordal instrument such as the organ, simply because there was no
need to notate music for monophonic instruments in score. It is much
more efficient to notate music for two lutes or other ensembles in parts,
a convention that in fact later became standard. Moreover, the Faenza
Codex includes alternatim Mass movements, the earliest such pieces
known. It is hard to imagine that such pieces could be played by anything but an organ. The chief argument against supposing the Faenza
Codex to be for organ involves the fact that in some pieces the two
voices cross, and there are occasional awkward simultaneities if the
music is played on a keyboard instrument with only one manual. Still,
while neither organs nor the newly invented stringed keyboard instruments of the time were supplied with a second manual, some Italian
organs had short pedal boards on which at least some of the tenors
could be played. The additional possibility of octave transposition in
one of the parts must not be overlooked.

What we can learn from the Faenza Codex, however, far transcends
any parochial arguments about the particular instrument or group of
instruments for which it was intended. The manuscript serves as our
chief witness to the practice of instrumentalists in general in the fourteenth and early fifteenth centuries, be they solo organists, harpists,
or harpsichordists, or pairs of musicians playing two lutes, portative
and lute, lute and harp, or one of the combinations ubiquitous in
fourteenth-century works of art: gittern and fiddle, or gittern and lute.
The Faenza Codex demonstrates the important role intabulations of
polyphonic secular song played in an instrumentalist's repertory; it
instructs us about the way instrumentalists arranged vocal music, and
about the kinds of musical textures they habitually used—information
we can scarcely learn so convincingly from any other source. To the
normal texture of Trecento vocal music—a fast-moving cantus and
a slower moving tenor—instrumentalists, if the Faenza Codex is to be
believed, habitually added cascades of additional ornamental notes,
leaving the tenor unchanged, or (more rarely) combining and con-
densing the lower voices, where there was more than one, into a
single simple part ('solus tenor'). Instrumentalists adopted this texture
whether they were arranging secular songs, inventing a cantus part

---

[70] For two possible estampies and further historical considerations, see Strohm,
Rise, 90–2.

to fit with a plainchant cantus firmus or a dance tenor, or freely composing abstract instrumental music.

The unchanged or simplified lower lines in the Faenza Codex inevitably recall the later fifteenth-century practice of associating a virtuoso player of gittern and lute like Pietrobono of Ferrara with his tenorista, a second instrumentalist who may normally have played lute or fiddle and accompanied the soloist.[71] One manuscript now in the Bibliothèque Nationale de France, Paris (MS nouv. acq. fr. 4379, part III) may preserve the repertory of such a tenorista. It contains tenor lines extracted from many of the compositions in the large early fifteenth-century anthology now in the Bodleian Library in Oxford (MS Canonici misc. 213). These tenors could have been used by a lutenist or fiddler to accompany another musician in the performance of secular music; they could, of course, also have provided the foundation upon which a discantus player improvised, or for a solo, even monophonic, performance.

The evidence which the Faenza Codex provides about the repertories and musical styles of instrumentalists is augmented by the other major source of information on fifteenth-century instrumental techniques: the German keyboard tablatures. A number of relatively small fragments of manuscript music make up the bulk of the German repertory, along with the gigantic Buxheim Organ Book, Munich, Bayerische Staatsbibliothek, Cim. 352b (*olim* Mus. Ms. 3725).[72] The music in these tablatures resembles that in the Faenza Codex in many ways. The compilers placed the same emphasis on arrangements of vocal music: French chansons (by Binchois, Dufay, and their contemporaries) appear in substantial numbers in the German sources, representing an international repertory of high art music everywhere in

---

[71] On Pietrobono and his tenorista, see Lewis Lockwood, 'Pietrobono and the Instrumental Tradition at Ferrara', *Rivista italiana di musicologia*, 10 (1975), 115–33, and id., *Music in Renaissance Ferrara*, 98–108. For a different interpretation of the role of the tenorista, see Strohm, *Rise*, 364–6.

[72] See the listing and descriptions in *New Grove*, xvii. 724–5, and Strohm, *Rise*, 367–74. Most of the smaller sources are discussed and edited in *Keyboard Music*, ed. Apel. For descriptions of other fragments, see Maria van Daalen and Frank Ll. Harrison, 'Two Keyboard Intabulations of the Late Fourteenth Century on a Manuscript Leaf now in the Netherlands', *TVNM* 34 (1984), 97–107; C. Meyer, 'Ein deutscher Orgeltraktat vom Anfang des 15. Jahrhundert', *Musik in Bayern*, 29 (1984), 43–60; and Martin Staehelin, 'Münchner Fragmente mit mehrstimmiger Musik des späten Mittelalters', *Nachrichten der Akademie der Wissenschaften in Göttingen, I. Philologisch-historische Klasse*, 6 (1988), 167–90. The Buxheim manuscript has been edited by Bertha A. Wallner, *Das Buxheimer Orgelbuch*, 3 vols. (Das Erbe deutscher Music, 36–8; Kassel, 1958); Eileen Southern, *The Buxheim Organ Book* (Brooklyn, 1963) and Hans Rudolf Zöbeley, *Die Musik des Buxheimer Orgelbuchs* (Tutzing, 1964) are studies of the collection. See also Marie Louise Göllner (ed.), *Bayerische Staatsbibliothek: Kataloge der Musikhandschriften*, vol. v/2 (Munich, 1979), 159–71.

Western Europe. There are also other kinds of secular music, especially German lieder, and intabulations of motets. There is, in addition, a sizeable group of chant arrangements, and a series of keyboard exercises showing how to extemporize over given material (*fundamenta*). A further important segment of the repertory consists of *praeambula*: improvisatory toccata-like pieces, the earliest examples of such kinds of pieces that have survived. The fundamenta and praeambula will be discussed below.

The arrangements of given polyphonic compositions exhibit relatively standard procedures. The original tenors are normally maintained, except for characteristic alterations to allow for more effective and up-to-date cadential formulae. The outline of the original contratenor is sometimes retained, but sometimes discarded or replaced with newly written material. The contratenors, too, are constructed to fit into the cadential formula motion of the tenors, modifying the original outlines where necessary. The effect of the texture, as in the Faenza codex, is to emphasize the difference between the ornamental melody and the slower-moving supporting structure. Unlike Faenza, the Buxheim tablature notates some low parts for pedal, so that there is the possibility of playing the original tenor and contratenor chordally. On the other hand, the slower motion of the lower parts, and the constant repetition of cadential formulae, would make a sound remarkably like that of a melody supported by a tenorista. As in the Faenza Codex, the intabulators of the Buxheim Organ Book and the other German sources often decorate the upper voice, although they use an entirely different repertory of ornamental melodic formulas. Sometimes such decoration is lacking, which raises the question whether the instrumentalists at work here performed at times with very little ornamentation. Conrad Paumann's polyphonic song *Wiplich figur*, for example, appears in an almost pristine version, with little decoration—and this is by no means a rare example.[73] Intabulation was not synonymous with embellishment.

Apart from these keyboard tablatures, few manuscripts reveal just what music other kinds of instruments might have played, or how they played it. The Buxheim Organ Book includes one composition (an intabulation of Binchois's *Je loe amours*) marked 'In Cytaris vel etiam in Organis', which some scholars have interpreted to mean that the piece could be played by two lutes or by a harp as an alternative to the organ.[74] One further source, Vienna, Österreichische

---

[73] See Polk, *German Instrumental Music*, 150–1.
[74] Howard Mayer Brown, 'Instruments and Voices in the Fifteenth-Century Chanson', in J. W. Grubbs (ed.), *Current Thought in Musicology* (University of Texas, 1976), 89–137 at 129–30

Nationalbibliothek, MS 5094, contains arrangements of Dufay's *Ce jour le doibt* and his *Seigneur Leon* which are especially striking. The version of *Ce jour le doibt* is untexted, notated in score, with the discant on one system and the tenor and contratenor *together* on another in a peculiar kind of schematic notation with barlines. Arguably, this provides an illustration of how a tenorist in a lute duo, for example, might have functioned. The setting dates from about 1440–50, and Theodor Göllner has suggested that it was most probably intended for keyboard performance.[75]

The earliest unambiguous written examples of polyphonic lute music are a fragment now in the University Library in Bologna and a manuscript in the Biblioteca Oliveriana in Pesaro, both of the late fifteenth century.[76] Earlier sources are unlikely to surface, because it seems that lutenists began to use their fingers rather than a plectrum to pluck their strings—and thus started to cultivate a polyphonic repertory—not much before the time these manuscripts were compiled. Besides lute music, the Pesaro manuscript also includes the only known written music for the lira da braccio, of a later date. All these manuscripts support the view that fifteenth-century instrumentalists shared a common repertory: intabulations of vocal music, dances, and abstract instrumental music.

MUSIC FOR INSTRUMENTAL ENSEMBLES

Music arranged in score or tablature for keyboard (or, as some scholars would argue, for plucked instruments) is the first large repertory of polyphonic music designated for instruments. The other major category of supposedly instrumental sources, now to be discussed, consists of manuscripts containing polyphonic music written out in parts just like vocal music, for example in normal 'choirbook' format. These sources are included here only insofar as there is some reason to believe that they were mostly or entirely intended for instruments, or used by instrumentalists.

n. 22, presents the case for the alternative of the harp. David Fallows, '15th-Century Tablatures for Plucked Instruments: A Summary, a Revision and a Suggestion', *Lute Society Journal*, 19 (1977), 7–33 at 31–2, argues for lutes, as does Polk, *German Instrumental Music*, 219 n. 45.

[75] See Göllner, 'Notationsfragmente aus einer Organistenwerkstatt des 15. Jahrhunderts', *Archiv für Musikwissenschaft*, 24 (1967), 170–7 at 172; a facsimile of the piece is given as ill. 2; see also Polk, *German Instrumental Music*, 160. The collection comprises, furthermore, the motet *Apollinis eclipsatur* arranged in what appears to be a keyboard score. See Reinhard Strohm, 'Native and Foreign Polyphony in Late Medieval Austria', *Musica disciplina*, 38 (1984), 205–30 at 212–13 and 227–8.

[76] On these manuscripts, see Fallows, '15th-Century Tablatures'.

Since there is sufficient iconographic evidence to show that professional instrumentalists did not normally use written music when performing in an ensemble, the case for the existence of manuscript sources of instrumental ensemble music may appear weak at first. There are, however, several important exceptions. First, by no means all extant music manuscripts—even vocal ones—were actually used in performance; many must have served as mere repositories, as complimentary copies for patrons, as archival copies, or for the purposes of composition, transmission, and training only. This may particularly be the case where instrumental performance was concerned. Much of this particular written material has doubtless been lost, for example because of wear and tear. We do know that some instrumentalists owned written repertories. Thus, about 1390, King John I of Aragon tried to recruit 'Johan dels orguens' (probably Jean de Visée of Flanders, employed at the Burgundian court) and he asked that Jean bring the book in which he had notated the *estempides* and other works he knew how to play on keyboard instruments.[77] As for ensemble performances, the fictitious character Solazzo in Simone Prodenzani's poem *Il Saporetto* (*c*.1425) performs with his friends vocal and instrumental music, only later revealing to his audience the manuscript roll—not used in the performances—where he has written 'all these and more pieces'.[78] We shall see that some fifteenth-century wind bands, too, possessed written anthologies of the music they played. Secondly, some scholars would argue that certain fifteenth-century song manuscripts were intended for instrumental use, or at least contain music regularly played by instrumentalists. In such a case, the extant, often calligraphic manuscript may have been little more than a 'libretto' for the patron who followed the performances, or indeed a copy he or she used to join in if desired. By the end of the fifteenth century, there is considerable evidence, arising from archival as well as iconographic sources, of amateur instrumental performance with the help of written notation. Thirdly, the fifteenth century as a whole witnessed an increase in literacy among musicians, and also an increase of complex polyphonic music in the repertories of instrumentalists. It is clear that some instrumentalists played written polyphony, learning it and transmitting it with the help of written copies. The written, and perhaps most significant part of their repertory consisted of music which today is regarded as strictly vocal: Mass movements, motets, chansons, and polyphonic

---

[77] Wright, *Music at the Court of Burgundy*, 116–17.
[78] See Reinhard Strohm, 'The Close of the Middle Ages', in James McKinnon (ed.), *Antiquity and the Middle Ages* (London, 1990), 269–312 at 280.

songs in various vernacular languages. The importance of vocal polyphony for keyboard players is already demonstrated by the contents of the Faenza Codex and the German keyboard tablatures discussed above; ensemble players seem to have developed analogous preferences. It would of course be an oversimplification to suggest that instrumentalists played monophonic music mostly or entirely until a certain time, and then switched mostly or entirely to polyphonic music, learning to master musical notation at that point. It seems more plausible to suppose that instrumentalists—like singers—mixed their repertories throughout our period, and that their literacy and use of music writing varied greatly.

A few fragments from the earlier fifteenth century reveal aspects of instrumental practice. The scribe of the so-called Mondsee–Vienna song manuscript (Vienna, Österreichische Nationalbibliothek, MS 2856, of *c*.1420), for example, explains that some written parts of the songs are appropriate for instruments, adding the rubric 'gut zu blasen' ('apt for winds') against one lower voice that is virtually a drone.[79] Brass instruments might have joined vocal performers more often than we know today, for example in festive performances of sacred music. A number of Mass compositions of the early fifteenth century exist with low parts labelled 'trompetta', 'ad modum tube', or similarly, suggesting that a brass instrument (a slide trumpet or early type of trombone), if not actually participating, was being imitated in its melodic idioms by the singers. The Czech theorist Paulus Paulirinus (*c*.1460) described such a type of vocal pieces under the name of *trumpetum*.[80]

There are a few manuscripts of vocal music containing clusters of pieces that may rather have been collected for instrumental performance, for example a section in Trent Codex '87' (= Trento, Museo Provinciale d'Arte, MS 1374 *olim* 87). Several three-part pieces—settings of dance tunes and other songs—assembled here by the organist and chaplain Johannes Lupi of Bolzano (*c*.1440–5) are possibly suited for ensemble performance.[81] Lupi was not only a collector of vocal polyphony but also of instruments: portative organ, clavichord,

---

[79] The piece is conveniently available in Christopher Page, 'German Musicians and their Instruments, a 14th-Century Account by Konrad of Megenberg', *EM* 10 (1982), 192–200 at 198.

[80] On this repertory and the complex question of performance, see Vivian Ramalingam, 'The *Trumpetum* in Strasbourg M 222 C 22', in *La Musique et le rite—sacré et profane. Actes du XIIIᵉ congrès de la SIM, Strasbourg, 1982* (Strasburg, 1986), ii. 143–60; Strohm, *Rise*, 108–11, 115, 177. See also below on trumpet bands and loud wind bands.

[81] See Crane, *Materials*, 62–7; Strohm, *Rise*, 360–1; Polk, *German Instrumental Music*, 159, with examples.

exchiquier (*schaffpret*), harpsichord, and two lutes are mentioned in his will of *c*.1455.[82]

The Glogauer Liederbuch of *c*.1478–80 (formerly in Berlin, Preußische Staatsbibliothek, Mus. Ms. 40098, now in the Biblioteka Jagiellońska in Kraków) is a set of three partbooks containing 292 compositions; among them are clusters of textless pieces, some with fanciful titles, many relating to animals (such as the fox tail, the silken tail, the cat's paw, the donkey's crown) that may well have been intended for performance on instruments and perhaps for dancing. Apparently the oldest of them, entitled 'Peacock's Tail' (*Pfawenschwantz*), is attributed to the Franco-Flemish composer Barbingant (fl. *c*.1450); it has a pre-existent tenor also used in another composition and its other three voices are elaborated in the manner of a written-out extemporization. Few of the other 'animal' pieces in the Glogau collection follow this example stylistically, but several are straightforward copies of Franco-Flemish polyphonic songs without words. These copies seem to reflect a practice of ensemble performance, whether vocal, instrumental, or mixed, which characterized German civic, intellectual, and monastic communities keen to appropriate an international repertory.[83] Similarly, the 'Schedel Songbook' of *c*.1460 contains 'Italian'—actually, French—dance tunes (see above), and the Augsburg Liederbuch of *c*.1510 (Augsburg, Staats- und Stadtbibliothek, Ms. 2° 142A) adds some Italian dances to its lieder and chansons.[84]

A manuscript in Maastricht (*c*.1505) may reveal the repertory of a late fifteenth-century town band.[85] The fragmentary collection includes parts to some polyphonic chansons and Flemish popular songs as well as a Marian motet suitable for performance at a Salve service, along with a handful of plainchants that might have served the Flemish minstrels either as a cantus firmi for polyphonic improvisation or as melodic material for elaboration during processions or other church-related services. And Fragment 'E' in the library of San

---

[82] Peter Wright, 'On the Origins of Trent 87-I and 92-II', *EMH* 6 (1986), 245–70 at 270.

[83] The relevant Glogau repertory is edited by H. Ringmann and J. Klapper, *Das Glogauer Liederbuch*, 4 vols.; *Kraków, Biblioteka Jagiellońska: Glogauer Liederbuch*, ed. Jessie A. Owens, 3 vols. (Renaissance Music in Facsimile, 6; New York, 1986) is a facsimile edition of the manuscript. See also Strohm, *Rise*, 362–4 and 501–3.

[84] Luise Jonas, *Das Augsburger Liederbuch*, 2 vols. (Berliner musikwissenschaftliche Arbeiten, 21; Munich, 1983) includes an edition of the Augsburg collection; see Polk, *German Instrumental Music*, 141–2 for a brief discussion of the dances.

[85] The manuscript is described, with facsimiles of the original, in Jozef Smits van Waesberghe, 'Een 15de eeuws muziekboek van de stadsminstrelen van Maastricht?', in Jozef Robijns (ed.), *Renaissance Muziek 1400–1600: Donum natalicium René Bernard Lenaerts* (Leuven, 1969), 247–73; see also Polk, *German Instrumental Music*, 133 and 243 n. 8.

Petronio in Bologna (*c*.1490) contains a Mass possibly intended for the wind players of the basilica.[86]

Several late fifteenth- and early sixteenth-century Italian anthologies of secular polyphony have been identified with the repertories used by the wind bands of Italian courts and cities. Most notable is the 'Casanatense Chansonnier' of *c*.1480 (Rome, Biblioteca Casanatense, MS 2856), apparently used at the court of Mantua; and there is an early sixteenth-century collection which almost certainly contains a repertory performed by the town band of Bologna (Bologna, Civico Museo Bibliografico Musicale, MS Q 18).[87]

The evidence that the Casanatense Chansonnier was meant for Mantua's court band is only circumstantial, but it is nevertheless persuasive. The anthology was presented to the young Isabella d'Este of Ferrara about 1480 as a betrothal present when she was pledged to marry Francesco Gonzaga of Mantua. Presumably, the Ferrarese wind band was so good that her family thought she would want to have their repertory available to her when she moved to the poorer and more provincial town of Mantua. Lewis Lockwood identifies the manuscript with an item described in court records as containing 'cantiones a la pifaresca' ('Songs in the manner of the wind band'). To demonstrate that the chansonnier served instrumental, not vocal, performances, Lockwood shows that its music has been partially recomposed to make it fit better on combinations of instruments tuned a fifth apart. The editor of the manuscript (or the players themselves) paid special attention to the lowest voices in the predominantly three-part polyphony, rewriting some of the counterpoint to avoid notes not available at the bottom of the ranges of shawm and sackbut players.[88] It must be understood that the manuscript itself, which has a beautifully illuminated opening page, was perhaps not physically used by the wind players but only by Isabella herself. Bologna Q 18, a manuscript compiled several decades later than Isabella's anthology, contains a similar kind of repertory, although its chansons and other compositions are mostly of a later date. Almost certainly, neither Bologna Q 18 nor the Casanatense Chansonnier gives us a comprehensive account of the repertory of fifteenth-century wind bands, of course, for they doubtless included other kinds of music—and espe-

---

[86] See Charles Hamm, 'Musiche del Quattrocento in S. Petronio', *Rivista italiana di musicologia*, 3 (1968), 215–32.

[87] Lockwood, *Music in Renaissance Ferrara*, 224–7 and 269–72, discusses the Casanatense manuscript. For details concerning the Bologna collection see Susan F. Weiss, 'Bologna Q18: Some Reflections on Content and Context', *JAMS* 43 (1988), 63–101.

[88] Lockwood, *Music in Renaissance Ferrara*, 269–71.

cially improvised polyphony that did not get written down—in their programmes.

The central part of the repertory, however (if these manuscripts may indeed be used as a guide) consisted of vocal pieces, especially French chansons, which were often but not always arranged for instrumental use. The songs, whether appearing with or without adjustments in the manuscripts, would most probably have been played in improvised embellished versions.

From these and other contemporary sources,[89] it can be deduced that the professional, mostly German wind players employed in Italian courts and cities also performed 'songs without words' of various kinds, as well as instrumental arrangements of motets and Mass movements, and especially those sections of the Mass, like the Pleni and the Benedictus, where the cantus firmus drops out and which are arguably more 'instrumental' in style. There are, furthermore, arrangements of popular monophonic tunes (such as the various settings of *Tandernaken* or *Scaramella*) found in anthologies intended for instruments, and pieces with florid voices against a sacred or secular cantus firmus that may have had the same destination. Alexander Agricola, for example, wrote several settings of Hayne van Ghizeghem's *De tous biens plaine* and other chanson tenors or superius parts. This type of song elaboration—often only in two parts, one of which is the borrowed song line and the other a virtuosic counterpoint to it—is found in manuscript sources as far apart as Segovia, Trent, Wroclaw, and England.

There are also a number of pieces evidently conceived in the first place for instruments and never associated with a text. The Casanatense manuscript includes, for example, several pieces called *La Martinella* and several described as *Fuga*; and Bologna Q 18 adds a number of others: *La Morra* of Isaac, *La Bernardina* of Josquin, the anonymous *La Quercia*, Obrecht's *La Tortorella*, and two settings of the basse dance tenor *La Spagna*. Titles such as these—feminine nouns, usually referring to a personal, animal, geographic, or otherwise characteristic name—are already typical of dance tunes in the earlier fifteenth century, and were presumably given to instrumental dances (feminine: *la danse*) favoured by particular personalities in the courtly and civic dance ceremonies.[90]

[89] On the various repertories, see Warwick Edwards, 'Songs without Words by Josquin and his Contemporaries', in Fenlon, *Music*, 79–92; Louise Litterick, 'On Italian Instrumental Ensemble Music in the Late Fifteenth Century', ibid. 117–30; Reinhard Strohm, 'Instrumentale Ensemblemusik vor 1500: Das Zeugnis der mitteleuropäischen Quellen', in Salmen (ed.), *Musik und Tanz*, 89–106; Strohm, *Rise*, 354–5, 364–70, 535–6, 567–70.
[90] See Strohm, *Music in Late Medieval Bruges*, 115–16.

To argue the instrumental destination of such pieces from their titles does not remove the difficulty of distinguishing an instrumental from a vocal style of writing in the late fifteenth century. Many of the pieces do have features—sequential and motivic patterning, passage-work, pedal-points, and ostinatos—that may today be considered as an abstract instrumental style, but are equally well known from the vocal polyphony of the period. A more central concern of these compositions seems to be to establish, in the absence of words, a purely musical coherence. Some pieces begin, for example, with a long expository point of imitation, or they are built on two or three large sections, or they make extensive use of sequences to lead to important cadences. None of these features, however, is unique to instrumental style either. Obviously many vocal pieces begin with imitation, and rondeaux and ballades will exhibit a two- or three-part structure. We may find striking the degree to which the features of abstract 'instrumental' style coherently mark off the musical structures. We must admit, however, that definitive criteria dividing vocal from instrumental music continue to elude us.

Some scholars have conjectured that many of the fifteenth-century anthologies of secular music, and especially those compiled in Italy, were intended primarily for instrumentalists; others have argued the seemingly incompatible point that fifteenth-century chansons were usually performed without accompanying instruments.[91] As so often happens, the truth may well lie somewhere in the middle. The question is wide open to what extent any song collection of the time might have been used by instrumentalists at least intermittently, or whether ensemble performances in amateur circles could not include one or more instrumentalists at least from the later fifteenth century onwards. As regards the evidence of the manuscripts themselves, the absence or partial absence of text is unfortunately an ambiguous criterion. That the text is often written only under the top voice of a chanson may merely have been a scribal convention, although it might reveal how the songs were performed. In many Italian manuscripts, moreover, the French texts were hopelessly garbled, which may imply that they were never sung, although it might simply mean that performers took their texts from other sources. The same kinds of arguments also apply to

---

[91] The case for instrumental performance is made by Louise Litterick, 'Performing Franco-Netherlandish Secular Music of the Late 15th Century', *EM* 8 (1980), 474–85; a quite different interpretation is suggested by Christopher Page, 'The Performance of Songs in Late Medieval France', *EM* 10 (1982), 441–50. Note that some of the most prominent collections were evidently presentation manuscripts, and show no signs that they were ever used in performance. Other sources which do bear the evidence of wear, however, are cast in exactly the same format.

the earliest printed anthologies. Ottaviano Petrucci's three volumes of secular music, beginning with the *Odhecaton* of 1501, contain no texts: is it likely that Petrucci (or his editor) intended them for instrumentalists? These were representative selections of secular music, mostly of foreign origin: perhaps they were presented without texts for users who did not know French, or because of the technical difficulty of printing the words in the correct places under the notes. Conceivably, the contents of the Petrucci volumes are to be sung or played as the users of the volumes deemed fit.

To sum up, the written evidence of instrumentalists' repertories between 1300 and 1520 concerns two main areas. The first area is that of independent instrumental music: it existed as early as the fourteenth century—if the Italian istanpitte can in fact be described in that way—but large repertories of such pieces appear in written sources only in the fifteenth century, including cantus-firmus settings and keyboard preludes in the Italian, English, and German tablatures, elaborations of dance tunes, and certain 'named' pieces without words (*La Morra*, *La Alfonsina*, *La Bernardina*, and the like) in anthologies of secular music. The second area is the practice of instrumental playing of any music, whether vocal or instrumental, monophonic or polyphonic in origin. Because of this practice, we cannot precisely categorize fifteenth-century music as vocal or instrumental: the difference between vocal and instrumental music was not always inherent in the notes, but could simply be a matter of performance.

PERFORMANCE FROM MEMORY, IMPROVISATION, AND ORNAMENTATION

However important the written sources are in discovering what instrumentalists played, we must nevertheless reckon that much instrumental music heard in the fourteenth and fifteenth centuries, and especially that segment that was characteristic of minstrels (as opposed to upper-class amateurs or organists), remained unwritten or was not written down in the specific arrangements made by instrumentalists. We shall probably only be able to speculate about the extent to which minstrels improvised abstract instrumental music, or about the techniques they used to extend and rework simple dance tunes to the length appropriate for social dancing. The nature of the minstrels' monophonic repertories also remains uncertain—although they must have included sacred plainsong, because that was the music usually performed in processions, an archetypal form of public performance for minstrels.

Improvisation (or extemporization), without any doubt, played an important role in the everyday professional lives of fourteenth- or fifteenth-century minstrels. One of their most important techniques—inventing contrapuntal lines against a cantus firmus—may be reflected in two kinds of written documents: the practical exercises (*fundamenta*) added to some of the German keyboard tablatures, and more general treatises on counterpoint, which were in the first place written for singers, but which may describe more or less closely the practice also followed by instrumentalists.

Some German keyboard tablatures include so-called *fundamenta* ('basic lessons') consisting of sets of examples to teach players how to improvise counterpoint against a cantus firmus, and how to decorate a melodic line. The Buxheim Organ Book, for example, contains among its 256 numbers four such *fundamenta*, including two by the blind organist Conrad Paumann.[92] Paumann's exercises are organized systematically. His first *fundamentum* in the Buxheim Organ Book begins with examples of alternative ways to harmonize a tenor that goes stepwise up an octave and then returns.[93] He proceeds to shorter formulas for harmonizing tenors that move *cdeedc*, *deffed*, *efggfe*, and so on, and then he offers examples of harmonizing tenors that move *cedc*, *dfed*, *egfe*, and so on. From there Paumann proceeds to various other stereotyped melodic formulas. He gives examples in two and three parts, showing both how to play a single line against a cantus firmus, and how to improvise a three-part texture with two slow-moving lines and a florid cantus. The players who used these guides to performance were evidently meant to work the examples into their fingers and memorize them. Since the tenors consisted of the melodic formulas most often found in chant, the players could then improvise two- or three-part plainchant settings by stringing together the appropriate segments from the *fundamenta*.

The *fundamenta* are instructive, too, in showing how German keyboard players ornamented melodies. Even many of the stereotyped melodic formulas that appear in the tenors have been lightly decorated, suggesting, among other things, that fifteenth-century musicians thought of music in terms of a decorated surface over a deeper level of structure. The *fundamenta* and, in fact, many of the compositions in the Buxheim Organ Book (or in other German tablatures) can be used to categorize the melodic formulas that players used to ornament any given melodic line. One fifteenth-century manuscript from Winsem (the original was destroyed in the Second World War) even

[92] Christoph Wolff, 'Conrad Paumanns Fundamentum organisandi und seine verschiedenen Fassungen', *Archiv für Musikwissenschaft*, 25 (1968), 196–222, describes the various sources of the *fundamenta*.
[93] *Buxheimer Orgelbuch*, ed. Wallner, ii. 234–6.

offers a table of ornamental formulas.[94] The German organ tablatures, as well as the Faenza Codex, suggest that keyboard players embellished at will the top line of whatever vocal piece they performed. (Note, however, that a number of pieces in Buxheim and Faenza are without ornamentation, suggesting that players would, in some performances, play a piece preserving the original melodic lines as written.) In any case, if this keyboard music can be taken as characteristic of fifteenth-century practices in general, we may also assume that the ability to add more or less florid ornamentation to a given melody was one of the qualities most highly prized in an instrumentalist.

As we have seen, keyboard players were not the only instrumentalists able to improvise in the fourteenth and fifteenth centuries. Members of wind bands would also have needed to know how to add contrapuntal lines against a cantus firmus in order to play polyphonic basses dances and very probably other improvised portions of their repertory. Players of soft instruments may also have needed such skills in order to pursue a professional career. We cannot know for certain how any instrumentalist (except keyboard players) learned to add counterpoint at sight against a cantus firmus, for no treatises or other written documentation survive to explain such techniques as they applied to instrumentalists. On the other hand, sixteenth-century theorists such as the Spaniard Domingo Marcos Durán in his *Súmula de canto de órgano* (published in Salamanca about 1507) explicitly state that the rules of counterpoint apply to playing as much as singing.[95] In fact, the German *fundamenta* seem to proceed according to the same contrapuntal rules as are set down in treatises intended primarily for singers. Singers employed at cathedrals and collegiate churches also had to be able to sing a contrapuntal line against a chant at sight, and some treatises explicitly teach such techniques, even defining 'counterpoint' as an art embracing improvised performance as well as written composition.[96] Thus we can perhaps come close to imagining what fifteenth-century improvised instrumental polyphony was like from reading treatises such as Johannes Tinctoris's *Liber de arte contrapuncti* of 1477, the most complete and perhaps the best book on the subject from the period.[97]

---

[94] Printed in *Keyboard Music*, ed. Apel, 22–3.

[95] Robert Stevenson, *Spanish Music in the Age of Columbus* (The Hague, 1960), 69.

[96] Concerning vocal improvisation and singing *super librum*, see Ch. 7 in this volume.

[97] Conveniently available in a translation by Albert Seay, *The Art of Counterpoint* (American Institute of Musicology, 1961).

Tinctoris and other writers of the period normally taught the rules of counterpoint systematically, starting with note-against-note counterpoint in two and then three voices (based on a cantus firmus). Only after the fundamentals were mastered was the student encouraged to go on to learn subtleties of florid counterpoint, conceived as the embellishment of the simple fundamental substructure. Improvised three-part florid counterpoint (still based on a foundation cantus firmus) was clearly harder to master, since it required a high degree of cooperation between the two improvising singers or players, although easier techniques involving extensive use of parallel motion, like fauxbourdon, also flourished in the fifteenth century.[98]

There is reason to believe not only that singers and players shared a common vocabulary of contrapuntal rules but that players of various instruments—organs, lutes, and fiddles, for example—shared a common vocabulary of ornaments. To judge from the surviving written records, the superius usually received the most florid ornamentation. The one or two lower parts moved more slowly and served as support (if two parts were present, however, the tenor was almost invariably the foundation voice). Either the tenor, or the contratenor (if present), could be ornamented, but only when the superius was less active.

In short, instrumentalists in the fourteenth and fifteenth centuries seem to have adopted a very flexible attitude towards the idea of a fixed composition. Whereas many instrumentalists appear to have known and performed a large repertory of written polyphonic compositions—including chansons from the international repertory—they used these texts as raw material from which to fashion a full-fledged performance.

PART III: Instruments: Their Groupings and their Repertories

In the following paragraphs, we shall consider the kinds of instruments in common use in the period *c*.1300–*c*.1520: what they were, how they were played, who played them, and what music was best suited to them.

Not much can be learnt from the study of actual instruments of the time, for very few survive from before the sixteenth century. Frederick

---

[98] Timothy McGee, *Medieval and Renaissance Music—A Performer's Guide* (Toronto, 1985), 186–200, describes how the rules might be put into practice. On fauxbourdon and other similar techniques, see Strohm, *The Rise*, 179–81, 207–10.

Crane has attempted to list them all.[99] His catalogue shows not only that few physical artefacts last for six or seven hundred years, but also that most of those which do are exceptional in character. Many of the surviving instruments were either made of a substance that resisted decay, or they survived in a climate or under circumstances that helped to preserve them. Thus metal instruments from Scandinavia have been found in bogs that kept them intact. A number of children's whistles have been dug out of the earthworks surrounding Russian cities. The earliest surviving recorder, from the fifteenth century, was found at the bottom of a well in the Netherlands; there is not much reason to suppose that it was actually intended to perform polyphonic art music.

Some instruments survive because they were evidently considered extraordinary at the time they were made. Almost certainly, for example, the elegant fourteenth-century stringed instrument now in the Metropolitan Museum in New York (it is not entirely clear just what kind of an instrument it is: a citole, gittern, or mandora) was made as a luxurious artefact to be admired for its superb workmanship rather than played on a regular basis. And the same conclusion seems to be justified for the very similar instrument in the British Museum. The fifteenth-century fiddle/rebec now in the Corpus Domini Monastery in Bologna, on the other hand, must regularly have been played. It is preserved because it was the personal instrument of Saint Caterina de' Vigri, in whose shrine it now rests.[100] None of the other instruments can be considered typical of their times; they were not normally used to perform the music found in fourteenth- and fifteenth-century manuscripts.

To identify the instruments in common use between about 1300 and 1520, we must instead rely on written and pictorial evidence. Romances and other works of fiction, chronicles, histories, and pay records report on the musical life of their times. And paintings, sculpture, and manuscript illuminations not only give us details about the construction of particular instruments but also often reveal the social contexts in which they were used. Because the principal evidence is so indirect, we need to assess its meaning very cautiously. Literary and iconographical sources from the same time and place surely offer views from slightly divergent angles of the same society. We should attempt to reconcile what they tell us, rather than rejecting one kind of

---

[99] See Frederick Crane, *Extant Medieval Musical Instruments: A Provisional Catalogue by Types* (Iowa City, 1972).

[100] See Marco Tiella, 'The Violeta of S. Caterina de' Vigri', *Galpin Society Journal*, 28 (1975), 60–70.

evidence or another. Not all the work necessary to form a clear picture of the musical life of the fourteenth and fifteenth centuries has yet been done, and so some of the hypotheses offered below must be considered very tentative attempts at a synthetic view.

Writers about music from the period differentiate between two large classes of instruments: *haut* and *bas*, loud and soft.[101] This distinction was made as early as the late fourteenth century; it maintains its usefulness throughout the fifteenth century; and it begins to lose its relevance in the early sixteenth century. The following survey adopts this division into *haut* and *bas* categories, concentrating at first on the principal loud instruments, trumpets and shawms. It describes various other loud instruments as well, including some that came into common use only at the very end of the period and do not fall clearly into either category. It continues with keyboard instruments, which had enough of an independent life to warrant separate treatment, and concludes with soft instruments, above all the strings that were the centrepiece of courtly music, but including also the soft winds, which came gradually into more common use as the fifteenth century progressed.

TRUMPET BANDS

Throughout the period between about 1300 and 1520, there were two basic types of trumpet: a thin cylindrical instrument roughly six to eight feet in length, ending with a small flare—the so-called field trumpet, or buisine, and a shorter wider bored instrument with a fairly pronounced conical flare in its final segment, which ended with a clearly defined bell—the so-called watchman's horn or Thurner horn.[102] The watchman's horn was a relatively simple signalling instrument, which played no role in the musical life of the times. The field trumpet underwent radical changes in its shape and function in the course of the fourteenth and fifteenth centuries. For example, some straight trumpets began to be made on which higher harmonies could be played: the so-called clareta (later more commonly called clarino). By the middle of the fifteenth century some players even began to spe-

---

[101] See Edmund A. Bowles, 'Haut and Bas: The Grouping of Musical Instruments in the Middle Ages', *Musica disciplina*, 8 (1954), 115–40.

[102] On the background of trumpets in the Middle Ages see Anthony Baines, *Brass Instruments: Their History and Development* (New York, 1981), 81–93 and Edward Tarr, *The Trumpet* (London, 1988), 35–78. Edmund Bowles, 'Eastern Influences on the use of Trumpets and Drums during the Middle Ages', *Anuario musical*, 26 (1972), 3–28, examines the introduction of trumpets into Europe *c.*1300. While the views of Peter Downey, 'The Renaissance Slide Trumpet: Fact or Fiction', *EM* 12 (1984), 26–33, have been sharply questioned, his discussion of trumpets themselves remains quite useful: see id., 'The Trumpet and its Role in Music of the Renaissance and Early Baroque' (Ph.D. diss., Queen's University of Belfast, 1983).

cialize in the development of a clarino technique. These three types are those distinguished in the first survey of instruments, Sebastian Virdung's *Musica getutscht* of 1511. He calls them *Felttrumpet*, *Clareta*, and *Thurner horn*.[103]

As technology changed, some field trumpets began to be made in shapes that enabled them to be played more conveniently. By the fourth quarter of the fourteenth century, some trumpets were built in S-shapes, and by about 1400 others were folded (in the manner of a modern bugle, but longer). Slide trumpets, with a slide that enabled the player to change his fundamental and thus obtain more diatonic notes, were invented, conceivably as early as the first decades of the fifteenth century.[104] Slide trumpets seem not to have been very efficient. They eventually died out, and their musical function was taken over by the newly invented trombone (sackbut, *prusun*, *busaun*, or *posaune*, the last three terms also used on occasion to mean trumpet). Trombones, however, normally played with shawm bands in the fifteenth and sixteenth centuries rather than with ensembles of trumpets and drums.

Nakers, small kettledrums normally played in pairs and strapped around the waist of the drummer, often accompanied ensembles of trumpets in the performance of ceremonial or martial music. Nakers can also be seen accompanying shawms or other instruments in contemporary pictures. Occasionally, artists depicted larger kettle-drums, either laid on the ground to be played or held by a second person.

Trumpet bands (with or without drums) were a sign of prestige and power during this period. Kings and emperors maintained the right to their own corps of trumpeters.[105] Some civic corporations, too, hired their own bands of trumpets. The city of Florence had six trumpeters on their payroll by about 1380, and Siena had about eight trumpeters

[103] For Virdung's illustrations, and a recent translation of the text, see *Musica getutscht: A Treatise on Musical Instruments (1511) by Sebastian Virdung*, trans. and ed. Beth Bullard (Cambridge, 1993); for the implications of clarino for 15th-c. performance practice, see Polk, *German Instrumental Music*, 46–50.

[104] The classic essay on the slide trumpet remains Heinrich Besseler, 'Die Entstehung der Posaune', *Acta musicologica*, 32 (1950), 8–35, with important additional information in Vivian Safowitz, 'Trumpet Music and Trumpet Style in the Early Renaissance' (Master's Thesis, University of Illinois, 1965). Downey, 'The Renaissance Slide Trumpet', proposed that the instrument in fact never existed, but Ross Duffin, 'The Trompette des Menestrels in the 15th-century Alta Capella', *EM* 17 (1989), 397–402, and Herbert Myers, 'Slide Trumpet Madness: Fact or Fiction', *EM* 17 (1989), 383–9, convincingly refuted this. Polk, *German Instrumental Music*, 60–70, examines the possible origins of the instrument and its development within the context of the shawm bands in the 15th c.

[105] For trumpet ensembles of the nobility in the 15th c. see Polk, *German Instrumental Music*, 87–103.

by the 1420s.[106] Venice already owned their famous set of silver trumpets in the fifteenth century, which they used in processions and on other state occasions.[107] In general, trumpet bands seem to have grown larger as time went on.[108] There is evidence of various kinds that two or three trumpets made up a normal trumpet band in the mid-fourteenth century, whereas as many as twelve trumpets were suitable for a king or emperor about 1500. It is not clear just how these trumpets functioned together.

Michael Praetorius' description of how to use a band of trumpets in the performance of church music, in the second volume of his *Syntagma musicum* (1619), suggests that trumpet bands then played with a mixture of drones, repeating figures, and simple tunes to produce a sound not unlike that of the toccata in Monteverdi's *Orfeo*. Although seventeenth-century practice has, of course, no direct application to the conventions of the fourteenth and fifteenth centuries, Praetorius' characterization of polyphonic ceremonial music is highly suggestive, also considering that corps of trumpeters are apt to have been extremely conservative in passing on their traditional way of playing. Praetorius' general guidelines explaining how civic trumpeters played are compatible with the musical style of early fifteenth-century *trumpetum* compositions imitating trumpet sounds, as described by Paulus Paulirinus (see above) and as represented by Dufay's *Gloria ad modum tube*. (As said, these pieces were apparently not intended to be performed by trumpets, but only to imitate their sound.)

Burgundian court records in the fifteenth century distinguish between *trompettes de menestrel* and *trompettes de guerre*.[109] The difference between the types may have corresponded to their construction, the minstrels' trumpet being supplied with a slide. Whatever the technical distinction, however, these notices suggest that trumpets fulfilled at least two different functions. On the one hand, they were used

---

[106] The size of the Florentine trumpet band was documented in the Statutes of the city of 1415, but six trumpet players had figured in city records for many years; see Polk, 'Civic Patronage', 66–7. On Siena's trumpeters' corps in the 15th c., see D'Accone, *The Civic Muse*, 438–80.

[107] The destruction of Venetian records in the late 16th c. has made the study of instrumental forces of Venice much more difficult than is the case for Florence. We do know, however, that the Venetian ensemble of silver trumpets was considered a key ingredient in civic ceremonies. See Edward Muir, *Civic Ritual in Renaissance Venice* (Princeton, 1981), 264–5 for documentation of the costly instruments in the 15th c. One peculiar feature of trumpet ensembles is that they were more local in make-up than was the case with other wind players. The trumpet ensembles of both Ferrara and Florence in the late 15th c., for example, were made up almost exclusively of Italian players—at a time when shawmists and trombonists were often German.

[108] See Polk, *German Instrumental Music*, 47–8 and 87–103.

[109] See Wright, *Music at the Court of Burgundy*, 41.

as signalling instruments for various courtly, military, and civic occasions, such as battles, jousts, hunting expeditions, and ordinary and extraordinary ceremonial events, like the formal appearance of a king or emperor. It is possible that the construction of most signalling trumpets was such that only the first few harmonies could be played, making the signals in general rather lower pitched than the sounds we associate with modern trumpets.

On the other hand, minstrels' trumpets may also have played other kinds of repertory. For example, there is evidence that some trumpets were used for dancing, although it is not clear just what sort of dance music they could play.[110] A wall-painting in the Torre dell'Aquila in Trento shows a dancing scene accompanied by shawms, nakers, and long straight trumpets; in this case, the trumpets might well have supplied a drone, if they were intended to be playing at all. Other trumpets, however, might well have played melodies. With the development of the clarino, at least some instruments were capable of playing higher harmonics and therefore even scale segments.

LOUD WIND BANDS

The shawm band (*alta capella*) constituted one of the most important features of musical life in court and city during the fourteenth and fifteenth centuries. In 1482–3 Tinctoris described the standard wind band as consisting of three instruments: discant shawm, bombard (that is, tenor shawm), and sackbut (that is, trombone). He even specified that the shawm played the cantus part, the bombard the cantus firmus in dances, and the trombone the contratenor.[111] Tinctoris suggested, in other words, the primacy of the discant/tenor duo in three-part compositions (or improvisations), the two shawms being responsible for the scaffolding voices, a scheme we can probably take as representative throughout most of the history of shawm bands.

So as far as we now can tell, the double reed in most shawms of the period was encircled by a *pirouette*, a small wooden disc against which the player rested his lips. Contact with the disc resulted in less

---

[110] Documents of 1393, referring to a visit of members of the Burgundian court to Ypres, mention a 'dance au son des trompettes': Edmond Vander Straeten, *Les Ménestrels au Pays-Bas* (Brussels, 1878), 188. In 1459 a Burgundian embassy report from Milan noted 'Et n'y dansoient ... que danses à cours, au son de clarons': Marix, *Histoire*, 77. In 1439 the Nuremberg city accounts record that a trumpeter of the Margrave of Brandenburg had performed 'at several dances' ('zu ettlichen tentzen trumetet'): Nuremberg, Bayerisches Staatsarchiv, Repertorium 54/9, fo. 64[r].

[111] Baines, 'Fifteenth-Century Instruments', 20–1.

muscle fatigue, allowing the performers to play at full power for long periods. Most shawms ended with a flared bell, but some in the fourteenth century were constructed with a rather long cylindrical end, a shawm that fell out of use in the early fifteenth century (it is not clear how these instruments differed from others in sound). Some tenors were supplied with one or two keys protected by a cover (called a *fontanelle*). Discant and tenor sizes of shawm were probably normally tuned about a fifth apart. They had an effective range of about two octaves, although their highest notes were doubtless only securely available to the best players. Shawms possess a considerable amount of flexibility of tone and volume, and they can easily play fast notes.[112]

The shawm band underwent many changes before it became fixed at three particular instruments in the second half of the fifteenth century. Works of art and archival documents both suggest that in the fourteenth century one or two shawms played with or without nakers, and that when a third wind instrument joined an ensemble, it was apt to be a bagpipe.[113] Quite possibly many (or most) fourteenth-century bagpipes were fitted with drones that could not be detached, and so we must imagine two shawms of different sizes either playing heterophonically, or more likely, a kind of rudimentary two- or three-part counterpoint (for the chanter of the bagpipe could also conceivably add a polyphonic line) over a drone. The limitations of this arrangement may have caused the shift about 1400 towards using a slide trumpet as the third instrument, and eventually, after it was invented—possibly for this very purpose—the trombone. In the course of the fifteenth century, moreover, the bagpipe came to be more and more closely identified with peasants, beggars, and members of the lowest classes, although it can still be seen in works of art of the period playing for upper-class dancing.

Whereas shawm bands seem normally to have performed in three parts in the fifteenth century, some archival notices record larger ensembles of five and even six instruments, especially among the more prestigious courts. Nevertheless, it was not until the late fifteenth or early sixteenth centuries that shawm bands regularly involved four rather than three players in performances, doubtless

---

[112] On the shawm see Anthony Baines, *Woodwind Instruments and their History* (New York, 1957), 232–4 and 268–72. See also Polk, *German Instrumental Music*, 50–4.

[113] On the documentation provided by illustrations of shawms see Edmund Bowles, 'Iconography as a Tool for Examining the Loud Consort in the Fifteenth Century', *Journal of the American Musical Instrument Society*, 3 (1977), 100–21.

as a result of a general shift in musical style away from counter-point against a cantus firmus to a four-part texture emphasizing melody and bass.[114] The four-part shawm band normally involved three shawms and a trombone, although the combination of two shawms and two trombones was not unknown.

Shawm bands were regularly employed at courts to supply the ruler and his courtiers with music at mealtimes, for dancing after dinner, and for other similar occasions. Cities also regularly hired their own shawm bands, who doubtless played at regular times in the town square or some other suitable place, took part at important civic occasions, and participated in various other annual or occasional civic festivities. In many larger towns and cities of Europe, there were free-lance musicians as well who formed shawm bands to play for whoever would hire them at weddings, banquets, and other kinds of celebra-tions. So far as we can tell, all these various groups shared a common repertory.

We know very little about the music which a loud wind band of the fourteenth or early fifteenth centuries would have played. The *canzonette tedesche* of London 29987 and several fifteenth-century cantus firmi for dances would be suitable for use in dance music per-formed by the band. Also some other pieces from the period around 1400 have been put forward because of the way they seem to fit spe-cific instruments.[115] We are at least certain that loud wind bands played for dancing, and it seems just as certain that the principal repertory of *haut* instruments was largely improvised until the first half of the fifteenth century.

From about 1440, however, there is increasing evidence that shawm bands participated in performances of the standard repertory, as we have already seen from the scattered sources mentioned above, includ-ing the manuscripts probably related to the court bands of Mantua and Ferrara, and the town bands of Bologna and Maastricht; the latter seems to have included Marian motets in its repertory. Contracts and archival notices make clear that shawm bands performed both sacred and secular music. The city officials of Bruges commissioned a special set of motets to be played by the wind band of the city.[116] The wind band of Venice played motets by Obrecht and Busnois

---

[114] On the interrelationships of the parts within the wind ensemble, see Polk, *German Instru-mental Music*, 50–70 and 79–83.

[115] See Strohm, *Rise*, 108–11.

[116] Nicasius de Brauwere, succentor of St Saviour's church, was commissioned to write motets for the town minstrels in 1484/5. We know that the ensemble performed settings of *Ave regina celorum* and *Salve regina* on 5 April 1488. See Strohm, *Music in Late Medieval Bruges*, 86–7.

especially arranged for them.[117] Thus it seems clear that by the fourth quarter of the fifteenth century the best wind players participated fully in the art music of the time. We can hypothesize that the repertory of a late fifteenth- and early sixteenth-century shawmist or trombonist consisted of at least the following five kinds of music: (1) dance music, much of it doubtless improvised or semi-improvised, (2) settings of popular tunes and local repertory items, (3) abstract instrumental music (bicinia, tricinia, and so on), (4) chansons from the central courtly repertory, and to a lesser extent songs in other vernacular languages, and even (5) ceremonial sacred music.

Moreover, at least a few wind players accompanied singers in the performance of sacred music by the late fifteenth century. Thus, the court chapel of Savoy, for example, regularly hired an instrumentalist, possibly a trombonist (even though his instrument is described as a *trompette*) who had to play cantus firmi with the singers (or to double them) in the performance of sacred music.[118] The extent to which wind players participated in the liturgy in the fifteenth century is not at all clear. It was not until the second half of the sixteenth century, for example, that Italian cathedrals and churches began regularly to hire instrumentalists; the strictures against using instruments except organs in church remained strong throughout the fifteenth and early sixteenth centuries. Probably, winds were used for special occasions such as weddings, or, especially in the north, to play for 'Salve' services, in effect sacred concerts after Vespers or Compline that grew out of the custom of singing a Marian antiphon at the end of the day.[119] Pictorial and documentary evidence suggests that trumpets were quite regularly heard in church on especially festive events such as royal coronations, sometimes in connection with the *Gloria in excelsis*.[120]

At least two other instruments in common use in the fifteenth century can also be associated with loud winds: the three-holed pipe played with a tabor and the Swiss fife played with a side drum.

---

[117] As shown by two letters written by Giovanni Alvise Trombon, allegedly a member of the civic ensemble of Venice, to Francesco Gonzaga, the first in 1494, the second in 1505. On these documents, see Prizer, 'Bernardino Piffaro', 161–2. Baroncini, 'Voci e strumenti', has established that Alvise was in fact a member of the Venetian civic wind ensemble during this period.

[118] See M.-T. Bouquet, 'La cappella musicale dei duchi di Savoia dal 1450 al 1500', *Rivista italiana di musicologia*, 3 (1968), 233–85 at 236–9, 251.

[119] On instruments in the Salve services, see Strohm, *Music in Late Medieval Bruges*, 85–6; Kristine Forney, '16th-Century Antwerp', in Iain Fenlon (ed.), *The Renaissance* (London, 1989), 361–78 at 364; Barbara Haggh, 'Music, Liturgy and Ceremony in Brussels, 1350–1500' (Ph.D. diss., University of Illinois, 1968), i. 401; and Polk, *German Instrumental Music*, 122.

[120] See Žak, *Musik als 'Ehr und Zier'*.

Whereas the three-holed pipe may not have been in itself very loud, it may often have functioned in place of *haut* instruments. Many courtly musical establishments seem regularly to have employed a pipe and tabor player, whose job it may have been to play monophonic tunes for the entertainment of the courtiers and to accompany dancing when a larger ensemble like a shawm band was either not available or not appropriate.[121] The combination of fife and drum, on the other hand, must have been loud enough to be heard over the sound of marching soldiers. The players of these instruments were regularly attached to Swiss mercenary units in the fifteenth and sixteenth centuries. They also played for civic processions and led infantrymen into battle (trumpets and drums being reserved for the higher-class cavalrymen). Some works of art show fifes and drums being used, too, to play for both upper- and lower-class dancing.[122]

In the late fifteenth century, moreover, the palette of instrumental sounds was enlarged by the addition of various new wind instruments. Both the crumhorn and the cornetto properly belong to the history of sixteenth-century instrumental music, although they first appear in the late fifteenth century. The crumhorn is related to the shawm only because both use double reeds; but the double reed of the crumhorn is enclosed in a wooden cylinder, giving it a very limited range. Crumhorns seem mostly to have been played in consorts of like instruments. Their limited usefulness probably explains why they fell out of favour by the seventeenth century.[123] An instrument related both to the crumhorn and the bagpipe, the bladder pipe (Platerspiel), in which the double reed is enclosed by a bladder, is associated chiefly with Germanic countries and with lower-class music.[124]

Various kinds of cornetto—straight, curved, leather-covered, or made from plain wood—also came into widespread use in the late fifteenth or early sixteenth centuries. Cornetti regularly played with

---

[121] The pipe and tabor has been little studied by modern historians. Wim Bosmans, *Eenhandsfluit en trom in de Lage Landen* (Peer, 1991), deals mostly with the period after 1520, but devotes some space to the medieval instrument. See also D. Hoffmann-Axthelm, 'Zu Ikonographie und Bedeutungsgeschichte von Flöte und Trommel in Mittelalter und Renaissance', *Basler Jahrbuch für historische Musikpraxis*, 7 (1983), 83–118; Walter Salmen, 'Zur Verbreitung von Einhandflöte und Trommel in europäischen Mittelalter', *Jahrbuch des österreichischen Volksliedwerkes*, 6 (1957), 154–61; and Gabriele Busch-Salmen, *Ikonographische Studien zum Solotanz im Mittelalter* (Innsbruck, 1982), 38–43, with further examples and discussion.

[122] On the fife and drum see Brown, 'Instruments', in *Performance Practice: Music before 1600* (Norton/Grove Handbooks on Music, ed. Howard M. Brown and Stanley Sadie, 1; London, 1989), 167–84 at 176–7, and Busch-Salmen, *Ikonographische Studien*, 40–3.

[123] For further information see Bara Boydell, *The Crumhorn and other Renaissance Windcap Instruments* (Buren, 1982), and Kenton T. Meyer, *The Crumhorn* (Ann Arbor, 1983).

[124] See Polk, *German Instrumental Music*, 54–6.

trombones as independent instrumental ensembles or to accompany singers in the performance of sacred music. Such groups served in a sense as domesticated versions of shawm bands, cornetti substituting for shawms when singers were involved. The versatility and flexibility of the cornetto made it also an ideal instrument on which to play solo lines. Its adaptability explains the rise of virtuoso cornetto players in the later sixteenth and seventeenth centuries, musicians who were adept at adding rapid passaggi and who were able to master the highly expressive styles of the early Baroque era.[125]

KEYBOARD INSTRUMENTS

As we have seen, music for keyboards survives from the fifteenth century in specially prepared anthologies, a circumstance that justifies treating the instruments as a special category. Stringed keyboard instruments were invented in the fourteenth century, and various kinds of organs were in common use from 1300 to 1520.

To judge from countless works of art, and from their association with famous men like Landini, portatives were more common in the fourteenth century than any other sort of organ. Held on the lap (or by a strap hung around the shoulders) while the player pumped the bellows with his or her left hand and fingered the keys with the right, portatives were almost certainly best equipped to play single lines. Indeed, they may never have been used to play more parts at once, although some were built with towers on one end which suggest the presence of one or more drones that could be disengaged. Moreover, an instrument small enough to be held while being played must have sounded at two-foot pitch. In short, it is highly unlikely that any of the surviving keyboard music was intended for portative organs. It is much more likely that they played whatever repertory was appropriate for any other soft instrument, and that included, of course, single top parts of polyphonic pieces such as Trecento madrigals. In the fourteenth century portatives were used by various classes of musician; it was an instrument that cut across social boundaries. It was certainly an instrument associated with upper-class music-making, but it can also be seen, for example, in one fourteenth-century manuscript illumination in the hands of a street musician of Paris.[126] In the course of the fifteenth century the portative organ gradually fell out of use.

[125] On the zinck, see Polk, ibid. 71–3.
[126] For the latter, see Kimberly Marshall, *Iconographic Evidence for the Late-Medieval Organ in French, Flemish and English Manuscripts* (New York, 1989), ii, pl. 22.

The most likely organ type for which most of the surviving keyboard music was intended was the positive, a free-standing instrument portable enough to be carried from one performance venue to the next. In common use in the fourteenth as well as the fifteenth century, the positive had but a single manual and one to three ranks of flue pipes. Playing it required a second person to pump the bellows. There is some evidence that positive organs were carried into churches when they were needed; their participation in sacred music including polyphony, particularly in services held in side chapels, is amply documented by about 1400. The famous Ghent altarpiece by Hubert and Jan van Eyck (*c.*1430) shows a positive organ being played polyphonically together with soloist singers. Nevertheless, the instruments were not used exclusively—or perhaps even chiefly—for the performance of sacred music, as the many secular pieces in fifteenth-century tablatures make clear.

Large organs could be found in churches by the tenth century, even though no evidence survives from before the thirteenth century to suggest that they were supplied with keyboards mechanically sophisticated enough to allow the performance of the kind of music found in the earliest tablatures. It may have been the invention of a practical keyboard that inspired the installation or rebuilding of a great many large organs in churches during the fourteenth century. The cathedral of Notre Dame in Dijon may have had an organ at the time of its dedication in 1334; a contract for the organ in the cathedral of Barcelona dates from 1345; Fra Domenico of Siena built an organ for the Church of the Santissima Annunziata in Florence in 1379 after plans by Landini; and so on.[127] It is conceivable that some of the surviving keyboard music—like the alternatim Mass movements in the Faenza Codex or a few of the plainsong settings in the English and German anthologies—was playable on instruments of this sort, but in fact we have very little idea of the function of large church organs during this period. They may have been used to play preludes, interludes, and postludes at sacred services; a document from Bruges, 1384, records the playing of a 'motet' on the organ in a ceremony.[128] They certainly performed plainsong in alternation with the choir, or accompanied the singers on occasion. Many church organs were installed over the west door, whereas the singers performed from the choir at the other end; a number of documents,

---

[127] See Hans Klotz, *Über die Orgelkunst der Gotik, der Renaissance und des Barock* (Kassel, 1975), i. 10–11.

[128] Strohm, *Music in Late Medieval Bruges*, 18.

however, suggest that the great organ alternated with the choir in processions outside the choir.[129]

Stringed keyboard instruments only gradually came into widespread use in the course of the fifteenth century.[130] Nevertheless, in
addition to the exchiquier and clavichord, which were probably the
oldest stringed keyboard instruments, also the invention of the harpsichord (*clavicymbalum*) happened before 1400. The Paduan lawyer
Giovanni Lambertacci reports in a letter written in 1397 that he had
made the acquaintance of the German physician and musician Hermann Poll, who claimed to have invented an instrument which he
called 'clavicembalum'; this term is consistent with other, shortly later
uses which seem to refer to a similar or the same instrument, for
example the North German poet Eberhard von Cersne in his poem
Der Minne Regel of 1404. There may well be a connection between
the introduction of the harpsichord and the sudden appearance of
keyboard tablatures in northern Italy (Faenza Codex and other
sources) around 1400.[131]

The most detailed knowledge we have about fifteenth-century
stringed keyboard instruments comes from a mid-century manuscript
treatise by Henri Arnaut de Zwolle, physician to the dukes of
Burgundy and later the kings of France.[132] Arnaut furnishes the earliest known technical descriptions of the harpsichord and clavichord,
as well as a somewhat mysterious *dulce melos*, and he includes in his
diagrams schemes for hammer actions as well as the plucking mecha-
nisms he found preferable (and which obviously prevailed).

The earliest anthologies of 'harpsichord' music are the seven
volumes published by Pierre Attaingnant in Paris in 1531, intended
for 'orgues, espinettes, manicordions, et telz semblables instrumenz
musicaulz'. They show us that even by 1531 no very strong distinction

---

[129] See Strohm, *Rise*, 272.

[130] Concerning early keyboard instruments, see Edmund Bowles, 'On the Origin of the Keyboard Mechanism in the Late Middle Ages' *Technology and Culture*, 7 (1966), 152–62; Edwin
M. Ripin, 'Towards an Identification of the Chekker', *Galpin Society Journal*, 28 (1975), 11–25;
Christopher Page, 'The Myth of the Chekker', *EM* 7 (1979), 482–9; Wilson Barry, 'Henri Arnaut
de Zwolle's *Clavichordium* and the Origin of the Chekker', *Journal of the American Musical
Instrument Society*, 11 (1985), 5–13; and Edwin M. Ripin, 'The Early Clavichord', *MQ* 53 (1967),
518–38.

[131] See Standley Howell, 'Medical Astrologers and the Invention of Stringed Keyboard Instruments', *Journal of Musicological Research*, 10 (1990), 3–17; Reinhard Strohm, 'Die private Kunst
und das öffentliche Schicksal von Hermann Poll, dem Erfinder des Cembalos', in Monika Fink,
Rainer Gstrein, and Günter Mössmer (eds.), *Musica Privata: Die Rolle der Musik im privaten
Leben. Festschrift zum 65. Geburtstag von Walter Salmen* (Innsbruck, 1991), 53–66; Strohm, *Rise*,
92.

[132] See Arnaut de Zwolle, in G. Le Cerf and E. R. Labande, *Les Traités d'Henri-Arnaut de
Zwolle et de divers anonymes (Paris: Bibliothèque nationale, ms. Latin 7295)* (Paris, 1932; repr.
1972).

was made by musicians to differentiate harpsichord or clavichord music from organ music (although one of Attaingnant's volumes does contain music exclusively for church organ), and that the repertory of a keyboard player at that time was the same as in earlier times: mostly intabulations of every conceivable genre of 'vocal' music as well as dances and a few abstract instrumental pieces.

One other stringed keyboard instrument needs to be included among those in common use between 1300 and 1520. By 1300, the hurdy gurdy (bowed with a resined wheel, and in some cases supplied with one or more drone strings) had already had a long and distinguished history (though earlier it was more commonly called organistrum) as a theoretical instrument, a kind of monochord. The organistrum was chiefly used to demonstrate the scientific basis for the location of pitches, and possibly to give the pitch to singers in churches. Probably already by the fourteenth century, but certainly by the fifteenth, however, the hurdy gurdy had lost whatever social standing it had once possessed and had become an instrument associated with beggars and members of the lower classes.

SOFT INSTRUMENTS

Whereas loud instruments played mostly in fixed ensembles (that is, the corps of trumpets and drums, shawm bands, and eventually ensembles of cornetti and trombones), soft instruments in the fourteenth and fifteenth centuries seem to have been used in a much more flexible way. Musicians specializing in soft instruments could use them to accompany themselves while singing, or they could play in a wide variety of mixed ensembles. They could also possibly accompany singers in the performance of secular, and even perhaps some sacred, music. We can see the difference between the way *haut* and *bas* instruments were used from the surviving pay records at various courts. Whereas players of *haut* instruments were hired to fill particular vacancies (and therefore to perform specific functions), chamber musicians appear to have been hired for their individual ability. The composition of the chamber musicians (how many there were and what they played) thus changed from court to court and from time to time at the same court.[133]

Moreover, so far as we now can see, soft instruments do not appear to be standardized in the fourteenth and fifteenth centuries.[134] To judge

[133] See Polk, 'Patronage', 152–5.

[134] A wide range of soft and keyboard instruments, some of them enigmatic, was described *c.*1460 by Paulus Paulirinus: see Standley Howell, 'Paulus Paulirinus of Prague on Musical Instruments', *Journal of the American Musical Instrument Society*, 5–6 (1979–80), 9–36.

from iconographical evidence, for example, neither fiddles nor lutes seem to have been built in only one or two conventional sizes (or even shapes). Their variety leads us to suppose they were tuned, therefore, to a variety of pitches. Even Jerome of Moravia's tunings for the fiddle and the rebec, the most explicit technical evidence that survives from the fourteenth century, appear to indicate the intervallic relationships between strings rather than fixed pitches.[135] And he proposes various alternative tunings for the same instruments. Even in the sixteenth century, when various kinds of instruments came to be constructed in families (most of them consisting of three conventional sizes), some commentators, like Martin Agricola, point out that good intonation can only be ensured if the consorts are made at the same time and by the same maker. Thus, Agricola reminds us that pitches were not standardized.[136] Soft instruments must have been built to sound together in an individual and ad hoc way.

The principal soft instruments used for the performance of courtly or upper-class music throughout the fourteenth and fifteenth centuries consisted chiefly of strings: fiddle, gittern, harp, lute, psaltery, and possibly rebec. There is not much reason to suppose that other kinds of soft instruments (except small organs and stringed keyboard instruments) were in widespread use for the performance of upper-class secular music before the mid-fifteenth century. Each of these instruments needs to have its detailed history written before we can begin to understand how each changed in the course of two hundred years, and what music each played. In the meantime, however, some preliminary observations can clarify the chief characteristics of the principal representatives of the categories of plucked and bowed strings. Finally, we need to consider the soft winds that may have come into common use in ensembles of chamber musicians only relatively late in the fifteenth century.

Both the psaltery and harp belong to the category of plucked strings that use one string (or course) per pitch. To judge from the way they are shown being played in works of art, both were capable of performing either single lines or polyphony. Psalteries were built in various shapes—rectangular, triangular, like a pig's snout, and so on— each of which may have been associated with a particular repertory of music or class of performer (in fourteenth-century Italy, for example, the pig-snout psaltery appears to have been associated with

---

[135] Christopher Page, 'Jerome of Moravia on the *Rubeba* and *Viella*', *Galpin Society Journal*, 32 (1979), 77–98.

[136] For further information see Howard M. Brown, 'Notes (and Transposing Notes) on the Viol in the Early Sixteenth Century', in Fenlon, *Music*, 61–78.

minstrels, and the more common rectangular psaltery with amateurs as well as professionals). Most psalteries must have had a fairly limited range, not more than a tenth or a twelfth, but nevertheless big enough to play most single lines, and many polyphonic pieces (or at least two parts of three-part pieces). In the fifteenth century artists began to depict psalteries struck with small hammers, that is, dulcimers, which seem to have come into existence just at a time when the psaltery was already going out of fashion as an instrument appropriate for the performance of upper-class music.[137]

Fourteenth- and fifteenth-century harps probably had considerably larger ranges than most psalteries. Some of them may even have been able to play all the diatonic notes in the Guidonian hand, that is, two octaves and a sixth. One central problem, however, in imagining how either instrument could be used in the performance of the surviving music involves the difficulty of playing accidentals. To some extent, a player could adjust his instrument for particular pieces, tuning only those notes that required inflection, which may explain why so many literary documents describe harp players as tuning at length before playing (especially before playing an unfamiliar instrument). It may be, too, that some technique was developed of raising a string by a half step through pressing the finger against it. A fully chromatic harp seems to have been an invention of the mid-sixteenth century.

Many members of the nobility could play the harp. Both Charles d'Orléans and his mother, Valentina Visconti, for example, were harpists, and the list of aristocratic players could easily be multiplied. Clearly, the harp was an instrument appropriate for the performance of whatever repertory was associated with the upper classes. The instrument was also cultivated by minstrels. Those professional players who specialized in soft instruments and who worked at courts would, of course, have shared some of their repertory with their noble patrons. Nevertheless, harps can be documented in so many different kinds of social situations in the fourteenth and fifteenth centuries that the repertory must have encompassed a wide variety of composed and improvised, monophonic and polyphonic music.[138]

Lutes and gitterns were the principal representatives of the category of plucked instruments fitted with relatively few strings, each of which

[137] See Brown, 'Instruments', 176.

[138] For further information on the harp, see Heidrun Rosenzweig, 'Zur Harfe im 15. Jahrhundert', *Basler Jahrbuch für historische Musikpraxis*, 8 (1984), 163–82; Howard M. Brown, 'The Trecento Harp', in Stanley Boorman (ed.), *Studies in the Performance of Late Medieval Music* (Cambridge, 1983), 35–73; Reinhard Strohm, '"La harpe de melodie" oder Das Kunswerk als Akt der Zueignung', in H. Danuser et al. (eds.), *Das musikalische Kunstwerk: Festschrift Carl Dahlhaus zum 60. Geburtstag* (Laaber, 1988), 305–16.

was required to supply more than one pitch. Some musicians in the fourteenth and fifteenth centuries played various other kinds of plucked strings as well: the citole, the rotta, and various forerunners of the sixteenth-century cittern, for example. Most of these instruments, however, had their heyday in the thirteenth century and were gradually dying out. By the fourteenth century their use was limited and mostly confined to particular localities. So far as we can tell, the citole, the rotta, and other ancillary plucked strings had become instruments of lesser minstrels by the fourteenth century and they were therefore unlikely to have been called for in the performance of upper-class music.

Today we are inclined to think of the lute as a solo instrument par excellence, and the principal plucked string instrument of the late Middle Ages and the Renaissance. That view, however, really stems from the place of the lute in sixteenth-century musical life. It is probable that the lute had only recently been introduced to most Western European countries at the beginning of the fourteenth century, presumably from Arabic countries (Spain was exceptional in having been so open to North African influence at a much earlier time than other European countries). During the fourteenth century, the lute may have served mostly in an accompanying role, playing tenor parts, or taking part in ensembles of two or three lutes. Although we have no firm idea of how the instrument was tuned in the fourteenth century, we can guess that it was in some combination of fourths and thirds.

The lute, like the gittern, was normally played with a plectrum until the mid-fifteenth century, a playing technique that severely limited the instrument's ability to cope with polyphony. It was the widespread adaptation of the technique of plucking the instrument with the fingers that enabled players to differentiate for the first time among several contrapuntal parts. The change from plectrum to finger technique liberated the instrument and allowed it to assume its position of importance as accompanying and solo instrument in the sixteenth century.[139]

The gittern was an instrument in common use in Western Europe long before the lute was introduced. Together with the fiddle, it was among the few thirteenth-century instruments that continued an active existence into the fourteenth. Works of art normally depict the gittern

---

[139] On the lute in the fifteenth century, see Crawford Young, 'Zur Klassifikation und ikonographischen Interpretation mittelalterlicher Zupfinstrumente', *Basler Jahrbuch für historische Musikpraxis*, 8 (1984), 67–103. See also Fallows, '15th-Century Tablatures'; Vladimir Ivanoff, 'Das Lautenduo im 15. Jahrhundert', *Basler Jahrbuch für Historische Musikpraxis*, 8 (1984), 147–61; and Prizer, 'The Frottola'.

with four double courses and frets. Its short string length indicates that it was relatively high pitched, capable mostly of playing cantus parts (if in fact it ever participated in the performance of composed polyphony) or treble melodies.[140] Notices about the virtuoso gittern player Pietrobono of Ferrara in the fifteenth century suggest, too, that the instrument was especially apt for florid passage-work. The same notices reveal that Pietrobono often played with a tenorista, presumably a musician who supplied a supporting voice on lute or fiddle, to Pietrobono's virtuoso top part.[141] Also other evidence indicates that gitterns were often accompanied by some other instrument. Although it is seldom possible to be certain of the social destination of any instrument from this period, it would appear that the gittern was an instrument primarily associated with minstrels, including such courtly minstrels as Pietrobono (if he can be described in that way). While being a widespread instrument, the gittern was less suitable than harp or fiddle for participation in the performance of composed polyphony, even if it was an instrument often accompanied by a tenorista.

The development of both the lute and gittern blur towards the mid-fifteenth century. Whereas they had previously been distinct instruments (the gittern being smaller, with a shorter, fretted fingerboard, and the lute larger, unfretted, and with a longer neck), evidently by about the mid-fifteenth century they became in essence two sizes of a similar instrument; the lute developed into a fretted instrument with a shorter neck. By about 1500 this process had run its course and we find numerous illustrations in which two and three players are shown, with the lower part(s) played by large lutes, and the discant clearly being played on a small lute, not a gittern.[142] Such a change was gradual, of course, with what appears to have been many decades of overlap. We may probably assume that the players themselves would have preferred some consistency. A professional player, even if noted for his skill as a sopranist, would certainly have played a larger instrument from time to time. These doublings would obviously have been much more workable if, for example, the tuning systems were consistent between the instruments. Another factor working in favour of the lute was that the instrument was being made in different sizes by about

---

[140] On this point and its implications for performance practice, see Howard Mayer Brown, 'St. Augustine, Lady Music and the Gittern', *Musica disciplina*, 38 (1984), 25–65; concerning the gittern in general see Laurence Wright, 'The Medieval Gittern and Citole: A Case of Mistaken Identity', *Galpin Society Journal*, 30 (1977), 9–42; and Mary Remnant, 'The Gittern in English Mediaeval Art', *Galpin Society Journal*, 18 (1965), 104–9.

[141] See Lockwood, *Music in Renaissance Ferrara*, 100.

[142] Ensembles which include two and three lutes, with small lutes, not gitterns, are shown e.g. in *The Triumph of Maximilian I*; see Polk, *German Instrumental Music*, 35–6.

1450. Tinctoris, at any rate, makes comments suggesting that changes had occurred which made it possible to play lower than had been the case previously, which would imply a larger instrument.[143] Once this notion had taken hold with instrument-makers, they would also have experimented with the idea of small lutes, as the production of instruments in consorts of various sizes was clearly the thrust of instrument-making towards the end of the fifteenth century.

Chief among the bowed strings, and arguably the most versatile instrument of the entire period between *c*.1300 and 1520, the fiddle should be considered the true workhorse among the instruments of the fourteenth and fifteenth centuries. As the theorist Johannes de Grocheio wrote in his treatise of *c*.1300, the fiddle could play any and every sort of piece that existed then.

Fiddles are shown in works of art with several different body outlines: oval, waisted, or figure-of-eight, for example, with or without bouts. Artists gave the instrument varying numbers of strings, although they are mostly depicted with five, the number that Jerome of Moravia about 1300 also considered standard. The evidence of the pictures and of Jerome suggests, too, that some fiddles had among their five strings one or two that did not run over the fingerboard. These off-board drones could either be plucked by the left thumb of the player, or bowed from time to time. Two of Jerome's three tunings for the fiddle seem best suited to an instrument playing a melody with drones. Only his third suggests that the inner strings of the fiddle could also be bowed separately and the instrument used to play single lines. So far as we now know, fiddles at that time did not have sound posts, so that their tuning and fittings could be changed more or less at will. Perhaps, then, the same instrument could be fitted with a more flattened bridge for polyphonic play (or more accurately melody with drones), or with a more arched bridge if it was necessary to play single lines: individual voices in a polyphonic composition, for example.[144]

Among their many uses, fiddles accompanied singer-poets who declaimed long narrative stories, both on street corners for the entertainment of the citizenry and at courts for the entertainment of the aristocracy. Indeed fiddles appear to have been the principal instruments to which the *improvvisatori* sang their tales of chivalry and high

---

[143] Baines, 'Fifteenth-Century Instruments' 22–4; see also Polk, *German Instrumental Music*, 26, and particularly Stradner, 'Zur Ausbildung', 177–9.

[144] Despite its position as the central instrument for minstrels at least in the 14th c., a thorough study of the fiddle remains overdue. For the available bibliography see Brown, 'Instruments', 35, esp. nn. 35–42.

romance. In time a special kind of fiddle evolved, evidently ideally suited for this particular kind of musical function. The poets called this new offshoot of the fiddle, with its body shaped rather like a violin, and with seven strings, the lira da braccio, an obviously classicizing name. The lira was the only fiddle that continued to be in widespread use into the sixteenth century, when it came to be the instrument almost invariably associated with the *ottave rime* improvised by gods and goddesses at Italian theatrical occasions.[145]

Although the fiddle was invariably held under the chin in the fifteenth and sixteenth centuries, some works of art from the thirteenth and fourteenth centuries show the instrument being played on the knees, and bowed underhand. Some scholars therefore refer to the instruments as medieval viols, by which they mean the very same instrument as the fiddle, being played in a different way.[146]

The only other bowed string instrument important in the fourteenth and fifteenth centuries, the rebec, was shaped like a bowl or a pear, and fitted with two or three strings, tuned in fifths according to Jerome of Moravia. The instrument had an ambiguous social position in the fourteenth and fifteenth centuries.[147] Like the gittern, the rebec appears to have been a thirteenth-century instrument that continued to be played in later times. By the fourteenth century, however, it seems to have sunk to the status of an instrument for use by lesser minstrels, peasants, and members of the lower classes. A few notices, however, contradict that assessment. In the later fifteenth century, for example, Tinctoris calls it one of his favourite instruments and singles it out for praise for its versatility; and it took part in some of the courtly *intermedii* organized for Medici weddings in the sixteenth century.[148]

At the end of the fifteenth century, the viola da gamba was developed in Italy from a Spanish prototype.[149] The new instrument soon spread from Italy to Germany and France. The history of the viol properly belongs to the sixteenth century, as does the history of the violin family, invented shortly after the viol, probably in the first decades of the sixteenth century. At the beginning of their existence, violins mostly played dance music, as a sort of string equivalent of the shawm band.

---

[145] On the lira da braccio see Howard M. Brown, 'Lira da braccio' in *New Grove*.

[146] See Woodfield, *Early History*, 9–14.

[147] See M. A. Downie, 'The Rebec: An Orthographic and Iconographic Study' (Ph.D. diss., West Virginia University, 1981).

[148] Baines, 'Fifteenth-Century Instruments', 24–5.

[149] The evidence for Spanish primacy in the development of the viol is described and discussed in Woodfield, *Early History*.

The principal difficulty in knowing which soft wind instruments were in common use in the fourteenth and fifteenth centuries comes from the ambiguity of the literary evidence used to describe them. In the first place, there is a question of terminology. Just what, for example, is a 'flute', and how does it relate to 'fleuste brehaingne', 'fistule', 'flajolle', 'flajos', 'flajos de Scens', 'pipe', and 'souffle', to name only the obvious names for whistle flutes and (possibly) transverse flutes, in a single fourteenth-century list of musicians who entertained the lover and his lady in Machaut's *Remède de Fortune*?[150] A idea of the soft wind instruments of the time would arise first from combining the information found in both literary and iconographical documents, and then from an investigation of the social context (and hence, the hypothetical repertory) of each instrument.

Some fourteenth-century poems include long lists of instruments. Guillaume de Machaut, for example, enumerates those he purports to have heard not only at the banquet in *Remède de Fortune*, but also at a banquet in his *La Prise d'Alexandrie*. Machaut tells us these were the instruments played by the minstrels who entertained the guests after dinner, but he may simply reflect the late medieval penchant to be encyclopedic, and name all the instruments known to him. At any rate, it is difficult to imagine courtly minstrels playing some of the things Machaut gives them, such as willow flutes, Alsatian reed pipes, and straw pipes, and it is impossible to reconcile his diverse lists with other kinds of evidence. Machaut may well have combined courtly instruments with those more commonly associated with children, peasants, simple citizens, and other classes of society.

It is most likely that only three soft winds were in widespread use between about 1300 and 1520: the transverse flute, the recorder, and the somewhat mysterious douçaine or dolzaina. The history of the transverse flute during this period can only dimly be reconstructed, mostly from iconographical evidence. There are one or two pictures of the instrument from before the fourteenth century. Flutes do, however, appear in more than one illumination in the well-known Manesse manuscript of Minnesang, in a courtly context, and so we must accept the possibility that they were used in the performance of courtly music in thirteenth- and fourteenth-century Germany.[151] Pictures of flutes also can be seen in late fourteenth- and early fifteenth-century manuscripts prepared in northern Europe and in England. It may be that

---

[150] Concerning lists of instruments in Machaut's works, see J. Godwin, ' "Mains divers acors": Some Instrument Collections of the Ars Nova Period', *EM* 5 (1977), 148–59.

[151] The illumination is available in Brown, 'Instruments', 30.

the artistic tradition travelled down the Rhine and into England during that period, but it is also possible that the instrument itself followed the same path. There seems to be some historical justification, in short, for calling the transverse flute German. Pictures of flutes in chamber contexts are rare in the fifteenth century. Not until the sixteenth century does the instrument seem to come into its own. It is described as a standard part of the instrumentarium both by Virdung and by Agricola, and Attaingnant in Paris published chansons especially apt for the instrument.[152]

Recorders—or rather whistle flutes of various kinds that cannot really be described as recorders—can be seen in any number of works of art from the thirteenth and fourteenth centuries, but they are shown in the hands of shepherds or peasants. Works of art showing courtiers or courtly minstrels playing recorders do not begin to appear until the mid-fifteenth century. And it may be that the 'flutes' provided for the losers in a tournament organized by the hero in the fifteenth-century prose romance of *Cleriadus et Meliadice* were in actuality recorders, an early indication that such instruments were by then an option for those members of the upper classes who cultivated music as a social accomplishment.[153] Like the flute, the recorder became a regular part of the instrumentarium by the early sixteenth century.[154]

One curious exception must be made to the statement that recorders were not yet a part of the regular instrumentarium of the fourteenth century. A number of works of art show double whistle flutes, two separate and unconnected tubes, each with a recorder-like mouthpiece, being played simultaneously by the same person. In most of them, each tube has a closed end, and only enough finger holes for a single hand. These double pipes, mentioned by Tinctoris in 1482–3 as old-fashioned and no longer very useful, appear to have been exclusively the province of minstrels. Although it seems curious that such a cumbersome and musically inefficient whistle flute should have existed before the altogether simpler and more versatile recorder, that is precisely the conclusion suggested by the available evidence.[155]

The nature of the douçaine, mentioned by Machaut and others in the fourteenth century, is not yet entirely clear. It was probably a soft double-reed instrument—a kind of 'still shawm' as it was

---

[152] See Jane Bowers, '*Fla[ü]ste Traverseinne* and *Flute d'Allemagne*': The Flute in France from the Late Middle Ages up through 1702', *Recherches sur la musique française classique*, 19 (1979), 7–49.

[153] Page, 'The Performance', 441–50.

[154] A detailed survey of the role of the recorder before 1500 has not yet been written. For an overview of the bibliography see Brown, 'Instruments', 36 and 183–4.

[155] On Tinctoris and the double pipe, see Baines, 'Fifteenth-Century Instruments', 21.

later called in England—that may well have taken part in the performance of upper-class music. One task of scholarship is to collect all
fourteenth- and fifteenth-century references to the instrument, and to
attempt to identify it in works of art at the time. Only then will we
begin to have a more concrete idea of the nature of the still mysterious douçaine.[156]

ENSEMBLES OF INSTRUMENTS AND OF VOICES AND INSTRUMENTS

Even from this brief survey of the instruments in common use in the
fourteenth and fifteenth centuries, we can see how much work remains
to be done—especially in relating instruments to the people who
played them and thence to the music they probably played—before we
can begin to understand the role of instruments in the musical life of
the late Middle Ages and the Renaissance. Nevertheless some tentative hypotheses can be advanced. For the entire period from *c.*1300 to
1520 we should probably attempt to divide instruments into roughly
three groups: those played by the upper classes (which they may have
shared with courtly minstrels), those associated exclusively with minstrels, and those associated primarily with members of the lower
classes, peasants and shepherds.

In the fourteenth century, aristocrats, courtiers, and courtly minstrels who specialized in soft instruments seem mainly to have played
stringed instruments. The poet and moralist Francesco da Barberino
(1264–1348), for example, who writes about the behaviour proper to
various classes of women, approves of the idea that genteel women
should learn to play harp, lute, or fiddle, instruments that do, in fact,
seem to have been those most closely associated with the performance
of upper-class music.[157] When the hero of the romance of Gerard de
Nevers wishes to disguise himself as a minstrel, he requests the help
of a professional, who offers him a choice of the instruments he
himself plays: harp, fiddle, lute, and psaltery, presumably a list of
instruments typical of those played by courtly minstrels.[158] We may

---

[156] For current notions as to the meaning of the term douçaine see Brown, 'Instruments', 36
and 184.

[157] Howard M. Brown, 'The Trecento Fiddle and its Bridges', *EM* 17 (1989), 308–29; concerning Francesco and contemporary ideas on the education of women, see John Larner, *Culture
and Society in Italy, 1290–1420* (New York, 1971), 191–2.

[158] Gerard de Nevers, *Prose Version of the Roman de la Violette*, ed. Lawrence F. H.
Lowe (Princeton and Paris, 1928), 31–2. See also Howard M. Brown, 'Songs after
Supper: How the Aristocracy Entertained Themselves in the Fifteenth Century', in
Monika Fink, Rainer Gstrein, and Günter Mössmer (eds.), *Musica Privata: Die Rolle der
Musik im privaten Leben. Festschrift zum 65. Geburtstag von Walter Salmen* (Innsbruck, 1991),
37–52 at 41–3.

then conclude that professional musicians shared some instruments (and repertories) also cultivated by the upper classes, but that they also played music on instruments inappropriate to the upper classes, most obviously in the case of players of trumpets, drums, shawms, bagpipes, slide trumpets, and trombones, but also including stringed instruments such as the gittern and the rebec, and wind instruments like the double pipe. It may also be true that the few soft winds in common use in the fourteenth century—and especially the transverse flute and the douçaine—were the province of courtly minstrels. We can perhaps adopt that scheme as a paradigm, too, for the fifteenth century. Around 1400, the fiddle, the gittern, and the rebec appear to have been in use for at least a century, whereas others, notably the lute, may have been introduced into Western Europe very recently. The major innovations in the practice of instrumental music in the fourteenth century include the installation of large organs into various churches, and the invention of stringed keyboards.

The fifteenth century witnessed yet other innovations in instrumental practice. The shawm band became a fixed and more or less stable ensemble, for example, after musicians had rejected the bagpipe as a viable third instrument, found the newly invented slide trumpet to be inefficient, and eventually settled on the newly invented trombone.[159] The harpsichord and clavichord came more and more to be a regular part of the musical life of the times, and so did the recorder, whereas a number of instruments—the rebec, the psaltery, the double pipe, the hurdy gurdy, and so on—either gradually disappeared, came to be more and more associated with the music of the lowest classes, or were transformed into new instruments, like the change from psaltery to dulcimer, and the development of the lira da braccio from the fiddle.

Towards the end of the fifteenth century and the beginning of the sixteenth, radical changes took place in the standard instrumentarium and in the way instruments were used. A number of new wind instruments, notably the crumhorn and the cornetto, expanded instrumental timbres. The viola da gamba family and soon thereafter the violin family transformed the sound of string music. And instruments began regularly to be built in families, normally of three sizes.[160] But these and other changes belong more properly to the history of sixteenth-century music, outside the concerns of the present chapter.

Ensemble practices were, it appears, remarkably consistent throughout Europe. They were not always exactly the same in all places, but

[159] See Polk, *German Instrumental Music*, 50–68.
[160] On the development of instrumental consorts see Stradner, 'Zur Ausbildung', 177–82.

archetypes established in leading centres would soon be imitated in more outlying areas. We have already seen that some ensembles were more or less fixed during the fourteenth and fifteenth centuries. Trumpets alone or trumpets and drums, for example, constituted an ensemble appropriate for ceremonial occasions and for military signalling. Patterns of support followed a strikingly similar pattern everywhere as the instrument retained an aura of privilege and of very high station. As we have seen, two or three trumpets satisfied the ceremonial needs of most high authorities in the early fifteenth century, while by about 1450 at least six trumpets were felt to be the minimum for an adequate ensemble.[161] By 1500 most of the highest nobility (the emperor Maximilian, the king of France, and the duke of Milan, for example) boasted ten or even more, which by then were routinely coupled with kettle drums.

Analogous consistency characterized the patterns of support of the wind bands. In the fourteenth century, a loud wind band consisted of shawms alone or shawms with bagpipe. In this case, the paradigms were similar in both courts and cities. Courts in Spain, France, the Low Countries, Italy, and Germany, for example, normally supported groups of three players of similar design, either three shawms (i.e. two shawms and a bombard) or two shawms (shawm and bombard) and a bagpipe. Many cities also supported three players (with the same configurations), but many also made do with a duo of shawm and bombard. This was true, for example, of cities in Italy, southern Germany, and the Low Countries.[162]

Between about 1400 and 1430 a new combination evolved, which was based on a trio of shawm, bombard, and slide trumpet. Some of the wealthier courts could supplement the fundamental wind trio with an additional shawmist or two, probably to provide relief for the players of the very tiring soprano part (as was the case at the court of Burgundy). Most courts and cities, however, supported only a three-part ensemble, again with remarkable consistency in various corners of the Continent. In the second half of the century one difference

---

[161] More than two or three trumpets of any particular prince were seldom recorded at any one performance, although the princes may well have supported a larger band. Both Florence and Bologna supported ensembles of six players in about 1400, which suggests that if they were imitating the higher nobility (which was apparently the case) then those bands were also as large. Cities, it should be added, seldom attempted to match the nobility, but a few of the largest harboured such ambitions; Venice and Ghent (in addition to Florence and Bologna) are examples of large, wealthy centres which could command the resources necessary to field trumpet ensembles. For further on the trumpet bands, see Polk, *German Instrumental Music*, 46–8.

[162] For comparative tables of ensembles of courts and cities in the 15th c. see Polk, 'Patronage', 163–5.

between court and city ensembles became increasingly clear, which was
that the wealthiest courts and cities were expanding the number of
players available to five and six (as, for example, at the Burgundian
and the Habsburg courts, in Ghent, Bruges, and Antwerp, and in such
Italian centres as Venice and Ferrara). The city pattern was similar in
Ghent and Bruges, in Nuremberg and Augsburg, and in Florence and
Siena.[163]

It is only partially correct to say that ensembles of soft instruments
were much less fixed during most of the period between about 1300
and about 1520. It is true that chamber musicians appear to have been
hired on an ad hoc basis, not for their fixed functions within a group,
but for their personal virtuosity. Thus Conrad Paumann seems to have
been engaged in Bavaria without any necessarily precise role within
the ensembles of the court, and this also appears to have been the case
when Pietrobono joined the musical forces of the court in Ferrara (in
1446, whereas his tenorista was not added until later: see below). It is
also true that in the years just after 1400 the emphasis seems to have
been on hiring players of general competence. Archival documents
reveal that the pair of Burgundian *bas* minstrels (Cordoval and
Fernandez), as well as those in Germany and Italy, seem to have
shifted easily from fiddle to lute, to gittern, to portative and even harp
as the particular performance conditions required.[164] Iconographical
sources from this time also support the notion of a flexible approach
to instrumental combinations. That is, when soft minstrels would
perform a two- or three-part piece they had relative freedom to blend,
for example, lutes, bowed stringed instruments, harps, keyboard
instruments, or recorders to meet the demands of the moment (the
shawm ensemble, in contrast, was more fixed). It may be added that
these sources also suggest that these flexible consorts were capable of
accompanying singers in the performance of chansons and other
secular music (combinations of voices with loud instruments were
quite rare, of course).[165] On the other hand, certain standard ensembles of soft instruments do recur in the records of the fourteenth and
fifteenth centuries. In the earlier part of the period, for example, duos
playing gittern and lute or gittern and fiddle can be seen in many works
of art, and they may well be the sorts of ensembles described in

---

[163] For documentation on these developments see Polk, ibid. For a discussion of the situation
in Italy see Prizer, 'Bernardino Piffaro'; for the general scene in the north see Polk, *German
Instrumental Music*, 50–75.

[164] See Polk, *Instrumental Music*, 13–15.

[165] On voices performing with instruments see Brown, 'Instruments and Voices' (which
includes a discussion of iconographical evidence). On the flexibility of soft minstrels see Polk,
German Instrumental Music, 13–15.

various literary sources as the soloist and his tenorista. The combination of gittern and lute cannot accurately be described as an ensemble of like instruments, for each has an independent history and character. Moreover, later in the fifteenth century patronage patterns relating to soft music seem everywhere to have become more specific. Lute duos, for example, were established throughout Germany by 1450 (these were termed lute duos in the account books, but they may well have been made up of either two lutes or a gittern and lute), and the analogous situation may be seen in Ferrara by at least 1449 when a certain Zanetto tenorista was added to the rolls of musicians to provide accompaniment for Pietrobono.[166] A distinctive pairing of players of viola (probably fiddles), was added in Ferrara in 1467.[167] Contrary to the situation with the pairs of players hired by courtly patrons earlier in the century, these Ferrarese players were specialists more exclusively on bowed stringed instruments. The model of specialized string players, too, was imitated elsewhere—a quartet of viols, for example, was retained by Maximilian I shortly after the turn of the century.

Specialization also extended to keyboard practices. Paumann was the dominant organist of his time, but frequently performed on other instruments. Paul Hofhaimer, the leading player in the next generation, was apparently exclusively an organist. The groups of stringed instruments reveal yet another apparently uniform line of development, in that consorts of recorders were also documented frequently in the decade or two just before 1500.[168] These cases demonstrate that unmixed consorts of instruments were commonly heard in the fifteenth century, even before there is evidence that such consorts were built regularly by instrument-makers. Pay records of such consorts begin to show an increase in the number of four-part ensembles by 1500, and again in such diverse locations as Mechelen, Augsburg, and Verona. Finally, patronage of soft ensembles, especially in the fifteenth century, seems everywhere to have been the domain of the courts. Very few European cities, at any rate, attempted to compete with the courts in this particular arena. In sum, what strikes us is the geographic spread of similar ideas. Modern criticism has emphasized the differences between north and south in such matters as painting, intellec-

---

[166] Lockwood, *Music in Renaissance Ferrara*, 100. Concerning the pairings of the 14th c., see Brown, 'St. Augustine'; on the lute duos in the 15th c., see Ivanoff, 'Das Lautenduo', and Polk, *German Instrumental Music*, 25–7.

[167] Lockwood, *Music in Renaissance Ferrara*, 97, 318 gives the date as 1466.

[168] See Keith Polk, 'Ensemble Instrumental Music in Flanders—1450–1550', *Journal of Band Research*, 11 (1975), 12–27 at 18; Stradner, 'Zur Ausbildung'; and Polk, *German Instrumental Music*, 40–1.

tual styles, and the functioning of patronage itself.[169] What is remarkable in music is consistency of patronage patterns not only north and south, but east and west of the Rhine as well.

In considering instruments, instrumentalists, and their repertories between 1300 and 1520, we should above all strive to avoid oversimplifications. Even to identify an instrument as belonging to the province of minstrels does not necessarily exclude it from the sphere of written compositions, for there were many kinds of minstrels, and a wide variety of practices over more than two hundred years. Nor should we exaggerate the gulf between the musician educated at a cathedral school and the minstrel trained by a master player. There were many points of contact between them, and between some professional musicians and their noble patrons, who cultivated music as a social accomplishment. Even though no large body of independent instrumental music survives from before the later fifteenth century, there is every reason to believe that a colourful palette of instrumental sound enlivened musical life from 1300 onwards.

ADDENDUM

Several relevant books and articles have been published since this chapter was written: Andrew Ashbee, *Records of English Court Music*, vii (1485–1558) (Aldershot, 1993); Ross W. Duffin, 'Shawm and Curtal', in Jeffrey T. Kite-Powell (ed.), *A Performer's Guide to Renaissance Music* (New York, 1994), 69–75; Herbert Myers, 'Recorders', ibid., 41–55; Fiona Kisby, 'Royal Minstrels in the City and Suburbs of Early Tudor London: Professional Activities and Private Interests', *Early Music*, 25 (1997), 199–219; Timothy McGee, 'National Style in 15th-Century Embellishment', *Yearbook of the Alamire Foundation*, 2, ed. Eugeen Schreurs and Henri Vanhulst (Leuven–Peer, 1997), 131–46; Gretchen Peters, 'Urban Minstrels in Late Medieval Southern France: Opportunities, Status and Professional Relationships', *Early Music History*, 19 (2000), 201–35; Martin Kirnbauer, 'Der Kasseler Lautenkragen (D-Km 2: Ms. Math. 31), der Regensburger Traktat (D-Rp Ms. Th. 98 40) und das "Königsteiner Liederbuch" (D-Bs Ms. germ. qu. 719): Die frühesten deutschen Quellen für Lautentabulatur', in Martin Kirnbauer and Crawford Young (eds.), *Sources of Early Lute Music/Quellen früher Lautenmusik* (Winterthur, 2001).

---

[169] See e.g. Weissman, 'Taking Patronage Seriously' (above, n. 30).

IV

DANCES AND DANCE MUSIC, *c*.1300–1530

By WALTER SALMEN

INTRODUCTION

THOSE who lived in the period between the fourteenth and the early sixteenth century were caught up in conflicting tendencies of judging the world and human life, albeit with chronological and regional variations. These currents gravitated between the admonition 'memento mori', denying all things corporeal, and the life-affirming invitation 'iuvat vivere'. Dance, whether conceptualized transcendentally as the Dance of Death, or taking the practical form of performance, was ubiquitous, a manifestation of life; apart from its broad social significance, it possessed a heavenly, cosmic, indeed universal meaning (see Pl. III). Dancing is thus an essential signifier of the world-view of late medieval and Renaissance society. Despite the disruptive effect of the Reformation it retained a central function both in public and in private life. Dancing was held to be both a right, differentiated according to social rank, and a duty; consequently both admonitions and prohibitions with regard to dancing were issued. Scarcely any ceremony, tournament, parliament, or wedding took place, whether among Christians or non-Christians, without the accompaniment of dancing.[1] Thus a chronicler in Nuremberg in 1433 could record on the occasion of the coronation of the emperor Sigismund: 'all the world dances: squires, youths, maidens, and respectable women, and young fellows without number'.[2] His observation that 'all the world' participated in this joyous dance is a reflection of historical reality: it was in fact the case that at that time everyone danced, from the emperor downwards: princes, bishops, burghers, and peasants, monks, beggars, and lepers, each according to his social degree.

[1] A. Mailly, *Deutsche Rechtsaltertümer in Sage und Brauchtum* (Vienna, 1933), 225 ff.
[2] 'alle welt tantzet: knaben, knecht, mait, und erber frawen und gesellen an zal'. Christoph Petzsch, 'Nachrichten aus deutschen Städtechroniken des 14. bis ins 16. Jahrhundert', *Musikethnologische Sammelbände*, 51 (1981), 69.

To cite one example: in 1490, in the chronicle of the south German town of Nördlingen, a social distinction was drawn between the courtly dance ('hove dantz'), the townsmen's dance ('bürger dantz'), and the peasants' dance ('buren dantz'). Elsewhere distinctions were drawn between round dances ('rayen') and other 'täntzen', 'dansses, notes et baleries'. Clear distinctions were drawn between high and low, pacing and leaping, narrow and widely paced movements. On the other hand, there were broad generic distinctions between children's dances, healing dances, armed dances, church dances, and mourning dances. Life's sorrows and joys met again and again in the dance, in a context rich in emotional, social, and religious tensions.

Although dancing was an integral part of most areas of life, there was no lack of impediments, prohibitions, and condemnations. St Augustine's dictum 'chorea est circulus, cuius centrum est diabolus' (the dance is a circle, in the midst of which is the Devil) lived on, quoted literally or in modified form (for example in the 'Sermones vulgares' of Jacques de Vitry). Both the established Church and various sects objected to dancing, regarding it as the Devil's own festivity. Dancers were indicted as servants of the Devil ('des tufels diener'); dancing was condemned as a mortal sin in penitentials and sermons.[3] The Hussites opposed dance with a stringency equal to that of the many synods, councils, and capitularies which campaigned against these 'vanities'.[4] Above all these opposed chain dances which took place in an anti-clockwise direction as 'a procession of the Devil' ('processio dijabuli', Georg v. Giengen, before 1465). The practical effect of these theologically motivated condemnations was that every priest was given the authority to forbid dancing (every 'luttpriester hat das Recht, das er mag verbieten zu tanczen', St. Peter im Schwarzwald, second half of the fifteenth century), and that both civic and manorial authorities had at their disposal countless restrictive measures. It was only in the context of mysticism that the round dance, performed clockwise as a spiritual act, in a sublime state of ecstasy, came to be viewed positively, in that it was identified with the concept of angels dancing in heaven, with Christ as their leader in the round dance (Pl. V).

SECULAR DANCE LOCATIONS

Dances, including round dances ('reigen'), were performed both in the

---

[3] Vienna, Österreichische Nationalbibliothek, MS Cyp. 3009, 'Was schaden tantzen bringt' ('What harm dancing causes').

[4] J. Ilg, 'Gesänge und mimische Darstellungen nach den deutschen Konzilien des Mittelalters', 9. *Jahresbericht des bischöflichen Gymnasiums 'Kollegium Petrinum' in Urfahr* (1906).

open air and within four walls, in festive company. The choice of locale
was not random, but depended upon the meaning and purpose of the
occasion, the social rank of those involved, the number of participants, and the choreography.

In the open air dancing took place on mounds ('Tanzbüheln'), in
meadows ('plan des danses', 'tanzplan' in Frankfurt am Main; from
1441 on the banks of the Pegnitz in Nuremberg), under lime trees (or
in France 'soz l'ormel'), in the streets ('uff offener gassen', Basle 1492),
in cemeteries and over the graves of one's ancestors,[5] sometimes even
on board dance ships. The places where dances were held normally
served for the holding of courts of parish assemblies. Thus a wedding
dance held under the village lime tree was an obligatory ceremony,
possessing legally binding significance (for example in Krems, Lower
Austria, in 1403).

In villages, especially in winter, granges and barns came into play,
as as did gaming rooms, taverns, or bath houses. Sometimes ad hoc
dance bowers ('tanzlauben') were erected (Vienna, 1349); dance huts
were made out of twigs with floors consisting of wooden planks. Or
dances took place in houses of entertainment (also termed *ballatoria*
or *choraria*) made of wood, structures belonging to the local community which generally stood near the village church or near a lime tree.[6]
These were erected in square proportions on pillars, the floorboards
sometimes at chest height (e.g. those erected in the Ringplatz in Prague
in 1456).

In the fortresses and castles of the nobility *salons de danse* were constructed to meet the needs of courtly dances ('hofedaunce', 1390).
These rooms, also known as 'Rittersäle', were generally longer than
they were wide, measuring about 12×30 yards (e.g. in the Wartburg
near Eisenach, or in the Kaiserpfalz of Gelnhausen). From the fifteenth
century onwards court dancing achieved increasing prominence; as a
result in some princely residences ballrooms were specially designed (for
example, on the upper floor of the west wing of the castle in Vienna),
or dance houses ('dantze hus', Schloß Gottorf, 1430) might be built.

In the towns the citizens' needs for dancing on the occasion of weddings, royal visits, and Shrovetide festivities were met by spacious rooms
in warehouses and guild chambers, and also by the 'domus consulum',
which thus not infrequently came to be known interchangeably as

[5] See Walter Salmen, 'Zur Praxis von Totentänzen im Mittelalter', in Franz Link (ed.), *Tanz
und Tod in Kunst und Literatur* (Berlin, 1993), 119–26.
[6] Karl S. Bader, *Studien zur Rechtsgeschichte des mittelalterlichen Dorfes*, ii (Cologne
and Graz, 1962), 402 ff.; *Schweizer Archiv für Volkskunde*, 17 (1913), 117–18; K. H. Burmeister,
'Die alten Gerichtstätten in Vorarlberg', *Österreichische Zeitschrift für Volkskunde*, 30 (1976),
268–74.

either council or dance house, or house of entertainment ('spelhus', Wernigerode, 1427; Darmstadt, and elsewhere). These were multi-purpose buildings, with halls on several floors, whose upper storeys provided long rooms for festivities, with anterooms for catering purposes. If the landed gentry wanted to celebrate on a larger scale, organizing dances befitting their aristocratic pretensions but for which their own rooms were inadequate, then they would hire these council chambers to 'hold court' ('hof halten', Delitzsch, 1432). In order to accommodate changing practices in the accompaniment of dancing, from the fifteenth century onwards balconies ('scaffolds', 'hourdys', 'palco'), sometimes called pipers' seats ('Pfeiferstühle'), were specially built, for example in Nuremberg, Leipzig, Amberg, and elsewhere.[7] The Hanssaal in the Cologne city hall of c.1360 measured 28.7×7.25 m., with a height of 9.8 m.;[8] in Wasserburg am Inn the town hall of 1459 measured $27 \times 13 \times 7.5$ m., that in Leipzig 43.5×12 m. These were, therefore, rooms with dimensions of $3:1$, which was of some import for the choreography of estampies or basses danses, which might require up to thirty-two consecutive steps in a single direction.

Where finances permitted or there was a particular need, dance houses of solid stone were built to stand next to the council chambers. This practice began in the twelfth century among the Jewish communities ('bet hatunnot') living in the ghettos, for example in Cologne, Trier, Erfurt, Eger, Speyer, and Worms. Before the pogrom of 1349 the Jews' dance halls ('der Juden Tantzhus') also existed in Ulm, Frankfurt am Main, and Augsburg.[9]

Dance houses owned by the townsmen of the local Christian community ('domus tripudialis') can only be documented from the second half of the fourteenth century. In Augsburg such a stately building to accommodate 'conventicula' stood until 1632, its dances frequently visited by emperors, kings, noble families, and also by the poet-singer Oswald von Wolkenstein—'I came to the dance hall there' ('do kom ich auf das tanzhauss dar').[10] These houses, furnished for burghers' dances ('bürger tantz'), richly ornamented with depictions of dancers and other decoration, were to be found, for example, in Cologne

---

[7] Walter Salmen, *Tanz im 17. und 18. Jahrhundert* (Musikgeschichte in Bildern, 4/iv; Leipzig, 1988), 144–51, and id., 'L'Iconographie des lieux de la danse et de son accompagnement musical avant 1600', *Imago musicae*, 4 (1987), 99–109.

[8] F. Mühlberg, 'Der Hansasaal des Kölner Rathauses', *Wallraf-Richartz-Jahrbuch*, 36 (1974), 65–80.

[9] Walter Salmen, 'Jüdische Hochzeits- und Tanzhäuser im Mittelalter', *Aschkenas*, 5 (1995), 107–20.

[10] In 'Wol auf, gesellen', l. 14 in MS A, fo. 33ʳ. *Oswald von Wolkenstein, Handschrift A: Vollständige Faksimile-Ausgabe des Codex Vindobonensis 2777 der Österreichischen Nationalbibliothek* (Codices Selecti, 59; Graz, 1977).

(Gürzenich, Pl. IV),[11] Arnhem, Heidelberg, Nördlingen, Görlitz, Innsbruck, and elsewhere. The interiors of the dance halls were barrel vaults, for the most part without any supporting pillars. Benches for the spectators were placed along the walls, with the seats of honour at the front, so that the choreography of the dances could be specifically oriented in that direction. The dance hall of the Münsterplatz in Basle accommodated, among other occasions, a conclave for a papal election in 1439.

DANCES IN AND AROUND CHURCHES

Dance rites were of great and varied significance in many churches of eastern and western Europe.[12] The physical surrender to a state of transcendence, personified by the dancing body, led to a wide range of expression in gestures, both where solo and round dance were concerned. Ritual dances took place in the cathedral of Dubrovnik prior to 1425, as they did in English cathedrals, in Notre-Dame in Paris, in Saint-Leonard in Limoges. In the cathedral of Seville, in an unbroken tradition instituted in 1439 by Pope Eugene IV, still today 'los seises' (the choirboys), clad in luxurious processional garments, sing and dance before the high altar accompanied by castanets, constituting an integral part of the liturgy.[13] The late medieval Church remained therefore in many places an 'ecclesia saltans', following in the footsteps of the celestial angels performing their symbolic round dance.[14]

Dance customs in and around churches ranged from the devout bending of the knee, devotional gestures of prayer, processional steps, and the circumambulation of places of worship, to the dancing accompaniment of sequences and tropes, and round dances about the Christmas crib or around the altar. People danced in the proximity of the altar, in the atrium (in Osnabrück, for example), and in cemeteries (e.g. in Narbonne). The preferred occasions were the high feasts of Christmas, Easter, Whitsun, and Ascension, the feasts of patron saints, and the first Masses of newly ordained priests. During Advent and Lent no dances were permitted ('nulla stampita ivi fo intesa'; Simone Prudenzani, c.1420). It was by no means the case in every dio-

---

[11] M.-L. Schwering, *Der Kölner Gürzenich* (Mönchengladbach, 1964); Walter Salmen, 'Das Freiburger "tantzhus oder kornhus"', in Hans Schadek (ed.), *Der Kaiser in seiner Stadt: Maximilian I und der Reichstag zu Freiburg 1498* (Freiburg, 1998), 186–97.

[12] Yvonne Rokseth, 'Danses cléricales du XIIIᵉ siècle', *Mélanges III, Études historiques 1945* (Publications de la Faculté des Lettres de l'Université de Strasbourg, 106; Paris, 1947), 93–126; Jacques Chailley, 'Un document nouveau sur la danse ecclésiastique', *Acta musicologica*, 21 (1949), 18–24.

[13] Renato Torniai, *La danza sacra* (Rome, 1950), 276–80.

[14] Reinhold Hammerstein, *Die Musik der Engel* (Berne, 1952), ills. 81 and 85.

cese that dance rites in worship—whether performed by clerics or laymen—were appreciated: councils and synods repeatedly sought to prohibit all *tripudio* and *cantilenae et runtelli* (London, 1308; Prague, 1412; Basle, 1435; Dubrovnik, 1425).

Ritual dancing was above all an expression of joy and devotion. It therefore accompanied sequences such as *Rex coeli, Victimae paschali, Veni sancte spiritus*, or *Alme virginis*; the latter was provided in the office of the Spanish Church with the rubric 'ad accedentes' (= with movements). Of responsories it is recorded that 'ad processionem in navi ecclesiae precentor debet ballare', that is, that the precentor also had to act as the leader in the dance.[15] Kyrie tropes, sung as the processions entered the place of worship, also indicated dancing music 'cum tripudio' ('Te decet laus cum tripudio'); secular dance songs shared with these texts exclamations such as 'eia et eia'. In Lisbon in 1500 the royal court danced on Christmas morning to the 'Gloria in excelsis Deo' in the church. A processional of the fourteenth century from Notre-Dame in Paris shows that on Christmas Eve after the consecration of the holy water a procession took place, and then the antiphon *Alma redemptoris* was performed 'per choream', as a round dance. This antiphon was also sung, accompanied by a round dance, during the Whitsun procession, at the Purification of the Virgin, at the Nativity of the Virgin, and at the procession in honour of St Denis. The way in which this was probably performed ('ad gaudium magnum') is indicated by Pl. V, from the Notre-Dame MS F. This miniature introduces paradigmatically the last section of this important source, which contains sixty *rondelli* for dancing; it shows four clerics in a row, with arms linked for dancing, but their hands free.

Christmas and Corpus Christi were predominant among the many feasts which were celebrated 'cum karola' in monasteries and cathedrals by the singing of antiphons, tropes, conducti, and rondeaux. Christmas was accorded special importance in Central Europe because the popular custom of the cradling of the Christ Child was carried out during Vespers. Nuns processed around the altar, or a crib that had been furnished for the purpose, to the accompaniment of *Resonet in laudibus* or the hymn *Magnum nomen Domini*, as for example in the nunnery of Preetz in Schleswig-Holstein, or in Franconia: 'iuvenes cum puellis per circuitum tripudiantes choreas agant'.[16] In Christmas plays of the fifteenth century one frequently finds

---

[15] Jacques Handschin, 'Zur Geschichte von Notre Dame', *Acta musicologica*, 4 (1932), 49–55 at 51; a Stephanus trope records: 'Invice nos Stephani Dominum pulsando canemus: eia'.

[16] Johannes Boëmus, *Omnium gentium mores, leges et ritus* (Freiburg i. Br., 1540).

directions such as 'Joseph et servus corisant' or 'we shall joyfully dance around' ('woln in freuden ringen'), or 'leap around the cradle' ('umb die wiege springen'), with *In dulci iubilo*, *Verbum caro factum est*, or *Puer nobis nascitur* as sung accompaniment.[17]

The feast to celebrate Corpus Christi, inaugurated in 1264, was elaborately enhanced by religious dances, by 'praying with the feet' (Cervantes), particularly in Spain, and from 1295 in Portugal. As a token of Christian respect, or induced by sheer pleasure at the spectacle, Christians supposedly danced alongside 'los iudíos e moros' on this occasion (Ávila, 1481).[18] In 1313, in Tauste near Saragossa, Rabbi Hacen Ben Salomo is said to have given instruction in ritual dancing, even within the walls of the Church of St Bartholomew. To judge from the words of the Spanish poet Diego Sánchez de Badajoz (first half of the sixteenth century):

> Venite todas naciones
> con bailes y con canciones . . .
>
> Come all nations
> with dances and with songs

such dances were in the spirit of an 'ecclesia saltans', which had no objection in principle to the honouring of God by means of rhythmic movement. After all, did not David dance before the Ark?

DANCING AS A THERAPEUTIC AID

Dancing as a tribute or religious veneration, or as a sign of intercession, directed at saints such as St Vitus (15 June), John the Baptist (24 June), or St Willibrord (apostle of Frisia, 7 November), had its complement in dancing for therapeutic effect. The dance of healing calmed, consoled, or might stimulate a state of ecstasy; in these divergent ways it offered a stimulus towards the alleviation of psychosomatic illnesses. Throughout the late Middle Ages dancing triggered mass hysteria (tarantism, flagellantism, St Vitus' dance); psychopathic individuals might perform hysterical circles, capable of entering into a state of trance through their stamping and cavorting. Dancing psychoses frequently spread like epidemics—often linked with religiously

---

[17] L. Berthold, 'Die Kindelwiegenspiele', *Beiträge zur Geschichte der deutschen Sprache und Literatur*, 56 (1932), 208 ff.; L. Prautzsch, 'Das Christkindlewiegen in Hessen', in *Beiträge zur Geschichte der evangelischen Kirchenmusik und Hymnologie in Kurhessen und Waldeck* (Kassel, 1969), 131 ff.

[18] Jaime Moll, 'Música y representaciones en las constituciones sinodales de los Reinos de Castilla del siglo XVI', *Anuario musical*, 30 (1975), 209–43 at 227. See also Detlef Altenburg, 'Die Musik in der Fronleichnamsprozession des 14. und 15. Jahrhunderts', *Musica disciplina*, 38 (1984), 5–24 at 23.

motivated illusions. In a state of intoxication deep layers of the sub-conscious emerged ('half-naked, the women garlanded their heads', *seminude sertis capita cingebant*, in the Rhineland, 1374). In many places, as far afield as southern Italy or Scandinavia, brotherhoods or sects were formed in order to bring about a state of ecstasy in the *chorea maior* (St Vitus' dance), or the healing of epilepsy, uraemia, hysteria, etc. Ecstatic dances accompanied by rattling, the clicking of shells suspended from the body, clapping, stamping, and calling were even on occasion decreed by the authorities and subsidized; for example, in 1518 in Strasburg there were 'people specially commissioned, for wages, who had always to dance [with the sick], with drums and pipes' ('bestellte eigene leutt umb lohn, die mußten stets mit ihnen [den Kranken] tanzen mit trummen und pfeiffen'). In Zurich in 1452, and later in Basle, musicians and drum-beaters ('trommenslaher') employed by the municipality were paid to accompany St Vitus' dances for the specific purpose of the temporary alleviation of hysterical states.[19] People danced for healing purposes both around objects regarded as sacred (altars, trees), and 'over the bridge' ('over een brugge', Avignon, Utrecht, and elsewhere), symbolizing transition from a state of fear and weakness to the salutary bank of healing and salvation.[20]

DANCING IN SECULAR AND RELIGIOUS DRAMAS

Late medieval society derived pleasure or edification from a wide range of plays, performed both in town and country; these took the form of a *processio* (= *scenae mutae*), *ludus*, *repraesentatio*, *historia*, *miraculum*, or *misterium*. In all these mummeries or *entremets* of sung dramas, dances on the part of individuals or groups constituted an integral part of the action, or made for diverting entertainment (for example, the 'disguysings' at the Tudor court around 1500). From the *Jeu de Robin et Marion* of Adam de la Halle onwards, in which 'Robin danse en branlant le chef' or 'Robin dansant fait le touret', to French plays of the early sixteenth century in which basses danses are specified, there runs a rich vein of dancing tradition, oriented towards the spectator and intended to encourage his participation in the dance.[21] Masquerades in England

---

[19] Fritz Ernst, 'Die Spielleute im Dienste der Stadt Basel im ausgehenden Mittelalter', *Basler Zeitschrift für Geschichte und Altertumskunde*, 44 (1945), 204; W. Salmen, *Musikleben im 16. Jahrhundert* (Musikgeschichte in Bildern, 3/ix; Leipzig, 1977; 2nd edn., Leipzig, 1983), fig. 103.

[20] A. Martin, 'Geschichte der Tanzkrankheit in Deutschland', *Zeitschrift für Volkskunde*, 24 (1914), 113 ff.; E. Louis Backman, *Den religiöse dansen inom Kristen Kyrka och folkmedicin* (Stockholm, 1945).

[21] Howard M. Brown, *Theatrical Chansons of the Fifteenth and Early Sixteenth Centuries* (Cambridge, Mass., 1963), 64 ff.

were accompanied 'with morishes' (1527); in miracle plays such as the *Mystère d'Adam* (fifteenth century), the Fall of Adam and Eve was accorded a visual accompaniment of a symbolic 'magnum tripudium'. In a *Mystère de la Passion* performed in Mons in 1501, Salome, the daughter of Herod, was instructed to dance a 'morisque' at the banquet to the sound of the tambourine.

The actors of the commedia dell'arte and earlier plays in Italy also danced, for example in the *Rappresentazione di Abramo e Isacco*, which was performed in 1449 in Florence,[22] and in diverse interludes (e.g. 'Ballo di satiri et baccanti') and other festivities. In Central Europe there were Christmas plays, in one of which it is recorded: 'and thus the servant and Joseph dance about the crib singing *In dulci iubilo*' ('et sic servus et Joseph corisant per cunabulum cantando: In dulci iubilo'), and Passion plays with the instruction 'in which we will dance and leap' ('darin woll wir tanczen und springen'), that is, in hell.[23] The appearance on stage of characters such as Mary Magdalene (Donaueschingen Passion play, *c.*1480), or heathens and Jews, of the Devil or of angels, lent themselves particularly to the inclusion of dances.[24] On occasion the rubric even reads: 'then the Saviour comes, dancing' ('deinde venit Salvator saltans'). In Latin-German scholastic dramas such as the *Spiel von fünfferley betrachtnussen* ('The Play of Five Kinds of Contemplation') by Johann Kolros of Basle (1532), a youth issues the command:

> Spilman, mach auff den schwarzen knaben
> So welle wir frölich vmbher traben ...

> Minstrel, play the Black Boy [the title of a dance],
> And we will merrily prance around ...

Shrovetide plays and Neidhart plays required particularly large numbers of dance scenes and were sometimes referred to as morris dances ('moriskentanz') in consequence.[25] These were held in high esteem because they presented the spectators with both 'chorea et ludus'. Frequently they called for 'fiddlers or pipers where danc-

---

[22] Wolfgang Osthoff, *Theatergesang und darstellende Musik in der italienischen Renaissance*, 2 vols. (Tutzing, 1969), i. 30–5.

[23] Joseph Eduard Wackernell, *Altdeutsche Passionsspiele aus Tirol* (Graz, 1897), 348.

[24] H. Colin Slim, 'Mary Magdalene, Musician and Dancer', *EM* 8 (1980), 460–73; Walter Salmen, 'Zur Choreographie von Solotänzen in mittelalterlichen Spielen', in Katrin Kröll und Hugo Steger (eds.), *Mein ganzer Körper ist Gesicht: Groteske Darstellungen in der europäischen Kunst und Literatur des Mittelalters* (Freiburg im Breisgau, 1994), 343–55.

[25] E. Simon, 'The Staging of Neidhart Plays, with Notes on Six Documented Performances', *Germanic Review*, 44 (1969), 16. D. Huschenbett, 'Die Frau mit dem Apfel und Frau Venus im Moriskentanz und Fastnachtspiel', in *Volkskultur und Geschichte: Festgabe für Josef Dünninger* (Berlin, 1970), 585.

ing is to take place' ('Geyger oder Pfeiffer an dem Ort da man
zů Tanntz machet, bestellt', Sterzing play script, after 1500). Round
dances (*rayen*) were performed, or 'a step after my old father's
fashion' ('tretten ainen tritt | nach meines alten vaters sytt',
Großes Neidhartspiel, l. 325; fifteenth century). Traditional peasants'
dances sometimes made way for the fashionable 'Portingal'
style, or:

> Ain hüpschen stoltzen trit
> Der ist nach newen hofsitt
> Si tritten hyn auff den zehen
> Dz sy nit gen auff die versen
> Jr sporen die klingen
> Jre lied dy sy singen
> Die machen manigs hertze fro
> Si tritten nider vnd tritten hoch
> Ich wais wol das kain ritter kan
> Den newen tritt den wir han
> Darumbe wisse man für war
> Wir wellen klaider vnd har
> Dar zu sprintzen und sprantzen
> Vnd wellen mit freüden tantzen.

. . . a proud, courtly step, | according to the new court custom. | They
prance in on their toes | —by no means upon their heels! | Their spurs
they jangled, | their songs they sang, | which make many a heart
rejoice. | They steppèd low and steppèd high. | I know full well
no knight can master | the new step that we have; | and so let it
be common knowledge: | our clothes and hair | we'll spruce and
preen, | and joyfully we'll dance.[26]

SOLO DANCES

Chrétien de Troyes writes: 'les baleresses baler et les tumeresses tumer'.
He is referring to female dancers, also called 'carolleresse' (Valenciennes, 1429), 'springerin', or 'jongleresse', who generally performed
solo. Their mode of performance can be traced back to classical times,
and to models from Christian tradition, such as Salome, the daughter
of Herod, who was represented as an acrobat, who 'turned somer-
saults' ('in sprungen überwarf', *Der Saelden Hort*, 1298, l. 2883). The
somersault, the acrobatic bending of the torso, handstands, even
doing the splits, all formed part of the favoured repertoire, along with

---

[26] *Großes Neidhartspiel*, ll. 1956–69 in *Neidhartspiele*, ed. John Margetts (Graz, 1982), 27
and 78.

dances with veils and the skilful juggling of goblets on the head.[27] Stylized arm and hand gestures, the rolling eye, long hair, and the fold of the clothes all characterized these performances, which had a rhythmic accompaniment of rattling rings, bells, chains, cymbals, handbells, or castanets (see Pls. VI and VII). Male solo dancers also employed swords, knives, or sticks in their dances. They showed a preference for dancing bare-headed, in simple belted tunics or short cloaks without any belts, smocks with long sleeves, or the garment of fools or jesters. On feasts they performed at the tables of those dining. Solo dances were also performed in religious dramas (by actors playing Salome, Miriam, or the Magdalen), or at fairs, by tightrope walkers. Given the obvious sensual appeal of such lascivious display of bodily charms, the authorities frequently sought to prevent 'women, above all, from leaping' ('den Weibspersonen füran das Springen', Bavarian prohibition of 1520), particularly when their charms were recompensed with disproportionately high wages, as for example those of a certain 'Margarita, anglesa, juglaresse' in the fourteenth century, or the dancer Graciosa de Valencia at the court of Navarre.

Among these dancers were some 'joglars', Poles, Hungarians, or gypsies, who took with them on their travels dancing bears or other trained animals, which they obliged to 'dance' at popular feasts, processions, or in the vicinity of castles and monasteries. The monastery accounts of Baumburg in Bavaria for 1504, for example, note that 'the Poles were here with a bear and danced' ('dy polackn sein hye gewesen mit ainem pern vnd [sind] gesprungen').[28]

From the fourteenth century onwards such companies consisting of actors and male dancers who made their way across the continent, from Portugal to eastern Europe, were sometimes known by the name of morris dancers. These were skilled performers who sought to capture the attention of audiences by hopping, leaping, or dragging their feet, with eccentric gestures and twists and vigorous motions of their arms and legs. Variously known as 'la murista' (Fribourg, 1443), 'maruska' in Poland, the 'morischkotanz' in Nuremberg in 1479, the 'mourisca' in Lisbon (see Pl. VIII), these dances constituted courtly entertainments, Shrovetide pantomimes, or wild, grotesque fairground displays. Some danced in an assumed frenzy of passion to woo Lady Venus, who proffered an apple or a ring as a prize for the best per-

---

[27] Gabriele Ch. Busch, *Ikonographische Studien zum Solotanz im Mittelalter* (Innsbruck, 1982), 44–50.

[28] See also R. Hiestand, 'König Balduin und sein Tanzbär', *Archiv für Kulturgeschichte*, 70 (1988), 343–5, and W. Salmen, 'Zur Geschichte der Bärentreiber und Tanzbären', *Studia instrumentorum musicae popularis*, 3 (Stockholm, 1974), 56, fig. 1.

formance; others showed their skill in fencing and leaping over swords, inspired by the ringing of bells, music-making jesters, drums, or pipes (see Pl. IX). There was no fixed sequence of steps.[29]

In his *Orchésographie* of 1588 Thoinot Arbeau describes the 'morisques' of his youth as a dance performed with blackened faces, in the 'mesure binaire' (duple time):

Originally they were executed by striking the feet together, but because the dancers found this too painful they tried striking the heels only while keeping the toes rigid. Others wished to dance them with *marque pieds* and *marque talons* intermixed. The practise of any of these three methods, especially the one involving tapping the feet, has been proven by experience to lead eventually to podagra and other gouty affections, wherefore this dance has fallen into disuse.[30]

ROUND DANCES

Reigen, round dances, are stylized sequences of movements, performed in groups of four or more people. These existed almost everywhere in Europe; they could be performed with steps, paces, hops, or leaps, among all age groups, and in all social classes. As late at the age of Maximilian I even kings and emperors took the lead in such round dances. The round dance thus retained its dominance among stylized dance movements, a tradition reaching back into classical times. It was only with social changes in the sixteenth century that these groupings gave way to the more individualized dances of couples. One authority, the clergyman Johann Adolf Köster (known as Neocorus), writing about the North Sea region of Dithmarschen, even gives us a precise date for this change: 1559. It was then that, at least in this region populated by peasants, dancing in couples, the 'Biparendantz', came into fashion, and what were known as 'langen Dentz' ('long dances' = round dances) were no longer the custom ('in Gebruke').

In medieval sources round dances are denoted by words such as *chorea, carolo, quirola, kirola, carola, chorella, corola, chacota, rey, querolle*, and *ronde*. In the linguistic usage of many peoples a clear distinction is drawn between the nouns 'round dance' and 'dance' ('reien und tanz', Styria, thirteenth century), 'carole and dance' (England, 1390), 'danse, carolle' (France, fourteenth century), or between the corresponding verbs: 'dance in the round' ('tanzen reien', Gottfried von Neifen, thirteenth century), 'round dancing or dancing' ('reien oder tanzen', Neidhart von Reuental), 'sprynge and carole' (England,

---

[29] Salmen, *Musikleben im 16. Jahrhundert*, 56, fig. 1.
[30] *Orchesography*, trans. Mary Stewart Evans (New York, 1948), 177.

c.1426), 'danse et querole' (France, beginning of the thirteenth century). A threefold subdivision of movements is also frequently indicated, such as 'run, dance, and leap' ('treten, tanzen, springen', Monk
of Salzburg), 'dancent et balent et querolent' (France, thirteenth
century), 'daunces, sprynges, reyes' (England, 1380). It was therefore
the custom in the late Middle Ages to distinguish terminologically
between solo jigs, dancing in pairs and threes, and the various kinds
of round dance. From the fifteenth century onwards these divisions
are no longer clearly marked linguistically, and it is commonly the case
that hybrid terms are employed such as 'Ringentanz' (Switzerland,
1548), 'reigen eines tanzes' ('dancing in the round'), or 'tanzreihen'
(1586).

Round dances could be executed in three different ways: (i) in a
closed circle (= ronde, chaîne fermée); (ii) in an open circle; and (iii)
as a chain (= chaîne ouverte).[31] The circles could be paced or leapt in
single file, or as double circles in the same direction or two different
directions, or in three distinct circles; a sermon of Savonarola records
this, for example, in Florence in 1497. Open circles at court festivities
or during the performance of folk customs in the towns could often
be of considerable length (= 'Langtanz').

Round dances were performed by day or night, in all localities.
Churches, monasteries, cemeteries, lime trees beneath which tribunes
were held, the courtyards of castles, gardens, roads, streets, open
fields—all these are frequently named as sites.

The majority of round dances must have been performed in the
open air in the spring or summer, accompanied by singing and led by
a 'foreman' ('Vortänzer') bearing a rod ('leitestap', *Virginal*, l. 1090.5)
or torch in his hand, or by one or more minstrels. 'Caroles' were in
the first instance round dances accompanied by a song and refrain,
which could also be performed without musical accompaniment. Literary expressions such as 'carole and synge so swetely' (England, 1369)
point to this custom, as does the line in the Colmar Songbook: 'gesanc
daz zieret manigen wünneclichen rei' ('song, that embellishes many a
delightful round dance'), or the round-dance song no. 42 in the
Lochamer-Liederbuch of 1460: 'I leap in this round dance' ('Ich spring
an disem ringe'). On occasion round dances—perhaps predominantly
in courtly society—were linked with ball games.

Round dances could be performed 'tres noble' (Pl. X), but also with
unrestrained vulgarity. No clear distinction according to class may be
drawn; on the one hand conventions might be respected both in town

---

[31] For a detailed analysis see Walter Salmen, 'Ikonographie des Reigens im Mittelalter', *Acta
musicologica*, 52 (1980), 14–26.

and country, while coarse excesses might occur in court circles. It was generally the case that the social classes were divided when it came to round dancing, and any mixing of genders was frowned upon or even forbidden, especially in Jewish communities.

More important than any social distinction is the marked subdivision of round dances into those performed by children, by men (Pl. IX), and by ladies ('dames et puceles', or only 'puelle'), and on the other hand those which were performed by both sexes together. The steps and leaps might be foot movements only, or be linked with hand gestures, mime, and other improvised effects. Round dances could have a narrow or a wide ambitus; the dancers could maintain their distance from one another or join hands, or link elbows; other dances involved the employment of kerchiefs, swords (Pl. IX), hoops, etc. The texts yield very little information concerning the tempo or mode of performance.

The Minnesänger of Sachsendorf (thirteenth century) mentions a woman who 'twisted like a willow wand' ('want alsam ein wîdegerte'); in Konrad von Würzburg's *Trojanerkrieg*, a round dance, a 'reige', is described in the following way:

> sie wunden sich dan unde dar
> und brachen sich her unde hin
>
> hither and thither they twisted,
> breaking off in this and that direction[32]

'Slîfen' with the 'füezen', dancing with a gliding motion of the feet, was followed by 'balde springen' ('bold leaps'), just as later the first and second section of a dance were combined (*Trojanerkrieg*, ll. 28206–7). Neidhart also describes the way in which the dancer moves but 'doesn't drag the feet over the ground on tip-toe' ('uf der erde niht gesiffel[t] mit den zehen').[33] More specific terminology sometimes occurs in the texts, such as the 'crooked circle' ('krumbe rei', Neidhart von Reuental), the 'crowned ring' ('gekrönte rei', Heinrich von Mügeln), or the 'firlifanz' (Oswald von Wolkenstein), the latter surviving into the recent past as an open chain, known as the 'Schwabentanz' ('Swabian dance').

Each round dance constituted at least three distinct phases: the introductory formation, the execution of one or more movements, and the dissolution of the grouping. The latter is typified by a Middle High

---

[32] *Trojanerkrieg*, ed. A. von Keller (Stuttgart, 1858), ll. 28200–1.
[33] Siegfried Beyschlag, *Die Lieder Neidharts* (Darmstadt, 1975), 54; Ann Harding, *An Investigation into the Use and Meaning of Medieval German Dancing Terms* (Göppingen, 1973), 213.

German source: 'when the dance was over, each man and woman
went to sit as separate couples on the grass' ('da sich der ray zerlie,
ye ain man und ain frowe gie und sassent sunder in daz gras'; cf.
Grimm, *Deutsches Wörterbuch*, viii. 644). A French miniature of the
fifteenth century shows people forming the round dance (Paris, Bibliothèque Nationale de France, MS ital. 9754, fo. 10ᵛ). Led by a player
of the bagpipes, six ladies dressed in long robes reaching to the
ground enter and form a round. Where round dances were concerned
the number of participants was not limited by convention, in contrast
to dance movements in pairs, and thus it was possible to make a
belated entry into a circle already in motion (Oxford, Bodleian
Library, MS Douce 195, fo. 7ʳ, c.1490), or to leave such a circle pre-
maturely. The introductory formation could take the form of a
closed circle with or without bows, with joining of hands, elbows, or
shoulders ('commenchierent leurs mains a tendre', Jean Froissart, 14th
century). If an accompanying minstrel were required, he could either
stand or sit outside this circle, or dance along with the others in the
round.

In an open circle, the leader of the round dance could demonstrate
the function that distinguished him visually, by swinging his arms
(New York, Pierpont Morgan Library, MS M 372, fo. 6ᵛ, 14th century). He could make manifest 'his power among the many maidens'
('sin gewalt under den kinden manicvalt') by acting as 'vortanzel'
('dance leader'), as Neidhart von Reuental confirms. In this function,
as also in chain dances, he was often distinguished by a staff, a green
branch, or the emblem of his group, for example the sign of a guild
of artisans, or by other accoutrements.

The round dance could be performed with elegant, measured paces,
side by side, with swords hanging from belts and long cloaks; but it
was also fashionable for couples to twist and turn, as a two-couple
round dance of French origin shows (Pl. X; also Paris, Bibliothèque
Nationale de France, MS fr. 1665, fo. 7ʳ). The spine might bend, the
hips sway, configurations being performed with a hopping gait, with
a vigorous 'swish' ('umbeswanke'), which could even lead to clothes
being torn.

Circles were turned inwards and outwards; arches were formed by
raised arms for people to leap or dance through. This is clearly to be
seen in a fresco of the early fourteenth century in the Palazzo Pub-
blico of Siena,[34] which shows not only the movement through such an
arch but also the role of the lead singer with her tambourine; this is

---

[34] Edmund A. Bowles, *Musikleben im 15. Jahrhundert* (Musikgeschichte in Bildern, 3/viii;
Leipzig, 1977), fig. 157.

also shown in a Swedish woodcut of 1555 in Olaus Magnus' *Historia de gentibus septentrionalibus*. In sword dances this movement took the form of the figure known as the 'bridge', an arch formed by swords through which the dancers leapt (Pl. IX).[35] Open round dances were performed in wave-like movements, narrow or broad, or could progress at a measured pace; they could also progress towards a spiral formation.

PAIRED DANCES

Peasants' Dances

For dancing in couples the evidence for country areas is for the most part limited to iconography. No choreography or detailed descriptions of 'dörperlich' ('peasant', 'boorish') dancing have survived. It is nevertheless certain that until *c.*1400 people danced in large units side by side ('aneinander', Ulm, 1406), hand in hand in a round, but that from the fifteenth century dancing in pairs became increasingly common practice among peasants, shepherds, and hirelings, and, copying the fashions of the upper classes, was performed with greater variation. Dancing in couples was particularly common at betrothal feasts ('lobetanz'), weddings, harvest festivals, at Shrovetide, and at public 'evening dances' ('Abendtänze'). At weddings there were, for example, dances of honour performed by the bridal couples (with 'Tanzkerzen', 'dance candles', in their hands), by the parents of the bride, the lord of the manor with the bride, etc. Either the dancer led his partner 'bei der Hand', at his side, or he pulled her along behind him. This leading could take place at a fast run in 'boorish and indecorous fashion' ('pawerische vnd vnformlich weise'), or at a measured walk, 'according to good, respectable custom' ('nach guter erbarlicher sitten'). In Heinrich Wittenwiler's *Ring* a parodistic description is to be found:

> Offenstek do fürher sprang
> Und nam fro Jützen an die hand.
> Er tanzt da hin, sie vegt im nach,
> Die andern auf und an vil gach.
> Daz gzöder michel ward und lang.
> Ieder sunderleichen sprang
> Auf und nider in dem traum
> Sam die äpfel von dem paum.[36]

---

[35] With regard to Pl. IX, it is furthermore worthy of note that as early as the 16th c. ring dances of European origin, including sword dances and morris dances, found their way to Africa, Asia, and America with the colonists.

[36] Heinrich Wittenwiler, *Der Ring, Frühneuhochdeutsch/Neuhochdeutsch. Nach dem Text von Edmund Wießner ins Neuhochdeutsche übersetzt und herausgegeben von Horst Brunner*

Offenstek led the dance, taking Lady Jutze by the hand. He danced
along, she swept after him, the others up and after them in a hurry. The
train grew big and long. Each and every one of them danced up and
down, in a trance, like apples falling from a tree.

People indulged in embraces ('halsen' or 'umbfahen') or twirled in
front of one another ('vordrehen') or threw (their partners) around
('herumbwerffen'). Difficult figures such as 'twisting' ('Wickeln') or
hoisting the female partner into the air were popular.[37]

Townsmen's Dances

In the *Roman des Sept Sages* of the twelfth century we read:

> Li jongleours vont vielant
> Et les borjoises karolant

The jugglers go playing their vielles and the townsmen dancing in the
round

whereas in a chanson set to music by Clément Janequin in 1530:

> Chantés, dancés, jeunes filettes,
> Bourgeoyses et bourgeoys.

Thus among townsfolk too the tendency was for the round dance to
give way to dancing in couples. In the urban bath houses, in town halls,
at banquets in 'bonne compagnie', after court sessions (for example
in Bremen in 1430), in the hostelries of merchants and elsewhere,
dancing was encouraged, with clerics, monks, and nuns frequently
participating, 'baylando e dançando' (Lisbon, 1400). Sometimes such
dances were decorous, sometimes less so—'cum grandissima lascivia'
('with the greatest voluptuousness', Bressanone, 1492).[38] Rank-based
distinctions were accordingly drawn between the 'common' dances
(Hildesheim, 1503) of the lower and middle townsfolk and the more
distinguished, exclusive patrician dances, in which noblemen and
princes frequently participated. Participation in the latter was by
special invitation, by messengers known as 'tanntzlader' (Nuremberg,
1500) or 'hochzeitlader'.[39] Overseers were paid to direct and supervise

---

(Stuttgart, 1991), ll. 6201-8. See also Edmund Wießner, *Heinrich Wittenwilers Ring* (Leipzig,
1931), 219.

[37] *MGG* viii. 56; Salmen, *Musikleben im 16. Jahrhundert*, figs. 13 and 17.

[38] J. Riedman, 'Eine Reise durch Tirol im Jahre 1492', *Das Fenster*, 23 (1978), 234.

[39] Georg Schünemann, 'Volksfeste und Volksmusik im alten Nürnberg', in *Musik und Bild:
Festschrift für Max Seiffert* (Kassel, 1938), fig. 2; Reinhard Strohm, *Music in Late Medieval
Bruges* (Oxford, 1985), 85.

the sequence of the dances, the succession of dancing couples, and the observation of all conventions.[40] Among such duties were the exclusion of couples who did not meet with approval,[41] of prostitutes and mothers with illegitimate children, or people whose clothing defied convention.

Townsfolk went to the dance 'bene ornata' (Siena, 1465), well adorned ('ghesmukket also wol', Rostocker Liederbuch, c.1470, song no. 10). Long trains, 'swense', were worn, which could be gathered up ('reffen'). Veils and masks made of cloth were donned, a wreath of roses ('ain rosen krantz') might be placed on the head (Hugo of Montfort), people danced in long cloaks with daggers or swords at their belts, wearing gloves and crakow shoes (with long pointed toes), which were forbidden, for example in Speyer in 1356, as evidence of overweening pride. Even the Augsburg cornettist Baruch, who in 1493 married a baker's daughter, appeared for the dance of honour in a green cloak with long crakows and a large gold brooch on his hat, in order to demonstrate his social pretensions, for 'fine feathers make fine birds'.[42]

The kinds of dances in which the townspeople indulged can only be deduced in vague terms, in view of the lack of sufficient sources. This is in part to be explained by the fact that in this social stratum a distinct tendency to rapid changes in fashion was present, and there were moreover considerable local and regional variations, for which there is no documentation. In 1429 in Lisbon, for example, visitors from Burgundy were 'dansans selon leur guise', but it is not clear what the regional peculiarities of their dances were at that time. Many references to dances take the form of 'olde daunce' (Chaucer) and 'nieuwe dansen', or even 'unusual dances' ('ungewöhnliche thänz'), and we cannot find out how they were performed. What did, for example, a 'trarat' mean in Danzig in 1515, what did a 'tortiglione' mean in the fifteenth century, or 'de dancer sur le nouvel art' or 'la Basse dance nouvelle' in France? What is one to understand by the 'piva' or 'calata' in Italy, the 'turdión fatto a proporzione' in Spain, the 'Spanieler' in South Germany in 1513, or the 'Swingenvuoz' of Rhenish origin in Lower Austria? What distinguished a 'welschen dantz' ('Italian dance', Hans Judenkünig, 1523) from 'windisch treten' ('Wendish steps') in Slovenia, or a 'Pauana alla Venetiana', as opposed to other 'trettenden tencz' ('step dances', Munich, 1429), which were differentiated

[40] Salmen, *Tanz im 17. und 18. Jahrhundert*, 148–51.

[41] Theodor Aign, *Die Ketzel: Ein Nürnberger Handelsherren- und Jerusalempilgergeschlecht* (Neustadt/Aisch, 1961), 103 ff.

[42] Salmen, *Tanz im 17. und 18. Jahrhundert*, 142–3.

from 'reschen', 'leapt'? The parliament assembled in Augsburg in 1530 held dances almost daily, alternating between German and Italian fashion ('auf deutsche und welsche Art'); there was also a Dutch dance, one 'à la Spagnuola', Hungarian ('vngerische') fashions,[43] 'saltarelli' (Florence, 1459), diverse 'balli', or in Reval in 1532 the shepherd's dance and four double dances ('den schaffer Dantz unde IIII dubbelde dentze').[44] There therefore existed an abundant range of dances, among which the best known are 'la trisca' (Juan Ruiz, first half of the 14th century), 'la stampita', or the 'bassas dansas' (Raimon de Cornet, c.1320).[45] The latter were in fashion for more than two hundred years, for as late as 1531 Thomas Elyot writes in his *Boke named the Governour* (ch. 20): 'we have nowe base daunsis, bargenettes, pavions, turgions and roundes'.

Courtly Dances

The distinction between ordinary dances and a 'proper court dance' ('einem rehten hovetanz'; 'hovedaunce', England, c.1390; 'danses à cours', France, fifteenth century) reaches back into the thirteenth century, as does the differentiation between low dances and 'alles hoghes' ('all things high', Wendische Chronik, 1311), or dancing 'proud and courtly' ('stolz vnde hovisch', Carmina Burana, no. 148a).[46] And what was known since the late fourteenth century as the 'court dance' ('hoff dantz') was thus both a kind of dance and a manner of dancing determined by rank, a controlled sequence of 'genteel steps' ('leisen trittn'), taken at a slow pace. The nobility expressed itself in a disciplined way, in 'gentyl behavying'. In festive clothing (long, trailing clothes, cuffed sleeves), wearing jewellery, processing in hierarchical order, high society announced its claims to exclusivity. The courtly dance, performed with dignity and honour ('mit tzuchten und mit eren', Peter Suchenwirt, 1377), and demonstratively accompanied by trumpets and shawms ('trompen ende met

---

[43] In 1534 a fiddler was required in Gries am Brenner who could play German, Italian, and French dances in succession! See also Walter Salmen, '"Alla tedesca" oder "welsch" tanzen', in Paolo Chiarini and Herbert Zeman (eds.), *Italia–Austria: alla ricerca del passato comune* (Rome, 1995), 207–18.

[44] Hans Joachim Moser, 'Zur mittelalterlichen Musikgeschichte der Stadt Cöln', *Archiv für Musikwissenschaft*, 1 (1918), 134–44 at 139.

[45] Elizabeth Aubrey, 'References to Music in Old Occitan Literature', *Acta musicologica*, 61 (1989), 110–49 at 119; Francisco Carreras y Candi, *Folklore y costumbres de España* (Barcelona, 1934), p. vii; Claudia Celi, 'La danza aulica italiana nel XV secolo', *Nuova rivista musicale italiana*, 16 (1982), 218–25; Robert Mullally, 'French Social Dances in Italy, 1528–9', *Music and Letters*, 65 (1984), 41–4.

[46] Harding, *An Investigation* (above, n. 33), 121.

scalmeyen') was an indispensable part of court custom ('hovesite'). It both served as pastime ('kurzwil') and conferred honour in the narrow confines of an elite. The courtly dance was designed to be performed before lords and ladies ('herren und frouwen'), manifesting a delight in luxury. For the proper execution of these dances long rooms were built in the castles, such as that in the castle of Kiel, called the 'Lange Kammer'.

The dances of courts and princes were not accompanied by singing. Strict ceremonial forbade this, as it did dances characterized by excessively lively leaping; thus in Innsbruck in 1516 the following prohibition was issued: 'Item no *Kerab*[47] is to be danced; it is not the custom amongst princesses' ('Item man sol keinen Kerab tanzen, ist nicht der gebrauch bei den Fürstinnen'). Courtly dances could be danced in pairs ('in uno homo e una dona', Italy, 15th century) or in threes (see Pl. XI). Choreographically, the 'haut monde' had at its disposal processional movements ('je veux mener ma demoiselle', Guillaume Coquillart, *c*.1480), the estampie, the diverse choreographies of the 'base dance' (England, 1500) without a fixed sequence of steps, contrasting with the manner of the 'alte danza', or the pavans. The 'famiglia di bassadanza' (Antonio Cornazano, *Libro dell'arte del danzare*, 1455) embraced five distinct types of step: R = reverence, b = branle, ss = simple, d = double, r = reprise, c = congé.[48] These dances were, however, by no means the restricted privilege of the aristocracy; in 1473, for example, a rich merchant paid an English harper at Calais for instruction in 'ffottyng off bass daunssys'.

DANCING MASTERS AND TREATISES

The *ars saltatoria* which emerged in the fourteenth century established itself as a gymnastic art, intended to distinguish between those who were well educated and possessed of better manners on the one hand, and on the other the 'meccaniche plebei' with their indisciplined activities. The complex of rules that belonged to this *ars*, bound by the conventions of class, could no longer be communicated purely on the basis of custom and tradition. Instead it called for the professional, scholarly activity of 'maestri di ballo' or 'professori di ballo', 'esperti' also termed 'magister de danser' or 'magister corearum' (Barcelona,

---

[47] 'Kehraus' in modern German, the last dance of a ball; here evidently a rather indecorous dance.

[48] Frederick Crane, *Materials for the Study of the Fifteenth-Century Basse Danse* (Brooklyn, 1968), 114 ff.; W. Brunner, *Höfischer Tanz um 1500* (Berlin, 1983); A. William Smith, *Fifteenth-Century Dance and Music*, i (New York, 1995), 83–107, with a complete bibliography since 1970, 301–8.

1503). These presided over 'escolas de dança', in which elegant bearing
and the choreography of favoured dances such as the 'mourisca'
(Lisbon, 15th century) or the 'balli et bassadançe' were taught. This
task was performed both by minstrels (for example in the service of
English kings) and by dance leaders equipped with a staff ('leitestap'),
who bade the learners step or leap after them ('nachtreten', 'nach-
springen'); 'dançatori' versed in the subject could fulfil the same function. It was in northern Italy, northern Spain, and Bohemia that the
first trend-setting centres of these 'arte di ballare et danzare' were
established, and from the fifteenth century onwards treatises recorded
their teachings in writing. These 'libri ballarum' took pains to point
out to the enemies of this social activity its noble nature, and proffered descriptions of the norms that obtained with regard, for
example, to 'dançar longo', 'dançar corto', 'dançare con mantellino',
or 'choreas ducendi'.[49] Other important aspects were: 'memoria,
misura, maniera, aiere, movimento corporeo', and 'partire del
terreno'.[50] All the authors were concerned not only to preserve standards but also to impart 'novi modelli', their personal inventions 'di
molto belle mutanze'.

The dancing instructors, although their duties were expressly to
educate the upper strata of society, 'sol per dignissime Madonne et
non plebeje' (Cornazano, 1455), were of diverse social backgrounds.
Many were Jews from the ghettos, others belonged to the middle class,
forming for example in Rouen in 1454 a 'corporation des joueurs,
faiseurs d'instruments de musique et maîtres de danse'. Some entered
service as court dancing masters, such as one engaged in Innsbruck in
1531 for the entertainment ('kurzweyl') of the royal children.[51] The
income of such as these was relatively high. A 'saltatorum princeps'
such as Domenico da Piacenza (1395–1470) was paid 20 lire a month
at the court of Ferrara. His colleague Guglielmo Ebreo da Pesaro,[52]
organizer of 'gran feste' at the courts of the Sforza, the Medici, and
other dynasties, enjoyed equally high favour.[53] Some of these teachers
acquired an international reputation, with the result that the art of

---

[49] F. Alberto Gallo, 'Il "ballare Lombardo" (circa 1435–1475)', *Studi musicali*, 8 (1979), 61–84;
more details are to be found in Walter Salmen, *Der Tanzmeister: Geschichte und Profile eines
Berufes vom 14. bis zum 19. Jahrhundert* (Hildesheim, 1997).

[50] Madeleine Inglehearn, 'A Little-Known Fifteenth-Century Italian Dance Treatise', *Music
Review*, 42 (1981), 174–81.

[51] Tiroler Landesarchiv Innsbruck OÖ. Kammer-Kopialbücher, vol. 23 (1531), fo. 125ᵛ.

[52] Guglielmo Ebreo of Pesaro, *On the Practice or Art of Dancing*, ed. and trans. Barbara Sparti
(Oxford, 1995).

[53] See Patrizia Castelli, Maurizio Mingardi, and Maurizio Padovan (eds.), *Mesura et
arte del danzare: Guglielmo Ebreo da Pesaro e la danza nelle corti italiane del XV secolo* (Pesaro,
1987).

Italian dancing ('wellschen tentz') was adopted north of the Alps in the fifteenth and early sixteenth century. Albrecht Dürer took dancing lessons during his period of training in Venice; in 1494 Bianca Maria Sforza taught Lombard dance fashions to court society in Innsbruck; and in 1517 translations from the Italian of descriptions of dances reached Nuremberg.[54]

DANCE SONGS

The municipal decrees of Saalfeld in the fourteenth century make the following concession to the townsfolk: 'Wer an der vasnacht reige wil, mag er nicht spilemanns gehabe, so sal her suvirliche und hubische lit vorsinge' ('If round dances are to be held at Shrovetide and no minstrels be present, then proper and courtly songs may be sung'). There were therefore the alternatives of minstrels accompanying dances or 'reigen' instrumentally, or singing led by lead singers. Both happened, but the singing accompaniment was still dominant throughout Europe, in all strata of society, and both where laymen and the clergy were concerned. There are countless examples of dance songs ('tancgesanc', 'tanzliet') composed, improvised, and intoned by 'dance rhymers' ('tanzrimer'), in the anticipation that all the dancers would join in the refrains.

The majority of the 'cantilenae de chorea' were modelled on refrain songs. Refrains at the end or in the middle of songs, interpolated exclamations along the lines of 'arriva là' or 'hoi ho' are among the characteristics of this genre,[55] as in the seven-line catalogue song entered in 1460 in the Lochamer-Liederbuch:

> Ich spring an disem ringe,
> des pesten, so ichs kan
> von hübschen frewlein singe,
> als ichs geleret han.
> he—!
> Ich rait durch fremde lande,
> do sach ich mancher hande,
> do ich die frewlein fand.[56]

---

[54] Salmen, '"Alla tedesca" oder "welsch tanzen"', 213. Ingrid Brainard, 'The Art of Courtly Dancing in Transition: Nürnberg, Germ. Nat. Mus. MS. 8842, a Hitherto Unknown German Source', in Edelgard E. DuBruck and Karl Heinz Göller (eds.), *Crossroads of Medieval Civilization: The City of Regensburg and its Intellectual Milieu* (Medieval and Renaissance Monograph Series, 5; 1984), 61–79.

[55] Christoph Petzsch, 'Rufe im Tanzlied', *Zeitschrift für deutsches Altertum und deutsche Literatur*, 95 (1966), 204–12.

[56] *Das Lochamer-Liederbuch*, ed. Walter Salmen and Christoph Petzsch (Wiesbaden, 1973), no. 42.

I leap in this ring as best I can, sing of pretty maidens as I have learnt. Hey! I rode through foreign lands, many things I saw there, when I found maidens fair.

Male or female lead singers ('vorsanger', 'vorsengerinne'), 'pucelles', or tambourine players performed these functional 'cançons de carolle' in the manner of rondeaux (AB aA ab AB), virelais, ballades, ballate, stampenies, carols, and 'roundels' (Chaucer),[57] or rounds ('Singradel'). It was the custom to distribute the lines of the song in the pattern 'diu sank vor, die andern sungen alle nach' ('one sang first, the others all after'), so that a rondeau might for example be performed in the following format: AB = the jongleur or lead singers, a = one of the dancers, A = all, ab = the individual dancer, AB = all. It often happened even as late as the sixteenth century that the leading singer's part was taken by a duke, a king, or an emperor, great honour being thereby conferred upon the dance; such round songs could thus be amongst the 'carmina incondita', as well as a constituent part of the high art of the troubadours or the professional urban singers. Thus in *Sir Gawain and the Green Knight*, written probably in the last quarter of the fourteenth century, we read:

> Justed ful jolilé thise gentyle knightes
> Sythen kayred to the court caroles to make (ll. 42–3)

and

> Dansed full drezly wyth dere carolez (l. 1026)

In noble circles in Scandinavia the singing in company of dance songs (= ballades) in the great halls or courtyards of castles was a common pursuit, for up to the sixteenth century the genre of the ballad was still frequently linked with the performance of dance (*ballare*). 'Reien' was a genre and form of performance which generally had recourse to primitive types of melody, in duple or triple rhythm,[58] such as are contained, for example, in the section called 'ethlich rayen vnder weltlichen rayen noten' ('some round dances with secular round-dance notation') in the Hohenfurter Liederbuch of *c*.1460: 'Nun hört zy disem rayen, den ich euch hie vorsing' (Now hark to this round dance, which I here sing to you') (see Ex. 4.1).[59] Many

[57] L. Jordan, 'Der Reigentanz Carole und seine Lieder', *Zeitschrift für romanische Philologie*, 51 (1931), 335 ff.

[58] Walter Wiora, 'Elementare Liedtypen als Abschnitte mittelalterlicher Liedweisen', in *Miscelánea en homenaje a Mons. Higinio Anglés* (Barcelona, 1961), 993–1009.

[59] Wilhelm Bäumker, *Ein deutsches geistliches Liederbuch mit Melodien aus dem XV. Jahrhundert* (Leipzig, 1895), 56.

Ex. 4.1. Song for a round dance ('rayen') in the Hohenfurter Liederbuch
(*c*.1460)

Nun hört zu di-sem ray - en, den ich euch hie vor-sing...

of these songs began with calls to join in the dance such as 'Ralons a
la balerie,—qui n'aime, n'i viegne mie', issuing invitations to commu-
nal action:

> Nu willen wyr alle frolich syn
> in ehren.
> wir willen frolich, fruntlich sin,
> singen, springen, hei wuchhei,
> in zucht und ehren.[60]

Now let us be all merry with honour. We will be merry, friendly, sing,
leap, ho ho! with decorum and honour.

Dance songs were to be heard at weddings, at evening dances on the
feast of St John with the intention of earning a garland of roses as a
mark of distinction, and sung in the colleges by students 'cum tripudio' with Latin lyrics ('Filia vis militem bene equitantem?'),[61] but also
very often during processions or pilgrims' journeys. Evidence for this
is supplied, for example, by the fourteenth-century *Llibre Vermell* from
Montserrat,[62] as well as by various chronicles which describe the activities of the flagellants, particularly in the year 1349. In the region of
the pilgrim centre of Montserrat it was the custom that pilgrims
'volunt cantare et trepudiare', that they gave voice to 'cantilenae . . .
ad tripudium rotundum', some taking the form of rounds (= caça),
for example 'Ad mortem festinamus, peccare desistamus, peccare desistamus' (see Ex. 4.2). The groups of flagellants who indulged in self-
castigation for the purpose of penance, inspired by the mass hysteria
originating in Italy from the middle of the thirteenth century onwards,
refrained from instrumental music and from 'amatorie cantilenae';
they did, however, as they travelled through the lands, perform 'leisen'
and 'reie' (Magdeburg, 1349), accompanied by singing of the simplest

[60] 'ein dantzlied' (a dance song'), Darfelder Liederhandschrift, *c*.1550, ed. R. W. Brednich
(Münster, 1976), no. 104.
[61] Cf. Friedrich Ranke and Joseph Müller-Blattau, *Das Rostocker Liederbuch* (Halle, 1927),
269.
[62] Higinio Anglés, 'El "Llibre Vermell" de Montserrat y los cantos y la danza sacra de los
peregrinos durante el siglo XIV', *Anuario musical*, 10 (1955), 45–78 at 68–70.

Ex. 4.2. Pilgrim's dance song from the *Llibre Vermell* of Montserrat, fos. 26ᵛ–27ʳ (after Anglès, 'El *Llibre Vermell*', 661)

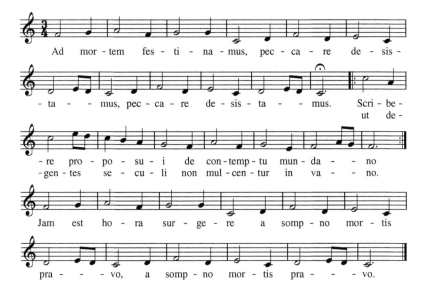

Ad mor - tem fes - ti - na - mus, pec - ca - re de - sis -

- ta - - mus, pec - ca - re de - sis - ta - - mus. Scri - be -
                                                              ut de -

- re pro - po - su - i de con - temp - tu mun - da - - no
- gen - tes se - cu - li non mul - cen - tur in va - - no.

Jam est ho - ra sur - ge - re a somp - no mor - tis

pra - - - vo, a somp - no mor - tis pra - - - vo.

kind.[63] Inspired by their processions, girls and women in the Lausitz in 1349 are said to have behaved in insane fashion, dancing and rejoicing ('danzen und jubilieren') before an image of the Virgin Mary which they imagined to have spoken to them. The spectrum of dance songs in the later Middle Ages was thus very broad.

DANCE ACCOMPANIMENTS

In the fifteenth-century French romance *Cleriadus et Meliadice* (London, British Library, Royal 20.C.ii, fo. 127ʳ) a festival is described with an unusual sequence of dances, some accompanied by minstrels, others by 'hommes et femmes' singing: 'quant la compaignie fut traueillée de danser aux menestrelz ilz se prinrent a danser aux chanchons'. Dancing 'aux menestrelz' thus alternated with dancing 'aux chansons'. Gian Giorgio Trissino (1478–1550), in his *Poetica*, describes dance music in terms of 'i piffari, i liuti e gli organi e gli altri suoni e canti'. Evidence such as this leads to the question of what minstrels played what instruments, what was the composition of the accompanying groups that conferred upon dances 'sentiment et mesura' (*Libro de caballeria*,

---

[63] A. Hübner, *Die deutschen Geißlerlieder* (Berlin, 1931).

1460). The written and pictorial evidence suggests that this complex of questions may be answered as follows:

For solo dances the customary accompaniments were rattles ('tablettes'; Pl. VII), cymbals, tambourines, bells, and fiddles. During the fourteenth century the practice of a single fiddler (who also joined in the dance) accompanying female solo dances (Pl. VI) was particularly dominant. Round dances were accompanied—depending upon the social rank of the dancers—by pipes and tabors, portative organs,[64] lutes, bagpipes and shawm, fiddle and shawm; or even 'drie vor im gîgen, und der vierde pheif' ('three fiddled before him, and the fourth piped'; Neidhart von Reuental).[65] Generally speaking, until the sixteenth century people were content to be accompanied by solo musicians or small ensembles.

Dances for couples, on the other hand, developed a tendency from the fourteenth century onwards towards more complex accompaniment, involving large bodies of up to eight trumpeters (in Marburg castle, 1497) or 'trompes, pipes, and with a fristele', intended to impress by 'lowde shallys' (John Lydgate). A clear distinction was drawn between the playing of 'les trompettes et ménestreux' (Jean de Fevre), and the different grades of accompaniment by 'bas Instrumens' or 'haulx menestriers', who might on occasion be positioned on a separate dais, in order to wait in attendance or pay court ('hofieren').[66] Effort and expenditure varied, depending upon the specific occasion for the dance, the dimensions of the room(s) available, and the location. At the court of Maximilian I c.1500, for example, duos of pipe and tabor were still clearly dominant, whereas such a modest accompaniment would at that time be regarded in the Hansa city of Tallin (Estonia) as suggestive of poverty.[67] The nobility, the burghers, and the common people all sought to outdo one another, particularly with regard to wedding dances. To exert a degree of control over such competition, many towns proclaimed limitations on the number of minstrels permitted. Thus in Kraków c.1336 the richer burghers were permitted eight minstrels, whereas in Zwickau in 1348 only four were allowed, in Ulm in 1400 three, in Lübeck in 1454 between six and nine, and in Breslau in 1480 two pair ('zwei par'). Dances were accompanied by specialist pipers and organists ('tanczpfeifer', 'tanzorganisten'). Bagpipes, piva, rebec,

[64] *Revue de l'art*, 47 (1980), 54, fig. 1.
[65] *Die Lieder*, ed. S. Beyschlag (Darmstadt, 1975), 254.
[66] Salmen, 'L'Iconographie des lieux de la danse', 109.
[67] Rainer Gstrein, 'Tanzmusik-Ensembles zur Zeit und am Hofe Kaiser Maximilians I.', in *Muziek aan het Hof van Margaretha van Oostenrijk = Jaarboek van het Vlaamse Centrum voor oude Muziek*, 3 (1987), 79–96 at 89.

trumpet marine, glockenspiel, buisine, krummhorn, cornett, and rectangular hammered dulcimer were among the accompanying instruments. After 1470 there was also a discernible increase in the employment of instruments such as lutes and harps, and distinguished
gatherings came to be graced by combinations of shawm, bombard,
and trumpet, or trombone (= *alta capella*, consisting of trumpets and
pipes, 'trompete en pepen'; see Pl. XII), for the polyphonic interpretation of dance music based on a cantus firmus.[68]

INSTRUMENTAL DANCE MUSIC

Until the sixteenth century all kinds of functional dance music were
improvised in character, not requiring a fixed notation that determined
all melodic lines and variants. None of the many depictions of the
dances of the nobility or of the peasants shows musicians reading
from sheet music. Their performances, often executed 'more lascivio'
(Robertus de Handlo), were more skill than art. Music performed
according to the rules of art music was rarely in demand, for often it
sufficed if a rhythmic 'grant noise' was made by the minstrels, when
the 'misura' of the dance was proclaimed. Only in the course of the
fifteenth and early sixteenth century did taste demand that dance
music be elevated from the realm of 'musica usualis' to that of 'musica
artificialis', with, if nothing further, the fixed mensuration of 'tenori'
(Cornazano, 1455).[69]

   Prior to this minstrels passed on to one another the practice of striking up a dance on stringed instruments ('ufstrichen' or 'ufslahen'),
following 'noten' (= dance melodies; Konrad von Würzburg) by
'leren' ('teaching'), i.e. precept and imitation. They employed the
techniques of doubling, of drones (sustained notes of the same or
varying kinds), the ornamentation of the cantus prius factus, variation, and harmonizing according to the possibilities offered by
the instruments to hand. The various 'compagnie di piffari', for
example, played over melodic frameworks or rhythmic patterns in
differentiated techniques ranging from monophony to harmony
and polyphony. The 'noten' might be linked to texts, such as songs
and Leichs, or they could be entirely instrumental. The evidence

   [68] Edmund A. Bowles, 'Iconography as a Tool for Examining the Loud Consort in the
Fifteenth Century', *Journal of the American Musical Instrument Society*, 3 (1977), 100–21
at 116; id., *Musikleben*, 52–3 and 57 ff.
   [69] Walter Salmen, 'Bemerkungen zum mehrstimmigen Musizieren der Spielleute im Mittelalter', *Revue belge de musicologie*, 11 (1957), 17–26; id., 'Ikonographische Aspekte zur instru-
mentalen Mehrstimmigkeit im Mittelalter', in *Le polifonie primitive in Friuli e in Europa: Atti
del Congresso internazionale Cividale 1980*, ed. Cesare Corsi and Pierluigi Petrobelli (Rome,
1989), 417–34.

attests that such dances, performed monophonically or polyphonically, served as functional music to accompany dances or as independent performances from the thirteenth century onwards, particularly
on the occasion of ceremonial banquets (for example in 1454 at
the court of Duke Philip the Good, played by four flutes and three
tambourines).[70]

The beginnings of the notation of melodies intended as dance
accompaniment date from the end of the fourteenth century.[71] From
this point onwards 'rundeli' without texts are attested, as well as
indications of melodic phrases in chansons, such as 'dansez la mi fa
la ré'.[72] Dance melodies that are in vogue crop in literature, as for
example the basse dance in the *Monologue Coquillart* of Guillaume
Coquillart (*c*.1475):

> Tabourin! à mon appetit;
> Branslez, 'le petit Rouen'.

Whereas the oldest dance treatises restrict themselves to indications of
the tune and accommodate the dance steps to these cantus prius facti,
during the second half of the fifteenth century the communication of
'notes' in the form of melodic patterns becomes necessary, as for
example in *L'art et instruction de bien dancer* with 'plusieurs basses
dances' of 1488, printed by Michel Toulouze in Paris.[73] These model
tenors for *balli* and for other dances are generally in a notation which
is abbreviated and lacks rhythmicization, thus being available for
double employ, 'en double emploi', i.e. for a performance in duple or
triple metre (first and second section).[74]

[70] Gilbert Reaney, *The Manuscript London, British Museum, Additional 29987* (facs. edn.,
Rome, 1965); Walter Salmen, 'Tafelmusik im hohen und späten Mittelalter', in *Atti del VII Convegno di Studio, Viterbo* (1983), 171–202.

[71] V. Plocek, 'Zur Problematik der ältesten tschechischen Tanzkompositionen', *Studia musicologica*, 13 (1971), 16ff.; Walter Salmen, *Der Spielmann im Mittelalter* (Innsbruck, 1983),
127–30; *Medieval Instrumental Dances*, ed. Timothy J. McGee (Bloomington and Indianapolis,
1989); see also Joan Rimmer, 'Medieval Instrumental Dance Music', *Music and Letters*, 72
(1991), 61–8.

[72] Frederick Crane, '15th-Century Keyboard Music in Vienna MS 5094', *JAMS* 18 (1965),
237–43; Helene Wagenaar-Nolthenius, 'Wat is een rondeel?', *TVNM* 21 (1969), 61–7; Christoph
Petzsch, 'Ein Nachtanz aus dem spätmittelalterlichen Ottobeuren', *Die Musikforschung*, 32
(1979), 417–19; Jacques Handschin, 'Das Weihnachts-Mysterium von Rouen als musik-
geschichtliche Quelle', *Acta musicologica*, 7 (1935), 97–110.

[73] Repr. Geneva, 1985; see also Barbara Sparti, 'The 15th-Century *Balli* Tunes: A New
Look', *EM* 14 (1985), 346–57; Frederick Crane, 'The Derivation of Some Fifteenth-Century
Basse-Danse Tunes', *Acta musicologica*, 37 (1965), 179–88; Ewald Jammers, 'Studien zur
Tanzmusik des Mittelalters', *Archiv für Musikwissenschaft*, 30 (1973), 81–95; Ernest Closson, *Le
Manuscrit dit des basses danses de la bibliothèque de Bourgogne* (Brussels, 1912); Daniel Heartz,
'The Basse Dance: Its Evolution circa 1450 to 1550', *Annales musicologiques*, 6 (1958–63),
287–340.

[74] Erika Schneiter, 'Tanz in der historischen Musikpraxis', *Basler Jahrbuch für historische
Musikpraxis*, 10 (1986), 245–64.

Here the longa serves as a unit of movement, corresponding to a double pace in the dance. The notation could be treated as the upper voice and the basis for variation, or as a tenor voice, surrounded polyphonically by discant and countratenor parts. The latter, artistically more demanding procedure was the preferred practice of accompanying trios or quartets, consisting of woodwind and brass instruments. Only town or court musicians, versed in mensural music, were capable of the like. Intabulations of 'branles', 'gaillardes', 'pauanes' in scores for keyboard or plucked instruments, stylized adaptations of dance pieces such as the 'Peacock's Tail' (*Pfauenschwanz*) in the Glogau Songbook, or an 'Aragonian' (*Arragonier*) in the Buxheim Organ Book (fos. 21 and 65) broaden the range, as do adaptations of dance melodies in, for example, the *Missa La basse danse* of Guillaume Faugues or in compositions of Johannes Martini, such as *Nenciozza mia* or the *Missa Coda de pavon*, or the early French parody noel, *c.*1530.[75] By this point in time dance music had achieved an emancipated position as an autonomous instrumental genre in the field of *musica composita*.[76]

---

[75] Guillaume Faugues, *Gesamtausgabe der Werke*, ed. George C. Schuetze (New York, 1960), 47 ff.; *New Grove*, xi. 727; Adrienne Fried Block, *The Early French Parody Noël* (Ann Arbor, 1983), 80.

[76] More details are to be found in Walter Salmen, *Tanz und Tanzen vom Mittelalter bis zur Renaissance* (Hildesheim, 1999) and id., *Spielfrauen im Mittelalter* (Hildesheim, 2000).

V

POLYPHONIC MUSIC IN
CENTRAL EUROPE, *c.*1300–*c.*1520

By TOM R. WARD

INTRODUCTION

THE fifteenth century saw the rapid development of musical institutions and the expansion of musical activity in the region east of the
Rhine and north of the Alps, specifically that part of Europe now
made up of Germany, Poland, the Czech Republic, and Austria (see
Map 4). The picture of this region during the fifteenth century found
in much of the literature of music history of the twentieth century is
generally that it is backward, undeveloped, and well behind the times
in comparison with northern France, the Italian city-states, and
England. In terms of the totality of musical activity in each of these
areas and significant figures in the development of music in the fifteenth century, this view is somewhat accurate—there was more activity and there were more major composers in other parts of Europe.
Unfortunately, this view has, until quite recently, also influenced
research to the extent that only in the last two decades have scholars
begun to identify the composers, repertories, and institutions of the
region that did indeed exist and thrive during the fifteenth century.
Recent research has shown that this region, while not possessing a
musical life the equal of that found in major centres in northern
France or in Italy, did have developed musical institutions and a significant number of people engaged in the composition, performance,
and discussion of music. These institutions (and in some cases, private
individuals) were aware of the works of the major composers of the
period rather soon after their creation. In addition, indigenous musical
forms and styles, some of which intentionally adopted or retained
relatively simple and, in some cases, archaic practices, continued to be
cultivated throughout the fifteenth century, and in some regions even
into the sixteenth. By the second half of the century, however, the
court of the Emperor and, slightly later, other courts, such as that of

the Elector of Saxony, had achieved positions of prominence, in terms of repertory performed and composers resident, that were on a par with the major centres of France and Italy.

The view of the period has been, understandably, coloured by the sources that have transmitted the repertory of the period to us. In a general way, these can be divided into two categories: those exclusively concerned with polyphonic music and those primarily concerned with monophony, but including a small number of compositions for more than one voice. The major polyphonic sources generally have, in addition, certain features characteristic of the region—mixed sacred and secular repertory, a high incidence of contrafacta, particularly substitution of Latin, or less frequently of German, for French secular texts, and musical and liturgical compositional types exclusively or more frequently encountered in this region than elsewhere, for example the cantio and the Proper of the Mass. The mixed mono-phonic/polyphonic manuscripts have a much more varied content. Some, such as the Wolkenstein manuscripts,[1] contain almost exclusively secular music. Others, such as Vyšší Brod V 42, are a mixture of standard Mass and Office genres and devotional texts, the latter in both Latin and the vernacular. Finally, by the end of the period, manuscripts, particularly those compiled in Bohemia, show a much greater propensity to retain works by composers active two or more generations earlier than do manuscripts compiled at the same time in France or Italy.

There are, however, additional means to discover more of the musical repertory cultivated in the region. Besides the music manuscripts, there are a number of treatises on music theory that use real compositions as examples for musical forms or notational devices. Many of the compositions included in these treatises are found in manuscripts originating in the region, but those that can only be identified through concordances in sources from other parts of Europe must be considered as once having been available. By considering all these works one can put together a relatively significant number of compositions that were enough a part of musical life in central Europe to have been usable as examples in writings about music. Through an investigation of the contents of these musical sources and of the individuals and institutions of the period, a picture of the musical life of the region results that is characterized by the cultivation of both 'native and foreign' polyphony and the production of

---

[1] Vienna, Österreichische Nationalbibliothek, MS 2777 and Innsbruck, Universitätsbibliothek, MS without signature. Both have been published in facsimile: *Oswald von Wolkenstein, Abbildungen zur Überlieferung*, i: *Die Innsbrucker Wolkenstein-Handschrift B*, ed. H. Moser and U. Müller (Litterae, 12; Göppingen, 1972), and *Oswald von Wolkenstein, Handschrift A: Vollständige Faksimile-Ausgabe des Codex Vindobonensis 2777 der Österreichischen Nationalbibliothek* (Codices Selecti, 59; Graz, 1977).

native monophonic forms in the context of institutions that share traits with their western European counterparts, while retaining their own unique features.

MUSICAL REPERTORIES AND INSTITUTIONS OF THE EARLIER FIFTEENTH CENTURY

Musical repertories current at the beginning of the century can be identified in manuscript collections from the east, south, and west of the region. These are comparatively few in number and, for the most part, small in size and extraordinarily varied in nature, ranging from the South-Bohemian cantional Vyšší Brod, Klásterní Knihovna, MS V 42, and Warsaw, Biblioteka Narodowa, MSS III.8054 and F.I.378, to the Wolkenstein codices from the Tyrol and the Strasburg Bibliothèque municipale MS 222 C 22 from the region around Basle. The first and fourth items in this list are primarily sources of monophonic song, sacred and secular, respectively. The second and third manuscripts contain Mass movements by leading composers of the period, Ciconia, Grossin, and Antonio Zacara da Teramo, along with similar works by a native Pole, Nicolaus of Radom. The last introduces a repertory that includes works by German composers of the region of its origin alongside works of major western European composers of the early fifteenth century. Examination of the repertory contained in these manuscripts can thus give a broad overview of the kinds of music being created and imported into central Europe and of the nature of the activities of musical institutions there during the first decades of the century.

Besides the collections of music, precious evidence of musical practices in the early part of the century exists in a number of musical treatises.[2] The treatises come from several different places, but share important traits apart from the repertory of works used as examples. The notational system is, in principle, identical with French mensural

---

[2] See the lists in Tom R. Ward, 'A Central European Repertory in Munich, Bayerische Staatsbibliothek, Clm 14274', *EMH* 1 (1981), 324–43; Martin Staehelin, 'Beschreibungen und Beispiele musikalischer Formen in einem unbeachteten Traktat des frühen 15. Jahrhunderts', *Archiv für Musikwissenschaft*, 31 (1974), 237–42; Lorenz Welker, 'Ein anonymer Mensuraltraktat in der Sterzinger Miszellaneen-Handschrift', *Archiv für Musikwissenschaft*, 48 (1991), 255–81; *Tractatulus de cantu mensurali seu figurato musice artis (Melk, Stiftsbibliothek, 950)*, ed. F. Alberto Gallo (CSM 16; Rome, 1971), 9–10, and Charles Brewer, 'The Introduction of the *Ars Nova* into East Central Europe: A Study of Late Medieval Polish Sources' (Ph.D. diss., City University of New York, 1984), 180–217. The treatise of Paulus Paulirinus has been published in part by Josef Reiss, 'Paulus Paulirinus de Praga Tractatus de musica (etwa 1460)', *Zeitschrift für Musikwissenschaft*, 7 (1924–5), 259–64, and Renata Mužíková, 'Pauli Paulirini de Praga Musica mensuralis', *Acta universitatis carolinae, Philosophica et historica*, 2 (1965), 57–87. The frequency with which works named in the treatises appear in Strasburg, Bibliothèque de la Ville, MS 222 C 22 and Prague, Státní Knihovna SSR—Universitní Knihovna, MS XI E 9 should be particularly noted.

notation of the fourteenth and fifteenth centuries.[3] The treatises as a
group provide definitions for common genres, such as motet, rondeau,
virelai, and ballade, as well as for less common ones like trumpetum,
khatschetum (facetum), rotulum, stampania (stampetum [estampie]),
and fuga. For these works the anonymous authors provide specific
compositions as examples, many of which can be traced to manuscript
sources of the period, in some cases to a particular group of copies
of the particular composition. For example, the ballade *A discort*
appears as an example of this type of song, but with the text *Virginem
mire* in two treatises, and is cited by both texts in a third. It is also
found with the latter text in several music manuscripts copied in
central Europe.[4] The musical examples for the treatises demonstrate
chronological layers in the penetration of Western European music.
The Harburg/Philadelphia treatise uses primarily works by Machaut
for its examples.[5] The other treatises use a slightly later repertory, with
some of the works datable in the last quarter of the fourteenth century
and possibly in the first decades of the fifteenth.[6] Thus, while there is
no reason to believe that Machaut's service to the Luxembourgs ever
brought him to central Europe, his music clearly was known there,
possibly transmitted through intermediaries in the court. The music
included as examples in the other treatises is a cross-section of French
and possibly one or two Italian works, many of which are among the
most widely known compositions of the period.

Other evidence of now lost sources is provided by some of the contrafacta of Oswald von Wolkenstein and other creators of contrafacta
in the region. Oswald was a member of the Tyrolean nobility in the
service of King Sigismund, and, as such, he travelled widely (including Constance and parts of France) and was thus in contact with many
of the leading centres of political power and cultivation of the arts.
His music and poetry were well known in his lifetime and, thanks to
the manuscript anthologies he had prepared, to us as well. In one very
important regard, he is different from the other, largely anonymous,

---

[3] That theorists in central Europe were concerned with both French and Italian music and
notation is shown in the verse treatise Michaelbeuern, Bibliothek des Benediktinerstiftes, Codex
man. cart. 95, which distinguishes between the two and which was prepared in 1369 in the environs of the University of Prague. See Renate Federhofer-Königs, 'Ein Anonymer Musiktraktat
aus der 2. Hälfte des 14. Jahrhunderts in der Stiftsbibliothek Michaelbeuern/Salzburg', *Kirchenmusikalisches Jahrbuch*, 46 (1962), 43–60.

[4] See Ward, 'Central European', 330–1.

[5] See the editions by Andres Briner, 'Ein anonymer unvollständiger Musiktraktat des 15.
Jahrhunderts in Philadelphia, USA', *Kirchenmusikalisches Jahrbuch*, 50 (1966), 27–44 for the
treatise on monophony and a description of the other contents of the manuscript, and Staehelin, 'Beschreibungen und Beispiele', for an edition of the treatise on forms and identification of
the works cited.

[6] See Ward, 'Central European', 328–9.

makers of contrafacta in the second through fifth decades of the fifteenth century. They preferred Latin sacred texts to German secular
ones, and their works, with very few exceptions, seem to have had
limited circulation. Oswald, on the other hand, produced musical settings of poetry that may have been the primary influence for the development of German song, a genre that became a staple of the secular
repertory and continued to be cultivated long after the practice of
making Latin contrafacta had disappeared.

The early view of the absence of a tradition of performance of
Western European art music in central Europe lead to the assumption
that Oswald could only have learned of the polyphonic works he
retexted during his travels. More recent research has uncovered additional examples of contrafacta among his polyphonic works and, at
the same time, has demonstrated that the reading Oswald used is
without exception closer to a central European source than to a
western European one, when concordant readings from both areas
exist. Oswald's method in setting his words to existing songs involved
texting the tenor rather the superius and frequent modifications of the
music itself, particularly subdividing longer notes to fit the text. This
means that it is extremely unlikely that the central European concordant copies could have been created from Oswald's works, and that
Oswald must have used a central European copy of each of these
works as his model. Because of the chronology established for the texts
and for the copying of the two principal sources of his music, it can
be shown that some copy of the composition, no longer in existence,
but predating any preserved copy, must have served as his model and
must have remained available to others involved in the line of transmission of the work in this region.

The resultant picture is of a region with a number of centres of the
practice of music, both monophonic and polyphonic, and of practitioners who were knowledgeable about the practice of Western
European music and were familiar with works by both major and
minor figures of the era. A significant number of these people seem
to have been associated with monasteries such as St. Emmeram in
Regensburg,[7] or with universities in Vienna[8] and Leipzig.[9] Others, like

[7] See Ward, 'Central European', and Ian Rumbold, 'The Compilation and Ownership of the
"St Emmeram" Codex (Munich, Bayerische Staatsbibliothek, Clm 14274)', *EMH* 2 (1982),
164–235 on Hermann Pötzlinger.

[8] See the discussions of the university statutes in Josef Mantuani, *Die Musik in Wien: Von
der Römerzeit bis zur Zeit des Kaisers Max I.* (Geschichte der Stadt Wien, iii/1; Vienna, 1907;
repr. Hildesheim, 1979), 281–90.

[9] See my 'Music in the Library of Johannes Klein', in John Kmetz (ed.), *Music in the
German Renaissance: Sources, Styles and Contexts* (Cambridge, 1994), 54–73, and 'Music in the
University: Leipzig, Universitätsbibliothek, MS 1084', in Martin Staehelin (ed.), *Gestalt und*

Wolkenstein, were members of secular courts, such as the Imperial court or the Tyrolean court at Innsbruck.[10] In fact, the line between monastic and university traditions is a difficult one to draw. Many of the important members of both the Augustinian[11] and Benedictine orders had studied in Prague or Vienna and later in Kraków or Leipzig. Some of the theory treatises are preserved in collections of texts of various kinds, in some cases implying the sort of collection apt for a member of a university community—texts on mathematics and astronomy—or of a religious community: collections of sermons or other religious writings. In addition, many people moved freely within church, university, court, and civic institutions, finding employment in one instance because of musical skill and in another because education enabled service at court.[12] During the first decades of the century, in the period during which the major courts were making only the first steps towards establishing chapels capable of regular performance of polyphonic music, this art was practised in schools and monasteries.

THE BOHEMIAN CANTIO

A monastic manuscript whose contents represent some of the earliest copies of polyphonic works in the fifteenth century is Vyšší Brod V 42.[13] It was copied in 1410 by a member of that Cistercian community named Pribik who also copied several other books for the monastery during this period. The repertory contained is rather heterogeneous: antiphons and responsories for processions, Mass Ordinaries (many with locally common tropes and including mensural Credos), alleluias, prefaces and responses for Mass, settings of the Benedicamus Domino with tropes, sequences, devotional songs for Mary (called 'antiphonae seu cantica'), and cantiones in both Latin and Czech. The manuscript also contains thirteen works that are wholly or partially set for two voices. This mixture of chant having specific Mass or Office assignment with cantiones and devotional texts for Mary and other saints, as well as the mixture of languages and of notational forms (the cantiones use mensural forms; the other works

Entstehung musikalischer Quellen im 15. und 16. Jahrhundert (Wolfenbüttler Forschungen, 83; Quellenstudien zur Musik der Renaissance III; Wiesbaden, 1998), 21–34.

   [10] Strohm, *Rise*, 252–3 and 518–20.

   [11] On possible musical activities in the Augustinian St Dorothy cloister in Vienna, see Reinhard Strohm, 'Native and Foreign Polyphony in Late Medieval Austria', *Musica disciplina*, 38 (1984), 205–30.

   [12] Hermann Edlerawer provides a good example of someone with connections to university, church, and court and the city in Vienna. See Rumbold, 'Compilation', 169–76.

   [13] A facsimile edition with an index and discussion of the contents is *Die Hohenfurter Liederhandschrift (H 42) von 1410: Facsimileausgabe*, ed. Hans Rothe (Cologne, 1984).

German chant notation), and of monophony and polyphony is typical of many manuscripts of this period from this region, but is not commonly found in those from western Europe.

The proper items taken from the standard liturgy for the Mass and Office represent only portions of the services for major feasts, with particular emphasis on Mary and the Easter season. Mass Ordinary settings are, on the other hand, rather numerous, possibly implying that these were more frequently sung by the intended owner of the manuscript than were Mass Propers and antiphons and responsories of the Office.

The cantiones in this and other manuscripts can be rather diverse in origin and form.[14] Ordinarily a cantio is a rhymed and strophic text clearly related to a particular feast or season, but without a fixed place in the liturgy. The cantiones may have stronger ties to the laity than to the clergy, and they are less regular and more diverse in origin than liturgical chant. Many seem to have been derived from Benedicamus Domino tropes with the specific omission of the line(s) containing the words identifying the source. Others seem to have been originally conductus intended to be performed as the Lector moved to his place to deliver a reading and include phrases such as 'Lector lego'. Still others may have originated as tropes, such as *Dies est letitiae*, which occurs as a Gloria trope. A large number of later works seem to have come into existence as strophic poems, much like hymns, but lacking a doxology.

The majority of the cantiones use rhyme and regular line scansion. A number also have a formal structure not unlike that of the ballade: two lines (or pairs of lines), each identified as a verse, are sung to a repeated musical phrase to form the first section; this is followed by a repetitio that has a new phrase, followed by a repetition or variation of the first phrase. In a few cases only the first phrase of the first section is notated. Other cantiones have no internal repetitions. Additional text for the first section and occasionally alternative texts for the repetitio are usually written beneath the music. Several of these texts (and their Czech paraphrases/translations) are found in polyphonic settings with some frequency later in this period.[15] At the beginning of the century the content of a cantionale tends to be similar in both German-speaking regions and Bohemia. These similarities tend to dwindle during the century as the Bohemian cantionale,

---

[14] Karl Heinz Schlager, 'Cantionale', in *Geschichte der katholischen Kirchenmusik*, ed. K. G. Fellerer, 2 vols. (Kassel, 1972), 286–93 provides a clear summary of the genre.

[15] See e.g. the settings of *Cedit hiems eminus* listed in RISM B/iv.3–4 along with variant Latin and Czech texts.

under the influence of both Hussite and Utraquist practice, tends more and more towards cantiones with Czech text and a repertory with many more texts than tunes, leading to multiple texting and instructions that a text is to be sung to a particular melody.

The variety of styles within the monophonic repertory is paralleled by differences among the polyphonic works. Two use chant notation in score in an organal style. The others use mensural notation, in some cases with separate voices on separate lines, in others with both voices on a single stave distinguished by ink colour.[16] The polyphonic compositions also vary as to whether the entire work or only a portion is set for two voices. In the cantiones, this may involve only momentary separation into two voices at cadences, as shown in Ex. 5.1, the first phrase of *Sampsonis honestissima*, a cantio for Easter. The melisma on the first syllable is embellished by a two-voice cadence.

The setting of the entire first text line which follows is *a 2*, and the final line is set in the manner of the first, dividing into two voices for the last five breves. Other cantiones use comparatively more or less two-part writing: *Surrexit Christus hodie* (fo. 151ᵛ) is written on two staves with the rubrics 'superior nota' and 'inferior [nota]'. *Resurrexit Dominus* is written in parallel fifths except for the setting of the first two and last words. The notation is often quite ambiguous; in *En etas iam aurea* voices appear to be written successively in red and black for at least two phrases, and alignment of the red and black notes is elsewhere not at all clear. The contrapuntal style is one that seems to both allow parallels and to prefer contrary motion, with writing of the latter sort the more common, particularly at cadences.

The implication for all these cantiones is that most of the work is sung in unison by the two performers with divisions into two voices as indicated. The nature of the two-voice sections, particularly those involving cadences, is such that one might hypothesize that in actual practice the pieces included more two-voice writing than explicitly notated. For example, *Dywo flagrans numine* begins with the melisma *d′ c′ e′ c′ d′* (B SB SB B B). A red breve *e′* appears above the fourth note. This sort of momentary cadential embellishment could have been inserted in performance of other works that are notated here as monophony.

A few of the works in this manuscript are also found in later sources from Bohemia, often in slightly modified form. They represent, however, along with the monophonic cantiones and the mensural Mass and Office chants, a distinctive tradition that will continue to

---

[16] The use of red ink to distinguish an additional voice is listed as one of the functions of red notes in the Breslau Anonymous. See Johannes Wolf, 'Ein Breslauer Mensuraltraktat des 15. Jahrhunderts', *Archiv für Musikwissenschaft*, 1 (1918–19), 329–45, at 337.

Ex. 5.1. *Sampsonis honestissima resurgentis cum gloria*. Vyšší Brod, Klásterní Knihovna, MS 42, fos. 152ᵛ–153ʳ

appear in sources from this region throughout the fifteenth and sixteenth centuries. The cantionale became, in effect, a kind of collection of works of a general nature, borrowing at times from the Graduale or Antiphonale, but most importantly including relatively new texts and music whose specific function, when it can be determined, often fell outside, or better, alongside the regular liturgy. The number of these books preserved from the fifteenth and sixteenth centuries is very large and their contents have yet to be systematically studied or inventoried.[17]

OSWALD VON WOLKENSTEIN

A significant representative of German secular song in this period was Oswald von Wolkenstein. He has been called the 'last Minnesinger', but this term does not fully capture his position as a transitional figure between medieval Minnesang and the Tenorlied. Oswald's life centred around his native Tyrol, but included extensive travels as a youth, going as far as the Holy Land, and as an adult in the service of King Sigismund through much of western Europe, including the Council of Constance, and much of central Europe. Some of his texts provide biographical details or are on topics readily relatable to his life. He

---

[17] See below, n. 83.

was sufficiently self-aware of his place as poet and composer that he had manuscripts of his works compiled.

His 133 songs include thirty-seven for two or more voices.[18] His monophonic songs, composed throughout his life, show a wide variety of styles, ranging from works in chant-like notation to highly rhythmic mensural works. His text setting is largely syllabic, with frequent use of melismas at phrase beginnings and endings. He provided a number of his monophonic songs with additional poems.

Fifteen of his thirty-seven polyphonic songs are contrafacta of works by other composers, and the recent identification of four of these sheds significant light on Oswald's sources for music and his technique in adding his own newly created texts.[19] Oswald's readings of all the contrafacta are clearly related to versions found in central European sources, and the new identifications show that he followed this practice throughout his creative life. How these songs came to be known to him is not absolutely clear. Early opinions, based on the assumption that Austria had little or no musical activity in this period, held that Oswald had to have come to know these works during his travels over much of western Europe. More recent research, showing the relationships among readings of these works,[20] has demonstrated that he could have acquired this music without the travel. There is also the possibility that for some of the music Oswald himself was the conduit in the line of transmission.

His treatment of his models is of interest not only for its own sake, but also for later developments in German song. In addition to retexting the superius of the borrowed music, that is the voice carrying the text in the original work, Oswald often added his poetry to the tenor voice, subdividing values where necessary to fit all of the new and longer text. (The breaking up of longer values to accommodate text also occurs in *Virginem mire*, a contrafactum frequently encountered in this region.) Assignment of the text to the tenor voice is even more

---

[18] The songs have been edited by Karl Kurt Klein and Walter Salmen in *Die Lieder Oswalds von Wolkenstein* (Altdeutsche Textbibliothek, 55; Tübingen, 1962). An edition of the polyphonic songs with readings from concordant sources is found in Ivana Pelnar, *Die mehrstimmigen Lieder Oswalds von Wolkenstein*, 2 vols. (Münchner Veröffentlichungen zur Musikgeschichte, 32; Tutzing, 1982).

[19] Lorenz Welker, 'New Light on Oswald von Wolkenstein: Central European Traditions and Burgundian Polyphony', *EMH* 7 (1987), 187–226 summarizes the prior literature on contrafacta in Oswald's oeuvre and adds two new identifications of works by Grenon and Fontaine, composers contemporary with Oswald, in contrast to the previously known contrafacta of late 14th-c. works. David Fallows, 'Two Equal Voices: A French Song Repertory with Music for Two New Works of Oswald von Wolkenstein', *EMH* 7 (1987), 226–41 provides identification of two additional models from the post-1420 repertory.

[20] Erika Timm, *Die Überlieferung der Lieder Oswalds von Wolkenstein* (Germanische Studien, 242; Lübeck, 1972).

common among the works that have not as yet been identified as contrafacta. This habit established a texture of a texted tenor with surrounding instrumental parts (or in the frequent two-voice settings, with a higher instrumental part), a texture to be encountered again in the Tenorlied repertory of the later fifteenth century.

Oswald's practice of retexting existing music is one that will be found throughout the fifteenth century in central European sources. The reasons for this practice are not at all clear, but the number of compositions involved is considerable. A few of these works involve replacing one Latin sacred text with another. The most common occurrence, however, is that a French or Italian secular work will appear with a Latin text. Martin Staehelin has suggested that the use of Latin may be due to two factors: French was not well known during the period in central Europe, and many of the scribes involved in the production of these manuscripts had church or university connections that would have given them a high level of familiarity with Latin.[21]

THE IMPERIAL CHAPEL BEFORE 1450

The Holy Roman Empire of the German Nation controlled central Europe and the region that is now modern Germany throughout the Middle Ages and Renaissance. Originally seen as the secular counterpart of the papacy and claiming holdings on both sides of the Alps, the Empire was by the fifteenth century limited to northern Europe and from the 1430s onward the title was a hereditary one for the Habsburg family, although the seven Electors did continue to meet and vote. The far-flung nature of the Empire, and the presence within it of secular authorities who could and often did assert their independence, meant that the Emperor often resided in various cities according to the needs of the moment. These included Vienna and Wiener Neustadt in the hereditary Habsburg lands, but also, at various times, Augsburg and Innsbruck.

The earliest evidence for the existence of a musical chapel serving the Imperial court comes from the period of the Council of Basle, a council existing under Imperial guarantees with which the court maintained ongoing contact.[22] It also seems very likely that the initial recruitment of musicians for the Imperial chapel took place at the council itself. Johannes Brassart, who had served in the papal chapel

---

[21] 'Zur Begründung der Kontrafakturpraxis in deutschen Musikhandschriften des 15. und frühen 16. Jahrhunderts', in *Florilegium musicologicum: Hellmut Federhofer zum 75. Geburtstag* (Mainzer Studien zur Musikwissenschaft, 21; Tutzing, 1988), 389–96.

[22] Strohm, *Rise*, 251–3.

in 1431 and in the chapel of the Council of Basle from June 1433,[23] may have entered the service of Sigismund as early as 1432,[24] but is first mentioned as serving the Emperor on 10 December 1434.[25] Two motets provide further evidence of his service in this chapel as well as information concerning the other members of the chapel.[26] His *O Rex Friderice* celebrates Friedrich III as King of the Germans. The motet *Romanorum Rex* on the death of King Albrecht II in 1439 by Johannes de Sarto[27] names Erasmus Adam, Johannes Tirion, Johannes Martin, and Johannes Galer, in addition to himself and Brassart, as members of the chapel. Both of these compositions are large, isorhythmic motets, the performance of which would require the services of rather capable singers, an indication that by the 1430s and 1440s the Imperial chapel had been developed to provide musical performances on a level appropriate to the political position of its patron. Published documents concerning Brassart imply that the primary function of the chapel was the performance of Mass and Office.[28]

This supposition finds support in the repertory of music by Brassart and de Sarto that has been preserved in manuscripts copied in Basle and in or near the Imperial court.[29] These works include a number of Introits and Mass Ordinary movements, music that seems to have been preferred for the celebration of the Mass liturgy at the Imperial chapel. These works, in their use of chant as the basis for the superius in a treble-dominated setting and fauxbourdon, are not at all unlike the works of similar function by leading composers like Dufay and Binchois. If these works were indeed written for the Imperial chapel, it had reached an important stage of development by the 1430s—it was performing the same sort of polyphonic settings based on the corresponding chants of the Mass as was any other major

[23] Keith E. Mixter, 'Johannes Brassart: A Bibliographical and Biographical Study', *Musica disciplina*, 18 (1964), 37–62; 19 (1965), 99–108.

[24] Hellmut Federhofer, 'Die Niederländer an den Habsburgerhöfen in Österreich', *Anzeiger der phil.-hist. Klasse der österreichischen Akademie der Wissenschaften*, 7 (1956) (Mitteilungen der Kommission für Musikforschung, 6; Vienna, 1956), 102–20 at 102–5.

[25] Mixter, 'Johannes Brassart', 48–9.

[26] For a discussion of these works see ibid. 55–8.

[27] See *A Correspondence of Renaissance Musicians*, ed. Bonnie J. Blackburn, Edward E. Lowinsky, and Clement A. Miller (Oxford, 1991), 663–4.

[28] See the letter by Friedrich to Bishop Johann Loos of Liège in which he requested preference in the award of benefices for members of his chapel who came from the diocese of Liège and for Brassart to hold positions in absentia. In the course of the letter reference is made to serving the king in performance of the Mass and Hours. See Mixter, 'Johannes Brassart', 59–60.

[29] These include: Aosta, Seminario maggiore, MS 15 (olim A 1° D 19): see Marian Cobin, 'The Aosta Manuscript' (Ph.D. diss., New York University, 1979); Trent 92 I: see Tom R. Ward, 'The Structure of Manuscript Trent 92-I', *Musica disciplina*, 29 (1975), 127–47; and Trent 87 and 92 II: See Peter Wright, 'The Related Parts of the Trent Museo Provinciale d'Arte, Mss 82 (1374) and 92 (1379): A Paleographical and Text-Critical Study' (Ph.D. diss., University of Nottingham, 1986).

chapel. In fact, the Introits attributable to Brassart and de Sarto could be viewed as representing a portion of a larger collection of chant-based settings of the Introit, a collection that might have spanned the liturgical year in the manner of Dufay's hymn cycle. If this is so, the existence of such a collection in the repertory of the Imperial chapel can be taken as an indication that the chapel habitually sang the Introit and some or all of the Ordinary in polyphonic settings as early as the 1440s. The preservation of this music in manuscripts that may have come into existence in close proximity to the chapel and thus may contain some of its music is significant.[30] Similar kinds of repertory, but more complex musically and more extensive in their inclusion of settings of other Propers of the Mass, form a prominent part of the contents of the Trent manuscripts 88–91 and 93, regarded by some as presenting the repertory of the Imperial chapel during the middle portion of the fifteenth century.[31]

Additional evidence for the cultivation of the performance of polyphonic music can be drawn from other manuscripts compiled during the 1430s and 1440s. Johannes Lupi, who was later active in Trent, copied much of Trent 87 and the latter part of Trent 92 in Austria, possibly while in the service of Duke Friedrich IV, Count of Tyrol.[32] Lupi may also have owned Trent 92-I, which contains music that may have originated in or around Basle and which in any case contains music that can be connected to that area. It also contains a complete and several partial plenary Masses, further indication of the cultivation of composition of both Mass Ordinary and Mass Proper in the German-Austrian region.

PÖTZLINGER'S MUSIC COLLECTION: A CROSS-SECTION OF EUROPEAN MUSIC

A major portion of the manuscript Munich, Bayerische Staatsbibliothek, clm 14274 has been shown to have been copied by its original owner, Hermann Pötzlinger, during the period including and immediately following his student years in Vienna from 1436 until 1439, that is, between 1436 and the early 1440s.[33] Its contents provide a

---

[30] See Ward, 'Trent 92-I'.

[31] See Adelyn Peck Leverett, 'A Paleographical and Repertorial Study of the Manuscript Trento, Castello del Buon Consiglio, 91 (1378)' (Ph.D. diss., Princeton University, 1990).

[32] See Peter Wright, 'On the Origins of Trent 87$_1$ and 92$_2$', *EMH* 6 (1986), 245–70, esp. 255–9, and Strohm, *Rise*, 251–4, for discussion of several of the manuscripts and composers mentioned here.

[33] Rumbold, 'Compilation', esp. 204–5. Rumbold's suggestion that Pötzlinger may have remained in Vienna after 1439 would be consistent with the practice of recent degree recipients remaining at the university to lecture during the period immediately following completion of the degree.

microcosmic view of the kinds of music in circulation in Vienna in the second quarter of the fifteenth century. This collection reinforces the impression of the repertory of sacred music of the Imperial chapel gained from the preserved output of Brassart and de Sarto, suggests that services in which polyphony was performed included Vespers as well as Mass, and perhaps implies that polyphony was cultivated in other Austrian institutions as well. The manuscript not only includes nearly 100 independent Mass Ordinary[34] and Mass Proper settings as well as two settings of the Responses of the Mass, but also shows that the Magnificat, hymns, and Psalms were also a part of the sacred performance tradition.

The more than 270 compositions copied into this book are representative of three distinct repertories of music present in central Europe during the 1430s: (i) works by major composers active in France and/or Italy; (ii) works by central European composers in a style clearly derived from that of the works in category (i), and (iii) works in a musical style native to central Europe, often using notational devices peculiar to this region. The composers represented in group (i) include the major composers of the 1430s, Guillaume Dufay, Gilles Binchois, John Dunstaple, and Leonel Power, as well as a number of less prominent French and Italian musicians. In this regard, this portion of the manuscript's contents differs little from that found in other major sources of the period, no matter what their place of origin. In addition, the works of these composers seem to have become available to Pötzlinger and his collaborators very soon after their composition. For example, Dufay's *Supremum est mortalibus* is generally assumed to have been composed in 1433 in celebration of a treaty between Eugene IV and Sigismund.[35] It appears to have been copied into Munich 14274 in 1440 or 1441, less than a decade after its creation.[36] The manuscript, however, also carries a characteristic sign of central European musical sources from this period: it is much more inclusive of much earlier music than are manuscripts copied outside central Europe during the 1430s. It includes music by the fourteenth-century composers Machaut, Landini, and Vaillant, composers not represented in a manuscript copied about a decade earlier, Bologna,

---

[34] At least one cyclic Mass, that on *Rex saeculorum* attributed to both Dunstaple and Power, appears, but in the form of a single movement. Thus, the cyclic Mass Ordinary seems to have been available, but was seemingly not recognized as an entity in this period. The scribe of Trent 92-I, when he was assembling Introit/Mass Ordinary cycles for this manuscript, separated movements of this Mass and assigned them to different cycles. See Ward, 'Trent 92-I', 129–33.

[35] Charles Hamm, *A Chronology of the Works of Dufay Based on a Study of Mensural Practice* (Princeton, 1964), 57.

[36] Rumbold, 'Compilation', 201 gives a date of 1440 for the paper of folios 107–9 on which the piece appears.

Civico Museo Bibliografico Musicale, Q 15, a manuscript that otherwise includes a very similar repertory by French and Italian composers. This tendency to retain older music in what appears to be the
active repertory is characteristic of central European sources through
much of the fifteenth century. The sense of a current repertory seems
to develop in Austria by the 1460s, but, as will be shown below, only
sometime after 1500 in Bohemia.

There is also a sizeable group of works by composers known to have
been active in central Europe, or in some cases, known only by the
attribution to them of works preserved in central European sources.
For all save two of these, the music is the only knowledge we have of
their activity.[37] The majority of these compositions are clearly modelled on the works of contemporary French composers, particularly
Dufay, and, while they are certainly not of the same artistic quality,
they are competent compositions. Among these composers, Hermann
Edlerawer is the only one whose life can be traced in any detail.[38]
His name first appears in the 1413–14 matriculation lists of the University of Vienna, probably indicating a birthdate just prior to the turn
of the century. His place of origin is given as Mainz and he is assessed
the maximum matriculation fee, ordinarily a sign that the student
comes from a somewhat well-to-do family. There are documents providing information about Edlerawer from this point until 1457. Some
simply indicate his presence in the city of Vienna, but others show that
he had gained a variety of positions and privileges. In 1427 he was
granted a coat of arms by King Sigismund, a grant renewed and
coupled with the right to appoint ten notaries in 1431. This latter type
of grant appears to have been a common method of augmenting the
income of members of the court—the grantee could extract a fee from
each of the notaries he appointed. The possession of a coat of arms
and a seal bearing these arms lead to the existence of several documents for which Edlerawer served as witness or for which he provided
his seal. One of these, dated 1437, also informs us that he was in the
employ (*diener*) of Duke Albrecht V of Austria. This connection
can be established, if not defined, as early as 1434 by the appearance of Edlerawer's name on the back of a letter sent on to the
court by its original addressee, Francesco Foscari, Doge of Venice,
from Austrian pilgrims to the Holy Land imprisoned in Cairo. This

---

[37] Details concerning these composers may be found in Rumbold, 'Compilation', and Dagmar
Braunschweig-Pauli, 'Studien zum sogenannten Codex St. Emmeram: Entstehung, Datierung
und Besitzer der Handschrift München, Bayerische Staatsbibliothek, Clm 14274 (olim Mus. ms.
3232a)', *Kirchenmusikalisches Jahrbuch*, 66 (1982), 1–48.

[38] Documents concerning his life are discussed and reproduced in Rumbold, 'Compilation',
169–76 and 210–14.

connection with the Imperial court continued after the accession of Friedrich IV, as is shown by the granting of a *littera familiaritatis* in 1444. In the meantime, documents show that Edlerawer had acquired the position of cantor in the cathedral of St Stephen's by 1439 and that he held the position until at least 1443. Later documents show him enjoying positions of some responsibility within the city of Vienna and in the employ of Count Ulrich II of Cili and Reinprecht von Wallsee.

Hermann Edlerawer, whom we know as a composer, seems then to have spent only approximately four years in a position having to do to some extent with the practice of music. Significantly, these four years coincide with the period of compilation of Munich 14274, the principal source for his music.[39] The position of cantor at St Stephen's appears to have had as much to do with administration and education as with music.[40] No one of the preserved works by Edlerawer can be shown to relate in any particular way to the cathedral, but all could have been used in the celebration of the liturgy there, or, given his other connections, in the Imperial chapel. Ian Rumbold rightly observes that the somewhat informal attribution of two works by the initials 'H. E.' might indicate a level of familiarity between the scribe and composer, or, possibly, the assumption that anyone in the immediate circle in which the work was being copied would be able instantly to resolve the abbreviation, a not unreasonable assumption if the scribe and likely users of the book were resident in Vienna. It should also be noted that the largest ornamental initial in the manuscript appears with his setting of *Que corda nostra*.[41]

Edlerawer's seven known works include three sequences, *Lauda Sion*, *Verbum bonum*, and *Sancti Spiritus assit nobis gratia*, a Communion, *Beata viscera*, a Kyrie, a Credo, and a textless work that appears to be secular. These compositions mirror the genres represented in Munich 14274: primarily music for the Mass, including both

---

[39] Edlerawer's output consists of seven works, all of which are found in Munich 14274 and only one of which has a concordant reading in another manuscript (his *Lauda Sion* appears in Trent 93 without attribution and is one of the works not copied into Trent 90). It should be noted here that Trent 93 also contains the only concordance for Petrus Wilhelmi's Kyrie found in Munich 14274—it was entered twice and was copied into Trent 90—and that it contains the only preserved work by Othmar Opilionis, one of the singers of the Archbishop of Kraków recorded in the matriculation lists of the University of Kraków. This could be dismissed as a fortuitous coincidence were it not for the number of instances in which compositions from this region seem to have 'travelled together'.

[40] The following is drawn from Rumbold, 'Compilation'.

[41] This may be fortuitous, but the descender of the letter 'Q' flows down the margin to the fifth of the seven staves on the leaf. The next largest initials have descenders reaching only the third stave. (Examples in Rumbold, 'Compilation', 196–7.) For most of the manuscript initial letters fill only the initial portion of the first stave of the voice, if they are in fact that large.

Proper and Ordinary, with secular music present in a lesser proportion, but without any vernacular text.[42] The musical style is likewise reflective of the works of the second category described above. Compositions are for two or three voices. Fauxbourdon appears with the ordinary indication and by implication: both the Patrem Dominicale and the setting of the even-numbered verses of *Sancti Spiritus* are written almost exclusively in parallel sixths with minimal rhythmic differentiation between the voices other than at cadences, precisely the behaviour of the notated voices of the eleventh verse of his *Lauda Sion* and his *Verbum bonum*, both of which have the fauxbourdon rubric. While simplistic, this sort of writing is found in much of the music 'a faux bourdon' that was produced by composers other than Guillaume Dufay. His three remaining works, all for two voices, are characterized by brief bits of imitation at the beginnings of phrases—every phrase of the textless work—and by differentiation in movement between the voices, both in direction and rhythmic activity.

Besides Edlerawer at least three additional composers are known either exclusively or primarily because of the preservation of their music in Munich 14274. These include B(W)iquardus who may be the Arnold Pikart who was employed in the Imperial chapel,[43] Urbanus Kungsperger, Sweikl (not Sweitzl, as the name occasionally appears in modern writings), Rudolffi, and Johannes Waring. Their music is like Edlerawer's in that it displays craftsmanship, if not artistry. But, in viewing this region in comparison with the rest of western Europe, this is about all that one can really expect to find in dealing with composers who were in some cases, such as Edlerawer's, engaged professionally in musical activities for only a portion of their careers. They are to be compared with the members of major chapels for whom we know only two or three compositions, not with Dufay and Binchois.

The third category of music found in Munich 14274 includes a number of works in a style and using a notation that is commonly encountered only in central European sources. The most readily recognizable aspect of this repertory is the mensuration signs used to indicate major and minor prolation: a vertical stroke followed by a vertical row of either three or two dots. This system of indicating mensuration is described in a number of music-theory treatises written in the region.[44] The system itself testifies to the existence of a distinct regional musical practice, testimony supported by the nature of the

---

[42] Other works provide only the secular incipit or the secular incipit and a complete Latin substitute text.

[43] Rumbold, 'Compilation', 176–7.

[44] See Ward, 'Central European Repertory', 328–9 for a list of the treatises and editions.

music in which it is used, much of which, because it moves almost exclusively in semibreves and minims, requires only the indication of prolation for performance. Other indicators of central European origin are the texts and, in some cases, associated cantus firmi. Finally, general aspects of musical style, gleaned, in part, from the characteristics of pieces identified using the other criteria, can imply a central European origin.

Music-theory texts describing this system for indicating the mensuration of a particular composition are relatively numerous. A core repertory of works showing the use of these signs has been established, and new discoveries have augmented this group of works. For present purposes, the appearance of this system in a particular composition is very helpful since this is not only an indication of central European origin, but also of copying no later than 1450 or 1460, when the system seems to have fallen out of use.[45] A number of compositions in Munich 14274 use the system, as do compositions found in three other manuscripts.[46]

Texts such as 'Cedit hiems eminus', 'Veni rerum conditor', or 'Jesus Christus nostra salus' are not found in French, English, or Italian sources of this period, whereas they appear frequently in central European ones.[47] A striking tradition of the texts set in this repertory is the abundance of settings that use the initial letters of the first few words to spell out a name (acrostic). A fondness for this textual device seems to be especially strong in the region, and the tradition has two distinct branches. One, by far the most frequently encountered, names the saint who is the subject of the poem. This type is particularly common with music for St Martin and St Nicholas, two saints whose veneration was not only extensive in this area, but also tied closely to popular religious practices. One also finds works for Thomas, Ignatius, and Paulus. A subset of this type presents a different sort of information related to the remainder of the text, e.g. 'Levat authentica zelorum agmina rectori vivo summo' (Munich 14274, fos. 51^v–52^r), spells Lazarus and appears in a Latin prelude to the text 'Christ der ist erstanden'. The Latin text tells a portion of the Easter story, but also includes references to the act of the singing of the story, the latter a trait not uncommon in some of these texts. The acrostic adds emphasis by linking the precursor Lazarus and the Resurrection. A final use of this literary device is as a signature, the common means used by

[45] According to the statement in Anonymous XII (CS iii. 483).

[46] Kraków, Biblioteka Jagiellońska, MS 2464; Warsaw, Biblioteka Narodowa, MS F.I.378, and Ústí nad Orlicí, Okresní Archív, MS A 3.

[47] See RISM B/iv.3–4.

Petrus Wilhelmi to sign his work, as will be seen below. This use of the device is indicated when the name spelt by the first letters of the opening words of the text does not directly or indirectly relate to the subject of the text.[48]

Melodic traditions are likewise distinctive in this region, for example, the employment of mensural chant as the cantus firmus in settings of the Mass Ordinary, particularly the Credo. Indeed, the setting in Munich 14274, fos. 44^v–45^r appears at first to be *a 2*, but closer examination shows that the cue in the tenor refers to a mensural Credo that appears in the second gathering of the manuscript among other Mass Ordinary chant melodies. The three voices begin in unison, separating on the fifth note. Since the Credo melody is mensural, it can be fitted into the texture without having to be redone in a new notation, as can be seen in Ex. 5.2. Recently composed, mensural chant for the Mass, particularly Credos, as well as mensural cantiones are an important portion of the monophonic repertory in central Europe and appear in significant numbers in several manuscripts from this region.[49]

A clear preference for composition for two voices is also a common feature of this repertory. In many cases this involves two composed parts, one of which may be based on a pre-existent melody. In a few cases the work involves the composition of a counterpoint to a chant cantus firmus that appears in chant notation. Munich 14274 contains in its third gathering a number of Kyries that demonstrate this practice. Interestingly, these are intermixed with several Kyries by Dufay. The *Kyrie fons bonitatis / Sacerdos summe* (fos. 30^v–31^r) provides a good example of locally produced music in the central European style. This piece, shown in Pl. XIII, has been characterized as 'heterophony but not polyphony' by Theodor Göllner.[50] The two voices share the same range and clef (c^3). One voice is notated in German chant notation, each sign of which has the value of a semibreve. The counterpoint uses solid mensural notation, semibreves and smaller values with longs as final pitches of phrases, and both voices employ the

---

[48] For example, the text 'Tonicat hylariter' (Berlin, Staatsbibliothek zu Berlin — Preußischer Kulturbesitz, MS Theol. Lat 4° 100, fo. 122^r) spells the name Thomas in the first six words of a text dealing with St Nicholas and is therefore probably a sign of authorship. The extraordinary popularity in central Europe of texts using this device requires additional investigation.

[49] See e.g. the so-called Tegernsee mensural Choralschrift (Munich, Bayerische Staatsbibliothek, clm 19558) or the many Credos listed in Tadeusz Miazga, *Die Melodien des einstimmigen Credo der römisch-katholischen lateinischen Kirche: Eine Untersuchung der Melodien in den handschriftlichen Überlieferungen mit besonderer Berücksichtigung der polnischen Handschriften* (Graz, 1976).

[50] Theodor Göllner, 'Critical Years in European Musical History: 1400–1450', *Report of the Tenth Congress of the IMS, Ljubljana, 1967* (Kassel, 1970), 60–6 at 62.

Ex. 5.2. Credo. Munich, Bayerische Staatsbibliothek, clm 14274, fos. 44ᵛ–45ʳ

characteristic prolation signs described in treatises on mensural music from this region. The counterpoint at times slavishly follows the cantus firmus so closely that it appears to be a simultaneous ornamented version of the chant melody. At other times, the counterpoint is clearly independent and proceeds primarily in contrary motion to the cantus firmus. The basis of this kind of counterpoint can be found, among other places, in the treatise 'Ad sciendum artem cantus',[51] which probably originated somewhere in the Austrian/Bavarian region in the mid-fifteenth century. The instructions for *contrapunctus fractus* work out

---

[51] Munich, Bayerische Staatsbibliothek, clm 24809, fo. 134ʳ⁻ᵛ and 16208, fos. 148ʳ–149ᵛ, in both instances as the third part of the anonymous treatise. In the former copy the section on counterpoint is followed by an independent chart setting out the mensuration system and employing both the normal dot within the circle or half-circle and the central European vertical stroke with two or three dots. This section of the treatise is also described in Sachs, *Contrapunctus*, 153–4.

from note-against-note writing. The succession of intervals given in the rubrics for the examples refers to the interval at the beginning of each semibreve. Successions of like intervals are permitted and patterned motion in the counterpoint seems to be preferred (at least in the examples). One result is that the voices often move together at a particular distance, one voice simply, the other floridly, until the approach to the end of the phrase when the motion becomes contrary. If the voices are in the same range the constant interval can be the unison, with the resulting impression of simultaneous performance of the cantus firmus and the ornamented cantus firmus. The similarity of the Kyrie and the treatise examples can be seen in Ex. 5.3.

This Kyrie is possibly a notated version of what may have been an improvisatory practice. This would extend the sort of examples provided by numerous organ *Fundamenta*[52] to the vocal repertory. The possibility that this sort of improvisation was a part of performance in Vienna or in the larger region from which Munich 14274 drew its repertory is suggested by the briefly sketched psalm tones in fauxbourdon found on fos. 25[v], 26[r], 34[r], 35[r], and 91[r]. These suggest that only the difficult portions, intonation and differentia, needed to be notated, with the remainder of the psalm performed by the three voices maintaining the intervallic relationship achieved in the notated segment. The possibility of improvisation being employed in performance of the Kyrie is suggested by one of the recommendations made in a visitation report for the Augustinian house in Munich by Berthold of Regensburg in 1421. He recommends that a 'magister' be employed to teach the novices, who are to be trained to sing the Kyrie in the Mass with the priests.[53] Since the novices would have been trained to sing chant in any case, the singling out of the Kyrie is suggestive. The conjunction between a performer of discant and the teacher of the novices, that is the *rector scolarium*, is demonstrable in the case of Hermann Pötzlinger, who held that position in Regensburg and was the owner and principal compiler of Munich 14274, which contains a number of two-voice Kyries. At least one other fifteenth-century

[52] See those in the Buxheimer Orgelbuch and Lochamer Liederbuch as well as the much earlier treatise published in Theodor Göllner, *Formen früher Mehrstimmigkeit in deutschen Handschriften des späten Mittelalters* (Münchner Veröffentlichungen zur Musikgeschichte, 6; Tutzing, 1961), 155–94. This method of either improvising or composing by means of counterpoint against a part moving up or down by a particular interval is part and parcel of the instrumental tradition in this period. It has been adduced as a peculiarly German trait by Martin Just in his discussion of late 15th-c. music of German origin in his *Der Mensuralkodex Mus. ms. 40021 der Staatsbibliothek Preußischer Kulturbesitz Berlin*, 2 vols. (Würzburger musikhistorische Beiträge, 1; Tutzing, 1975), particularly i. 131 ff.

[53] Vienna, Österreichische Nationalbibliothek, MS 5094, fo. 141[v]: 'addiscant cum sacerdotibus in missa dicere Kyriel[eison]'. It should also be kept in mind that the contrapuntal examples given above are preceded by the statement 'totius biscantus' emphasizing the close connection between the term and this sort of music in central Europe during this period.

Ex. 5.3. *Kyrie fons bonitatis pater ingenite*. Munich, Bayerische Staatsbibliothek, clm 14274, fos. 31ᵛ–32ʳ; clm 24809, fo. 134ʳ

musical source, Munich, Bayerische Staatsbibliothek, MS 5023, was owned and possibly produced by a teacher employed by a monastery, Johannes Greis, *rector scolarium* at Benediktbeuern, and Johannes Wiser, the scribe responsible for much of the copying of the later group of Trent manuscripts, held that position in Trento.

Thus it can be seen that this source, Munich 14274, provides a very accurate cross-section of the repertory in circulation in south Germany and Austria during the first half of the fifteenth century. This repertory included both relatively new and relatively old works by composers active in France and Italy such as those of Dufay, probably composed no more than ten years earlier, as well as works by Machaut and Landini; works by composers active only within this region, but attempting works in the mainstream style; and works involving locally generated and perpetuated styles that are distinct from the mainstream in a number of ways, including contrapuntal style and notation. That Vienna should be home to music relating to Emperor Sigismund (Dufay's *Supremum est*) should not be surprising, nor should one be surprised that music from composers associated with the Council of Basle, held under the protection of the Emperor, should come to be known in the territories of his Habsburg successors.

EARLY FIFTEENTH-CENTURY MUSIC IN POLAND

Musical developments in the Kingdom of Poland are documented by three major manuscript sources of polyphonic music dating from around the end of the first third of the fifteenth century or slightly later. Two, Warsaw 8054 and 378, are possibly connected with the Polish court at Kraków, while the third, Kraków 2464, seems to stem from the university. The court books present a mixture of music of the first two decades of the century by Italian and French composers and a few more recent works by a native Pole, Nicolaus of Radom.[54] The principal composers represented are Antonio Zachara da Teramo, Étienne Grossin, and Johannes Ciconia. The music, principally Mass Ordinary settings, includes some of the most widely known works of these composers, such as the *Et in terra* with trope 'Gloria laus et honor' by Zachara da Teramo that is found in five other sources, as well as the *Patrem* by Ciconia that is found only in these two manuscripts. The works of Grossin are slightly more recent than the above-mentioned and his Kyrie (Warsaw 8054, fo. 181^v) may have been the means by which the practice of fauxbourdon was introduced into the region. A work well known in central European practical and theoretical sources as *Virginem mire* and in French sources as *A/En discort* also appears.

These two relatively contemporaneous manuscripts suggest that there was, in fact, a considerable amount of music by western European composers available to musicians in Poland, as was shown to be true in Austria and south Germany. These two books contain a number of works in common, but neither was copied from the other. As has been noted by Miroslav Perz,[55] this may indicate that a number of earlier manuscripts existed and were used as models in the copying of these two. The two manuscripts preserve music quite similar to the earlier repertorial layer of Bologna Q 15, but are probably nearly a decade more recent. The pattern emerging with these sources, as with

[54] All three are reproduced in facsimile and transcribed in *Sources of Polyphony up to c. 1500*, ed. Miroslaw Perz, 2 vols. (Antiquitates musicae in Polonia, 13 and 14; Graz, 1973–6). The repertory is discussed there and in the dissertation by Charles Brewer cited above.

[55] Miroslav Perz, 'Die Einflüsse der ausgehenden italienischen Ars Nova in Polen', in *L'ars nova italiano del Trecento: secondo convegno internazionale* (Certaldo, 1971), 465–83.

Munich 14274, discussed above, is one in which the time required for the acquisition of works by major figures in France and Italy is comparatively short. The works by Nicolaus of Radom seem to derive from the style of the mainstream repertory found in these manuscripts much in the same way that the music of Edlerawer takes its salient features from the music of Dufay, demonstrating that the time required by local musicians to assimilate characteristics of musical style is also relatively brief.

There is no certain information available on the life of Nicolaus of Radom.[56] It seems very likely, based on the prominence of his music in Warsaw 8054 and 378, particularly his setting of the text on the birth of Prince Kazimierz in 1426, *Hystorigraphi aciem*, that he was connected in some manner with the Polish royal court. He has been identified with the Nicholas described as clavicembalista and organista in documents from the royal court from 1422 and 1425. He may also be the Nicolaus Johannis de Radom who matriculated in the University of Kraków in 1420, in the same year as Stanisław Ciołek, chancellor of the Polish royal court and author of the text 'Hystorigraphi aciem', and two other men mentioned with Nicholas clavicembalista in the document of 1422.[57] His activities, other than composing the works found in these two manuscripts, remain unknown. One might view the musical activity as having occupied him only in his youth during or immediately following university training, before he went on to some other vocation or to a position perhaps earned through his service as a musician. Something of this nature seems to have been true in the case of Hermann Edlerawer, whose professional musical activity may have been limited to the period as cantor of St Stephen's, occurring as an interlude in a life otherwise centred on some kind of employment at the Imperial court or in a noble household.

The ten preserved works by Nicolaus of Radom show him to have absorbed the principal techniques of Ciconia, Zacara da Teramo, Zacharie, and Grossin. In his Mass movements he employs repeated material much as does Nichola Zacharie as a means of achieving some structural unification in a longer work.[58] He borrows the specific setting of the word 'pax' in his Gloria (Warsaw 8054, no. 22) from Antonio Zacara's *Gloria Anglicana*.[59] He also borrows from this

---

[56] Brewer, 'The Introduction', 263–8 provides a summary of available information.

[57] See ibid. 265. On the identification of two men with this name see Mirosław Perz, 'Il carattere internazionale delle opere di Mikołaj Radomski', *Musica disciplina*, 41 (1987), 153–9 at 154–5.

[58] See Brewer, 'The Introduction', 285–6.

[59] See *Sources*, ed. Perz, 14, pp. 282 and 413.

composer the use of overlapping, sequential repetitions of short rhythmic patterns in all voices, in one instance using not only the device, but also the same pattern.[60]

It has also been suggested, with good reason, that his Gloria and Credo copied in succession in Warsaw 8054 and related by clef, mensuration, cadence pitches, and other devices are intended to function as a Mass pair, a genre commonly found in the French repertory of the 1420s.[61] There is also a refreshing variety among his Mass movements. One or all of the voices may be provided with text; the voices may be rhythmically similar or, at least in certain passages, divided by consistent use of longer or shorter values. Imitation plays an occasional role at the opening of a movement, but is not a device of real significance. In two Mass settings, a Gloria and Credo, he contrasts duos for a divided superius with sections for three parts, a device used in a Credo by Zacharie copied immediately preceding his work in Warsaw 378.[62] His Magnificat[63] employs fauxbourdon, a device possibly borrowed from Grossin's Kyrie, found immediately preceding it in Warsaw 8054, but also possibly learned of through contact with other music of the late 1420s and 1430s. He uses similar durations in the superius and tenor except for the approach to the cadence, a practice not often used by Dufay but followed by many composers. It is also of interest to note here that the technique is applied to a Magnificat, a genre quite often set in this manner in the West. Strangely, the scribe of Warsaw 8054 managed to give at least three different marginal verbal canons for the realization of the piece, not one of which is conventional or clearly leads to a successful realization. The textless work attributed to Nicolaus[64] is in ballade form, a form favoured in this pair of manuscripts, and makes some use of the technique of overlapping rhythmic sequences described above in a passage repeated in the outer sections of the piece. His *Hystorigraphi aciem*, also in ballade form, sets a text by the chancellor Stanisław Ciołek that refers to Prince Kazimierz and may have been written for his christening on 2 June 1426.[65] Ciołek is also the author of the text of *Cracovia civitas*, a motet without attribution in praise of the city of Kraków and of the court. The work appears in both Warsaw 8054 and 378, and in the latter source the characteristic signs of the central European notational system are used to indicate prolation in the

---

[60] See *Sources*, ed. Perz, 290 and 413–14.
[61] Brewer, 'The Introduction', 285.
[62] See *Sources*, ed. Perz, AMP 14, pp. 443–8 and 387–94 for the Gloria and Credo, respectively, by Nicolaus of Radom, and 311–21 for the Credo by Zacharie.
[63] See ibid. 252–60.
[64] Ibid. 270–2.
[65] See Brewer, 'The Introduction', 293.

tenor, which moves primarily in longer values and thus lacks the semi-breve/minim patterns that would otherwise identify the mensuration, whereas in Warsaw 8054 the notation is standard mensural notation, indicating a sort of co-existence of the two practices, at least in certain circles in the region.

The anonymously preserved *Breve regnum* establishes a connection with the University at Kraków in its references to student celebrations. It is a relatively straightforward setting for two voices.

The manuscript Kraków 2464, a book containing a few leaves of music within a manuscript of texts on grammar and theology, certainly came into existence within the context of the university rather than the court.[66] Its contents, settings of Latin texts, all but two of which are for one or two voices, are generally much simpler in compositional organization than works in Warsaw 8054 and 378.[67] Discussion of musical style of the music is made difficult by the rather poor standard of the copying of the music. Stems are omitted, as are some clefs and almost all dots of division. Although in some instances small vertical strokes seem to replace dots of division, visual grouping of minims and semibreves seems to prevail. Numerous ligatures are misdrawn or were improperly copied, often resulting in situations in which more than two notes in ligature must be interpreted as semibreves, even though notated as breves. Occasionally dots are used to indicate the number of semibreves contained in a larger value, including one instance of a seven-semibreve *brevis* (or possibly *longa*), neither of which is rational. These problems seem to have led to the signed criticism of someone named Rambowski attached to the tenor of *Altitonanti cantica*, which lacks all of the necessary stems to identify its minims.[68]

From the music that can be transcribed, a style somewhat similar to that found in Vyšší Brod 42 can be discerned: voices move at times

---

[66] For a description of its contents see *Sources*, ed. Perz, 13, pp. xxi–xxii.

[67] Brewer, 'The Introduction', 365 ff. applies the description 'popular polyphony' to this repertory and to a very large number of compositions preserved in more than fifty manuscripts from central Europe. This term is in many ways as problematic as those it would replace. 'Retrospective, peripheral, archaic, and primitive' are admittedly pejorative, but 'simple' has the value of being an accurate description without connotations of artistic worth, relative modernity, or level of artistic sophistication. There is another aspect of the music to which these terms are applied that is not often considered, namely its function as defined by the text. Although one can find the same texts set in this repertory and in the high art repertory, e.g., those of the Mass Ordinary, to a very large extent the texts set are different and one has to consider the possibility that the function of the piece was a significant determinant of the musical style. An instructive example of this function-determined style can be seen in the repertory found in western European sources: works intended for performance at the Elevation, such as Josquin's *Tu solus qui facis mirabilia*, are not at all similar in complexity to his other motets or Mass movements.

[68] Following 'tenor huius' another hand has added 'sed falsus ergo asinus tza quia hoc videtur fore de racione bestialitatis. Rambowsky.'

in parallel fashion, but also in contrary motion. The parallels include perfect intervals and momentary unisons. The style also seems to admit very striking dissonances, seconds and sevenths. Imperfect intervals are found most frequently as cadential preparations, the most common being sequences of two or more parallel sixths (or thirds) leading to an octave (or unison) at phrase endings. The voices are in similar ranges and often cross, although there seems to be a clear distinction in rate of movement between the two voices with longer values occurring more frequently in the voice labelled tenor.

All but one of the works are unica. Only three of the twenty-five works have a possible attribution and in every instance the likely composer is Petrus Wilhelmi of Grudencz. His works, with one exception,[69] have their attribution recorded in the first letters of the first six words of the text, employing the acrostic device so well liked in this region. The three pieces exhibit this particular acrostic.[70] The presence of Petrus' music in this manuscript is very probably the result of his presence at the University of Kraków from his matriculation in 1418 through his receipt of the baccalaureate in 1425 and promotion to the master of arts in 1430.[71] This period of study would make it likely that he had some acquaintance with Nicolaus of Radom, if the identification of the composer with the matriculating student of 1420 cited above is correct. In any case, the nature of Petrus' Latin texts with their neologisms and borrowed words, particularly at the opening where the acrostic is formed, can only be linked to an environment like the university in which there would be some likelihood that the texts would be understood.

Petrus seems also to have had some contacts with the Imperial court. Direct evidence is his *Pontifices ecclesiarum* requesting Friedrich's aid for the Council of Basle.[72] There is little specific evidence for his activities after 1430 except for Friedrich III's grant of a *littera familiaritatis* and a safe-conduct in May 1442, in which

---

[69] The exception is the *Kyrie fons bonitatis* attributed to Magister Petrus Wilhelmi on fos. 11ᵛ–12ʳ of Munich, Bayerische Staatsbibliothek, clm 14274.

[70] The identity of the composer and the works to be attributed to him were discovered by Jaromír Černý and presented in two articles, 'Petrus Wilhelmi of Grudziądz—an Unknown Composer of the "Age of Dufay"', *Musica antiqua Europae orientalis IV: Bydgoszcz 1975* (Bydgoszcz, 1975), 90–103, and 'Petrus Wilhelmi de Grudencz', *Hudební věda*, 12 (1975), 195–238. The key to the recognition of the composer and to linking him with a historical personage was Černý's discovery of the complete name as three acrostics in a polytextual motet.

[71] Černý, 'Petrus Wilhelmi de Grudencz', 196.

[72] The poem uses a formal procedure similar to Petrus' musical settings, a series of stanzas followed by a refrain marked 'Repeticio'. His *Proclivi eius temporis* for St Elizabeth appears in Göttingen, Universitätsbibliothek, MS Theol. 200ⁱ, a manuscript of material for the feast of this saint compiled in Magdeburg in 1517. It is also completely possible that he never set, nor intended to set, some of his poetry.

document he is described as a master of arts and cleric of the diocese of Chełmno.[73] One might, however, assume that a portion of this period was spent in Bohemia since it is in sources from this region that the majority of his works are preserved, some in several sources, with both the original texts and as contrafacta. In any case, his works show a clear indication of a composer completely versed in the stylistic conventions of the central European motet, both mono- and polytextual, and with Western European traditions. The latter is indicated by his Kyrie and by his *Prodigiis eximiis tropheo refulgenti virtutum sanctimoniis*, which employs fauxbourdon. He could well have learned both the native and the foreign styles during his studies in Kraków.

Some type of association between musicians active in universities in central Europe is also suggested by the source distribution of his music. His works are found in at least four sources, all of which can be shown to have been copied in a university environment or owned by a member of a university community. In addition to Kraków 2464, these are Munich 14274, already described above, and two manuscripts once owned by Johannes Klein of Löbau, a student and teacher at the University of Leipzig in the second half of the fifteenth century.[74] The association of musicians with the universities of central Europe has yet to be fully explored and explained, but evidence is accumulating that suggests that some type of association was not an uncommon practice. Hermann Edlerawer, Petrus Wilhelmi, and possibly Nicolaus of Radom all were enrolled in a university, as were Hermann Pötzlinger and Johannes Klein. Within this small group, the range of connections can be extended to monastic institutions through Pötzlinger's employment as *rector scolarium* at St. Emmeram in Regensburg. In 1440 six singers of the Bishop of Kraków, Zbigniew Oleśnicki, entered the University of Kraków.[75] The purpose of these matriculations and of Hermann Edlerawer's in Vienna is by no means

---

[73] J. Chmel, *Regesta chronologico-diplomatica Friderici III. Romanorum Imperatoris (Regis IV)* (Vienna, 1859), 66. The connection between Petrus and the copying of the Glogauer Liederbuch suggested by Černý on the basis of the Petrus acrostic in *Probitate eminentem*, which contains a reference to the local Glogau figure Andreas Ritter, is a bit tenuous: there is no direct evidence linking him to Glogau or Sagan, and his age, at least 75 by the late 1470s, would have to be dealt with. In addition Miroslav Perz, in 'The Lvov Fragments', *TVNM* 36 (1986), 26–51 has pointed out that the crucial reference to Andreas Ritter is absent from the Lvov manuscript, possibly indicating that whoever copied the piece into the Glogauer Liederbuch used the name of a local figure, as could readily, and possibly intentionally, be done.

[74] The manuscripts are now in the University Library as MS 1084 and MS 1236. Each contains works by Petrus, including the fauxbourdon setting of *Prodigiis eximiis tropheo refulgenti virtutum sanctimoniis* in MS 1084.

[75] See Gerhard Pietzsch, *Zur Pflege der Musik an den deutschen Universitäten bis zur Mitte des 16. Jahrhunderts* (Hildesheim, 1971), 44 and Brewer, 'The Introduction', 100.

clear: none of these men seems to have received a degree. It is conceivable that some connection with a university provided the possibility of gaining a particular type of position.[76] In some of the central European universities, benefices in local churches were linked with positions at the university. At St Stephen's in Vienna, the subcantor had the responsibility of teaching if he possessed a university degree or arranging for an assistant if he did not.[77] It is thus very likely that tangible benefits could come to a musician with some relationship to a university or to a member of a university community with some skill in practical music and that this possible benefit is as satisfactory an explanation of the conjunction of music and the university as is the citation of private inclinations of members of the university community.

MENSURAL POLYPHONY IN BOHEMIA

Musical developments in Bohemia from the early fifteenth century through the sixteenth are distinguished from developments throughout the rest of the region and western Europe by several factors. The most striking of these are the apparent attitude towards the definition of what can be described as a current repertory and the continued cultivation and development of older formal types.[78] Works that came into circulation, that is, works that entered the repertory, tended to remain in it. A result of this is that sources copied in the sixteenth century often contain music composed in the 1420s and 1430s. Motets with multiple texts and conductus-like motets, two genres derived from earlier models, continue to be composed and, in some cases, modified during at least the first half of the fifteenth century. These works also use the central European notational system described above in some of their earliest sources and, even when this notational system is discarded, the copies continue to be made in solid notation well into the sixteenth century. Certain aspects of the later form of solid notation are also eccentric. For example, minims are sometimes notated with flags, thus appearing to be semiminims. The interaction of this practice of retention of older compositions that were themselves modelled on even earlier practices further emphasizes the stylistic dichotomy of surviving early sixteenth-century sources: works by Josquin and Isaac co-exist with compositions created in the mid-fifteenth century on

---

[76] See Ian Rumbold, 'The Compilation', 171, where it is noted that the statutes of the University of Vienna specified that those holding particular positions were required to matriculate.

[77] Ibid. 175–6 and sources cited there.

[78] Černý has set out the compositional types and their interrelationships in the series of articles cited in the following footnotes.

fourteenth-century models that are notated in a different form of the mensural system.

The situation in Bohemia is also different from that found in other parts of central Europe in that there are a significant number of musical sources preserving fifteenth-century repertory. This can be contrasted in particular with the source situation in Poland and Hungary. The provenance of the manuscripts is also quite unlike that of sources copied in other regions in that they seem to have been compiled by and for the use of groups of laymen acting in a religious context, rather than for a court or ecclesiastical chapel. These manuscript sources can be quite extensive and they preserve a large number of works in common. Jaromír Černý has noted this body of common repertory in a group of sixteenth-century manuscripts and has suggested that it may owe its existence to the fact that the Hussite and later Utraquist practice that replaced the Roman Catholic at the beginning of the fifteenth century allowed the performance of music to fall to the laity, to Literary Brotherhoods made up of members of the middle class.[79] These groups seem to have regarded the earlier repertory as worthy of retention, perhaps as a reminder of the beginnings of their denomination. The Speciálník Codex, copied sometime around 1500, contains music by Josquin, Isaac, Agricola, Ghiselin, and others, music that is as up-to-date as that being copied into manuscripts then being produced from the Netherlands to Italy. It also contains a significant number of works in solid notation that date from as early as the 1420s. This split repertory demonstrates that the Literary Brotherhood in Prague for which it was made chose to collect and perform both the most recent and the old repertory, each probably for different reasons. The earlier music was clearly different, even in notation, but it seemed to have retained some level of importance to this group for reasons other than modernity or comparability to the Netherlandish model. It may have been that it was regarded as an important element of their religious tradition and that the preservation of the tradition was more important than contemporary views about currency of style or aesthetic value.[80] This group of composi-

---

[79] Černý, 'Zur Frage der Entstehungs- und Verwandlungsprozesse der mehrstimmigen Repertoires in Böhmen', in *Trasmissione e recezione delle forme di cultura musicale: Atti del XIV Congresso della Società Internazionale di Musicologia*, ed. Angelo Pompilio *et al.*, 3 vols. (Turin, 1990), i. 168–74 at 170–1.

[80] There are other instances of the retention of a clearly older work within more recent repertories. See e.g. Wreede's setting of the hymn *Pange lingua* which first appears in Spanish sources of the late 15th c. but continues to be copied throughout the 16th c. and into the early 17th c. (Tom R. Ward, *The Polyphonic Office Hymn from 1400–1520: A Descriptive Catalogue* (Neuhausen-Stuttgart, 1980), no. 489), or Jacob Handl's *Ecce quomodo*, which remains in the Lutheran tradition until at least the 18th c.

tions is found in a number of other Bohemian sources, often copied on successive folios, as though its different character, or perhaps different function, was clearly recognized.[81] In any case, the different circumstances surrounding the cultivation of music and the production of manuscripts resulted in a very different view of what constituted a worthwhile collection of music.

The manuscript sources for the fifteenth-century repertory also show some traits in common that distinguish them from manuscripts from western Europe and from, for example, contemporary Austrian manuscripts. Graduals containing only a few polyphonic pieces are very common,[82] as are manuscripts that mix monophonic cantiones with polyphonic works.[83] Books whose contents are exclusively polyphony are relatively rare until well into the late sixteenth century. The Speciálník Codex[84] is the best-known manuscript from this region, but it is not really typical. Speciálník has far more in the way of mainstream repertory than any other manuscript from the region and a significant number of compositions bear attributions. The Franus Cantional is of interest for the number of polyphonic works contained, but it has only two works that concordances identify as being by western European composers and provides no attributions for any of its polyphonic music. Its most significant content consists of a large number of monophonic cantiones and other similar monophonic works.

One of the more striking genres found in Bohemian sources is one of these older compositional types, the polytextual motet. These compositions, sometimes described in relation to the motets of the Engelberg manuscript,[85] were out of fashion in most of Europe after the beginning of the fifteenth century and, with only a few exceptions, do not appear in any of the other manuscripts described above as presenting the music common to this region. This repertory also includes works that either have concordances with fourteenth-century

---

[81] See Černý, 'Zur Frage', 171.

[82] See e.g. *Census-Catalogue*, iii. 55–68, for a number of Graduals, now in Prague, that have fewer than ten polyphonic works.

[83] The best-known of these is the 'Franus Cantional' (Hradec Králové, Krajske Muzeum, MS II A 6), which contains a large repertory of monophonic cantiones, a smaller number of polyphonic compositions of local origin, and a very small number of western European works. There is not as yet firm bibliographical control over the cantio repertory, but lists of sources can be found in *Analecta hymnica*, ed. Clemens Blume and Guido Dreves, vols. 1, 2, 15, 20, 33, 45, and 46 (Leipzig, 1895–1904), and Bruno Stäblein, *Schriftbild der einstimmigen Musik* (Musikgeschichte in Bildern, 3/iv; Leipzig, 1975), 75.

[84] Hradec Králové, Krajske Muzeum, MSS II A 7.

[85] Engelberg, Stiftsbibliothek, MS 314. See *Engelberg Stiftsbibliothek Codex 314*, ed. Wulf Arlt and Manfred Stauffacher (Schweizerisches Musikdenkmäler, 11; Winterthur, 1986). The manuscript was copied in 1372/73 and was in use into the 15th c.

manuscripts[86] or are clearly related to earlier works in that they use the same tenor melody (pitch and durations), occasionally with a change from perfect to imperfect prolation, or are based on both voices of an earlier work.[87]

These motets often use tenors that repeat, either coinciding with repetitions of the upper voices, producing a varied strophic form, or, occasionally, without any relationship to the shape of the upper voices. They also generally require some repetition of all of the voices of some or all of the work, often noted only by cues at the end of the voice parts. There are also what appear to be examples of a gradual expansion of a work from two to three or four voices, sometimes involving a change or, possibly, an expansion of meaning and relationships within the text. *Exordium quadruplate* is an example of this sort of development.[88] The two voices *Verbum caro* and *Concrepet* have a relationship commonly found between the tenor and motetus in the thirteenth and fourteenth centuries: the first text is a Christmas Responsory and the second can be seen as providing an expansion on its meaning. The third voice, *Nates nate dei*, adds further to this expansion by reference to the community of clerics, but the fourth voice specifically refers to the performance of this four-voice motet, without mentioning the Christmas theme of the other texts.

The repertory is not static throughout the period. Earlier works can be separated from later ones and differences in contrapuntal and harmonic style identified. The earliest works have a clear preference for fifths and octaves and tend to have few thirds and sixths except as cadential preparation for perfect intervals. This practice leads to not infrequent successions of parallel perfect intervals and to occasional, brief unison passages, not unlike those found in Vyšší Brod 42. The later works in the repertory show a growing preference for complete triads in both root position and first inversion, but retain occasional parallel fifths and octaves. The only composer identified by name is Petrus Wilhelmi. Indeed, his identity was discovered through the extended acrostic in *Veni veri illustrator / Pneuma eucharistiarum /*

---

[86] *Voce cordis / Pulchre Sion* is found in the Engelberg manuscript and in Ústí nad Orlicí, Okresni Archív, MS A 3.

[87] For example, *Stirps regalis / Salve mundi Domina / Gloriose Domine*, found in three 16th-c. Bohemian sources, is based on an *a 2* setting in Munich, Bayerische Staatsbibliothek, Cod. germ. 716. See Černý, 'K nejstaršim dějinám moteta v českých zemich', *Miscellanea musicologica*, 24 (1971), 7–90, esp. the transcriptions, 66–9. A similar situation exists for *Ave Jesu / O premium*, a motet much more widely disseminated in 14th-c. sources in and outside of central Europe. It appears in 15th-c. sources with one or two added voices and texts and with modifications to the durations of the common voices. See Černý, 12–14 and 47.

[88] The following discussion is based on Černý, 'Zur Frage' and 'K nejstaršim dějinám moteta'. Černý admits that the successive versions are not preserved, but argues convincingly that the additive process is likely given other examples.

Paraclito tripudia / Dator eya gratiarum that provided not only his first name, as do several other works, but also the remainder of his name and his birthplace.[89]

Petrus' music shows aspects of both the earlier and later style (see Ex. 5.4). His *Veni veri* initially moves from an open sonority to a root-position triad which is followed by a measure emphasizing parallel movement in thirds and sixths. In bar 7, however, there are completely exposed parallel fifths and octaves between the upper three voices. He also follows earlier works in his use of brief motifs in a mosaic-like manner as though working with standard figures from consonance to consonance. These patterns, generally notated in minims, reappear throughout the work. One device that is not as frequently encountered is his treatment of the Repetitio in this work and in his five-voice *Panis ecce angelorum*.[90] This section uses one text in all four or five voices in a homorhythmic setting in perfect prolation, providing both textural and rhythmic contrast with the body of the work. In both cases, he also alternates shorter and longer cadential patterns to provide shape to this section, that is, the phrases end either minim, semibreve, set syllabically, or employ more notes, set melismatically. In *Panis ecce angelorum* Petrus also makes imaginative use of very brief passages in semiminims in the middle three voices to connect the four segments of six breves each into which the piece is divided by rests in the outer voices. In addition, the lowest voice provides four iterations of the same pattern of durations, drawing perhaps on isorhythmic models. The primary fault one could find with Petrus is the too frequent occurrence of parallel perfect intervals. They seem in part to be a result of his attempting to fit four or even five voices in the total range of an octave plus a fifth or a sixth, but it could well be that the style simply permits this. A number of these works are found with alternative texts, replacing the at times rather involved poetry of Petrus with less complicated texts in either Latin or Czech. It may be that as the works moved from Petrus' initial sphere of activity, which may have been the university, into the middle-class Literary Brotherhoods, the artfully contrived texts with their neologisms lost their appeal and were replaced by others that were more serviceable in the current circumstances, whatever their literary merits.

An anonymous motet for three voices with three Christmas texts, *Unde gaudent*, demonstrates additional aspects of the motet style.[91]

[89] Černý, 'Petrus Wilhelmi de Grudencz', 195–6.
[90] Černý, 'K nejstaršim', 78–83 for transcriptions of both works.
[91] See ibid.

The voice ranges are narrow, spanning only a fifth or a sixth, and the total range is only a tenth. Text-setting is largely syllabic, with syllables assigned to semiminims, which are often repeated pitches. Paral-

Ex. 5.4. (*a*) *Veni, veri illustrator*; with (*b*) second section *Paraclito tripudia*. Transcription after Černý, 'K nejstarším dějinám'

lel fifths and octaves occur frequently on almost any durational value. Passages in shorter notes reminiscent of onomatopoeic imitations of trumpets and drums are frequently found. All these characteristics are found to a greater or lesser extent in the multi-textual motets as well as in the songs and conductus-like works of the period.

Two additional compositional types can be found in this repertory: song-like and conductus-like settings, both with Latin texts in their original form, or at least in their earliest copies. On the most obvious level the distinction between these two types and between the motet and these types has to do with the text. These works are distinguished from the motet by their use of a single text. They may be distinguished from each other according to whether the text is present in all voices or only in one. The conductus has one text present in all voices, with the result that all the voices move at about the same rate. The song-like compositions have the text only in the discantus and it is clearly the focal point of the work. Typical melodic figurations recur in some of these works to provide a shaping of the composition. The tenor (and other additional voices, if present) tends to move in longer notes and to provide harmonic support rather than further melodic interest.[92]

The conductus-like motet derives its texture of two (or three) texted voices declaiming their syllables more or less simultaneously from the thirteenth-century genre.[93] It also displays other characteristics of this model: melismatic preludes, interludes, and postludes in the manner of *caudae*, frequent use of brief melodic cells and common contrapuntal devices, and use of regular rhythmic patterns similar to modal patterns. It differs from the earlier model in its use of repetition. Many works are in AAB form. There are also occasional passages for one voice, often in alternation. *Paranimphus adiit* (Ex. 5.5), provides a typical example of this genre, showing a number of characteristic features. Contrapuntally, it moves between blatant parallel perfect intervals (see b. 7) and standard contrapuntal patterns (bb. 1–3), and approaches to cadences (bb. 14–16). Passages of each type are found elsewhere in this piece and in other compositions of this type.

The text, in praise of Mary, forms the name 'Paulus' by means of an acrostic in the initial letters of the first six words. The music also appears with another text, 'Paraclitus egrediens'. Contrafacta in both Latin and Czech are not uncommon in this repertory.[94] Another practice is the reduction of an *a 2* setting to a monophonic melody. It might be assumed that this is merely the result of the omission of one of the voices. Closer inspection, however, shows that the monophonic version includes material at different times from both voices of the polyphonic version, indicating that it was derived from the entirety of the polyphonic setting.

These types provide a sense of the general nature of this repertory, but a number of compositions defy simple categorization. They mix aspects of song and conductus by assigning text to all voices and/or lessening the distinctions among the voices. Others introduce moments of imitation, primarily at section beginnings, but also in the midst of the texture where it goes almost unnoticed. Still others show acquaintance with additional compositional techniques, some not represented in the types described above. An example is the motet *Ave coronata / Alme parens / Ave coronata*, which was composed around 1400.[95] In its origi-

---

[92] See the transcription of *Flos florum* in Jaromír Černý, 'Die Ars nova-Musik in Böhmen', *Miscellanea musicologica*, 21 (1970), 47–106 at 91.

[93] Jaromír Černý, 'Vícehlasé písne konduktového typu c českých pramenech 15.století', *Miscellanea musicologica*, 31 (1984), 39–142.

[94] For example, some musical settings appear as many as three times, each time with a different text, in a late copy of music from this tradition, Vodňany, Děkanský Úřad, MS without signature.

[95] The work is discussed and edited in Černý, 'Die Ars nova-Musik', 80–4 and 96–102.

Ex. 5.5. *Paranimphus adiit virginem letanter*. Hradec Králové, Krajske Muzeum, MS II a 6, fos. 321ᵛ–322ʳ

nal form it was an isorhythmic motet using the antiphon *Virgo pruden-tissima* as the *color* for its four *talea* statements. The copies of the work in the Speciálník Codex and Franus Cantional divide the long notes of the tenor into shorter, repeated pitches in order to allow the text of the superius to be underlaid in this voice as well. The middle voice, which moves primarily in longer values, does not seem to have been altered, except that the text underlaid here may not have been present originally. The result is that a work that was once a relatively typical isorhythmic motet with an active uppermost voice and two lower voices moving in longer values (and possibly without text) is presented with outer voices that function in the manner of a conductus with nearly simultaneous declamation of the same text. The piece may be one that was to be sung after the *Salve regina* on the Feast of the Assumption for a memorial service in the church of Mary Magdalene in Kraków, according to a document of 1472.[96] This would be appropriate since *Virgo prudentissima* is the Magnificat antiphon for this day.

The sources of the repertory discussed thus far are also important in that they show that Bohemia was not just a passive recipient of music composed in other regions. Manuscripts now in Trier and Merseburg show that music from Bohemia was copied in other parts of Europe.[97] Political relationships and the movement of people between institutions, particularly the universities, seem to have made connections and exchanges among Bohemia, Poland, and Austria relatively common. The music of Petrus Wilhelmi found in Bohemian sources may have been composed in Bohemia, but it is also found in manuscripts copied in Vienna, Leipzig, and Trent.[98] In these cases, it seems likely that musically literate students or faculty may have been the agents who carried the music with them as they moved to and from the universities in Kraków, Prague, Vienna, and Leipzig. This repertory, which came into existence in the first half of the fifteenth century, found its way into a wide variety of locations, but achieved its enduring place in the musical life of the Literary Brotherhoods of the Utraquist church, where it continued to be copied until the end of the sixteenth century.

There is a major late fifteenth-century manuscript that contains a very different musical repertory, one reflecting the musical practices of the cathedral or collegiate church, Prague, Památník Národního Písmnictví, Strahovská Knihovna, MS D.G.IV.47. This book was copied between 1460 and 1480 in Bohemia or Silesia (or possibly in Moravia). Its contents are primarily settings of items for the Proper and Ordinary of the Mass, hymns and Magnificats for Vespers, and motets. It shares a large number of works with the later Trent manuscripts (discussed below) and demonstrates as well the importation of music from major centres in western Europe. The motets show a number of features characteristic of central Europe and demonstrate the local cultivation of a universal compositional type with and without local characteristics.

POLAND AFTER 1450

Musical activity in Poland in the remainder of the fifteenth century is much more difficult to chronicle. The number of manuscripts pre-

[96] Georg Bauch, *Geschichte des Breslauer Schulwesens vor der Reformation* (Codex Diplomaticus Silesiae, 25; Breslau, 1909), 88.

[97] Trier, Stadtbibliothek, MS 322/1944 (see Rudolf Ewerhart, *Die Handschrift 322/1944 der Stadtbibliothek Trier als musikalische Quelle* (Regensburg, 1955)) and Merseburg, Domstiftsbibliothek, MS 13b (see Kurt von Fischer, 'Neue Quellen zur Musik des 13., 14. und 15. Jahrhunderts', *Acta musicologica*, 36 (1964), 79–87).

[98] Munich, Bayerische Staatsbibliothek, clm 14274; Leipzig, Universitätsbibliothek, MSS 1084 and 1236; and Trent, Museo Provinciale d'Arte, MSS 90 and 93.

served is relatively small and all are fragmentary in nature. Likewise
fragmentary is knowledge about musicians who were active there
during the second half of the century. The information available suggests that the musical establishment at the court of Kraków was of
some importance during this period. Although no records document-
ing expenditures for a chapel are preserved from the reign of Kazimierz IV (1447–92), it is known that the young Heinrich Finck was
sent there as a child to become a member of the chapel.[99] The only
published documents concerning the chapel have to do with Finck's
activities there and the only contemporary reference to his years in
Poland is that set out by his grand-nephew Hermann in the introduction to his *Practica musica* (Wittenberg, 1556), the remark 'bonus
cantor' in the notice of his matriculation at the University of Leipzig
in 1482, and the description of him in 1494–5 in a Torgau account
book as 'des königs von Polen singer'.[100] Finck's career also allows us
to discover a break in the royal support of the chapel from 1492 until
1498. Johann Albrecht (1492–1501), who succeeded his father as king
of Poland, seems not to have been interested in music, but his brother
Alexander, who became Grand Prince of Lithuania in 1492 and joined
to that title the one of King of Poland in 1502, did maintain a chapel,
and it was to his employ that Finck returned in 1498. Hoffmann-
Erbrecht has published records of payment to Finck as a member of
the chapel, possibly as its master, in the years 1498 to 1505.[101] The
possibility exists that he remained in this chapel until travelling to
Stuttgart in 1510.

The position can be taken that Finck's works found in sources of
the period up to about 1510 and in even later Polish collections were
very likely written for the chapel of Kazimierz or Alexander. These
include works found in the major manuscripts copied or completed
around the turn of the century—Berlin 40021, Leipzig 1494, Munich
3154, Warsaw 58, and Hradec Králové II A 7—and possibly all those
found in the series of manuscripts from Lutheran centres in Saxony
and Slovakia. The works found in these sources represent most of
the genres of sacred music: Mass Ordinary and Proper, Magnificat,
hymn, antiphon, and responsory. It is not readily believable that all
the music preserved in the earlier group of manuscripts was composed
in the four-year hiatus in his Polish service (1494–8) or that all that in
the later sources was composed between 1505 and his death in 1527

---

[99] Lothar Hoffmann-Erbrecht, *Heinrich Finck—musicus excellentissimus* (Cologne, 1982),
10–11.
[100] All references to documents are drawn from Hoffmann-Erbrecht, *Heinrich Finck*.
[101] Ibid. 28–30.

at the age of 82, or that Finck learned a new style and produced music in this new manner once out of Poland. One can, then, take these works, particularly the earlier ones, as examples of the kind of music that formed a part of the repertory of the Polish royal chapel in the last decades of the fifteenth century and first decade of the sixteenth. This view is strengthened by the recent discovery of a set of choir-book fragments in Lvov, fragments preserving Masses by Dufay, Domarto, and Josquin as well as motets, including one, *Probitate eminentem / Ploditando exarare*, that is attributed to Petrus Wilhelmi and is also found in the Glogauer Liederbuch.[102] This last work helps to counter the possibility that the original manuscript of which only these fragments remain was an imported one, not representative of local or regional practices. The combination of Finck's earlier output and the contents of the Lvov fragments also helps counter the impression of a relatively low level of artistic production that would result from the examination of the few fragmentary sources preserved and published. The state of affairs, then, at the end of the fifteenth century is not significantly different from that of the 1420s: music by leading western European composers is known and works are being produced by local musicians that are in a comparable style, if not of equivalent quality.

THE GERMAN-SPEAKING REGION AFTER 1450

The personnel of the chapel of Friedrich III during the fifteenth century have been identified, at least in part; however, none of them, other than Johannes Brassart and Johannes de Sarto, can be shown to have been active as a composer.[103] A considerable amount of information is available about members of the Imperial chapel during the second half of the fifteenth century, unfortunately not in the form of descriptions of musical activity, but rather as requests on their behalf by Friedrich III for preferment for ecclesiastical positions or other affairs not directly connected with music. An additional problem is that no music is attributed to any of these men identified as singers in any manuscript of the late fifteenth century. A number of hypotheses have been put forward recently that would not only increase the number of musicians associated in some manner with the Imperial chapel, but, more importantly, would also increase the number of composers and, in some cases, specific works with some connection to this institution.

---

[102] Perz, 'The Lvov Fragments'.
[103] Documentary data on the members of the chapel in the 15th c. has been summarized by Gerhard Pietzsch, *Fürsten und fürstliche Musiker im mittelalterlichen Köln* (Beiträge zur Rheinischen Musikgeschichte, 66; Cologne, 1968), 59–82.

The suggestion that the Trent manuscripts[104] contain music from the Imperial court has been made by a number of writers—often, it seems, for lack of another possibility.[105] The identification of Johannes Lupi as the scribe and original owner of manuscripts 87 and 92 (second section) by Peter Wright[106] and the association of the music of MS 91 (and by extension the other later manuscripts) with liturgical practices to be found in the Imperial chapel by Adelyn Leverett[107] have made it possible to discuss the nature of the activities of this chapel on the basis of the kind of music it produced and collected. Their identification of a large body of music that was not only known to the Imperial court, but of which a large portion was composed for use in the court or in its immediate environs, provides us with the example of a very active musical establishment that performed Mass and Vespers polyphonically on most of the relatively important feast days of the year. In terms of the frequency of performance of polyphonic sacred music implied by these collections, this is about as active a chapel as we know from the fifteenth century.

The collection of sacred music preserved in the Trent manuscripts is large and, in terms of liturgical categories represented, comprehensive. The nature and extent of the repertory support the interpretation of the performance of Mass and Office as including polyphony in Friedrich's letter to the bishop of Liège.[108] The majority of the works, particularly those in the later manuscripts, are preserved without attribution. This may be a result of the genres involved: cantus-firmus-based Mass Propers and hymns as well as Magnificats composed (or collected) in and for the use of the Imperial chapel might not have been regarded in the same way that large-scale works, such as cyclic Mass Ordinaries by a well-known composer, were. There is a very strong possibility that the music of composers such as Martini, Ockeghem, Touront, and Pullois was regarded as a special acquisition and worthy of attribution, as compared with the more everyday cantus-firmus elaborations.[109]

---

[104] Trent, Museo provinciale d'arte, MSS 87–92 and Archivio capitolare, MS 93, hereafter Trent 87–93. The manuscripts have been published in facsimile as *Codices musicales Tridentini* (Rome, 1969–70). Selected works are published in Denkmäler der Tonkunst in Österreich, 14/15, 22, 38, 53, 61, 76, and 120. Contents of the manuscripts are inventoried in RISM B/iv.5, 461–547.

[105] See e.g. Hellmut Federhofer, 'Trienter Codices', *MGG* xiii. 666–73.

[106] Wright, 'The Related Parts', and 'On the Origins'.

[107] Leverett, 'A Paleographical and Repertorial Study'.

[108] See above at n. 28.

[109] The underlying assumption here is that the repertory was gathered from the Imperial court by the scribes of the Trent manuscripts. While this is probably correct in general, for certain works it might be an oversimplification. That some of the music, e.g. Martini's, may have come to Trent by other routes is quite likely; see Leverett, 'A Paleographical and Repertorial Study', 112 ff. Martini's Mass on *In feuers hitz* perhaps shows that his stay in Constance brought him into contact with the tradition of Masses on German lieder.

The cantus-firmus-based works imply the existence of a calendri-
cally ordered repertory of settings of this type, providing a polyphonic
setting for every important feast of the year as well as for votive services. The nature of the content of such performances seems to have
evolved during the century: the earliest manuscripts, Trent 87 and
Trent 92, give particular emphasis to Introits. The later manuscripts
include more of the other Mass Propers, at times organized as cycles,
as in Trent 88,[110] or ordered liturgically but copied in groups by genre,
as in the collections of introits, sequences, and Mass Ordinary movements found in Trent 93. The hymns provide settings for most of the
feasts of the year and include examples of local adaptation, such as
the addition of the text for St Vigilius, the patron of Trent, to a setting
of *Ut queant laxis*, and of an awareness of differences in practice
between the source of the collection and Rome, as set out in the rubric
accompanying *Christe redemptor omnium* in Trent 88, fos. 340^v–341^r,
where the use of text and cantus firmus is explained by reference to
the 'romane curie'. The majority of the Mass Proper settings seem
to have been drawn from the Imperial chapel, particularly those
in manuscripts Trent 89–91.[111] It has been shown that Laurence
Feininger's generally ignored attribution of some of the cycles of Mass
Propers in Trent 88 to Dufay may, in fact, be correct, at least in part.[112]
The collections also show a change in musical style from the settings
attributable to Brassart or Dufay and unnamed contemporaries, which
ordinarily have the ornamented cantus firmus in the superius of a
three-voice setting, to three- or four-voice settings (sometimes with
provision for alternate three- or four-voice performance) with the
cantus firmus often in the tenor in equal values, sometimes set out
in chant notation. It has been suggested by Reinhard Strohm[113] that
the *Choralis Constantinus* of Isaac is the culmination and very formal
presentation of a practice of the Imperial chapel going back more
than five decades by the time of its composition and that it represents
the second complete replacement of the chapel repertory by 'modern'
settings.[114]

Few of the Mass Propers and hymns carry attributions. This
state of affairs is the rule for this kind of music during the fifteenth

[110] On these cycles see Alejandro E. Planchart, 'Guillaume Dufay's Benefices and his
Relationship to the Court of Burgundy', *EMH* 7 (1987), 117–71, esp. 143–69.

[111] See Leverett, 'A Paleographical and Repertorial Study', 73 ff.

[112] See David Fallows, 'Dufay and the Mass Proper Cycles of Trent 88', in Nino Pirrotta
and Danilo Curti (eds.), *I codici musicali trentini. Atti del Convegno Laurence Feininger: La
musicologia come missione* (Trento, 1986), 46–59, and the literature cited there.

[113] *Rise*, 525.

[114] Leverett, 'A Paleographical and Repertorial Study', 107.

century except in the case of a few unusual collections. It may well be
that this situation obtains because the music was never intended to be
performed outside the institution whose liturgy controlled its choice
of text and tune and whose customs as to use of polyphony called for
its existence. Hence, the pieces did not require labelling with the name
of their creator since he would ordinarily be present at their performance or known to the performers.

The musical nature of the cantus-firmus elaborations is quite
variable. The chant melody may be either in the superius or in the
tenor, it may be ornamented and elaborated, or it may be stated in
equal values. The other two or three voices may function imitatively;
if so, they may imitate the cantus-firmus-bearing voice or present
material totally unrelated to it. A number of the compositions have
five notated voices, including three contratenors labelled to indicate
that either one or two may be used to create a three- or four-voice
work. In a few of the introits the antiphon is *a 3* and the verse is *a 2*
or *a fauxbourdon*. A number of the introits lack a setting of the verse
or Doxology or both. This incompleteness may be illusory in that the
missing sections could have been improvised in fauxbourdon. The
marginal additions of psalm-tone intonations and differentia, identified by tone and without text, using this technique found in Munich
14274 can be taken as an indication of this practice with Office psalms,
a practice that would be readily transferable to the introit. That only
the portions of the tone in which the pitch changes are found in
Munich 14274 might indicate that the notator of these fragments was
only concerned with preserving the difficult portion of the procedure
and assumed that the easier portion, the recitation tone, need not be
notated.

In some of the later hymn settings the anonymous composer
has created a rather sophisticated, if relatively brief, composition.
In a work such as *Veni redemptor gentium* (Trent 89, fos. 303ᵛ–304ʳ)
the hymn melody is presented phrase by phrase in semibreves in
the tenor. Each tenor phrase is preceded by a statement of the tune
in ornamented form in shorter values in another voice. Individual phrases are set for two, three, or four voices with the long
values of the tenor alternately present or absent. Successive phrases
contain the hymn melody either in ornamented or unadorned
form. In this and in a number of compositions based on a chant
melody, the anonymous composer has created a lively, varied elaboration of a very familiar melody, a composition that goes well beyond
simply presenting the text and its traditional tune in a polyphonic
guise.

The strong preference for setting out the chant in longer, equal values is a characteristic of works from the German-speaking region[115] and is relatively rare in settings used in Italian centres. The very presence of Mass Propers, much less their large number, sets this collection apart from almost any made south of the Alps or west of the Rhine.[116] The repertory of the Trent manuscripts is found as well in the Strahov manuscript and in the Glogauer Liederbuch,[117] both in concordances and in the presence in all three of works very similar in style.[118] In addition, there are concordances linking the later works in these manuscripts with the repertory preserved in several manuscripts compiled in the general region just before and around 1500.[119]

The Mass repertory contained in the Trent manuscripts and the Strahov manuscript is very extensive and includes works by the major composers from Dunstaple and Power through Faugues, Martini, and Ockeghem.[120] The very size of the repertory and the familiarity with works by major composers documents the degree to which this music had penetrated the Empire. Of greater interest for present purposes are works that seem to show local and regional origin.

At least three types of Mass Ordinary seem to be very commonly found here and relatively uncommon in other sources. The first of these has been known for some time: the Mass cycle using German lieder as cantus firmi.[121] These works have in common the use of lieder

---

[115] See Strohm, *Rise*, 525–6.

[116] If all the details concerning Dufay's authorship of the Proper cycles in Trent 88 can be worked out and the nature of the collection reported to have been copied in Cambrai determined as polyphonic, this statement will have to be revised. One is still left with a situation in which almost every collection of sacred music for use in the Empire copied between 1430 and 1530 contains Mass Proper settings and few are found elsewhere until well into the 16th c.

[117] Prague D.G.IV.47 and Berlin, former Preußischer Staatsbibliothek, MS 40098, now in Kraków, Jagiellonian Library.

[118] Leverett, 'A Paleographical and Repertorial Study', i. 81–90 and ii. 41–53, makes a convincing case for the repertorial relationship between the Mass Propers of Trent 91 and the Glogauer Liederbuch.

[119] Munich, Bayerische Staatsbibliothek, MS Mus 3154 (edition by Thomas Noblitt, Das Erbe deutscher Musik, 80–3); Berlin, Bibliothek zu Berlin — Preußischer Kulturbesitz, MS 40021 (ed. Martin Just in Das Erbe deutscher Musik, 76–8); Leipzig, Universitätsbibliothek, MS 1494 (ed. Rudolf Gerber in Das Erbe deutscher Musik, 32–3, and Ludwig Finscher and Wolfgang Dömling, 34); Warsaw, Biblioteka Uniwersyteka, MS MF 2016.

[120] See Leverett, 'A Paleographical and Repertorial Study', 114–69 and 192–7 regarding the copies of these Masses in Trent 91 and questions about the authenticity of the Ockeghem attribution.

[121] See Louis E. Gottlieb, 'The Cyclic Masses of Trent Codex 89' (Ph.D. diss., University of California at Los Angeles, 1958), and Robert F. Schmalz, 'Selected Fifteenth-Century Polyphonic Mass Ordinaries Based upon Pre-existent German Material' (Ph.D. diss., University of Pittsburgh, 1971); Reinhard Strohm, 'Meßzyklen über deutsche Lieder in den Trienter Codices', in *Liedstudien: Wolfgang Osthoff zum 60. Geburtstag* (Tutzing, 1989), 77–106. Leverett, 'A Paleographical and Repertorial Study', 258–62 adds the *Missa Zersundert ist das junge Herze mein*. See also ead., 'Song Masses in the Trent Codices: The Austrian Connection', *EMH* 14 (1995), 205–56.

as pre-existent material but subject this material to a variety of procedures as a means of unifying the Masses. These works are found
in Trent 89–91 and the Strahov manuscript. The Masses on *Rozel im
gorten, Grüne Linden, Hilf und gib Rat, Sig säld und hail, Wünschliche
schöne, Zersundert ist das junge Herze mein*, and *Gross senen* are all
based on single German lieder. *Missa Christus surrexit* uses the melody
associated with *Christ ist erstanden*, and the Mass appearing in Trent
89, fos. 408^v–413^r, referred to in recent writings as the *Missa Deutscher
Lieder*, uses a number of identifiable lieder. The composer of only
one of these, the *Missa Hilf und gib rat*, can be identified. The Mass
carries an attribution to 'Philipus' in the Strahov manuscript, a
name otherwise unknown except for works found in the Strahov and
Speciálník manuscripts.[122] These Masses are significant for several
reasons. First, the use of German lieder ties their composition to some
centre in the Empire, a centre which can be shown to be the Imperial
court on the basis of source distribution. Second, several (*Sig säld,
Zersundert*, and *Wünschliche schöne*) at times make simultaneous
reference to the discantus as well as the tenor of the lied, making these
works approach the parody or imitation Mass technique, as do several
other works in the Trent collection. Others use relatively sophisticated
verbal canons to create different tenors from the original notation of
the model voice.

The conclusions to be drawn here are that composers, whose
identities are as yet unknown, but who were certainly working in or
near the Imperial court, were creating works that have been rightly
characterized as pioneering and central.[123] This is an extraordinarily
important matter in the face of the ordinary view of this region as
peripheral and the style of music produced here as derivative. Still to
be explored are the ramifications of the presence of many of the lieder
in the Glogau and Schedel songbooks, particularly the fact that several
of these songs are to be found in the Glogauer Liederbuch in quodli-
bets associated with Dunstaple's *O rosa bella*, itself the model for
Masses in the Trent manuscripts. Are these lieder, in ordinary form
and as quodlibet quotations, the popular standards of the court? A
related question is the source of the practice of simultaneous quota-
tion. There is the example of the Latin or German contrafacta of
secular songs, but that involves retexting of entire pieces in order to
change the function, not a momentary reference to the polyphonic

---

[122] Adelyn Leverett has set out evidence of possible attributions of the Masses on *Gross senen*
and *Sig säld und hail* to Touront and that on *Zersundert ist* to Vincenet in her dissertation,
234–60. See also her 'Song Masses in the Trent Codices'.
[123] Strohm, 'Meßzyklen', 102–3.

structure with a new text. A chronologically distant source could be seen in the works of a composer whose music, on the basis of pre-served sources, was relatively widely known in the region: Antonio Zacara da Teramo, who produced several Gloria and Credo move-ments based on his own secular songs.[124] Additional Masses using other kinds of pre-existent models and not yet securely attributed to any composer appear in the later group of Trent manuscripts and may also have a similar origin.[125] If these are ultimately linked to the Imperial court as their place of origin, we would have there a major centre for the production of new, innovative music. Even if these works can be shown to be from other parts of Europe, the Imperial chapel would remain a place very well informed about the most recent developments in the composition of cyclic Mass Ordinaries.

An additional Mass type has recently been identified as forming an important part of the Trent repertory: the three-voice Mass with low contratenor.[126] Whether the type originated in Austria, or was simply favoured (and collected) by the Imperial court, is not at present deter-minable. The large number of these works and the use of this scoring in two of the Masses on German songs does make it an important element of the regional repertory, regardless of its origin. There is another group of Masses in repertory shared by the later Trent manuscripts and the Strahov manuscript: the Mass-motet cycle. These works are a Mass Ordinary (sometimes lacking a Kyrie) and a motet, all of which are based on the same cantus firmus.[127] The specific use of this kind of work is not completely clear, although the existence of several of them suggests not only that they had a place in the

---

[124] Kurt von Fischer, 'Kontrafakturen und Parodien italienischer Werke des Trecento und frühen Quattrocento', *Annales musicologiques*, 5 (1957), 43–59.

[125] For three Masses on Latin-texted cantus firmi for which evidence of an Austrian origin is presented, see Reinhard Strohm, 'Zur Rezeption der frühen Cantus-firmus-Messe im deutschsprachigen Bereich', in W. Konold (ed.), *Deutsch-englische Musikbeziehungen: Referate des wissenschaftlichen Symposions 'Musica Britannica' (1980)* (Munich, 1985), 9–38.

[126] Leverett, 'A Paleographical and Repertorial Study', 170–220. Caution must be applied in accepting the conclusions reached here. At least one of the works listed as part of a slightly later group found in German sources, the *Officium Auleni*, is found in two, not one, non-German sources (Barcelona, Biblioteca Central, MS 454, fos. 74–82 should be added to the list of sources), suggesting that it might be of Netherlandish rather than of German origin. This rein-forces questions about this group as representing a type of specifically Austrian origin raised by the attributions to Barbingant and Vincenet and by the concordances for other works in Italian manuscripts. These questions must not be permitted to discount the thesis, however. There is evidence of contact with Rome in this period and there is the additional musical evidence of a series of antiphons found in Trent 89 and Rome, Archivio San Pietro, MS B 80.

[127] These works were originally decribed by Robert Snow in his dissertation, 'The Manuscript Strahov D.G.IV.47' (Ph.D. diss., University of Illinois, 1967) and subsequently in 'The Mass-Motet Cycle: A Mid-Fifteenth-Century Experiment', in R. J. Snow (ed.), *Essays in Musicology in Honor of Dragan Plamenac on his 70th Birthday* (Pittsburgh, 1969), 301–20. More recently, Reinhard Strohm has suggested that several of the works are not six-movement cycles in his 'Meßzyklen', 87–9.

celebration of the Mass, but also that the practice in this region included the performance of a motet at the end of the Mass, raising interesting questions about some of the motets copied among the Masses in the manuscripts from this region.

In sum, the music just discussed would indicate that the chapel of the Emperor Friedrich III was an active, vital musical organization. Despite the political problems that seemed constantly to demand his attention, leading to the unwarranted assumption that he must have been left with little time for music, he must have invested some time in its development, or, at least, entrusted someone with the authority to work towards this end. Although little has been discovered and published to tell us about the membership of the chapel and its duties and functions, the preserved music does indicate an extensive performance schedule of polyphonic music within the liturgy. In addition, Friedrich was active in endowing musical activity, not clearly defined as monophonic or polyphonic, in a number of churches in his realm, particularly in proximity to his primary residence in Wiener Neustadt.[128] His son and successor, Maximilian I, received a highly developed tradition upon his accession.

THE IMPERIAL CHAPEL UNTIL THE DEATH OF MAXIMILIAN

The Imperial chapel under Maximilian has received far more attention than under his father. Maximilian travelled extensively, and determining what constituted the chapel that accompanied him is not without problems. His occasional periods of residence in the Low Countries have also raised questions about the origins of some of his musicians, that is, were they German or French? Maximilian seemed to understand the importance of a musical chapel in creating the proper image of a ruler for the influence he hoped to have. To this end he took singers from the Habsburg Netherlandish chapel with him to Frankfurt and Aachen in 1477.[129] In 1494 he met Frederick the Wise of Saxony in Mechelen, and documents refer to the performance of a Mass by his French and German singers.[130] It appears more likely that this statement means that his chapel had singers of both nationalities, rather than that he had two chapels. In 1498 he ordered the establishment in Vienna, a city he avoided as had his father, of a chapel under the administrative direction of Georg Slatkonia.[131] This group of

---

[128] See Rudolf Flotzinger and Gernot Gruber, *Musikgeschichte Österreichs*, 2 vols. (Graz, 1977), i. 189.
[129] Ibid. 196.
[130] Ibid. 199.
[131] Ibid.

musicians included Hannsen Kerner, who was a member of the chapel as early as 1496, as 'Singmaister', Heinrich Isaac as 'Hofkomponist',[132] and Paul Hofhaimer as organist.

The presence of a musician of the international reputation of Isaac marks a major point of development in the nature of the musical scene in the region. Numerous works by Isaac, most notably Books I and III of the *Choralis Constantinus*, but also several Masses and motets as well as German lieder, can be linked to this period of service or to Isaac's relationship with Constance or his casual employment by Frederick the Wise, Elector of Saxony. There is also good reason to associate the Mass Propers and works such as the *Missa Carminum* with earlier Imperial court traditions described above. Several of Isaac's motets have been linked to important events in Maximilian's rule.[133] One of them, *Virgo prudentissima*, is in six voices and combines references to Maximilian with Marian prayers. Any chapel that could have performed works such as this and the Mass Propers of the *Choralis Constantinus* at a level of quality that Maximilian would have understood as essential to the projection of his own image, would have been very highly skilled. In addition to the music that can be identified as having been composed within the court, specifically works by Isaac and Hofhaimer, manuscripts compiled for Maximilian in the Netherlands can also be identified.[134]

Maximilian visited Augsburg several times after 1500,[135] and it was here that the volume of motets *Liber selectarum cantionum* (RISM 1520[4]), which serves both as a memorial to him and to his musical establishment and as a sign of the importance of the city of Augsburg, was published. This collection presents a cross-section of music of the first decades of the sixteenth century that was apparently readily available in Augsburg. One of the leading humanists in the city, Konrad Peutinger, had a role in its production as well as in other musical and publication efforts in the city.[136] Besides the works of members of the chapel, one obvious path by which music came to this city was through the collecting activities of members of the Fugger banking family, with its ties to all parts of Europe, but particularly the Netherlands. Travel, employment of a composer of the rank of Isaac,

[132] Martin Staehelin, *Die Messen Heinrich Isaacs*, 3 vols. (Publikationen der Schweizerischen Musikforschenden Gesellschaft, ser. 2, vol 28; Berne, 1977), ii. 43–82, provides documents related to the composer's relationship to the Imperial court.

[133] Albert Dunning, *Die Staatsmotette: 1480–1555* (Utrecht, 1970), 39–45.

[134] See the description of Vienna, Österreichische Nationalbibliothek, MS 15495 in *Census-Catalogue*, iv. 96.

[135] Of particular interest are the Reichstage of 1500, 1510, and 1518, which would have brought the chapel to the city. See *MGG*, s.v. Augsburg.

[136] See also Louise Cuyler, *The Emperor Maximilian and Music* (London, 1973).

and acquisition of music created an institution that was by this time a part of the musical mainstream and very likely set the model for later emperors and other lesser rulers, such as the Wittelsbachs in Munich, in their hiring of some of the leading musicians of western Europe during the remainder of the sixteenth century.

As important as was the Imperial chapel's place in comparison with French and Italian chapels, equally important was the development of strong musical forces in other courts in Germany, particularly that of Frederick the Wise in Torgau/Wittenberg at the end of the fifteenth century and, to a lesser extent, Ulrich in the Württemberg court in Stuttgart at the beginning of the sixteenth.[137] Both of these chapels hired important composers—Frederick at various times in the 1490s had Adam von Fulda, Finck, and Isaac in his service, and Ulrich hired Finck in 1510. Frederick's travels took him over much of western Europe and he seems to have taken special pains to acquire music from the Netherlands, as is demonstrated by some of the presentation manuscripts now in Jena. By the time of the Reformation, musicians and religious leaders had in this court a very strong and active focal point for the production of music for the new liturgy, serving as a central source for dissemination of music. One must ask if this could have happened without the nearly forty years of sustained support for music at the Torgau/Wittenberg court.

The repertory of music known in Germany, Austria, and Silesia at the end of the fifteenth and beginning of the sixteenth century is documented by a series of large choirbooks, as well as a number of fragmentary sources, that show a significant number of works by the leading composers of the day, Josquin, Compère, Obrecht, and Agricola, among others, as well as numerous works that can be shown for various reasons to have been composed somewhere within the region.[138] The degree to which western European music had become commonplace in the region is shown, for example, by the extraordinarily important role of manuscripts from this area among the sources of the music of Jacob Obrecht.[139] Martin Just has provided an important discussion of aspects of this repertory in terms of imitation of mainstream models and identification of regional style trends. Among the latter is a discernable tendency in some compositions for the composer to work with contrapuntal elaboration around pairs of pitches

---

[137] On the former see Wilhelm Ehmann, *Adam von Fulda als Vertreter des ersten deutschen Komponistengeneration* (Berlin, 1936) and Karl Roediger, *Die geistlichen Musikhandschriften der Universitätsbibliothek Jena*, 2 vols. (Jena, 1935). On the latter, see Hoffmann-Erbrecht, *Heinrich Finck*.

[138] See note 119.

[139] See Chris Maas, 'Toward a New Obrecht Edition', *TVNM* 26 (1976), 84–108.

with at least the value of a breve, a practice already found in the 1430s.[140]

Throughout the second half of the fifteenth century, music-making became an ever more broadly practised activity in central Europe. An important change in the practice of music involves the venues in which this took place. Towards the beginning of the century monastic establishments, along with universities, were an important part of the production, performance, and transmission of music. In the middle of the fifteenth century the reforms of the Melk Congregation of the Benedictine order included a ban on the use of laymen in the performance of the liturgy and an apparent ban on polyphony as well.[141] The word 'apparent' is used because although the legislation was in place, music can still be associated with Benedictine institutions, particularly with various people holding the title 'rector scolarium'. It may be that the ban on use within the liturgy was adhered to, but that music continued to have a role in the schools sponsored by the monasteries. Universities continued to demonstrate that at least as it affected individual members of these communities, the production of collections of music was an ongoing activity.

GERMAN SONG FROM 1440 TO 1520

There are two gaps in the preserved repertory of German secular texts that present certain difficulties in providing a description of the development of this genre from the end of Wolkenstein's career through the extensive flowering of the genre in the printed song collections of the sixteenth century. The sources of German song begin with the three collections: the Lochamer (c.1455), Schedel (1460s), and Glogau (c.1480) songbooks.[142] All three contain other types of music: Lochamer includes organ tablatures as well as monophonic (35) and polyphonic (9) songs; Schedel has French and Italian secular music as well as motets, but just over half its contents are German songs; Glogau has close repertorial connections with the Trent manuscripts

---

[140] Just, *Der Mensuralkodex Mus. ms. 40021*, i. 131 ff.

[141] Joachim Angerer, *Die liturgische-musikalische Erneuerung der Melker Reform* (Vienna, 1973), and 'Die Begriffe *Discantus, Organa* und *Scolares* in reformgeschichtliche Urkunden des 15. Jahrhunderts', *Anzeiger der Österreichischen Akademie der Wissenschaften, Philosophish-Historische Klasse*, 109 (1972), 146–70.

[142] Berlin, Staatsbibliothek zu Berlin — Preußischer Kulturbesitz, MS 40613: *Locheimer Liederbuch und Fundamentum organisandi des Conrad Paumann*, ed. Konrad Ameln (Berlin, 1925); *Lochamer-Liederbuch und Fundamentum Organisandi des Conrad Paumann* (Kassel, 1972); Munich, Bayerische Staatsbibliothek, MS Germ. 810: *Das Liederbuch des Dr. Hartmann Schedel* (Das Erbe deutscher Musik, 84; Kassel, 1978); and Berlin, former Preußischer Staatsbibliothek, MS 40098 (currently in Kraków, Jagiellonian Library): *Das Glogauer Liederbuch* (Das Erbe deutscher Musik, 3, 4, 85, and 86; Renaissance Manuscripts in Facsimile, 6 (New York, 1986)).

in its large sacred repertory, which dominates the collection of nearly 300 works, but it also contains at least seventy German songs. There are a few works that are found in more than one of these sources, but the bulk of the music appears as unattributed unica. The polyphonic settings each seem to be based on a pre-existing monophonic melody, ordinarily appearing in either the tenor or superius in values longer than those found in the other voices. Text is usually set syllabically, or very nearly so, particularly in the voice carrying the cantus firmus. There is very occasional use of imitation, sometimes based on the tune, but the music generally tends to be ornamental counterpoint around the voice bearing the text and carrying the tune. The frequency with which only one voice is provided with text suggests that the intended medium is a mixed vocal/instrumental ensemble, not unlike the texture of some of Oswald von Wolkenstein's music. A few songs are set homophonically with the tune in the highest part. It is not clear whether the absence of any text beyond an incipit in the Schedel and Glogau collections is an indication that the words were well enough known and underlay was not complicated that their copying would be unnecessary or whether this is simply scribal inertia.

Songs appear in most of the major manuscripts from the end of the fifteenth century, but not in large numbers. This may reflect the nature of the collections more than anything else, since most of them are concerned primarily with sacred music. They do, however, include songs by Heinrich Finck, Adam von Fulda, and Paul Hofhaimer. These songs tend to be somewhat more complex than the preceding repertory. Finck, for example, generally writes for four voices, assigning the tune to the tenor, and imitates the opening contours of some of its phrases in the other three voices. In some of these songs, the tenor entry is delayed, much in the manner of the cantus-firmus-bearing voice in sacred music. In others the texture is much simpler, approaching homophony. Similar kinds of more involved contrapuntal activity are employed by the other composers as well. By the third decade of the sixteenth century the German lied was widely enough known that Glareanus could cite Adam's *Ach hülf mich leid* as being sung throughout Germany.

The more than thirty-year gap between the first song manuscripts and the first printed collections can be filled in part by references to songs in other genres.[143] There are Masses based on German lieder in the Trent and Strahov manuscripts that provide important evidence on this point. There is little purpose, it would seem, in constructing a

---

[143] This point was first explicitly made by Reinhard Strohm in 'Meßzyklen'.

Mass on a tune that no one has ever heard. Thus, these works would tend to indicate that the performance of German song was a relatively frequent occurrence. Likewise, some slightly later hymns that use songs as a second text and cantus firmus, generally with the effect of expanding upon the meaning of the hymn, show that these songs could claim a certain familiarity among those in attendance at a Vespers service.[144] These works that bring song into the context of liturgical music have the effect of multiplying the relatively few settings preserved in the sources compiled between 1480 and the appearance of the printed song books in the second decade of the sixteenth century.

The sudden appearance of five printed collections between 1512 and 1519 is striking. Together they present nearly 300 German songs, the vast majority of them secular, and a scattering of Latin-texted works, both sacred and secular. The *Liederbuch* published in 1512 in Augsburg by Erhard Öglin presents forty-two *a 4* Tenorlieder. Peter Schöffer's print prepared in Mainz in 1513, containing sixty-one secular songs and a setting of *Christ ist erstanden*, includes music by a number of composers active in this period in Stuttgart and may be based on the court repertory there, although the absence of any music known to be by Heinrich Finck, then employed there, raises doubts about this possibility. Additional publications by Öglin and Schöffer appeared in 1513 and 1515, respectively, but only the superius of each is preserved. The *Liederbuch* of Arnt von Aich printed in Cologne in 1519 includes music by Adam von Fulda, who was at the court of Torgau, as well as an early appearance of music by Adam Rener, a student of Ludwig Senfl. With the exception of some of the compositions in the 1513 print by Schöffer, none of the music is attributed within the collections. No additional printed collections of secular music appear until 1534, yet another interruption of the succession of sources.[145]

All these collections include settings of Hofweisen (courtly songs), works carrying on, in part, the Minnesang tradition, particularly in their choice of subjects and their structure. The poems tend to be in Bar form (AAB), to use short rhyming lines, and to use syllable count as a formal device. The poems tend to be limited to love songs or moralizing/didactic texts, with references to classical mythology sometimes appearing, particularly in the very popular songs of Adam von Fulda *Apollo aller Kunst* and *Ach Jupiter*. The less frequently encountered Gesellschaftslied, intended for a broader audience, appears as

[144] See Ward, *The Polyphonic Office Hymn*, nos. 112, 362, and 636.
[145] The repertory of Tenorlieder has been catalogued in *Das Tenorlied*, ed. Norbert Böker-Heil, Harald Heckman, and Ilse Kindermann, 3 vols. (Catalogus musices, 9–11; Kassel, 1979–86).

early as the Lochamer songbook but does not become at all popular until the 1530s. Its texts tend to be much more varied in subject matter, with narrative texts or texts extolling nature being very common. Both types seem to be based on melodies that had a currency in the monophonic repertory prior to becoming the tenor or superius of the polyphonic setting. It has been pointed out that, among other differences, the Hofweisen tend to have larger ranges than the Gesellschaftslieder.[146] Along with the delineation of these types, it is important to note that a large portion of the repertory displays characteristics of both forms. The settings show a preference for presentation of the melody in one voice, usually the tenor, but at times the superius. The other three voices generally move in smaller values and often imitate the initial notes of the traditional melody at the beginning of each phrase.

Broadly speaking, the stylistic preferences found in the various repertories of German song in the early sixteenth century are distinct from those in western Europe or in Italy and Spain, although most of the particular compositional techniques cultivated elsewhere are known in central Europe as well.

---

[146] Kurt Gudewill, 'Deutsche Liedtenores mit F-dur-Melodik und Oktavambitus', in *Festschrift für Walter Wiora* (Kassel, 1967), 269–77, and 'Beziehungen zwischen Modus und Melodiebildung in deutschen Liedtenores', *Archiv für Musikwissenschaft*, 15 (1958), 60–88.

VI

MUSIC THEORY OF THE FOURTEENTH AND EARLY FIFTEENTH CENTURIES

By Jan Herlinger

INTRODUCTION

THE modern study of medieval music theory began with the collections of treatises published during the eighteenth and nineteenth centuries by Gerbert, La Fage, and Coussemaker. Though Gerbert and particularly Coussemaker (in contrast to La Fage, who generally presented his texts on the basis of single sources) were sometimes aware of multiple copies of the treatises they published, they were often unfortunate in choosing which sources to present, inaccurate in transcribing them, and haphazard in reporting variant readings. Though the contributions of these scholars have been and remain indispensable for students of medieval theory, it is only in the last fifty years that critical editions of medieval theoretical works have begun to appear in quantity.[1] Even in these there is considerable variation in procedure and accuracy.

The cataloguing of theoretical sources has remained problematic. The first two volumes of the RISM series devoted to the theory of music in manuscript suffer from their arbitrary cut-off date of 1400 (1500, which marks the end of the manuscript tradition of music theory, would have been more sensible), from the selective exclusion of many fifteenth-century manuscripts that contain works dating from before 1400, from the omission of some pre-1400 sources, and from an unacceptably low level of accuracy in dating the manuscripts and recording their contents. Subsequent volumes rectify these problems, and revisions of the first two volumes are planned; meanwhile

---

[1] In addition to the many single volumes that have appeared, the main series are Corpus scriptorum de musica (CSM; American Institute of Musicology, since 1950), Divitiae artis musicae (Schola Palaeographica Amstelodamensis, 1975–85), and Greek and Latin Music Theory (University of Nebraska Press, since 1984); a revision of Gerbert's collections is under way: Bernhard's *Clavis Gerberti*. Note also the Music Theory Translation Series (Yale University Press, since 1963).

scholars must supplement the first two volumes with more general catalogues like those of Kristeller and Thorndike-Kibre.[2]

Contributing to the bibliographic problems is the question of authorship for many of the treatises; attribution is at least as great a problem for medieval theoretical treatises as it is for medieval musical compositions. Johannes de Muris, for instance, has been deprived of most of the treatises attributed to him in the collections of Gerbert and Coussemaker;[3] and even the existence of Philippe de Vitry's *Ars nova*—which gave its name to an epoch of music history—has been questioned.[4]

Two of the greatest problems facing the student of medieval theory have been the lack of a comprehensive dictionary of medieval musical terms and the lack of indexes of terms in most critical editions of medieval treatises (much less a comprehensive index for the entire period); this second problem has meant that those who wish to trace the evolution of a particular concept have had to rely on their own efforts and their memories. Now, however, the *Lexicon musicum Latinum medii aevi* has begun to appear. Moreover, since the Thesaurus Musicarum Latinarum, an evolving full-text database for music theory in Latin, *c*.600–*c*.1600, went on-line in 1990, scholars have been able to run computer-assisted searches of medieval musical terms on their own. Both enterprises should greatly facilitate the study of medieval music theory.

Given the problems that exist in the field, it should not be surprising that a reliable history of medieval and Renaissance music theory has been so long coming. The first two books of Riemann's *Geschichte der Musiktheorie*, which cover the Middle Ages and the Renaissance, suffer not only from the unreliability of the sources Riemann had to work with but from his bizarre perspectives (for instance, his treatment of just intonation as the norm; see for example p. 114 of the English translation); some but by no means all problems are dealt with by the translator. Smits van Waesberghe's *Musikerziehung* is less a comprehensive history than a collection of vignettes—very revealing vignettes, to be sure. The *Geschichte der Musiktheorie* edited by Frieder Zaminer promises to fill this gap; several of the projected fifteen volumes deal with music theory during the period of concern here.

[2] Paul Oskar Kristeller, *Iter Italicum: A Finding List of Uncatalogued or Incompletely Catalogued Humanistic Manuscripts of the Renaissance in Italian and Other Libraries*, 6 vols. and Index (London and Leiden, 1963–97); Lynn Thorndike and Pearl Kibre, *A Catalogue of Mediaeval Scientific Writings in Latin* (Publications of the Mediaeval Academy of America, 29; rev. and augmented edn., Cambridge, Mass., 1963).

[3] See Ulrich Michels, *Die Musiktraktate des Johannes de Muris* (Beihefte zum Archiv für Musikwissenschaft, 8; Wiesbaden, 1970), 16–55.

[4] See Sarah Fuller, 'A Phantom Treatise of the Fourteenth Century?—The *Ars Nova*', *Journal of Musicology*, 4 (1985–6), 23–50.

The subject matter of the present volume commences at about 1300. It is convenient to begin a short survey of music theory at that time, for by then the theory of notes, syllables, pitches, and their interrelations had coalesced, enabling a systematic theory of the modes of plainchant to develop; the classification of intervals had stabilized, enabling a coherent theory of counterpoint to develop;[5] and mensural notation had reached a sophistication that enabled rhythms to be written down without ambiguity. Given the enormous number of medieval treatises on music,[6] however, a comprehensive synopsis is not possible in the space available here. Rather, this survey will cover in succession the topics music fundamentals, mode, counterpoint, mensuration, and *musica speculativa*, touching on the most significant aspects of each.

FUNDAMENTALS

Music fundamentals, as conceived in the late Middle Ages, treated the basic scale, solmization, and mutation; intervals; tuning; and the extended scale. We shall discuss these in order.[7]

The Basic Scale, Solmization, and Mutation

The music theory of the fourteenth and early fifteenth centuries inherited a basic scale extending from G at the bottom of our bass staff to E at the top of our treble staff and including all the natural notes in that range plus the B♭s a second below and a seventh above our middle C (but not the B♭ on the second line of our bass staff), these notes being designated Γ A B C D E F G a b ♮ c d e f g aa bb ♮♮ cc dd ee[8] (in this chapter pitches will be designated according to this system) and organized into registers as follows:

low (*graves*)	Γ A B C D E F G
high (*acutae*)	a b ♮ c d e f g
very high (*superacutae*)	aa bb ♮♮ cc dd ee

On this set of notes had been imposed a series of interlocking hexachords, hexachord being defined as a set of six notes identified by the syllables *ut, re, mi, fa, sol, la* and separated by the five intervals tone,

---

[5] On these points, see Karol Berger, *Musica Ficta: Theories of Accidental Inflections in Vocal Polyphony from Marchetto da Padova to Gioseffo Zarlino* (Cambridge and New York, 1987), p. xiii.

[6] For an overview, see Michael Bernhard, 'Das musikalische Fachschrifttum im lateinischen Mittelalter', in Zaminer, iii. 37–103.

[7] For a more extended discussion, see Klaus-Jürgen Sachs, 'Musikalische Elementarlehre im Mittelalter', in Zaminer, iii. 105–61.

[8] The round b indicates B flat, the square ♮ B natural. The double letters representing each of the last six notes were usually aligned vertically rather than horizontally by medieval scribes. The earliest known treatise in which the seven letters A–G, reduplicated for higher octaves, are used with their present meaning is the anonymous *Dialogus* (*c*.1000) formerly attributed to Oddo.

Ex. 6.1. The basic scale

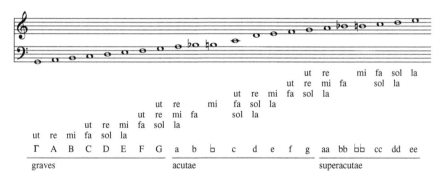

																					ut	re		mi	fa	sol	la
																			ut	re	mi	fa			sol	la	
																ut	re	mi	fa	sol	la						
									ut	re		mi		fa	sol	la											
							ut	re	mi	fa		sol	la														
					ut	re	mi	fa	sol	la																	
ut	re	mi	fa	sol	la																						
Γ	A	B	C	D	E	F	G	a	b	♮	c	d	e	f	g	aa	bb	♮♮	cc	dd	ee						

graves · acutae · superacutae

tone, semitone, tone, tone. In the basic scale hexachords could be built on Gs, Fs, and Cs (see Ex. 6.1); a hexachord built on G was said to be sung 'with the property of square ♭', one built on F 'with the property of round ♭', one built on C 'with the natural property' (Marchetto, *Lucidarium* 8.3).[9] To each letter name in the scale were attached the syllable names normally associated with it (the occurrence of B♮ as *mi* in the G hexachords and of B♭ as *fa* in the F hexachords accounts for the inclusion of two inflections of b—bfa, ♭mi):

> low: Γut, Are, Bmi, Cfaut, Dsolre, Elami, Ffaut, Gsolreut
> high: alamire, bfa♮mi, csolfaut, dlasolre, elami, ffaut, gsolreut
> very high: aalamire, bbfa ♭♭ mi, ccsolfa, ddlasol, eela[10]

Melodies exceeding the range of a single hexachord or using both B♭ and B♮ were accommodated by mutation, 'a change in the name of a syllable or note lying in the same space or on the same line and with the same pitch' (Marchetto, *Lucidarium* 8.2.2). A mutation could be made anywhere in the basic scale where two or three syllable names were attached to the letter name of a note. For instance, on Cfaut a change could be made from *fa* to *ut* or vice versa (Ex. 6.2) and on Gsolreut changes could be made from *sol* to *re* or *ut*, from *re* to *sol* or *ut*, or from *ut* to *sol* or *re* (Ex. 6.3).[11]

---

[9] The usual term for hexachord in this period was *deductio* 'a leading', qualified according to a *proprietas* 'property'.

[10] The familiar depiction of the notes on a hand can be traced to the end of the 11th c. (Joseph Smits van Waesberghe, *Musikerziehung: Lehre und Theorie der Musik im Mittelalter* (Musikgeschichte in Bildern, 3/iii; Leipzig, 1969), 126). So common was this depiction that the basic scale was commonly referred to as 'the hand' (sometimes but inaccurately 'Guido's hand') through the Renaissance.

[11] Smits van Waesberghe traces the theory of mutation back to the second half of the 11th c.; ibid. 116–17.

Ex. 6.2. Mutations on Cfaut (Marchetto, *Lucidarium*, ex. 15)

ut fa sol fa mi fa   fa mi re ut re ut
[re ut re fa sol fa   fa re ut re fa sol fa sol]

Ex. 6.3. Mutations on Gsolreut (Marchetto, *Lucidarium*, exs. 17, 18, 19)

re fa mi re mi re mi   mi re
[re ut fa sol   sol re ut re fa sol mi fa sol fa]

ut mi fa sol fa mi fa   fa mi re mi re ut
[re fa sol la sol   sol mi re fa re ut re]

ut mi fa sol sol fa la   la sol fa mi fa re ut
[ut re fa mi re ut re   re ut fa mi re ut re]

The restriction of mutation to syllable changes *on the same pitch* prevented mutation between *fa* and *mi* on bfa♮mi (i.e. between b♭ and b♮). But to accommodate the chromatic progressions that mark Italian music of the early fourteenth century, Marchetto of Padua introduced the technique of permutation, 'a change in the name of a syllable or note lying in the same space or on the same line but with a different pitch' (*Lucidarium* 8.1.2).[12] With the gradual disappearance of chromatic progressions from musical style over the next century or so, permutation gradually ceased to be an issue among theorists; the term survived in Marchetto's sense, however, in the works of Anselmi (1434), Gaffurio (1496), and even Lanfranco (1533),

---

[12] Marchetto is documented as master of the boys at Padua Cathedral, 1305–7. Between 1317 and 1319 he wrote his monumental treatises *Lucidarium in arte musicae planae* and *Pomerium in arte musicae mensuratae*. The first was enormously influential for its pioneering fractional division of the whole tone and especially for its theory of mode; the latter was the seminal treatise on Italian mensural notation. One composition of Marchetto's survives, the motet *Ave, regina celorum / Mater innocencie*. See F. Alberto Gallo, 'Marchetus in Padua und die "franco-venetische" Musik des frühen Trecento', *Archiv für Musikwissenschaft*, 31 (1974), 42–56, and Jan W. Herlinger, introduction to *The Lucidarium of Marchetto of Padua* (Chicago and London, 1985), 3–5.

and Ramos de Pareja (1482) used it as a synonym for mutation.[13] The more comprehensive term *disiuncta* took its place, defined in the Berkeley Treatise (1.2) as 'a violent transition from one hexachord to another, without whatever mutation of syllables might be possible there'.[14]

Intervals

The intervals between notes were identified originally on the basis of Greek-derived names like tonus, ditonus (with their combinations semitonium, semiditonus); later they came to be represented by Latin numeric designations like secunda, tertia, sometimes differentiated as major or minor. Often they were simply identified by solmization syllables, '*ut-sol*' for a fifth, etc. They were measured in terms of the number of whole tones and semitones they contain (see Table 6.1).

Tuning

Medieval theorists most often defined tuning for the basic scale through directions for the construction of a monochord, and though their routes through the notes of the scale vary, the goal is in the overwhelming majority of cases the same, a tuning system that has since come to be known as 'Pythagorean'.[15] This is a system in which

---

[13] *Georgii Anselmi Parmensis De musica*, ed. Giuseppe Massera ('Historiae Musicae Cultores' Biblioteca, 14; Florence, 1961), 3.46–50; Franchino Gaffurio, *Practica musicae* (Milan, 1496; repr. Bologna, 1972), 1.4; Giovanni Lanfranco, *Scintille di musica* (Brescia, 1533), 12; Bartolomé Ramos de Pareja, *Musica practica Bartolomei Rami de Pareia Bononiae*, ed. Johannes Wolf (Publikationen der Internationalen Musikgesellschaft, Beihefte, 2; Leipzig, 1901), 1.2.4, 5. Fernand Estevan, in his *Reglas de canto plano* of 1410 (in Karl-Werner Gümpel, 'Zur Frühgeschichte der vulgärsprachlichen spanischen und katalanischen Musiktheorie', *Spanische Forschungen der Görres-Gesellschaft*, 1st ser., 24 (1968), 257–336), p. 329, uses the term *mutança* for both mutation and permutation.

[14] The Berkeley Treatise is an anonymous five-part compilation of works on fundamentals and mode, discant, mensuration (this part a version of the *Libellus cantus mensurabilis secundum Johannem de Muris*), *musica speculativa*, and tuning, preserved in the Music Library, University of California, Berkeley. See *The Berkeley Manuscript: University of California Music Library, MS. 744 (olim Phillipps 4450)*, ed. Oliver B. Ellsworth (Greek and Latin Music Theory, 2; Lincoln, Nebr. and London, 1984). Its third part bears the date 1375 (and in a concordant manuscript an attribution to Goscalcus Francigena, possibly identical with the composer Goscalch known through one ballade in Chantilly, Musée Condé, MS 564). It is important for its exposition of the theory of hexachords built on notes other than C, F, and G; for its treatment of florid counterpoint; and as the earliest dated source of the *Libellus*.

[15] On the monochord, see Cecil Dale Adkins, 'The Theory and Practice of the Monochord' (Ph.D. diss., State University of Iowa, 1963); Christian Meyer, *Mensura monochordi: la division du monocorde (IXe–XVe siècles)* (Publications de la Société Française de Musicologie, 2nd ser., 5; Paris, 1996); and Jan Herlinger, 'Medieval Canonics', ch. 3 of *The Cambridge History of Western Music Theory*, ed. Thomas Christensen (Cambridge and New York, forthcoming). For practical purposes, the medieval theory of the monochord may be said to begin with the anonymous *Dialogus de musica* (c.1000). For tuning systems in general, see J. Murray Barbour, *Tuning*

TABLE 6.1 Intervals and their sizes

Greek-derived names[a]	Latin numeric names[b]	English names	Size[c]
unisonus		unison	
semitonium	secunda minor	minor second	1S
tonus	secunda maior	major second	1T
semiditonus	tertia minor	minor third	1T + 1S
ditonus	tertia maior	major third	2T
diatessaron	quarta minor	perfect fourth	2T + 1S
tritonus	quarta maior	augmented fourth	3T
diapente imperfectum	quinta minor	diminished fifth	2T + 2S
diapente	quinta maior	perfect fifth	3T + 1S
diapente cum semitonio	sexta minor	minor sixth	3T + 2S
diapente cum tono	sexta maior	major sixth	4T + 1S
diapente cum semiditono	septima minor	minor seventh	4T + 2S
diapente cum ditono	septima maior	major seventh	5T + 1S
diapason imperfectum	octava minor	diminished octave	4T + 3S
diapason	octava media	perfect octave	5T + 2S
diapente cum tritono	octava maior	augmented octave	6T + 1S

  [a] From Ugolino, *Declaratio*. Among variations in terminology are Prosdocimo's *semitritonus* for *diatessaron*, *diatessaron cum semitonio* for *diapente imperfectum*, and *bisdiatessaron cum semitonio* for *diapason imperfectum*, and Marchetto's *exadem minus* and *maius*, *eptadem minus* and *maius* for the sixths and sevenths.
  [b] From Prosdocimo, *Tractatus musice speculative*. In his *Contrapunctus* Prosdocimo calls the three varieties of octave *octava minor*, *maior*, and *maxima*.
  [c] T = tone; S = semitone. These semitones are the minor semitones of the Pythagorean system.

intervals between any two notes are defined as ratios of two whole numbers (these numbers understood as representing the relative lengths of the two string segments that produce the notes of the intervals) and in which the perfect octave is defined as the ratio 2:1 and the perfect fifth as the ratio 3:2. When so defined, the sizes of those two intervals are 1,200 and 702 cents respectively;[16] and given the sizes of the perfect octave and perfect fifth, the sizes of the other intervals can be determined by addition and subtraction. Moreover, given the ratios of the perfect octave and perfect fifth, the ratios of the other intervals can be determined by multiplication and division (multiplication of their ratios corresponding to addition of their sizes, division of their ratios to subtraction of their sizes). Table 6.2 shows intervals of the Pythagorean tuning system along with their sizes in cents, their ratios, and one among the many possible means of deriving these.

and Temperament: A Historical Survey (East Lansing, Mich., 1953); for 16th-c. temperaments, Mark Lindley, 'Early Sixteenth-Century Keyboard Temperaments', *Musica disciplina*, 28 (1974), 129–51, and *Lutes, Viols, and Temperaments* (Cambridge, 1984).

  [16] A cent is 1/100 of an equally tempered semitone. Cents values of intervals in common tunings and temperaments are given by A. J. Ellis in his App. 20, section D of Hermann

TABLE 6.2 Intervals of the Pythagorean tuning system and their sizes

Interval	How size determined[a]	Size in cents	How ratio determined[a]	Ratio
Perfect octave (P8)		1200		2:1
Perfect fifth (P5)		702		3:2
Perfect fourth (P4)	P8 − P5	498	2:1/3:2	4:3
Major second (M2)	P5 − P4	204	3:2/4:3	9:8
Major third (M3)	M2 + M2	408	9:8 × 9:8	81:64
Minor second (m2)	P4 − M3	90	4:3/81:64	256:243
Augmented prime (A1)	M2 − m2	114	9:8/256:243	2187:2048
Ditonic comma	A1 − m2	24	2187:2048/256:243	531441:524288
Minor third (m3)	P5 − M3	294	3:2/81:64	32:27
Augmented fourth	P5 − m2	612	3:2/256:243	729:512
Diminished fifth	P4 + m2	588	4:3 × 256:243	1024:729
Minor sixth	P5 + m2	792	3:2 × 256:243	128:81
Major sixth	P5 + M2	906	3:2 × 9:8	27:16
Minor seventh	P5 + m3	996	3:2 × 32:27	9:16
Major seventh	P5 + M3	1110	3:2 × 81:64	243:128
Diminished octave	P8 − A1	1086	2:1/2187:2048	4096:2187
Augmented octave	P8 + A1	1314	2:1 × 2187:2048	2187:1024

[a] With the exception of the perfect fourth, sizes and ratios of the intervals could be derived through various other means. Derivations given are the most straightforward.

The intervals of the Pythagorean tuning system differ significantly from those of present-day equal temperament. Though the Pythagorean perfect fifth is the acoustically pure interval of 702 cents, only 2 cents larger than the equally tempered perfect fifth, the Pythagorean major second, which may be seen as the compound of two perfect fifths minus an octave, is 4 cents larger than the equally tempered major second, and the Pythagorean major third, which may be seen as the compound of four perfect fifths minus two octaves, 8 cents larger than the equally tempered major third. The Pythagorean major third, however, exceeds the pure major third (of 386 cents, ratio 5:4) by 22 cents, and consequently is quite dissonant;[17] its dissonance,

Helmholtz, *On the Sensations of Tone*, trans. Alexander J. Ellis (2nd edn., London, 1885; repr. New York, 1954).

[17] The English Benedictine Walter Odington, writing near the beginning of the 14th c., reports that singers narrow the major third (and widen the minor third correspondingly) in order to make it sound sweeter by approximating the pure interval (*Speculatio musicae* 2.10); a century and a half later Martin Le Franc lists *frisque concordance* in close connection with a style he terms the *contenance angloise* (his term may of course apply to compositional style as well as to tuning).

Walter's *Summa de speculatione musicae*, a treatise with a decided speculative slant, comprises chapters on number *per se*, on sound as related to number, on numerical proportions as realized in musical instruments (these three chapters draw heavily on Boethius and Isidore), on number in poetic metres, on music fundamentals and the modes of plainchant, and on mensuration. He also wrote on the other quadrivial arts and on alchemy.

which is somehow exacerbated in combination with a fifth, probably helps explain why composers of the period generally avoided the third in final cadences.

The Pythagorean system differs from equal temperament also in having two sizes of semitones, the minor second of 90 cents and the augmented prime of 114 (usually called minor semitone and major semitone by theorists of the time).

The narrowness of the minor second in Pythagorean tuning increases the tendency of the leading-note to lead. Indeed, in one standard cadential formula of the period (Ex. 6.4(a)), the dissonance of the penultimate minor triad, the narrowness of the melodic minor seconds, and the resonance of the pure harmonic fifth and octave in the final combination produce the effect of a powerful attraction of the penultimate combination to the final one, an attraction that is in no way lessened by the dissonant major triad that appears in the 'under-third' variety of this cadence (Ex. 6.4(b)).

Two fourteenth-century modifications of Pythagorean tuning (or perhaps alternatives to it) should be mentioned. Marchetto of Padua (*Lucidarium* 2.5–8) divided the whole tone into what he called 'diatonic or major' and 'enharmonic or minor' semitones of 3/5 and 2/5 tone respectively and into a 'chromatic' semitone and a 'diesis' of 4/5 and 1/5 tone respectively. In Ex. 6.5 the enharmonic or minor semitone falls between a and b♭, and between b♮ and c, the diatonic or major semitone between b♭ and b♮; the chromatic semitone falls between c♮ and c♯, the diesis between c♯ and d (this latter division is reserved for progressions involving a sharpened note in an imperfect consonance that moves to a perfect one). Since Marchetto's explicitly Pythagorean definitions of the octave, fifth, fourth, and whole tone demand a Pythagorean minor semitone between a and b♭, and between b♮ and c and a Pythagorean major semitone between b♭ and b♮, it seems evident that his diatonic and enharmonic semitones were intended as approximations of the Pythagorean semitones. Then his chromatic semitone is probably to be seen as an interval somewhat larger than the Pythagorean major semitone and his diesis as an interval correspondingly smaller than the Pythagorean minor semitone—but not necessarily as different from them as the fractions 4/5 and 1/5 imply. Be that as it may, the concept of dividing the tone fractionally, radical because the tone's ratio, 9:8, was not susceptible of geometric mediation in Pythagorean arithmetic, was an epochal step in the history of tuning.[18]

---

[18] See Jan W. Herlinger, 'Marchetto's Division of the Whole Tone', *JAMS* 45 (1981), 193–216. On a 15th-c. reaction to Marchetto's proposal, see below, pp. 298–9.

Ex. 6.4. Standard fourteenth-century cadence formulae

Ex. 6.5. Progressions from Marchetto, *Lucidarium*

Oliver Ellsworth finds in the Berkeley Treatise (part 5) a proposal for dividing the octave into nineteen equal parts, a system he calls an equal temperament. But as elsewhere this treatise advocates Pythagorean tuning, and as the text of the crucial passage is corrupt, the question must remain open; the Berkeley proposal may represent a modification of Pythagorean tuning somewhat like Marchetto's. In any case, a division of the octave into nineteen parts, producing narrow major thirds and wide minor seconds in Ellsworth's construction, would more conventionally be classified as a variety of meantone temperament than of equal temperament.[19] And not all listeners might find such a temperament as suitable for late-fourteenth-century music as Ellsworth does.[20]

The Extended Scale
By the period under discussion, of course, composers were using many notes outside what we have called the basic scale, and theorists of the fourteenth and fifteenth centuries were no less assiduous in exploring the new territory. The anonymous treatise *Videndum est de falsa musyca* (fourteenth or fifteenth century) states that every whole tone is divisible into two semitones;[21] Marchetto, writing in 1317 or 1318,

---

[19] Cf. Salinas's very similar '1/3-comma temperament'; Barbour, *Tuning and Temperament*, 33–5.
[20] See Oliver B. Ellsworth, 'A Fourteenth-Century Proposal for Equal Temperament', *Viator*, 5 (1974), 445–53, and introduction to *The Berkeley Manuscript*, 10; Jan W. Herlinger, 'Fractional Divisions of the Whole Tone', *Music Theory Spectrum*, 3 (1981), 74–83.
[21] Nigel Gwee, '*De plana musica* and *Introductio musice*: A Critical Edition and Translation, with Commentary, of Two Treatises Attributed to Johannes de Garlandia' (Ph.D. diss.;

reported the use of the low B♭ in plainchant and presented polyphonic examples including F♯, C♯, G♯, and D♮; Hugo Spechtshart of Reutlingen documented A♭ in his *Flores musicae* (2) of 1332/42.[22] Johannes Boen, in his *Musica* (3.51–162) of 1357, probed the intricacies of the extended scale through the progressions of Ex. 6.6.[23] In 1413 Prosdocimo de' Beldomandi constructed a monochord with E♭, A♭, D♭, and G♭ tuned by successive perfect fifths downward from B♭, and F♯, C♯, G♯, D♯, and A♯ tuned by successive perfect fifths upward from B♮, thus obtaining, in addition to the seven natural notes, five flats and five sharps not enharmonically equivalent to the flats:[24] since the fifths are pure intervals of 702 cents, each sharp lies 24 cents—one Pythagorean or ditonic comma—higher than the flat to which it would be enharmonically equivalent in equal temperament.[25] The monochord of Nicolaus de Luduno, which must date from about the same time, includes the same notes as Prosdocimo's plus C♭.[26]

Louisiana State University, 1996), 269–79. The text was printed also in CS i. 166–75 as part of the *Introductio musice secundum magistrum de Garlandia*.

[22] The versified treatise *Flores musicae* of the parish priest and schoolmaster Hugo Spechtshart of Reutlingen (d. 1359/60) includes chapters on solmization, the monochord (it is one of the earliest monochord discussions to mention five chromatic notes—B♭, E♭, A♭, F♯, and C♯—in addition to the seven natural ones), intervals, and modes; widely disseminated, it survives today in twelve manuscripts and four 15th-c. prints. See *Flores musicae (1332/42)*, ed. Karl-Werner Gümpel (Akademie der Wissenschaften und der Literatur, Mainz, Abhandlungen der Geistes- und Sozialwissenschaftlichen Klasse, Jahrgang 1958, 3; Wiesbaden, 1958). Hugo's *Chronicon* is the main source for 14th-c. German flagellant songs.

[23] The *Musica* of the Dutch priest Johannes Boen (d. 1367) contains chapters on the scale and its tuning, intervals smaller than the tone, the interrelationships among these, and consonances and dissonances; his *Ars (musicae)* deals with mensuration and music fundamentals. See *Ars (musicae) Johannis Boen*, ed. F. Alberto Gallo (CSM 19; n.p.: American Institute of Musicology, 1972), and Wolf Frobenius, *Johannes Boens "Musica" und seine Konsonanzenlehre* (Freiburger Schriften zur Musikwissenschaft, 2; Stuttgart, 1971), 32–78.

[24] Prosdocimo de' Beldomandi took the doctorate in arts at Padua in 1409, the licence in medicine in 1411; he was professor of arts and medicine at Padua from 1422 at the latest until 1428, the year of his death. His musical treatises cover French notation (two treatises, 1404? and 1408), ratios (1409), counterpoint, Italian notation, plainchant (all 1412), the monochord (1413), and *musica speculativa* (1425); he also wrote two treatises on arithmetic, nine on astronomy, and one on geometry. His works represent the interests of a typical Paduan doctor of arts and medicine (a common combination) of the day; the musical treatises in particular are notable for their concision, clarity, and rigour.

[25] The 13th-c. fragment *Sequitur de synemenis*, published by Coussemaker as an adjunct to the treatise of Anonymous IV, derives the same musica ficta notes as Prosdocimo; but this fragment appears only in two medieval British manuscripts and an 18th-c. copy, and seems to have had a marginal influence on later music theory. For the text, see Prosdocimo, *Monacordum*, in Prosdocimo de' Beldomandi, *Brevis summula proportionum quantum ad musicam pertinet* and *Parvus tractatulus de modo monachordum dividendi*, ed. and trans. Jan Herlinger (Greek and Latin Music Theory, 4; Lincoln, Nebr. and London, 1987), app. B; for an extended study, Christian Meyer, 'Le *De synemmenis* et sa tradition: contribution à l'étude des mesures du monocorde vers la fin du XIIIᵉ siècle', *Revue de musicologie*, 76 (1990), 83–95.

[26] Nicolaus uses A♯ only in the low register, C♭ only in the upper two registers. His monochord is depicted in tabular form in the frontispiece of GS iii and in corrected form in Koller, 'Aus dem

Ex. 6.6. Progressions from Boen's *Musica*

The *Tractatus monochordi* of Ugolino of Orvieto, an appendix to his *Declaratio musicae disciplinae*, is largely derivative from Prosdocimo's monochord theory.[27]

As the extended scale became established more and more firmly a terminology solidified to differentiate its notes from those of the basic scale: notes of the basic scale came to be known as 'regular' or 'true' music (*musica recta* or *vera*), notes of the extension as 'feigned' or 'false' music (*musica ficta* or *falsa*). Prosdocimo's definition of the latter term is telling: 'the feigning of syllables or the placement of syllables in a location where they do not seem to be—to apply *mi* where there is no *mi* and *fa* where there is no *fa*, and so forth' (*Contrapunctus* 5.1). *Mi* and *fa* are applied through use of the two chromatic signs available at the time, forms derived from the square ♮ and round b: 'Wherever a square ♮ is set down we sing *mi*; wherever a round b is

Archive des Benedictinerstiftes St. Paul im Lavantthal in Kärnten', *Monatshefte für Musikgeschichte*, 22 (1890), 22–9, 35–45, supplement; see also Joseph Levitan, 'Adrian Willaert's Famous Duo *Quidnam ebrietas*', *TVNM* 15 (1936–9), 166–233 at 227–9. A table similar to that of Nicolaus turns up in a Sicilian manuscript of 1473; see Prosdocimo, *Monacordum*, app. D. For a thorough study of these tables, see Lawrence Gushee, 'The *Tabula monochordi* of Magister Nicolaus de Luduno', in Graeme M. Boone (ed.), *Essays on Medieval Music in Honor of David G. Hughes* (Isham Library Papers, 4; Cambridge, Mass., 1995), 117–52.

[27] The cleric Ugolino of Orvieto was canon of Santa Croce, Forlì, from 1415 (in which year he represented the city at the Council of Constance), archdeacon from 1425; archpriest of the cathedral chapter of Ferrara from 1431 until his retirement in 1448. His *Declaratio musicae disciplinae*, in progress when he moved to Ferrara in 1431, is the most comprehensive work on music theory of the 15th c. Its five books cover fundamentals of music and the modes (following Marchetto), counterpoint (following Prosdocimo), mensuration (elaborating on the *Libellus cantus mensurabilis secundum Johannem de Muris*), ratios, and *musica speculativa*, all discussed with scholastic rigour in 427 chapters (plus ten for the pendant *Tractatus monochordi*). See *Ugolini Urbevetanis Declaratio musicae disciplinae*, ed. Albert Seay, 3 vols. (CSM 7; Rome, 1959–62). Lewis Lockwood suggests that the treatise, with numerous references to Aristotle's *Politics* in its prooemia, is in essence a justification of music in aristocratic education in mid-century Ferrara (*Music in Renaissance Ferrara, 1400–1505: The Creation of a Musical Center in the Fifteenth Century* (Cambridge, Mass., 1984), 77–85; see also 109–18). For further information on Ugolino's life, see Enrico Peverada, *Vita musicale nella chiesa ferrarese del Quattrocento* (Ferrara, 1991), 1–19; on the treatise, Cecilia Panti, 'Una fonte della *Declaratio musicae disciplinae* di Ugolino da Orvieto: quattro anonime *questiones* della tarda scolastica', *Rivista italiana di musicologia*, 24 (1989), 3–47.

set down we sing *fa'* (Marchetto, *Lucidarium* 8.1.9–10).[28] Thus when
a square ♭ is applied, say, to high cfaut, that note is sung as *mi*, which
(in Prosdocimo's words) is placed in a location 'where it does not seem
to be'; its placement there implies a semitonal (*mi–fa*) relationship
between it and the D just above it, the C♮ of cfaut being raised to the
C♯ of C *mi*. Likewise the application of round b to high elami indicates that the note should be sung as *fa*, which is also placed in a location 'where it does not seem to be'; its placement there implies a
semitonal relationship (*fa–mi*) between it and the D just below it, the
E♮ of elami being lowered to the E♭ of E *fa*. But note that the square
♭ and the round b do not necessarily indicate alteration of pitch. The
application of a round b to, say, high ffaut would indicate solmization
of the note as *fa* without altering its pitch, just as the application of
a square ♭ to high elami would indicate solmization of the note as *mi*
without altering its pitch. Thus a square ♭ may indicate the equivalent of a modern sharp or natural, the round b the equivalent of a
modern natural or flat, depending on the notes to which they are
applied.[29]

The presence of *mi* on C (i.e. C♯) implies *ut* on A, just as the presence of *fa* on E (i.e. E♭) implies *ut* on B♭, and, indeed, as early as
1375 the Berkeley Treatise uses the term *coniuncta* to refer to 'the
mental [*intellectualis*] transposition of any property or hexachord
from its own location to another location above or below' (1.3)
and explicitly describes hexachords built on various E♭s, As, B♭s, and
Ds in addition to hexachords on Cs, Gs, and Fs (1.4).[30] Such ficta
hexachords gradually became the common stock of music theory, as
did the term *coniuncta*, which eventually was used to designate any
musica ficta note.

MODE

Perhaps no aspect of the music theory of the fourteenth and early fifteenth centuries is so bound to earlier theory as the doctrine of mode.

---

[28] A similar rule appears in the 13th-c. Anonymous II's *Tractatus de discantu (Concerning Discant)*, ed. and trans. Albert Seay (Texts/Translation, 1; Colorado Springs, Col., 1978), 32, and resonates in music theory through the Renaissance.

[29] Ugolino's use of a round b in the position of G to indicate the sharpening of F (*Declaratio* 2.34.15 and ex. II-121) should be regarded as exceptional, as Berger has shown, *Musica Ficta*, 17–18.

[30] Theodore Karp discusses the implications of the Berkeley *coniunctae* for Gregorian chant in 'From the Aural to the Written Tradition: The *Coniunctae* of the Anonymous Berkeley Theory MS', in id., *Aspects of Orality and Formularity in Gregorian Chant* (Evanston, Ill., 1998), 181–223.

I. Office for St Dominic. Rome, Santa
Sabina, MS XIV.L1 (Humbert's Codex):
(*a*) First Vespers (first antiphon *Gaude felix
parens yspania*); beginning of Matins,
fo. 296ʳ

I (*b*). Matins (continuation), fo. 296ᵛ

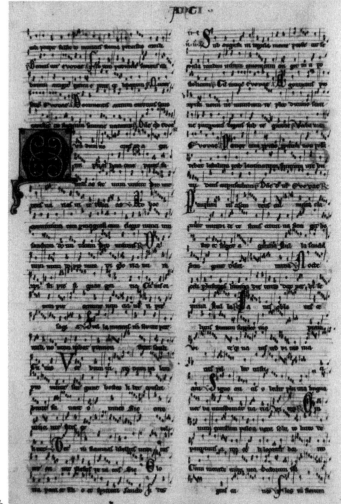

a

b

c

I (c). Matins (continuation), Lauds,
Second Vespers, fo. 297ʳ

I (d). Second Vespers (end) fo. 297ᵛ   d

II. Office for St Benedict: LA2 (Lauds, second antiphon) *Huic iubilate*.
Munich, Bayerische Staatsbibliothek, clm 4306, fo. 161[r-v]

III. Christ as fiddler and his
mother Mary as dancer (early
14th century). Antiphonal
Karlsruhe, Landesbibliothek,
Cod. St. Georgen 5, fo. 16ᵛ

IV. The Gürzenich in Cologne:
civic dance hall, erected
1441–7. Photograph taken
after 1930. Bildarchiv Foto
Marburg

V. Rondellus: clerics dancing
in a chain (13th century).
Florence, Biblioteca Medicea
Laurenziana, Plut. 29.1, fo.
463ʳ

VI. Female dancer and fiddler (14th century). Oven tile from Cologne. Kommern, Rheinisches Freilichtmuseum

VII. Female dancer with clappers (early 14th century). Wooden figure from the choir-stalls of Cologne cathedral, front row, seat N ii 8. Photograph: Bildarchiv Foto Marburg

VIII. Morris dancer (*c.*1500). Anonymous line drawing (10.6 ¥ 14.7 cm) from Basle. Basle, Kunstmuseum, Kupferstichkabinett, Inv. No. U. vii. 54

IX. Sword dance of Portuguese soldiers (before 1550). Tapestry from Brussels (355 ¥ 394 cm), no. 7 in the series 'Life and deeds of João de Castro'. Vienna, Kunsthistorisches Museum, tapestry collection, Inv. No. xxii/7

X. 'Carole' (c.1400). French miniature. Oxford, Bodleian Library, MS Douce 332, fo. 8r

XI. 'Bassa danza', 1463. Miniature from Guglielmo Ebreo da Pesaro, *De practica seu arte tripudii vulgare opusculum*. Paris, Bibliothèque Nationale de France, fonds it. 973, fo. 21ᵛ

XII. Betrothal at the court of King Huon of Gascogne, 1468–70. Miniature from the studio of Loyset Liédet. Paris, Bibliothèque de l'Arsenal, MS fr. 5073, fo. 117ᵛ

XIII. *Kyrie fons bonitatis / sacerdos summe.* Munich, Bayerische Staatsbibliothek, clm 14274, fos. 30ᵛ–31ʳ

Early plainchant treatises like the *Dialogus de musica* (*c*.1000), the *Micrologus* of Guido of Arezzo (early eleventh century), and the *Musica* of Berno of Reichenau (d. 1048) continued to be copied through the end of the fifteenth century, some of them even beyond. To take only Guido's *Micrologus* as a case in point, nineteen of its seventy-seven extant manuscripts date from the fourteenth or fifteenth century. Of these nineteen, moreover, ten present it along with fourteenth- or fifteenth-century treatises, suggesting that these manuscripts' compilers saw it not as a work of merely antiquarian interest but as part of the living tradition. One manuscript of the late fifteenth century even presents a digest of Marchetto's *Lucidarium* (itself the most innovative plainchant treatise of its time) in a version that coordinates the conventional doctrine of mode with Marchetto's point by point. To a great extent, the modal theory of this period *was* the theory of earlier times, and we shall begin our survey of the theory with the eleventh century.[31]

The Dialogus de musica, *Guido*

The primary elements through which modes were differentiated in music theory as it was received at the dawn of the fourteenth century were final, range, initial notes, and choice of B♭ or b♮; secondary elements, not discussed here, include psalm tones and notes that end phrases (*distinctiones*).

Final

The *Dialogus de musica* presents a system of eight modes organized into four pairs, the two modes of each pair sharing a final (D, E, F, or G). The four pairs are named protus, deuterus, tritus, and tetrardus; each pair contains an authentic and a plagal mode, the authentic of each pair occupying a higher range than the plagal. The modes are numbered 1 through 8 or named as follows:[32]

[31] Around 1000 is a convenient starting point for a survey of modal theory, as from about that time letter names for the notes were fixed in the manner we still know today. On *Micrologus* manuscripts and their contents, *Guidonis Aretini Micrologus*, ed. Joseph Smits van Waesberghe (CSM 4; n.p.: American Institute of Musicology, 1955), 4–71. The version of *Divina auxiliante gratia*, the digest of Marchetto's *Lucidarium*, appears in Bergamo, Biblioteca Civica 'A. Mai', MS M. A. B. 21 (*olim* Σ 4.37), fos. 69ʳ–89ᵛ. The most comprehensive history of modal theory to date is Harold S. Powers, 'Mode', in *New Grove* xii. 376–450. For a recent collection of essays, see Ursula Günther, Ludwig Finscher, and Jeffrey Dean (eds.), *Modality in the Music of the Fourteenth and Fifteenth Centuries* (MSD 49; Neuhausen-Stuttgart, 1996).

[32] The designations Dorian, Hypodorian, Phrygian, Hypophrygian, etc., though they occasionally appear in medieval treatises—e.g. the *Alia musica* and the *Musica enchiriadis*—were rare.

Number	Name	Final
1	Authentic protus	D
2	Plagal of the protus	D
3	Authentic deuterus	E
4	Plagal of the deuterus	E
5	Authentic tritus	F
6	Plagal of the tritus	F
7	Authentic tetrardus	G
8	Plagal of the tetrardus	G

For Guido, the crucial factor was the arrangement of whole tones and semitones above and below the final. Accordingly, he allowed the first pair of modes to be located either on A or D, the second pair either on B or E, the third pair either on C or F—the arrangement of whole tones and semitones above and below the final being the same in either case (*Micrologus* 7).

Range

The treatment of mode in the *Dialogus de musica* begins by giving the limits of the ranges of the authentic modes as a note below the final and the octave above it and limits of the ranges of the plagals as the perfect fifths below and above the final, or sometimes the sixth above it (*Dialogus* 9). In the subsequent discussion of the modes one by one (*Dialogus* 10), however, the stated ranges are somewhat different:

1	C–d	2	A (or Γ)–b♭
3	D (or C)–e	4	C (or B or A)–c
5	F–f	6	C–d
7	F (or E)–g	8	C–e

Guido, on the other hand, stated that authentic melodies, which rarely descend beyond one note below their finals (like the author of the *Dialogus*, he explained that the authentic tritus rarely descends below the final at all because of the semitone found there), may ascend to the octave, ninth, or tenth above their finals, and that plagal modes may ascend and descend to the fifth from the final; but then he stated that some authorities allowed the plagals to rise to the sixth above their finals by analogy to the ninth or tenth of the authentics, implying that the octave was the normal upper limit for the authentics (*Micrologus* 13).

Initials

If finals were seen by most theorists as the most important elements in determining the mode of a chant, by the eleventh century initial

notes had taken on a certain importance as well. Guido stated only
that initial notes are to harmonize with the finals by the 'consonances'
minor second, major second, minor third, major third, perfect
fourth, and perfect fifth)—except for the c allowable for an E-mode
melody (*Micrologus* 11). The author of the *Dialogus*, however, went
into much greater detail, though contradicting Guido's general principle only with respect to the c of third mode (which he allowed as an
initial note): he listed from four to six possible initials for each mode
(citing a specific chant as an example for each initial in each mode),
and even pointing out which initials are most common, which
least common—in mode 1, for instance, the permissible initials are C,
D, E, F, G, and a; of these D is most common, E least common
(*Dialogus* 11–18).

B♭

Treatment of b♭ became critical already in the eleventh century;
according to Guido, the two inflections b♮ and b♭ are never used in a
single *neuma*, a term here to be understood probably as 'melodic
gesture' (*Micrologus* 8). The author of the *Dialogus* made the use
of b♭ a distinguishing characteristic of modes 1, 2, 4, 5, and 6
(*Dialogus* 11–16). Guido explained why: b♭ is used in chants in
which F appears prominently (*Micrologus* 8). The *Dialogus* author
argued specifically against the use of b♭ in mode 7 or 8, as the b♭ would
convert the melodies to mode 1 or 2 by altering the arrangement of
tones and semitones with respect to the final (*Dialogus* 17–18), thus
implying that a melody can be transposed to various notes without
altering its mode as long as its characteristic arrangement of tones
and semitones is preserved. Guido said much the same: with b♭, G
sounds as protus, a as deuterus, and b♭ as tritus. These are important
early statements of the doctrine of modal affinity—'the similarity
of melodic movement shared by certain tones of the gamut'
(*Micrologus* 8).[33]

Ambiguous Cases

These considerations were not always sufficient to determine the mode
of a melody unambiguously. The *Dialogus* goes into considerable detail
in explaining how to differentiate each authentic mode from its plagal
partner if the melody in question stays in the range common to both. In
the case of modes 1 and 2, for instance, the author stated that if the

---

[33] On modal affinities, see Dolores Pesce, *The Affinities and Modal Transposition* (Music:
Scholarship and Performance; Bloomington and Indianapolis, 1987). She traces the origins of
the concept back to Hucbald (d. 930).

melody does not ascend to a and b, it belongs to mode 2; if it begins on a, or touches a and b many times, it belongs to mode 1; if it begins lower, and ascends to a and b only rarely, it belongs to mode 2 (*Dialogus* 12). The author referred to an authentic mode being 'mixed' with its plagal partner when a melody in the authentic mode occasionally drops to the low notes of the plagal partner (*Dialogus* 16).

Berno

Though he retained most of the elements of his predecessors' modal theory, Berno's most significant contribution was the classification of modes according to their construction from three species of the tetrachord and four of the pentachord:[34]

	Tetrachord	*Pentachord*
1st species	T S T	T S T T
2nd species	S T T	S T T T
3rd species	T T S	T T T S
4th species		T T S T

He then described each mode as consisting of a pentachord species plus a tetrachord species either above or below it:[35]

Mode	*Definition*
1	1st species of pentachord, 1st species of tetrachord above
2	1st species of pentachord, 1st species of tetrachord below
3	2nd species of pentachord, 2nd species of tetrachord above
4	2nd species of pentachord, 2nd species of tetrachord below
5	3rd species of pentachord, 3rd species of tetrachord above
6	3rd species of pentachord, 3rd species of tetrachord below
7	4th species of pentachord, 1st species of tetrachord above
8	4th species of pentachord, 1st species of tetrachord below

---

[34] Intervals are to be read upward; Berno spelled them downward.

[35] In Berno's theory, the range of a mode is not limited to the octave composed of its pentachord and tetrachord species, but may range a note or so beyond it in either direction.

Thus Berno's system may be seen as a systematization of the earlier doctrine that it was the arrangement of tones and semitones that defined a mode. Berno's system appears abstract in comparison with that of the *Dialogus*: his upper limit of mode 4 is b♮, a fifth above the final, with c as a rare exception, whereas the *Dialogus* simply gives c as the upper limit; Berno also made no mention of the use of b♭ in any mode, whereas for the *Dialogus* (as has been pointed out) it is a distinguishing feature of modes 1, 2, 4, 5, and 6; Berno allowed b♮ as an initial in modes 3, 5, 7, and 8, whereas the *Dialogus* never allows b♮ as an initial; and unlike the author of the *Dialogus*, Berno never cited specific melodies as examples for the various initial notes he specified.

Like Guido and the author of the *Dialogus*, Berno discussed the problem of differentiating between an authentic mode and its plagal partner. If a melody neither ascends to the fifth above its final nor descends below the final it is plagal; if it ascends to the fifth and does not descend below the final it is 'common' (Berno parenthetically differentiated twelve modes, four authentic, four plagal, and four medial—these last for melodies limited to the pentachord common to the authentic and plagal partners); if it ascends beyond the fifth and does not descend below the final it is authentic; if it ascends beyond the fifth and below the final, the mode is determined by whether the ascent beyond the fifth or the descent below the final is greater (GS ii. 73a). Like his predecessors, too, Berno discussed modal affinities, but unlike them he named chants that must be ended not on their proper finals but on notes a fourth or a fifth above (GS ii. 74–6).

Marchetto and his Impact

Such was the modal doctrine inherited by the greatest innovator of the fourteenth century, Marchetto of Padua. Marchetto regularized the criteria for definition of the modes while at the same time expanding and systematizing the exceptions to these criteria. And he cited specific chants for almost every exception mentioned.

Marchetto adopted the traditional doctrine of eight modes divided into four pairs sharing the common finals D, E, F, and G. As standard ranges for the authentic modes he set a tone below the final to an octave above it;[36] for the plagal modes, a fourth below the final to a sixth above it (*Lucidarium* 11.2.20–5). But to accommodate melodies that either do not fill the normal ranges of their modes or

---

[36] Like some earlier theorists, Marchetto made an exception for mode 5: as he put it, melodies in this mode rarely descend below their final because of the semitone that lies there; but when they do they may descend to D (*Lucidarium* 11.4.168–9).

exceed them—or show other anomalies, such as the use or avoidance of b♭—he introduced the constellation of terms 'perfect, imperfect, pluperfect, mixed, and intermixed (*perfectus, imperfectus, plusquam-perfectus, mixtus, commixtus*)'. The perfect mode is that whose melodies fill its normal range; the imperfect that whose melodies do not fill its normal range; the pluperfect that which, if authentic, exceeds the upper limit of its range or, if plagal, the lower limit; the mixed mode that which, if authentic, exceeds the lower limit of its range (thus touching the low range associated with its plagal counterpart, hence 'mixed' with it)[37] or, if plagal, exceeds the upper limit of its range (thus touching the high range associated with its authentic counterpart, hence 'mixed' with it); the intermixed that which is combined with a mode other than its authentic or plagal counterpart (*Lucidarium* 11.2.10–35).

Marchetto described tetrachord and pentachord species that are like Berno's, but applied the doctrine of species less restrictedly and with finer distinctions than had Berno. Here is Marchetto's array of modes on the basis of these species (*Lucidarium* 11.4 *passim*):

Mode	Definition
1	1st species of pentachord, 1st species of tetrachord above
2	1st species of pentachord, 1st species of tetrachord common and below
3	2nd species of pentachord, 2nd species of tetrachord above
4	2nd species of pentachord, 2nd species of tetrachord common and below[38]
5	3rd species of pentachord in ascent, 4th in descent; 3rd species of tetrachord above
6	3rd species of pentachord in ascent, 4th in descent; 3rd species of tetrachord common and below
7	4th species of pentachord, 1st species of tetrachord above
8	4th species of pentachord; 3rd species of tetrachord common, or 1st species of tetrachord below

[37] Because of its exceptional nature as indicated in the previous note, the fifth mode is more than normally difficult to classify when its melodies descend to D. In that case the mode is said to be either perfect above and below, if the melody ascends to the octave above the final, or pluperfect above and mixed below, if it ascends past the octave above the final (*Lucidarium* 11.4.168–72).

[38] Marchetto stated that the fourth mode rarely uses the species of tetrachord below the final, *Lucidarium* 11.4.124.

New here is the 'common' species of the tetrachord, which Marchetto defined as the tetrachord that extends upward from the final, noting that 'the common species may be used in both authentic and plagal modes,[39] though more frequently in the plagal' (*Lucidarium* 11.4.89–90; cf. 11.4.218); what Marchetto was saying in effect was that melodies lacking the upper tetrachord and in which the note a fifth above the final is also lacking or relatively unimportant are more likely to be plagal than authentic.

New also is the distinction in pentachord species in modes 5 and 6 depending on ascent or descent; the distinction as stated, in fact, calls for b♮ in ascent, b♭ in descent in these modes. Indeed, Marchetto was much more explicit about the use of b♭ than any earlier theorist. Mode 1 is sung with b♮ if it ascends to d, so that the first species of the tetrachord above occurs in regular fashion; but if it does not ascend as far as d, then two possibilities must be considered. Either it ascends to b and no further, in which case it is sung with b♭ (and is said to be intermixed with mode 6); or it ascends to c, in which case two further possibilities must be considered. Either after touching b it ascends to c before it descends to F, in which case it is sung with b♮; or after touching b it descends to F before touching c, in which case it is sung with b♭ (*Lucidarium* 11.4.5–16). Mode 2, lacking the upper tetrachord, is always sung with b♭, to avoid the tritone with F (*Lucidarium* 11.4.96). Mode 3 is always sung with b♮ to avoid both the diminished fifth between b♭ and the final and the tritone between b♭ and the e an octave above the final (*Lucidarium* 11.4.110–12). Mode 4 is sung with b♮ unless F is prominent, as in the responsory *Jerusalem*, in which case b♭ is preferred (*Lucidarium* 11.4.126–7). Modes 5 and 6, as already stated, are sung with b♮ in ascent (so that the third species of the pentachord will occur in regular fashion),[40] but with b♭ in descent to avoid the tritone with the final (*Lucidarium* 11.4.140–50). Modes 7 and 8 are always sung with b♮, as b♭ would convert the characteristic G–d pentachord from fourth species to first, and thus convert seventh mode to first, eighth mode to second (*Lucidarium* 11.4.186, 201–2). But Marchetto added that thanks to the possibility of intermixing any mode with any other, either b♭ or b♮ could appear in any mode, though not necessarily in the proper form of the mode (*Lucidarium* 11.4.228).

---

[39] One recalls Berno's definition of 'common' melodies as those that stay within the common range of an authentic and plagal partner.

[40] Marchetto stated that fifth-mode melodies that circle around c without descending below a should be sung with b♮, but cited as exceptional the openings of the responsories *Ecce Dominus veniet* and *Ecce veniet Dominus*, which use b♭ in such cases.

Marchetto used the array of terms 'perfect, imperfect, pluperfect, mixed, intermixed' to refine the treatment of initial notes. Where the *Dialogus* and Berno had given the notes C, D, E, F, G, and a as the initials for mode 1 (the *Dialogus* singling out D as the most common and E as the least common), Marchetto explained that E occurs as an initial when mode 1 is intermixed with 3 or 4, as in the responsory *Annuntiatum est per Gabrielem* (*Lucidarium* 11.4.81–2); he added to the initials the notes A and b♭, as in the graduals *Gloriosus Deus* and *Salvum fac servum* respectively (*Lucidarium* 11.4.52–3, 59), explaining that they occur as initials when mode 1 is mixed with 2. And where the *Dialogus* had simply listed C as an initial for mode 8 and Berno had omitted it entirely, Marchetto explained that it occurred in the pluperfect form of the mode, as in the offertory *Elegerunt apostoli* (*Lucidarium* 11.4.205).

Marchetto's treatment of modal affinities is likewise more refined than that of earlier theorists. He stated that a mode could be located anywhere in the hand where its species can be constructed, and worked out a system of classification for the various possibilities. A regular mode is one built on its proper final. An irregular mode is one built on its cofinal (the note a fifth above its final), like the second-mode gradual *Nimis honorati sunt*, which must be built on a because of the occurrence of a note that can then be notated as b♭ (were it built on D, the note would have to be spelt as E♭, a note outside the basic scale). An acquired mode is one built on a note other than its final or cofinal, like the third-mode communion *Beatus servus*. If this melody were built on its proper final, E, F♯s would occur, and if built on its cofinal, B, f♯s would occur; but its construction on a turns the former into bs and the latter into es.[41] An artificial mode is one that involves a whole tone where it does not occur 'by nature', that is, where it does not lie in the basic scale, like the first-mode gradual *Salvum fac servum*, a melody that begins a major third below its final and, according to Marchetto, should be sung beginning on B♭, thus producing a tone with the following C where a tone does not lie in the basic scale (*Lucidarium* 11.4.36–48, 59–80).[42]

[41] This particularly problematic melody had been discussed earlier by Berno and Johannes 'Cotto'. See also Gustav Jacobsthal, *Die chromatische Alteration im liturgischen Gesang der abendländischen Kirche* (Berlin, 1897), 99–123; Charles Atkinson, 'From *Vitium* to *Tonus acquisitus*: On the Evolution of the Notational Matrix of Medieval Chant', *Studia musicologica Academiae Scientiarum Hungaricae*, 31 (1989), 181–97; and Karp, 'From the Aural to the Written Tradition'.

[42] Marchetto rejected the alternative of beginning on F and ending on a, because that solution would require frequent f♯s whereas the b♭/D solution requires b♭s in only two instances. His choice, here and elsewhere, is the transposition that involves the fewest anomalies, i.e. notes outside the basic scale. On *Salvum fac servum*, see Karp, 'From the Aural to the Written Tradition'.

Marchetto also described characteristic melodic gestures spanning fourths, fifths, and wider intervals that he labelled as 'initial' and 'terminal' according to function; as 'proper' to an authentic mode or its plagal counterpart or 'common' to both; as 'simple' when spanning either a fourth or fifth or 'composite' when spanning a combination of the two; as 'conjunct' or 'disjunct', etc. (*Lucidarium* 11.4.212–30). He further presented examples of the first-species pentachord intermediated ('interrupted') in various ways, each appropriate to a particular mode or group of modes. The intermediation consisting of all notes of the pentachord (that is, of the intervals T–S–T–T read upward) is characteristic of modes 1 and 8; the intermediation T–P4, of mode 4; the intermediation T–m3–T, properly of mode 4, often of mode 2; the intermediation P4–T properly of mode 2, occasionally of mode 1; the intermediation m3–M3 of modes 1 and 8 (or, if built on A, of mode 2); the intermediation T–S–M3 occasionally of mode 1, often of modes 2 and 8, sometimes of modes 4 and 6; the intermediation m3–T–T of modes 1 and 8, sometimes of 6 (or if built on A, of mode 2); and perhaps most importantly, the intermediation that consists simply of the perfect-fifth leap D–a, which, according to Marchetto, is a sign of mode 1 rather than mode 2 even if the melody does not rise beyond a fifth above the final at all, as is the case in the responsory *Sint lumbi vestri praecincti* (*Lucidarium* 11.4.231–48).[43]

Marchetto's theory of mode had an enormous impact on later theorists. Prosdocimo de' Beldomandi, highly critical of other aspects of Marchetto's thought, wrote that 'where he turned to the practice of plainchant he wrote uncommonly well, so that there he was beyond reproach'; and Prosdocimo, indeed, incorporated most aspects of Marchetto's modal theory into his own *Tractatus plane musice* of 1412.[44] Powers calls Book I of Ugolino's *Declaratio musicae disciplinae* of the 1430s 'an enormously expanded and rationalized commentary on Marchetto's work'.[45] In particular, the classification of modes as 'perfect, imperfect, pluperfect, mixed, or intermixed' became the common coin of Italian music theory in the fifteenth century, eventually (through Tinctoris's manuscript treatises and especially Gaffurio's

[43] On this topic, see Jay Rahn, 'Marchetto's Theory of Commixture and Interruptions', *Music Theory Spectrum*, 9 (1987), 117–35.

[44] Prosdocimo's *Tractatus plane musice* includes a discussion of psalm tones, ignored by Marchetto. His discussion of choosing b♭ or b♮ differs from Marchetto's: he simply advocated the choice of whichever note would cause the fewest mutations (2.23), a principle that brings him close to Guido's dictum that both b♭ and b♮ do not occur in a single melodic gesture. He also chose not to differentiate between mixed and intermixed modes (2.5). The present writer is preparing an edition and translation of this previously unpublished treatise; the excerpt translated here appears in Lucca, Biblioteca Governativa, MS 359, fo. 51ᵛ.

[45] Powers, 'Mode', 392.

prints) entering the pan-European tradition. The *Lucidarium* spawned
many offspring, including two digests of Marchetto's modal doctrine,
each of which developed its own manuscript tradition during the
fifteenth century, and numerous abridgements and collections of
excerpts. Reminiscences of the *Lucidarium* pepper Italian theoretical
manuscripts of the fifteenth century.[46] The concept of modal mixture and intermixture proved useful for later writers attempting
to explain polyphonic music in terms of modality; Powers, indeed,
characterizes the *Lucidarium* as the seminal modal treatise of the later
Middle Ages.[47]

Polyphony

At the beginning of the fourteenth century Johannes de Grocheio had
explicitly denied that mode was applicable to polyphonic pieces;[48]
and indeed the only references to mode in polyphony from the
period under consideration here seem to be those of the Berkeley
Treatise of 1375 (1.5, 1.8). The treatise states only that the modes
of motets, ballades, rondeaux, virelais, and the like should be judged
by their final notes; that such pieces, when plagal, may have wider
ranges than monophonic pieces in the plagal modes; and that their
tenors should conform to the nature of plainchants, though they may
begin differently from them (perhaps, that is, having a wider choice
of initial notes) so long as they end like them. There are no further
discussions of mode in polyphony until the time of Tinctoris (see
below, Ch. 7).

But Reinhard Strohm has argued that it is demonstrable that modal
conceptions were significant in fifteenth-century polyphony; specifically, that modal applications can be detected in polyphonic works

---

[46] The five-part modal classification ('perfect, imperfect', etc.) appears, along with discussions
of construction of modes by pentachord and tetrachord species, in Anonymous of Vallicelliana
C 105 (a manuscript of the late 14th or early 15th c.); in the *Compendium musicale* (1415) of
Nicolaus of Capua, who may have been priest at Treviso around 1440; and in the *Palma choralis*
8 (1440–3) of Johannes de Olomons, who dedicated the treatise to Cardinal Branda, founder of
a school for Ambrosian chant at Castiglione Olona (near Varese). The *Lucidarium* digests are
Sciendum quod antiquitus, preserved in three sources, and *Divina auxiliante gratia*, preserved in
five (Jay Rahn is preparing an edition of the first, the present writer of the second; for an edition
of the first based on a single source, see Raffaello Monterosso, 'Un compendio inedito del
Lucidarium di Marchetto da Padova', *Studi medievali*, 3rd ser., 7 (1966), 914–31). On all these,
and the manuscript reminiscences, see Klaus Wolfgang Niemöller, 'Zur Tonus-Lehre der italienischen Musiktheorie des ausgehenden Mittelalters', *Kirchenmusikalisches Jahrbuch*, 40 (1956),
23–32, and Herlinger, 'Marchetto's Influence: The Manuscript Evidence', in André Barbera (ed.),
Music Theory and its Sources: Antiquity and the Middle Ages (Notre Dame Conferences in
Medieval Studies, 1; Notre Dame, Ind., 1990), 235–58, and introduction to *Lucidarium of Marchetto*, 10–12.

[47] Powers, 'Mode', 392–406.

[48] *Musica*, in *Die Quellenhandschriften zum Musiktraktat des Johannes de Grocheio*, ed. Ernst
Rohloff (Leipzig, n.d.), 219.

(including secular songs) of Du Fay and Binchois; that theorists'
general silence on the subject of mode in polyphony may result from
their having treated the subject so thoroughly in plainchant treatises
that further discussion would have been redundant.[49] Karol Berger,
too, in his survey of musica ficta theory (see below), holds that the
theorists' rules for application of accidentals in polyphony must be
interpreted in the context of a prevailing mode.[50] Certainly this problematic topic demands further consideration.

COUNTERPOINT

Though theorists of the fourteenth and early fifteenth centuries did
not develop a full-blown theory of composition like Tinctoris's late in
the fifteenth century, they did establish general principles that may be
seen as steps towards such a theory. They discussed not only note-
against-note counterpoint in two parts, devoting special attention to
the treatment of accidentals, i.e. musica ficta, but florid counterpoint
as well.[51]

Note-against-Note Counterpoint in Two Voices

The short treatise *Quilibet affectans* of *c.*1330 may be taken as representative of the earliest stage of fourteenth-century counterpoint
theory. Occupying only about one page in Coussemaker's edition, it is
nonetheless, with its twelve sources (in all but one of which it is attributed to Johannes de Muris), the most widely disseminated fourteenth-
or fifteenth-century counterpoint treatise in manuscript.[52] The treatise
begins by defining all intervals larger than the octave as reiterations,
replications, or reduplications and by stating that within the octave
there are three perfect consonances, the unison, the fifth, and the
octave itself, and three imperfect ones, the minor third, the major
third, and the major sixth.[53] The omission of the minor sixth recalls
the discant theory of the thirteenth century, in which the minor sixth

---

[49] Reinhard Strohm, 'Modal Sounds as a Stylistic Tendency of the Mid-Fifteenth Century:
E-, A-, and C-Finals in Polyphonic Song', in Günther, Finscher, and Dean (eds.), *Modality in
the Music of the Fourteenth and Fifteenth Centuries*, 149–75 at 152–5.

[50] Berger, *Musica Ficta, passim*.

[51] The history of contrapuntal theory in the 14th and 15th cc. is traced by Sachs, *Contra-
punctus*; 'Die Contrapunctus-Lehre im 14. und 15. Jahrhundert', in Zaminer, v. 161–256; and
'Counterpoint', *New Grove*, iv. 833–43, sections 1–11; and by Claude V. Palisca, 'Kontrapunkt:
II, Mittelalter', in *MGG*², Sachteil, v. 598–603.

[52] On the date, see Sachs, 'Contrapunctus-Lehre', 178; on manuscripts, Sachs, *Contrapunctus*,
217. Coussemaker published this work along with two others under the single rubric 'Ars contrapuncti secundum Johannem de Muris'; Giuliano Di Bacco is preparing a critical edition.
Titles of anonymous counterpoint treatises discussed in this chapter are those introduced by
Sachs, *Contrapunctus*.

[53] The differentiation of perfect consonance, imperfect consonance, and dissonance is basic
to all contrapuntal theory of the 14th and 15th cc., though theorists' terminology varies.

was catalogued as more dissonant even than the minor seventh.[54]
Quilibet affectans next takes these six consonances one by one, explaining to which consonances each tends to move. Two examples will suffice:

The first perfect species, that is, the unison, naturally demands after itself the semiditone, that is, the minor third. The semiditone is *re fa*, *mi sol*, or vice versa. It can have another species, perfect or imperfect, after itself, and this for the sake of variety. . . .

The dyapente plus tone, an imperfect species, naturally demands after itself the dyapason, that is, the octave. It can have another species, perfect or imperfect, for the reason given. It can have a fifth when the tenor ascends a ditone or a semiditone and not otherwise.

The treatise closes with a group of general principles:

Any melody ought to begin and end in a perfect consonance [with the tenor]; and a melody should never ascend or descend into a perfect consonance with the tenor[55] unless by a tone or a semitone.

Two identical perfect consonances should never be made in succession, although two, three, or four identical imperfect consonances may be made in succession.

When the tenor ascends the melody ought to descend, and vice versa.

Obviously, the treatise is practical and didactic, not to say elementary; it is designed to teach beginners how to connect one interval to another. The attribution to Johannes de Muris, one of the most distinguished schoolmen of his age, accordingly seems improbable.[56] Nonetheless *Quilibet affectans* appears to have influenced later discussions of counterpoint, notably the Berkeley Treatise (2.1), Theodonus de Caprio's *Regule contrapuncti*, and at least part of the fragment *Sex sunt species principales* often associated with the putative *Ars nova* of Philippe de Vitry.[57]

Marchetto, for instance (*Lucidarium* 5.6.2–4), called a perfect consonance *consonantia*, an imperfect one *dissonantia compassibilis auditui* (a dissonance compatible to the ear); Ugolino (*Declaratio* 2.3.37–40) reported a system that calls a perfect consonance *consonantia*, an imperfect one *dissonantia*, and a dissonance *discordantia*.

[54] See e.g. Franco, *Ars cantus mensurabilis*, ed. Gilbert Reaney and André Gilles (CSM 18; n.p.: American Institute of Musicology, 1974), 11.13–17, and Johannes de Garlandia, *De musica mensurabili* 9.25–34.

[55] i.e. in similar motion with the tenor.

[56] Reimer accepts the attribution (*Die Musiktraktate des Johannes de Muris* (Beihefte zum Archiv für Musikwissenschaft, 8; Wiesbaden, 1970), 40–2); Gushee ('Jehan des Murs', *New Grove*, ix. 588) and Sachs (*Contrapunctus*, 183) question it.

[57] Sachs, *Contrapunctus*, 67–70. In 'Contrapunctus-Lehre', 178, Sachs calls *Quilibet affectans* 'apparently the most influential counterpoint treatise of the fourteenth and fifteenth centuries'. Theodonus de Caprio (d. 1434) was prior of the Benedictine abbey at Capua; his treatise was

The treatise *Cum notum sit*, which appears in various manuscripts as an adjunct to *Quilibet affectans*, represents a later stage in the development of counterpoint theory. Though its date is uncertain, Sachs believes it was known to Johannes Boen when he wrote his *Musica* in 1357.[58] The number of consonances is considerably expanded—unison, third, fifth, sixth, octave, tenth, twelfth—with major and minor inflections of the thirds, sixths, and tenths not differentiated, so that the minor sixth (as the examples confirm) has taken its place as a legitimate consonance alongside the major sixth. Unlike the rules in *Quilibet affectans*, which deal only with the connection of one interval with the next, the examples in *Cum notum sit* extend over as many as nine intervals in succession; and the author's rules, though generally confirming those of *Quilibet affectans*, are more detailed, and are sometimes provided with rationales (rules 4–9 follow; the first three rules concern the definition of counterpoint, the enumeration of the consonances, and their classification as perfect or imperfect):

4. The counterpoint (i.e. the melody added above the tenor) should begin with a perfect consonance; an imperfect consonance should follow it.[59]

5. The counterpoint should not present two twelfths, two octaves, two fifths, or two unisons adjacently; a twelfth may move to an octave, an octave to a fifth, and a fifth to a unison, but it is better if one interval is perfect and the next imperfect.

6. The counterpoint should present (only) two or at most three imperfect consonances in succession, after which a perfect consonance should follow.

7. The counterpoint should not present two identical notes in succession (while the tenor moves), for then the tenor would appear to function as the contrapuntal voice.

8. The penultimate consonance should be imperfect, for the sake of euphony.

9. As the counterpoint should begin with a perfect consonance, so should it end with one; otherwise the soul, not hearing a perfect sound, would remain suspended, and the end of the composition would not be indicated.

copied into Vatican City, Biblioteca Apostolica Vaticana, Barb. lat. 307 in 1431. *Sex sunt species principales* is attributed (probably incorrectly) to Philippe de Vitry in Paris, Bibliothèque Nationale de France, f. lat. 7378A. Attributions of treatises to Philippe will be discussed below in the section on mensuration.

[58] Sachs, *Contrapunctus*, 83–8, and 'Contrapunctus-Lehre', 183–5.

[59] The consonances are those between the counterpoint and the tenor, which in discussions of counterpoint is generally assumed to be given.

Cum notum sit shows considerably more refinement than *Quilibet affectans*, particularly with regard to a balanced alternation of perfect and imperfect consonances. Where *Quilibet affectans* merely requires a counterpoint to begin and end with a perfect consonance, *Cum notum sit* proposes that the initial perfect consonance should be followed by, and the final one preceded by, an imperfect one; where *Quilibet* merely prohibits successive identical perfect consonances, *Cum notum* recommends the insertion of an imperfect consonance between perfect consonances of any sort; where *Quilibet* allows as many as four successive identical imperfect consonances, *Cum notum* advises against more than three successive imperfect consonances of any sort. But like *Quilibet*, *Cum notum* is clearly a didactic work.

The contrapuntal theory in the *Contrapunctus* (1412) of Prosdocimo de' Beldomandi is closely related to that of *Cum notum sit*. After listing the intervals (of which he points out there is an infinite number, thanks to octave duplications) and cataloguing each as consonant or dissonant, then cataloguing each consonance as perfect or imperfect (*Contrapunctus* 3)—which are the topics of the first three rules of *Cum notum sit*—Prosdocimo presents six rules, each of which he provides with a rationale (*Contrapunctus* 4):

1. Discords are not to be used in [note-against-note] counterpoint in any way, because, on account of their dissonance, they are deeply hostile to harmony and nature, which seem to be the ultimate goal of this art.

2. Counterpoint ought to begin and end only with perfect intervals; the reason for this is that if the listener is to be charmed by these harmonies, he should at first be moved by the harmonies that are sweeter and more amicable by nature. . . . Finally, the listener ought to be sent away with the sweetness and harmony delectable to nature.

3. We ought never to ascend or descend in identical perfectly concordant intervals with the melody above or below which we make counterpoint though we may well do so in different perfectly concordant intervals. The reason for this is that one voice would sing the same as the other, which is not the purpose of counterpoint; its purpose is that what is sung by one voice be different from what is pronounced by the other,[60] and that this be done through concords that are good and properly ordered.

---

[60] This rule recalls traditional definitions of counterpoint or discant, such as that of the anonymous English treatise *Quatuor principalia* 4.2.11: 'Discant is the consonance of some *different* melodies (Discantus est aliquorum diversorum cantuum consonantia)'.

4. We ought not continually to make counterpoint with imperfectly concordant intervals without inserting any perfectly consonant intervals, because it would then be hard to sing; for no harmony whatever would be found in the counterpoint, and harmony seems to be the ultimate goal of music.

5. In perfectly consonant intervals we ought never to place *mi* against *fa* or vice versa, because we would straight away make the perfectly consonant intervals minor [i.e. diminished] or augmented, which forms are discordant.

6. a. We may ascend or descend in major or minor intervals imperfectly consonant with the melody above or below which we make counterpoint, occasionally inserting perfectly concordant intervals. The reason for this is that from this procedure arises a different melody—not identical to the other—on account of the lack of conformity that nature has in these imperfectly consonant intervals.

   b. Between any two successive perfect consonances there should fall an imperfect one: between a unison and a fifth there should fall a third, between a fifth and an octave there should fall a sixth, and between an octave and a twelfth there should fall a tenth, and so forth. When an approach is made from one of these imperfect consonances to some one of the perfect ones among which the imperfect interval is placed, there results an extremely charming style of singing.

Prosdocimo agreed with *Cum notum sit* in requiring perfect consonances at the beginnings and ends of counterpoints (rule 2) and in prohibiting parallel perfect consonances (rule 3). Like *Cum notum sit*, he recommended the insertion of an imperfect consonance between perfect ones (rule 6(*b*), in which he called the progression from an imperfect consonance to a perfect one 'extremely charming') and the avoidance of too many imperfect ones in succession (rule 4). But unlike *Cum notum sit*, Prosdocimo did not specifically limit the number of imperfect consonances that may occur in succession, nor did he prohibit repetition of a note in the contrapuntal voice—indeed, Prosdocimo's sole example (see Ex. 6.8, below) contains a repetition in the upper voice while the lower one—which ends like a tenor though it is not so labelled—moves). If in its greater generality his treatise is less practical for the novice, that is surely because it is not primarily a didactic work but a survey of contrapuntal practice viewed as *subiectum* by a Paduan professor who devoted treatises to all aspects of music (plainchant theory, counterpoint, French and Italian mensuration, tuning, *musica speculativa*)—and to arithmetic, astronomy, and geometry as well.

Among the many elements of counterpoint discussed by Ugolino of Orvieto in Book II of his *Declaratio* (dating probably from the 1430s) is a set of rules clearly derived from Prosdocimo's. Missing only is Prosdocimo's rule that counterpoint should begin with a perfect consonance;[61] and indeed the extended examples of 'composed counterpoint' in *Declaratio* 2.27, though they always end with perfect consonances (a point on which Ugolino agreed with Prosdocimo), sometimes begin with imperfect ones.

Thus theorists of the fourteenth and early fifteenth centuries established a catalogue of consonances and developed principles that held for centuries: that parallel perfect consonances are to be avoided; that a perfect consonance should not be reached through similar motion unless the upper voice moves stepwise; that counterpoint should generally begin and always end with a perfect consonance; that not too many imperfect consonances should be used consecutively without the insertion of perfect ones; and that the motion from a perfect consonance to an imperfect one, and yet more so that of an imperfect consonance to a perfect one, was particularly satisfying.

Musica Ficta

As noted above in the section on Fundamentals, theorists of the fourteenth and early fifteenth centuries generally defined musica ficta or falsa as consisting of those notes outside the basic scale (which consisted of the natural notes from Γ to ee inclusive, plus the B♭s above and below middle C). The term also refers to the alteration, by accidentals, of notes of the basic scale: 'Musica falsa occurs when we make a semitone of a tone.'[62] Since the rules governing the use of accidentals are primarily (though not exclusively) contrapuntal, discussion of accidentals typically occurs in counterpoint treatises.

The theorists agree that accidentals are to be introduced for two primary reasons, the first being to make simultaneously sounding fifths, octaves, and the like perfect where they would be augmented or diminished without the accidentals. As Prosdocimo put it (*Contrapunctus* 5.6):

For understanding the placement of these two signs, round b and square ♮, it must be known that these signs are to be applied to octaves, fifths, and similar intervals as it is necessary to enlarge or diminish them in order to

---

[61] For a point-by-point comparison of Prosdocimo's and Ugolino's contrapuntal doctrines, see Prosdocimo, *Contrapunctus*, ed. and trans. Jan Herlinger (Greek and Latin Music Theory, 1; Lincoln, Nebr. and London, 1984), app.

[62] *Videndum est de falsa musyca*; Gwee, 269. Cf. CS i. 166.

make them good consonances if they earlier were dissonant, because such intervals ought always to be major [i.e. perfect] or consonant in counterpoint.

The rule appears as early as the thirteenth century, and remains current throughout the period under consideration here. Example 6.7 shows diminished fifths and octaves corrected by accidentals, as given in the anonymous treatise *Quot sunt concordationes*, dating probably from the late fourteenth century.[63] Note that the author used both sharps (or naturals) and flats to correct the bad intervals. In this he is typical of theorists of the time; but as Berger has shown, late in the fifteenth century it became normal for theorists to correct such intervals with flats only.[64]

The second primary rule is that accidentals are to be introduced to alter imperfect consonances so that they lie as close as possible to the perfect ones to which they move. Prosdocimo again (*Contrapunctus* 5.6):

These signs are to be applied to imperfectly consonant intervals—the third, the sixth, the tenth, and the like—as it is necessary to enlarge or diminish them to give them major or minor inflections as appropriate, because such intervals ought sometimes to be major and sometimes minor in counterpoint; and if you wish to know the difference—when they should be major and when minor— you should consider the location to which you must move immediately after leaving the imperfect consonance; then you must see whether the location you leave is more distant from that location which you intend immediately to reach, making the imperfect consonance major or making it minor: for you should always choose that form, whether major or minor, that is less distant from that location which you intend immediately to reach, and you should, by means of the signs posited above, make a major interval minor or, contrariwise, a minor one major as appropriate. There is no other reason for this than a sweeter-sounding harmony. Why the sweeter-sounding harmony results from this can be ascribed to the sufficiently persuasive reason that the property of the imperfect thing is to seek the perfect, which it cannot do except through approximating itself to the perfect. This is because the closer the imperfect consonance approaches the perfect one it intends to reach, the more perfect it becomes, and the sweeter the resulting harmony. . . . [Ex. 6.8]

Similar rules appear in many treatises of the time.[65] Note that closest-approach progressions employ alteration of one voice only; altering

---

[63] The round b and square ♮ are represented by flat and sharp. Coussemaker presented *Quot sunt concordationes* as part of the 'Ars discantus secundum Johannem de Muris'; Sachs (*Contrapunctus*, 180–1; cf. Michels, *Musiktraktate*, 43) dismissed the attribution to Muris, but dated the treatise to the 14th c. The discussions of intervals as wide as two octaves plus a third suggest that it dates probably from the latter part of the century.

[64] *Musica Ficta*, 115–18.

[65] For instance, Marchetto, *Lucidarium* 5.6.2–7; Petrus dictus Palma ociosa, *Compendium de discantu mensurabili* (1336), 513–15 (Petrus was a Cistercian monk at Cherchamps, diocese

Ex. 6.7. Diminished fifths and octaves corrected by accidentals (*Quot sunt concordationes*)

Ex. 6.8. Accidentals producing the closest approach (Prosdocimo, *Contra-punctus*)

both voices simultaneously, one with a sharp, the other with a flat, would produce augmented or diminished intervals that would no longer be consonances. Prosdocimo's example actually shows three types of progression involving alteration by accidentals—of an imperfect consonance expanding or contracting stepwise in both parts to the nearest perfect consonance (M6–P8 and m3–unison; M3–P5, though not shown here, would also be possible); of an imperfect consonance moving in similar motion (stepwise in one part) to a perfect consonance (m6–P8); and of an imperfect consonance moving to another imperfect consonance (m6–m6).[66] Four of the five instances use a sharp to effect the closest approach, only one a flat. Berger, in fact, has found that fourteenth-century theorists preferred the sharp to the flat in such cases,[67] and this is certainly true for Prosdocimo.

When used in music of three or more parts the closest-approach principle in its formulation involving stepwise contrary motion accounts for one of the most characteristic progressions of fourteenth- and early fifteenth-century music, that involving the so-called double leading-note (see Ex. 6.4 above, where the F is sharpened to produce a major sixth that moves to a perfect octave and the C is sharpened to produce a major third that moves to a perfect fifth).[68]

---

of Amiens); *Quilibet affectans*, 59b; *Quot sunt concordationes*, 72a–73a; Ugolino, *Declaratio* 2.6.7, 9.

[66] Berger reports only one other treatise that recommends alteration of an imperfect conso-nance to make it lie closer to an ensuing imperfect consonance, Giovanni del Lago's *Breve intro-duttione de musica misurata* (Venice, 1540); Berger, *Musica Ficta*, 124.

[67] *Musica Ficta*, 140, 143.

[68] As no treatments of counterpoint in three or more parts seem to date from the period under consideration in this chapter, it is not discussed further here.

Though most musica ficta rules involve harmonic or contrapuntal considerations, purely melodic considerations, which theorists typically presented in discussions of plainchant rather than counterpoint, also play their part. Among these is the avoidance of the direct chromatic progression (prevented by the proscription of mutation between b♮ and b♭) and of melodic tritones (for which theorists proposed the use of b♭ rather than b♮). But note that contrapuntal considerations may override these melodic considerations, especially during the fourteenth and early fifteenth centuries. The chromatic progressions for which Marchetto invented the term *permutatio* most frequently occur in connection with the closest approach from an imperfect consonance to a perfect one (see Ex. 6.9);[69] similarly, Prosdocimo introduced a melodic tritone in order to effect the closest approach from one imperfect consonance to another (see Ex. 6.8).[70]

Florid Counterpoint in Two Voices

Though fourteenth- and early fifteenth-century theorists universally forbade the use of dissonances in note-against-note counterpoint, these were allowed in florid counterpoint by the handful of theorists who discussed it. According to Petrus dictus Palma ociosa (1336), 'although we may not dwell on . . . dissonances at any length, we may ascend or descend through them briefly' on the way to consonances. The treatise *Volentibus introduci* states of dissonances, 'We do not use them in counterpoint except where a note is divided into three parts; then one of those parts may be discordant, namely, the middle part . . .'.[71] Antonius de Leno's rules for 3 : 1 counterpoint are like those of *Volentibus introduci*. But in the examples he gave (as Sachs points out), the middle note is more often consonant than dissonant; when it is dissonant it always moves stepwise to a consonance, though it may be approached by leap. Antonius further specified that in 2 : 1 counterpoint both notes must be consonant with the tenor, a rule that necessitates many leaps.[72] The treatise *De diminutione contrapuncti*, which never occurs except as an adjunct to *Quilibet affectans* and *Cum*

---

[69] *Quatuor principalia* 4.25 also shows a direct chromatic progression in connection with the closest approach of an imperfect consonance to a perfect one.

[70] On such unorthodox progressions, see Herlinger, 'What Trecento Music Theory Tells Us', in Eugene Narmour and Ruth A. Solie (eds.), *Explorations in Music, the Arts, and Ideas: Essays in Honor of Leonard B. Meyer* (Festschrift Series, 7; Stuyvesant, NY, 1988), 177–97.

[71] Petrus dictus Palma ociosa, *Compendium de discantu mensurabili*, 518; *Volentibus introduci*, version Pi, Sachs, *Contrapunctus*, 173. The version of *Volentibus introduci* Coussemaker published as part of the 'Ars contrapuncti secundum Philippum de Vitriaco' is less specific, stating only that one of the three parts may be dissonant.

[72] Antonius de Leno, *Regule de contrapunto*; see especially the example on p. 321b, partially transcribed in Sachs, *Contrapunctus*, 143. Sachs (p. 141) dates Antonius to the 14th c.; Leno is near Brescia. The treatise is in Italian.

Ex. 6.9. Chromatic progressions from Marchetto's *Lucidarium* (ex. 5)

notum sit, presents many examples of florid counterpoint, but the rules its author presents concern not counterpoint but mensuration. In the examples in the treatise, however, dissonances occur only on minims (never on breves or semibreves), usually in unaccented metric positions, and usually in stepwise motion, with passing notes predominating over neighbour notes.[73]

But far more elaborate than any of these discussions of florid counterpoint is that from the Berkeley Treatise of 1375.[74] In discussing what he calls *verbulare*, or dividing notes in counterpoint, the Berkeley author states that when such a division is made, although it is allowable for the first combinations over adjacent tenor notes to produce identical fifths or octaves with it, such a practice is not 'masterful', thus in effect advising against (though not prohibiting) parallel fifths or octaves on successive beats; that the greater part, or in any case half, of the notes over a particular tenor note must be consonant with it;[75] that a group of notes over a single tenor note may begin or end with a dissonance, so long as the dissonance is shorter than half the value of the consonant notes over that tenor note (except in syncopation, where consonant and dissonant values may be equal); and that the final note over one tenor note may not create a parallel perfect consonance with the first note over the next tenor note. Sachs points out that the Berkeley author thus sought to produce a true theory of florid counterpoint, and that his discussion of this topic is the most extensive before Tinctoris's.[76]

MENSURATION

The most radical and most significant innovations of fourteenth-century music theory lay in the field of mensuration. Indeed, musicologists have named the period after 1300 the *Ars nova*, a term that

[73] As reported by Sachs, *Contrapunctus*, 145. For transcription of the examples, see ibid. 146–7; 'Counterpoint', 835.
[74] Berkeley Treatise 2.2 (pp. 130–47).
[75] The treatise also reports that according to some, consonance must predominate; according to others, the first note of a group over a single tenor note must be consonant (pp. 130–1).
[76] *Contrapunctus*, 149–50. It is unfortunate that the many examples of florid counterpoint in the Berkeley Treatise omit the tenor voice.

refers specifically to the new 'art', or technique, of mensural notation introduced at about that time. There were in fact two main strands of mensural theory during the period under consideration in this chapter. One emerged in Italy towards the end of the second decade of the fourteenth century, developed almost exclusively in that area, and was moribund by the first decades of the fifteenth. The other emerged in France just a few years later; more comprehensive and more systematic than the Italian, it spread throughout Europe and continued to develop through the sixteenth century.[77]

The Thirteenth-Century Background
The *Ars cantus mensurabilis* (*c.*1280) of Franco of Cologne was the foundation upon which fourteenth-century theorists built their doctrines of mensuration. Franco distinguished three basic values, the long, the breve, and the semibreve (Ex. 6.10), each of which existed in two or three durations. The long was either perfect (equal to three time units), imperfect (equal to two), or duplex (equal to six time units); the breve either regular (equal to one time unit) or altered (equal to two); the semibreve either major (equal to two-thirds of one time unit) or minor (equal to one-third). Franco's system was based on the perfect long and regular breve as divisible only into thirds. Thus an imperfect long occurred only in conjunction with a regular breve (or a group of semibreves together equal to a regular breve) preceding or following it; indeed, the breve was said to make the long imperfect. When two breves occurred between two longs, the second breve was to be altered—doubled in length—so that the two breves together then equalled a perfect long. Franco also gave straightforward rules for imperfection: a long was perfect if followed by another long (this rule accounts for the necessity of the altered breve, as the imperfect long—equal to it in length—could not be used before another long); a long was made imperfect by a single breve (or group of semibreves) preceding it or following it or by four or more breves following it; when

---

[77] On the history of mensuration, see Johannes Wolf, *Geschichte der Mensural-Notation von 1250–1460 nach den theoretischen und praktischen Quellen bearbeitet*, 3 vols. (Leipzig, 1904) and *Handbuch der Notationskunde*, 2 vols. (Kleine Handbücher der Musikgeschichte nach Gattungen, 8; Leipzig, 1913), and F. Alberto Gallo, 'Die Notationslehre im 14. und 15. Jahrhundert', in Zaminer, v. 257–356. On Italian mensuration in particular see F. Alberto Gallo, *La teoria della notazione in Italia dalla fine del XIII all'inizio del XV secolo* (Antiquae Musicae Italicae Subsidia Theorica; Bologna, 1966). Heinz Ristory, *Post-franconische Theorie und Früh-Trecento: Die Petrus de Cruce-Neuerungen und ihre Bedeutung für die italienische Mensuralnotenschrift zu Beginn des 14. Jahrhunderts* (Europäische Hochschulschriften, ser. 36: Musikwissenschaft, 26; Frankfurt and New York, 1988), surveys the transition from post-Franconian notation through the early stages of the Italian Trecento. Most of the Italian treatises between Marchetto and Prosdocimo are collected in *Mensurabilis musicae tractatuli*, ed. F. Alberto Gallo and Piero Paolo Scattolin, 2 vols. to date (Bologna, 1966–).

Ex. 6.10. Franco's duplex long, long, breve, and semibreve

a single breve fell between two longs it imperfected the preceding long,
not the following one; a group of three breves made neither a preceding nor a following long imperfect. These normal procedures, however, could be overridden by the use of a stroke called *divisio modi*
to group the breves in different ways. A regular breve equalled two or
three semibreves (in a group of three semibreves, all were minor; in a
group of two, the first was minor and the second major); an altered
breve equalled four to six semibreves in two groups of two or three; a
perfect long equalled six to nine semibreves in three groups of two or
three—with the groupings of the semibreves clarified by the *divisio
modi*. Franco also gave rules for recognizing the values of notes (i.e.
whether they were longs, breves, or semibreves) written contiguously
in ligatures. He called ligatures beginning with a breve 'with propriety', those beginning with a long 'without propriety', those beginning
with two semibreves 'with opposite propriety'; those ending with a
long 'with perfection' (or 'perfect'), those ending with a breve 'without
perfection' (or 'imperfect'). The various types were distinguished by
their shapes. The types of two-note ligatures are shown in Table 6.3;
in ligatures of three or more notes all internal notes are breves except
for the second note in a ligature with opposite propriety (distinguished
by the upward tail at the left of the ligature), which is a semibreve
(*Ars cantus mensurabilis* 4, 5, 7).

Even earlier than Franco's time theorists had entertained the possibility of binary division of the long and the breve alongside the
orthodox ternary,[78] and before the thirteenth century had run its
course they were investigating the possibility of dividing the breve into
more than three units. Jacques de Liège, writing probably in the 1320s
but looking back to an earlier time, attributed to Petrus de Cruce the
use of groups of four, five, six, and seven semibreves, each group in
the time of a breve; and to another person the use of groups of eight
and nine semibreves.[79] The mensural theory of the fourteenth century

---

[78] See Heinz Ristory, 'Ein Kurztraktat mit Binärmensuration und praefranconischem
Gepräge', *Studi musicali*, 15 (1986), 151–6.
[79] *Speculum musicae*, ed. Roger Bragard, 7 vols. (CSM 3; Rome, 1955–73), 7.17.7–11. Lefferts
suggests that the other person is the Johannes de Garlandia mentioned by the Englishman
Robertus de Handlo in 1326 (not the same Johannes de Garlandia mentioned earlier in this
chapter), and dates this Garlandia to 1300–20 (introduction to Robertus de Handlo, *Regule*, ed.

TABLE 6.3 Franco's two-note ligatures

Name	Ascending	Descending	Value[a]
with propriety, with perfection			(BL)
with propriety, without perfection			(BB)
without propriety, with perfection			(LL)
without propriety, without perfection			(LB)
with opposite propriety			(SS)

[a] B = breve; L = long; S = semibreve.

can be seen as an attempt to bring order to the profusion of shorter-valued notes and to coordinate emerging binary metres with the traditional ternary ones.

Italian Fourteenth-Century Mensuration

The earliest fourteenth-century mensural treatise to which a reasonably firm date can be assigned is Marchetto's *Pomerium in arte musice mensurate* of 1318–19,[80] which describes successive divisions of the breve into three or two parts, the divisions called *ternaria*, *senaria perfecta*, *duodenaria*, *novenaria*, *binaria*, *quaternaria*, *senaria imperfecta*, and *octonaria* (Table 6.4).[81] Within each of the divisions of the breve shown in Table 6.4 the semibreves represent the greatest number of notes possible within that division. When there are fewer notes in a division, the shorter notes fall at the beginning of the time unit, the longer notes at the end (an arrangement said to proceed

Peter M. Lefferts (Greek and Latin Music Theory, 7; Lincoln, Nebr. and London, 1991), 24–7). Nothing certain is known of the author of the *Speculum musicae*, the longest musical treatise of the Middle Ages. Its seven books deal respectively with the nature of music and its arithmetic foundation, the intervals and their ratios, the numerological properties of these, the consonances, tuning, plainchant, and mensuration; this last book is an attack on the innovations of the Ars nova. Michels has dated the treatise—or at least its seventh book—to 1323–5 (*Musiktraktate*, 50–5).

[80] Oliver Strunk's dating of the *Pomerium* has never been refuted, though it is often ignored ('On the Date of Marchetto da Padova', in id., *Essays on Music in the Western World* (New York, 1974), 39–43). For a summary of his and others' findings, see the introduction to *The Lucidarium of Marchetto of Padua*, 3–4.

[81] Marchetto mentioned the possibility of subdividing *senaria imperfecta* further into twelve or eighteen units (*Pomerium* 40.2–3), but did not discuss either division.

TABLE 6.4 Marchetto's *divisiones*

A. Division of the perfect breve into *ternaria*, *senaria perfecta*, and *duodenaria*

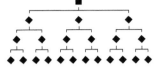

B. Division of the perfect breve into *ternaria* and *novenaria*

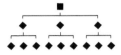

C. Division of the imperfect breve into *binaria*, *quaternaria*, and *octonaria*

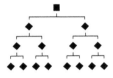

D. Division of the imperfect breve into *binaria* and *senaria imperfecta*

via naturae, in a natural manner) unless they are tailed downward or upward; in that case (an arrangement said to proceed *via artis*, in an artificial manner) downward-tailed notes are longer, upward-tailed notes the shortest values in *divisiones duodenaria*, *novenaria*, or *octonaria*—though the shortest values in these *divisiones* can also be represented sometimes by untailed semibreves. A few examples will suffice to show some possibilities within the perfect metres (Table 6.5).

Of the greatest interest is Marchetto's discussion of the differences between imperfect metres as read in the Italian and the French manner (*modo ytalico* and *modo gallico*): whereas the Italians placed the longer values after the shorter ones, the French placed them before (Table 6.6); Marchetto proposed the use of the letters Y and G in notated pieces to distinguish the two national styles. He also described the single-pitch ligatures (normally ligatures were used to represent only notes of different pitches) with which Italian scribes sometimes notated syncopation both within the breve unit and from one breve unit to the next (Ex. 6.11 shows such ligatures in Giovanni

TABLE 6.5 Some arrangements of notes within the perfect metres in Marchetto's system

A. *Divisio ternaria* (modern equivalents in 3/4)

B. *Divisio senaria perfecta* (modern equivalents in 3/4)

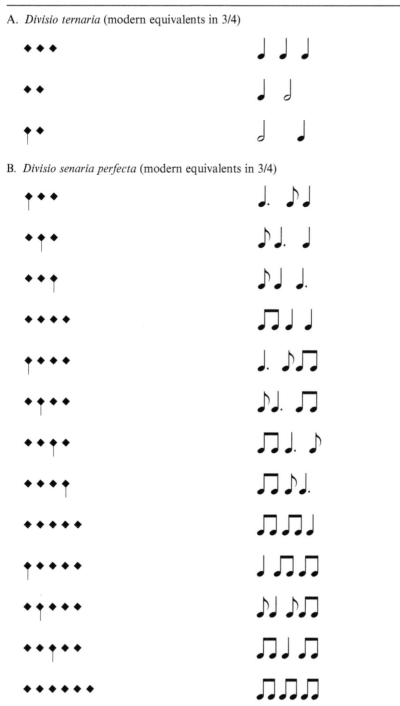

TABLE 6.5 (*cont.*)

C. *Divisio duodenaria* (modern equivalents in 3/4)

D. *Divisio novenaria* (modern equivalents in 9/8)

TABLE 6.6 Some differences between Italian and French styles, according to Marchetto

Notation	*Modus ytalicus*	*Modus gallicus*
◆ ◆ ◆		
◆ ◆ ◆ ◆		
◆ ◆ ◆ ◆ ◆		
◆ ◆ ◆ ◆ ◆ ◆		

Ex. 6.11. Use of single-pitch ligatures to represent syncopations in Giovanni da Firenze's madrigal *La bella stella*, Biblioteca Apostolica Vaticana, MS Rossi 215, fo. 23ᵛ. In the manuscript the clef sign is one line too high. Transcription from Marrocco, *Italian Secular Music*, 40

da Firenze's madrigal *La bella stella*, as it appears in the Rossi Codex).[82]

Over the course of the next century Italian theorists expanded and refined Marchetto's doctrine. The notational system Marchetto had described employed—depending on context—either upward-tailed on untailed semibreves to represent the shortest values in *divisiones duodenaria* and *novenaria*, a practice that produced a confusing note picture; in the last monument of Italian mensural theory, the *Tractatus practice de musica mensurabili ad modum italicorum* (1412; revised *c*.1425), Prosdocimo described a more consistent system in which the shortest values in these mensurations are always represented by

[82] On the *modus ytalicus* and *gallicus*, see *Pomerium*, ed. Giuseppe Vecchi (CSM 6; n.p.: American Institute of Musicology, 1961), 42–3. On single-pitch ligatures, see *Pomerium* 49–50, and Michael Long, 'Musical Tastes in Fourteenth-Century Italy: National Styles, Scholarly

TABLE 6.7 Comparison of Marchetto's and Prosdocimo's notational systems

Rhythm	Marchetto	Prosdocimo

A. *Divisio duodenaria*

B. *Divisio novenaria*

upward-tailed semibreves (Table 6.7). Marchetto had stated that a minim could shorten a semibreve only if placed next to it (*Pomerium* 30–1.17–18); Prosdocimo described a diagonal tail that prevented the shortening of a semibreve, thus shifting the reduction in value to a non-adjacent semibreve (Ex. 6.12). Last, Prosdocimo described the use of the letters *si, n, o,* and *d* to distinguish the *divisiones senaria imperfecta, novenaria, octonaria,* and *duodenaria* unambiguously.[83]

French Fourteenth-Century Mensuration

The French took a more systematic approach to the notation of rhythms than the Italians, organizing note values into a hierarchical system with the same principles governing note relationships at every level. The first monument of fourteenth-century French mensural theory is the *Notitia artis musice* written by Johannes de Muris in 1321. Johannes devoted Book 1 and the beginning of Book 2 to *musica spe-*

Traditions, and Historical Circumstances' (Ph.D. diss., Princeton University, 1981), ch. 5; Long (p. 16) also corrects a crucial error concerning such ligatures in Vecchi's edition of the *Pomerium*. The letters Y and G distinguish the two styles in the earliest major source of 14th-c. Italian polyphony, the Rossi Codex, which also shows single-pitch ligatures. Marchetto's discussion of semibreves in the *modus gallicus* is an important witness to the interpretation of French notation of the early 14th c. (like that of the *Roman de Fauvel*, compiled just a few years before the *Pomerium*).

[83] Many of the details of Italian mensural theory after Marchetto, however, betray the influence of contemporary French theory. Johannes Vetulus (*Musica*, ed. Frederick Hammond (CSM 27; n.p.: American Institute of Musicology, 1977), 54.1–4), for instance, followed the Italian fashion by writing two semibreves in perfect metres to show a rhythm in which the second note is twice the length of the first, but he adopted French terminology in calling the second semibreve 'altered'. And he notated the reverse of that rhythm with a breve and a semibreve in the French fashion, where the Italian system would have used a downward-tailed and an untailed semibreve. It is not certain whether the author is the Johannes Vetulus de Anagnia cited as notary in a document of 1372 from Frosinone.

Ex. 6.12. Use of diagonal tail to prevent shortening of a semibreve by an adjacent minim (Prosdocimo, CS iii. 238b)

Ex. 6.13. Johannes's maxima, long, breve, semibreve, and minim

culativa (see below), then turned to the principles of French mensural theory. The Franconian background is evident in the rules that a long before another long is perfect, that when a breve occurs between two longs it imperfects the preceding long rather than the following one, and that when two breves occur between two longs the second breve is altered (Johannes' second music treatise, the *Compendium musice practice* of *c*.1322, shows Franconian ligature forms). But the new system extends the Franconian relationships of long to breve to encompass notes called the maxima and the minim as well (Ex. 6.13),[84] thus establishing relationships on four levels: the maxima was equal to two or three longs, the long to two or three breves, the breve to two or three semibreves, and the semibreve to two or three minims. Franco's rules for imperfection and alteration at the long–breve level were extended to the maxima–long, breve–semibreve, and semi- breve–minim levels as well (Franco's *divisio modi* became a dot [*punctus*]). Also new was the concept of imperfection of a part of a note: thus a long could be imperfected not only by a breve (which reduced its value by one-third) but by a semibreve (which reduced its value by one-third of one of its constituent breves), and the breve by a minim. Johannes, however, ignored the musical contexts that called forth imperfection and alteration (devoting less discussion to them than had Franco) and dismissed the subject of perfect and imperfect metres with the barest mention; the *Notitia* is very much the work of a scholar examining the rational bases of a new mensural system rather than a musician showing how it actually

[84] The term *maxima* appears first in the *Compendium musice practice*; in the *Notitia* the imper- fect maxima (Franco's duplex long) is called *longior* and the perfect one *longissima*.

works. Indeed, as Johannes himself wrote (*Notitia* 2.7.5), 'There are many other innovations latent in music, which will appear clearly to later investigators.'[85]

Many of these latent possibilities were realized in the torso known as chapters 15–24 of Philippe de Vitry's *Ars nova*.[86] The author of this fragment, whether or not he was Philippe, defined *modus perfectus* and *imperfectus* explicitly as metres with three and two breves respectively to the long, *tempus perfectum* and *imperfectum* as metres with three and two semibreves respectively to the breve. He described the signs that indicate them as well: three lines for *modus perfectus*, two for *modus imperfectus*; circle for *tempus perfectum*, semicircle for *tempus imperfectum*. He also described the use of red notes (as opposed to black) to indicate, among several possible meanings, the imperfection of notes that would otherwise be perfect or vice versa, and described the semiminim (whose value is half the minim) alongside the maxima,

---

[85] Johannes de Muris, who received the Master of Arts degree between 1319 and 1321, probably at the Sorbonne, is the author of over twenty treatises on arithmetic, geometry, astronomy, and music. The earliest of the musical treatises is the *Notitia artis musice*, one of five treatises from that year that together cover all four branches of the quadrivium (Michels suggests that they represent his first round of lectures at the Sorbonne). The second book of the *Notitia* was printed separately in GS iii. 292–301. Through an idiosyncratic explicit in one manuscript it came to be known as the *Ars nove musice*; the date 1319, suggested by Coussemaker, is no longer tenable. See Michels, *Musiktraktate*, 2–8. The other musical treatises that can with certainty be attributed to Johannes are *Compendium musice practice* (*c.*1322) and *Musica speculativa* (1323, revised 1325). Attributions of the *Ars contrapuncti* and the *Libellus cantus mensurabilis* are discussed elsewhere in this chapter.

[86] Philippe de Vitry was born in Paris in 1291, educated at the Sorbonne, was attached to the French royal court for many years, became bishop of Meaux in 1351, and died in 1361. He was renowned in his time as one of the leading intellectuals, poets, and musicians of France. Roesner, Avril, and Regalado have presented circumstantial evidence that points towards Philippe as music editor of the *Roman de Fauvel* (introduction to *Le Roman de Fauvel*, 42). For other recent contributions to Philippe's biography, see Andrew Wathey, 'The Marriage of Edward III and the Transmission of French Motets to England', *JAMS* 45 (1992), 1–29 and 'The Motets of Philippe de Vitry and the Fourteenth-Century Renaissance', *EMH* 12 (1993), 119–50.

In the form in which the treatise called *Ars nova* appears in Biblioteca Apostolica Vaticana, Barb. lat. 307 (the form in which it was printed first by Coussemaker and later by Reaney, Gilles, and Maillard along with what they called other versions of the treatise; CSM 8; n.p.: American Institute of Musicology, 1964), its first thirteen chapters deal with fundamentals; they appear separately in other manuscripts and have been attributed to Johannes de Garlandia (Reimer, introduction to *Johannes de Garlandia: De mensurabili musica*, 2 vols. (Beihefte zum Archiv für Musikwissenschaft, 10–11; Wiesbaden, 1972), ii. 4–8). Reaney, Gilles, and Maillard questioned their attribution (and that of ch. 14 on musica ficta) to Philippe even as they published them as part of his treatise. Chapters 15–24 deal with mensuration, but begin *in medias res* with a discussion of minims in *tempus perfectum*. The text Reaney, Gilles, and Maillard present as a concordant version of chapters 17–24, from Paris, Bibliothèque Nationale de France, lat. 14741, differs so markedly from the Barberini text that it must be seen as a separate treatise that shares some material with the Barberini fragment. The four other 'versions of the *Ars nova*' Reaney, Gilles, and Maillard present differ even more. Fuller ('Phantom Treatise') questions whether these various 'versions' derive from a single ancestor, and indeed raises doubts whether there was a treatise called *Ars nova* written by Philippe de Vitry. The first thirteen chapters of *Ars nova* have recently been critically edited as one version of a treatise *De plana musica* perhaps by Johannes de Garlandia: Gwee, '*De plana musica and Introductio musice*'.

long, breve, semibreve, and minim. Where Johannes had described partial imperfection of the long by the semibreve and of the breve by the minim, this author described as well partial imperfection of the long by the minim. He also cited a number of pieces by name, some of them by Philippe de Vitry.

The first comprehensive mensural treatise of the French Ars nova is the *Libellus cantus mensurabilis*.[87] After enumerating the five note values (maxima, long, breve, semibreve, minim),[88] the author explicitly stated that each of them equals either two or three of the next smaller value; adopted the terms *modus perfectus* and *imperfectus* to indicate the relation of long to breve, *tempus perfectum* and *imperfectum* to indicate that of breve to semibreve; and introduced the terms *prolatio maior* and *minor* to indicate the relationship of semibreve to minim. The four basic metres that result from combining *tempus perfectum* or *imperfectum* with *prolatio maior* or *minor* are shown in Table 6.8, along with the symbols that represent them in the *Libellus* and most later sources.[89] The author discussed the rules of imperfection and alteration exhaustively (codifying in the process the various sorts of partial imperfection), detailed the musical contexts in which they operate, and surveyed unorthodox practices among contemporary composers, one of whom, Guillaume de Machaut, he named. He also devoted chapters to the dots of perfection and division, time signatures (alongside those of the Ars nova he introduced three dots to represent *prolatio maior*, two dots to represent *prolatio minor*), rhythmic modes (thereby acknowledging a debt to thirteenth-century theory), ligatures, syncopation, rests, diminution, and *color* (the last two phenomena function prominently in the archetypical genre of the time, the isorhythmic motet).[90]

---

[87] CS iii. 46–58. A critical edition has now appeared: *Ars practica mensurabilis cantus secundum Iohannem de Muris*, ed. Christian Berktold (Bayerische Akademie der Wissenschaften, Veröffentlichungen der Musikhistorischen Kommission; Munich, 1999).

[88] The semiminim is ignored, though the semiminim rest is mentioned near the end of the treatise.

[89] For the sake of brevity, the *modus* level is not represented in the table.

[90] Who wrote the *Libellus*? It is attributed to Johannes de Muris in the overwhelming majority of manuscripts, and none bears any other attribution. A number of writers of the 14th and 15th cc. regarded it as his, and none offered a conflicting attribution. Michels accepts it as a work of Johannes, and explains its considerable discrepancies from the *Notitia artis musice* of 1321 and the *Compendium music practice* of a year or so later as reflecting his response to the continuing developments in Ars nova practice over the twenty years or more that presumably intervened before he wrote the *Libellus* (*Musiktraktate*, 27–40). Yet the *Libellus* differs from the *Notitia* and the *Compendium* not only in substance but in outlook. The author of these two treatises dealt with his subject in the abstract, focusing on the possibilities of a new notational system while almost totally ignoring the details of actual practice; the author of the *Libellus* seems totally engaged with the practice of the time. Despite the manuscript attribution, it remains difficult to see him as the same person who wrote the *Notitia* and the *Compendium*.

TABLE 6.8 The four basic metres of French fourteenth-century notation with their signatures as given in the *Libellus* and in later sources

Division	*Libellus*	Later sources
A. *Tempus perfectum, prolatio maior*	⊙⋮	⊙
B. *Tempus perfectum, prolatio minor*	⊙⋮	○
C. *Tempus imperfectum, prolatio maior*	⊙⋮	⊙
D. *Tempus imperfectum, prolatio minor*	⊙⋮	⊂

The Ars Subtilior

Late in the fourteenth century a musical style arose that has been described as 'born of a time alive with the vigorous exploration of rhythmic and harmonic possibilities based on reasoned extensions of traditional mathematical and musical principles'.[91] Its intricate rhythms, unequalled in complexity until the mid-twentieth century, display extended syncopations and employ note values in addition to those described thus far. Both phenomena are amply documented in the theory of the time.

The rules of French mensural notation, as stated in the *Libellus cantus mensurabilis*, sometimes call forth syncopation. According to the *Libellus*, when in major prolation a minim falls between two semibreves it normally imperfects the preceding semibreve rather than the one following (rule 4 concerning imperfection). If the preceding semi-

[91] Philip Schreur, introduction to *Tractatus figurarum: Treatise on Noteshapes*, ed. and trans. Philip E. Schreur (Greek and Latin Music Theory, 6; Lincoln, Nebr. and London, 1989), 2. The repertoire is preserved primarily in two manuscripts of the early 15th c., Chantilly, Musée Condé, MS 564, and Modena, Biblioteca Universitaria e Estense, α.M.5.24.

Ex. 6.14. Imperfection of a semibreve by a minim: (*a*) by an adjacent minim; (*b*) by a non-adjacent minim

(*a*)

(*b*)

breve cannot be imperfected (for instance, because it has already been imperfected by a minim preceding it, or because its imperfection is prevented by a dot of division), the minim will imperfect the first note it can (rule 5); normally this will be the semibreve immediately following (Ex. 6.14(*a*)). But if that semibreve is followed by another it cannot be imperfected either, as a 'semibreve before a semibreve in perfect [i.e. major] prolation is always perfect' (rule 1); in such a case syncopation occurs (a dislocation of a perfect semibreve by the value of the one minim), and if a series of semibreves follows, the syncopation continues until an imperfectible semibreve occurs. That is the note the minim imperfects, and with which it is counted to make up a perfection, a figure equal in value to one perfect semibreve (Ex. 6.14(*b*), in which the minim is counted with the fourth—imperfected— semibreve). The definition of syncopation given in the *Libellus* is apt: 'the division of any figure into separate parts, which are brought together in counting units of perfection' (CS iii. 47–9, 56–7).

How did later theorists extend these principles? The author of the *Ars cantus mensurabilis mensurata per modos iuris* (the Anonymous V of CS iii), writing probably during the last quarter of the fourteenth century, gave a more complicated example of syncopation, which he said came from the motet *Ida capillorum* (Ex. 6.15).[92] As the author explains this passage, 'the first minim is brought together with two later ones, that is, the minim rest and the minim' (p. 212; my translation): a dot prevents the first minim from imperfecting the preceding

[92] *Ars cantus mensurabilis mensurata per modos iuris*, ed. and trans. C. Matthew Balensuela (Greek and Latin Music Theory, 10; Lincoln, Nebr. and London, 1994), 212. The motet *Portio naturel/Ida capillorum* contains rhythms similar but not identical to these; see *Motets of the Manuscripts Chantilly, Musée Condé, 548 (olim 1047) and Modena, Biblioteca Estense, α. M. 5, 24 (olim lat. 568)*, ed. Ursula Günther (CMM 39; n.p.: American Institute of Musicology, 1965),

Ex. 6.15. Examples of syncopation from *Ars cantus mensurabilis per modos
iuris* (Balensuela edn., p. 212). Each of the upward-tailed ligatures represents
two semibreves

semibreve; the dots surrounding the minim rest prevent it from imperfecting the preceding semibreve and prevent the second minim
from being altered. Johannes Vetulus de Anagnia explained several
syncopated examples as follows (*Musica* 57.19, 26):

[Ex. 6.16(*a*)]: The first part will be a minim, the second, because of the sign
of perfection [the dot] will be a syncopated note of the value of three minims.
The first minim is brought together with the first two minims after the syncopated note, and the second of the two remaining at the end is altered . . .
to recover the measure.

[Ex. 6.16(*b*)]: The first of these is a minim, the second is a minor semibreve
because it is imperfected by the preceding note; the third, standing alone, is
brought together with the last two, of which neither, because of the dot of
division, can be altered; the fourth will be a syncopated note of the value of
three minims.

Equally as striking as the syncopations of the Ars subtilior are its
rhythms cutting across the normal metric divisions—four equal notes
in the time of six minims in *tempus perfectum* with *prolatio minor*, or
four equal notes in the time of nine minims in *tempus perfectum* with
prolatio maior, etc. No treatise presents these in more exuberant profusion than the *Tractatus figurarum* (of which the earliest dated manuscript was copied in 1391)—notes with black, red, void, and semivoid
heads, upward and downward tails (some turned back), and solid and
void dots. Table 6.9 summarizes their meaning: complex rhythmic
relationships such as these were one of the seeds of the theory of

no. 14. On the basis of the musical examples in the treatise, Balensuela concludes that the *Ars
cantus mensurabilis mensurata per modos iuris* was written in Italy during the last quarter of the
14th c. (p. xi).

Ex. 6.16. Examples of syncopation from Johannes Vetulus

proportions that reached full flower in the treatises of Tinctoris, Gaffurio, and their contemporaries (see below, Ch. 7).

Yet the Ars subtilior, of which the *Tractatus figurarum* is one of the theoretical monuments, was a short-lived development centred in southern France and northern Italy that spent itself early in the fifteenth century. The theoretical source of the mainstream mensural notation cultivated all over Europe through the sixteenth century was the *Libellus cantus mensurabilis*. The *Libellus* was copied in France, the Low Countries, England, Germany, Austria, and Italy in a tradition extending into the sixteenth century. It was translated into French and Italian, adapted to evolving mensural practice, commented upon, and taken as the model for independent treatments of the subject; it was still being cited as late as 1532.[93] Indeed, it was recognized as the foundation of mensural theory until the

[93] Fifty-one sources for the *Libellus* survive today; the earliest is Berkeley, University of California Music Library, MS 744 (1375), the latest British Library, Add. MS 10336 (1526). A French translation appears in Cambrai, Médiathèque municipale, MS 920, Italian translations in Bologna, Civico Museo Bibliografico Musicale, MS A.48 and Florence, Biblioteca Medicea-Laurenziana, MS Redi 71. Adaptations include that of Antonius de Luca, who in his *Ars cantus figurati* added to the *Libellus*'s doctrine discussions of partially coloured ligatures and those with internal dotting (see especially the examples on p. 50 of Ristory's edition). Prosdocimo's commentary is his *Expositiones* (1404?); Ugolino's appears as Book 3 of his *Declaratio*. The *Libellus* served as model for the *Ars cantus mensurabilis mensurata per modos iuris* (discussed above) and for Prosdocimo's *Tractatus practice cantus mensurabilis* (1408 with later revisions). Giovanni del Lago mentioned it in a letter to Giovanni Spataro dated 22 Nov. 1532 (*A Correspondence of Renaissance Musicians*, ed. Bonnie J. Blackburn, Edward E. Lowinsky, and Clement A. Miller (Oxford, 1991), no. 47). See Gallo, 'Notationslehre', 300–3; Herlinger, 'A Fifteenth-Century Italian Compilation of Music Theory', *Acta musicologica*, 53 (1981), 90–105 at 92–3, 97–8; and Daniel Seth Katz, 'Earliest Sources for the *Libellus cantus mensurabilis secundum Johannem de Muris*' (Ph.D. diss., Duke University, 1989), 1–4, 9–13.

TABLE 6.9 Unusual note values in the *Tractatus figurarum*

A. In *tempus perfectum* with *prolatio maior*

2 equal notes as in *tempus imperfectum*
with *prolatio maior*:

4 equal notes as in *tempus imperfectum*
with *prolatio maior*:

3 equal notes over two *tempora*:

B. In *tempus imperfectum* with *prolatio maior*

3 equal notes as in *tempus perfectum*
with *prolatio minor*:

6 equal notes as in *tempus perfectum* with
prolatio minor:

9 equal notes as in *tempus perfectum*
with *prolatio maior*:

C. In *tempus perfectum* with *prolatio minor*

9 equal notes as in *tempus perfectum*
with *prolatio maior*:

2 equal notes as in *tempus imperfectum* with
prolatio maior:

6 equal notes as in *tempus imperfectum* with
prolatio maior:

4 equal notes as in *tempus imperfectum* with
prolatio minor:

D. In *tempus imperfectum* with *prolatio minor*

6 equal notes as in *tempus imperfectum* with
prolatio maior:

3 equal notes as in *tempus perfectum* with
prolatio minor:

[a] Brackets indicate red notes.

mensural system itself evolved into our modern one in the seventeenth
century.

MUSICA SPECULATIVA

Background

The topics discussed thus far—fundamentals, modes, counterpoint,
and mensuration—deal with the practice of music and were subsumed
during the Middle Ages as *musica practica* or *activa*. *Musica theorica*
or *speculativa*, on the other hand, treats music not as an activity to be
practised but as an object of contemplation (*speculatio*), contemplation that serves the moral edification of the soul as well as the
intellectual edification of the mind.[94] This appears very clearly in the
seminal treatise of the *musica speculativa* tradition, the *De musica* of
Boethius, the first chapter of which is titled 'Music forms a part of us
through nature, and can ennoble or debase character'.[95]

For the writers of the *musica speculativa* tradition the word music
does not signify merely the music we hear in our everyday life; it con-
notes harmony conceived broadly enough to encompass the relationships obtaining in the human body and psyche and governing the
motions of planets. Boethius indicated this very clearly in his distinction of the kinds of music:

There are three: the first is cosmic, whereas the second is human; the third is
that which rests in certain instruments. . . .

The first kind, the cosmic, is discernible especially in those things which
are observed in heaven itself or in the combination of elements or the diversity of seasons. For how can it happen that so swift a heavenly machine moves
on a mute and silent course? . . .

Whoever penetrates into his own self perceives human music. For what
unites the incorporeal nature of reason with the body if not a certain
harmony and, as it were, a careful tuning of low and high pitches as though
producing one consonance? . . .

---

[94] For an overview, see Michael Bernhard, 'Überlieferung und Fortleben der antiken lateinischen Musiktheorie im Mittelalter', in Zaminer, iii. 7–35, and Albrecht Riethmüller, 'Probleme
der spekulativen Musiktheorie im Mittelalter', ibid. 163–201.

[95] Boethius, *Fundamentals of Music*, trans. Calvin M. Bower (Music Theory Translation Series;
New Haven, 1989), 1. Anicius Manlius Severinus Boethius (d. 524/5) was one of the most important figures in the transmission of ancient learning to the Middle Ages. He translated and commented on the works that together came to be known as the Old Logic (Porphyry's *Isagoge*,
Aristotle's *Categories* and *On Interpretation*); the recovery of his translations of Aristotle's *Prior
Analytics*, *Topics*, and *Sophistical Refutations* (which along with the *Posterior Analytics*, translated
by James of Venice, complete the collection of Aristotle's logical works) was a milestone in the
history of philosophy. His *De institutione arithmetica* and *De institutione musica* (which survive in
183 and 137 manuscripts respectively), two volumes of a projected four on the arts of the quadrivium, laid the foundation for the study of those disciplines during the Middle Ages.

The third kind of music is that which is said to rest in various instruments. This music is governed either by tension, as in strings, or by breath, as in the aulos or those instruments activated by water, or by a certain percussion, as in those which are cast in concave brass, and various sounds are produced from these.[96]

Cassiodorus elaborated on the scope of music:

The discipline of music is diffused through all the actions of our life. First, it is found that if we perform the commandments of the Creator and with pure minds obey the rules he has laid down, every word we speak, every pulsation of our veins, is related by musical rhythms to the powers of harmony. Music indeed is the knowledge of apt modulation. If we live virtuously, we are constantly proved to be under its discipline, but when we commit injustice we are without music. The heavens and the earth, indeed all things in them which are directed by a higher power, share in this discipline of music, for Pythagoras attests that this universe was founded by and can be governed by music.[97]

If music is the knowledge of 'apt' modulation, precisely what sort of modulation is to be characterized as apt? Cassiodorus's correlative definition of music suggests the answer: 'The science of music is the discipline that deals with those numeric proportions that are found in sounds.'[98] It is number that lies at the heart of order, harmony, music; or as the ninth-century commentator Remi of Auxerre put it, 'Truth is contained in numbers'.[99] Those modulations are apt that reflect the numeric proportions underlying reality. Cassiodorus' reference to Pythagoras is telling; for Pythagoreanism may be defined as the doctrine that all being is governed by numbers. The Wisdom of Solomon admitted this pagan doctrine into Christian thought: 'Thou hast ordered all things in measure and number and weight' (11: 21). Augustine promulgated it in his *De Genesi ad litteram*:

In the sense that measure places a limit on everything, number gives everything form, and weight draws each thing to a state of repose and stability, God is identified with these three in a fundamental, true, and unique sense. He limits everything, forms everything, and orders everything. Hence, in so far as this matter can be grasped by the heart of man and expressed by his

[96] Boethius, *Fundamentals of Music* 1.2 (pp. 9–10; trans. Bower).

[97] Cassiodorus, *Institutiones* 2.5.2. (trans. in Strunk). This passage is quoted in part by Marchetto, *Lucidarium*, 1.3.8. Cassiodorus Senator (d. 575) was a praetorian prefect in the Roman court of the Ostrogothic kings; after retiring from public life, he founded a monastery, Vivarium, in southern Italy. The two books of his *Institutiones divinarum et humanarum litterarum* are devoted respectively to the exposition of the Scriptures and of the seven liberal arts; the latter became one of the major sources for medieval study of the arts.

[98] *Institutiones* 2.5.4; my translation.

[99] Remi of Auxerre, *Commentum in Martianum Capellam*, ed. Cora E. Lutz, 2 vols. (Leiden, 1962–5), 46.8.

tongue, we must understand that the words, *thou hast ordered all things in measure and number and weight*, mean nothing else than 'Thou hast ordered all things in Thyself'.[100]

Indeed, the medievals came to see numeric relationships behind virtually every aspect of nature, art, and thought—in the motions of the heavenly spheres, in the harmony of soul and body, in the relationships of man to Christ; in the dimensions of cathedrals and wood carvings, in the octagonal shape of baptismal fonts; in poetic structures, metres, and rhyme schemes; and in musical tuning, melody, harmony, counterpoint, and rhythm.[101]

The Fourteenth and Early Fifteenth Centuries

Johannes de Muris acknowledged the significance of number in music very clearly in his *Notitia artis musice* of 1321, Book 1 of which is devoted to the measurement of pitch. Here Johannes, beginning with the most basic principles of sound, derived from them the structure of the gamut in logical progressions. Chapter 1 begins by stating that 'because music consists of pitch related to numbers and vice versa, musicians have to consider both number and pitch'.[102] Because the generation of pitch requires that something strike something else, there can be no pitch without motion. Pitch in its turn is defined as the breaking up of air due to the impulse of that which strikes on that which is struck. Low pitch is generated from slower and less frequent motions, high pitch from faster and more compact motions; thus there is a greater number of motions in a high pitch than in a low one. A lesser quantity is related to a greater quantity by a number; therefore a low pitch is related to a high pitch as the number of motions in the one is proportionally related to the number of motions in the other.[103] This argument follows Boethius *De musica* 3 very closely; chapter 2

[100] Augustine, *De Genesi ad litteram* 4.3, in *Sancti Aurelii Augustini hipponensis episcopi Opera*, 12 vols. (Naples, 1854), iii, cols. 109–378, trans. John Hammond Taylor, SJ as *The Literal Meaning of Genesis*, 2 vols. (Ancient Christian Writers, 41–2; New York, 1982). Saint Augustine of Hippo (354–430) was arguably the most profound thinker among the Fathers of the Church. His *De Genesi ad litteram*, written to resolve the apparent contradictions between the scriptural account of Creation and the views of contemporary science, advanced the idea that mathematical laws were intelligible representations of immutable divine truth.

[101] On the doctrine of numbers in the Middle Ages, see Edgar de Bruyne, *Études d'esthétique médiévale*, 3 vols. (Bruges, 1946); D. W. Robertson, Jr., *A Preface to Chaucer: Studies in Medieval Perspectives* (Princeton, 1962); S. J. Heninger, Jr., *Touches of Sweet Harmony: Pythagorean Cosmology and Renaissance Poetics* (San Marino, Calif., 1974); and Umberto Eco, *Art and Beauty in the Middle Ages*, trans. Hugh Bredin (New Haven and London, 1986). But as a corrective to overly Pythagorean readings of medieval culture, see Christopher Page, 'Cathedralism', ch. 1 of *Discarding Images: Reflections on Music and Culture in Medieval France* (Oxford, 1993), esp. 11–18.

[102] *Notitia*, ed. Ulrich Michels (CSM 17; n.p.: American Institute of Musicology, 1972), 1.1.2.

[103] Parallel passages: Johannes de Muris, *Musica speculativa*, 8–13; Jacques de Liège, *Speculum musicae* 1.23; Ugolino, *Declaratio* 5.8.

enumerates the classes of proportional relationships obtaining among numbers, again following Boethius (*De musica* 1.4).[104] Chapter 3 relates these proportions to intervals by recounting Boethius' (*De musica* 1.10) tale of the discovery of the principles of harmony by Pythagoras, who noticed that musical intervals were produced by hammers whose weights were related in the proportionality $12:9:8:6$. $12:6$ (i.e. $2:1$), Pythagoras discovered, was the ratio of the octave; $12:9$ or $8:6$ (i.e. $4:3$) that of the perfect fourth; $12:8$ or $9:6$ (i.e. $3:2$) that of the perfect fifth; $9:8$ that of the whole tone.[105] The chapter also shows these intervals as scalar spans (the perfect fourth, two whole tones plus a semitone; the perfect fifth, three whole tones plus a semitone; the octave—as the combination of fourth and fifth— five whole tones plus two semitones). Chapter 4 is devoted to the demonstration that the semitone, whose ratio is $256:243$, is not half the whole tone (cf. Boethius, *De musica* 2.29; this proposition is one of the chief Pythagorean *topoi*).[106] Chapter 5 finally derives the gamut as consisting of seven interlocking hexachords.

Book 2 of the *Notitia*, concerning the measurement of time, continues the logical progression begun in Book 1. Chapter 1 relates motion and time: time is the measure of motion, that is, the measure of sound sustained with continuous motion. One unit of time is greater, another lesser; the greater is that which has a longer motion, the lesser that which has a shorter motion. Earlier writers rationally assigned the 'perfect' measure to that unit of time measuring sound which was susceptible of division into three parts, as they believed that all perfection consists in the number 3.[107] Only after this introduction does the treatise address matters pertaining to musical practice.

Johannes's *Musica speculativa*[108] is even more clearly Boethian than the *Notitia*; indeed, according to Johannes in his preface, 'It seemed to me a good thing to draw out of Boethius' *De musica* . . . a short

[104] Parallel passages: Marchetto, *Lucidarium* 7; Johannes de Muris, *Musica speculativa*, 12–21; Jacques de Liège, *Speculum musicae* 1.35–48; Ugolino, *Declaratio* 4.3–58.

[105] The story of Pythagoras is recounted also by Marchetto, *Lucidarium* 1.1; Johannes de Muris, *Musica speculativa*, GS iii. 258–60; Ugolino, *Declaratio* 5.31—among many others. The proportionality $12:9:8:6$ figures also in medieval theory independently of the Pythagoras legend; see e.g. the Berkeley Treatise, 4.2. For a study of late medieval and Renaissance accounts in which Jubal ('the father of them that play upon the harp and organ', Gen. 4: 21) replaces or is coordinated with Pythagoras, see James W. McKinnon, 'Jubal vel Pythagoras: Quis Sit Inventor Musicae?', *MQ* 64 (1978), 1–28.

[106] Parallel passages: Johannes de Muris, *Musica speculativa*, 90–113; Philippe de Vitry, 13.5; Jacques de Liège, *Speculum musicae* 2.42.1; Prosdocimo, *Tractatus musice speculative*, 732–33; Ugolino, *Declaratio* 5.12–13.

[107] Cf. Remi, *Martianus Capella* 44.5–12; Marchetto, *Lucidarium* 6.3.

[108] The *Musica speculativa* of Johannes de Muris (written 1323, revised 1325) is the most widely disseminated of the treatises whose attribution to him is unquestioned, surviving in forty-eight manuscript copies. It was frequently prescribed in medieval university curricula.

treatise in which I shall sincerely try to present, with clarity of thought and expression, the most beautiful and most essential conclusions pertinent to the art of music.' The first part of the treatise is devoted to the explication of twenty theorems based on Boethian principles (e.g. 'that the diapente exceeds the diatessaron by a tone'; 'that the tone cannot be divided into equal parts'); the second turns to division of the monochord.

What exactly is the relationship between *musica practica* and *musica speculativa*? Almost half of the *Notitia*, often treated as a practical work dealing with mensuration, is devoted to matters perhaps better regarded as *musica speculativa*; and the *Musica speculativa* turns at the end to division of the monochord, which might seem to be an aspect of *musica practica*. Indeed, it is impossible to discuss intervals and their tunings on the one hand or mensuration on the other without discussing numerical relationships; and even in discussions of modes and counterpoint theorists sometimes incorporate numerology to a great or a lesser extent. What distinguishes treatises of *musica speculativa* from those of *musica practica* is not so much their subject matter as the focus their authors bring to it: one treatise on, say, mensuration will concentrate almost exclusively on practical matters (the *Libellus cantus mensurabilis*, for example) where another will stress the numerological basis (the *Notitia artis musice*).

The mix of *musica practica* and *musica speculativa* is particularly evident in the treatises of Marchetto: though the *Lucidarium*, dealing with plainchant broadly defined, and the *Pomerium*, dealing with mensuration, are certainly works of *musica practica*, both have a markedly speculative cast. Marchetto began the *Lucidarium* by recounting Pythagoras' discovery of the ratios of the musical intervals (1.1). He defined music as 'that science which consists in numbers, proportions, consonances, intervals, measures, and quantities' (1.5.3), and paraphrased Remi: 'Truth in music lies in the numbers of proportions' (1.4.5; cf. Remi above, p. 294). His numerological orientation becomes quite clear in his explanation of why the first species of the pentachord, the basis of modes 1 and 2, begins on the second syllable of the hexachord, *re*, rather than the first, *ut*:

It is certain that music consists of notes, and that these notes consist of numbers; therefore the order obtaining among notes will be like that obtaining among numbers. But in numbers, 1 enumerates both 2 and 3, by means of which the other numbers are enumerated; and yet 1 is not a number.[109]

---

[109] The statement is standard in Pythagorean numerology. Cf. Macrobius, *Somnium Scipionis* 1.6.7: 'One is called *monas*, that is Unity, and is both male and female, odd and even, itself not a number, but the source and origin of numbers' (trans. Stahl); Isidore, *Etymologiae* 3.3.1:

Thus if we wish to constitute something in the first number we constitute
it in 2, which is called the first number even though 2 cannot be conceived
of without the conception of 1, which is not a number. It is the same in
notes, because *ut* is the first syllable or note that occurs in singing, and
it is a pitch; yet it produces no melody. The syllable that is closest to *ut* is *re*;
the first motion is made to it. Singing arises through motion, and without
motion there is no singing; if all notes were to lie on one line or in one
space no singing would result, but rather wailing. Guido writes aptly on
this point: 'Music is the motion of notes through *arsis* and *thesis*, that is,
through upward and downward motion' [cf. *Micrologus* 16.9–10]. Then
that syllable through which singing first becomes intelligible will be called
the first, just as that number which is founded on the binary is called the
first. From what has been said it is manifest that *re* is the first note or
syllable in singing.[110]

Marchetto also substantiated his unorthodox division of the whole
tone into fifths on the basis of numerology. The very idea of such a
division is anti-Pythagorean, as from an arithmetic point of view it
requires the insertion of a series of geometric means between the terms
of a superparticular ratio (one in which the two numbers differ
by 1; in this case, 9:8), a division impossible within the framework
of Pythagorean mathematics.[111] And though the division is anti-
Pythagorean, Marchetto's justification for it, which he argued intri-
cately, touches many of the standard Pythagorean topoi as presented
by such authorities as Boethius, Macrobius, Martianus Capella, and
Remi of Auxerre.[112] In the *Pomerium* (25.12–19), Marchetto applied
similar numerological principles to the exposition of standard mensural doctrines: that the altered breve follows the regular breve and
not vice versa; that the altered breve must be followed by a long.

The speculative aspect of Marchetto's *Lucidarium* called forth
one of the most vitriolic attacks of one medieval theorist on another,
Prosdocimo's *Tractatus musice speculative* of 1425. Recognizing
Marchetto's division of the whole tone into fifths as fundamentally
anti-Pythagorean, Prosdocimo dismissed it summarily, and disman-
tled block by block the numerological defence of the division
that Marchetto had so carefully constructed, criticizing the earlier
theorist for his deficient arithmetic, faulty logic, and unorthodox
terminology. Since the 'errors of this Marchetto', as Prosdocimo saw

---

'Number is a multitude made up of unities, for 1 is the seed of number, not [itself] a number';
Remi, *Martianus Capella* 285.14: 'Unity . . . is not a number but the progenitor of all numbers.'
Ugolino admitted that though 1 is by definition not a number ('unity is not a collection of
unities'), it is often taken improperly as a number (*Declaratio* 4.89).

[110] Marchetto, *Lucidarium* 9.1.54–66.
[111] See Boethius, *De musica* 3.11, 4.2; Jacques de Liège, *Speculum musicae* 3.51–2.
[112] See Herlinger, 'Marchetto's Division of the Whole Tone'.

them, had 'spread throughout Italy and beyond', he found it fitting 'that the evils, lies, and errors produced and disseminated by one Paduan might be removed by another, and thus that Italy might be purged of such errors'. Marchetto himself he dismissed as 'a simple performer [*simplex practicus*] totally devoid of theoretical or speculative knowledge, which he nonetheless thought he understood perfectly' (p. 731).

This last point brings us to a recurrent topos of speculative music theory, the distinction between *musicus* and *cantor*, between the theorist who examines the subject of music rationally and the performer who practises the art. Boethius had laid down the fundamental distinction in his *De musica*, but without using the word *cantor*:

Now one should bear in mind that every art and also every discipline considers reason inherently more honorable than a skill which is practiced by the hand and labor of an artisan. For it is much better and nobler to know about what someone else fashions than to execute that about which someone else knows; in fact, physical skill serves as a slave, while reason rules like a mistress. . . .

A musician is one who has gained knowledge of making music by weighing with the reason, not through the servitude of work, but through the sovereignty of speculation. . . .

There are three classes of those who are engaged in the musical art. . . .

Those of the class which is dependent upon instruments and who spend their entire effort there—such as kitharists and those who prove their skill on the organ and other musical instruments—are excluded from comprehension of musical knowledge, since . . . they act as slaves. None of them makes use of reason; rather, they are totally lacking in thought.

The second class of those practicing music is that of the poets, a class led to song not so much by thought and reason as by a certain natural instinct. For this reason this class, too, is separated from music.

The third class is that which acquires an ability for judging, so that it can carefully weigh rhythms and melodies and the composition as a whole. This class, since it is totally grounded in reason and thought, will rightly be esteemed as musical. That person is a musician who exhibits the faculty of forming judgments according to speculation or reason relative and appropriate to music concerning modes and rhythms, the genera of songs, consonances, and all the things which are to be explained subsequently, as well as concerning the songs of the poets.[113]

The distinction was expressed through the dichotomy *musicus/cantor* as early as the ninth century (Aurelian, *Musica disciplina* 7), and

---

[113] Boethius, *Fundamentals of Music* 1.34 (pp. 50–1; trans. Bower).

this dichotomy remained standard for centuries. Its classic statement comes from Guido's *Regulae rhythmicae* (early eleventh century):

> Great is the gap between musicians and singers;
> the latter [merely] sing, while the former understand what music involves.
> For he who does what he does not understand is termed a beast.[114]

By dismissing Marchetto as a *simplex practicus*, Prosdocimo clearly intended to rank him among the ignorant (a ranking belied by the profound influence of the *Lucidarium*, acknowledged even by Prosdocimo). Marchetto's own treatment of the *musicus/cantor* question is revealing. After quoting Boethius, this is how he closed the *Lucidarium*:

> The musician knows the power and nature of the musical proportions; he judges according to them, not according to sound alone. The singer is, as it were, the tool of that musician—who is an artisan in that he is occupied with a tool, but a musician inasmuch as he puts into practice what he has previously investigated through rational process.
>
> Thus the musician is to the singer as the judge to the herald. The judge sets things in order and commands the herald to proclaim them. So it is with the musician and the singer: the musician investigates, perceives, discerns, selects, orders, and disposes all things that touch on this science, and he commands the singer, who serves as his messenger, to put them into practice.[115]

Reimer has shown that the model of *musicus* and *cantor* Marchetto presented in the second paragraph quoted is appropriate to a teacher, to the head of a choral organization (both of which Marchetto seems to have been)—to one who sees himself as the *musician* who leads and the choristers in his charge as *singers* dependent on his judgement.[116] But the first paragraph suggests a union of musician and singer in one person: a musician who investigates his subject rationally and then puts into practice what he has learned. This, indeed, is the model of the *musicus-cantor* that was to become the ideal of the Renaissance.[117]

---

[114] Guido, *Regulae rhythmicae*, in *Guido d'Arezzo's* Regule rithmice, Prologus in antiphonarium, *and* Epistola ad Michahelem: *A Critical Text and Translation*, ed. and trans. Dolores Pesce (Musicological Studies, 73; Ottawa, 1999), 330–3; I have altered the second line of the translation.

[115] Marchetto, *Lucidarium* 16.1.4–11.

[116] Erich Reimer, 'Musicus und Cantor: Zur Sozialgeschichte eines musikalischen Lehrstücks', *Archiv für Musikwissenschaft*, 35 (1978), 1–32.

[117] This outlook is reflected by Jacques de Liège: 'Whoever understood both theoretical and practical music would be a better musician than he who understood only the second' (*Speculum musicae* 1.3.12).

VII

MUSIC THEORY AND MUSICAL THINKING AFTER 1450

By Bonnie J. Blackburn

INTRODUCTION

THE fifteenth century was a period of great ferment in musical ideas. It was the century in which a decisive change took place in the way music was generally composed, from the successive method, in which voices were successively added to a single part or a duo, to the method (sometimes termed 'simultaneous') in which the complex of voices was conceived as a whole—an innovation analogous to the discovery of perspective in art. Intimately linked with this change was a revolution in musical aesthetics. The judgement of the ear was allowed to take precedence over mathematical ratios.[1] While never losing its original place in the quadrivium, music also came to be considered part of the trivium, justifying its place among the linguistic arts through its expressive power.[2]

The scope of music theory widened considerably in the fifteenth century. Whereas treatises of the earlier centuries tended to concentrate either on the practical or the speculative aspect of music, beginning with Ugolino of Orvieto's *Declaratio musicae disciplinae* of *c*.1430 many theorists attempted to cover the whole field of musical inquiry. Some felt more comfortable with speculation, others with

---

[1] On the problem that Boethius left to posterity in his delicately balanced claim for the superiority of the *sensus intellectus*, while not neglecting the importance of the *sensus auditus*, see Klaus-Jürgen Sachs, 'Boethius and the Judgement of the Ears: A Hidden Challenge in Medieval and Renaissance Music', in Charles Burnett, Michael Fend, and Penelope Gouk (eds.), *The Second Sense: Studies in Hearing and Musical Judgement from Antiquity to the Seventeenth Century* (Warburg Institute Surveys and Texts, 22; London, 1991), 169–98, and also John Caldwell's article in the same volume, 'The Concept of Musical Judgement in Late Antiquity', 161–8.

[2] So at least it appeared to Jean Perréal, who placed Music in the company of Grammar, Logic, and Rhetoric in his fresco of the Liberal Arts at Le Puy, painted *c*.1500; it has been suggested that the figure of Tubal-Cain is based on Josquin. See Edward E. Lowinsky, 'Helmuth Osthoff's Josquin Monograph', in id., *Music in the Culture of the Renaissance and Other Essays*, ed. Bonnie J. Blackburn, 2 vols. (Chicago, 1989), ii. 531–4 at 531–2.

musica practica; some were at home in both. The last quarter of the century and the first decades of the next saw an explosion in writings about music. Italy was the main site, although only three of the six major theorists were native Italians.[3] The hot-headed Spaniard Bartolomé Ramos de Pareja published his *Musica practica* in Bologna in 1482. In it he took on the whole musical establishment, from Guido d'Arezzo, through Marchetto of Padua, down to his own contemporaries: Johannes Tinctoris, a Walloon who spent the major part of his career at the Neapolitan court, and John Hothby, the English Carmelite who taught music at Lucca Cathedral for the last twenty years of his life. Niccolò Burzio violently attacked Ramos, who was defended in turn by the most mordant tongue of all, that of his pupil Giovanni Spataro, whose own running controversy with Franchino Gaffurio erupted into print in 1520. In this flurry of treatises and counter-treatises, where serious musical arguments are mingled with *ad hominem* attacks, the burning musical questions of the day were aired. Among these were the recovery of ancient Greek writings on music and their relevance to contemporary practice (Gaffurio, Hothby), the dissatisfaction with Pythagorean intonation as the basis of the tuning system (Ramos, Gaffurio), the problem of rationalizing the existence of sharps, flats, and microtones outside the Guidonian system (Spanish theorists, Hothby, Aaron), the applicability of the modal system to polyphony (Tinctoris, Aaron), and the nature of music itself, especially as revealed in the changing concept of consonance and dissonance and the emergence of harmony as a technical musical concept (Tinctoris). All these questions were crucial to the future of music.[4]

In the fifteenth century, music reached out to other disciplines. Poets were just as interested as musicians were in the fabled effects of ancient Greek music, and when they declaimed their verses to musical accompaniment they saw themselves as imitating the Greeks. Artists envied

---

[3] All the proponents were then living in Italy; owing to loss of sources we know little about music theory in England and especially in France; apart from Tinctoris, Georg Erber's notes on proportions, made in Paris *c*.1460, are a notable exception; see Renate Federhofer-Königs, 'Ein Beitrag zur Proportionenlehre in der zweiten Hälfte des 15. Jahrhunderts', *Studia musicologica Academiae Scientiarum Hungaricae*, 11 (1960), 145–57. In England we have a rare witness in John Tucke's notebook, which reflects his personal interest in quite abstruse aspects of musical notation but is not likely to reflect the normal studies of an aspiring theorist. See Ronald Woodley, *John Tucke: A Case Study in Early Tudor Music Theory* (Oxford, 1993).

[4] On the new directions in music theory of the 15th c., see Edward E. Lowinsky, 'Music of the Renaissance as Viewed by Renaissance Musicians', in Bernard O'Kelly (ed.), *The Renaissance Image of Man and the World* (Columbus, Ohio, 1966), 129–77, repr. in Lowinsky, *Music in the Culture of the Renaissance*, i. 87–105, and id., 'The Concept of Physical and Musical Space in the Renaissance', in *Papers of the American Musicological Society, Annual Meeting, 1941*, ed. Gustave Reese (n.p., 1946), 57–84; rev. repr. in *Music in the Culture of the Renaissance*, i. 6–18.

music its position in the quadrivium, for painting, sculpture, and architecture did not belong to the liberal but the mechanical arts. Seeking to demonstrate the applicability of mathematical principles to artistic endeavours, Leon Battista Alberti derived architectural principles from the ratios of musical harmonies. Luca Pacioli, in his *De divina proportione*, made a specific comparison between music and perspective, and Leonardo, in his *Paragone*, claimed music as a sister of painting, arguing for the superiority of painting because 'music vanishes as it is born' and can never be grasped as a whole. All three use technical musical terms, and their writings reveal that musical thought was directly relevant to artistic concerns.

These new ideas were developed within a tradition that had changed little over the centuries. Beginning singers had to be taught to read music, to recognize intervals, to know where the semitone fell, to navigate melodies by mutating to new hexachords, to understand the modes, and to know the psalm-tone differences (see Ch. 6). To judge by the many fifteenth-century copies of treatises by Guido, the *Dialogus* once ascribed to Oddo, and multiple versions of Franco of Cologne's *Ars cantus mensurabilis*, the past was very much with fifteenth-century musicians: these were basic texts, still relevant. Boethius was required reading for university students, and the speculative tradition continued to be represented by more modern writers, of whom Johannes de Muris was the most influential. The common notion that theory lags behind practice can easily be demonstrated in the fifteenth century; but so can its opposite: Bartolomé Ramos anticipated the tuning system that was to be favoured in the sixteenth century; John Hothby envisaged a division of the monochord into six orders and built a keyboard instrument with quarter-tones long before Vicentino; Johannes Tinctoris and Franchino Gaffurio successfully championed reforms of the notational system.

GERMAN AND CENTRAL EUROPEAN THEORY

At our present state of knowledge, no more than a sketch can be given of German and Central European music theory in the fifteenth century; most of it is anonymous and remains in manuscript.[5] The orientation is predominantly practical; many of the sources originated in

---

[5] The extent of theoretical sources in Germany only became clear with the publication of the third volume in the RISM series *The Theory of Music*, which is devoted to sources in the then West Germany: Michel Huglo and Christian Meyer, *Manuscripts from the Carolingian Era up to c. 1500 in the Federal Republic of Germany (D-brd)* (Munich, 1986). Meyer has recently edited a selection of anonymous treatises: Anonymi, *Tractatus de cantu figurativo et de contrapuncto (c. 1430–1520)* (CSM 41; Neuhausen-Stuttgart, 1997). For Czech and Polish sources see *The Theory of Music, 5: Manuscripts from the Carolingian Era up to c. 1500 in the Czech Republic, Poland, Portugal and Spain*, ed. Christian Meyer, Elżbieta Witkowska-Zaremba, and Karl-Werner Gümpel (Munich, 1997).

monasteries and collegiate churches, and the emphasis is on the fundamentals of music and plainchant. Typically, the treatises appear as parts of compilations, side by side with theological, rhetorical, or astronomical works.[6] Tonaries continue to be copied.

A distinct group of related sources, in prose and metrical versions, apparently originating in the university towns of Prague, Kraków, and Leipzig, testifies to the early introduction and long-lasting influence of French Ars nova theory in Central Europe. John of Luxembourg, whom Machaut served as secretary, became King of Bohemia in 1310; his son, Charles IV, who had been educated in France, founded the University of Prague in 1348. In 1367 music became required study, and two years later the metrical version of the treatise was written; the prose versions date after 1400 and were copied as late as the 1460s. These treatises mainly transmit the notational theory of Johannes de Muris, codified in the *Libellus cantus mensurabilis* of *c*.1340, but with important differences: mensural signs for mode (only minor mode is discussed) are shown by the circle and semicircle, *tempus* by a dot or its absence, and prolation by a vertical line with two or three dots. The minim is treated as imperfectible.[7] The *Libellus* continued to be used for generations, being adapted to current notational practice as necessary.[8] In the version of the prose treatise copied in the monastery of Melk in 1462, the compiler mentions Johannes's five note shapes, but says that according to 'the moderns' there are fourteen: longissima, duplex longa (also called maxima), longa, brevis, semibrevis, minima, semiminima, fusiel, semifusiel, brevis plicata, 'cardinalis seu voluntaria' (i.e. fermata), oblonga, vacua, semivacua.[9] Some of these names sound rather old-fashioned—and the musical compositions referred to as example date from the fourteenth century—but other parts of the treatise are quite modern, especially the discussion of composition in more than two parts; indeed the definition of 'cantus copulatus' is similar to

---

[6] See e.g. the *Parvulus musice* owned by Johannes Klein of Löbau that he probably used in his university studies in Leipzig around 1450, discussed by Tom R. Ward in 'Music and Music Theory in the Universities of Central Europe during the Fifteenth Century', in *Atti del XIV Congresso della Società Internazionale di Musicologia: Trasmissione e recezione delle forme di cultura musicale*, ed. Angelo Pompilio *et al*. (Turin, 1990), i. 49–57.

[7] On these treatises and their notational system see Tom R. Ward, 'A Central European Repertory in Munich, Bayerische Staatsbibliothek, Clm 14274', *EMH* 1 (1981), 325–43. See also above, Ch. 5.

[8] A critical edition has been published by Christian Berktold; see above, Ch. 6 n. 87. Earlier we depended on Coussemaker's edition (CS iii. 46–58). There are also glossed versions by Prosdocimo de' Beldomandi and Ugolino of Orvieto. On the question of Johannes de Muris's authorship and influence see Ch. 6.

[9] The treatise has been edited by F. Alberto Gallo: *Tractatulus de cantu mensurali seu figurativo musice artis* (Melk, Stiftsbibliothek, MS 950) (CSM 16; n.p.: American Institute of Musicology, 1971). On the note shapes see pp. 16–18.

Tinctoris's definition of *res facta*, discussed below: *Cantus copulatus* ('linked song') is 'the sounding with each other of different melodies according to the manner and equivalence of consonances, diversified by figures and notes of various kinds throughout such melodies, duly proportioned in [mensural] modes by the number of *tempora* and in the concordance of sounds according to above and below'.[10]

In the second half of the fifteenth century another group of related treatises appears; the main representatives are known after Coussemaker's edition as Anonymi XI and XII, and probably date from the 1460s.[11] Anonymus XI is in fact a collection of treatises that most likely originated at different times and places; the compiler of the manuscript put together what he thought would have been needed by the student in the middle of the fifteenth century: the fundamentals of music, comprising definitions, the Guidonian hand, notes, mutation, and intervals; an explanation of *coniunctae* (another term for *musica ficta*, the notes outside the Guidonian hand); an exceptionally comprehensive tonary; a short section on counterpoint that also covers three-part composition;[12] and brief treatments of the mensural modes and proportions, showing how different mensurations are to be related. There are in fact two separate sections on relating note values through proportions, a subject that fascinated the fifteenth-century musician and was exploited by composers in the mensural transformations of a cantus firmus. Only lacking, it would seem, is a section on notation: this is supplied by Anonymus XII, in the same manuscript.[13] Here we find the same unusual signs for prolation as in the Central European sources, but they are said to be no longer in use; prolation is shown in the normal way by the presence or absence of the dot in a circle or semicircle. Proportions are also discussed, now with the inclusion of two-part music examples.

[10] 'Cantus copulatus est diversorum cantuum ad invicem secundum modum et equipollentiam consonantium concentus, diversarum specierum figuris ac vocibus per cantus huiusmodi varificatus, modis temporum numero ac sonorum concordantia secundum supra et infra debite proporcionatus'; ibid. 13. For other German treatises that discuss composition in more than two parts, see the edition by Meyer cited in n. 5, pp. 42–4, 59–62, 70–2, 75.

[11] CS iii. 416–75 and 475–95. Both are now available in better editions: Anonymus XI by Richard Joseph Wingell, 'Anonymous XI (CS III): An Edition, Translation, and Commentary' (Ph.D. diss., University of Southern California, 1973), and Anonymus XII by Jill M. Palmer, *Tractatus et compendium cantus figurati* (CSM 35; Neuhausen-Stuttgart, 1990). Another (partial) version, copied in his student days in 1490 by the future archbishop of Esztergom, László Szalkai, has been edited by Dénes Bartha, *Das Musiklehrbuch einer ungarischen Klosterschule in der Handschrift von Fürstprimas Szalkai (1490)* (Musicologica Hungarica, 1; Budapest, 1934).

[12] This section is discussed by Hugo Riemann, *History of Music Theory, Books I and II: Polyphonic Theory to the Sixteenth Century*, trans. Raymond H. Haggh (Lincoln, Nebr., 1962), 242–6.

[13] Originally in Trier, now British Library, Add. MS 34200.

One of the few identifiable German music theorists of the fifteenth century is Conrad von Zabern (d. between 1476 and 1481). After obtaining the bachelor's and master's degrees at the University of Heidelberg in 1410 and 1414, and earning a reputation as a preacher, he became an itinerant teacher with a mission: to improve choral singing in churches and monasteries. In his later years he taught at the universities of Heidelberg, Freiburg im Breisgau, Basle, and Ingolstadt.[14] His proposals for reform are embodied in his *De modo bene cantandi choralem cantum in multitudine personarum*, the first printed book on music (Mainz, 1474).[15] We know from church records all over Europe that singers of chant were constantly being admonished to sing more slowly and evenly, observing the proper pauses. Conrad lays down six requirements for singing well: *concorditer* (in unison, as if with one voice), *mensuraliter* (in even time), *mediocriter* (in the middle register), *differentialiter* (in a tempo appropriate to the feast), *devotionaliter* (without ornamentation and improvised discant; here he censures the use of secular melodies in masses and organ music, a diabolical practice 'alas, in many churches almost in daily use'); and *satis urbaniter* (in a refined manner). The last has to do with avoiding 'rustic' vocal production: the habit of aspirating vowels beginning a syllable, singing through the nose, distorting vowels, singing flat or sharp, and forcing the voice (especially in the high register). Conrad also has some unkind words for celebrants who pitch their intonations at will, not taking account of what has been sung before. Nor is it sufficient to sing well: deportment also is important. Conrad's principal teaching tool was the keyed monochord, whose virtues he praises in the *Opusculum de monochordo*; his university courses included practical instruction in building the instrument.[16]

---

[14] For his biography and an edition of his treatises, see Karl-Werner Gümpel, *Die Musiktraktate Conrads von Zabern* (Akademie der Wissenschaften und der Literatur, Abhandlungen der Geistes- und Sozialwissenschaftlichen Klasse, Jahrgang 1956, no. 4; Wiesbaden, 1956).

[15] The treatise is summarized and the last chapter translated in Joseph Dyer, 'Singing with Proper Refinement from *De modo bene cantandi* (1474) by Conrad von Zabern', *EM* 6 (1978), 207–27. A much condensed English translation is in Carol MacClintock (ed.), *Readings in the History of Music in Performance* (Bloomington, Ind., 1979), 12–16.

[16] Conrad directs readers wishing to acquire a monochord to an instrument-maker in Speyer 'who has been accustomed to make clavichords and other musical instruments—this man, having been taught by me, knows very well how to make monochords and always stands ready to make them for everyone' ('qui clavichordia et alia musicalia facere consuevit,—hic a me instructus optime scit facere monochorda omnibus ad faciendum semper paratus existens'). Alternatively, they may seek out Conrad's recent students, 'for I have lectured on music in three universities, demonstrating everything on the monochord, and I have passed on to my listeners in detail the manner of making it and have communicated the measurement' ('quia in tribus universitatibus publice legi in musica cuncta in monochordo ostendens meisque audientibus modum faciendi sic plene tradidi et mensuram communicavi') (ed. Gümpel, 256). Full instructions on building a

Towards the end of the century we begin to find the more systematic approach to music theory that characterizes Tinctoris's and Gaffurio's writings. Adam von Fulda's *Musica* of 1490 reflects his humanistic education with its citations of ancient authors, but also an awareness of the current state of music, and not just in Germany.[17] He praises Innocent VIII for his patronage of musicians, following in the footsteps of his predecessors, and also kings, princes, prelates, and private citizens throughout Italy, France, and Germany (the order is noteworthy, but there is an ulterior motive: Adam had just become a singer at the court of Frederick the Wise of Saxony). To the inventors of music in antiquity he adds Gregory, Isidore, Guido, Oddo, Berno, and Johannes de Muris. Then he mentions 'the most learned' Guillaume Dufay and Antoine Busnoys, as models to be imitated.[18] The former he credits with the extension of the range three notes beneath Γ and three above *e la*. And why, asks Adam, should music, which belongs to the quadrivium and rejoices in measure, number, and proportion, which have no limit, not apply that same proportion to harmonic voices and extend into infinity? The treatise is a curious mixture of straightforward instruction, frequently taken directly from medieval theorists (especially Guido, Johannes, and 'Oddo in Enchiriade'), ancient *dicta*, and personal observations. For example, ch. 15 of Book II begins with Guido's characterization of modal ethos, followed by a line from Ovid matching song to affect, from which he moves to the plagal and authentic ranges according to Berno and Oddo. Next he notes that originally there were only four modes, similar to the four seasons, as the Psalmist seems to indicate when he says 'psallite Deo nostro, psallite, psallite regi nostro, psallite' (Ps. 46: 7 Vulg.). This passage comes straight from Johannes 'Cotto' or Affligemensis, whose twelfth-century treatise *De musica*[19] continues to be a mainstay of music theory well into the sixteenth century, when he is sometimes cited as 'Johannes Pontifex', a confusion with the learned French Pope John XXII. But, continues Adam, since moderns are pleased by variety, in polyphony they are not bound to single modes but may use the paired modes, or one mode of the ancients. He does not discuss

monochord are also given in Conrad's third treatise, *Novellus musicae artis tractatus* (ibid. 207–11). On this instrument see Karl-Werner Gümpel, 'Das Tastenmonochord Conrads von Zabern', *Archiv für Musikwissenschaft*, 12 (1955), 143–66.

[17] The treatise is in GS iii. 329–81. The unique source, in Strasburg, Bibliothèque de la Ville, was destroyed by fire in 1870.

[18] '& circa meam aetatem doctissimi Wilhelmus Duffay, ac Antonius de Busna, quorum & nos sequaces esse volumus, verbis scilicet, utinam & factis' (ibid. 341).

[19] Ed. J. Smits van Waesberghe (CSM 1; Rome, 1950), 76. Translated in *Hucbald, Guido, and John on Music*, trans. Warren Babb, ed. Claude V. Palisca (Music Theory Translation Series; New Haven and London, 1978).

the problem of determining the mode in polyphonic music, perhaps because he lacked a modern term that would encompass the authentic and plagal ranges of each pair of modes. (Tinctoris, drawing on a long Italian tradition stemming from Marchetto of Padua, calls it 'mixtio tonorum'.)

Much of early sixteenth-century German theory is pedagogical; Johannes Cochlaeus, for example, wrote his *Tetrachordum musices* 'chiefly for instruction of the youth at the church of St Lorenz' in Nuremberg; he includes a section on vocal practice so 'they do not continue on to the priesthood without knowledge of music, always singing like laboring oxen'.[20] Other treatises were written for students in the Lateinschule; the large number of printed books testifies to their popularity. A typical example (though more comprehensive than most) is Andreas Ornithoparchus' *Musice active micrologus* (Leipzig, 1517). Ornithoparchus divides his treatise into four books: fundamentals, including the modes; notation, including proportions; ecclesiastical accents; and counterpoint. He undertook the treatment of ecclesiastical accents 'because either none or very few men have handled this point'.[21] While acknowledging his indebtedness to grammar, Ornithoparchus nevertheless distinguishes grammatical from ecclesiastical accent, which he defines (in Dowland's translation) as 'a melody, pronouncing regularly the syllables of any words, according as the naturall accent of them requires'. The discussion has much wider significance than the proper way of chanting lessons: it opens the whole question of the relationship between words and music that was to become of overriding importance in the sixteenth century.[22]

German theory was in advance of Italian in the recognition that there were only two basic scales: one with B♮, the other with B♭. Since

[20] From the title-page and preface; see the translation by Clement A. Miller (MSD 23; n.p.: American Institute of Musicology, 1970) (of the edition of 1511; earlier editions appeared in c.1504 and 1507). A facsimile exists of the 1512 edition (Hildesheim, 1971). Cochlaeus is heavily indebted to the *Opus aureum* of Nicolaus Wollick and Melchior Schanppecher and Gaffurio's *Practica musicae*. Wollick's treatise also went through several enlarged editions, published at Paris in 1509, 1512 (facs. Geneva, 1972), and 1521 under the title *Enchiridion musices*. He too borrows from Gaffurio, but also from Tinctoris.

[21] Andreas Ornithoparchus, *Musice active micrologus* (Leipzig, 1517); repr. in facsimile, together with John Dowland's English translation of 1609, ed. Gustave Reese and Steven Ledbetter (New York, 1973); see p. 187. He was preceded by Guillaume Guerson, *Utilissime musicales regule* (c.1495), and Nicolaus Wollick, *Enchiridion musices* (1509). Jean Le Munerat's brief treatise *De moderatione et concordia grammatice et musice* (1490) counters the criticisms of humanists of wrong word accentuation in music from a musician's point of view; see the edition and translation by Don Harrán, *In Defense of Music: The Case for Music as Argued by a Singer and Scholar of the Late Fifteenth Century* (Lincoln, Nebr. and London, 1989).

[22] On this tradition, which continues right through the 16th c., see Don Harrán, *Word–Tone Relations in Musical Thought: From Antiquity to the Seventeenth Century* (MSD 40; Neuhausen-Stuttgart, 1986), ch. 5.

all the notes of the gamut could be covered by the soft and hard hexachords, the natural hexachord was considered superfluous. And, since it was necessary only to know where the semitone *mi–fa* occurred in the scale, the whole cumbersome system of mutations fell by the wayside. Ornithoparchus still describes Guido's syllables and the three interlocking hexachordal properties, soft, natural, and hard, but when it comes to mutation, his explanation is so brief that novice singers would have been mystified. Significantly, there are none of the detailed lists of where mutations are made that we find in Tinctoris and Gaffurio and later Italian theorists.

SPANISH THEORY

Spanish theory of the fifteenth century shows distinctly original traits, but within the medieval tradition; it is largely untouched by Humanism.[23] Writing in 1410, Fernand Estevan praised his teacher, Remon de Caçio, for his many new discoveries, 'in which he was not anticipated by others, but demonstrated his own entire originality'.[24] Bartolomé Ramos de Pareja aroused the ire of his contemporaries for his dismissal of the venerable system of solmization in favour of a scale based on the octave and his new, more practical, division of the monochord. Francisco de Salinas, in 1577, was the first to show that the medieval modes were not the same as the Greek *harmoniai*.

Originality is a concept rarely encountered in music theory, which generally tends to consist of a compilation of previous knowledge, sometimes attributed, more often not. It is a characteristic of the medieval mentality to give great weight to authorities. Paradoxically (in view of the above), this tradition persisted in Spanish theory long past the Middle Ages: most treatises refer to a number of authorities, whether in a separate list, in marginalia, or in the treatise itself. It is tantalizing that so many of these names are hardly known today: Albertus de Rosa, Arnaldus Dalps, Johannes Goscaldus, Michael de

[23] Robert Stevenson's chapter on 'Foundations of Spanish Musical Theory: 1410–1535' in *Spanish Music in the Age of Columbus* (The Hague, 1960) remains the most comprehensive and accessible account of the subject. See also his 'Spanish Musical Impact beyond the Pyrenees (1250–1500)', in Emilio Casares Rodicio *et al.* (eds.), *España en la Música de Occidente: Actas del Congreso Internacional celebrado en Salamanca*, 2 vols. (Madrid, 1987), i. 115–64.

[24] Quoted in Stevenson, *Spanish Music in the Age of Columbus*, 52. Caçio's treatise (if it existed) has not come down to us; Estevan's has been partially edited by Gümpel, together with three anonymous treatises of similar content, in 'Zur Frühgeschichte der vulgärsprachlichen spanischen und katalanischen Musiktheorie', *Gesammelte Aufsätze zur Kulturgeschichte Spaniens*, 24 (Münster, 1968), 257–336. A complete edition may be found in M.a Pilar Escudero García: *Reglas de canto plano è de contrapunto è de canto de órgano. Primer tratado de música escrito en castellano de Fernand Estevan: Comentario, estudio, transcripción y facsímil* (Madrid, 1984). Estevan's work is incomplete: only the section on plainchant survives.

Castellanis, Johannes de Londonis, Johannes de Villanova, Blasius de Romero, Rubinettus, and Petrus de Venecia.[25]

We know from practical sources that the Spanish were much freer in their use of accidentals, and not just in polyphonic music. Their predilection for degree inflection in chant is already attested by Estevan, who argues that accidentals in plainchant are not only appropriate but also necessary, specifying, among others, the use of $B\flat$ in the responsories *Sancta et immaculata* and *Emendemus in melius*, $e\flat$ in the responsory *Gaude Maria*, and $f\sharp$ in the communion *Beatus servus*.[26] These same examples were used in the so-called Berkeley treatise of 1375, to show the locations of the *coniunctae*, the sharps and flats outside the Guidonian hand.[27] This treatise, written in Paris, was attributed to 'Goscalcus' in a later source; it seems to have been particularly influential in Spain: 'Goscaldus' (occasionally 'Johannes Goscaldus') continues to be cited as a reference as late as Bermudo's *Comiença el libro primero de la declaracion de instrumentos* (1549). Like Goscalcus, Estevan recognized ten *coniunctae*: $B\flat$, $c\sharp$, $e\flat$, $f\sharp$, $a\flat$, $c\sharp'$, $e\flat'$, $f\sharp'$, $a\flat'$, and $c\sharp'$.[28] By virtue of these, he can claim that in bfa♮mi six syllables can be found: *la* arising from the hexachord beginning on D, *sol* from the hexachord on E♭, *fa* by virtue of the flat, *mi* by virtue of the natural, *re* arising from the hexachord on A, and *ut* as the origin of a hexachord on $B\flat$.[29] Estevan is much more willing than Italian theorists to leave melodic tritones unaltered: if a melody rises from the lower ranges through *f* to *b*, then descends immediately to *f*, it is to be sung with $b\flat$, but if it touches *a* two or more times before reaching *f*, then $b\natural$ is to be sung (except in the fifth and sixth modes, commonly sung with a flat throughout). If the melody rises directly from *d* to *a* and then to *b*, descending immediately to *f*, $b\natural$ is also to be sung (this contravenes the 'una nota supra la' rule).[30] The five rules for deter-

---

[25] The last-named is possibly Petrus Castellanus, Petrucci's editor; for the evidence, see Bonnie J. Blackburn, 'Petrucci's Venetian Editor: Petrus Castellanus and his Musical Garden', *Musica disciplina*, 49 (1995), 15–45 at 26–7.

[26] See also above, Ch. 6, p. 264.

[27] *The Berkeley Manuscript: University of California Music Library, MS. 744*, ed. Oliver B. Ellsworth (Greek and Latin Music Theory, 2; Lincoln, Nebr. and London, 1984); see esp. 52–66.

[28] Goscalcus also mentions the low $A\flat$, but says it is not in common use; *Berkeley Manuscript*, ed. Ellsworth, 52–4.

[29] Gümpel, 'Zur Frühgeschichte', 329. Writing in 1525, Pietro Aaron thought he was presenting a new theory when he claimed that all six syllables could be found on every note of the hand (see below).

[30] Ibid. 305–7. Devised to mitigate the melodic tritone, the 'pseudo-rule' (as Karol Berger terms it; see *Musica Ficta: Theories of Accidental Inflections in Vocal Polyphony from Marchetto da Padova to Gioseffo Zarlino* (Cambridge, 1987), 77) of 'fa above la' goes back at least to the 13th c.: 'If [the melody] ascends above *la* on *e* or *e'*, it ascends by a semitone; in *a* and *a'* the first ascent is similarly by a semitone' ('Si ascendit ultra la in e gravi aut acutum, ascendit in semitonio. In a acutum et superacutum primus ascensus similiter est in semitonio');

mining whether to sing a flat or natural are capped with a surprising sixth rule: if the melody would be more beautiful ('mas fermosa') with the opposite note, then the rules may be disregarded.

Estevan's treatise was widely known in fifteenth-century Spain, to judge from anonymous manuscript versions and the undated and anonymous printed version, *Arte de canto llano*, and it is a fundamental source for a number of sixteenth-century treatises.[31] (It does not appear, however, to have influenced Bartolomé Ramos de Pareja, whose treatise was written and printed in Italy, and seems to have had little impact on the Spanish theorists who followed him.) In 1492 Domingo Marcos Durán published a brief treatise on fundamentals, *Lux bella*; it differs from similar non-Spanish manuals in that it lists *coniunctae*, now expanded to thirteen, provides a larger number of psalm intonations, and sets forth rules for reading plainchant written on a single line. In 1498 he issued an expanded version, *Comento sobre Lux bella*. His comments on plainchant performance are particularly interesting (see below). His *Súmula de canto de órgano* (undated, c.1504) is the first Spanish manual of polyphony ('canto de órgano', sometimes 'cantus organicus', was the normal Spanish term for polyphony). It covers both counterpoint, including improvised counterpoint, and composition, for which he provides a number of consonance tables. At the very end he includes eleven pages of vocal exercises: ornamentation of intervals from unison to the double octave, practice in smaller note values, varied rhythms, and syncopation, and a few proportions. He promises that these *verbos* and *passos fuertes*, if practised carefully, will make dexterous and excellent singers.[32] The manual makes explicit what often can only be inferred: that counterpoint treatises were directed mainly towards singers, not budding composers.

Rather than Ramos, it was the Catalan theorist Guillermo Despuig (de Podio) who was the fountainhead of sixteenth-century Spanish theory. Breaking with Spanish tradition, he wrote in Latin, reflecting his scholarly bent (and heavy dependence on Boethius). In fact his *Ars musicorum* (1495) seems to have been designed to return Spanish

---

Amerus, *Practica artis musice [1271]*, ed. Cesarino Ruini (CSM, 25; American Institute of Musicology, 1977), 29. For later formulations of the rule, see Berger, *Musica Ficta*, 77–9.

[31] See the list in Gümpel, 'Zur Frühgeschichte', 330. A facs. edn. of the *Arte de canto llano* was published in the series Viejos libros de música (Madrid, 1978), which also includes facsimiles of treatises by Ramos de Pareja, Domingo Marcos Durán, Guillermo Despuig, Cristóbal de Escobar, Bartolomé Molina, Diego del Puerto, Alfonso Spañon, Francisco Tovar, Gonzalo Martínez de Biscargui, Juan de Espinosa, and Gaspar de Aguilar.

[32] The term 'verbos' recalls the 'verbula' of the Berkeley theorist, who also gives musical examples illustrating these ornamentations in various mensurations; see *Berkeley Manuscript*, ed. Ellsworth, 134–47.

theory to a position of respectability; though Ramos is referred to only indirectly ('quidam ex nostris'), ridicule is cast upon his proposal to replace the Guidonian syllables, and great care is expended on the proper (Pythagorean) division of the monochord. Nor does Despuig always concord with his Spanish colleagues, maintaining that chant is not sung uniformly but according to its note shapes (see below). Most surprisingly, he vehemently objects to the *coniuncta*, both as name and as procedure.[33]

In Spain, much earlier than in Italy, flats are associated with the chromatic genus. Cristóbal de Escobar, in his treatise headed *Esta es una introduction muy breve de canto llano* (*c*.1498), begins his chapter on the genera as follows:

The genera according to the ancients are three: chromatic, diatonic, and enharmonic. Boethius considers these in his first book in the chapter beginning 'His igitur' [*Inst. mus*. i. 15]. But this meaning is very ancient and forgotten in practice. Therefore here we shall give an explanation not according to ancient doctrine but to a certain likeness of them given by Rubinetto in his third book in the chapter 'Illatio gravium ad acutas', by which should be understood the raising and lowering of sounds.[34]

He then proceeds to describe the chromatic genus as formed from the fourth species of diapente, 'giving colour' (*dando el color*) where the diatonic places the semitone. The outer notes of this diapente are said to be *fa*s and the middle is *fa* or *ut* or their equivalents. This explanation would be incomprehensible did we not know that he (like Durán) describes the first species of diapente as beginning on C rather than the customary D. The fourth species therefore runs F–G–A–B♮–C, and 'giving colour' (the literal meaning of 'chromatic') means replacing B♮ with B♭. By implication, every time that an ascending melodic tritone is encountered, it is to be changed to a perfect fourth by using a flat.[35]

---

[33] *Ars musicorum* (Valencia, 1495; facs. edn., Bologna, 1975; Madrid, 1976), Book V, ch. 5. Books VI and VIII were edited by Albert Seay: Guillermus de Podio, *Ars musicorum libri vi et viii* (Colorado College Music Press, Critical Texts, 8; Colorado Springs, Colo., 1978).

[34] 'Los generos segund los antiguos son tres, scilicet chromathico, diatonico, y enarmonico, los quales el Boecio considera en su primero libro capitulo His igitur. Pero esta consideracion es muy antigua y olvidada del uso. Pero aqui se dara alguna declaracion dellos aunque non segund la doctrina antigua: mas segund alguna semejança dellos dada por el Rubineto en su tercero libro capitulo Illatio gravium ad accutas [*sic*], con la qual las intensiones y remissiones del sonido se entiendan' (sig. a2ᵛ). Although the unknown Rubinetto's treatise is specified as the source, Escobar also lists as authorities for this section 'Goscaldus parte quarta' (chs. 5, 3, and 6), 'Guido prima parte. capi. ix', 'Gregorius libro de natura tonorum', and 'Johannes Illarius'.

[35] This explanation differs from that given in Stevenson, *Spanish Music*, 84, who thought that Escobar meant that sharps were used when the *fa–fa* diapente was transposed to other degrees. In Spanish theory, however, the chromatic genus applies only to flats. Cf. Durán, *Comento sobre*

Perhaps the most influential of the Spanish theorists, to judge from the number of editions his treatise went through, was Gonzalo Martínez de Bizcargui, *maestro de capilla* at Burgos Cathedral.[36] He owes much to Despuig, whom he quotes extensively, but he departs from his model on two issues, arousing the wrath of the theorist Juan de Espinosa.[37] Drawing on his experience with keyboard instruments, Martínez maintained that the *mi–fa* semitone was the major, not the minor semitone. He appealed not only to the distance observable between strings[38] but also to the sense of hearing. Espinosa contests this 'diabolical statement': not only is it contrary to mathematics, but the ear is fallible.[39] Martínez's practical bent is also shown by his insistence that the time-honoured name *bfa♭ mi* is incorrect; the note should be called *bfami*, that is, a name that includes both the fixed letter *b* and the mobile letter *b*, analogous to the letter *e*, which can be flat or natural.[40] Such a position was the more natural for Spanish theorists, who are almost unanimous in designating all flats as belonging to the chromatic genus; several even refer directly to the upper order of the keyboard. It would be easy to understand how the original meaning of *color* came to be transferred to the black notes of the keyboard.

Martínez devotes more space than any other theorist to the rules concerning flats and sharps, covered in twenty-six pages of the 1538 edition. These rules are far more specific than most of the rules given by Italian theorists, which are often couched in general terms and mainly apply to the use of a flat to correct tritones and diminished fifths. Like his Spanish contemporaries, and reflecting the heritage of the theory of the *coniuncta*, he gives all examples from plainchant, although he remarks that those with sharps are more applicable to

Lux bella, sig. c7ᵛ–8ʳ: 'El genero chromatico se atribuye a un sonido lasso remisso que no es boz rezia entera en su vigor mas quasi boz flaca submissa dulce melosa y blanda, que chroma es un color fengido de cantar . . . el bquadro es atribuido al enarmonio, natura al dyatonico, bmol al chromatico.'

[36] *Arte de canto llano y contrapunto y canto de organo* (Zaragoza, 1508); it was reprinted in various enlarged edns. up to 1550.

[37] *Tractado de principios de musica practica y theorica sin dexar ninguna cosa atras* (Toledo, 1520). Espinosa was archpriest at Toledo Cathedral in 1520 and later a colleague of Bizcargui as canon at Burgos Cathedral.

[38] Since he refers to an instrument 'bien templado' (1538 edn., sig. e4ᵛ), his understanding must be based on meantone tuning, where the sharp is lower than the flat. Espinosa retorts that organs and keyboard instruments are tuned in an ad hoc manner and never reach perfection ('todos andan a tiento y sin ningun concierto en el repartir delos tonos y semitonos enel diapason del organo que cada uno le traca de su manera sin concertar enlas cantidades uno con otro'; *Tractado de principios de musica*, sig. e1ᵛ).

[39] In Italian theory Martínez would have been likened to Aristoxenus, derided by Boethius for the very same reason, but Spanish theory did not take up this point; Aristoxenus is mentioned only by Despuig, *Ars musicorum*, fo. 3ᵛ.

[40] 1538 edn., sig. a5ᵛ–7ᵛ.

polyphony. (None of the rules is tied to a specific mode.) His rules and exceptions may be paraphrased as follows:[41]

Rule 1. *Every melody that rises from* f *to* b *or rises to* b *and returns to* f *is sung with* B♭, *to avoid a tritone.* He notes that some disregard this rule when the word has two consecutive vowels, for example in the introits *De ventre matris meae* at *meae* (*LU* 1499) and *Scio cui credidi* at *cui* (*LU* 1344). He disagrees, saying that B♮ is sung there because of the first exception to the first rule:

First exception: *If the passage coincides with a clausula on the note* a *at the end of a word,* B♮ *is sung, even if a tritone ensues:*

Ba - pti - zat   Au - gu - sti - num   sa - cer - dos

Thus the well-known introit *Gaudeamus* will be sung with B♮. Other theorists, beginning with Estevan, also specify B♮, but Martínez is the only one who cites the verbal structure as the reason.

Second exception: *If a melody rises to* b *but before descending to* f *touches* g *and/or* a *four or more times,* B♮ *is sung:*

De - us me - us   es   tu   ne   dis - ce - das

This rule too goes back at least to Estevan, who requires only two gs or *a*s.

Third exception: *If a melody rises from* g *or* a *to* b, *then descends to a clausula where* f *should be sharpened,* B♮ *is sung:*

Ne   a - ver   -   tas   fa - ci - em

[41] I cite only the beginning of the examples, enough to illustrate his points. The accidentals above the stave are in the original, but some have obviously been misplaced by the setter. In the first example the natural is over the following note; in the fourth example the natural is placed over the following *d'*.

Rule 2. *Every melody that ascends to c′ is sung with B♮*:

He notes that some (including Guillermo Despuig) believe that if B♭ has been sung previously, the passage should stay in that hexachord. He disagrees, though he acknowledges that B♭ must be sung so frequently in the fifth and sixth modes that it might as well be preserved (but according to taste, not art). B♭ will also be retained if the melody leaps to *f′* or requires a flat on *e′*.

Rule 3. *Every melody that descends from* f *to* B *or ascends from* B *to* f *must be sung with* B♭. (This rule avoids the melodic diminished fifth.)

Martínez next moves on to E♭, which will be required in similar circumstances to avoid the tritone or diminished fifth with B♭; by a similar chain-reaction A♭ is sometimes required. Since organs tune this note to G♯ instead, some believe a tritone should be sung, but Martínez affirms A♭, the human voice being more perfect.

There are no fixed rules for sharps (*semitonos mis sostenidos*), which are sung without mutating (that is, changing the solmization syllable); his examples show a subsemitone on C♯, F♯, and G♯. Some Spanish theorists transmit the rule that if a rising melody touches G or D three times, these become equivalent to *fa* and F or C is sharpened.[42] In discussing these passages, Martínez alludes to special note shapes used in chant notated on one line that clarify these intervals for the singer, the *punto cabeçudo* and *punto de semitono*.[43] He confirms that parish churches in his day still had chant-books in which the melodies were written on only one line. Durán, in his *Comento sobre Lux bella*, gives the most extensive explanation of how to recognize chants written on a single line, which differs according to the mode.

The Spanish preoccupation with plainchant (few treatises discuss mensural music) also allows insights into the rhythmic performance of chant, rarely vouchsafed in non-Hispanic sources of this time.[44]

[42] For examples see Gümpel, 'Gregorianischer Gesang und Musica ficta: Bemerkungen zur spanischen Musiklehre des 15. Jahrhunderts', *Archiv für Musikwissenschaft*, 47 (1990), 120–47 at 138–41.

[43] 1538 edn., ch. 26; for the signs see ch. 31.

[44] For examples, see John Caldwell, 'Plainsong and Polyphony 1250–1550', in Thomas Forrest Kelly (ed.), *Plainsong in the Age of Polyphony* (Cambridge, 1992), 6–31, esp. 7–14, and Richard Sherr, 'The Performance of Chant in the Renaissance and its Interactions

Curiously, there appears to be disagreement among the theorists. According to Durán, chant is sung evenly (*por compás*), but a note with two plicas takes up the value of two *compases*. In former times, he remarks, the alpha (oblique ligature) was sung as $1\frac{1}{2} + \frac{1}{2}$ *compases* (*Comento*, sig. e5^r). Guillermo Despuig, however, says that chant is not strictly measured; the notes are sung longer or shorter according to their shape, 'as the singer pleases' (*Ars musicorum*, bk. vi, ch. 36). Moreover, a breve at the beginning of a melody or the penultimate note in a descending clausula is pronounced as a long.

The performance of chant may have differed from region to region. In Toledo, a type of ornamented chant called *canto melódico* was sung by choirboys, a tradition that lasted well into the eighteenth century.[45]

BARTOLOMÉ RAMOS DE PAREJA

Ramos was a native of Baeza, in Andalucía. He studied with Johannes de Monte and, by his own evidence, lectured at the University of Salamanca before transferring to Italy, *c*.1465.[46] Apart from a possible stay in Florence,[47] he spent the major part of his career in Bologna, where he lectured publicly but failed to win appointment to the university lectureship in music, which bitterly disappointed him. His *Musica practica*, published in Bologna in 1482, was only the second full-scale music treatise to be printed (after Gaffurio's *Theoricum opus*, 1480) and the first in a long series that bore the word 'practica' in the title. Only part of it was published; according to his disciple, Giovanni Spataro, Ramos intended to finish it after moving to Rome, but his 'lascivious lifestyle' there led to his death, some time after 1491.[48]

with Polyphony', in Thomas Forrest Kelly (ed.), *Plainsong in the Age of Polyphony* (Cambridge, 1992), 178–208.

[45] See Karl-Werner Gümpel, 'El canto melódico de Toledo: algunas reflexiones sobre su origen y estilo', *Recerca musicològica*, 8 (1988), 25–45. A handwritten example in a Mozarabic missal of 1500 using semiminims is given on p. 13 of the article by Caldwell cited in the previous note.

[46] The most up-to-date consideration of Ramos's biography in English is Stevenson, *Spanish Music in the Age of Columbus*, 55–63, reprinted with additional material in 'Spanish Musical Impact', 125–35. Stevenson believes that he left Salamanca before 1465 because the chair of music was gained by Martín González de Cantalapiedra in that year.

[47] Suggested by Albert Seay, but on the basis of very tenuous evidence; see 'The *Dialogus Johannis Ottobi Anglici in arte musica*', *JAMS* 8 (1955), 86–100 at 91–2, and id., 'Florence: The City of Hothby and Ramos', *JAMS* 9 (1956), 193–5. However, Spataro says that Ramos consulted an old theoretical manuscript 'nella libraria della nunciata di fiorenza', i.e. SS. Annunziata; see *Johannis Spadarii . . . Bartolomei Rami Pareie eius preceptoris honesta defensio in Nicolai Burtii Parmensis opusculum* (Bologna, 1491) (repr. in Johannis Spatarii Opera omnia, 1; Bologna, 1967), fo. 8^v.

[48] The treatise is available in two facsimile edns. (Bologna, 1969; Madrid, 1983). It has been edited by Johannes Wolf (Leipzig, 1901), with errors, and more recently by Clemente Terni, together with a Spanish translation by Gaetano Chiappini and commentary (Madrid,

In style as well as thought Ramos represents a new departure in music theory. Unlike his more circumspect adversary, John Hothby, who clothed his novel ideas in enigmatic terminology, Ramos set out to demolish some very venerable names and systems in highly polemical style. Dismissing Guido as 'a better monk than musician', he proposed replacing the system of hexachords and mutations with a single set of syllables based on the octave, beginning on C: *psal-li-tur per vo-ces is-tas* (meaning 'it is sung with these syllables/pitches'). The impracticality of his proposal precluded its adoption,[49] but the fragility of the hexachordal system was becoming increasingly obvious with the recognition, and eventual use, of five flats and five sharps. Quoting with approval the otherwise unknown Johannes de Villanova, Ramos advised singers to ignore mutation when singing sharps: A C♯ D, for example, though presented as *ut mi fa* in his 'ordo accidentalis sinister' (a diagram showing the scale beginning on A), should simply be pronounced *re fa sol*, and G F♯ G *sol fa sol*.[50]

Ramos's iconoclastic attitude finds its most characteristic expression in his proposal to reform the tuning system, replacing Pythagorean intonation with a division of the octave approaching Ptolemy's syntonic diatonic, in which all intervals from the octave to the minor semitone are based on superparticular ratios. While this tuning provided pure major thirds (5:4) and minor thirds (6:5), it forced him to narrow one fifth, *g–d′*, and expand the corresponding fourth, *d–g*, and to accept two sizes of whole tones, 9:8 and 10:9. Further compromises were necessary for the minor thirds *B–d* and *g–b♭*, which meant that the *b♭–b♮* major semitone could not be tuned 15:14 but in fact was smaller (135:128) than the 16:15 minor semitone.[51] None of this bothered Ramos: his proposal, like his reform of the solmization system, was a purely practical one, meant to reflect the way singers actually sang thirds; he is vague about his sources ('early

1983). An English translation has been made by Clement A. Miller (MSD 44; Neuhausen-Stuttgart, 1993).

[49] Apart from the fact that a descending scale would be sung with the nonsensical *tas is ces vo*, etc., and that the semitone occurred between two different sets of syllables (*tur-per, is-tas—* and more, if accidentals were involved), the system would be of no help in determining the location of accidentals; see Hothby's criticism, below. For Ramos, however, the motivation for his new solmization was not so much to do away with the system of mutations as to vindicate the central importance in music of the octave, which he justifies on mathematical grounds as well, as a full and perfect number (the discussion is placed in ch. 8 of his first tractate not by accident).

[50] *Musica practica*, ed. Wolf, 43; trans. Miller, 93. Gaffurio too reports this practice, and the use of G♯ in the *Salve regina* motif; see *Practica musice* (Milan, 1496), bk. iii, ch. 13; trans. Clement A. Miller (MSD 20; n.p.: American Institute of Musicology, 1968), 146.

[51] Compare the sizes of these intervals (augmented prime and minor second) in Ch. 6, Table 6.2.

writers') and merely presents his division as 'very easy' for singers to understand. His pupil Giovanni Spataro stressed that this tuning was to be used for *musica activa*, or performance, whereas Pythagorean intonation remained the basis of *musica theorica*.[52] Ramos's proposal was put on a firmer theoretical footing in Lodovico Fogliano's *Musica theorica* of 1529, and by mid-century the general consensus among Italian theorists was that the tuning system in practical use was indeed Ptolemy's syntonic diatonic.[53]

In line with his emphasis on practical music, Ramos included interesting chapters on musical instruments, *musica ficta*, counterpoint (including an early description of *fuga*, or imitation), mensuration (reviewing different fifteenth-century usages of signs), and canonic inscriptions, mentioning some of his own compositions, now lost. Throughout the treatise he takes issue with many contemporary theorists, in often quite intemperate language. Ramos's broadsides inaugurated a new direction in music theory: theory as polemic, directed not against time-honoured verities but authors themselves. Those moved to respond were John Hothby, Niccolò Burzio, and Franchino Gaffurio. Spataro took up the defence of his master, in equally polemical terms, in a treatise directed against Burzio and a famous running controversy with Gaffurio, a pamphlet war that did not end with the latter's death in 1522.[54]

JOHN HOTHBY

In his *Musica practica* Bartolomé Ramos heaped ridicule on 'frater Johannes Ottobi anglicus carmelita' for claiming that there were three kinds of semitones: hard, soft, and natural, a doctrine Ramos supposed Hothby had from 'that Marchettist', that is, Marchetto of Padua. 'But it doesn't surprise me', says Ramos, 'because he is a follower of Guido. I wish to destroy the head so that the body, which is riddled with errors, may become a cadaver and cannot live any longer.'[55] This belligerent remark could have been directed at all Ramos's contemporaries.

---

[52] *Errori di Franchino Gaffurio . . . in sua deffensione et del suo preceptore Maestro Bartolomeo Ramis hispano subtilemente demonstrati* (Bologna, 1521), Error 39, fo. 45[r]. See also Palisca, *Humanism*, 232–5, and *A Correspondence of Renaissance Musicians*, ed. Bonnie J. Blackburn, Edward E. Lowinsky, and Clement A. Miller (Oxford, 1991), 67–8.

[53] In addition to Miller's translation of the treatise, a translation of Ramos's proposal for tuning the monochord is in Strunk, 201–4. For Fogliano, see the discussion in Palisca, *Humanism*, 235–42.

[54] Spataro transmits many personal asides about Ramos, as well as some of his teachings that are not included in the *Musica practica*, in his correspondence with Pietro Aaron and Giovanni del Lago; see *Correspondence of Renaissance Composers*, esp. 1009–11.

[55] *Musica practica*, ed. Wolf, 41–2; Miller, 92.

Among the more measured responses to Ramos's polemics was that of John Hothby, the English Carmelite friar who, after travelling in France, Germany, and Spain, had settled in Lucca, where he was chaplain and 'magiscolus' at the Cathedral of St Martin from 1467 to his death in 1487.[56] It took the form of a letter to Ramos, in which he quotes and refutes fourteen passages from the *Musica practica*.[57] A major part of the work is given over to the correct, Pythagorean, division of the monochord, opposing Ramos's more practical one. Hothby also devotes considerable space to the refutation of Ramos's proposal to do away with solmization by substituting the syllables *psal-li-tur per vo-ces is-tas*, pointing out that the *mi–fa* semitone must be sung with different syllables, *tur-per* and *is-tas*, but also *ces-vo* (i.e. A♭–G), and that the syllable *is* must serve for all Bs, whether flat or natural. He criticizes Ramos on the premiss of the medieval system, refusing to recognize any advantage in Ramos's innovations. As to the question of the three semitones, he defends Marchetto's use of the term (semitone meaning 'an incomplete tone'), but not its application. Furthermore he complains that Ramos has misunderstood him: he does not claim that the semitones belong to different genera and therefore are of different sizes but they are called soft, hard, and natural according to the quality of the B they contain, just as a house built of white stones is called a white house.

Hothby had special cause (and also justification) to be offended at Ramos's remarks because he had not published any of his works. Following Horace's injunction, he had kept them back—not just nine, but twenty years. What Ramos must have seen, he says in his *Excitatio*, is notes taken down by his students, far different from what he would

[56] Hothby, who was licensed to lecture in sacred theology, was installed as chaplain of the altar of St Regulus in Feb. 1467, with the express obligation of teaching plainchant and polyphony to priests and clerics of St Martin. In 1469 the canons and chapter of the cathedral petitioned the city council to contribute to Hothby's salary, noting that he also taught grammar and arithmetic. In 1486 he was called back to England by Henry VII; he died there in Nov. 1487. The only firm knowledge we have of Hothby's career is derived from his treatises and documents in the Lucca cathedral and city archives, most of which have been published by Luigi Nerici, *Storia della musica in Lucca* (Lucca, 1879). In addition, a letter to Lorenzo de' Medici of 17 Nov. 1469 suggests that he had been in Florence (requesting a favour on behalf of a friend, he praises Lorenzo's 'great humanity, with which I know you have always regarded me'); see Seay, 'Florence: The City of Hothby and Ramos', 193. The belief that Hothby studied at Oxford in 1435 rests on a mistaken identity: see A. B. Emden, *A Biographical Register of the University of Oxford to A.D. 1500*, 3 vols. (Oxford, 1957–9), ii. 969. He may be the John Otteby, a Carmelite in the Oxford convent, who was ordained a subdeacon in Northampton in 1451 (ibid. 1409).

[57] The *Excitatio quaedam musicae artis per refutationem* has been published by Albert Seay in *Tres tractatuli contra Bartholomeum Ramum* (CSM 10; Rome, 1964), 17–57. This edition (which must be used with caution: there are many misreadings) also includes the *Dialogus Johannis Octobi anglici in arte musica* and a letter in Italian to an unnamed cleric, only the latter of which deals with Ramos's criticisms.

have written.[58] This remark explains the confused transmission of
Hothby's treatises, which exist in multiple versions, with different titles
and in different arrangements of material, partly Latin and partly
Italian.[59] No one version is authoritative, nor can we tell (unlike in the
case of Tinctoris) in what order Hothby taught his pupils. But they
would have learnt the following:

1. Notation.[60] Going beyond the *Libellus* attributed to Johannes de
Muris, his students were taught that there were eight note shapes,
the new ones being semiminima, croma, and semicroma. (Others
can be invented at will, but their shapes should be similar to those in
use.) Mensuration signs are introduced immediately; they form
an important part of Hothby's teachings, for he was the proponent of
the system that shows minor *modus* with *tempus* by a circle or semicircle combined with a figure 2 or 3, a usage favoured by practical
musicians, but opposed by Tinctoris and Gaffurio. In pieces measured
according to major *modus*, the mensuration is shown with a sign and
two figures. To demonstrate its use, Hothby wrote a motet, *Ora pro
nobis*, where O22 appears at the beginning of the tenor.[61] This work
also illustrates various temporal proportions, another subject taken up
in the notational treatises, though not in the systematic manner of
Tinctoris and Gaffurio. Although not explained in his treatises,
the mode signs also indicate diminution: *proportio dupla* in minor
mode, *proportio quadrupla* in major mode; such usage is the inverse
counterpart of treating the sign of major prolation as indicating
augmentation.

---

[58] 'Praeterea opera mea nec tu nec alius umquam vidisti, fortasse tamen quae a meis disci-
pulis excepta sunt et valde diversa' (*Tres tractatuli*, 55). (This explains the Italian phonetic
spelling 'Fich' of the English composer Thick; see Reinhard Strohm, *Music in Late Medieval
Bruges* (Oxford, 1985), 123.)

[59] It confirms Gilbert Reaney's thesis that many of these treatises derive from lecture notes;
see 'The Manuscript Transmission of Hothby's Theoretical Works', in Michael D. Grace (ed.),
A Festschrift for Albert Seay (Colorado Springs, Colo., 1982), 21–31. Reaney traces the network
of relations between Hothby and Johannes Gallicus (Hothby calls him 'Johannes Legiensis',
from the diocese of Liège [*not* 'Legrense', a misreading by Seay]; they were fellow students at
Pavia), Niccolò Burzio (Gallicus' student), and Johannes Bonadies (a fellow Carmelite, who
copied nine of Hothby's compositions into the Faenza Codex, and was the teacher of Gaffurio), and the copyists of some of Hothby's treatises, one of whom, Matheus de Testadraconibus,
expressly says that he studied with Hothby in Lucca in 1471. Reaney gives an overview of
Hothby's treatises in 'The Musical Theory of John Hothby', *Revue belge de musicologie*, 42
(1988), 119–33.

[60] Five different versions of his treatise have been edited by Reaney in Hothby, *Opera omnia
de musica mensurabili* (CSM 31; Neuhausen-Stuttgart, 1983).

[61] Hothby's nine musical works (all unica) have been edited by Albert Seay, *The Musical Works
of John Hothby* (CMM 33; n.p.: American Institute of Musicology, 1964). In some versions of
his treatises one sign is placed within another.

2. Proportions.[62] The explanation is purely mathematical, based on Boethius' *De arithmetica*, and covers the relation of numbers in the five species.

3. Counterpoint.[63] These treatises exist in quite different versions, and are mostly in Italian; Hothby's pupils may have used them as teaching tools. The emphasis is on the theory of 'gradi' (degrees), a form of improvised counterpoint that can be learnt with a minimum of theoretical background. For each of the four degrees (unison, fourth, fifth, and octave, referring to the hexachord of the counterpoint in relation to the tenor's hexachord) the student memorizes the range of notes available against each note of the tenor's hexachord. Against *ut* in the 'grado di pari' (unison), for example, one may sing *ut, sol, mi*, and *la*; against *re* one may have *re, la*, and *fa*. Since the range is limited to the hexachord, only when *mi* is reached can one sing beneath the tenor; for *la* one may sing at the unison, but the remaining notes are fifth, sixth, and third beneath.[64] Compared with the treatment of counterpoint by Tinctoris and Gaffurio, Hothby's is quite elementary.

4. *Calliopea legale*.[65] This is the most idiosyncratic of Hothby's treatises. It is divided into four sections: hexachords and mutation; melodic movement (shown in chant notation); rhythmic movement (in chant and mensural music, including rules of notation); and intervals. Although it would seem to cover the fundamentals of music, it presupposes considerable knowledge. For anyone not acquainted with

[62] Gilbert Reaney has published three separate versions of a treatise on proportions in *Opera omnia de proportionibus* (CSM 39; Neuhausen-Stuttgart, 1997). Not yet published is *Quid est proportio* in London, British Library, Add. 10336, fos. 58ʳ–62ᵛ, and Lambeth Palace, MS 466, fos. 19ʳ–22ᵛ.

[63] Five versions are edited by Reaney in Hothby, *De arte contrapuncti* (CSM 26; Neuhausen-Stuttgart, 1977). However, the treatise 'secundum venerabilem Priorem Dominum Johannem de Anglia', published by Reaney in two different recensions (pp. 25–42 and 43–9) is heavily dependent on an early 15th-c. treatise, *Ad avere alcuna notitia del contrapunto*, and is probably not by Hothby. It has been edited by Albert Seay in *Anonymous (15th-Century), Quatuor tractatuli italici de contrapuncto* (Colorado College Music Press Critical Texts, 3; Colorado Springs, Colo., 1977), 17–24.

[64] The theory of *gradi*, sometimes known as the *manus* or *palma contrapunctorum*, has a long tradition. The earliest source is the Berkeley treatise of 1375, where it is set out in tabular form and called 'contrapunctus', the 'fundamentum discantus' (ed. Ellsworth, 116–20). The consonance tables of 16th-c. theorists are a late manifestation of the same teaching. The most extended treatment of the subject is Pier Paolo Scattolin, 'La regola del "grado" nella teoria medievale del contrappunto', *Rivista italiana di musicologia*, 14 (1979), 11–74. See also the section on Guilielmus, below, and Klaus-Jürgen Sachs, sect. 5, 'Gradus-Lehre und Sight-Lehre', in 'Die Contrapunctus-Lehre im 14. und 15. Jahrhundert', in Zaminer, v. 208–24.

[65] Modern edition, with French translation, in Edmond de Coussemaker, *Histoire de l'harmonie au moyen âge* (Paris, 1852), 297–349. New critical edition and English translation by Timothy L. McDonald, *La Calliopea legale* (CSM 42; Neuhausen-Stuttgart, 1997). See also Anton Wilhelm Schmidt, *Die Calliopea legale des Johannes Hothby: Ein Beitrag zur Musiktheorie des 15. Jahrhunderts* (Leipzig, 1897) (partial transcription with explanation).

Hothby's teachings, the *Calliopea* is bewildering, for Hothby uses his own terminology; nor are the terms applicable to the concepts that one expects. For example, 'voce' is not *vox* (= syllable of the hexachord or pitch, the sound represented by that syllable) but letter. The three 'ordini principali delle voci' are not the three properties of the hexachord, hard, soft, and natural, but the three orders of the letters: natural (equivalent to the white keys on the keyboard), flat (equivalent to the black keys tuned as flats, but including F and C from the first order), and sharp (equivalent to the black keys tuned as sharps, but including E and B from the first order). The three orders are set out in the following table:

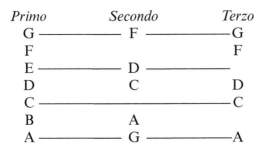

Primo	*Secondo*	*Terzo*
G ———————— F ———————— G
F		F
E ———————— D ————————
D	C	D
C ———————————————————— C
B	A	
A ———————— G ———————— A

From this it can be seen that Hothby has named all the flat notes in the second order by the next lower natural note: B♭, for example, is 'A del secondo ordine'. The reason must stem from his conception of the scale in terms of the keyboard, since B♭s fall between A and A♯.[66] Accidentals are described in terms of the letter B 'painted' in three different ways: ♮ *diritto*, or straight square b, which has the form of the modern natural sign; b *rotondo*, or round b, the flat; and ⌐ *quadro iacente*, slanting square b, the sharp. The notes of the gamut ('le voci famose') are classified according to function: *principe* (B and E in the first order), *comite* (C and F in the first order), and *demostratore* (A, D, and G in the first order). While one might understand these as princes, counts, and demonstrators, they make better sense as leaders (they are leading-notes), followers, and pointers. In imagery recalling that of Fortune's wheel, leaders of the first order become followers with respect to the third order (A♯–B, D♯–E). The leaders and followers govern all the 'nomi officiali' in their 'schiera', that is, the syllables in the hexachord. Only after this point does Hothby start using the Guidonian syllables: leaders are *mi*, followers are *fa*. He reinforces the notion of function when he says that *mi* should be pronounced

---

[66] Hothby's conception of the gamut in terms of the keyboard, which has antecedents in Prosdocimo, is an important point made by Karol Berger in *Musica Ficta*, esp. 32–7 and 42–3.

'cordially and very sharp, because there is a large space between *re* and *mi*, but *fa* should be pronounced moderately, because between *mi* and *fa* there is less space than half the other'; they are 'closely entwined, as good companions should be'.[67] (This narrow leading-note is what Tinctoris calls a 'chromatic semitone'; it is related to Marchetto of Padua's diesis, a fifth of a tone.) Mutation is then explained in terms of the Guidonian hexachords. Adding the hexachords involving flats and sharps ('schiere promiscue') makes it possible to sing all six syllables on each degree of the gamut.

5. *Tractatus quarundam regularum artis musice.*[68] This is Hothby's most developed treatise. A major component is the division of the monochord—a subject rarely treated by Hothby's time, but central to his thought since it includes divisions yielding not only his second and third orders, but also his fourth and fifth orders, not discussed in the *Calliopea*. The fourth order is found by dividing the distance between G and A♭ in half (and from this note generating the remaining notes as in the first order), the fifth order by dividing the distance between G♯ and A in half and generating the rest of the notes similarly. The notes in these orders are to be shown by the *b quadro iacente* with a dot in the centre, 'but up to now', he says, 'they have not been used either in plainsong or in polyphony'.[69] In one version of this treatise he even envisaged a sixth order, splitting the comma into two schismata.[70] His interest in these matters was evidently piqued by reading Boethius, *De institutione musica* iii. 8, on Philolaus' division of the tone, since he uses the same terminology: schisma for half the comma, and diaschisma for half the minor semitone (however, his preferred term for the latter was diesis, which Philolaus used for the minor semitone; Hothby—following later theory—calls it limma).

[67] 'Mi ascendendo debbe essere proferito cordialmente, et molto aciuto, perche intra re et mi e grande spatio. Ma il fa debbe essere proferito moderatamente, perche intra mi et fa e meno spatio della meta de laltro. . . . sono strettamente insieme abraciati, si chome debbono essere li buoni compagni'. *Calliopea*, ed. McDonald, 25 (Coussemaker, 306–7).

[68] This is the title in Florence, Biblioteca Nazionale Centrale, MS Pal. 472, fos. 9ʳ–15ʳ. Other versions go under the titles *De musica intervallosa* and *Ars plane musice*; for sources see Seay, 'Hothby', *New Grove*, viii. 730. It is not yet available in a modern edition. To some extent the treatise duplicates the *Calliopea*, which is only in Italian and 'reducta in brevità'.

[69] 'Tutte le voci del quarto ordine et del quinto debbano essere dipinte per b quadro iacente con uno puncto in meço, ut puta ⬚, a differentia del terzo, benche facilmente possano essere cogniosciuti per li principi et comiti delli ordini principali, conciosia cosa che sempre cadeno intra loro. Ma infino a qui mai sono stati dipincti, ne in legale ne in chorale'; Florence, Pal. 472, fo. 13ᵛ.

[70] 'Chisma minor fit inter A secundi et A sexti, quequidem A sexti ordinis habetur divisionem comatis in duas partes equales'; ibid., fo. 10ᵛ. This would not have produced an equal temperament, since the tone remains at 9:8 and the minor semitones B–C and E–F at 256:243, but it would have come very close to it: whereas the exact half of a 9:8 tone is 101.955 cents, the combination of a minor semitone with Hothby's minor and major schisma would yield respectively 101.92 and 101.99 cents.

The *Tractatus* also includes an extended discussion of intervals and
their species and a thorough treatment of modes, based on the teachings of Guido, Johannes 'Cotto' or Affligemensis (Hothby, like Adam
of Fulda, identifies him with Pope John XXII), and Marchetto. After
listing the ethos of each mode, he advises that great care should be
taken in matching the modes with the words, even going so far as to
suggest moving from Hypodorian to Phrygian when the words change
from narrative to interrogative.[71] Many fifteenth-century treatises pay
lip-service to the concept of modal ethos, which was to be taken up
seriously only in the next century.[72]

Hothby is commonly considered a conservative. He certainly was
conservative insofar as he venerated Boethius and Guido, the two
pillars upon which his teaching rests, but he clothed his avant-garde
ideas in terminology so enigmatic that the full extent of his revolu-
tionary thought is still not appreciated. (This may have been deliberate, in view of Ramos's experience as an innovator, not least at
Hothby's hands.) Even in his own time he was not understood: Pietro
Aaron thought that he had discovered something new when he proposed that it was possible to demonstrate the six syllables on each note,
yet he did not go as far as Hothby since he only showed flats.[73] In his
Tractatus Hothby anticipates the intent, if not the exact theory, of
Nicola Vicentino's 'ancient music adapted to modern practice', *L'antica musica ridotta alla moderna prattica* (Rome, 1555),[74] to recreate
the substance of the ancient Greek tunings for the modern musician.
And, like Vicentino, he did not stop at theory. Although the monochord as described in his *Tractatus* is not keyed,[75] Hothby did own a

---

[71] 'Et in quelle parti unde si muta, si de fare commixto secondo la diversita della materia . . .
se in qualche parte è narrativo, si de pigliare una specie del secondo tono. Cioè el diatessaron in
luogho del diapente, et se in qualche parte è interrogativo, si debbe usare in quello luogho la
seconda specie del diapente overo del diatessaron'; Florence, Pal. 472, fo. 12[v]. This remark is not
found in the other versions.

[72] There was little agreement among theorists as to the ethos of each mode; for some
lists, ranging from Hermannus Contractus (mid-11th c.) to Hermann Finck (1556), see
Harold Powers, 'Mode', *New Grove*, xii. 398–9. A comparison of classical and Renaissance
sources is given in Claude V. Palisca, 'Mode Ethos in the Renaissance', in Lewis Lockwood and
Edward Roesner (eds.), *Essays in Musicology: A Tribute to Alvin Johnson* (n.p.: American Musicological Society, 1990), 126–39. Hothby's effects are closer to those transmitted by Gil de
Zamora (c.1240), which Ramos follows; Palisca suggests they were based on plainchant
experience (131–2).

[73] See below, n. 118. But see Estevan's precedent, discussed above. Both Aaron and Estevan
base their demonstration on the note name, e.g. A can be either A♮ or A♭. Hothby, however, uses
one pitch, to which he relates notes a semitone distant on either side.

[74] Facs. edn. with a postface by Edward E. Lowinsky (Documenta musicologica, 17; Kassel,
1959); trans. Maria Rika Maniates and ed. Claude V. Palisca, *Ancient Music Adapted to Modern
Practice* (Music Theory Translation Series; New Haven and London, 1996).

[75] Hothby describes it thus: 'Monocordum est lignum concavum et longum ad modum synphonie habens unam cordam tantum supra se extensam ab uno capite lineis rota que volvitur

keyboard instrument that had quarter-tones, shown by red keys.[76] Perhaps he would have found a way of including the sixth order, evidently developed after the *Epistola* was written.[77] His treatises are silent on the practical application of this instrument, but since it was based on Pythagorean intonation, it was more useful for teaching purposes than for polyphonic music. His compositions show no adventurous accidentals.

JOHANNES TINCTORIS

In a succession of treatises, written mostly in the 1470s, Johannes Tinctoris surveyed fifteenth-century music theory with magisterial thoroughness. A composer as well as a theorist, he was above all interested in practical music; his discussion of the modes, counterpoint, and proportions is especially valuable because it reflects the ferment in the music of his time. No stranger to controversy, he did not hesitate to criticize the outstanding composers of the day when they did not measure up to his norms. Much of his criticism stems from an effort to set music theory on a more rational basis, and his reforms of mensural practice, supported by Franchino Gaffurio, largely took hold.

Tinctoris was born *c.*1435 in Braine-l'Alleud, about 10 km. north of Nivelles.[78] Briefly a singer at Cambrai Cathedral (April–July 1460), by July 1462 he had matriculated in law at the University of Orléans; concurrently he was succentor at the church of Sainte-Croix. As a subject of the Emperor he was a member of the university's German Nation, even though his native language was French; in April 1463 he

sub corda reddens voces debitas cum synphonie musice', i.e. the single string is sounded by a rotating wheel in the manner of a hurdy-gurdy, while a moveable bridge ('punto') sets the length of the vibrating string (Florence, Pal. 472, fo. 9^v). Since the pitches were marked, it would have been fairly easy to produce a melody.

[76] 'I have an instrument that has it [the enharmonic genus with its 'smallest semitones'] throughout, for otherwise that genus would have been invented in vain' ('Io [ho] uno instrumento il quale lo [the enharmonic genus with its 'semitonii minimi'] ha interamenti, che altramenti tal generatione sarebe indanno trovata'). The remark is made in passing in his explanation of the division of the tone in the enharmonic genus in his *Epistola* to an unnamed cleric; in the diagram the keys are labelled 'biancho', 'rosso', and 'nero' (*Tres tractatuli*, 85).

[77] Vicentino too has six orders (in two keyboards) on his *archicembalo*, but they were divided differently. The first order, like Hothby's, was diatonic. The second included the black keys in common use (both sharps and flats), the third their counterparts, plus B♯ and E♯. The fourth order stood a quarter-tone above the first, the fifth a quarter-tone above the flat notes of the second and third orders, and the sixth a comma above the first order. But where Hothby retained Pythagorean intonation, Vicentino not only divided the tone into five dieses, but used a meantone temperament. On his instrument, see Maniates, pp. xlviii–li, and Henry W. Kaufmann, 'More on the Tuning of the *Archicembalo*', *JAMS* 23 (1970), 84–94.

[78] The most recent and thorough treatment of Tinctoris's life is Ronald Woodley, 'Iohannes Tinctoris: A Review of the Documentary Biographical Evidence', *JAMS* 34 (1981), 217–48, on which this account is based. Some dates are problematic; Woodley discusses the evidence.

was elected its procurator. Either before or after his period in Orléans he was, according to his *De inventione et usu musicae*, master of the choirboys at Chartres Cathedral.

Had Tinctoris remained in France, he might well have been no more than a shadowy figure today, owing to the dearth of fifteenth-century French musical and theoretical sources. But, like many northern singers, he went south. By the early 1470s he was a singer and chaplain of Ferdinand I (Ferrante), king of Naples, where he spent the major part of his career. What was probably his first treatise written at the court, the *Proportionale musices*, was dedicated to the king, as was the last of his didactic treatises, the *Liber de arte contrapuncti*, completed 11 October 1477. Three treatises and two motets were dedicated to the king's young daughter Beatrice, to whom he probably taught music. It is not known when he left Ferrante's service; he was in Rome in 1492 (where a motet of his in honour of Pope Alexander VI was sung) but was not a member of the papal chapel. He died in 1511, after retiring to Nivelles. He was sufficiently well known to have merited an entry in Johannes Trithemius' *Cathalogus illustrium virorum Germaniae* (1495), where he is called 'doctor of both laws, formerly *archicapellanus* and *cantor* of King Ferrante of Naples, a man very learned in all respects, an outstanding mathematician, a musician of the highest rank, of a keen mind, skilled in eloquence, [who] has written and is writing many remarkable works', including 'many remarkable letters to various personages'.[79]

Tinctoris was a born teacher. His treatises show the great care he took to present the material in logical order, with each point illustrated, where feasible, by a musical example. The pedagogical treatises, written during the 1470s, are found in the following order in a presentation copy:[80]

---

[79] The full article is translated in Gustave Reese, *Music in the Renaissance* (New York, 1954; rev. edn., 1959), 138, who gives an excellent summary of Tinctoris's treatises on pp. 139–49. Only one of the letters is extant, to Giovanni Marco Cinico; see Ronald Woodley, 'Tinctoris's Italian Translation of the Golden Fleece Statutes: A Text and a (Possible) Context', *EMH* 8 (1988), 173–244 at 236–44.

[80] Valencia, Biblioteca Universitaria, MS 835. The same order is followed in the two other 'collected works' copies, Bologna, Biblioteca Universitaria, MS 2573 (prefaced with the motet *Virgo Dei throno*) and Brussels, Bibliothèque Royale, MS II. 4147 (which adds at the end the *Diffinitorium* and an incomplete copy of the *Complexus*). These treatises, originally published by Coussemaker (iv. 1–200), are now available (with the exception of the *Diffinitorium*) in Tinctoris, *Opera*. This edn. must be used with caution, and even more so Seay's translations: 'The *Expositio manus* of Johannes Tinctoris', *Journal of Music Theory*, 9 (1965), 194–232; *Concerning the Nature and Propriety of Tones* (Colorado College Music Press Translations, 2; Colorado Springs, Colo., 1967); *The Art of Counterpoint* (MSD 5; American Institute of Musicology, 1961); and 'The *Proportionale musices* of Johannes Tinctoris', *Journal of Music Theory*, 1 (1957), 22–75; rev. in *Proportions in music (Proportionale musices)* (Colorado College Music Press Translations, 10; Colorado Springs, Colo., 1979). The *Complexus* is now available in a new

Expositio manus
Liber de natura et proprietate tonorum
Tractatus de notis et pausis
Tractatus de regulari valore notarum
Liber imperfectionum notarum musicalium
Tractatus alterationum
Liber de punctis musicalibus
Liber de arte contrapuncti
Proportionale musices

This arrangement does not reflect the order of writing (the book on modes is dated 6 November 1476, that on counterpoint 11 October 1477; the rest were completed earlier) but a didactic one: the fundamentals of music (the explanation of the Guidonian hand, clefs and locations of pitches, hexachords, mutation, and intervals), the modes, mensural notation, counterpoint, and proportions.

A comparison with the order and contents of Ugolino's *Declaratio musicae disciplinae* is instructive.[81] Ugolino divided his treatise into five books: the fundamentals (*musica plana*, which also includes a treatment of the modes and a tonary), counterpoint, mensural notation (an extended gloss on the *Libellus cantus mensurabilis*), proportions, and speculative music (an inquiry into the subject of music in decidedly philosophical terms, acoustics, and mathematical proportions of intervals). Ugolino is firmly rooted in the medieval scholastic tradition: throughout, the emphasis is on the theoretical aspect of music, with no mention of composers or compositions. The book on counterpoint (the shortest), is restricted to note-against-note writing in two parts, and that on proportions treats only mathematical ratios with reference to intervals, not to mensuration. Tinctoris has very little interest in speculative music (aspects of it are treated in his last treatise, *De inventione et usu musicae*).[82] His orientation is not just towards practical music, but to polyphony. The treatises on counterpoint and

edition and translation in *On the Dignity and the Effects of Music: Egidius Carlerius, Johannes Tinctoris, Two Fifteenth-Century Treatises*, trans. and ann. J. Donald Cullington, ed. Reinhard Strohm and J. Donald Cullington (Institute of Advanced Musical Studies Study Texts, 2; London, 1996).

[81] On Ugolino, see above, Ch. 6.

[82] The complete treatise does not survive; six chapters were published in Naples *c.*1481–3, and another five have been recovered in a manuscript in Cambrai. For the former, see Karl Weinmann, *Johannes Tinctoris (1445–1511) und sein unbekannter Traktat "De inventione et usu musicae"*, ed. Wilhelm Fischer (Tutzing, 1961), for the latter Ronald Woodley, 'The Printing and Scope of Tinctoris's Fragmentary Treatise *De inventione et usu musice*', *EMH* 5 (1985), 239–68, including an edition of the new chapters. From the latter we discover that the *Complexus effectuum musices*, omitted from the two presentation copies of Tinctoris's works, was included in a revised form in the *De inventione*, where it formed ch. 5 of the first book.

proportions are illustrated with numerous examples of from two to five voices. The examples in the treatises on notation are melodic as well as rhythmic (but monophonic, unlike Gaffurio's examples). Ugolino was able to discuss counterpoint before notation because he taught only note-against-note movement; Tinctoris covers florid counterpoint as well, which entails an extended discussion of allowable dissonances— a topic barely mentioned by theorists up to that time. Even Tinctoris's treatise on the modes, seemingly concerned almost exclusively with plainchant, was primarily undertaken for the understanding of modes in polyphonic music.[83] He is the first to state that the mode is to be judged according to the tenor, as the principal part and foundation of the relations between the voices; nor are the modes applicable only to sacred music, since the example he cites is Dufay's chanson *Le serviteur*.

Many fifteenth-century theorists were also composers: we have works by Ugolino, Hothby, and Gaffurio, and we know that Ramos composed as well, although all his compositions are lost.[84] But none was of the calibre of Tinctoris, who emphasizes that the student must constantly keep in practice by singing counterpoint against a plain-chant and composing, imitating the best authors, among whom he counted Dufay, Faugues, Regis, Busnoys, Ockeghem, and Firmin Caron (despite criticizing many of them in his treatises on counter-point and proportions). Characteristically, Tinctoris summed up his teachings on notation and proportions in a pedagogical motet (as Gaffurio termed it), *Difficiles alios delectat pangere cantus*, copiously annotated in the unique source.[85] The motet also illustrates the touch-stone of Tinctoris's precepts on composition, the last of his eight rules of counterpoint: variety. Noting that the type and amount of variety is dependent on the genre of the composition, Tinctoris says that the best composers write 'now with one quantity, now with another, now with one perfection, now with another, now with one proportion, now with another, now with one interval, now with another, now with syn-copation, now without, now with imitation, now without, now with

---

[83] After listing the possible beginning notes for each mode, Tinctoris says: 'Which I say chiefly in respect of the beginning notes of the modes in polyphonic compositions, which were my first and main concern in embarking on this treatise' ('Quodquidem dico praecipue quantum ad prin-cipia tonorum cantuum compositorum favore quorum primo et principaliter tractatum hunc aggressus sum'; *De natura et proprietate tonorum*, ch. 19).

[84] Unless the circular canon at the beginning of Florence, Biblioteca Nazionale Centrale, Banco rari 229, is his, as the inscription seems to suggest. The lost works are mentioned in his *Musica practica*, in the chapter on canonic inscriptions.

[85] This composition, which must date from the early 1470s, although it is not mentioned in any of Tinctoris's treatises, came to light only in 1981. See Bonnie J. Blackburn, 'A Lost Guide to Tinctoris's Teachings Recovered', *EMH* 1 (1981), 29–116, which includes a modern edn.

rests, now without, now with diminutions, now note-against-note'
(*Liber de arte contrapuncti*, bk. iii, ch. 8).

For those not familiar with Tinctoris's writings, the terms 'quantity'
and 'perfection' will not be entirely clear—indeed, much fifteenth-
century musical terminology needs explanation because of the
great changes that have taken place between then and now, both in
notation and in the way music is discussed. On a smaller scale, the
same was true in the fifteenth century itself, and the problem did
not escape Tinctoris's attention. To him we owe the first comprehensive dictionary of musical terms, the *Terminorum musicae diffinitorium*, printed in Treviso, probably in 1495, although its genesis was
in the 1470s, and quite possibly earlier.[86] In it he defines 'quantity' as
'that according to which it is understood how large a piece is', that
is, the mensuration of a piece according to *modus, tempus*, and *prolatio*.[87] 'Perfection' has two meanings, 'the demonstration in which
way a note remains perfect' and (its meaning in the passage cited)
'the recognition of the completion of the whole work or of its parts',
that is, final and internal cadences.[88] Cadences come under scrutiny
in the counterpoint treatise, where perfection has two more meanings:
a mensural unit (usually the breve, whether itself perfect or imperfect)
and the presence of perfect intervals, fifth and octave. When the
tenor voice makes 'a descent into a perfection', special rules for suspension dissonance come into play, which sharpen the focus on the
cadence, itself distinguished (in Tinctoris's music at any rate) by
the absence of a third, an imperfect interval. (Tinctoris is very precise
in his use of terms: a 'perfection' may not include any imperfect
interval.)

[86] On the dating, determined on bibliographical grounds (none of the exemplars carries
a date), see the essay by James B. Coover in Tinctoris, *Dictionary of Musical Terms by
Johannes Tinctoris*, trans. Carl Parrish (New York and London, 1963), 101–8. The treatise was
dedicated to Beatrice, before her marriage to Matthias Corvinus in 1476. I suspect that it was
largely written before Tinctoris came to Naples, perhaps for the use of his choirboys in Orléans
or Chartres.

[87] In the 15th c. sacred pieces were normally measured on the *modus* level, comprising the
division of the maxima into longs (*modus maior*) and the long into breves (*modus minor*), as well
as *tempus* and prolation. The sixteen possible species that result from the combination of the
four mensurations, each of which could be duple or triple, are the subject of the *Tractatus de
regulari valore notarum*. While compositions in perfect minor mode (often with the mensuration
sign O2) are frequent, use of perfect major mode is rare; Tinctoris himself used it only in the
tenor of his *Difficiles alios*.

[88] The *Diffinitorium* is available in two facsimile edns. and has been translated into English,
French, German, and Italian. Despite its usefulness, it is deficient in a number of respects and
does not reflect the stage of thought Tinctoris had achieved by the mid-1470s. That it does not
appear in the two presentation copies gives grounds for belief that Tinctoris either rejected it or
had plans to revise it; on this point, see *Correspondence of Renaissance Musicians*, 215–16. (It
is present in the Brussels manuscript in a somewhat different form.)

The detailed treatment of dissonance sets Tinctoris's treatise apart from all its predecessors. Dissonance is tied to the basic note value of the particular mensuration, the *mensurae directio* or measuring-note, and is dependent on its rhythmic and melodic context. For pieces in major prolation, the measuring-note is the minim; for those in minor prolation it is the semibreve. Unstressed dissonances are allowed against the second half of a measuring-note or, if it is divided, against the second part of each half (see the notes marked with a cross in Ex. 7.1). Stressed dissonances, against the beginning of a measuring-note, occur in the form of prepared suspensions, and are allowed only when approaching a 'perfection' (see the places marked with an arrow). If the last note before a perfection in the tenor is equivalent to two basic units, it usually receives a dissonance (see b. 2); if it is equivalent to one unit and is preceded by a stepwise descent of a similar value, both notes may be dissonant on the first half (see b. 6). Note that no dissonant suspension occurs in the penultimate bar: the tenor does not descend and the final measure is not a perfection because of the third in the superius; this cadence marks the end of the first section, not the conclusion of the piece.[89]

Tinctoris's treatise on counterpoint might just as well have been called a treatise on harmony, were it not that the term 'harmony' had not yet acquired the technical musical meaning it has today.[90] It has a bearing on the meaning of the puzzling term *res facta*, first used as a Latin term by Tinctoris, for which various interpretations have been offered. He contrasts it with singing *super librum*, 'over the book', that is, improvising counterpoint above a plainchant (usually measured).[91] The distinction is not entirely between written and improvised music, nor between written and sung music composed according to

[89] Tinctoris's rules for dissonance technique are admirably elucidated in Sachs, *Contrapunctus*, 154–69, and summarized in his article on 'Counterpoint' in *New Grove*, iv. 833–43. For a discussion of Tinctoris's dissonance precepts in the context of 15th-c. theory, see Bonnie J. Blackburn, 'On Compositional Process in the Fifteenth Century', *JAMS* 40 (1987), 210–84 at 233–46. See also ead., 'Did Ockeghem Listen to Tinctoris?', in *Johannes Ockeghem: Actes du XLᵉ Colloque international d'études humanistes. Tours, 3–8 février 1997*, ed. Philippe Vendrix (Paris, 1998), 597–640.

[90] A brief survey of its meanings and a more extended discussion of Spataro's and Zarlino's conception of the term is given in Blackburn, 'On Compositional Process', 224–33. On Gaffurio's definition, see ead., 'Leonardo and Gaffurio on Harmony and the Pulse of Music', in Barbara Haggh (ed.), *Essays on Music and Culture in Honor of Herbert Kellman* (Paris, 2001) 128–49.

[91] See in particular Ernst T. Ferand, 'What is *Res Facta*?', *JAMS* 10 (1957), 141–50, who discerned two contradictory meanings, (i) 'a written, not improvised, composition in plain or florid counterpoint' and (ii) 'florid, not plain, counterpoint, whether written or improvised' (p. 150), and Margaret Bent, '*Resfacta* and *Cantare Super Librum*', *JAMS* 36 (1983), 371–91, who viewed *res facta* and singing *super librum* as two different stages, one usually written, the other sung, though carefully prepared, of the same process of counterpoint, following the rules of consonance and dissonance.

Ex. 7.1. Tinctoris's rules for dissonance illustrated in his *Salve martyr virgoque Barbara*

the same rules, but between composition and counterpoint. In composition (*res facta*) all the voices must obey the rules of counterpoint ('the law and order of concords') in relation to each other; in singing *super librum* the added voices are only required to harmonize properly with the tenor, though Tinctoris prefers the singers to agree beforehand not to duplicate their counterpoints. Here lie the roots of the distinction (first discussed specifically by Pietro Aaron in 1516) between 'simultaneous' conception and successive composition (see below). For Tinctoris, however, the method by which the result is achieved is less significant than the result itself. *Res facta* could equally well be composed in the successive manner, and then refined, since a higher degree of harmonic relations is required in order to consider the composition an *opus perfectum et absolutum*, as Listenius was to term it in 1537. For this reason I have proposed to call the process 'harmonic composition' rather than 'simultaneous conception'.[92] *Res facta*, the Latin equivalent of 'chose faite' (a term used in literary sources of the time), denotes a finished work, one that exists apart from its performance.

For Tinctoris, the music of his day had reached the pinnacle of perfection. The 'new art', ushered in by Dunstable, Dufay, and Binchois, had blossomed in the works of the 'moderns', Ockeghem, Busnoys, Regis, and Caron. Yet for all the subtlety and ingenuity of their compositions, they (and 'many other famous composers whom I admire') 'are either wholly ignorant of musical proportions or indicate incorrectly the few that they know', a defect that stems from ignorance of arithmetic, 'a science without which no one becomes eminent, even in music, for from its innermost parts all proportion is derived'.[93] Hence the treatise on proportions, undertaken not only to instruct the ignorant but to bring order into a mensural system whose inconsistencies Tinctoris deplored.[94] Using mathematics as a model, he regarded the minim as the basic unit of counting, of equal value in all mensurations. Therefore a breve in perfect *tempus*, with six minims, was one-half longer than a breve in imperfect *tempus*, with four. As a consequence, only notes of equal value could be compared in proportions, and the relationship could only be indicated (except in the case of coloration) by two figures, the upper one showing the number of notes in the new section being compared with the number of like notes either in the previous section or in another voice. Using this method, it was possible to indicate such abstruse proportions as 17:8. The problem

---

[92] This interpretation is argued in Blackburn, 'On Compositional Process'. Because of changes that take place in the course of composing, it is difficult to determine how a given piece of music has been composed, unless there are clashes between the upper parts. It flies in the face of reason to suppose that composers of earlier eras did not conceive the voices to some degree simultaneously; surely they were able to hear in their heads the sound of two—and not just two—voices at the same time. Daniel Leech-Wilkinson has proposed that Machaut, in composing his four-part mass, had in mind the chord-progressions, though not the individual voices, at a very early stage, and that he may even have used a single-stave score as a working tool; see *Machaut's Mass: An Introduction* (Oxford, 1990), ch. 3.

[93] See the preface to his *Proportionale musices*, trans. in Strunk, 193–6 (Strunk², 291–3). Tinctoris adds Faugues to the list of great composers in the preface to his *Liber de arte contrapuncti* (Strunk, 197–9). On Tinctoris's rhetorical strategies in this treatise, see Ronald Woodley, 'Renaissance Music Theory as Literature: On Reading the Proportionale Musices of Iohannes Tinctoris', *Renaissance Studies*, 1 (1987), 209–20. See also below, Ch. 8.

[94] Musicians of course were long familiar with the proportions governing musical intervals (see the discussion of *musica speculativa* in Ch. 6); many theoretical treatises of the 15th c. include sections explaining proportions in abstract mathematical terms (as, for example, the treatise by Hothby mentioned above). These had been applied to the mensural system since the late 14th c. and were first treated theoretically by Prosdocimo (see Anna Maria Busse Berger, *Mensuration and Proportion Signs: Origins and Evolution* (Oxford, 1993), esp. ch. 6). Inconsistencies arose in practice because they were commonly indicated not by ratios but by mensuration signs, which were subject to varying interpretation.

was that this logical system did not fit the mainstream of musical practice at Tinctoris's time. Many other theorists, and most composers,
believed that the central note in the mensural system was not
the minim but the breve, that longs and maximas were aggrega-
tions of breves, and semibreves and minims were divisions of
the breve. Their system had the drawback that minims (and semibreves
in the same prolation) could have different lengths. But it also
meant that mensuration signs could be used to indicate proportions.
C followed by O meant *sesquialtera* (3:2) between semibreves, C
followed by Ȼ *sesquialtera* between minims. But mensuration signs
were ambiguous: the reversed C, for example, could mean *sesquiter-
tia*, 4:3, or *proportio dupla*, 2:1. Other aspects of this system to which
Tinctoris objected were the use of signs of major prolation to mean
augmentation (unless an explanatory canon, such as 'crescit in triplo',
was added) and signs of minor *modus* to mean diminution. Dufay
'wondrously erred' in two respects in the 'Qui cum patre' of his *Missa
Sancti Antonii* in the passage shown in Ex. 7.2: not only did he produce
sesquialtera by equating three perfect breves with two imperfect breves,
he used a sign of *modus* (O3) to indicate diminution. According to
Tinctoris, he should have written O^9_4, to indicate a *dupla sesquiquarta*
(9:4) relation between minims.[95] All Tinctoris's criticisms of composers in the *Proportionale* stem from the clash of the two notational
systems.[96] Whether by force of his authority (and that of Gaffurio,
who agreed with him in these matters) or a general decline of interest
in mensural complexities, Tinctoris's reforms prevailed.[97]

FRANCHINO GAFFURIO AND MUSICAL HUMANISM

Unlike Tinctoris, whose interests turned from *musica practica* to
musica theorica only in his later years, Franchino Gaffurio
(1451–1522) started out with a keen interest in speculative music. His
Theoricum opus musice discipline, printed in Naples in 1480, was the
first fully-fledged music treatise to be published. Reprinted in a revised
edition in Milan in 1492 under the title *Theorica musice*, it was followed by another speculative treatise, the *De harmonia musicorum
instrumentorum opus* (1518). In between appeared his *Practica
musicae*, which attained wide fame for the theorist after its initial

[95] *Proportionale*, bk. iii, ch. 6. For the passage, see Guillaume Dufay, *Opera omnia*, ii, ed.
Heinrich Besseler (CMM 1; Rome, 1960), 60.
[96] For Tinctoris's criticisms of Ockeghem and his possible response, see Blackburn, 'Did
Ockeghem Listen to Tinctoris?'.
[97] The view of Tinctoris as reformer of the mensural system has only emerged in recent
years, principally in the work of Anna Maria Busse Berger. See her *Mensuration and Proportion
Signs*.

Ex. 7.2. Dufay, 'Qui cum patre' from *Missa Sancti Anthonii*. Trent, Museo Provinciale d'Arte, Castello del Buon Consiglio, MS 90, fos. 401ᵛ–402ʳ

publication in 1496; a somewhat different Italian version (despite its Latin title) of 1508, *Angelicum ac divinum opus musice*, anticipating some of the chapters of the *De harmonia*, was aimed at those who could not read Latin.[98]

For a theorist with a speculative bent, Gaffurio lived in exciting times.[99] Having mastered Boethius and absorbed all the stories about music in antiquity that he could get his hands on (all through secondary, mostly literary, sources), he wrote the *Theoricum opus*; by the time the revised edition was published he had become acquainted with Plato in Marsilio Ficino's translation, Pseudo-Aristotle's *Problems* in Pietro d'Abano's translation, and Themistius' *Paraphrases* on Aristotle's *De anima* (transmitting the theory of sound and hearing), translated by Ermolao Barbaro. These allowed him to correct and supplement Boethius, but they did not change the basic character of the book, which, owing to his habit of juxtaposing disparate quotations, is somewhat of a patchwork quilt.[100] Only after 1492 did the wider world of

[98] The most comprehensive treatment of Gaffurio remains the collection of essays by Alessandro Caretta, Luigi Cremascoli, and Luigi Salamina, *Franchino Gaffurio* (Lodi, 1951). Gaffurio also published three pamphlets in answer to Giovanni Spataro's criticisms of his treatises. Two early works, written in Verona, are lost. For the list of his works, see Caretta *et al.*, 134–5, to which should be added the early version of Book II of the *Practica musicae* in the Houghton Library, Harvard University (see *Correspondence of Renaissance Musicians*, 166–73). Facsimile edns. are available of all Gaffurio's major treatises. The *Practica musicae* and *De harmonia* have been translated by Clement A. Miller: MSD 20 (American Institute of Musicology, 1968), and MSD 33 (American Institute of Musicology, 1977). The *Theorica musice* has been translated by Walter Kreyszig: Music Theory Translation Series (New Haven and London, 1993).

[99] The following section is based on Palisca's indispensable *Humanism in Italian Renaissance Musical Thought*, esp. ch. 2, 'The Rediscovery of the Ancient Sources', and ch. 9, 'Gaffurio as a Humanist'.

[100] The characterization is Palisca's; see *Humanism*, 195. Kreyszig has traced the references with considerable success.

humanist scholarship become available to him. In 1497 Giorgio Valla published a Latin translation of Euclid and Cleonides; Carlo Valgulio did the same for Pseudo-Plutarch's *De musica* in 1507. But much more lay in manuscript. In 1433 Ambrogio Traversari had reported seeing among the books of Vittorino da Feltre in Mantua (at whose school Johannes Gallicus was transformed from a singer into a scholar) music treatises by Aristides Quintilianus, Bacchius Senior, and Ptolemy. In 1468 Cardinal Bessarion donated to the library of St Mark's manuscripts that included treatises by Ptolemy, Aristides Quintilianus, Bryennius, Porphyry, Nicomachus, and Bacchius Senior and the Aristotelian *Problems*, later adding Aristoxenus, Alypius, and Gaudentius. Unfortunately, this world of learning was largely closed to Gaffurio because he knew little or no Greek. Not deterred, he sought out translators. Between 1494 and 1497 Giovanni Francesco Burana translated for him Aristides Quintilianus, the three Bellermann Anonymi, Bacchius Senior, and Bryennius. In 1499 Niccolò Leoniceno produced a translation of Ptolemy's *Harmonics* for him.[101]

Gaffurio absorbed these treatises rapidly, for by 1500 he had already completed the manuscript of his *De harmonia musicorum instrumentorum*, though publication had to wait eighteen years until he found a patron, Jean Grolier, treasurer of the King of France and a famous book-lover.[102] Perhaps the dedicatees were disappointed that the work did not deal with musical instruments, as the title suggests. To a certain extent the *De harmonia* duplicates the earlier theoretical treatises: definitions, intervals, the proportional system, consonances, modes, and the Greek genera are treated in both, but the emphasis is different. The *De harmonia* reflects Gaffurio's newly acquired knowledge in its enlarged discussion of the Greek genera, this time including the tunings of Archytas, Aristoxenus, and Ptolemy.[103] It also expands the treatment of arithmetic, geometric, and harmonic means. The harmonies of the universe and the harmonious relations of the human body and soul—*musica mundana* and *musica humana*—form the final chapters, from which it becomes clear what Gaffurio had in mind by the title of the book.

The treatise also has a more practical bent, probably reflecting

[101] See F. Alberto Gallo, 'Le traduzioni dal Greco per Franchino Gaffurio', *Acta musicologica*, 35 (1963), 172–4, and Palisca, *Humanism*, 111–22.

[102] Three beautifully illuminated presentation copies, addressed to three different prospective patrons, document the difficulties Gaffurio had in finding someone who would subsidize the printing of what must have seemed a very esoteric work, requiring numerous woodcut diagrams; see the introduction to Clement Miller's translation and Palisca, *Humanism*, 200–3, who has brought to light two new exemplars. The Lodi manuscript shows that Gaffurio continued to revise the treatise until 1514.

[103] For the specifics, see Palisca, *Humanism*, 208–25.

Gaffurio's experience as *maestro di cappella* at Milan Cathedral, a post
he obtained in 1484 and held till his death: he discusses the temperament of perfect fifths and the practice of slightly lowering the very
sharp Pythagorean major thirds and sixths, accepting that in practice
a certain divergence from theoretically correct temperament is permissible, according to the judgement of the ear. But in the *De harmonia* he attacks Ramos de Pareja for advocating a 5:4 major third and
6:5 minor third, even though he is charmed by the superparticular
ratios of Ptolemy's syntonic diatonic, which, arranged in an arithmetic
progression, 6:5:4:3:2:1, form the series of minor third, major third,
fourth, fifth, and octave.[104] Gaffurio was, in fact, the first to give a complete exposition of Ptolemy's division (imperfectly transmitted in
Boethius' fifth book), a tuning that would become central in the sixteenth century. Yet all his new-found knowledge did not help him elu-
cidate the difference between the ancient Greek system of modes and
the modern one—indeed, to have done so, as Claude Palisca points
out, would have 'made the entire Book IV irrelevant to modern harmonics'—but he provided so much information about ancient learning that he stimulated both musicians to attempt to recover the
marvellous effects of Greek music (Vicentino) and theorists to ratio-
nalize the modern modal system (Glareanus and Zarlino).[105]

At the time Gaffurio was writing his *Theoricum opus musice* he had
in mind to follow it with a treatment of practical music. Early versions
of three of the four books that were eventually published as *Practica
musicae* in 1496 show him heavily influenced by Tinctoris; the two had
been friends in Naples, 1478–80.[106] The printed version reflects his
studies during the intervening years in its more historical (and less personal) orientation.[107] The treatise is divided into four books, covering
fundamentals, the mensural system, counterpoint, and proportions.[108]
In the context of the discussion of modes in Book I Gaffurio presents
examples from both the Ambrosian and Gregorian rites, giving valuable insights into the use of Ambrosian chant at the time he was
choirmaster in Milan. Book III, on counterpoint, is organized quite
differently from Tinctoris's treatise. Dissonance treatment is covered
in one chapter, with two further chapters on the use of the fourth.

---

[104] Palisca, *Humanism*, 222.

[105] Ibid. 298.

[106] See Clement A. Miller, 'Early Gaffuriana: New Answers to Old Questions', *MQ* 56 (1970),
367–88. On the early version of Book II, not known in 1970, see above, n. 98.

[107] In addition to ancient authors, Guido, and Johannes de Muris, Gaffurio cites Giorgio
Anselmi, whose treatise of 1434 he owned and annotated. See the edition by Giuseppe Massera,
De musica ('Historiae musicae cultores' Biblioteca, 14; Florence, 1961).

[108] See Clement A. Miller, 'Gaffurius's *Practica musicae*: Origin and Contents', *Musica disciplina*, 22 (1968), 105–28.

Gaffurio lays more stress on rules and procedures; unlike Tinctoris, he discusses composition in three or more parts, the use of *musica ficta*, and proper decorum in singing. Book IV, on proportions, offers an even more complete treatment than Tinctoris's. Gaffurio's last example of the *genus submultiplex superpartiens* includes a passage in 4:19; further examples are left 'to the investigation of diligent musicians'.[109] It was the last full treatment of proportions, which rapidly dropped out of favour in composition, with a few notable exceptions such as Isaac's *Choralis Constantinus*.

The *Practica musicae* was reprinted in 1497, 1502, 1508, and 1512, and became a standard source for later theorists throughout Europe; Henricus Glareanus borrowed many of its examples in his *Dodeka-chordon* of 1547. Its success was due not only to its availability in print but also to the thorough and thoughtful presentation of its subject, with its more than 150 polyphonic music examples.

GUILIELMUS MONACHUS AND 'ENGLISH COUNTERPOINT'

The curious compendium on the art of music by the otherwise unknown Guilielmus Monachus, *De preceptis artis musicae*, dating perhaps 1480–90, is mainly concerned with proportions and mensuration signs.[110] Three sections, however, deal with English contrapuntal practice, characterized as such. One, 'which is called the faulxbordon manner', describes how to improvise a soprano and contratenor over a tenor. The soprano proceeds as if in thirds under the tenor but transposes up an octave, producing parallel sixths; the contratenor moves in parallel thirds above the tenor. This method of 'sighting' is now characterized as 'English discant'; it is related to the theory of 'gradi' discussed by Hothby (see above). 'These English', remarks Guilielmus, 'have another method called gymel'; the description is puzzling, but the example shows parallel thirds with the tenor, sometimes above, sometimes below; a contratenor can also be added.[111] Guilielmus also gives

---

[109] *Practica musicae*, trans. Miller, 233.

[110] It has been edited by Albert Seay (CSM 11; n.p.: American Institute of Musicology, 1965). The unique source is a late 15th-c. Italian manuscript, Venice, Biblioteca Nazionale Marciana, Lat. 336 (= 1581), which includes Antonio de Leno's *Regulae de contrapunto* (ed. Albert Seay in Colorado College Music Press Critical Texts, 1; Colorado Springs, Colo., 1977) and a brief treatment of text underlay; on this manuscript see Don Harrán, 'In Pursuit of Origins: The Earliest Writing on Text Underlay (*c.* 1440), *Acta musicologica*, 50 (1978), 217–40, and id., 'Intorno a un codice veneziano Quattrocentesco', *Studi musicali*, 8 (1979), 41–60. Although Guilielmus has been regarded as Italian because he distinguishes between practices 'apud Anglicos' and 'apud nos', his word order in Latin and the constant use of 'nos' as a subject (e.g. 'nos debemus incipere et finire contrapunctum per speciem perfectam', p. 34) sound more English (or northern) than Italian.

[111] The subject of English discant, faburden, and fauxbourdon is still a vexed one, as are most questions that deal with improvisation. For a lucid explanation of faburden and fauxbourdon,

instructions for improvising in three voices using parallel tenths against a tenor and in four voices, producing the English equivalent of *falsobordone* in root-position chords. All these methods are quite formulaic, and do not yield as artistic a result as Tinctoris's examples of counterpoint *super librum*. Nevertheless, they testify to the widespread use of improvisation over plainchant melodies, a practice that flourished particularly in the next century.[112]

That English practice was known on the Continent is not surprising, in view of the large number of English pieces found in Continental manuscripts. Niccolò Burzio speaks of 'singers' counterpoint, that "ultramontanes", especially the French, use', again involving sights.[113] This method was discussed as late as 1540; Giovanni del Lago calls it 'contrapunto ad videndum'.[114]

PIETRO AARON

Throughout the fifteenth century, the major theorists were men of letters, some with advanced degrees in theology (Hothby) or law (Tinctoris). Pietro Aaron (*c*.1480–after 1545), by contrast, seems to have been largely self-educated; he prides himself on being a Florentine, yet we have no knowledge of his early life or training in Florence. By 1516 he was a priest and living in Imola, where he later sang and taught music at the Cathedral. He spent the major part of his career in Venice, where his circle of friends and correspondents included the theorists Giovanni del Lago and Giovanni Spataro.[115]

Aaron began writing on music theory at a critical juncture. He attempted to apply the standard teachings on mode, counterpoint, and *musica ficta* to the music he knew at a time when it was becoming increasingly difficult to do so: the classification of modes had been

---

see Brian Trowell, *New Grove*, vi. 350–4. On English discant and sights, see Ernest Sanders, *New Grove*, v. 492–5, and Trowell, *New Grove*, xvii. 307–8. See also Sachs, 'Die Contrapunctus-Lehre', 208–24.

[112] See Klaus-Jürgen Sachs, 'Arten improvisierter Mehrstimmigkeit nach Lehrtexten des 14. bis 16. Jahrhunderts', *Basler Jahrbuch für historische Musikpraxis*, 7 (1983), 166–83.

[113] *Florum libellus*, ed. Massera, 126–7; *Musices opusculum* (1487), trans. Clement A. Miller (MSD 37; Neuhausen-Stuttgart, 1983), 87–8.

[114] *Breve introduttione di musica misurata* (Venice, 1540; facs. edn. Bologna, 1969), [35–6].

[115] The most recent treatment of Aaron's life, including his correspondence, is in *Correspondence of Renaissance Musicians*, ch. 4. Aaron's five treatises are all available in facsimile: *Libri tres de institutione harmonica* (Bologna, 1516; facs. edn., New York, 1976); *Toscanello* (Venice, 1523; rev. edns. 1529, 1539; 1529 edn. repr. Bologna, 1969); *Trattato della natura et cognitione di tutti gli tuoni di canto figurato* (Venice, 1525; facs. edn., Utrecht, 1966); *Lucidario in musica* (Venice, 1545; facs. edn., Bologna, 1969); *Compendiolo di molti dubbi, segreti et sentenze intorno al canto fermo, et figurato* (Milan, *c*.1545; facs. edn., Bologna, 1970). The most extended discussion of his theoretical works is Peter Bergquist, 'The Theoretical Writings of Pietro Aaron' (Ph.D. diss., Columbia University, 1964). Bergquist has also made an English translation of the *Toscanello* (Colorado College Music Press Translations, 4; Colorado Springs, Colo., 1970).

devised for monophonic music, the theory of counterpoint was mostly limited to note-against-note writing for two voices, and the practice of *musica ficta* presupposed a tonal system that rarely left the confines of the Guidonian hand. He promised, in his first treatise, *Libri tres de institutione harmonica* (1516), to include 'many of the secret chambers of this art, never heretofore revealed' (fo. 7ʳ). Although his lack of rigorous training shows both in his unsystematic approach and the occasional errors that mar this and his next treatise, the *Toscanello in musica* of 1523 (reprinted with an *Aggiunta* in 1529 and 1539), the faults are more than offset by the insights these writings afford into musical practice at his time.

Aaron was the first to distinguish between the older method of composing, one voice at a time (the additive method, characterized by Tinctoris as *contrapunctus*), and the method of the 'moderns', in which all voices were taken into consideration at the same time, leading to a more harmonious composition (a description similar to Tinctoris's characterization of *res facta*). His remarks do not in fact apply to the method of composition but underline the necessity for precompositional planning. Nor did he develop a method for composing in the new manner, contenting himself with the older teachings (and a rather cursory exposition, at that), though counselling the student to follow the moderns in leaving an adequate space for each voice-part.[116] In truth, only so much could be taught by rule. Good composers, as his friend Spataro insisted, were born just as poets were; whoever wished to proceed beyond the rudiments needed not only inborn talent but the help of a teacher.[117] The *Toscanello*, in Italian rather than the Latin customary in the fifteenth century, proved a popular book; it was reprinted in 1529 and 1539. The ability to purchase books on music as well as music itself, facilitated by the burgeoning output of music printers, was an important factor in the spread of musical learning in the sixteenth century.

Aaron's most original treatise, the *Trattato della natura et cognitione di tutti gli tuoni di canto figurato* (1525), concerns 'the nature and understanding of all the modes in polyphony'.[118] In it Aaron tried to apply Marchetto of Padua's modal theory to polyphonic music,

---

[116] The topic is covered in the *Libri tres* (bk. iii, chs. 7–13) and the *Toscanello* (bk. ii, chs. 16–17). On the interpretation of these passages, see Blackburn, 'On Compositional Process', 212–19.

[117] See his remarks in a letter to Aaron of 6 May 1524 (*Correspondence of Renaissance Musicians*, 295; a similar statement is on p. 364). Spataro and Aaron exchanged their own compositions and subjected them to a critical evaluation of considerable interest; see ibid., ch. 5.

[118] Chapters 1–7 have been translated in Strunk, *Source Readings*, 205–18. On Aaron's use of musical examples in this treatise, see Cristle Collins Judd, 'Reading Aron Reading Petrucci: The

citing numerous pieces in the contemporary repertory. He follows Tinctoris in determining the mode by the tenor's final, range, and species of fifths and fourths. Endings on *a*, *b*, and *c* (which did not fit Marchetto's system) he explained as confinals and psalm-tone differences; the dependence on the latter produced some contradictory results: a composition ending on *c'* (with or without flat signature), for example, could be assigned to the fifth mode, but not to the sixth, despite the presence of the requisite confinal, since only the former had a difference on *c'*. Nevertheless, his is the first systematic attempt to categorize the modes of polyphonic works, and it points to a revived interest in modes at a time when the incursions of *musica ficta* were beginning to narrow the differences between them: far from being irrelevant, the modes were to gain new life both in theory (Glareanus and Zarlino) and in practice (cycles of works organized in modal order).[119]

In the 'Aggiunta' to the 1529 edition of the *Toscanello*, Aaron reconsidered some remarks he had made on the nature of the sharp and the question of indicating accidentals, prompted by Spataro's criticism.[120] Running counter to the traditional notion of the application of *musica ficta* as a performer's art, Aaron, at Spataro's urging, counsels that all accidentals be written, likening them to signposts at crossroads. He cites with approval compositions by Mouton, Josquin, Févin, and others where flats have been written to mitigate tritones and diminished fifths. But sometimes correcting one will produce the other: in such cases (the examples are from masses by Josquin) Aaron prefers the melodic tritone solely for the convenience for the singer, who would find it very awkward to sing the leap of a diminished fifth; however, he notes that in general it is a lesser error to commit a diminished fifth than a tritone.[121] Indeed, in the *Lucidario* he devotes considerable space to the demonstration of permissible infringements of the '*mi* contra *fa*' rule prohibiting harmonic tritones and diminished fifths.

Music Examples of the *Trattato della natura et cognitione di tutti gli tuoni* (1525)', *EMH* 14 (1995), 121–52.

[119] For a critical evaluation of Aaron's thought, see Harold Powers, 'Is Mode Real? Pietro Aaron, the Octenary System, and Polyphony', *Basler Jahrbuch für historische Musikpraxis*, 16 (1992), 9–52, esp. 22–45. See also Cristle Collins Judd, 'Modal Types and *Ut, Re, Mi* Tonalities: Tonal Coherence in Sacred Vocal Polyphony from about 1500', *JAMS* 45 (1992), 428–67.

[120] For Spataro's remarks, on bk. ii, ch. 20 of the *Toscanello*, see *Correspondence of Renaissance Musicians*, letter 12. In ch. 26 of the treatise on the modes Aaron showed how it was possible to find the six solmization syllables on every note of the hand; Spataro faulted him for showing only flats and offered to demonstrate the sharps as well (letter 31). In 1531 Aaron published an untitled pamphlet (later reprinted in his *Lucidario*) that remedied his faulty exposition; see ibid. 438–9.

[121] See Margaret Bent, 'Accidentals, Counterpoint, and Notation in Aaron's *Aggiunta* to the *Toscanello*', *Journal of Musicology*, 12 (1994), 306–44.

The pragmatic approach, with examples drawn from contemporary practice, characterizes all Aaron's treatises: as he develops as a theorist he becomes increasingly interested in problems and their solution, a format he used in his last major treatise, the *Lucidario* of 1545, the origins of which may be traced in his correspondence with Giovanni Spataro, where the two discussed (sometimes in disagreement) problems of notation, modal theory, counterpoint, composition, and accidentals.[122] He stands at the threshold of a new era.

MUSIC THEORY AND THE ARTS

The very same numbers that cause sounds to have that *concinnitas*, pleasing to the ears, can also fill the eyes and mind with wondrous delight. From musicians therefore who have already examined such numbers thoroughly, or from those objects in which Nature has displayed some evident and noble quality, the whole method of outlining is derived.

Thus did Leon Battista Alberti introduce the method of proportioning private buildings in his *De re aedificatoria* of about 1450, first printed in 1486.[123] He went on to give a thumbnail sketch of the phenomenon of sound and the intervals produced by ratios of string lengths, using the terms *diapente/sesquialtera*, *diatessaron/sesquitertia*, *diapason*, *diapason diapente*, *disdiapason*, and *tonus/sesquioctavus*. Architects, he says, employ these numbers in pairs when laying out flat areas, but in threes when designing three-dimensional space, where height should be proportioned harmoniously to length and width. For Alberti, as for generations after him, that which was true was beautiful: he defines beauty as 'that reasoned harmony of all the parts within a body, so that nothing may be added, taken away, or altered, but for the worse'.[124] That this notion was connected above all

---

[122] Only nine of Aaron's letters have survived, but much of Spataro's side of the correspondence has been preserved. See *Correspondence of Renaissance Musicians*.

[123] I quote from *On the Art of Building in Ten Books*, trans. Joseph Rykwert, Neil Leach, and Robert Tavernor (Cambridge, Mass., and London, 1991), 305 (from bk. ix, ch. 5). Christine Smith is sceptical of a musical theoretical interpretation of Alberti's use of *concinnitas*, believing that his notion of harmony reflects *heard* music, and relates it therefore to rhetoric; see *Architecture in the Culture of Early Humanism: Ethics, Aesthetics, and Eloquence, 1400–1470* (New York, 1992), 89, 91–4. While not denying this aspect, it seems to me that Alberti was knowledgeable enough to know that pleasing harmonies were based on simple mathematical ratios—the very ones he names in this passage.

[124] *On the Art of Building*, 156 (bk. vi, ch. 2). The fundamental study of this idea, as expressed in architecture, is Rudolf Wittkower, *Architectural Principles in the Age of Humanism* (2nd edn., London, 1952). Michael Baxandall, *Painting and Experience in Fifteenth Century Italy* (Oxford, 1972) offers valuable insights into the role of mathematics in art, especially the practical application of proportions using the 'Rule of Three' (pp. 86–102). He also makes a highly interesting comparison between the technical terms used in Domenico da Piacenza's treatise on the art of dancing—*aere, maniera, misura, misura di terreno, memoria*—and contemporary painting (pp. 77–81).

with music is shown in a remark that he made to the architect of
S. Francesco at Rimini that if the proportions of the pillars were
altered, its music would be thrown into discord ('si discorda tutta
quella musica').[125]

Alberti is the most eloquent fifteenth-century spokesman for the
fundamental relationships between music and architecture (reducible
of course to mathematics), but he was not the only one, nor was the
connection original with him, for Vitruvius had included a section on
music in his famous *Ten Books on Architecture*. In chapter 4 of Book
V he explains (following Aristoxenus) the science of harmonics, 'an
obscure and difficult branch of musical science, especially for those
who do not know Greek', and he apologizes for using Greek names,
since there are no Latin equivalents.[126] When Cesare Cesariano came
to translating Vitruvius in the sixteenth century, he consulted Franchino Gaffurio on this chapter, and his ample commentary includes
two diagrams taken from Gaffurio's *De harmonia musicorum instrumentorum*.[127] Cesariano retains Vitruvius' Greek names for intervals,
but the note names have also been translated into modern terminology, e.g. trite diezeugmenon is C sol fa ut. Cesariano also found
Cleonides' *Harmonic Introduction* (in Giorgio Valla's translation) and
Politian's *Panepistemon* helpful.[128]

The insistence on the mathematical basis of architecture has an
underlying motive: to elevate architecture to the status of a liberal art.
The argument is similar to that of the distinction between the *cantor*
and the *musicus*: those who think out the structure of buildings on the
basis of reason are deserving of the status of theoreticians. (But for
Alberti, as for Vitruvius, practice was not to be scorned, just as for
Tinctoris the *musicus* is the practitioner who operates on the basis of

---

[125] Cited in Wittkower, *Architecture*, 103.

[126] Vitruvius, *The Ten Books on Architecture*, trans. Morris Hicky Morgan (Cambridge, Mass.,
1914; repr. New York, 1960), 139. While Alberti's emphasis is on proportions, Vitruvius' is on
the harmonic system itself. Its application becomes clear when the context of the chapter is considered: it follows one on the construction of theatres and precedes one on 'Sounding Vessels in
the Theatre', the bronze vessels tuned to produce the boundary notes of the tetrachords, which
acted as resonating chambers. Vitruvius in fact is more concerned with the modular construction of buildings, based on the symmetry of the parts of the human body, than with the
Pythagorean proportions.

[127] Published Como, 1521 (by the printer of Gaffurio's book, Gotardo da Ponte); facs. edn.,
with an introduction and index by Carol Herselle Krinsky (Munich, 1969). The commentary is
not limited to the exposition of the harmonic system; on fo. 4[r], betraying the visual orientation
of the artist, Cesariano compares minims and semiminims ('which appear to be fragments of
the proportions') in a composition to furniture, which must be arranged harmonically and sym-
metrically in a room.

[128] On this work, written in 1490–1 and based on Ptolemy and Aristides Quintilianus, whom
Politian of course read in Greek, see Fiorella Brancacci, 'L'enciclopedia umanistica e la musica:
il *Panepistemon* di Angelo Poliziano', in Piero Gargiulo (ed.), *La musica a Firenze al tempo di
Lorenzo il Magnifico* (Florence, 1993), 299–316.

reason.) The case was more easily arguable for architects than for painters. However, by drawing together the cosmological speculations about the relationship between the harmony of the spheres and the harmony of the human body and soul—*musica mundana* and *musica humana*—the Renaissance fused, in the words of Erwin Panofsky, 'the cosmological interpretation of the theory of proportions, current in Hellenistic times and in the Middle Ages, with the classical notion of "symmetry" as the fundamental principle of aesthetic perfection'.[129] Mathematical relationships could be demonstrated to underlie painting—especially with the newly invented art of perspective—as well as architecture.

Luca Pacioli, in his *De divina proportione* (Venice, 1509), felt so strongly about the equal claim of music and perspective to belong to the quadrivium that he wished either to remove the former or include the latter: among his reasons he points to music's 'sonorous number and measurement by the *tempus* of its prolations', perspective's natural number according to definition and the measurement of the visual line, as well as music's harmonic, perspective's arithmetic and geometric, proportions. 'Alas!', he remarks on the unfairness of excluding perspective, 'who on seeing a graceful figure with its well-disposed lineaments (design), in which it appears that only breath is lacking, would not judge it more divine than human'?[130] Earlier, in the dedicatory letter to Guidobaldo, duke of Urbino, of his *Summa de arithmetica, geometria, proportioni et proportionalità* (Venice, 1494), he had listed all the arts that were dependent on the knowledge of numbers and proportions for the practical application of the artist's or artisan's skill, beginning with architecture and painting, the latter for its use of perspective. Music comes next, which 'clearly gives us the laws of number, measure, proportion, and proportionality'—and here he offers a compliment to Guidobaldo's 'celebrated chapel of most excellent singers and players', headed by his fellow Franciscan, frate Martino.[131] Boethius' *De musica* is one of his primary sources; the harmonic mean, he states, is found only in 'suoni e canti', and 'is

---

[129] Erwin Panofsky, 'The History of the Theory of Human Proportions as a Reflection of the History of Styles', in *Meaning in the Visual Arts* (Garden City, NY, 1955), 55–107 at 89.

[130] Part I, ch. 3. See Arnaldo Bruschi, Corrado Maltese, Manfredo Tafuri, and Renato Bonelli (eds.), *Scritti rinascimentali di architettura* (Milan, 1978), 67–8.

[131] 'La musica chiaro ci rende lei del numero. misura. proportione. e proportionalità esser bisognosa. Dela cui melodia V. ornatissima corte de ogni genere virtutum è piena. Maxime per lo culto divino. La celeberrima capela de dignissimi cantori e sonatori. Fra liquali el venerabil padre nostro conterraneo per habito fratello frate Martino non immeritamente è connumerato' (fo. 2ʳ). Not much is known about musicians at the court of Urbino in the 1490s. Frate Martino is possibly the Fra Martino who served as organist at the Duomo in 1475; see Bramante Ligi, 'La cappella musicale del Duomo d'Urbino', *Note d'Archivio*, 2 (1925), 38.

as it were a mixture of the continuous and the discrete, as is music with respect to time in its rests and prolations and with respect to number in its divisions of notes [i.e. mensuration]'. In perspective, he continues, number applies to the size of the figures and continuous quantity to line.[132] Knowledge of proportions is useful not only to architects but also to tailors, shoemakers, carpenters, shipbuilders, weavers, and—his main readers—merchants.

Leonardo believed that painting was not numbered amongst the sciences for lack of writers on the subject; but since painting 'is the sole imitator of all the manifest works of nature' and 'nothing can be found in nature that is not part of science', and furthermore since it draws upon the lines and points of geometry, and perspective depends on arithmetic (discontinuous quantity) and geometry (continuous quantity), painting can rightly be considered a science.[133] In his famous *Paragone* Leonardo compared the arts of poetry, painting, and music. Because the eye, 'which is said to be the window of the soul', is superior to the ear, painting is superior to poetry and to music. The poet is limited because his descriptive words 'are separated from one another by time, which leaves voids between them and dismembers the proportions'.[134] Music, by contrast, 'composes harmony from the conjunction of proportional parts',[135] but it 'is constrained to arise and die in one or more harmonic intervals'. Thus painting 'is superior in rank to music, because it does not perish immediately after its creation'; moreover, the eye can grasp the whole simultaneously. Therefore, if music is amongst the liberal arts, 'either you should place painting there or remove music'.[136]

One of Leon Battista Alberti's colleagues in papal service was Guillaume Dufay. When Eugenius IV moved the papal court to Florence in 1434, Alberti became friends with the architect Filippo Brunelleschi, who was just then engaged in his great project of completing the cupola of the cathedral. From these years date Alberti's *Della pittura*, 'the first systematic exposition (and indeed the first

---

[132] 'L'armonica solo in suoni e canti se ha aritrovare. E questa e quasi mista de la continua e discreta si commo essa musica a respeto al tempo ne le sue pause e prolationi e al respetto al numero ne le divisioni de le note. Si commo el prospettivo el numero in quanto la sua figura ha esser longa o larga. 3. o 4. bracia. E a la continua in quanto a la linea' (fos. 69ᵛ–70ʳ).

[133] *Leonardo on Painting*, ed. Martin Kemp, selected and trans. Martin Kemp and Margaret Walker (New Haven, 1989), 13–15. I discuss Leonardo at greater length in 'Leonardo and Gaffurio'.

[134] *Leonardo on Painting*, 20, 24.

[135] Ibid. 34. Leonardo means chords ('harmonic intervals'), for singing the parts of a polyphonic composition singly 'cannot result in that grace of proportioned harmony which is contained within harmonic intervals' (ibid. 37).

[136] Ibid. 34, 35, 37. See also Emanuel Winternitz, *Leonardo da Vinci as a Musician* (New Haven, 1982), ch. 12, 'The *Paragone*: The Role of Music in the Comparison of the Arts'.

written exposition) of the rules of painter's perspective',[137] and one of Dufay's most impressive isorhythmic motets, which truly could be called architectural music. In 1973 Charles Warren suggested that *Nuper rosarum flores*, composed for the consecration of the cathedral on 25 March 1436, was constructed using the proportions of the church itself, the four *taleae* in the proportion 6:4:2:3 corresponding to the length of the nave, the width of the transept, the length of the apse, and the height of the dome.[138] This theory has faltered on Warren's measurements, which accord neither with that of the original design nor with known Quattrocento measurements.[139] A different architectural model for Dufay's motet has been proposed by Craig Wright: the Temple of Solomon. Not only do its biblical dimensions correspond to those of the motet, but the number seven, a structural feature of *Nuper rosarum*, is also stressed in the biblical description of the dedication.[140] Since the Temple figures prominently in the ceremony for the dedication of a church, the analogy carries greater weight.

Although we know of no direct link between Dufay and Alberti, their acquaintance, if not friendship, is very likely, especially in view of Alberti's interest in music. The same may equally well be true of other musicians or theorists and writers on the arts: Gaffurio was in Milan at the same time as Luca Pacioli and Leonardo da Vinci. Tracing analogies between the arts is problematic at best and likely to be mistaken when carried very far. Yet when the disciplines share an underlying kinship—whether it be mathematical or aesthetic—it is likely that the practitioners will wish to learn from each other. If we cannot document personal connections, we can point to shared terminology and, in the case of the three figures discussed above, the direct comparison of music with art and architecture.

[137] Joan Gadol, *Leon Battista Alberti: Universal Man of the Early Renaissance* (Chicago and London, 1969), 6–7.

[138] See Charles W. Warren, 'Brunelleschi's Dome and Dufay's Motet', *MQ* 59 (1973), 92–105.

[139] See the critique by Christine Smith, *Architecture in the Culture of Early Humanism*, 94. However, Warren's other suggestion, that the overlapping construction of the two tenor parts, not quite canonic, may reflect Brunelleschi's ingenious double-shell construction of the cupola, remains attractive.

[140] See Craig Wright, 'Dufay's *Nuper rosarum flores*, King Solomon's Temple, and the Veneration of the Virgin', *JAMS* 47 (1994), 395–441, esp. 404–7.

VIII

MUSIC, HUMANISM, AND THE IDEA OF A 'REBIRTH' OF THE ARTS

By REINHARD STROHM

In memory of Hans Strohm (1908–98)

INTRODUCTION

THE following contribution seeks to identify the beginnings of the idea of a musical 'Renaissance' by evaluating testimonies of fifteenth-century humanists and musicians. That European music experienced a 'Renaissance' comparable to that of literature and the other arts is a proposition both familiar and controversial.[1] It will be argued here that this idea originated as a by-product of humanist reflections on the arts in the fifteenth and early sixteenth centuries; its anchorage in musical repertoires and discussions is more speculative. The earliest statements apparently suggesting a musical 'renewal', those of Martin Le Franc (*c.*1410–61) and Johannes Tinctoris (*c.*1435–1511), are well known. The former wrote (in *c.*1440–2) about a 'novel practice' (*nouvelle pratique*) of music; the latter, writing in 1477, welcomed a 'new art' (*ars nova*) of composition which had originated about forty years

---

[1] See Paul Oskar Kristeller, 'Music and Learning in the Early Italian Renaissance', *Journal of Renaissance and Baroque Music*, 1 (1947), 255–74; also in id., *Renaissance Thought II: Papers on Humanism and the Arts* (New York, Evanston, and London, 1965), 142–62; Leo Schrade, 'Renaissance: The Historical Conception of an Epoch', in *International Musicological Society, Report of the Fifth Congress, Utrecht 1952* (Amsterdam, 1953), 19–32; Heinrich Besseler, 'Das Renaissanceproblem in der Musik', *Archiv für Musikwissenschaft*, 23 (1966), 1–10; Edward E. Lowinsky, 'Music in the Culture of the Renaissance', in Lowinsky, *Culture*, i. 19–39; id., 'Music of the Renaissance as Viewed by Renaissance Musicians', in Lowinsky, *Culture*, i. 87–105; Willem Elders, 'Humanism and Early Renaissance-Music: A Study of the Ceremonial Music by Ciconia and Dufay', *TVNM* 27 (1977), 65–101; Lewis Lockwood, 'Renaissance', *New Grove*, xv. 736–41; Kurt von Fischer, 'Language and Music in 14th-Century Italy: On the Question of an Early Renaissance', in id., *Essays in Musicology*, ed. Tamara S. Evans (New York, 1989), 76–92; Palisca, *Humanism*; Klaus Hortschansky, 'Musikwissenschaft und Bedeutungsforschung: Überlegungen zu einer Heuristik im Bereich der Musik der Renaissance', in id. (ed.), *Zeichen und Struktur*, 65–86; Jessie Ann Owens, 'Music Historiography and the Definition of "Renaissance"', *Notes*, 47 (1990), 305–30; Klaus Wolfgang Niemöller, 'Zum Paradigmenwechsel in der Musik der Renaissance: Vom "numerus sonorus" zur "musica poetica"', in *Abhandlungen der Akademie der Wissenschaften in Göttingen, Phil.-Hist. Klasse*, 3. Folge (Göttingen, 1995), 187–215.

earlier, *c.*1437. Despite their notoriety, these statements have not been convincingly interpreted; their relationship with each other and with their common cultural background remains to be clarified. This background is a well-documented historiographical and philosophical discourse among humanists about the rebirth of Antiquity in eloquence and various arts.[2] A new appreciation of this discourse may facilitate critical and informed choices between challenging and supporting the Renaissance concept in music.

Nineteenth- and twentieth-century discussions of culture in the Renaissance record what may be called an 'evolutionist' view, which regards medieval (particularly fourteenth-century) precedent as a necessary preparation, and a 'revivalist' one, which accepts the humanist idea of a more or less sudden rebirth of Antiquity. According to a wide modern consensus, this humanist tendency of thought, whether a product of self-definition or arising from self-deception, was in itself real enough to justify the notion of a historical epoch called the 'Renaissance'.[3] But despite this and other intermediate solutions which have been proposed, the basic conflict between 'evolutionism' and 'revivalism' has remained unsettled.[4] It assumes a special significance in the field of music. In the light of the fact that ancient music could not be recovered, can a case be made at all for a 'rebirth' of music along with literature and the other arts in the fifteenth century? Has it been made by contemporaries, and if so, how might this affect our understanding of a musical 'Renaissance'?

References to *musica* are fairly frequent in the prose writings of Italian humanists. Before the early sixteenth century, however, most

---

[2] On humanist debates about the rebirth of the arts, see Franco Simone, 'La coscienza della rinascita negli umanisti', *La Rinascita*, 2 (1939), 838–71; 3 (1940), 163–85; Herbert Weisinger, 'Renaissance Theories of the Revival of the Fine Arts', *Italica*, 20 (1943), 163–72; id., 'Renaissance Accounts of the Revival of Learning', *Studies in Philology*, 45 (1948), 105–18; orig. publ. in *Papers of the Michigan Academy*, 30 (1945), 625–38; trans. as 'Die Erneuerung der Bildung in Selbstzeugnissen der Renaissance', in Buck (ed.), *Zu Begriff und Problem*, 228–55; Wallace K. Ferguson, *The Renaissance in Historical Thought: Five Centuries of Interpretation* (Cambridge, Mass., 1948) (an indispensable survey); Paul Oskar Kristeller, 'The Modern System of the Arts: A Study in the History of Aesthetics', *Journal of the History of Ideas*, 12 (1951), 496–527; also in id., *Renaissance Thought II: Papers on Humanism and the Arts* (New York, Evanston, and London, 1965), 163–227; B. L. Ullman, 'Renaissance—the Word and the Underlying Concept', *Studies in Philology*, 49 (1952), 105–18; Ernst H. Gombrich, 'The Renaissance Conception of Artistic Progress and its Consequences', in id., *Norm and Form* (London, 1966), 1–10 and 137–40 (first publ. in Congress Report, *XVIIᵉ Congrès d'Histoire de l'Art*, Amsterdam, 1952); Erwin Panofsky, *Renaissance and Renascences in Western Art* (Stockholm, 1960); Eugenio Garin, *Italian Humanism: Philosophy and Civic Life in the Renaissance*, trans. P. Munz (Oxford, 1965); August Buck, 'Über die Beziehungen zwischen Humanismus und bildenden Künsten in der Renaissance', in id. (ed.), *Die humanistische Tradition in der Romania* (Bad Homburg, Berlin, and Zürich, 1968), 243–52; id. (ed.), *Zu Begriff und Problem der Renaissance* (Darmstadt, 1969).

[3] Panofsky, *Renaissance*, ch. 1: ' "Renaissance"—Self-definition or Self-deception?', 1–41.

[4] Ferguson, *Renaissance*; Jacob Burckhardt, *Die Kultur der Renaissance in Italien* (18th edn., Leipzig, 1928), 161–6 (III. Abschnitt, 'Vorbemerkungen').

of them concern the ancient or academic status of music, its scientific or philosophical significance, or occasionally its modern daily practice as a pleasurable activity. The historiographical trope of the 'rebirth' (*rinascita*) of the arts and letters was at first not applied to music. Those who wrote about the 'rebirth' of an art, for example of poetry or of sculpture, assumed a historicizing position towards it, imagining its history as exemplified in memorable achievements or surviving 'works'. To acknowledge the innovative achievements of composers in the same way, and to consider musical pieces as lasting products commanding the attention, at their own time or later, of listeners or readers, meant awarding music the status of an *ars poetica*— a work-creating discipline. This conceptual change happened, in fact, in the course of the fifteenth century. A case was made for a 'renewal' of the standards of music although no technical comparisons with ancient music were possible; compositional innovation and progress were applauded, and the humanist concept of the *ars poetica* was applied to musical compositions, leading to the idea of the 'complete and transmittable (musical) work'—the *opus perfectum et absolutum* of Listenius.[5]

In order to illustrate this momentous conceptual change, a selection of contemporary writings will be considered: by authors who were primarily concerned with literature and the fine arts (see Appendix, Testimonia 1–12), and by those few who wrote specifically on music (Testimonia 13–17).

First of all, let us hear the testimony of an outsider. In 1408 the French humanist Nicolas de Clamanges (1355?–1437) wrote in a letter to Gontier Col that he accepted the Italian renewal of arts and letters as a model for his own country. Out of patriotism he had attempted to revive Latin eloquence in France:

I have endeavoured to achieve, to some extent, a rebirth of eloquence, which had long been buried in France, and to make it sprout again with new flowers, even if they cannot be compared with the original ones. I wished that France, as it is not inferior to other regions in other achievements, might also have some rhetorical skills, so that it could never be said to be devoid of them, even if it did not equal others.[6]

---

[5] See Peter Cahn, 'Zur Vorgeschichte des "Opus perfectum et absolutum" in der Musikauffassung um 1500', in Hortschansky (ed.), *Zeichen und Struktur*, 11–26, mentioning (pp. 20–3) the term 'res facta' with reference to Margaret Bent, 'Resfacta and *Cantare super librum*', *JAMS* 36 (1983), 371–91, and Bonnie J. Blackburn, 'On Compositional Process in the Fifteenth Century', *JAMS* 40 (1987), 210–84. See also Peter Cahn, '*Ars poetica* und *musica poetica*—Quintilian und Horaz in der Musiktheorie und Kompositionslehre des 15. und 16. Jahrhunderts', in F. R. Varwig (ed.), *AINIGMA: Festschrift für Helmut Rahn* (Heidelberg, 1987), 23–33. Further on *ars poetica* and the 'work concept' in music, see Niemöller, 'Zum Paradigmenwechsel'; Strohm, *Rise*, 423.

[6] '. . . eloquentiam diu sepultam in Galliis quodammodo renasci novisque iterum floribus, licet priscis longe imparibus, repullulare laboravi, ut, sicut in ceteris laudibus Gallia etiam his tem-

He added the general consideration:

The arts usually originate in an imperfect state, and are refined little by little through usage and expansion; thus they reach perfection when they have been more precisely elaborated and polished. The first inventor of the art of stone-masonry sculpted in a primitive manner, not with the same elegance of shape as did an Euphranor or Polyclitus.[7]

The first paragraph articulates nothing less than the humanist idea of a 'rebirth' of classical letters. It had already been formulated by the Florentines Petrarch, Boccaccio, and Salutati in the fourteenth century. Nicolas de Clamanges, their follower and emulator, uses the Latin verb *renasci*, 'to be reborn', to express exactly what his fellow-countryman Jules Michelet four and a half centuries later was to call 'la Renaissance'.[8] Nicolas agrees with the early Italian humanists when choosing *eloquentia*, the classical art of refined speaking and writing, as the tradition he wishes to revive. In the second paragraph, he suggests a general model of how perfection in art is reached, taking as example the development of Hellenic sculpture. This shows his humanist belief that eloquence and the fine arts have common or analogous histories. Since he confines his potted history of sculpture to Antiquity and does not mention later decline and renewal, his picture of a seamless development of sculpture by constant use and expansion (*usu et incremento*)[9] to some extent contrasts with his history of eloquence, which is being 'reborn' after having been 'buried'. Furthermore, Nicolas sees himself as a protagonist on behalf of the civilization of his own country. It is his belief in a bond between the arts that makes him wish to add eloquence to the other achievements of his country. These three ideas—the emphasis on a renewal of

---

poribus ceteris regionibus non inferior est, ita etiam oratorie virtutis aliquid haberet, quo etsi aliis non fortassis equaretur, prorsus tamen expers esse argui non posset . . .'. Nicolas de Clamanges, Letter 'Cum omnibus', cited after Dario Cecchetti, ' "Florescere—Deflorescere": in margine ad alcuni temi del primo umanesimo francese', in *Mélanges à la mémoire de Franco Simone: France et Italie dans la culture européenne* (Geneva, 1980), 143–55 at 146. See also Ullman, 'Renaissance', 116–17.

[7] 'Solent artes ab imperfecto oriri paulatimque usu et incremento excoli, sicque accuratius exculte atque expolite ad perfectionem venire. Ruditer primus artis quadratorie inventor sculpsit, non ea figurae elegantia quam Eufranor aut Policletus.' Cecchetti, ' "Florescere" ', 146.

[8] Jules Michelet, *Histoire de France*, pt. 7: 'Histoire de France au seizième siècle (Renaissance)' (Paris, 1857). On the 19th-c. 'Renaissance' concept before Michelet, see Jan Huizinga, 'Das Problem der Renaissance', in id., *Parerga*, ed. W. Kaegi (Amsterdam, 1945), 87–146; Ullman, 'Renaissance'; Kristeller, 'Modern System'; Reinhart Koselleck, ' "Neuzeit": Zur Semantik moderner Bewegungsbegriffe', in id., *Vergangene Zukunft: Zur Semantik geschichtlicher Zeiten* (Frankfurt am M., 1992), 300–48.

[9] The passage recalls Quintilian's surveys of the history of painting and sculpture (*Institutio oratoriae* 12. 10. 3–9), which mention both Polyclitus and Euphranor. On this developmental model, see Gombrich, 'Renaissance Conception', 3 and n. 4.

classical eloquence, the belief in a common bond between the arts, and the ideal of a national culture—are primary topics of early humanist literature.

Let us consider these issues one by one (see Testimonia (hereafter abbreviated 'T.') 1–12).

THE IMAGERY OF DECLINE, REBIRTH, AND SURVIVAL

The notion of an organic rise and decline in culture, associated with imageries of light and dark, the seasons, plant life, and human life, is widely used in history. But it took on a special meaning for Renaissance humanists, who extended it to imply a total rebirth or resurrection of culture, denying the finality of death or darkness.[10] This idea was essentially compatible with Christian dogma and could be regarded as one of the philosophical links between Renaissance humanism and Christianity. The idea of a rebirth was in competition, however, with actual survival: the physical presence of objects surviving from the past, whether of medieval churches and codices or of classical statues and architectural monuments, required interpretation. Although Horace had dismissed the crude longevity of works of the 'mechanical' arts with his authorial and authoritative claim 'Monumentum exegi aere perennius' ('I have erected a monument more perennial than bronze'), many Renaissance humanists were interested in the material conditions of survival, including that of manuscripts. A famous letter written in 1416 by Poggio Bracciolini to Guarino da Verona reporting his rediscovery, at St Gall, of precious codices of Valerius Flaccus, Cicero, and Quintilian,[11] depicts heartbreaking scenes in which these Latin authors themselves, languishing in exile and left to perish in the monastery's horrid dungeon, were physically rescued from certain death. This story offered a successful model for narratives of survival and rebirth: barbaric medieval conditions had threatened the afterlives of the ancient monuments and documents. Enea Silvio Piccolomini, in turn, adduces the death-like or inhuman appearance of medieval art as evidence to condemn it (T. 4*a*), probably inspired by a remark by Filippo Villani on medieval wall-paintings which documents the decline of the arts with physical examples (T. 1).

[10] Ferguson, *Renaissance, passim*; Ullman, 'Renaissance'; Cecchetti, '"Florescere"'; Simone, 'Coscienza'; Gombrich, 'Renaissance Conception'. Alamanno Rinuccini (see Gombrich) confutes the theory of a general biological decline of humanity and ageing of the world. See also Lilio Gregorio Giraldi's formula 'hanc aetatem non senio languidam atque defectam', quoted in Weisinger, 'Renaissance Theories', 164–5.

[11] *Prosatori latini del Quattrocento*, ed. Eugenio Garin (Milan and Naples, 1952), 240–7.

The idea of a rebirth of classical learning was always connected with issues of personality, fame, and invention. The classical authors themselves had described history in such terms. Particularly influential were Cicero's considerations of the development of rhetoric in the preface of *De oratore* (see below) and Quintilian's (*Institutio oratoria* 12. 10) short sketches of the development of painting, sculpture, and oration, mentioning many names of authors and 'inventors' of arts. Humanist writers praised Petrarch as an originator, whether by ascribing to him the idea of a renewal of classical letters, or by crediting him with this achievement itself. Dante Alighieri was soon associated with this claim as well. Giovanni Boccaccio and Filippo Villani added the names of the painters Cimabue and Giotto (T. 1). By the end of the fourteenth century, the credit for the recovery of classical studies as well as the arts was firmly located with these great Florentine luminaries.[12]

Some later writers retained this specifically Florentine topos of Giotto and Petrarch as the heroes of their respective arts; Enea Silvio (T. 4*a* and 4*c*) and Albrecht Dürer (T. 12) refer to it.[13] An alternative topos is formed, however, in the generation of Leon Battista Alberti and Lorenzo Valla, both writing *c*.1435–44 (T. 2 and 3). They locate the rebirth in their own time, as something they have observed personally. Erasmus echoes them 'eighty years later' in 1518 (T. 11). Vespasiano da Bisticci (T. 7) and Antonio Manetti (T. 8) concur by relating the rebirth to the lifetimes of Valla, Traversari, and Brunelleschi. Filarete's (T. 5) slightly earlier date (*c*.1400–10) might reflect a wish to honour papal or Visconti patronage. Antonio Manetti and Alberti are particularly conscious of Brunelleschi's masterwork, the dome of S. Maria del Fiore in Florence, consecrated in 1436 by Pope Eugenius IV; the performance of Dufay's motet *Nuper rosarum flores* took place on this occasion. Humanist awareness of this event is documented.[14] Marsilio Ficino (T. 10) uses the unspecific temporal

[12] As formulated e.g. in a letter by Coluccio Salutati of 1 Aug. 1395: 'Emerserunt parumper nostro seculo studia litterarum; . . . emerserunt et ista lumina florentina; ut summum vulgaris eloquentiae decus et nulli scientia vel ingenio comparandum qui nostris temporibus floruit, aut etiam cuipiam antiquorum, Dantem Alligherium, pretermittam; Petrarca scilicet et Bocaccius, quorum opera cuncta, ni fallor, posteritas celebrabit . . .'. Francesco Novati (ed.), *Epistolario di Coluccio Salutati* (Rome, 1896), iii. 84 (no. 9); here cited after Weisinger, 'Renaissance Accounts', tr. 'Erneuerung', 231. Further on Florentine self-interpretations, see Ullman, 'Renaissance', 108–14; Panofsky, *Renaissance*, 12–15.

[13] Ferguson, *Renaissance*, 19–22; Buck, 'Über die Beziehungen', 246; Cesare Vasoli, 'Umanesimo e rinascimento', in *Storia della critica*, ed. Giuseppe Petronio, vii (Palumbo, n.d.), 25–7. Dürer's first estimate of a date around 1373, later corrected to *c*.1323, may reflect uncertainty about Giotto's lifetime.

[14] Sabine Žak, 'Der Quellenwert von Giannozzo Manettis Oratio über die Domweihe von Florenz 1436 für die Musikgeschichte', *Die Musikforschung*, 40 (1987), 2–32. A famous bronze

category 'seculum' but is explicit about the place of the renewal, Florence. This again suggests a connection with the consecration of S. Maria del Fiore in 1436, which also saw the beginning of a regular choir school at the cathedral, celebrated in the famous choir balconies by Donatello and Luca della Robbia.[15] The date of these events strikingly matches Tinctoris's idea of a musical *ars nova* originating about 1437.

The letter of Nicolas de Clamanges quoted above is not concerned with music, but touches upon a crucial problem of musical historiography. His evolutionist model of artistic development, although classical in origin, does not harmonize with the concept of a 'rebirth'. Had Nicolas used music as an example, he would surely have described its history in evolutionist terms. In fact, no known writer in his time stated that music was 'buried' and needed a rebirth. The regular appearance of musical innovations was, of course, taken for granted in specialized circles, as is shown by titles such as *Ars nova*, *Ars nove musice*, or *Musica nova*, which were casually applied to the latest descriptions of mensural rhythm, and (negatively) by the anti-innovation bull concerning church music issued by Pope John XXII in 1324–5.[16] There are similar uses of the term 'new' in contemporary literature, as with Dante's collection *Vita nuova*, or his characterization of a *dolce stil novo* in poetry. In painting, the tale how Cimabue's fame was eclipsed by the innovations of Giotto was told by Dante himself in the *Purgatorio*; it was taken up by many later writers.[17] Boccaccio and Villani also mention musicians, including Francesco Landini, but do not place music in a historiographical framework. Something like a historical perspective is occasionally found, however, in contemporary French treatises on motet composition, which distinguish between the achievements of successive generations of composers. The Dutchman Johannes Boen claimed that musical performance was reaching ever greater perfection, and that the progress of music since the days of Pythagoras, as well as the present differences between national performance styles, predicted further progress

door relief by Filarete at St Peter's, Rome, refers to another event celebrated by Dufay's music: the meeting of Pope Eugenius IV and King Sigismund in 1434, for which the motet *Supremum est mortalibus bonum* was written. See David Fallows, *Dufay* (rev. edn., London, 1987), 34.

[15] See Frank D'Accone, 'The Singers of San Giovanni in Florence during the Fifteenth Century', *JAMS* 14 (1961), 307–58; id., 'Music and Musicians at Santa Maria del Fiore in the Early Quattrocento', in *Scritti in onore di Luigi Ronga* (Milan, 1973), 99–126.

[16] Sarah Fuller, 'A Phantom Treatise of the Fifteenth Century? The *Ars Nova*', *Journal of Musicology*, 6 (1985), 23–50; Kurt von Fischer, 'Der Begriff des "Neuen" in der Musik von der Ars Nova bis zur Gegenwart', in *Report of the Eighth Congress of the IMS, New York, 1961*, 2 vols. (Kassel, 1961), i. 184–95; Strohm, *Rise*, 34–5.

[17] For Villani's (T. 1) and Boccaccio's comments on Cimabue and Dante's *Purgatorio*, see Panofsky, *Renaissance*, 12–15; Buck, 'Über die Beziehungen', 245–6.

in musical 'subtlety'.[18] Boen, who studied at the University of Paris a generation before Nicolas de Clamanges, may be just another adherent of the classical theory of the gradual and necessary evolution of art towards perfection. But since his view reflects the music of his time, its capability and achievement of renewal, there is a question whether he represents an early 'Renaissance' historiography of musical development. If so, this historiography would be a French, evolutionist one.

COMMON HISTORY AND THE SYSTEM OF THE ARTS

Early Renaissance humanists almost habitually supported their stories of decline and rebirth of classical eloquence with evidence taken from other arts and disciplines. They came to believe, in the words of E. H. Gombrich, 'that the state of eloquence and the state of the arts are somehow bound up and that both are an index to the greatness of an age. It is this conviction which colours the outlook of so many Renaissance humanists and still influences our view of their age.'[19] The idea of a 'sisterhood of the arts', expressed in several texts cited from Valla and Enea Silvio to Erasmus, was of course conditioned and influenced by the traditional groupings of arts and disciplines in the academic and philosophical systems. But these systems were in a process of change.

The late antique and medieval academic system of the *artes liberales* was still alive when Italian humanists developed a new grouping of *studia humanitatis* which was determined not so much by categorical characteristics as by classical precedent. Coluccio Salutati, for example, commented on the basis of Cicero and other authorities that 'the humanistic studies are connected',[20] and Gasparino Barzizza revalued Cicero's opinion that 'all the arts which concern humanity have a certain common bond and are related to each other in a kind of family relationship'.[21] Barzizza went on to emphasize the significance of this common bond for the concept of human dignity—a normative and historical rather than systematic approach to art theory. These earlier humanists confined the *studia humanitatis* to grammar,

---

[18] Strohm, *Rise*, 38–40.

[19] Gombrich, 'Renaissance Conception', 3.

[20] Richard J. Schoeck, ' "Lighting a Candle to the Place": On the Dimensions and Implications of *Imitatio* in the Renaissance', *Italian Culture*, 4 (1983) (Binghamton, 1985), 123–43 at 128.

[21] *Pro Archia poeta* 1. 2: 'Omnes artes quae ad humanitatem pertinent habent quoddam commune vinclum et quasi cognatione quadam inter se continentur'; quoted in Barzizza's *Oratio in principio quodam artium* (1407?), in *Reden und Briefe italienischer Humanisten*, ed. Karl Müllner (Vienna, 1899; new edn., B. Gerl, Munich, 1970), 57, and *Prosatori*, ed. Garin, 306; similar statements are found in Horace and Quintilian. See also Garin, *Italian Humanism*, 56; Schoeck, ' "Lighting a Candle" ', 139–40 n. 21.

rhetoric, and poetry, later admitting moral philosophy and history.[22] This grouping was particularly supported by classical authority; as Kristeller has demonstrated, classical writers did not usually include the fine arts; when music was associated by them with other arts or disciplines, it was usually with the sciences.[23]

Other humanist writers of the earlier fifteenth century went in a different direction. They reinterpreted and widened the academic system of the liberal arts itself to include moral philosophy, poetry, architecture, painting, and other creative arts among the *studia humaniora*. Leon Battista Alberti promoted painting and sculpture, showing how various fine arts and sciences, including music, were associated in their times of flowering in Antiquity (T. 2*b*: 28) and in their later decline (T. 2*a*). Although there was no classical precedent for this grouping, a well-attested link between poetry, music, and the fine arts was the concept of imitation or *mimesis* of nature.[24] It is the ability of paintings to narrate 'stories' (*historiae*) drawn from nature which allows Alberti to compare painting with poetry, redirecting the focus of Horace's formula *ut pictura poesis* (*Ars poetica* 361) to the former art.[25] Such 'bilateral' associations probably helped to transform the academic system as well, whether by bridging the trivium and the quadrivium, as in the later comparisons of rhetoric and music,[26] or by associating rhetoric or music with a 'mechanical' art, as in Alberti's famous parallels between music and architecture in *De re aedificatoria*, for which Bonnie J. Blackburn has established a classical precedent and contemporary context.[27]

Some writers must have felt that there was not only philosophical but historical evidence for the sisterhood of the arts in the simultaneous renewal of painting and literature, led by Giotto and Petrarch, which had happened in fourteenth-century Florence. I suggest that this observation, based on the experience of life in a city where a

[22] Benjamin G. Kohl, 'The Changing Concept of the *studia humanitatis* in the Early Renaissance', *Renaissance Studies*, 6 (1992), 185–209.

[23] Kristeller, 'Modern System', 166–71.

[24] Ibid. 171–2.

[25] Alberti, *On Painting and Sculpture: The Latin Texts of 'De Pictura' and 'De Statua'*, ed., with trans. and notes, Cecil Grayson (London, 1972), Book ii. 37–42; and introduction.

[26] See Brian Vickers, 'Rhetoric and the Sister Arts', in id. (ed.), *In Defence of Rhetoric* (Oxford, 1988), 340–74. On the special association of music and poetry in writings from *c.*1500, see Niemöller, 'Zum Paradigmenwechsel', and (critically) Fritz Reckow, 'Zwischen Ontologie und Rhetorik: Die Idee des *movere animos* und der Übergang vom Spätmittelalter zur frühen Neuzeit in der Musikgeschichte', in W. Haug and B. Wachinger (eds.), *Traditionswandel und Traditionsverhalten* (Tübingen, 1991), 145–78.

[27] See above, Ch. 7. Generally for Alberti's thoughts on music, see Paul-Henri Michel, *Un idéal humain au XVᵉ siècle: la pensée de Leon Battista Alberti (1404–1472)* (Paris, 1930), *passim*; Nanie Bridgman, *La Vie musicale au Quattrocento et jusqu'à la naissance du madrigal (1400–1530)* (Paris, 1964), 104–5.

variety of skills was at hand and living conditions depended on collaboration, was then conjecturally transferred to ancient civilization,
projecting also the fine arts and music into a prominent position
within the imagined classical communities. Not so much the philosophy as the rhetorical and poetic literature of the ancients, which consistently presents the fine arts and music as educated pursuits of high
social status, now permitted them to be considered as belonging to the
studia humaniora.[28]

How the fine arts and architecture came to be identified as 'Arts' in
our modern sense is another issue. The difficulties of painters or sculptors in raising their status above that of mere *mechanici* are documented throughout our period. Nevertheless, fourteenth-century
representations of various arts such as the bas-reliefs of Giotto's Florentine campanile have been interpreted as signs that these arts had
gained some public recognition, and Filippo Villani (1382) paralleled
the achievements of Giotto with those of Petrarch. By the time of
Leonardo da Vinci, the acceptance of the fine arts into the humanist
Parnassus was almost completed.[29]

References to music occur in the related testimonies of Pontano
(T. 9) and Ficino (T. 10). Both affirm the restoration of music to the
standards and the dignity which it had possessed among the ancients.
Ficino implies that music experienced the same rebirth as many other
arts. He also mentions 'singing upon the Orphic lyre' as a separate discipline; Pontano speaks only of the latter. Both writers seem to claim
that this particular type of ancient music, forgotten or decayed during
the intervening age, was being revived in their time. Pontano gives it
a background in contemporary rural music: his performer (*lyricen*) is
a man of the common folk who has trained himself to recite classical
bucolic verse in music. This fusion of the 'rebirth' idea with pastoral
nostalgia had an enormous influence on the arts of the sixteenth
century and later. Also noteworthy is Pontano's concept of *imitatio*,
which he describes as the transmission of skills from teacher to
student.

COMPETITION AND EMULATION

The subject of competition in its various forms mushrooms in humanist literature. The debate between contesting parties, the typical pro-

---

[28] On the rhetorical function ascribed to the fine arts in 14th-c. Florence, see Michael
Baxandall, *Giotto and the Orators: Humanist Observers of Painting in Italy and the Discovery of
Pictorial Composition, 1350–1450* (Oxford, 1971).

[29] See Anthony Blunt, *Artistic Theory in Italy 1450–1600* (11th, paperback edn., Oxford,
1991), 1–20 and 55–6.

fessional occupation of the orator, was a hugely significant literary mode, whether it took the form of verbal aggression in the exchange of 'invectives', or of platonic or academic dialogues between friends. Poets liked the contest between allegorical figures such as Fortune and Misfortune (Petrarch) or Fortune and Virtue (Le Franc: see below). An important stimulus for competition was regional pride, as often found in Florentine writers (Villani, Alberti, Ficino, and others). And, ever since Petrarch had hailed *Italia* as a nation overarching the various cities and territories, national competition was rife at least with the French. Lorenzo Valla, in the prefatory oration of his *De elegantiis linguae latinae*, addresses his readers/listeners as 'Quirites' (ancient Roman citizens) and challenges them to throw off Gallic domination in political matters as well as in literature.[30] Enea Silvio Piccolomini (T. 4*a*) invites the Germans to follow the Italian example in the renewal of eloquence and the arts. Antonio Manetti condemns the political domination of Italy by the Northerners during the dark ages, identifying medieval architecture with 'modi Tedeschi' (T. 8).[31] Some of these identifications of art and literature with national interests were perhaps paralleled by the competitive relationships then emerging in European trade and industry.

There was competition and emulation also between the disciplines, and between the moderns and the ancients. The most fundamental competition, which extended well beyond this period, was that between philosophy and rhetoric for a leading position in the humanities.[32] The climate of rivalry intensified as time went on; the criteria changed too. For example, Alberti's *De pictura* of 1436 attempted to demonstrate the dignity of painting not with its superiority over other disciplines but with examples of its high social status in classical Antiquity and its significance in modern life; but Leonardo da Vinci, in comparing painting, poetry, and music, argued on aesthetic and philosophical grounds for the superiority of painting.[33]

---

[30] Valla, *Elegantiarum linguae latinae libri sex* (Lyons: Seb. Gryphius, 1544), i. 9–10. Valla refers to the political rivalry which then (*c.*1435–44) concerned both the heritage of the Roman Empire and the leadership of the Church.

[31] An anthology of further examples is in Vasoli, 'Umanesimo', 25–7.

[32] See Eugenio Garin, 'Rhetorica e "studia humanitatis" nella cultura del Quattrocento', in Brian Vickers (ed.), *Rhetoric Revalued: Papers from the International Society for the History of Rhetoric* (Medieval & Renaissance Texts & Studies, 19; Binghamton, NY, 1982), 225–39 and other contributions on 'Rhetoric and Philosophy' in the same volume, 201–81.

[33] In his *Libro della Pittura*; see Rudolf Kuhn, 'Lionardo's Lehre über die Grenzen der Malerei und der Musik gegen die Dichtung und die Grenzen der Malerei gegen die Musik', in N. Dubowy and S. Meyer-Eller (eds.), *Festschrift Rudolf Bockholdt zum 60. Geburtstag* (Pfaffenhofen, 1990), 65–79.

Personal or national fame was locked into a 'dialectic' relationship with the rhetorical precept of *imitatio*.[34] The assessment of literary works and the construction of narrative histories relied on notions such as the imitative transfer of an idea or technique from one author to another, or from one country to another. In practice, the imitation of forerunners and teachers, and indeed of the classical world, was tied to the principles of education and moral formation. Humanists pondered whether imitation of Antiquity was harmful to personal fame and originality (a criterion welcome to them); they had to decide whether to reiterate actual procedures or styles used by the ancients, or merely to aim at restoring perceived classical standards. Especially in painting and music, the recovery of ancient precedent amounted at first to little more than certain uses of terminology, while the model of the ancients served as a critical yardstick for entirely contemporary debates.[35]

For the early Renaissance humanists, the distinction between rebirth and novelty was more a matter of emphasis, as long as the claim of medieval antecedents was rejected. When Villani characterized Giotto as 'superior to the ancients in knowledge and talent' (T. 1),[36] it does not seem that he suggested a rivalry: his praise was simply hyperbolic. Likewise, Alberti's seemingly anti-classicist statement that Florentine artists of his time had 'found unheard-of arts and sciences without any teachers or models' must be read in context.[37] Alberti contrasts the abundance of visual models and instruction which had been available to artists in classical times with the poor situation in which his contemporaries had to operate. Thus he is, of course, a 'revivalist'. It is only in the later fifteenth century that stronger denials of ancient precedence were heard. Among them was Alamanno Rinuccini's dismissal of those who 'decried the manners of their own time' (T. 6); Marsilio Ficino's description of his own century as a 'Golden Age' (T. 10) similarly affirms standards achieved only recently. It is probably no coincidence that the first musician to join the debate, Johannes Tinctoris, came forward at the historical moment when the view of Rinuccini and Ficino had begun to dominate. It is also significant that he came from France.

[34] The role of *imitatio* for literature and art of the Renaissance has been extensively discussed. A summary is in Schoeck, '"Lighting a Candle"'.

[35] The tension between imitation and innovation later engendered the notorious battles between 'the ancients and the moderns' in European culture. See Kristeller, 'Modern System', 193–6; Gombrich, 'Renaissance Conception', 140 n. 2; Schoeck, '"Lighting a Candle"', 130–1.

[36] 'Knowledge and talent' (*arte e ingegno*), used twice in this statement, are a rhetorician's main qualities. Already in 1396 Pier Paolo Vergerio had proposed Giotto as a model to be imitated by contemporary painters: see Panofsky, *Renaissance*, 13 n. 2.

[37] '. . . se noi sanza preceptori, sanza exemplo alchuno truoviamo arti et scientie non udite et mai vedute.' *On Painting*, 33.

THE STATUS OF MUSIC

Musica was an uncontroversial subject matter for erudite discussions as far as its moral, philosophical, or performative aspects were concerned. These 'timeless qualities' of music were perceived to be the same as they had been in the ancient world. Lorenzo Valla, for example, in his *De voluptate et vero bono* (1431), praises the appeal of music's pleasures to an Epicurean mind.[38] A mythological platform where *musica* conversed with other disciplines was the panel of the nine Muses—an evocative symbol of the sisterhood of the arts.[39] Another strong tradition, ancient as well as medieval, concerned the mythical figures of Orpheus or Timotheus. The musical bard at the dinner table of the great ones was a motif often chosen by writers and artists; Pontano's *lyricen* is such a bard. These figures usually symbolized the power of music over the soul.[40]

The academic status of music was more ambiguous, despite or perhaps because of its established place among the liberal arts. *Musica* as an academic discipline was fostered by some humanists, for example Pope Nicholas V, who in 1450 instituted a chair of music at Bologna, although it appears not to have been filled. Universities such as Padua and Pavia/Milan were centres of musical learning in the late fourteenth and early fifteenth centuries. But the great achievements of Italian philologists in the recovery of ancient music theory and aesthetics were still to come, although some of them had started to grow out of the traditional academic system.[41] University humanists often mentioned music among the liberal arts and *studia* in their inaugural

---

[38] *De voluptate et vero bono*, in Mario Dal Pra (ed.), *Antologia di testi filosofici del Quattrocento* (Milan, 1964), 22.

[39] The iconography of the nine Muses was unstable throughout Antiquity and the Middle Ages. More than one of the Muses were in turn connected to the art of sound. In a letter of 5 Nov. 1447 to Marquis Leonello d'Este, Guarino da Verona designed the iconographic programme of a painting of the nine Muses, stressing his individual choice in assigning the various functions: Euterpe is depicted as the inventor and teacher of flutes. Melpomene has invented song and vocal melody, therefore she holds a book with musical notation. Terpsichore has designed the rules of dancing and leads the boys and girls in the dance. Guarino adds two sets of 'carmina de musis' as explanatory captions for the paintings which also stress the intellectual aspect of music. Remigio Sabbadini (ed.), *Epistolario di Guarino Veronese*, 3 vols. (Venice, 1915–19), ii. 498–500 (no. 808). See also below on Martin Le Franc and the Muses.

[40] A successful contemporary representative seems to have been Binchois—if it is he who is portrayed in Van Eyck's famous 'Tymotheos' panel; see Edward E. Lowinsky, 'Jan van Eyck's *Tymotheos*: Sculptor or Musician? With an Investigation of the Autobiographic Strain in French Poetry from Ruteboeuf to Villon', *Studi musicali*, 13 (1984), 33–105, repr. in Lowinsky, *Culture*, 351–82, and Strohm, *Rise*, 191–3. Another surely was Pietrobono de Burcellis; see Nino Pirrotta, 'Music and Cultural Tendencies in 15th-Century Italy', *JAMS* 19 (1966), 127–61. Guarino da Verona even compares a humble church organist, Gioacchino da Ferrara, with Orpheus; see Enrico Peverada, 'Vita musicale nella cattedrale di Ferrara nel Quattrocento: note e documenti', *Rivista italiana di musicologia*, 15 (1980), 3–30 at 30.

[41] See Palisca, *Humanism*.

orations;[42] some of these are aesthetically perceptive, but apparently none speaks of music as a work-creating practice with its own history.

If the testimony of contemporary chroniclers and archival sources can be believed, the status of practical music in Italian society equalled that of the other arts.[43] Patrons of music began to demonstrate not their power but their musical education and taste. The founding of chapels and hiring of singers, the accumulation of repertories of polyphonic song, mass, and motet, the sponsorship of courtly and civic performers—these were grandiloquent gestures in the imagined theatre of a reborn civilization.[44] They helped transform the art at a pace that must have seemed contrary to experience and expectation. This process was independent of humanist interpretations.

Much has been made of an alleged reluctance of humanists to appreciate written polyphonic music.[45] The known evidence before the 1490s, however, unanimously suggests that humanists accepted music in all its forms, including that of written polyphonic works. Fifteenth-century examples include the Paduan circle described by Margaret Bent or the visits of foreign composers such as Arnulfus Giliardi and John Hothby to the garden academies of the Medici family.[46] Florentine polyphony under Lorenzo de' Medici was so variously connected with the pulsating social and intellectual life of the city that any attempt to separate it entirely from the pursuits of humanists would seem a futile endeavour.

The most striking aspect of this music, however, the amazing development of harmonic composition,[47] perhaps did not fit well together with the idea of a rebirth. It could be claimed that this development was centred outside Italy. Erwin Panofsky has described the relationship between the fifteenth-century renewal of the various arts in Italy

---

[42] As collected in *Reden und Briefe*, ed. Müllner; an oration (no. XVI/2, pp. 182–91) by Gregorio Tiphernas—in Paris, 1456?—is particularly explicit about *musica*.

[43] Lowinsky, 'Music . . . Viewed' proposes essentially the same evaluation.

[44] See Nanie Bridgman, 'Mécénat et musique', in *Report on the Eighth Congress of the IMS, New York, 1961*, 2 vols. (Kassel, 1961), ii. 19–30; Lewis Lockwood, 'Strategies of Musical Patronage in the Fifteenth Century: The Cappella of Ercole I d'Este', in Fenlon, *Music*, 227–48; Lewis Lockwood, *Music in Renaissance Ferrara, 1400–1505* (Cambridge, Mass., 1984); Strohm, *Rise*, 597–605.

[45] Pirrotta, 'Music and Cultural Tendencies'.

[46] See Margaret Bent, 'Humanists and Music, Music and Humanities', in *Tendenze e metodi nella ricerca musicologica: Atti del Convegno Internazionale, 27–29 settembre 1990*, ed. Raffaele Pozzi (Florence, 1995), 29–38. The Medici gardens mentioned in Strohm, *Rise*, 318, were in fact the 'Medicean Academy'. Priapus was celebrated in Tuscan musical gardens as well: see Howard M. Brown, 'A Guardian God for a Garden of Music', in Sergio Bertelli and Gloria Ramakus (eds.), *Essays Presented to Myron P. Gilmore* (Florence, 1978), ii. 371–81.

[47] On the technical aspects of this development, see Blackburn, 'On Compositional Process'.

and the Low Countries as a 'chiastic' one: in Italy, where the influence of Antiquity prevailed, architecture and decorative arts underwent 'maximal' but music 'minimal change'; the Netherlands witnessed a 'renewal without Antiquity' in which music was transformed the most and architecture the least.[48] In most histories of Renaissance culture, in fact, north-western Europe remains as peripheral to the map as music marginal to the argument.

Nevertheless, Italy contributed significantly to the development of harmonic composition as well as other forms of music.[49] But since the influence of Antiquity upon this process was originally minimal, Panofsky's formula 'renewal without Antiquity' would be quite appropriate for Italian music. As mentioned, there was no classical precedent for the conception of music as a work-creating discipline. Traditional medieval practices, for example solmization, modal chant classification, or 'Pythagorean' tuning, were not fundamentally challenged before the 1480s, when Bartolomé Ramos de Pareja published his *Musica practica*.[50] For all the achievements of Italian music, the idea of associating it with the reborn *studia humaniora*, if put forward at that time, was bound to be problematic. Could it really be demonstrated that music had been reborn along with other arts and approximately at the same time? At the least, its relationship to eloquence needed to be shown. Great creators and models in the field of music had to be identified, comparable to Homer and Virgil, or Petrarch and Giotto, or Alberti and Brunelleschi. It also had to be argued that music contributed in a significant way to civic or national glories, or to great ceremonial occasions evoking the memory of classical civilization.

TINCTORIS

Rising to this challenge, Johannes Tinctoris, in his early treatises of the 1470s, presented modern polyphonic compositions as proof of superior achievement, likening them to the literary and artistic glories of classical Antiquity. He asserted a 'rebirth' in music, to which certain European nations had contributed more than others (see T. 13–15). His initiative raises questions of motivation and purpose. Since music in all its forms had a foothold in Italian society, what was gained if it

---

[48] Panofsky, *Renaissance*, 162–8.

[49] Italian polyphony is surveyed in Strohm, *Rise*, 570–94.

[50] Johannes Gallicus (not 'Legrense' but 'Legiensis': see Ch. 7, n. 59) from Namur, who had studied with Vittorino da Feltre, attempted (*c.*1460) a comparison of the medieval tone system with the Greek system as transmitted by Boethius. He did not correctly evaluate the Greek musical system, as almost suggested in Palisca, *Humanism*, 7; a more convincing interpretation is Lowinsky, 'Music . . . Viewed'.

was also proven to have been 'reborn', and could therefore be accepted into the fold of the *studia humaniora* along with eloquence or painting? Was there really a need for a hagiographic history of musical works and great composers, such as Giorgio Vasari was to write of the painters?

Certain general motivations to integrate music into the 'rebirth' mythology can be posited. First, there might simply have been a desire for theoretical roundedness: music had to conform to the other arts. Secondly, the integration of music into the *studia humaniora* seemed to fit the idea of human dignity and of a comprehensive, balanced education. Thirdly, a hagiography of musical creators would have reflected the courtly atmosphere of competition among professionals of different arts and studies. Musicians perhaps felt the same competitive urge which still motivates musicology today: the claim that, if literature and the other arts experienced a 'Renaissance', music was entitled to have one, too. With its projection into the past and future, this abstract claim was to become a historical agent because it transformed cultural expectations.

That Johannes Tinctoris emulated humanist values is not surprising from a biographical point of view. In his position as a chaplain and secretary at the Aragonese court,[51] he was competing with some of the leading humanists of his generation, and could only benefit from having his musical profession acknowledged among the *studia humaniora*. Having acquired a familiarity with classical Latin, probably before his arrival in Italy, he wished to apply it to his own field of study. Tinctoris was one of the first *musici* to have some of his writings printed; his treatises seem to have circulated together with humanist literature, in and outside Italy. He had access to classical and humanist texts which he could emulate. Quintilian's *Institutio oratoria*, for example, was first printed in Rome in 1470;[52] Cicero's *De oratore* was printed in Italy in 1465 and 1468, in Paris in 1471. Among the modern writers, Alberti's *De pictura*, Valla's *De elegantiis linguae latinae*, and the letters of Enea Silvio Piccolomini were especially well circulated, also in France and the Low Countries.[53] Guillaume Fichet's

---

[51] For biographical matters, see Ronald Woodley, 'Iohannes Tinctoris: A Review of the Documentary Biographical Evidence', *JAMS* 34 (1981), 217–48.

[52] Cahn, 'Zur Vorgeschichte', 25. Quintilian is repeatedly mentioned in the *Liber* and the *Complexus*.

[53] On Alberti, see Cecil Grayson, 'The Text of Alberti's *De Pictura*', *Italian Studies*, 23 (1968), 71–92, and Alberti, *On Painting*, introduction. The Flemish music theorist Nicasius Weyts was familiar (1464) with the *Elegantiae* and Enea Silvio's letters: see G. G. Meersseman, OP, 'L'Épistolaire de Jean van den Veren et le début de l'humanisme en Flandre', *Humanistica Lovaniensia*, 19 (Louvain, 1970), 119–200 at 164–5, and Reinhard Strohm, *Music in Late Medieval Bruges* (rev. edn., Oxford, 1990), 44. This complex is not absorbed in Jozef IJsewijn, 'The Coming of

Rhetorica, based on a work by George of Trebizond—a student of Barzizza—was printed at the Sorbonne, and dedicated to Pope Sixtus IV, in 1471.[54] The opinions of other famous men such as Filarete, Rinuccini, or Ficino may have reached Tinctoris through connections with Florence, Rome, or Milan. He personally knew Giovanni Pontano, the Neapolitan orator, and may well have shared with him the idea of 'national' performance styles.[55] When emulating these authors, Tinctoris could follow classical and humanist traditions of praising one's own subject of study, for example by illustrating its dignity and humane effects. He did write a treatise on this subject— the *Complexus effectuum musices*—but he did not stop there.

In the proemium of the *Proportionale musices* (*c*.1472–3), in the conclusion of the *Complexus effectuum musices* (*c*.1475), and in the prologue of the *Liber de arte contrapuncti* (1477) (T. 13–15), Tinctoris attempts to demonstrate that music is a work-creating practice (*ars poetica*) with its own history and protagonists. First, he documents the appreciation and flourishing of music among the ancient Jews and Greeks, citing the names of its most famous cultivators, including philosophers, poets, and princes. (The list of Greek musicians in the *Liber de arte contrapuncti* is better informed than the two earlier lists.) The idea of such a gallery of famous specialists, and the evocation of classical civilizations fostering the arts, is shared with Alberti's *De pictura*. In the *Proportionale*, however, Tinctoris also emphasizes the esteem in which music was held by Christian authorities from Ambrose to Johannes de Muris, and describes its flourishing in the Church. This is a far cry from the usual humanist condemnations of the dark ages and their institutions. Tinctoris then applauds—but only in the earlier two treatises—the courtly and ecclesiastical cultivation of music in modern times, which fires the ambition of budding musicians and thus stimulates musical achievement. He stresses the role of music in education and its contribution to a happy life (T. 13: 3–5;

the Humanities to the Low Countries', in Heiko A. Oberman and Thomas A. Brady, Jr. (eds), *Itinerarium Italicum: The Profile of the Italian Renaissance in the Mirror of its European Transformations* (Leiden, 1975), 193–301, where the enthusiasm for Italian humanism in the Low Countries is probably underestimated.

[54] The letters of Gasparino Barzizza were printed at the Sorbonne in 1470, his *De orthographia* in 1472; see R. G. G. Mercer, *The Teaching of Gasparino Barzizza, with Special Reference to his Place in Paduan Humanism* (London, 1979), 97–8, and Franco Simone, 'Per una storia dell'umanismo francese: i tempi e i modi di un periodo storico', *Romanic Review*, 59 (1968), 174–84. Robert Gaguin's dedicatory distichs for Fichet's *Rhetorica*, and Fichet's own congratulatory address to the editor of Barzizza's letters, Johannes (Heynlin) de Lapide, are splendid eulogies of the rescue of books and *eloquentia* from darkness and decay. See Franco Simone, 'Le Moyen Âge, la Renaissance et la critique moderne', *Revue de littérature comparée*, 18 (1938), 411–35.

[55] See Ronald Woodley, 'Renaissance Music Theory as Literature: On Reading the *Proportionale musices* of Iohannes Tinctoris', *Renaissance Studies*, 1 (1987), 209–20 at 217–18.

T. 14: 161–4). The assiduous artist derives glory and riches from his expertise (T. 13: 9–11; T. 14: 165–9). These arguments closely reflect passages in *De pictura* on the educational value of art and on the status of painters (T. 2*b*: 27–9).[56] Then, the greatest modern composers are named in all three treatises (T. 13: 11; T. 14: 166; T. 15: 16), although their appearance is differently motivated.

In the *Proportionale* and the *Complexus*, Tinctoris explains, perhaps in deference to his own royal patron, the astonishing growth (*mirabile incrementum*) of music in his time with the sponsorship of princes who follow classical and biblical precedent (T. 13: 9–10; T. 14: 16). The wording recalls the formula *usu et incremento* in Nicolas de Clamanges. The achievement of the modern musicians named— all known composers—is measured in terms of successful written works, and the glory of the renewal is attributed to the competing nations, England and France. But Tinctoris does not define the development of the musical art in his time as a rebirth of Antiquity ending the dark ages. On the contrary, these ages fill his *Proportionale* with almost the same number of glorious forerunners as does Antiquity.

The idea of a previous neglect of the art appears first in the *Liber de arte contrapuncti*, of 1477 (T. 15). Here, the praise of contemporary artists is not introduced by a eulogy of princely patronage, but by a condemnation of all music older than about forty years. The implications of this often-quoted 'quantification' of the renewal can now be unravelled.

First of all, Tinctoris's date matches Alberti's and Valla's accounts of the rebirth, clearly concurring with their date of *c*.1435–44. For this reason alone, Tinctoris's rejection of older music can hardly result, as has been claimed, from an involuntary 'loss of a musical past'.[57] His date of *c*.1437 is not entirely derivative, however. It coincides with important musical circumstances which humanists had noted: Dufay's last years in Italy, his great isorhythmic motets, linked with works by Filarete and Brunelleschi, the Roman and Florentine ceremonial performances of the papal chapel, the Council of Basle, and the high point of English influence on Continental music. All these events

[56] For example, the artist may obtain 'praise, riches, and everlasting fame' (T. 2*b*, 29); 'good painters were always maintained in high esteem and honour among all' (T. 2*b*, 27). See also Blunt, *Artistic Theory*, 7 and 49.

[57] Owens, 'Music Historiography', notes progressive misunderstandings or ignorance of the musical past among Tinctoris's followers in the 16th c. and later. I cannot agree when she applies the same criticism to Tinctoris himself, giving as reasons 'lack of access to sources and difficulty in deciphering unfamiliar notations' (p. 325). Tinctoris's own report about 'incompetently composed' old songs (T. 15: 14) suggests that his view of the musical past was probably not blurred by major difficulties in reading earlier notation.

could also be imagined as the type of ceremonial occasions which had made the arts so noteworthy in Antiquity.

Secondly, the condemnation of older music, which underscores the need for a 'rebirth', reproduces the humanist topos of the 'ineptitude' or 'coarseness' of medieval arts and letters. Tinctoris proves his point with tangible, written compositions (he has 'held them in his hands', and is 'reporting what he saw and heard') and thus echoes Enea Silvio's and Villani's demonstrations of the inferiority of medieval art with extant specimens. Thirdly, when expressing bewilderment at the unknown sources of genius (T. 15: 16), the author reflects a growing Renaissance concern with artistic inspiration and genius. The notion was at home in Ficino's Platonic Academy, and it reflected classical statements about the relative weight of *ars*, *ingenium*, and, possibly, *imitatio* in the formation of the successful orator.[58] Tinctoris, abandoning his earlier admiration for a patronage-led expansion of the art (*mirabile . . . incrementum*), now adopts the extreme rhetorical pose of astonishment and total inability to explain the contrast between earlier neglect and sudden rebirth (T. 15: 15, *neque . . . satis admirare nequeo*). The formula recalls Alberti's surprise when, on arrival in Florence in 1434, he found that the sudden achievement of a Brunelleschi or Donatello belied his expectation of a languishing state of the arts. The new rhetorical figure of bewilderment (*nescio an . . . an*) also recalls Valla's *Nescio cur . . . aut . . . aut* (T. 3) and Enea Silvio's *Mirabile dictu est* (T. 4c), used in analogous contexts.

That Tinctoris imitates the linguistic forms of humanist prose is no surprise. His use of a classical Latin colloquialism—'by Hercules!'— and his frequent citations of classical authors suggest that he is addressing humanist readers in any case. For the benefit of this audience he adopts, for example, a famous Homeric expression on the effects of the Sirens' songs (T. 15: 18: 'I never hear them . . . without coming away the happier and wiser')—poignantly using these very words when describing the effects of great composers on himself.[59] What is more, Tinctoris seems to emulate the genres of Latin expository writing with his musical treatises as a whole, aspiring to compile the typical oeuvre of a grammarian and rhetorician. His earlier writings are generically comparable, for example, to the corpus of

---

[58] On divine inspiration, see Cahn, 'Zur Vorgeschichte'; Lowinsky, 'Musical Genius', in Lowinsky, *Culture*, i. 40–66. *Ars et ingenium* are mentioned by Villani (T. 1: *d'arte e d'ingegno superiore*); Alberti (T. 2b: 29: *si ingenium studio auxissent*), and Enea Silvio (T. 4b: *ingenium* is a connecting link between the arts).

[59] See Leofranc Holford-Strevens, 'Tinctoris on the Great Composers', *Plainsong and Medieval Music*, 5 (1996), 193–9.

grammatical and rhetorical works by Gasparino Barzizza (d. 1430), the Paduan teacher of early humanists, whom Bartolomeo Facio (1456), Enea Silvio, and later writers credited with the reawakening of Latin eloquence.[60] Tinctoris also knows the genre of academic orations praising the arts, mentioned above. In effect his various prefaces and epilogues praising music, and his eulogies (*encomia*) of ancient or recent musicians,[61] demonstrate not only the value of music in itself, but also how a humanist orator might deliver a eulogy of music just as well as of literature.

Ronald Woodley has argued that the proemium of the *Proportionale* is directly based on the prologue of Cicero's *De oratore* (i. 6–23),[62] both in stylistic forms (as he demonstrates with aspects of the vocabulary)[63] and in historiographic terms. For Woodley, Cicero's enquiry into the origin of rhetoric among the Greeks, and its second flourishing among the Romans, is re-created in Tinctoris's tale of English and French musical innovations. In truth, Cicero investigates why rhetoric in his own times has so few excellent representatives,[64] and narrates its traditions—which he compares with those of other arts, including music—ostensibly only to refute easy answers to this question. Also Quintilian's potted histories of rhetoric, painting, and sculpture (see above), which emphasize the rivalry between the 'Attic' and 'Asian' schools of rhetoric, may have inspired Tinctoris's story of a rivalry of nations. But the influence of Cicero's famous book on the *Proportionale* is undeniable,[65] and the attempt to write at least his preface in a style worthy of such ancestry is admitted in the conclusion of the treatise: 'This is what your Tinctoris has written about the musical proportions . . . , although he has not dyed them with the strongest rhetorical colours *except for the arguments put forward in*

---

[60] His works include *De orthographia*, *De compositione*, *De punctis*, *Lexicographia*, and letters. See Mercer, *Teaching* (n. 54 above), especially 96, and Robert Paul Sonkowsky, 'An Edition of Gasparino Barzizza's "De compositione"' (Ph.D. diss., University of North Carolina, Chapel Hill, 1958).

[61] Besides the passages quoted here, the conclusion of the *Liber de arte contrapuncti* (III. viii. 7) praises the composers Dufay, Faugues, Regis, Busnois, Okeghem, and Caron for their use of *varietas*: see Tinctoris, *Opera*, ii. 155–6.

[62] Woodley, 'Renaissance Music Theory'.

[63] The triad of music's rewards, 'honore, gloria, divitiis afficiuntur', is closer to Alberti's 'ars affert . . . laudem, divitias ac perpetuam famam' (T. 2b: 29) than to Cicero's 'sunt exposita praemia vel ad gratiam vel ad opes vel ad dignitatem'. All three authors agree, of course, that these rewards can inspire young people to study the art.

[64] A point reiterated by Alberti (T. 2a).

[65] Sentence 3 ('. . . quod teste Tullio . . . comprehenderint') quotes *De orat.* i. 10: '. . . quin omnem illarum artium paene infinitam vim et materiem scientia et cognitione comprehenderit?' Cicero claims that he who has fully studied music or grammar has also 'fully researched and understood the almost endless scale and substance of these disciplines', but that the same is not possible in oratory, as this field is even larger. See also Woodley, 'Renaissance Music Theory', 217.

the proemium' (my emphasis).[66] Another model for the proemium can be found in Guillaume Fichet's *Rhetorica*. In the British Library copy of the print (Paris, Sorbonne press, 1471), the painted dedication miniature has a caption closely resembling the dedicatory words of the *Proportionale* (although they are to some extent a cliché).[67] The first and fourth paragraphs of Tinctoris's proemium begin with the same significant conjunctions ('Quamquam' and 'Quo fit ut', respectively) as do the first two paragraphs in Fichet, who explains: 'This is why in the city of Paris, in no other respect inferior to immortal Athens, nobody has yet mastered and taught rhetorics with philosophy as did Aristotle and other Greeks.' No doubt: besides the ideas of *De oratore* and the lament of a past decline of the art, also the ambition and national pride of Nicolas de Clamanges and the Sorbonne scholars are absorbed in Tinctoris.

The *Proportionale* and the *Liber* also discuss the break of musical traditions between Antiquity and modern times, although from different viewpoints. The earlier treatise begins with an overlong explanation (T. 13: 3–4) that ancient music, despite its high status in its own age, cannot be considered a relevant tradition, since neither the performance nor the composition [*sic*] of the ancients is known at all. The Christian Church has filled this gap with a written tradition (theological tracts, sacred chant, and music theory) which is available in 'widely disseminated codices'; this is one of the preconditions for the perfection of the present age.

In the later treatise, however, the assertion that it is quite unknown how the ancients 'arranged their harmonies or composed with them' sounds more dismissive. No tears are shed over a lost tradition: Dunstaple, Dufay, and other modern composers have rescued the art, without any mediating models (cf. Alberti's formula *senza esempio alcuno*), from a previous state of ineptitude, just as Alberti and Valla did with eloquence and the fine arts. The modern composers equal not the musicians but the most famous poets of antiquity, in written compositions, exuding the typical sweetness of an excellent oration.[68] But

---

[66] 'Haec ... de proportionibus musicis ... licet eas non summis rhethoricae coloribus tinxerit praeter causas in prohemio positas, tuus Tinctoris tractavit': III. viii; see Tinctoris, *Opera*, iia. 60. A charming rhetorical 'colour' is the pun on the author's own name, 'Dyer'.

[67] Compare British Library IA. 39009, fo. 1ʳ: 'Sanctissimo patri Sixto Quarto pontifici maximo, Guillermus Fichetus minimus theologorum Parisiensium doctorum devota pedum oscula' with: 'Sacratissimo ac invictissimo principi divo Ferdinando, ..., Johannes Tinctoris, inter musicae professores suosque capellanos minimus pedum osculotenus humili atque servilem obedientiam.'

[68] Fragrance ('suavitudinem ... redolent') as a quality of eloquence is amply attested in Cicero, *Brutus*, and elsewhere. Classical precedent is also obvious in the cited letter 'Cum omnibus' by Nicolas de Clamanges (see above, n. 6), who laments that the fragrant flowers of eloquence of earlier French authors have withered ('... flores illi, qui annis felicioribus tam

their music imitates the ancients only insofar as it achieves the same praiseworthy effects on its own imitators: enjoyment, edification, admiration, imitation, and praise.

Alamanno Rinuccini's claim that this modern age can be appreciated for its own artistic achievements is therefore justified also in music. And, as Pontano describes, it is the process of *imitatio* which assures continuing success. Tinctoris's near equation of musical with literary works, and his emphasis on a written musical tradition also in the intervening times (the 'inept' old songs came to him as written copies), makes music appear just as susceptible of imitative procedures as is literature. The motive of national rivalry in the *Proportionale* is replaced by that of peaceful teacher–student relationships—the generation of Okeghem derives 'glory' from counting Dunstaple, Dufay, and Binchois as their masters. Okeghem's generation, in turn, is another model for Tinctoris. This two-tiered process of imitation follows the example of Virgil who, in imitating Homer, became himself a model.

The emphasis on *imitatio* in the latest of these texts has its problems.[69] Although the principle of *imitatio* had been endorsed by Aristotle, by the *Rhetorica ad Herennium* (then believed to be Cicero's), and to a lesser extent by Quintilian's *Institutio oratoria*, early humanists such as Alberti were not particularly emphatic about it, even when they described the rebirth of eloquence in Cicero's and Quintilian's terms. They feared to admit that many modern achievements had more direct models in the dark ages—in music, Boethius and Isidore, for example. In the *Liber de arte contrapuncti*, Tinctoris plays down the significance of these forerunners and concentrates on very recent models, so that the procedure of *imitatio* is repeated within modernity alone. Even here, he recommends not so much the imitation of a certain style as the praiseworthiness of the models and the imitative procedure itself.

Whereas Tinctoris treats music as an *ars poetica*, likening it to Homer's and Virgil's poetry, he does not compare the history of music to that of another art, in contrast to Enea Silvio's or Filarete's explicit comparisons of the arts. Tinctoris does not mention painting or architecture, nor does he reflect Alberti's warm recommendation of music

---

suaviter ibi redoluerunt suosque fructus perpererunt, iam pridem inde evanuerint . . .', cited after Cecchetti, ' "Florescere—Deflorescere" ', 146). I cannot therefore agree with a proposal that Tinctoris's use of this particular word suggests a strong link with synaesthesia as perceived by the medieval tradition: see Christopher Page, 'Reading and Reminiscence: Tinctoris on the Beauty of Music', *JAMS* 49 (1996), 1–31.

[69] Honey Meconi, 'Does *Imitatio* Exist?', *Journal of Musicology*, 12 (1994), 152–78, challenges Tinctoris's construction; see also below under 'Critique'.

in *De re aedificatoria*. Perhaps he felt encouraged by these other writers to come forward with his humanist praise of music, but did not wish to incite a direct comparison between the 'arts', fearing the effects of rivalry. It may be for a similar reason that his references to competing nations make no mention of Italy.

As is well known, Tinctoris's idea of a musical hagiography of authors and works, his praise of musical innovation, and in particular his association of music with rhetoric and poetry as an *ars poetica* had lasting effects.[70] To some extent, however, his status in music history seems to be the result of subsequent elaborations and interpretations (see also below under 'Critique').

Conversely, Tinctoris as a witness of fifteenth-century musical thought seems more isolated in his own time. To place him as a musical theorist within his own sphere is difficult: unlike John Hothby or Bartolomé Ramos, for example, he shuns direct reference to contemporary debates or to recent forerunners.[71] Nevertheless, the passages at hand do open windows on a learning process in the author, and on a wider discourse among contemporaries in the field of music. The search for this wider discourse among musicians must accompany the recognition of Tinctoris's individual humanist background.

MARTIN LE FRANC

When contemplating music in his poem *Le champion des dames* of *c*.1440–2, Martin Le Franc (*c*.1410–61) coined a few lines whose later reputation he may not have foreseen (T. 16). Music historians know him almost exclusively as the author of these few lines, but remain in the dark about the remainder of this 24,000-line epic. Moreover, *Le champion des dames* is but one of the many works by Le Franc—Latin and French, philosophical, rhetorical, and poetic—and perhaps not the most characteristic one. The musical descriptions in Book IV are

[70] In modern literature, the association of music with rhetoric is rarely dated before *c*.1500, except for unconvincing suggestions in Elders, 'Guillaume Dufay as Musical Orator', *TVNM* 31 (1981), 1–15, and id., 'Humanism'. More importantly, see Howard M. Brown, 'Emulation, Competition, and Homage: Imitation and Theories of Imitation in the Renaissance', *JAMS* 35 (1982), 217–66; Cahn, 'Zur Vorgeschichte'; Meconi, 'Does *Imitatio* Exist?'; Klaus Wolfgang Niemöller, 'Die musikalische Rhetorik und ihre Genese in Musik und Musikanschauung der Renaissance', in Heinrich Plett (ed.), *Renaissance Rhetorik* (Berlin, 1993), 285–311; id., 'Zum Paradigmenwechsel', and Reckow, 'Zwischen Ontologie und Rhetorik'. Reckow provides a noteworthy reminder of medieval links between music and rhetoric.

[71] For Tinctoris's dependence on Egidius Carlerius for his *Complexus effectuum musices*, see Egidius Carlerius and Johannes Tinctoris, *On the Dignity and the Effects of Music: Egidius Carlerius, Johannes Tinctoris, Two Fifteenth-Century Treatises*, trans. J. Donald Cullington, ed. Reinhard Strohm and J. Donald Cullington (Institute of Advanced Musical Studies Study Texts, 2; London, 1996).

believed to refer to the wedding celebrations of Louis of Savoy and Anne de Lusignan in February 1434, at Chambéry (see below). These stanzas (T. 16) have often been associated with the statements of Johannes Tinctoris on the *ars nova* and the rebirth in music, with which they appear to be partly congruent. David Fallows's critical edition and discussion of the passage clarifies its immediate context and lexicographic problems.[72] Biographic and philological research concerning Le Franc as a French poet and churchman adds contemporary and local flavour;[73] but this fascinating personality must be viewed from an even wider angle to reveal the significance of his comments about contemporary music.

Stanzas 2 and 3 of T. 16, which praise and apparently describe the *nouvelle pratique* of Dufay and Binchois, can obviously be related to Tinctoris's concept of *ars nova*. If Le Franc meant that the primary reason for Dufay's and Binchois's success was their followership (*imitatio*) of the *contenance Angloise* and especially of Dunstaple, then the scenario of an English-led renewal is the same in both authors, with the same protagonists and distribution of roles. This scenario, then, forms the most important link of a longer narrative chain in either text—a story of innovation, imitation, and emulation which extends across two generations into each author's personal reach and memory. Le Franc begins by reporting from hearsay about music datable *c*.1400 (Tapissier), then advances to matters of personal observation, and finally to experiences datable in the 1430s which are shared by his interlocutor ('Tu as ouy'). He mentions the flageolet-player Verdelet who has already died,[74] and then the blind Burgundian musicians who are alive, adding strength to his evidence as his proofs become more tangible. Tinctoris takes a similar path one generation further down the line, from Dunstaple (*c*.1380–1453) to himself. The common patch of the two stories is the renewal of music in the 1430s; the common viewpoint is the superiority of a

---

[72] Fallows, 'The *Contenance angloise*: English Influence on Continental Composers of the Fifteenth Century', *Renaissance Studies*, 1 (1987), 189–208 at 195–208; still indispensable is Charles van den Borren, *Guillaume Dufay* (Brussels, 1926), 53–4. See also Massimo Mila, *Dufay* (Turin, 1972), 21–5.

[73] Significant biographic contributions are Gaston Paris, 'Un poème inédit de Martin Le Franc', *Romania*, 16 (1887), 383–437; Arthur Piaget, *Martin Le Franc, prévôt de Lausanne* (Lausanne, 1888, repr. Caen, 1993); Max Bruchet, *Le Château de Ripaille* (Paris, 1907); Alphonse Bayot, *Martin Le Franc: 'L'Estrif de Fortune et de Vertu': Étude du manuscrit 9150 de la Bibliothèque Royale de Belgique, provenant de l'ancienne 'librairie' des Croy de Chimay* (Paris, Brussels, and New York, 1928).

[74] Jeanne Marix, *Histoire de la musique et des musiciens de la cour de Bourgogne sous le règne de Philippe le Bon (1419–1467)* (Collection d'études musicologiques, 28; Strasburg, 1939), 106 and 116, tentatively identifies him with Jean Boisard fils, 'menestrel du roy des menestrelz' serving the Comte de Richemont who in 1435 attended the congress of Arras—as did Le Franc.

living present over a not-too-distant past. Of course, Le Franc's glorious present is the 1430s, whereas for Tinctoris it has begun in the 1430s but has meanwhile lasted forty years. Both *nouvelle pratique* and *ars nova* have a pre-history on a higher temporal plane: the remote past of biblical and classical Antiquity and (only in the *Proportionale*) the Christian tradition. Le Franc imagines, after Jubal's mythical invention of music, a continuous arrival of new improvements with successive generations. These gradual improvements he describes not only in music but also in other arts and disciplines (see below). Tinctoris, by contrast, admits a change of leadership only once, and subsequently to the rebirth: from the English to the French.[75] In the terms coined above, Tinctoris is the revivalist, Le Franc the evolutionist.

Their musical interests, too, coincide only partly. Tinctoris, while praising performers, unambiguously identifies *composition* (albeit not necessarily written composition alone) as the musical practice in which the rebirth happened, and famous composers as its protagonists. Likewise, Le Franc's 'ont prins de la contenance Angloise et ensuy Dunstable' probably means that Dufay and Binchois took as their models certain compositions embodying the English countenance, not just performance manners or notational techniques. The passage occurs, in fact, in those two stanzas of the narrative which speak of composers and vocal music. Stanza 2 also says—not metaphorically—that the composers sing their own works, which is not what Tinctoris implies. The following three stanzas of *Le champion*, however, emphatically turn to the subject of musical performance, as they deal with instrumental music and harp-accompanied song, connected with Orpheus. None of these is addressed by Tinctoris. Le Franc offers a vast panorama of musical practices reinforcing his central observation: the progress of musical culture at the court of Burgundy (the poem was dedicated to Duke Philip the Good). Unfortunately, his technical vocabulary, which should tell us more about the actual music he has in mind, is difficult to unravel.[76] Perhaps it is only a rhetorical strategy that he lets the minstrels outclass the composers, demonstrating rivalry as well as imitation.

---

[75] Mila, *Dufay*, 33–4, appropriately quotes the stanza in the *Purgatorio* which says how Giotto superseded Cimabue (see also n. 17 above); but he relates this *topos* only to Tinctoris's narrative, not to Le Franc's.

[76] See Fallows, 'Contenance', 197 and 201–5. I am not convinced that the various technical terms ('frisque concordance', 'pause', 'fainte', 'muance') all denote aspects which individually underwent a change; the *nouvelle pratique* may have affected some aspects more strongly than others.

Le Franc's verses, embedded in an overlong French poem of medieval orientation,[77] seem a far cry from the music theorist's Latin rhetoric. The two authors belonged to different cultural spheres: if they shared a central thesis, it might have been shared by other contemporaries as well. But if Tinctoris copied the idea from Le Franc, his testimony may be considered worthless. Did he know *Le champion*? Fallows's suggestion that Guillaume Dufay was the common source for both writers is compatible with what we know about their respective biographies. But even if this were the case, there is a more obvious parentage between them.

The biography of Martin Le Franc should help our understanding of his views.[78] Most of his earlier life can only be reconstructed from his own remarks in *Le champion des dames*—just as the datable historical events mentioned in the narrative help to establish a *terminus post quem* for the completion of the poem itself (*c*.1440–2). Le Franc was born *c*.1410 in Aumale (Normandy). He studied in Paris, probably under Thomas de Courcelles, acquired a master's degree, and became a priest. He travelled to the Netherlands and Italy. In 1435 he attended the peace negotiations of Arras between Burgundy, France, and England. It is unknown at present just why he dedicated *Le champion des dames* to Philip the Good, except that the poem addresses the duke as a protector of the honour of ladies, as which he was officially (and undeservedly) regarded. Biographers mention an apparent lack of appreciation of *Le champion* in Burgundian circles, perhaps due to its political and moral views; the author refers to this in a prefatory poem for a later copy (Arras, 1451) of the work.[79] That Pope Felix V sent him as apostolic legate to Burgundy in 1447 suggests an appreciation at that court which was not necessarily based on his book; his second large-scale poem, *L'estrif de Fortune et de Vertu* (1447–8), was also dedicated to Philip the Good.

Le Franc is first mentioned at the court of Savoy on 11 April 1439, when a payment record attests his activity for the whole preceding year as a translator (from Latin into French and vice versa) for Duke Amadeus VIII at his new residence, the Château de Ripaille near

---

[77] Fallows, 'Contenance', 195: '*Le champion des dames* belongs to a genre of poems continuing the debate on the *Roman de la Rose* . . .'. The name of Le Franc's protagonist, Franc-Vouloir, is already found in Eustache Deschamps's poem *Le miroir de mariage*: see Piaget, *Martin Le Franc*, 56.

[78] Unless indicated otherwise, biographical data are derived from Piaget, *Martin Le Franc*.

[79] On this matter, see also Otto Cartellieri, *Am Hofe der Herzöge von Burgund* (Basle, 1928), esp. 191.

Thonon on the lake of Geneva.[80] Around this time, he also contributed
to a French translation of the Vulgate Bible for the court. On 5
November 1439, Amadeus was elected (anti-)Pope Felix V by the
Council of Basle, and he appointed Le Franc at Basle as his papal secretary and protonotary. For his chapel, the new pope borrowed at least
nine chant-books from the Sainte-Chapelle of Chambéry, which were
catalogued by Le Franc.[81] The pope's chapel singers were hired from
the Savoyard and conciliar chapels; in 1444–5 they included Robert
Guillot, Jacques Villette (de Villa), and Nicholas Merques; compositions by Merques and Villette are extant.[82]

Guillaume Dufay served the Savoy court from at least February
1434,[83] when he directed the chapel for the wedding festivities at
Chambéry—apparently mentioned by Le Franc—in the presence of
Duke Philip the Good and his large retinue, which included Binchois
and the blind minstrels Jean Cordoval and Jean Fernandes. Dufay
obtained a curateship of Versoix, near Geneva, by August 1434, but
continued for the moment to be a member of the papal chapel of
Eugenius IV. In the years 1437–9, however, he was at Basle (as dele-
gate of the Cambrai Cathedral chapter) and in Savoy; a peace treaty
signed at Berne, 3 May 1438, between Duke Amadeus' quarrelling
sons, Counts Louis and Philip, was celebrated with the performance
of Dufay's motet *Magnanimae gentis/Haec est vera fraternitas*. Martin
Le Franc, given his position at the court, could well have been asked
to write the Latin texts for the motet.

Apparently as a reward for his services to Felix V, he was made
canon of Lausanne cathedral on 6 May 1443 and provost on 24 September of the same year; from then on, historical records usually
mention him as 'prévôt de Lausanne'. He also acquired a curateship
at Andilly near Geneva, to be exchanged in 1447 for that of Saint-
Gervais in the city, and canonries at the cathedrals of Turin and
Geneva. The years 1443–7 were mostly spent in the Geneva–Lausanne
area, where the papal court usually resided. Le Franc was involved in
the negotiations which led to the honourable abdication of Felix V; he
countersigned the abdication document, dated Lausanne, 7 April
1449. The new pope, Nicholas V (the humanist Tommaso Parentu-

[80] Max Bruchet, *Le Château de Ripaille* (Paris, 1907), 375. Earlier records may be lost; but
suggestions that Le Franc had been in Savoy service, or at the Council of Basle, as early as 1431
are unlikely.

[81] Sheila Edmunds, 'The Medieval Library of Savoy', *Scriptorium*, 24 (1970), 318–27.

[82] Robert J. Bradley, 'Musique et musiciens à la cour de Félix V', in B. Andenmatten,
A. Paravicini Bagliani, and N. Pollini (eds.), *Amédée VIII—Felix V: premier duc de Savoie et
Pape (1383–1451)* (Bibliothèque historique Vaudoise, 103; Lausanne, 1992), 447–55.

[83] See Fallows, *Dufay*, 32–51; Louis Binz, *Vie religieuse et réforme ecclésiastique dans le diocèse
de Genève pendant le Grand Schisme et la crise conciliaire (1378–1450)* (Geneva, 1973), 310.

celli), continued to employ him as protonotary apostolic.[84] After the
death of Amadeus VIII in 1451, Le Franc served his son Louis I of
Savoy as *maître des requêtes*; he helped negotiate a treaty between
Duke Louis and King Charles VII of France, signed in 1452 at Le
Cleppé-en-Forez.[85] In 1452–6 Dufay was again closely linked to the
Savoy court; the composer's only surviving letter was written in 1455
or 1456 from Geneva. In 1459, Le Franc became titular abbot of the
Piedmontese abbey of Novalesa; he died on 8 November 1461.

In the years 1438–47 the focal points of his activities were the
Church Council and the papal court of Felix V—intellectual and ceremonial environments that are incompletely researched today. One of
the little-known subjects is the sacred ceremonial in which Le Franc
had to involve himself as a papal secretary.[86] Enea Silvio Piccolomini
reports in a well-known letter to Juan of Segovia that at the coronation ceremony of Felix V on 24 July 1440 in Basle the papal advocates
and secretaries had to sing responds to the chants of the cardinal cele-
brant, but did this so badly that they aroused laughter and tears in
the 50,000-strong audience. Enea admits that he, as a conciliar secretary of Felix V, contributed with his singing to the bad effect, but
excuses himself with his lack of training.[87] Even more than in ceremonies, the papal secretaries were involved in legal and political
debates over the Council and its position towards Pope Eugenius IV.
The superiority of the Council over the pope is the subject of Enea
Silvio's *Libellus dialogorum de generalis concilii auctoritate*, completed
before November 1440.[88] This virtuosic piece of prose takes the form
of a double dialogue, conducted by a pair of 'advocates'—the famous
conciliar canonists Nicholas of Cusa and Stefano Caccia of Novara—
and a pair of 'secretaries'—the poets Enea Silvio and Martin Le
Franc. They all meet in the pastoral meadows along the river Rhine
near Basle. Stefano and Nicholas argue about the authority of the

[84] Barthélemy Chuet, a singer ('contre') in the Savoy chapel and ducal councillor, 1444–62 (see
Marie-Thérèse Bouquet, 'La cappella musicale dei duchi di Savoia dal 1450 al 1500', *Rivista italiana di musicologia*, 3 (1968), 233–85 at 244–7), is mentioned as a protonotary of Pope Calix-
tus III (r. 1453–8) in Trier, Seminary Library, MS 44, a miscellany assembled in Flanders
c.1460–70.

[85] Édith Thomas, 'Une mission dipomatique de Martin Le Franc, prévôt de Lausanne',
Romania, 56 (1930), 593–5.

[86] But see Bernhard Schimmelpfennig, 'Zum Zeremoniell auf den Konzilien von Konstanz
und Basel', *Quellen und Forschungen aus italienischen Archiven und Bibliotheken*, 49 (1969),
273–92.

[87] The irony of the report seems to resonate with Dufay's apparently satirical composition
Iuvenis qui puellam, which may date from 1438: see Fallows, *Dufay*, 49; Ernest Trumble, 'Auto-
biographical Implications in Dufay's Song-Motet "Juvenis qui puellam"', *Revue belge de musicologie*, 42 (1988), 31–82. The author of Dufay's text is not known.

[88] *Analecta monumentorum omnis aevi Vindobonensia*, ed. Adam Franciscus Kollarius (Vienna,
1761–2), ii. 686–790.

Council (Stefano tries to persuade his German partner to return to a pro-conciliar stance), whereas the two others, hidden at first behind a bush, talk mostly about literature (Virgil, Cicero, Quintilian), history, the arts, and ultimately music. Martin admits that the chanting of hymns and psalms in church may be good for monks but that he conforms to it unwillingly, preferring to read the Bible. In contrast to Enea Silvio's weightier books on the subject of the Council, the *Libellus* focuses on a circle of colleagues and their personal interests.[89] Enea Silvio's famous correspondence confirms the triangular relationship between himself, Stefano Caccia, and Martin Le Franc. In *c.*1443 Stefano's nephew Gasparo da Caccia wrote to Enea: 'I recently composed a poem, which I called eclogue, in which I introduced Martinus Gallus Felicianus, your co-secretary, as your dialogue partner; I had in fact chosen him as my master and had got hold of him for a few days, but then he had to leave Basle in a haste with our Felix. Then I asked my uncle Stefano to adjudicate your debate. . . .'[90] Whatever the young man's poetic creation may have amounted to—a dialogue or a pastoral poem or both—it seems to have used appropriate interlocutors. We know that Le Franc composed Latin eclogues (pastoral poems in the vein of Virgil's *Bucolica*), as Guillaume Dufay had a volume of them in his possession when he died.[91]

The Savoyard orbit provided the poet with yet another range of contacts. He must have known the personal advisers of Amadeus VIII, Jean de Grolée, Provost of Montjoux, and the court chancellor Guillaume Bolomier, who is said to have been responsible for the duke's 'pontifical adventure' in 1439; the learned and ambitious Bolomier, a *homo novus*, fell victim to a conspiracy of Savoyard nobility and was executed in 1446.[92]

The famous humanist Francesco Filelfo calls Martin one of his 'first friends' in a Latin ode addressed to his son, Gian Mario. This ode may have been written in 1451, in the context of a visit of Gian Mario

---

[89] See Georg Voigt, *Enea Silvio de' Piccolomini, als Papst Pius der Zweite, und sein Zeitalter* (Berlin, 1856), i. 238–44; Cecilia M. Ady, *Pius II (Aeneas Silvius Piccolomini): The Humanist Pope* (London, 1973), 291–7.

[90] *Der Briefwechsel des Eneas Silvius Piccolomini*, ed. Rudolf Wolkan, 3 vols. (Vienna, 1909–18), i, no. 53, 150–1. Stefano Caccia was archdeacon of Turin from 1439 and vicar-general of Geneva from 1449: thus he remained in contact with Le Franc, a canon of Geneva since 1447 (Binz, *Vie religieuse*, 486). Late in life, Stefano also became chaplain of Francesco Gonzaga. Among Enea Silvio's other regular correspondents in the 1440s and 1450s, potential acquaintances of Le Franc, were the archbishop of Milan, Francesco Pizzolpasso, the Milanese court secretary Guiniforte Barzizza, son of Gasparino, the papal secretary Pietro da Noceto of Lucca, and Bishop Johannes Hinderbach of Trent.

[91] Fallows, *Dufay*, 81–2; another volume then owned by Dufay was a 'Virgil'—perhaps including the *Bucolica*.

[92] On him, see Bruchet, *Le Château de Ripaille*, 119–27 and *passim*.

Filelfo to Savoy, where he was to receive the 'couronne poétique' from Duke Louis I.[93] Perhaps this is an example not only of Italian–Savoyard cultural relations but also of another triangle of Latin poetry-writing. A further notable Italian probably known to Le Franc was Francesco Sassetti, the Florentine banker who in 1448–59 directed the Medici bank in Geneva and Lyons. He was a benefactor of Geneva Cathedral and especially of its 'Florentine chapel' ('Notre-Dame des Florentins').[94] Dufay says in his letter from Geneva mentioned above that Sassetti 'helped him in the court of Rome'. In his famous library, Sassetti had a manuscript of comedies of Terence, which had formerly belonged to Martin Le Franc. Its erased ex-libris reads 'Martinus Le Franc s[anctissi]mi d[omini] n[ostri] pape Felicis quinti secretarius prepositus Lausanen[sis]' which dates the possession in the years 1443–9. The codex (now in the Biblioteca Medicea Laurenziana, Florence) had been copied in Italy in 1436, but was in Geneva by 1442, when somebody recorded in it a visit of the King of the Romans, Frederick III, to Geneva on 23 October of that year.[95] This was a few months before Enea Silvio Piccolomini became Frederick's secretary.

Books were at the centre of Le Franc's interests.[96] We do not know which French books were in his library; notable items mentioned in *Le champion des dames* are 'the book [of poems] which [Duke Charles d'Orléans] had made in England'[97] and the poetry of Jamette de Nesson, living at the court of Charles VII, whom he praises as 'another Minerva'.[98] As for Latin works, he also owned a codex of Cicero's *Orationes* (now MS 101, University Library of Geneva). It was copied in a humanist hand in Italy, c.1436–40, and probably taken to Basle by Pietro Donato, bishop of Padua and a known patron of humanists, who was then presiding over the Council.[99] The codex may have come into Le Franc's hands at Basle. Three other extant manuscripts, copied 1436–7 for Italian humanists at Basle, must be mentioned here because their initials or frontispieces were painted by

[93] Paris, 'Un poème inédit', 399; Piaget, *Martin Le Franc*, 17–18.

[94] Binz, *Vie religieuse*, 79.

[95] Albinia de la Mare, 'The Library of Francesco Sassetti (1421–90)', in Cecil H. Clough (ed.), *Cultural Aspects of the Italian Renaissance: Essays in Honour of Paul Oskar Kristeller* (Manchester and New York, 1976), 160–201.

[96] I am not sure whether this applies to a 10th-c. codex of Ioannes Cassianus, *De institutis et regulis monachorum* (MS I. II. 13, Biblioteca Universitaria, Turin) which calls him on a fly-leaf 'administrator of this abbey of Novalesa'; see Paris, 'Un poème inédit', 399.

[97] Paris, 'Un poème inédit', 418.

[98] See Barbara L. S. Inglis, *Le Manuscrit B. N. nouv. acq. fr. 15771* (Bibliothèque du XVᵉ siècle, 48; Geneva and Paris, 1985), 48–9.

[99] Sheila Edmunds, 'Catalogue', in *Les Manuscrits enluminés des Comtes et Ducs de Savoie*, ed. Agostino Paravicini Bagliani (Turin, [1992]), 195–218 at 216.

Perronet Lamy, the court illuminator of Amadeus VIII and his son Louis I.[100] Lamy, who often worked at Ripaille, also painted the frontispiece of Le Franc's dedication manuscript of *Le champion des dames* for the court of Burgundy (now MS 9466, Bibliothèque Royale, Brussels). The poet may well have been involved in the illuminating and transfers of the other manuscripts as well. This would connect him with Italian humanist circles at Basle as early as 1436, particularly if he indeed acquired his Cicero from Pietro Donato.

In later years, Le Franc may have had some influence on the development of the court library of Savoy.[101] The *c*.20 extant illuminated codices which were completed in Savoy during his lifetime include Petrarch, *De remediis utriusque fortunae*, Boccaccio, Terence's comedies, Boethius, Flavius Vegetius, Christine de Pisan, Alain Chartier, Cicero's *Epistolae ad familiares* (apparently once owned by a Piccolomini), Lucan, and Livy; manuscripts copied after 1461 which may still reflect the interests of the former secretary are Gian Mario Filelfo's *Consolatoria* (1477), Guillaume Fichet's *Rhetorica* as well as his *Orationes* (1471), and the well-known musical chansonnier Cordiforme (*c*.1460–75).[102]

Martin Le Franc's own writings divide, as far as we know today, into four groups: translations, French poetry, Latin poetry, and Latin prose works.

The translations, among which there is a French version of St Jerome's prologue to the Bible, have apparently not been studied yet. Outside the two enormous poems, *Le champion des dames* of *c*.1440–2 and *L'estrif de Fortune et de Vertu* of *c*.1447–8, almost no French poetry is extant. A manuscript of *Le champion* also contains the 'Complainte du livre du champion des dames a maistre Martin le Franc son auteur', a sixty-stanza 'debate' in itself. A single love song,

---

[100] They are a lectionary, annotated by Pietro Donato and copied by his Paduan scribe Giovanni Monterchio at Basle in 1436; a copy, made at Basle in 1436 for Pietro Donato, of the *Notitia dignitatum Imperii Romani* (a famous historical source from late Antiquity) of which a Carolingian codex had been found in 1426 at Speyer Cathedral; and yet another copy of the *Notitia*, apparently copied for the humanist Pier Candido Decembrio in 1437—by a scribe who in 1436 also completed three further manuscripts at Basle for Archbishop Francesco Pizzolpasso of Milan. See Sheila Edmunds, 'The Missals of Felix V. and Early Savoyard illumination', *Art Bulletin*, 46 (1964), 138–40; ead., 'New Light on Bapteur and Lamy', *Atti della Accademia delle Scienze di Torino*, II classe, 102 (1967–8), 501–54; J. J. G. Alexander, 'The Illustrated Manuscripts of the *Notitia Dignitatum*', in R. Goodburn and P. Bartholomew (eds.), *Aspects of the Notitia Dignitatum: Papers . . . Oxford, 1974* (British Archeological Reprints, suppl. ser. 15, 1976), 11–24; Edmunds, 'Catalogue', 217.

[101] See Edmunds, 'Catalogue'.

[102] Did Le Franc have anything to do with manuscripts of polyphonic music? On a fragment of an English motet book (*c*.1450) in the library of Lausanne, see Martin Staehelin, 'Neue Quellen zur mehrstimmigen Musik des 15. und 16. Jahrhunderts in der Schweiz', *Schweizer Beiträge zur Musikwissenschaft*, 3 (1978), 57–83.

the rondeau 'Le jour m'est nuyt', occurs in two rather divergent versions in three contemporary manuscripts and the printed collection *Le Jardin de plaisance* (1503).[103] No musical setting—for which this kind of poem would often have been intended—is extant. *L'estrif* contains no fewer than thirty-three self-contained poems, mostly in complex forms not usually employed for music at the time.[104] A sacred poem, the strophic *oraison* 'O escarbuncle reluisant, nuit et jour sans obscurité'—with a strange thematic resemblance to the rondeau—has been published from the records of Lausanne Cathedral and of the convent of Sainte-Claire at Orbe.[105] This is, unexpectedly, the one text by Le Franc which also survives as a musical composition: two musical settings, one for three and one for four voices, are notated in the miscellaneous French manuscript Copenhagen, Ny kgl. Saml. 1848 2°.[106]

Le Franc's Latin eclogues are unfortunately lost. A useful if somewhat repellent example of his Latin versification is a 'Poème invective sur le Coran' in elegiac couplets ('In tenebras dense fumantis abissi . . .'), credibly attributed to him in a manuscript largely copied, it seems, from exemplars in the library of Duke Charles d'Orléans at Blois.[107]

The following Latin prose writings are known at present:

1. Two letters, written to Duke Amadeus VIII of Savoy and to his secretaries, respectively (discussed below).

2. [*Dialogus*] *de bono mortis* (Dialogue on the rewards of death), dedicated to Pierre Héronchel, a collaborator of Le Franc and Jean Servion, on the translation of the Bible.[108]

3. *Oratio in funere Philiberti de Ruppis habita* (Philibert de Roche, canon of Lausanne, d. before 1456).[109] This funeral oration is written

---

[103] Inglis, *Manuscrit* (n. 98 above), 40–1 and no. LVII.

[104] Harry F. Williams, 'La Poésie inédite de Martin Le Franc', in *Saggi e ricerche in memoria di Ettore Li Gotti*, iii (Centro di studi filologici e linguistici Siciliani: Bollettino, 8; Palermo, 1962), 468–78.

[105] Piaget, *Martin Le Franc*, 228; Virgile Rossel, *Histoire littéraire de la Suisse Romande dès origines à nos jours*, 2 vols. (Geneva, 1889), 85–6.

[106] See Nanie Bridgman, 'La Vie régionale française dans un manuscrit danois du début du xvie siècle', in *Arts du spectacle et histoire des idées: recueil offert en hommage à Jean Jacquot* (Tours: CESR, 1984), 193–200. The possibility that the source is somehow connected with Martin Le Franc may deserve investigation.

[107] Paris, Bibliothèque Nationale de France, MS lat. 3669; see *Catalogue général*, vi. 489–90; Pierre Champion, *La Librairie de Charles d'Orléans* (Paris, 1910), 70–1. I have not seen the full poem, which may bear comparison with the *invectivae* by Alain Chartier.

[108] Dole, Bibliothèque Municipale, MS 55–57, pp. 265–88. See Marc-René Jung, 'Rhétorique contre philosophie? Un inédit de Martin Le Franc', in B. Vickers (ed.), *Rhetoric Revalued*, 241–6 at 245 n. 2. I have not seen this text.

[109] Basle, University Library, MS A II 25, fos. 298^r–299^r; see Martin Steinmann, *Descriptions of the Medieval Manuscripts, University Library of Basle* (typescript); Max Reymond, *Les Dignitaires de l'Église Nôtre-Dame de Lausanne* (Lausanne, 1912), 431.

in an elegant Latin style. It cites, among others, Cato, Seneca, 'noster Cicero', Plato, Pliny, and figures from the *Iliad*.

4. *Sermo de dominica passionis factus in Concilio Basiliensi per M. Martinum de Francia, sacr[ae] theol[ogiae] doct[orem]*.[110] Considering the conventional diction and the ascription formula, this sermon for Passion Sunday held at the Council of Basle may be by a different author.

The only source of the two undated Latin letters is a manuscript miscellany, copied *c*.1450–70 by one humanist hand, of orations and letters by Poggio Bracciolini and the Ferrarese circle around Guarino da Verona.[111] As the only items of non-Italian provenance, Le Franc's two letters may have entered this collection through personal contacts, perhaps between an Italian humanist and the court of Savoy.

In both letters, Le Franc introduces himself as an exponent of classical learning and eloquence, such as any Italian humanist would then have done when aspiring to the role of a courtly 'orator' or ambassador. In the letter to the duke, which is headed 'De laudibus Illustrissimi gloriosissime [*sic*] que principis A. Sabaudie ducis', the poet calls himself a 'disciple of Archesilas', a Greek philosopher. He delivers a eulogy of the qualities of Duke Amadeus VIII's reign: 'peace, humanity, generosity, justice, strength, and modesty' ('pax, humanitas, liberalitas, iustitia, fortitudo, modestia'). In a postscript ('Forsitan mirabere'), the writer implores the prince: '. . . and let me be a servant among your lowest ones' ('tuorumque minimorum servum me esse velis'). This has been interpreted as a request for employment in Savoy, and would therefore be datable in 1438 or earlier. It does not belong in the same biographic context as the second letter, addressed 'to their outstanding Lordships, secretaries of the most illustrious and glorious Duke of Savoy, etc.' (T. 17). Here the writer hints in poetic language that he has visited the ducal secretaries at court—presumably in Chambéry—and has been impressed by their eloquence. One of these secretaries was the Savoyard chancellor Guillaume Bolomier (d. 1446), whose eloquence and fame the letter praises in exaggerated terms. The concluding address formula,

---

[110] Basle, University Library, MS A VII 52, fos. 2ᵛ–10ᵛ (in a group of thirty sermons, some dated in the 1430s); see Steinmann, *Descriptions*.

[111] Wolfenbüttel, Herzog August Bibliothek, Cod. Guelf. 83.25 Aug.2°, fos. 62ʳ–65ᵛ (Heinemann Cat. 2859). Both letters are copied by the main hand; each is subscribed (in red ink): 'martin le franc'. First discussed in Jung, 'Rhétorique', then by Martin Staehelin in *Musikalischer Lustgarten: Kostbare Zeugnisse der Musikgeschichte*, ed. U. Konrad, A. Roth, and M. Staehelin (Exh. cat., Herzog August Bibliothek, 1985; Wolfenbüttel, 1985), 37–8. See also Fallows, 'Contenance', 199.

'ex ripa dulcis equoris' ('from the shore of the sweet water-plain') is probably a poetic metaphor for Ripaille (lat. *Ripalia*) on the lake of Geneva. Le Franc was there in 1439 and probably other times with Amadeus VIII/Felix V. The letter makes no allusion to a request for employment; if it postdates Le Franc's appointment as ducal secretary, it may have been written in 1439 at Ripaille, but presumably not after November 1439, when Amadeus would have been mentioned as Pope.

In the introduction (1–8), Le Franc describes how his wanderings in search of true wisdom have finally led him to the true 'Pegasean' fountain of eloquence on the Helicon of Savoy,[112] comparing his earlier visits to various 'gymnasia of philosophy' with the mythical travels of Pallas Athena, Plato, Pythagoras, and 'many other philosophers'. He has written an earlier letter to the secretaries, in which he could not yet ask for a gift from their eloquence, nor say a generous farewell. Now, he requests instruction from them (9) and raises a problem of rhetorical theory (*rhetoricam iactans questionem*) to initiate a discussion (10–11). He names the major subdivisions of the art of eloquence described by Cicero, but specifically asks which of the three means by which to acquire eloquence—*ars, exercitatio*, or *imitatio*—is the most important (12). What follows is a short, well-balanced treatise on this central question of classical oratory (13–48).

Set up in this way, the discussion sought by Martin might well resemble an academic debate, for example at the humanist *studia* of Padua or Milan/Pavia under Gasparino Barzizza or his followers Francesco Filelfo and Antonio da Rho.[113] Italian humanists of this generation accepted the triad of *ars* (doctrine), *usus* or *exercitatio* (practice), and *imitatio* (imitation), endorsed mainly by the influential *Rhetorica ad Herennium*.[114] Cicero himself, Quintilian, and the Greek orators had also included *natura* (talent, genius) or even preferred it to *imitatio*. To raise a question of preference between the three elements while including *imitatio* was, therefore, a fairly explicit invitation to assess the significance of *imitatio* itself for the education of the orator. This is indeed Le Franc's main purpose, as he introduces various arguments in favour of each of the three elements *ars, exercitatio*, and *imitatio* in turn.

[112] The metaphor of the fountain of wisdom refreshing the ardent throat of the thirsty man has both a classical and a biblical ancestry.

[113] See *Reden und Briefe*, ed. Müllner, 56–9 and 164–73, respectively. Antonio da Rho (Antonius Raudensis), a pupil and successor of Gasparino at Milan, whose work *De imitatione eloquentiae* was criticized by Valla, has many references in common with Le Franc.

[114] Jung, 'Rhétorique', 244–5 and n. 9.

What is the poet's own contribution to this old question? His lists of inventors or famous representatives of poetry (18) and oratory (19) are traditional, as is the notion that their fame was based on newly invented artistic principles (*praecepta*) or modes of expression (*novos dicendi modos*). His strict analogies between oratory, painting, and music, however (22–6), imply a contemporary discourse. The arts of drawing and painting are especially used to illustrate the benefits of *exercitatio* (25), which leads to an example taken from music: just as practice is essential in painting, so the exercise of the 'vocal arteries' in many different sounds (pitches?) is more useful to musical training than when the specialists 'profusely debate' their interval proportions (26). This anti-quadrivial and anti-Pythagorean statement sounds isolated in its time, at least in the context of a learned discourse. Le Franc's criticism is twofold: he rates practice higher than theory, and he associates the art of 'sweet harmonists' (he does not say *musica*) with the mechanical, non-academic, art of painting. Some ancient examples for strenuous practice follow. That of C. Gracchus (30–1) has musical implications: whereas in Cicero's *De oratore* (3. 225) a servant's pipe (*fistula*) keeps the orator in his rhythm, it has now become an ivory horn, keeping his intonation and pitch.[115] *Imitatio* is introduced with an almost ironic-sounding remark on the model character of Cicero or Livy in recent times (34); the imitation of such authors provides any modern effort with a pleasant fragrance.[116] But the continuation quickly confirms Le Franc's high esteem for these classics (35–9). That Virgil imitated Homer to the point of borrowing his verses (40) is a topos which Tinctoris (T. 15: 18) found equally useful. The well-worn example of the imitative relationships between Phidias, Praxiteles, Zeuxis, and Apelles (43)[117] prepares the climactic passage on living composers (44). Already the language equates Dufay and Binchois with Cicero and Virgil. Dufay benefits as much from superlatives as do Cicero and the Savoy secretaries in the remainder of the letter.[118] The particular quality of sweetness is attributed to Binchois's songs, to the Muses themselves, and to Virgil's poetry.[119] Heavenly influence aligns Dufay's 'celestial harmonies' with the 'divine

---

[115] Jung, 'Rhétorique', 245 n. 3.

[116] For Tinctoris's analogous use of *redolere*, see T. 15: 17, and n. 68 above.

[117] All four are quoted together—plus Polyclitus—by Enea Silvio (T. 4*a*). The survival of originals by Phidias and Praxiteles in Rome had been asserted by Petrarch (*Fam.* 6. 2, 13): see Jung, 'Rhétorique', 245 n. 5.

[118] Dufay is called *superegregius* and *modestissimus*—cf. *eloquentissimus omnium Cicero* (33); *Ciceronem vel probatissimos* (35); *studiosissime volumina lectitavit* (39); Bolomier and the Savoy secretaries earn superlatives in (1–2), (9–11), and (45).

[119] Cf. *suavissima carmina* (44), *Musarum dulcissonis carminibus* (4), and *dulciloquentem Maronem* (36).

precepts' of Zeuxis and Apelles. The unusual term 'to make similar' (*similifacit*), a high point in this evaluation of *imitatio*, seems to say that also the models—Binchois's songs and Dufay's harmonies—are 'works' (*res factae, choses faictes*).[120] Reaching the goal of his argument,[121] Le Franc praises eloquence in the Savoy secretary Bolomier—a subject involving his partners personally (45). Already when mentioning the composers, he had migrated from ancient to contemporary examples, equating ancient and modern uses of imitation ('Also today . . .') and strengthening his case with personal, contemporary proofs just as in *Le champion des dames*. Dufay and Binchois were known to the Savoy secretaries; their functions in the rhetorical strategy of both texts are analogous.

Le Franc concludes by suggesting that *imitatio* is not the least among the three elements, precisely because it is so important also outside the art of speech (46); he rests his case with the judgement of the secretaries (47). In an afterthought, he surprisingly introduces himself (48): he hopes to imitate the Greek orator Carneades in the art of debating in favour of both sides (*in utramque partem disputasset*).[122] As Marc-René Jung suggests, the author of two major 'débats', *Le champion des dames* and *L'estrif de Fortune et de Vertu*, probably articulates a special interest here.[123] The epilogue of the letter, a general praise of eloquence, says that philosophers, geometers, and artists are frequent, but eloquent speakers are rare. This complaint is not only found in Cicero and Nicolas de Clamanges,[124] but also in Alberti's preface to *De pictura* (T. 2a), where the observation is extended to artists of all sorts. The mention of 'geometers' in Alberti's and Le Franc's texts seems directly concordant.

This Latin letter sheds much light on the 'musical stanzas' of *Le champion des dames*. It certainly demonstrates the poet's humanist

---

[120] For literature on this issue, see above, n. 5.

[121] A similar climax is found in Giannozzo Manetti's *De dignitate et excellentia hominis*; the author arrives at the subject of literature ('Sed, ut ad altiora et liberaliora ingenuarum artium monumenta ascendamus, quid de poetis . . . commemorabimus?'), having praised the works of Zeuxis, Apelles, Euphranor, the Pyramids, Praxiteles, Giotto's frescoes, and Brunelleschi's dome; see Eugenio Garin, *Filosofi italiani del Quattrocento* (Florence, 1942), 236.

[122] Le Franc's authority for this sentence, and for aspects of the letter as a whole, is perhaps Antonio da Rho with '. . . attingere perpaucorum, paene dixi nullorum est quippe qui tunc natura mirabili quadam accedente ipsa exercitatione et arte, ut ait Cicero [*ad Her.* 1. 2, 3] imitationeque in utramque partem possent de quacumque re data eleganter, ornate, graviter, copiose dicere [*De orat.* 1. 64]': *Reden und Briefe*, ed. Müllner, 168–9.

[123] Jung, 'Rhétorique', 243. According to Jung, there is no classical tradition for the statement that Carneades, banished by the Romans, still found the time to praise the city in a great farewell speech to the Senate. The story is indeed unlikely. Jung also constructs an analogy between Carneades' political situation in Rome and that of Bolomier, or Le Franc himself, at the court of Savoy.

[124] *De orat.* 1. 6–14; 1. 94. See also Jung, 'Rhétorique', 243 and n. 8.

credentials: this author is keenly interested in the classical tradition and its particular debates. There are equally strong ties between Le Franc's French poems and Italian humanism—from the use of Boccaccio's *De claris mulieribus* in *Le champion des dames* and the emphatic reliance of *L'estrif de Fortune et de Vertu* on Petrarch's *De remediis utriusque fortunae* to small but striking concordances of his thoughts with current humanist literature.[125]

Le Franc's arguments in *Le champion* (T. 16) and the Latin letter (T. 17) are perfectly congruent. Both times, he attempts to show that progress in art or eloquence is made possible by imitation and emulation, and that this principle operates analogously in more than one discipline, whether rhetoric, painting, or some other art. His assertion 'From the ancients we got art, practice, and modelling' ('Car des anciens nous avons / L'art, l'experience et l'espreuve': T. 16, stanza 0) indeed refers to the three rhetorical elements *ars*, *exercitatio*, and *imitatio*. The poet arrives at this subject in the following way. Earlier in Book IV of *Le champion*, Franc-Vouloir argues that the end of the world is near—a frequently discussed idea at the time—and tries to demonstrate this by the 'subtlety of intelligences' of his day which has produced perfection in the arts.[126] Even children nowadays seem more intelligent than their elders. Such intellectual progress is possible because Nature, in her wisdom, knows that no one individual will live too long. But there is also another reason: the triad of doctrine, practice, and imitation, inherited from the ancients. The history of musical techniques follows in stanzas 1–6 (starting with music's inventor Jubal), as the first example of the development of an art. The last two lines of stanza 1 draw an explicit analogy with rhetoric. After the extended musical passage, the author cites the mechanical arts of painting, manuscript illumination, lace-making, tapestry, 'pleterie',

---

[125] For Boccaccio, see Anna Slerca, 'L'utilizzazione del "De claris mulieribus" in due testi della "querelle des femmes": il "Champion des Dames" di Martin Le Franc (1440) e il "Jugement poetic de l'honneur femenin" di Jean Bouchet (1538)', in Dario Cecchetti *et al.* (eds.), *L'Aube de la Renaissance* (Geneva, 1991), 47–65. For Petrarch, see Oskar Roth, 'Martin Le Franc et le "De remediis" de Petrarque', *Studi francesi*, 15 (1971), 401–19; Pierre-Yves Badel, 'Le Débat', in Daniel Poirion (ed.), *La Littérature française aux XIV*^e *et XV*^e *siècles* (Heidelberg, 1988), 55–110 at 107–8. As for other points of contact, Le Franc's version of the myth of Hercules and the two ladies in *L'estrif* (127–8) shares, according to Roth, unique details with two letters written by Enea Silvio Piccolomini in Nov.–Dec. 1442. The episode is prominent in Philostratus' *Vita Apollonii Tyanei*, translated by Rinuccini in 1473 (see T. 6). *Le champion* deserves further thematic investigation; the poet's fondness for mythical women (nymphs, Sibyls, and especially Muses, who are more musical in *Le champion* than elsewhere) is demonstrated in Françoise Joukovsky-Micha, *Poésie et mythologie du XVI*^e *siècle* (Paris, 1969), *passim*. The same author states that Le Franc is the only French medieval writer who mentions the Greek singer Arion: see Françoise Joukovsky, *Orphée et ses disciples dans la poésie française et néo-latine du XV*^e *siècle* (Geneva, 1976), 116.

[126] 'Le champion evince et declare que la legierete des engins de maintenant argue la fin du monde. et sur ce parle de la perfection des arts presentes.'

and military techniques as well as sciences and theology, before arriving at a long section on literature, thus observing the same order as in his letter.[127]

Le Franc seems to focus on three interrelated issues. The first is the question of human progress within a world which, in his theocentric view, has to come to an end. He rejects apparently fashionable legends of human longevity or even immortality—but equally the fear that modern lives are getting shorter. These themes were familiar to humanists. Alberti, in the preface to *De pictura*, had admitted his fear that Nature had grown tired and was no longer producing the same giants of intellect as in Antiquity—until the experience of the 'rebirth' changed his view. Alamanno Rinuccini optimistically claimed that lives were not getting shorter and that there was progress in the arts. This problem was related to the Hippocratean formula *ars longa, vita brevis*, and thus to the concepts of imitation and emulation.[128] For Le Franc, the general brevity of life and subservience to Nature and God's will counteracts any excesses of cumulative progress. His second concern is the question of the wellsprings of great works. *Ars, exercitatio, imitatio* are constantly challenged by the Platonic notion of *natura, ingenium*, or 'genius', possibly implying divine inspiration.[129] Le Franc meets this challenge by assessing the contribution of 'l'engin', *ingenium*, to artistic progress. The inherited gifts observed in children are for him precious evidence in this regard. Thirdly, he firmly believes in a common history of the arts. 'Mechanical' and quadrivial disciplines are for him analogous to eloquence and history. He enjoys drawing various arts into the discourse; his view of music is that of a practical, creative art of composers and performers—'works' are explicitly mentioned in the Latin letter. The 'nouvelles pratiques' of all these arts, and not only of music, arise from know-how, practice, and imitation, not from a beginning *ex nihilo*.

David Fallows rightly says that Tinctoris 'would scarcely have accepted Martin Le Franc's views on the evolution of musical history'.[130] But the difference between their views is more one of philosophical attitude than of musical judgement, and it is enhanced by the temporal distance between them. Le Franc, like Clamanges, was still responsive to the forerunners, accepting an evolution by *usus et incrementum*. Tinctoris makes it a *mirabile incrementum*, then

---

[127] The court of Burgundy is not identified as the home of these other arts; but there is a reference to the tapestries of Arras.

[128] Gombrich, 'Renaissance Conception', 2–4. See also above, n. 10.

[129] See above, n. 58.

[130] Fallows, 'Contenance', 198.

drops the medieval ancestors, and in 1477 rejects older music. If we subtract these more aggressive views, which are possibly influenced by Rinuccini, Ficino, or Pontano, Tinctoris continues Le Franc's narrative of a musical renewal, largely relying on the same humanist models.

The background of Le Franc's story about a 'nouvelle pratique' is, in my reconstruction, a circle of humanists at the Council of Basle and the Savoy court which discussed the rebirth of the arts. Literary sources, hearsay, and matters of personal experience were brought into the debate, including, for example, recollections of the wedding of 1434. Leading participants were Enea Silvio Piccolomini and Martin Le Franc. Like other 'secretaries' at the Council and in Savoy, they were then experiencing performances of the music of Dunstaple, Dufay, Binchois, and their followers; several of these musicians were known to them personally. Given these personal relationships—the manuscript of Martin Le Franc's 'Eclogues' later found in Dufay's possession may speak volumes—it is tempting to suggest that musical creators such as Dufay himself may have been vaguely inspired by Ciceronian ideals of humanist studies and rhetoric. They may, in turn, have influenced the discourse of the 'nouvelle pratique'. The known interlocutors took different attitudes to it. For Enea, the Tuscan humanist, music probably remained a pleasurable diversion. The Frenchman and colleague of Dufay, however, admitted music to his poetic 'contest' of the work-creating arts.

A generation later, these ideas reached Tinctoris, perhaps via Guillaume Dufay himself, as Fallows has suggested. In addition, at least two other musicians qualify as transmitters: the composer Éloi d'Amerval, a Savoy chaplain in 1455–7, who later met Tinctoris at Orléans,[131] and Jacques Villette, a bachelor of law of Cambrai, singer of the Savoy court and Geneva Cathedral, who in the 1470s was employed at the court of Naples.[132] Not that a professional musician was really needed to relate this story to Tinctoris; by 1470 it may already have been commonplace in Cambrai, Paris, Tours, Blois, and Orléans. Accretions stemming from this sphere perhaps included the partisan rumour that the English had stopped developing their composition. Finally, Tinctoris took the new myth to the heart of Italian humanism. The musical *ars nova* of the fifteenth century was a French

---

[131] On him, see Paula Higgins, 'Antoine Busnois and Musical Culture in Late Fifteenth-Century France and Burgundy' (Ph.D. diss., Princeton University, 1987), 262–9; Bouquet, 'Cappella musicale', 240–1 and 283.

[132] Bouquet, 'Cappella musicale' 251, 254, 285; Allan W. Atlas, *Music at the Aragonese Court of Naples* (Cambridge, 1985), 43–4; Strohm, *Rise*, 439.

nationalist idea, sparked off by contact with Italian humanism in 'Switzerland', cultivated in France, and then reformulated in Italy under renewed humanist influence.

CRITIQUE

Our interest in the idea of a musical Renaissance looks at a musical history of 500 years with accumulated self-consciousness and through a maze of interpretations. De-mystification seems a key priority, and it ought to question not only the results but also the origins of an investigation or interest. We may well ask with Jessie Ann Owens whether the idea of a musical 'rebirth' was due to original misunderstandings, or with Ronald Woodley whether the uncovering of classical models for Tinctoris or of humanist biases in Le Franc has put their narratives in doubt.[133] But issues of understanding and credibility take on a different shape once a historical narrative has interacted with the cultural products themselves. The idea of a 'rebirth' inspired sixteenth-century and later musicians; whatever its relevance for Dufay, we are not free to ignore its influence.

Let us first question the extent of this influence. The narratives of Le Franc and Tinctoris lack several aspects that are almost automatically associated with the 'Renaissance' concept today. In their musical thinking, principles of Latin eloquence have a normative rather than descriptive function. Literary historians have observed that *imitatio* gains descriptive relevance only when we focus on stylistic norms and traditions. But when Tinctoris says that he has imitated the 'composing style' of his models (T. 15: 18), he probably refers to contrapuntal techniques only and in any case avoids a closer definition of the stylistic issues. It may be so difficult to identify the stylistic characteristics of a 'contenance Angloise' precisely because Le Franc was unable to enter into questions of style.

Le Franc's Ciceronian concept of *imitatio*—the following of great forerunners—differs from that of Alberti, who had paralleled painting and rhetoric on account of their *mimesis* of nature—the Aristotelian and Horatian concept. Neither Le Franc nor Tinctoris transfers the idea of imitating nature from rhetoric to music—a significant 'omission' when considering the later role of *mimesis* in musical aesthetics. Nor do they attempt to locate descriptive rhetorical notions (*inventio*, *dispositio*, etc., or *color*, *ornatus*, etc.) in musical works; this was begun by the next generation. Word-relatedness of

---

[133] See, respectively, Owens, 'Music Historiography', and Woodley, 'Renaissance Music Theory', 217: 'Does the existence of the rhetorical model undermine the credibility of the narrative?'

music, a sort of imitation of nature, is for modern writers almost the epitome of a 'Renaissance' style in music; it is altogether absent from Le Franc and Tinctoris, and seems to have no foothold in their thinking. There is a suspicion that word-generated music was not at all a 'Renaissance' innovation.[134]

As regards the historiographic concept of the 'rebirth', for fifteenth-century humanists it was not identical with a historical 'epoch' denoting a recurrent time-span, which is what we understand by 'Renaissance'.[135] Humanists of this generation still perceived their present state as that of an arrival, distinguished from the past by quality rather than chronology. The very feeling of closeness to Antiquity prevented—at first—an appreciation of the intervening age (the *media aetas*) as its transmitter. To conceive of the rebirth as a period among others would have required such an appreciation. Nevertheless, the relationship of this event to other historical notions needed to be reconsidered as time went on: the paradigm of progress and the momentum of stylistic modelling which the musical *ars nova* had promoted later made the musical rebirth appear as a more gradual, ongoing phenomenon. The difficulties within Tinctoris's own statements suggest that the idea of evolution, and even the appreciation of a preceding age, were tempting options for him as a musician and Frenchman. Some sixteenth-century musical commentators moved their *exempla* along with themselves in time, rarely looking back to models older than two generations.[136] This idea of a 'repeatable renewal' also coalesced with a notion of organic growth in music, not evident in Le Franc or Tinctoris and apparently first introduced by Glareanus.[137] It could be argued, furthermore, that it was a factual step beyond the *ars nova* when principles such as rhetoric and imitation began to infiltrate the sounding body of music, affecting, for example, musical form and harmony. The perception of the dark ages was

---

[134] For discussions of musical rhetoric in a descriptive sense, see above, n. 70.

[135] Schrade, 'Renaissance', 30: 'The term "Ars nova" Tinctoris introduced was not intended to be discarded after it had fulfilled a specific purpose. It embodied the belief in a lasting epoch. In contrast to any previous use of such a term, the Ars nova of Tinctoris was meant to stay, and so it did.' Despite his use of the term 'epoch', Schrade presumably intended to mean that the *ars nova* was not felt to be a period among others, but a point of arrival or a 'golden age' (Ficino's term, T. 10).

[136] On the musical theorists who followed Tinctoris with similar statements about the rebirth, see Schrade, 'Renaissance', 29–31; Lowinsky, 'Music . . . Viewed'; Owens, 'Music Historiography'; Ludwig Finscher, 'Einleitung', in *Die Musik des 15. und 16. Jahrhunderts*, ed. L. Finscher (Laaber, 1989), i. 1–21. The need for ongoing renewal is emphasized by Sebald Heyden (sig. A1ᵛ) in Owens, 'Music Historiography', 314 n. 26.

[137] Schrade, 'Renaissance', 30, cites Glareanus' (1547) concept of organic growth dialectically implying decline, but seems to underrate the contradiction between this image and Tinctoris's concept of *ars nova*.

presumably sweetened by sixteenth-century confessionalism, which proposed to revive the word-relationship of sacred chant and the legend of modal ethos.[138] On the other hand, the humanism of the Camerata and later scholars offered so many opportunities for musical 'rebirths' that it inevitably devalued the one hailed by Tinctoris. For all these reasons, the notion of a musical 'rebirth' in the early fifteenth century has not settled as well as Tinctoris the humanist may have wished—but he did set a historiographical paradigm which has become almost indispensable to Western musical writing and indeed composing.

Now for the more important issue: the validity of the interpretation itself. The writing of history is conventionally understood to imply the task of interpreting historical facts, and the fluctuation of such interpretations is thought to be an inevitable reflection of history itself. Historical critique may thus be effective as it replaces one inter- pretation with another. On this conventional assumption, the uncov- ering of a common humanist background for Le Franc and Tinctoris is an effective piece of historical critique, as it identifies their stories as more or less wilful interpretations of facts which by themselves would not have required a 'revivalist' explanation. The idea of a musical 'rebirth' is shown to be a prejudice, imposed on the actual compositions from outside. This idea does not hold up in the mirror of fact which the musical works provide; it was but an interpretation from the beginning, a discourse initiated by certain identifiable per- petrators—including perhaps the 'maker' of such music, Guillaume Dufay himself.

But are 'fact' and 'interpretation' not separated too strictly here? Only because 500 years of music-historical reception have privileged a kind of narrative which would separately identify Dufay's music with fact and Le Franc's words with interpretation, can the recognition that the 'facts' and their 'interpretations' were created by the same circle of individuals have such a sobering effect. The separation of fact and interpretation is in itself an ideology of our age; we should rather accept that the historian does not just interpret given facts, but decides in the first place what are facts and what are interpretations, distrib- uting the burden of proof as is convenient. Under this assumption, the discourse of a 'rebirth' of the arts, and the prejudicial terms 'nou- velle pratique' and 'ars nova', become heuristically equivalent to the supposed facts, works, or events of history: the mirror turns opaque again. If the historian may decide what are facts and what are

[138] But see Harold S. Powers, 'Modal Representation in Polyphonic Offertories', *EMH* 2 (1982), 43–88 at 44 and 84.

interpretations, so may the historical subject; whether we are now convinced or not that a rebirth of music happened, its perpetrators have made posterity believe it did, creating a fact/interpretation/discourse well beyond critical verifiability. History is not a real dialogue, it is a fictitious one. We cannot question our historical interlocutors, we can only question how much our own response may be influenced by what they have already said.

APPENDIX: TESTIMONIA

1. Filippo Villani, *Le vite d'uomini illustri Fiorentini* (1382), preface:[1]

... il primo fu Giovanni chiamato Cimabue, che l'antica pittura, e dal naturale già quasi smarrita e vagante, con arte e con ingegno rivocò; perocché innanzi a questo la greca e latina pittura per molti secoli avea errato, come apertamente dimostrano le figure nelle tavole nelle mura anticamente dipinte. Dopo lui fu Giotto di fama illustrissimo, non solo agli antichi pittori eguale, ma d'arte e d'ingegno superiore. Questi restituì la pittura nella dignità antica ...

The first [of the great Florentine painters] was Giovanni called Cimabue, who with knowledge and talent recaptured the ancient art of painting, which had strayed far from naturalness and had almost been lost; before him Greek and Latin painting had been vagabond for many centuries, as is shown by the figures in the wall-paintings made in those times. Giotto, after him, was of outstanding fame, and not only equal to the ancients, but superior in knowledge and talent. He restored painting to its ancient dignity ... (tr. R.S.)

2. Leon Battista Alberti, *De pictura* (Florence, 1435–6)[2]
(a) From the preface:

Io solea maravigliarmi insieme e dolermi che tante ottime e divine arti e scienze, quali per loro opere e per le istorie veggiamo copiose erano in que' vertuosissimi passati antiqui ora così siano mancate e quasi in tutto perdute: pittori, scultori, architetti, musici, ieometrici, retorici, auguri e simili nobilissimi e maravigliosi intelletti oggi si truovano rarissimi e poco da lodarli. ...
Ma poi che io dal lungo essilio in quale siamo noi Alberti invecchiati, qui fui in questa nostra sopra l'altre ornatissima patria riducto, compresi che in molti ma prima in te, Filippo, et in quel nostro amicissimo Donato, Nencio e Luca e Masaccio, essere a ogni lodata cosa ingegno da non posporli a qual sia stato antiquo e famoso in queste arti.

I used to be surprised and simultaneously saddened that so many excellent arts and sciences which flourished in those ingenious times of the past, as we can see from their works and from the historical accounts, are now gone and almost totally lost; painters, sculptors, architects, musicians, geometers,

---

[1] Cited after Weisinger, 'Renaissance Theories', 163–4.
[2] Alberti, *On Painting*, 32–3 (preface) and 62–3 (Bk. II). Alberti wrote the work in Latin, *c*.1435; in 1436 he translated it into Italian, also adding an Italian preface dedicated to Filippo Brunelleschi.

rhetoricians, augurs and similarly noble and admirable minds are found extremely seldom today, or deserve little praise ... But when I returned from the long exile in which we Albertis have grown old, and arrived in our native city, so splendid above all others, I realized that there was in many men but first of all in you, Filippo [Brunelleschi], and in our dearest friend Donato [Donatello], in Lorenzo [Ghiberti], Luca [della Robbia], and Masaccio, a genius for every praiseworthy thing, such as would have equalled whoever was famous in these arts in Antiquity. (tr. R.S.)

(b) Book II, 27–9:

27. Multa praeterea huiusmodi a scriptoribus collecta sunt, quibus aperte intelligas semper bonos pictores in summa laude et honore apud omnes fuisse versatos, ut etiam nobilissimi ac praestantissimi cives philosophique et reges non modo pictis rebus sed pingendis quoque maxime delectarentur ... Longum esset referre quot principes quotve reges huic nobilissimae arti dediti fuerint ... Sunt quidem cognatae artes eodemque ingenio pictura et sculptura nutritae.

  28. ... eoque processit res ut Paulus Aemilius caeterique non pauci Romani cives filios inter bonas artes ad bene beateque vivendum picturam edocerent. Qui mos optimus apud Graecos observabatur, ut ingenui et libere educati adolescentes, una cum litteris, geometria et musica, pingendi quoque arte instruerentur. Quin et feminis etiam haec pingendi facultas honori fuit ...

  29. Itaque voluptatem haec ars affert dum eam colas, laudem, divitias ac perpetuam famam, dum eam bene excultam feceris. Quae res cum ita sit, cum sit pictura optimum et vetustissimum ornamentum rerum, liberis digna, doctis atque indoctis grata, maiorem in modum hortor studiosos iuvenes ut, quoad liceat, picturae plurissimam operam dent. Proxime eos moneo, ... qui si ingenium studio auxissent, in laude facile conscendissent, quo in loco et divitias et voluptatem nominis accepissent.

27. Much further evidence of this kind has been collected by the writers, from which you can clearly see that good painters were always held in the highest esteem and honour by all people, so that even the highest-born and most excellent citizens, philosophers, and kings took great delight not only in pictures but in the activity of painting itself ... It would take too long to report how many princes and how many kings were devoted to this most noble of arts ... Painting and sculpture are, in any case, related arts, and nourished by the same spirit.

  28. The matter developed to the point that Aemilius Paulus and several other Roman citizens educated their children in painting, among the other fine arts leading towards a good and happy life. This excellent custom had been observed by the Greeks, where free-born and liberally educated adolescents were taught, together with letters and language, geometry, and music as well as the art of painting. Indeed the ability to paint was highly regarded in women too.

29. Therefore, this art brings enjoyment to you if you cultivate it, and praise, wealth, and everlasting fame when you have worked it out to perfection. Since this is so, and since painting is the best and loveliest ornament of material things, worthy of free people, cherished by the learned and the uneducated, I invite with greater emphasis studious youth to devote, as is possible, the greatest efforts to painting. Next, I admonish those [less successful ones] who, if they had added practice to talent, would easily have arrived amidst praise at a place where they would have obtained riches and an enjoyable reputation. (tr. R.S.)

3. Lorenzo Valla, *De elegantiis linguae latinae* (written between 1435 and 1444). From the preface:[3]

Et multae quidem sunt prudentium hominum, variaeque sententiae . . . cur illae artes quae proximae ad liberales accedunt, Pingendi, Scalpendi, Fingendi, Architectandi, aut tandiu tantoque opere degeneraverint, ac pene cum litteris ipsis demortuae fuerint, aut hoc tempore excitentur, ac reviviscant: tantusque tum bonorum artificum tum bene literatorum proventus efflorescat.

The reasons given by wise men are many and varied . . . either why those arts that are closest to the liberal arts—painting, sculpting, clay-modelling and architecture—had been for so long and so much in decline, and were, with literature itself, almost dead; or why they are being aroused and brought to life again in this time, and why such a large harvest of good artists as well as good writers is flourishing. (tr. R.S.)

4. Enea Silvio Piccolomini, later Pope Pius II (†1468).
(a) Letter to Gregor Heimburg, 31 January 1449[4]

. . . ante centum ferme annos et antea trecentis quadringentisque non invenisses qui per Italiam sermonem habuerit tersum et lucidum. Sic pingendi sculpendique accidit arti. Si ducentorum trecentorumque annorum aut sepulturas intueberis aut picturas, invenies non hominum sed monstrorum portentorumque facies. Priscis vero seculis Apellem atque Zeuxim, Polycletum, Phidiam et Praxitelem magnos fuisse comperimus . . . Sed ecce jam revixerunt sculpendi pingendique discipline! Revixit etiam eloquentia et nostro quidem seculo apud Italos maxime floret. Spero idem in Theutonia futurum . . .

One hundred years ago and three or four hundred years before that, you would not have found anyone in Italy who had a polished and clear expression. The same problem affected the art of painting and sculpting. If you regard the tombs or paintings made two or three hundred years ago, you find the faces not of humans but of monsters and supernatural beings. In early ages, on the other hand, we learn of the greatness of Apelles and Zeuxis,

---

[3] Valla, *Elegantiarum*, praefatio (Bk. I), 9; Panofsky, *Renaissance*, 16 n. 3.
[4] Cited after Piccolomini, *Briefwechsel*, ed. Wolkan, ii, no. 25, 79–80; Piccolomini, *Ausgewählte Texte*, 294–6.

Polyclitus, Phidias, and Praxiteles . . . But already the disciplines of sculpting and painting have been revived. Eloquence, too, has come alive again, and in our century at least, it flourishes, especially in Italy. I hope that the same will happen in Germany . . . (tr. R.S.)

(b) Letter to Niklaus von Wyle, Vienna, *c.* July 1452[5]

(Having congratulated him on his letter, his calligraphy, and his painting:)

. . . ingenium pictura expetit, ingenium littere exquirunt, uno eloquentia et pictura fonte prodeunt et passe sunt easdem calamitates easdemque felicitates. Olim eloquentia mirum in modum floruit, postea jacuit multis annis ab Augustino et a Jeronymo usque ad Petrarcham. Deinde extollere caput cepit et jam ita elucet, ut Ciceronis temporibus equata videatur. Sic et prisca etate, dum Romana republica in summo fuit, pictura ingens erat, deinde cecidit usque ad Jobtum, qui eam reparavit seu reformavit. Postea multi creverunt et jam in summo ars est, ut surgere et cadere cum eloquentia pictura videatur.

Painting requires natural ability, and so does literature; eloquence and painting originate from the same wellsprings and have undergone the same adversities and times of happiness. At one time, eloquence blossomed marvellously; thereafter it was depressed for a long period lasting from Augustine and Jerome to Petrarch. Finally, it began to raise its head, and is already so illustrious that it might seem to have reached the standard of Cicero's times. Similarly, painting was great in early times, when the Roman Republic was at its peak, but afterwards it declined until Giotto, who healed and reformed it. Since then, many [painters] have grown up and now the art is at a peak, so that painting seems to rise and decline together with eloquence. (tr. R.S.)

(c) *Opera* (Basle, 1571), 646, no. CXIX[6]

Amant se artes hae [eloquentia ac pictura] ad invicem. Ingenium pictura expetit, ingenium eloquentia cupit, non vulgare, sed altum et summum. Mirabile dictu est, dum viguit eloquentia, viguit pictura, sicut Demosthenis et Ciceronis tempora docent. Postquam cecidit facundia, iacuit et pictura. Cum illa revixit, haec quoque caput extulit. Videmus picturas ducentorum annorum nulla prorsus arte politas. Scripta illius aetatis rudia erant, inepta, incompta. Post Petrarcham emerserunt literae; post Iotum surrexere pictorum manus; utramque ad summam iam videmus artem pervenisse.

These arts love one another with mutual affection. A mental gift, and not a low but a high or supreme one, is required by eloquence as well as painting. Wonderful to tell, as long as eloquence flourished, painting

---

[5] Piccolomini, *Der Briefwechsel*, ed. Wolkan, iii, no. 47; Piccolomini, *Ausgewählte Texte*, ed. Widmer, 298.

[6] Piccolomini, *Der Briefwechsel*, ed. Wolkan, ii, no. 100. Some of this narrative is based on Boccaccio: see Panofsky, *Renaissance*, 15–17 and n. 1; Buck, 'Über die Beziehungen', 246.

flourished, as can be learned from the times of Demosthenes and Cicero. When the former revived, the latter also raised its head. Pictures produced two hundred years ago were not refined, as we can see, by any art; what was written at that time is [equally] crude, inept, unpolished. After Petrarch, letters re-emerged; after Giotto, the hands of the painters were raised once more. Now we can see that both these arts have reached perfection. (tr. Panofsky)

5. Antonio Averlino detto il Filarete, *Treatise on Architecture* (*c.*1460–4)[7]
(On architectural customs and tastes introduced by the *tedeschi* and *francesi:*)

Come le lettere mancarono in Ytalia, cioè che s'ingrossorono nel dire e nel latino, e venne una grossezza, che se non fusse da cinquanta o forse sessanta anni in qua, che si sono asottigliati et isvegliati gl'ingegni. Egli era, come ò detto, una grossa cosa; e cosi è stata questa arte.

Just as letters declined in Italy, that is to say, as people became gross in their speech and in their [use of] Latin, and general coarseness ensued (so that it is not until fifty or perhaps sixty years ago that minds came to be resubtilized and awakened). That general use [of language] was, as I said, a coarse thing, and so was this art [of architecture]. (tr. Panofsky, rev. R.S.)

6. Alamanno Rinuccini, dedicatory letter to Federigo da Montefeltro, for his translation of Philostratus' *Vita Apollonii Tyanei* (1473)[8]

... Cogitanti mihi saepenumero, generosissime princeps Federice, et aetatis nostrae viros cum veteribus conferenti, eorum opinio perabsurda videri solet, qui veterum quaeque dicta factave pro maximis celebrantes, non satis digne ea laudari posse arbitrantur, nisi temporum suorum mores accusent, ingenia damnent, homines deprimant, infortunium denique suum deplorent quod hoc seculo nasci contigerit ...

Mihi vero contra gloriari interdum libet qui hac aetate nasci contigerit, quae viros paene innumerabiles tulit, ita variis artium et disciplinarum generibus excellentes, ut putem etiam cum veteribus comparandos.

Whenever I have looked at the men of our own age and compared them with those of the past—my most generous Prince Federigo—I have always found the opinion of those utterly absurd who think they can never adequately praise the exploits and the wisdom of the ancients unless they decry the manners of their own time, condemn its talents, belittle its men and deplore their misfortune which made them be born in this century ...

As for me, I sometimes like to glory in the fact that I was born in this age, which produced countless numbers of men who so excelled in several

[7] Antonio Averlino detto il Filarete, *Traktat über die Baukunst*, ed. W. von Oettingen (Quellenschriften für Kunstgeschichte, NS 3; Vienna, 1890), ix. 291 and xiii. 428. See also Panofsky, *Renaissance*, 22–3 and n. 3.

[8] Alamanno Rinuccini, *Lettere ed orazioni*, ed. Vito R. Giustiniani (Florence, 1953), 104–6; Gombrich, 'Renaissance Conception', 1–2 and 139–40; Vito R. Giustiniani, *Alamanno Rinuccini 1426–1499* (Cologne and Graz, 1965), 198–203.

arts and pursuits that they may well bear comparison with the ancients. (tr. Gombrich)

7. Vespasiano da Bisticci, *Le vite d'uomini illustri fiorentini* (c.1475)[9]
(Vespasiano says that Latin had been dead and buried for 1,000 years, but was then revived by Brother Ambrogio [Traversari] and Leonardo [Bruni] Aretino, favouring the period c.1420–40 in preference to that of Petrarch.)

8. Antonio di Tuccio Manetti, *The Life of Filippo Brunelleschi* (c.1480?)[10]
(Manetti states that Gothic architecture, 'modi Tedeschi', lasted until the time of Filippo Brunelleschi, 'durarono insino al secholo nostro al tempo di Filippo'.)

9. Giovanni Pontano, *Dialogus Antonius* (Naples, 1491)[11]
(The guests of Antonius invite a *lyricen*—'lyre-singer'—to sing something 'worthy of this new and revived discipline' of music, and then thank him for his performance of a Latin bucolic poem:)

Plenos voluptatis nos relinquis ac bonae spei, suavissime homo; nam quanquam multum tibi aetas debet nostra, qui ex agresti illa musica sic emerseris, debituri tamen plura multo sunt posteri, si qui te volent imitari. Fore enim speramus, si quos tui similes reliqueris, uti pristinam in dignitatem excellentiamque restituatur.

You leave us full of pleasure and also of hope, you charming fellow; for although our age already owes you a great deal, since you have emerged from [your background of] rustic music in this way, the next generation will owe you much more, if anybody shall decide to imitate you. We hope that, if indeed you leave followers behind who are like yourself, it will be restored to its ancient dignity and excellence. (tr. R.S.)

10. Marsilio Ficino, Letter to Paulus van Middelburg, 13 September 1492[12]
Si quod igitur seculum appellandum nobis est aureum, illud est proculdubio tale, quod aurea passim ingenia profert. Id autem esse nostrum hoc seculum minime dubitabit, qui praeclara saeculi huius inventa considerare voluerit. Hoc enim seculum tanquam aureum, liberales disciplinas ferme iam extinctas reducit in lucem, grammaticam, poësim, oratoriam, picturam, sculpturam, architecturam, musicam, antiquum ad Orphicam lyram carminum cantum. Idque Florentiae.

---

[9] *The Vespasiano Memoirs (Le vite d'uomini illustri fiorentini)*, ed. W. George and E. Waters (New York, 1926), 211; Weisinger, 'Renaissance Accounts', tr. as 'Die Erneuerung', 232.

[10] Antonio di Tuccio Manetti, *The Life of Brunelleschi*, ed. Howard Saalman (University Park, Pa. and London, 1970), 63.

[11] Giovanni Pontano, *Dialoge*, ed. and tr. Hermann Kiefer *et al.* (Humanistische Bibliothek II, 15; Munich, 1984), 242. I am most grateful to Dr Michael Fend for drawing my attention to this passage.

[12] *Opera omnia* (Basle, 1576), repr. ed. P. O. Kristeller (Turin, 1962), i. 944. The date of 1484, given by several authors, seems to be erroneous. See also Ferguson, *Renaissance*, 28.

If therefore we are to call any age a 'golden' one, that is without any doubt the age that produces a series of golden talents. Whoever wants to consider the outstanding innovations of our present century will have no doubt that it is indeed the one. Like a golden age, this century has returned to light the liberal disciplines which had almost been extinct: Grammar, Poetry, Oratory, Painting, Sculpture, Architecture, Music, and the ancient art of singing poems upon the Orphic lyre. [All] this happened in Florence. (tr. R.S.)

11. Erasmus of Rotterdam rarely mentions the fine arts in his writings, but in a letter to Cornelius Gerard (June 1489), he describes how the *bonae litterae* and the neighbouring arts of painting, sculpture, and architecture were raised from the grave, crediting Lorenzo Valla and Francesco Filelfo.[13] In a letter to Bonifacius Amerbach (31 August 1518), Erasmus cites the renewal of the *studia humanitatis* and 'all branches of study (under the favour of the Muses)', including medicine and jurisprudence. He suggests that a good use of Latin and the vernacular languages is the main factor in this rebirth, which began in Italy only about 'eighty years ago'.[14]

12. Albrecht Dürer, *Four Books on Human Proportions*, draft preface (1523)[15]
(Dürer says that 'the present revival', 'die itzige Wiedererwachsung', had its inception one and a half centuries ago. In a slightly later version of the preface, the revival is pushed back to 'two hundred years ago'.)

II. JOHANNES TINCTORIS ON THE REBIRTH OF MUSIC

13. Johannes Tinctoris, *Proportionale musices* (*c*.1473–4), prohemium[16]

3. Quamquam, o sapientissime rex, a tempore prothomusici Jubalis, cui Moyses tantum tribuit, ut eum in Genesi patrem canentium organis et cithara dixerit, plerique viri percelebres velut David, Ptolomeus, Epaminondas, principes Judeae, Egypti et Graeciae, Zoroastres, Pythagoras, Linus Thebeus, Zethus, Amphion, Orpheus, Museus, Socrates, Plato, Aristoteles, Aristoxenus, Timotheus, ingenuae arti musicae operam adeo dederunt, quod teste Tullio paene vim omnem ac materiam eius infinitam cogitatione comprehenderint, quo nonnullos eorum, praecipue Pythagoram, musicae primordia invenisse multi Graecorum voluerunt, 4. tamen qualiter pronunciaverint aut composuerint scripto nobis minime constat, verum elegantissime id eos fecisse verisimillimum est. 5. Summam etenim in hac scientia, quam Plato vocat potentissimam, eruditionem ponebant, itaque eam omnes antiquitus

---

[13] Erasmus, *Opus epistolarum Erasmi*, ed. P. S. Allen (Oxford, 1913), 78–80; cited after Ferguson, *Renaissance*, 43–4. See Panofsky, *Renaissance*, 17 n. 1; Weisinger, 'Renaissance Theories', 164.

[14] *Opus epistolarum Erasmi*, 383; Desiderius Erasmus, *Collected Works*, tr. R. A. B. Mynors and D. F. S. Thomson (Toronto, etc., 1982), vi. 100–2.

[15] Panofsky, *Renaissance*, 30 n. 4.

[16] Tinctoris, *Opera theoretica*, iia. 9–10 (slightly emended).

discebant, nec qui nesciebat satis excultus doctrina putabatur. . . . (T. then mentions supposed mysterious powers of music.)

8. At qui postquam plenitudo temporis advenit, quo summus ille musicus Jesus Christus, pax nostra, sub proportione dupla fecit utraque unum, in eius ecclesia miri floruere musici, ut Gregorius, Ambrosius, Augustinus, Hilarius, Boethius, Martianus, Guido, Johannes de Muris, quorum alii usum in ipsa salutari ecclesia canendi statuerunt, alii ad hoc hymnos canticaque numerosa confecerunt, alii divinitatem, alii theoricam, alii practicam huius artis, iam vulgo dispersis codicibus posteris reliquerunt. 9. Denique principes Christianissimi quorum omnium, rex piissime, animi, corporis fortunaeque donis longe primus es, cultum ampliare divinum cupientes more Davidico capellas instituerunt in quibus diversos cantores per quos diversis vocibus, non adversis, Deo nostro iocunda decoraque esset laudatio, ingentibus expensis assumpserunt. 10. Et quoniam cantores principum si liberalitate, quae claros homines facit praediti sint, honore, gloria, divitiis afficiuntur, ad hoc genus studii ferventissime multi incenduntur. 11. Quo fit ut hac tempestate facultas nostrae musices tam mirabile susceperit incrementum quod ars nova esse videatur, cuius, ut ita dicam, novae artis fons et origo apud Anglicos quorum caput Dunstaple exstitit, fuisse perhibetur, et huic contemporanei fuerunt in Gallia Dufay et Binchois, quibus immediate successerunt moderni Okeghem, Busnoys, Regis et Caron, omnium quos audiverim in compositione praestantissimi. 12. Nec eis Anglici nunc, licet vulgariter iubilare, Gallici vero cantare dicantur, veniunt conferendi, illi etenim in dies novos cantus novissime inveniunt, ac isti, quod miserrimi signum est ingenii, una semper et eadem compositione utuntur.

3. Although, wisest of kings, since the times of Jubal, the first musician (to whom Moyses, in Genesis, pays the honour of calling him the father of all those playing the organ and cithara), a host of very famous men (as for example David, Ptolemy, Epaminondas, the Judaean, Egyptian, and Greek princes, Zoroaster, Pythagoras, Linus the Theban, Zethus, Amphion, Orpheus, Museus, Socrates, Plato, Aristotle, Aristoxenus, and Timotheus) have so devoted themselves to the inspired art of music that they, as Cicero testifies, penetrated with their thoughts almost all the power and the infinite substance of it, which is why many Greeks claimed that one or the other of them, and especially Pythagoras, did originally invent music, 4. it has not at all come down to us in writing how they performed or composed, although it is most probable that they did it brilliantly. 5. For indeed they invested the highest degree of training in this science, which Plato calls the most powerful, and from ancient times on they all learned it, while somebody who ignored it was regarded as being insufficiently educated. . . .

8. But when the time had finally come that the supreme musician, our redeemer Jesus Christ, made two into one in a duple proportion, admirable musicians flourished in his Church, such as Gregory, Ambrose, Augustine,

Hilary, Boethius, Martianus, Guido, Johannes de Muris, some of whom established the use of singing in the Holy Church herself, while others composed for that purpose numerous hymns and canticles; and in widely disseminated codices, some transmitted the spiritual, others the theoretical, yet others the practical aspects of this art to posterity. 9. Finally, the Christian princes of whom you, most pious of kings, are by far the most gifted in mind, body and fortune, instituted chapels in David's manner to enhance the divine services. In these chapels they appointed, at immense cost, various singers through whose diverse but not adverse voices 'pleasurable and beautiful praises be given to our God'. 10. And since singers, if they are treated by their princes with the generosity which makes men famous, acquire honours, fame, and riches, many people are strongly incited to take up this kind of study. 11. So it happens that in this age the discipline of our music took such a marvellous development that it might seem a novel art. The wellspring and origin of this novel art, as I might call it, is believed to have been with the English whose head was Dunstaple; his contemporaries in France were Dufay and Binchois, followed on the heels by the moderns Okeghem, Busnoys, Regis and Caron—the foremost composers of all those I have heard. 12. Nor can the English now be compared with them (although it is said that they jubilate, whereas the French only sing), because the latter invent new songs in novel ways every day, whereas the former keep using the self-same manner of composition, which is a sign of an impoverished mind. (tr. R.S.)

14. Johannes Tinctoris, *Complexus effectuum musices* (*c*.1475)[17]
(The nineteenth effect:)

(161) Et quoniam olim in Graecia summa musici afficiebantur gloria . . . , (162) non modo praestantissimi viri philosophi operam illi impenderunt, ut Socrates, Pictagoras, Plato, Aristotiles, sed et bellicosissimi principes, ut Epaminondas et Achilles; (163) 'Themistoclesque, cum in epulis recusaret liram, habitus est indoctior.' (164) Immo vero et cum hoc Cicero ponit in prologo *Quaestionum Tusculanarum*: 'Discebant id omnes, nec qui nesciebat satis excultus doctrina putabatur.' (165) Nostro autem tempore experti sumus quanta plerique musici gloria sint affecti. (166) Quis enim Johannem Dunstaple, Guillelmum Dufay, Egidium Binchois, Iohannem Okeghem, Anthonium Busnois, Iohannem Regis, Firminum Caron, Iacobum Carlerii, Robertum Morton, Iacobum Obrechts non novit? (167) Quis eos summis laudibus non prosequitur, quorum compositiones per universum orbem divulgatae Dei templa, regum palatia, privatorum domos summa dulcedine replent? (168) Taceo plurimos musicos eximiis opibus dignitatibusque donatos, quoniam et si honores ex hiis adepti sunt, famae immortali quam primi compositores sibi extenderunt, minime sunt conferendi. (169) Illud enim fortunae, istud autem virtutis opus est.

---

[17] Carlerius/Tinctoris, *On the Dignity*, 60–1 and 76 (ch. 20, 159–70); Tinctoris, *Opera theoretica*, ii. 176–7 (ch. 19, 6–8).

(161) And since in Greece long ago musicians won supreme glory . . . , (162) not only did the most illustrious men of philosophy devote their attention to music, such as Socrates, Pythagoras, Plato, and Aristotle, but even the most warlike leaders, such as Epaminondas and Achilles; (163) 'and Themistocles was regarded as rather uneducated when he declined to play the lyre at a banquet'. (164) Indeed, together with this Cicero also asserts in the preface to the Tusculan Disputations: 'Everybody learned music, and anyone ignorant of it was thought educationally deficient.' (165) In our own day, though, we have observed what great glory numerous musicians have achieved. (166) For who does not know of John Dunstable, Guillaume Dufay, Gilles de Binche dit Binchois, Johannes Okeghem, Antoine Busnois, Johannes Regis, Firmin Caron, Jacobus Carlerii, Robert Morton, Jacob Obrechts? (167) Who fails to bestow the highest accolades on those whose compositions, circulated throughout the civilised world, fill God's churches, kings' palaces and private houses with supreme sweetness? (168) I pass over numerous musicians who have been granted uncommon riches and honours, since whatever prestige they have gained from these is not in the least comparable with the undying fame which the foremost composers have amassed for themselves. (169) For the former is the work of providence, the latter of excellence. (tr. J. D. Cullington)

15. Johannes Tinctoris, *Liber de arte contrapuncti* (1477), Prologus[18]
(He rejects the theory of the harmony of the spheres, quoting Aristotle, Averroes, and 'our modern philosophers':)

13. Concordantiae igitur vocum et cantuum quorum suavitate, ut inquit Lactantius, aurium voluptas percipitur, non corporibus caelestibus sed instrumentis terrenis cooperante natura conficiuntur, quibusquidem concordantiis, licet veteres etiam musici ut Plato, Pythagoras, Nicomachus, Aristoxenus, Philolaus, Archytas, Ptolomaeus ac alii numerosi, ipse quoque Boethius, operosissime incubuerint, tamen qualiter eas ordinare componereque soliti sint nobis minime notum est. 14. Et si visa auditaque referre liceat nonnulla vetusta carmina ignotae auctoritatis quae apocrypha dicuntur in manibus aliquando habui, adeo inepte, adeo insulse composita ut multo potius aures offendebant quam delectabant. 15. Neque quod satis admirare nequeo quippiam compositum nisi citra annos quadraginta extat quod auditu dignum ab eruditis existimetur. 16. Hac vero tempestate, ut praeteream innumeros concentores venustissime pronuntiantes, nescio an virtute cuiusdam caelestis influxus an vehementia assiduae exercitationis infiniti florent compositores, ut Johannes Okeghem, Johannes Regis, Anthonius Busnois, Firminus Caron, Guillermus Faugues, qui novissimis temporibus vita functos Johannem Dunstaple, Egidium Binchois, Guillermum Dufay se praeceptores habuisse in hac arte divina gloriantur. 17. Quorum omnium omnia fere opera tantam suavitudinem redolent ut, mea quidem sententia, non modo hominibus heroibusque verum etiam Diis immortalibus dignissima censenda sint. 18. Ea

[18] Tinctoris, *Opera theoretica*, ii. 12–13.

quoque profecto numquam audio, numquam considero quin laetior ac doctior evadam, unde quemadmodum Virgilius in illo opere divino *Eneidos* Homero, ita iis, Hercule, in meis opusculis utor archetypis. 19. Praesertim autem in hoc in quo, concordantias ordinando, approbabilem eorum componendi stilum plane imitatus sum.

13. The harmonies, then, of voices and songs whose sweetness, as Lactantius says, brings enjoyment to the ears, are not created by heavenly bodies but by earthly instruments, with the collaboration of Nature. And although musicians already of Antiquity such as Plato, Pythagoras, Nicomachus, Aristoxenus, Philolaus, Archytas, Ptolemy, and many others, let alone Boethius, have devoted so much effort to these harmonies, it is quite unknown to us how they arranged them and composed with them. 14. And, if it is permitted to report what I have seen and heard myself, some time ago I had in my hands a few ancient songs—of unknown authorship, or apocrypha, as they are called—that were so incompetently, so tastelessly composed that they rather offended the ears than pleased. 15. Nor is there, to my never-ending astonishment, anything composed except within the last forty years which the experts consider to be worth hearing. 16. In this age, however, even leaving aside the innumerable singers who perform so beautifully, an endless number of composers flourish (whether through some heavenly influence or through the impact of assiduous practice I do not know), for example Johannes Okeghem, Johannes Regis, Antoine Busnoys, Firmin Caron, Guillaume Faugues, who can boast that they had as their teachers in this divine art the recently deceased Johannes Dunstaple, Gilles Binchois, and Guillaume Dufay. 17. Almost all the works of all these [composers] exude such great sweetness that they should, in my opinion, be considered worthy not only of humans and heroes but of the immortal gods themselves. 18. And indeed, I never hear them, never study them without coming away the happier and wiser; therefore, just as Virgil used Homer as model in his divine work, the *Aeneid*, so do I use them, by Hercules, as models for my writings. 19. This is particularly true for the present work, where my arrangement of the harmonies is a straightforward imitation of their praiseworthy style of composition. (tr. R.S.)

III. MARTIN LE FRANC ON MUSIC AND ELOQUENCE

16. Martin Le Franc, *Le champion des dames* (*c*.1440–2), Book IV[19]

> 0. Et aussy aultre cause y treuve
> Car des anciens nous avons
> L'art l'experience et l'espreuve
> Et les choses prestes trouvons

[19] Stanza '0' after MS 9466, Bibliothèque Royale Albert Ier, Brussels, fo. 120[r]; stanzas '1–6' after Fallows, 'Contenance', 206–8.

Si n'est merveille se sçavons
Plustost ou plus qu'ils ne sçavoyent
Car encores nous adioustons
Beaucop aux choses qu'ils trouvoient.

1. Pour le temps du mauvais Cayn
Quant Jubal trouva la pratique,
En escoutant Tubalcayn,
D'acorder les sons de musique,
L'art ne fut pas sy autentique
Qu'elle est ou temps de maintenant;
Aussy ne fut la Rhetorique
Ne le parler sy avenant.

2. Tapissier, Carmen, Cesaris,
N'a pas long temps sy bien chanterent
Qu'ilz esbahirent tout Paris
Et tous ceulx qui les frequenterent;
Mais onques jour ne deschanterent
En melodie de tel chois,
Ce m'ont dit ceulx qui les hanterent,
Que G. Du Fay et Binchois.

3. Car ilz ont nouvelle pratique
De faire frisque concordance
En haulte et basse musique,
En fainte, en pause et en muance;
Et ont pris de la contenance
Angloise, et ensuy Dompstable;
Pour quoy merveilleuse plaisance
Rend leur chant joieux et notable.

4. Des bas et des haults instruments
A on joué le temps passé—
Doubter n'en fault tres doulcement—
Chacun selon son pourpensé;
Mais jamais on n'a compassé,
N'en doulchaine n'en flajolet
Ce qu'ung nagueres trespassé
Faisoit, appellé Verdelet.

5. Ne face on mention d'Orphee
Dont les poetes tant escripvent:
Ce n'est q'une droicte faffee
Au regard des harpeurs qui vivent,
Que sy parfaittement avivent
Leurs accors et leurs armonyes
Qu'il semble de fait q'ilz estrivent
Aux angeliques melodies.

6. Tu as les avugles ouy
Jouer a la court de Bourgongne
N'as pas? certainement ouy.
Fut il jamais telle besongne?
J'ay veu Binchois avoir vergongne
Et soy taire emprez leur rebelle.
Et Dufay despite et frongne
Qu'il n'a melodye sy belle.

17. Martin Le Franc, [*De eloquentia*]: Letter to the Savoy court secretaries (*c*.1439)[20]

Singularib(us) viris d(omi)nis Illustrissimi gl(ori)osissimique Sabaudie ducis etc. secretariis.
(1) Si cui mirum videatur cur vos, amplissime scientie viri, istis litteris praepediam, is primum opere perdite negligentieve accuset illum qui a fontibus faucibus aridis regreditur, atque existimet eum rusticitatis et insolentie plenum qui prudentias vestras insalutatas inhonoratasque relinquit. (2) Tum quoque iusta animadversione censebit me quem fama fulgentissima ad id loci ad elicona sacrumque pegaseumque fontem traduxit, labris illotis arentique gutture accedere non debere. (3) Sed scriptis dudum vocibus non licuit eloquentie vestre munus aliquid expetere valeque dicere generosum. (4) Pallada finxit periocundus naso eliconii montis antra lustrasse ut musarum dulcissonis carminibus oblectaretur. (5) Platonem scribit divinus Joannes itemque angelicus Aurelius egipti summa peragrasse loca. (6) Pictagoram quoque Samium venisse in oras ytalie. (7) Complures insuper magne auctoritatis et sapientie philosophos tradunt varias inisse terras ut vel aliis imbuerentur disciplinis vel moribus et ritibus novis assuescerent vel optimarum artium sanctorumque morum precepta perdocerent. (8) Ego vobis non ut qui equari velim sapientibus illis si confessus fuerim propter bonorum studiorum frugem decusque multa philosophie gymnasia visitasse non mentiar, atque postremo conscendisse ad vos ut vestre beate(?) facundie liquore proluerer non mentiar. (9) Quoniam igitur ut moris est sophistarum commovere doctissimos ad docendum novorum tironumque duces exercitus artibus imbellicis consulere pars modo mea sit. (10) Vos inter eloquentissimos rethoricam iactans quaestionem quantis vestris scriptis gravissimis ac sermonibus suavissimis disputarem! (11) Ego ipse sitibundus guttas a flumine sumam, munusculoque a vestris ditissimis thesauris accepto ditior recedam. (12) Vedendum itaque est cum noster Cicero benedicendi copiose artem quinque scilicet invencione, disposicione, elocucione, memoria, pronunciacione subsistere dixerit; easque res tribus comparari: arte, usu, imitacione, quid horum trium praeferendum putetis?
[marg.: *Ars*] (13) Arti plurimas partes tribuendum censent nonnulli, quid enim sine artis documentis effici potest? (14) ea quippe in omni re directrix

---

[20] Cod. Guelf. 83. 25 Aug. 2°, Herzog August Bibliothek, Wolfenbüttel, fos. 64ʳ–65ᵛ.

et regulatrix est agendorum. (15) qua sine convertitur ordo; posteriora
priora praecedunt, media confuse permiscentur. (16) qua vero cuncta eorum
quae fiunt manent et placent. (17) Et [fo. 64ᵛ:] cui si nil aliud preeminentiam
daret, quam quod in ea complectanda vires ingenii desudare fortius operatur,
iure potest ceteris praeferri. (18) Hinc eciam fit ut aput poetas orpheus,
museus, homerus, ysiodus, esopus celebratiores sint, quare longioribus
lucubracionibus poesis adinvenerint praecepta. (19) Quisque quoad decuit res
dicendas, aput quoque oratores laudibus digniores sunt Hermagoras,
Aristotiles, Gorgias Leontinus, noster Cicero, Quintilianus qui novos dicendi
modos expressere. (20) Atque in omnibus ita est quod qui artes educant,
mirabiliores habeantur hiis quos usus ac imitatio faciles facit in rebus
faciendis. (21) Nec supervacue addicitur quod nemo nominatur artifex nisi
fuerit artem complexus. (22) Ex quo fit ut pictorem a pictoria vocemus arte,
et scriptura scriptorem, non quare pingat ac scribat, sed quare pingendi
scribendique raciones non ignorat. (23) Harum itaque trium [ars, usus, imita-
cio] prior ars esse cernitur, coniectatur que non tam usui vel imitacioni
concedendum.

[marg.: *Exercitacio*] (24) *Exercitacioni* vero quaeque plurimum laudis
afferunt, cum ea sit per quam leviter et in procinctu quidquid habetur
arte fit, et quae si defuerit, nihil artis cito pulcreque patebit. (25) Videmus
enim quosdam multarum rerum racionem cognoscere sed usu non tritos
tamquam inexpertos in agendo remitti quemadmodum de lineamentis
corporumque figuris multam diiudicacionem parant, sed nisi crebro pin-
gendo usu extra formarint quod intus effigiatum est, pene in prima pro-
tractione deficient. (26) Nonnulli eciam de dyatesseron, de dyapente
deque musicis proporcionibus habunde disputant sed nisi vocales arterias
multis sonis accomodarint numquam predicabuntur suaves armonici. (27)
Ex quo evenit ut nulla iudicetur ars esse, nisi fuerit exercitacione conducta.
(28) Proinde usui et frequentacioni tantum tribuerunt prisci oratores
quantum ad adipiscendum nomen oratorium suffecit: (29) *Demostenes* quod
non habuit usu comparavit, ut enim in dicendo promptior esset et longiori
spiritu valeret, fertur nonnumquam lapillos in os coniecisse et per littora
quantum potuit exclamasse, et in continua versuum pronuntiacione multos
fecisse gradus, qua peracri exercitacione olim celeberrime fame habitus est.
(30) *Gracus*, aput romanos ut cuilibet sentencie suam vocem daret, dum con-
cionabatur et orabat, ad sonitum cornu eburnei suam pronuntiacionem
exercebat. (31) quo si lentiore spiritu diceret ac leviore familiaris eius tergo
inherens ipso cornu eum ad acutiorem citioremque reduceret. (32) Non ergo
absque causa tantopere invigilandum exercitacioni commonuit. (33)
Eloquentissimus omnium *Cicero* quidem viderit in ea totum munus
oratorium relucere.

[marg.: *Imitatio*] (34) *Porro quid de imitacione* tacemus, quae nunc temporis ita grata est quod nulla facundia nisi Ciceroniano vel Tituliviano
balsamo fuerit circumlota redolens putatur. (35) Quare si quispiam novo
dicendi genere peroraret, nec *Ciceronem* vel probatissimos sequetur,

quamquam polite graviterque diceret, non haberetur intra magnos oratores. (36) Vel si dulciloquentem *Maronem* vel Homerum quisque poeta non legisset carmina proferret insipida. (37) Quam ob rem cum primum ad dicendum vocem impellimus, id consilii legimus a maioribus relictum, ut alicui quidem eloquentissimo similes esse studeamus. (38) Quod et ipsum Tullium non neglexisse putandum est. (39) Audivit enim grecos oratores et romanos et studiosissime volumina lectitavit illorum, quos facundiores censuit nec Philonis divini libros contempsisse perhibetur. (40) *Mantuano* itemque poete alienum non fuit Homeri vestigia sequi et suos versus suis carminibus inserere. (41) Posteri quoque, Lucanus, Statius, Galtherus, quoad potuerunt visi sunt priorum actorum [fo. 65ʳ:] dictis sua dicta confirmare. (42) Nec Annaeo *Senecae* grave fuit in tradicione morum Socratem testari. (43) Praxitelles et Fidias quorum Rome adhuc extant opera satis sibi fidei in sua arte prestari debere crediderunt, cum Zeusis et Appellis divinorum statutorum imitatores se esse dicerent. (44) Nunc quoque qui celestibus armoniis nostri superegregii et omnium modestissimi musice professoris G. du Fay aut carminibus suavissimis Binchois sua similifacit, dicitur in arte prestare. (45) Vel primo quod nostre rei accomodatius est si quis in dicendis, conficiendis et componendis decenter ornateque rebus virum illum spectatissimum G. Bollomerii cuius fama pervigil usquequaque montes ambit et maria sequetur is sibi non parum nominis in benedicendo faciendoque conquireret. (46) Quoniam ergo non modo in arte dicendi potiores insequendum est, tum propter copiam preceptorum meliorum, tum quo severo sue auctoritatis vocabulo eorum imitaciones iactentur, profecto istarum trium imitacionem non esse ultimam coniecto. (47) Vestrarum itaque sit discretionum quantum decet unicuique deferre. (48) Sed ut imitacioni paulisper deserviam quam magnopere moderni probare videntur, Carneadem copiosissimum grecum oratorem persequar, qui cum coram patribus conscriptis de iusticia in utramque partem disputasset valefaciens urbi ipsam sua ornatissima oratione laudavit. (49) Siccine ego post iniectum proplemma vos qui eloquentie appositeque dictandi arti vestras operas et ingenia datis, demum ab eo collaudari iudico par equum? . . .[21]

(12) Let us see, then: since our Cicero has stated that the art of fine oratory consists of five things: invention, disposition, elocution, memory, and pronuntiation, and these five are acquired by three means—doctrine, exercise, and imitation—which of these three do you regard as preferable?

(13) *Art* (or doctrine), should, in the opinion of some people, claim the greatest respect, since what could be created without the guidance through

---

[21] Critical notes. I owe several of the following emendations and references to Hans Strohm and Leofranc Holford-Strevens. (1) fauces aridae *Persius Sat. I*; (3) scriptis dum *MS*; (4) Palida *MS* Pallada finxit *Metam.*; (5) Ioannes: *sc. Scotus Eriugena*; (5) peregisse *MS*; (8) quo equari *MS*; *first* non mentiar *probably redundant (dittography)*; (10) iacere *MS*; (12) Venandum *MS*; intencione *MS*; (24) aufferunt *MS*; (41) Galtherus: *(sc. of Châtillon)*; (44) Bruchois *MS*; (49) appositeque *MS*; dum ab eo *MS*. The translation as well as the text has benefited from the advice of Hans Strohm and Leofranc Holford-Strevens.

doctrine? (14) It is she who governs and regulates the action in every matter. (15) Without her, order is overturned, what is last becomes first, and the middle gets disturbed and mixed up. . . .

(24) Some reasons also support the superior merit of *practice* (or exercise), because it is through her that all the ingredients of art become easily accessible, whereas when she is missing, nothing can be made apparent quickly or enjoyably. (25) Certain people, we will observe, know the ins and outs of many things but since they have not steeped themselves in practice, they fail in the action as if they were inexperienced; or similarly, they bring a great deal of judgement to the outlines and shapes of bodies, but if they have not learned through frequent painting to externalise what they have internally envisaged, they will break down almost in the first attempt at drawing. (26) Some others profusely debate dyatesseron, dyapente, and musical proportions—but if they have not familiarized their vocal chords with many sounds they will never be judged to be pleasing harmonists. . . .

(34) Furthermore, we must not remain silent about *imitation*, which is so welcome today that no [rhetorical] ability is thought to be fragrant unless it is soaked in Ciceronian or Livian beauty lotion. (35) Thus if anybody were to hold a speech in a new manner without following Cicero or the other most accepted authors, he would not be reckoned among the great orators, however artful and dignified his speech. (36) Or, if a poet had not read the sweetly speaking Vergilius Maro or Homer, he would produce boring poems. (37) Therefore, from the moment we attempt our first speech, we read the advice left to us by our forebears that we must strive to resemble some most eloquent author. (38) There is reason to believe that even M. Tullius Cicero heeded this advice. (39) He did in fact hear Greek as well as Roman orators and eagerly read those of their books which he thought to be most eloquent, not despising—it is believed—even the books of the divine Philo. (40) Virgil the poet of Mantua, then, did not think it unsuitable to follow in the footsteps of Homer and to insert his verses into his own poems. (41) Also later writers such as Lucan, Statius, Walter of Châtillon, endeavoured as much as possible to strengthen their works with the words of earlier authors. (42) Nor did Annaeus Seneca find it burdensome to use Socrates as a witness in the teaching of morality. (43) Praxiteles and Phidias, whose works are still extant at Rome, were sure of obtaining a good deal of authority in their art, when they declared to be imitators of the divine principles of Zeuxis and Apelles. (44) Also today, whoever makes his songs similar to the celestial harmonies of our most eminent and utterly modest musical practitioner G. du Fay, or to the honey-sweet songs of Binchois, is said to be a leader in the art. (45) Or, to mention first what fits our subject more closely: if somebody, in the recitation, elaboration, or creation of speeches in a tasteful and artful manner, were to follow that distinguished man, Guillaume Bolomier, whose unsleeping fame will travel night and day across the mountains and seas, he would make a considerable name for himself in reciting and creating speeches.

(46) Since, therefore, we need to follow the better ones not only in the art of oratory—whether for the wealth of their better precepts, or because imitations of their art can gain acclaim from the verdict of their respected authority—I definitely suggest that imitation is not the least of the three elements. (47) Thus, let it be up to your judgement how much praise each of them deserves. (48) But if I may dwell for another moment on imitation which the moderns seem to appreciate so much: I would wish to follow Carneades, the ingenious Greek orator who, when taking both sides in an argument about justice in the Senate, said his farewell to Rome praising the city in an exquisite speech. (tr. R.S.)

BIBLIOGRAPHY

Introductory Note

The following bibliography consists of primary sources, reference works, editions, and a selection of the secondary literature cited in the individual chapters, but also includes standard reference works and suggestions for further reading. Works cited only by short title appear in the List of Abbreviations.

CHAPTER I MUSLIM AND JEWISH MUSICAL TRADITIONS OF THE MIDDLE AGES

(i) *Primary Sources, Reference Works, and Editions*

ADLER, ISRAEL, *Hebrew Writings Concerning Music* (RISM B ix/2; Munich, 1975).

AL-ḤASAN AL-KĀTIB, *La Perfection des connaissances musicales*, trans. Amnon Shiloah (Paris, 1972).

AL-MAGHRIBĪ, SAʿĪD, *al-Mughrib fī ḥula al-Maghrib*, ed. Shawqi Dayf (Cairo, 1953).

AL-MAQQARĪ, AḤMAD IBN MUḤAMMAD, *Nafḥ al-ṭīb*, ed. Iḥsān ʿAbbās (Beirut, 1968), iii. 122–33.

IBN EZRA, MOSES, *Kitāb al-muḥāḍara waʾl-mudhākara*, ed. and trans. A. Sh. Halkin (Jerusalem, 1975).

IBN KHALDŪN, *al-Muqaddima*, trans. F. Rosenthal, 3 vols. (Princeton, 1967).

SHILOAH, AMNON, *The Theory of Music in Arabic Writings* (RISM B x; Munich, 1979).

(ii) *Books and Articles*

ADLER, ISRAEL, 'Les Chants synagogaux notés au XIIᵉ siècle (ca 1103–1150) par Abadias, le prosélyte normand', *Revue de musicologie*, 51 (1965), 19–51.

ANGLÈS, HIGINI, 'La Musique juive dans l'Espagne medievale', *Yuval*, 1 (1968), 48–64.

ARMISTEAD, SAMUEL G., and SILVERMAN, JOSEPH, with musical transcription and studies by Israel J. Katz, *Judeo-Spanish Ballads from Oral Tradition* (Berkeley and Los Angeles, 1986).

BURNETT, CHARLES, 'European Knowledge of Arabic Texts Referring to Music: Some New Material', *EMH* 12 (1993), 1–17.

——'The Translating Activity in Medieval Spain', in Jayyushi (ed.), *The Legacy of Muslim Spain*, 1036–58.

ETZION, J., 'The Music of the Judeo-Spanish Romancero: Stylistic Features', *Anuario musical*, 43 (1988), 221–56.

FARMER, HENRY GEORGE, *A History of Arabian Music to the XIIIth Century* (London, 1929).

JAYYUSI, SALMA KHADRA (ed.), *The Legacy of Muslim Spain* (Handbuch der Orientalistik, i: The Near and Middle East, 12; Leiden, 1992).

KATZ, ISRAEL J., *Judeo-Spanish Traditional Ballads from Jerusalem: An Ethnomusicological Study*, 2 vols. (Brooklyn, 1971–5).

LIU, BENJAMIN, and MONROE, JAMES, *Ten Hispano-Arabic Songs in the Modern Oral Traditions: Music and Poetry* (University of California Publications in Modern Philology, 25; Berkeley and Los Angeles, 1989).

POCHÉ, CHRISTIAN, 'Un nouveau regard sur la musique d'al-Andalus: le manuscrit d'Al-Tifashi', International Conference of IMS, Madrid, 1992, Round Table iv, *Revista de musicología*, 16/1 (1993), 367–79.

SHILOAH, AMNON, *Jewish Musical Traditions* (Detroit, 1992).

—— *Music in the World of Islam* (London and Detroit, 1995).

—— 'Techniques of Scholarship in Medieval Arabic Treatises', in A. Barbera (ed.), *Music Theory and its Sources: Antiquity and the Middle Ages* (South Bend, Ind., 1990), 85–99.

WEICH-SHAHAQ, S., and ETZION, J., 'The Spanish and Sephardic Romances: Musical Links', *Ethnomusicology*, 32 (1988), 173–209.

WRIGHT, OWEN, 'Music in Muslim Spain', in Jayyushi (ed.), *The Legacy of Muslim Spain*, 555–79.

CHAPTER II   LATE MEDIEVAL PLAINCHANT
FOR THE DIVINE OFFICE

(i) *Primary Sources, Reference Works, and Editions*

AH; *AH Register*; *CAO*; *DMA*; GS

Birger Gregerssons 'Birgitta-officium', ed. Carl-Gustaf Undhagen (Svenska fornskriftsällskapet, ser. 2; Latinska skrifter, 6; Stockholm, 1960).

Epistola S. Bernardi: De revisione cantus Cisterciensis and *Tractatus scriptus ab auctore incerto Cisterciense: Cantum quem Cisterciensis ordinis ecclesiae cantare*, ed. Francis J. Guentner, SJ (CSM 24; American Institute of Musicology, 1974).

GERBERT, MARTIN, *De cantu et musica sacra* (St Blasien, 1774).

Historia rymowana o św. Jadwidze (Kraków, 1977) and *Historia rymowana o św. Wojciechu*, ed. Jerzy Morawski (Kraków, 1979) [*The Rhymed History of St Hedwig . . . St Adalbert*].

Hucbald, Guido, and John on Music: Three Medieval Treatises, trans. Warren Babb, ed. Claude V. Palisca (Music Theory Translation Series, 3; New Haven, 1978).

HUGHES, ANDREW, *Late Medieval Liturgical Offices: Texts* and *Sources and Chants* (Subsidia mediaevalia, 23–4; Toronto, 1993–6). (*LMLO*)

JULIAN OF SPEYER, *Vita e uffizio ritmico di San Francesco d'Assisi*, ed. Eliodoro Mariani (Vicenza, 1980).

Die liturgischen Reimoffizien auf den heiligen Franciscus und Antonius. Gedichtet und componiert durch Julian von Speier, ed. H. Felder (Freiburg i.d. Schweiz, 1901).

Matins, Lauds, and Vespers for St David's Day, ed. Owain T. Edwards (Cambridge, 1990).

Philippe de Mézière's Campaign for the Feast of Mary's Presentation. Edited from Bibliothèque Nationale Mss latin 17,30 and 14454, ed. William E. Coleman (Toronto Medieval Latin Texts, 11; Toronto, 1981).

RALPH OF TONGRES, *De canonum observantia liber*, in *Maxima bibliotheca patrum*, xxvi (Lyons, 1677), 289–320.

'Rosa rorans': Ett Birgittaofficium af Nicolaus Hermanni, ed. Schück Hermann (Meddelanden från det literaturhistoriska seminariet i Lund, 2; *Lunds universitets årsskrift*, 28 (1893)).

The Use of Sarum, ed. Walter Howard Frere, 2 vols. (Cambridge, 1898, 1901; repr. 1969).

(ii) *Books and Articles*
NOHM ii; NOHM ii[2]

AUDA, ANTOINE, *L'École musicale liégeoise au Xe siècle: Étienne de Liége* (Brussels, 1923).

BAILEY, TERENCE, *The Processions of Sarum and the Western Church* (Studies and Texts, 21; Toronto, 1971).

BERNARD, MADELEINE, 'Les Offices versifiés attribués à Léon IX (1002–1054)', *Etudes grégoriennes*, 19 (1980), 89–164 (incl. facs. pp. 122–64).

——'Un recueil inédit du xiie siècle et la copie aquitaine de l'office de saint Grégoire', *Études grégoriennes*, 16 (1977), 145–59 (with facs.).

BERSCHIN, WALTER, and HILEY, DAVID (eds.), *Die Offizien des Mittelalters: Dichtung und Musik* (Regensburger Studien zur Musikgeschichte, 1; Tutzing, 1999).

BJÖRKVALL, GUNILLA, and HAUG, ANDREAS, 'Text und Musik im Trinitätsoffizium Stephans von Lüttich', in Berschin and Hiley (eds.), *Die Offizien des Mittelalters*, 1–24.

BOYCE, JAMES, O.CARM., 'Cantica Carmelitana: The Chants of the Carmelite Office' (Ph.D. diss., New York University, 1984).

——'The Carmelite Feast of the Presentation of the Virgin: A Study in Musical Adaptation', in Fassler and Baltzer (eds.), *The Divine Office*, 485–518.

——'Die Mainzer Karmeliterchorbücher und die liturgische Tradition des Karmeliterordens', *Archiv für mittelrheinische Kirchengeschichte*, 39 (1987), 267–303.

BOYLE, LEONARD E., 'Dominican Lectionaries and Leo of Ostia's *Translatio S. Clementis*', *Archivum Fratrum Praedicatorum*, 28 (1958), 362–94.

BROWN, TERRY DAVID, 'Songs for the Saints of the Schism: Liturgy for Vincent Ferrer and Catherine of Siena' (Ph.D. diss., University of Toronto, 1995).

BRUNING, E., *Giuliano da Spira e l'officio ritmico di s. Francesco* (Edizioni 'Psalterium', Rome), extr. from *Note d'Archivio*, 1–4 (1927), 129–202.

——'Der musikalische Wert des Reimoffiziums zu Ehren des Antonius von Padua', *Gregorius-Blatt*, 55 (1931), 113–19.

BUKOFZER, MANFRED, 'Two Fourteenth-Century Motets on St Edmund', in *Studies in Medieval and Renaissance Music* (New York, 1950), 17–33.

CATTIN, GIULIO, *Music of the Middle Ages*, i (Cambridge, 1979).

CHARTIER, YVES, '*Clavis Operum Hucbaldi Elnonensis*: Bibliographie des Œuvres d'Hucbald de Saint-Amand', *Journal of Medieval Latin*, 5 (1995), 202–24.

——*L'Œuvre musicale d'Hucbald de Saint-Amand: les compositions et le traité de musique* (Cahiers d'études médiévales: Cahiers spécial, 5; Montreal, 1995).

CORBIN, SOLANGE, 'Le Fonds manuscrit de Cadouin', *Bulletin de la Société historique et archéologique du Périgord*, supplément, 81 (1954), 1–7.

——'L'Office en vers *Gaude mater ecclesia* pour la conception de la vierge', in *Congresso internazionale di musica sacra, Roma 1950*, ed. Iginio Anglès (Tournai, 1952), 284–6.

CROCKER, RICHARD, 'Matins Antiphons at St Denis', *JAMS* 39 (1986), 441–90.

DAMILANO, PIERO, 'Un antico "ufficio ritmico" della Visitazione nella biblioteca capitolare di Fossano', *Rivista internazionale di musica sacra*, 5 (1984), 133–63.

DELALANDE, FR DOMINIQUE, OP, *Le Graduel des Prêcheurs: vers la version authentique du Graduel grégorien* (Bibliotheque d'histoire dominicaine, 2; Paris, 1949).

DELAPORTE, YVES, 'Fulbert de Chartres et l'école chartraine de chant liturgique au XIᵉ siècle', *Etudes grégoriennes*, 2 (1957), 51–81.

EPSTEIN, MARCY J., '*Ludovicus decus regnantium*: Perspectives on the Rhymed Office', *Speculum*, 53 (1978), 283–333.

FALVY, ZOLTAN, 'Die Weisen des König Stephan-Reimoffiziums', *Studia musicologica*, 6 (1964), 207–69.

——'Drei Reimoffizien aus Ungarn und ihre Musik', *Musicologia hungarica*, NS 2 (Budapest, 1968).

FASSLER, MARGOT E., and BALTZER, REBECCA A. (eds.), *The Divine Office in the Latin Middle Ages: Methodology and Source Studies, Regional Developments, Hagiography* (New York, 2000).

FELDER, HILARIN, *Histoire d'études dans l'ordre de saint François*, trans. from the German by Eusèbe de Bar-le-Duc (Paris, 1908).

FLAHIFF, G. B., 'Ralph Niger', *Mediaeval Studies*, 2 (1940), 104–26.

Francesco d'Assisi (Catalogue of an Exhibition in Assisi), ed. Carlo Pirovano, 3 vols. i: *Chiese e conventi*; ii: *Documenti e Archivi. Codici e Biblioteche. Miniature*; iii: *Storia e arte* (Milan, 1982). Includes numerous articles on various aspects of St Francis, including Agostino Ziino, 'Liturgia e musica francescana nei secoli XIII–XIV' (i. 127–58).

GY, PIERRE-MARIE, 'L'Office du Corpus Christi et S. Thomas d'Aquin', *Revue des sciences, philosophie, et théologie*, 64 (1980), 491–507.

HAGGH, BARBARA H., 'The Celebration of the *Recollectio Festorum Beatae Mariae Virginis*, 1457–1987', *Studia musicologica*, 30 (1988), 361–74.

HALLER, ROBERT B., 'Early Dominican Mass Chants: A Witness to Thirteenth-Century Chant Style' (Ph.D. diss., Catholic University of America, 1986).

HARRISON, FRANK LL., *Music in Medieval Britain* (London, 1958).

HARTZELL, K. DREW, 'A St. Alban's Miscellany in New York', *Mittellateinisches Jahrbuch*, 10 (1975), 20–61.

HILEY, DAVID, 'The English Benedictine Version of the Historia Sancti Gregorii and the Date of the "Winchester Troper" (Cambridge, Corpus Christi College, 473)', *International Musicological Society Study Group Cantus Planus: Papers Read at the Seventh Meeting, Sopron, 1995*, ed. László Dobszay (Budapest, 1998), 287–303.

—— 'The *Historia* of St. Julian of Le Mans by Létald of Micy: Some Comments and Questions about a North French Office of the Early Eleventh Century', in Fassler and Baltzer (eds.), *The Divine Office*.

—— *Western Plainchant: A Handbook* (Oxford, 1993).

HUGHES, ANDREW, 'British Rhymed Offices: A Catalogue and Commentary', in Susan Rankin and David Hiley (eds.), *Music in the Medieval English Liturgy: Plainsong and Medieval Music Society Centenary Essays* (Oxford, 1993), 239–84.

—— 'Chants in the Offices of Thomas of Canterbury and Stanislaus of Poland', *Musica antiqua*, 6 (Bydgoszcz, 1982), 267–77.

—— 'Chants in the Rhymed Office of St Thomas of Canterbury', *EM* 16 (1988), 185–202.

—— 'Chantword Indexes: A Tool for Plainsong Research', in *Words and Music*, ed. Paul Laird (Acta, 17; Binghamton, 1993), 31–49.

—— 'Echoes and Allusions: Sources of the Office for St Dominic', paper delivered at the Conference on *Liturgie, musique et culture au milieu du XIIIᵉ siècle. Autour du Ms. Rome Santa Sabina XIV.L.1, prototype de la liturgie dominicaine*, Rome, March 1995 (to be published).

—— '*Fons hortorum*—the Office of the Presentation: Origins and Authorship', in Berschin and Hiley (eds.), *Die Offizien des Mittelalters*, 153–77.

—— 'Literary Transformation in Post-Carolingian Saints' Offices: Using all the Evidence', in Sandro Sticca (ed.), *Saints: Studies in Hagiography* (Medieval and Renaissance Texts and Studies, 141; Binghamton, 1996), 23–50.

—— *Medieval Manuscripts for Mass and Office: A Guide to their Organization and Terminology* (Toronto, 1982; rev. paperback edn., 1995).

—— 'Modal Order and Disorder in the Rhymed Office', *Musica disciplina*, 37 (1983), 29–52.

HUGHES, ANDREW, 'The Monarch as the Object of Liturgical Veneration', in Anne J. Duggan (ed.), *Kings and Kingship in Medieval Europe* (King's College London Medieval Studies, 10; London, 1993), 375–424.

——'Offices (new liturgical)', *The Garland Encyclopedia of Medieval England* (New York, 1998).

——'Research Report: Late Medieval Rhymed Offices', *Journal of the Plainsong and Mediaeval Music Society*, 8 (1985), 33–49.

——'Rhymed Offices', *DMA*.

——'Word Painting in a 12th-Century Office', in Bryan Gillingham and Paul Merkley (eds.), *Beyond the Moon: Festschrift Luther Dittmer* (Musicological Studies, 53; Ottawa, 1990), 16–27.

HUGLO, MICHEL, 'Règlement du xiiie siècle pour la transcription des livres notés', in Martin Ruhnke (ed.), *Festschrift Bruno Stäblein zum 70. Geburtstag* (Kassel, 1967), 121–33.

HUSMANN, HEINRICH, 'Zur Überlieferung der Thomas-Offizien', in *Organicae Voces: Festschrift Joseph Smits van Waesberghe* (Amsterdam, 1963), 87–8.

JAMMERS, EWALD, 'Die Antiphonen der rheinischen Reimoffizien', *Ephemerides liturgicae*, 43 (1929), 199–219, 425–51; 44 (1930), 84–99, 342–68.

JANCEY, MERYL (ed.), *St Thomas Cantilupe, Bishop of Hereford: Essays in his Honour* (Hereford, 1982).

JONSSON, RITVA, *Historia: Études sur la genèse des offices versifiés* (Acta Universitatis Stockholmiensis Studia Latina Stockholmiensis, 15; Stockholm, 1968).

KERN, ANTON, 'Das Offizium *De Corpore Christi* in Österreichischen Bibliotheken', *Revue bénédictine*, 64 (1954), 46–67.

KIRK, DOUGLAS KARL, '*Translatione corona spinea*: A Musical and Textual Analysis of a Thirteenth-Century Rhymed Office' (Ph.D. diss., University of Texas, 1980).

LEBEUF, ABBÉ, *Traité historique et pratique sur le chant ecclésiastique* (Paris, 1741; repr. Geneva, 1972).

MATHIESEN, THOMAS J., 'The Office of the New Feast of Corpus Christi in the *Regimen Animarum* at Brigham Young University', *Journal of Musicology*, 2 (1983), 13–44.

OESCH, HANS, *Berno und Hermann von Reichenau als Musiktheoretiker* (Publikationen der Schweizerischen Musikforschenden Gesellschaft, ser. 2, 9; Berne, 1961).

PATIER, DOMINIQUE, 'L'Office rythmique de sainte Ludmila', *Études grégoriennes*, 21 (1986), 51–96.

——'Un Office rythmique tchèque du xivème siècle: étude comparative avec quelques offices hongrois', *Studia musicologica*, 12 (1970), 41–131.

PIKULIK, JERZY, 'Les Offices polonais de saint Adalbert', in id. (ed.), *État des recherches sur la musique religieuse dans la culture polonaise* (Warsaw, 1973), 306–72.

ROBERTSON, ANNE WALTERS, 'Benedicamus Domino: The Unwritten Tradition', JAMS 41 (1988), 1–62.

SCHEEBEN, H.-CHR., 'Petrus Ferrandi', Archivum Fratrum Praedicatorum, 2 (1932), 329–47.

SCHLAGER, KARLHEINZ, 'Reimoffizien', in Geschichte der katholischen Kirchenmusik, ed. Karl Gustav Fellerer (Kassel, 1972), i. 293–7.

SHARPE, RICHARD, 'The Date of St Mildreth's Translation from Minster-in-Thanet to Canterbury', Medieval Studies, 53 (1991), 344–54.

——'Goscelin's St. Augustine and St. Mildreth', Journal of Theological Studies, NS 41 (1990), 502–16.

——'Words and Music by Goscelin of Canterbury', EM 19 (1991), 93–7.

STÄBLEIN, BRUNO, Schriftbild der einstimmigen Musik (Musikgeschichte in Bildern, 3/iv; Leipzig, 1975).

STEINER, RUTH, 'Gruppen von Antiphonen zur Matutin des Afra-Offiziums', in Berschin and Hiley (eds.), Die Offizien des Mittelalters.

STEVENS, DENIS, 'Music in Honor of St. Thomas of Canterbury', MQ 56 (1970), 311–48 (with 2 facs.).

STEVENS, JOHN, Words and Music in the Middle Ages: Song, Narrative, Dance and Drama, 1050–1350 (Cambridge Studies in Music; Cambridge, 1986). Reviewed by David Hughes in JAMS 52 (1989), 403–10; Jeremy Yudkin in Speculum, 64 (1989), 765–9.

THOMSON, RODNEY M., 'The Music for the Office of St Edmund King and Martyr', Music and Letters, 65 (1984), 189–93.

TONETTI, P. OTTONE, OFM, 'L'Uffizio ritmico di san Francesco d'Assisi di fra Giuliano da Spira', Rivista internazionale di musica sacra, 3 (1982), 370–89.

TROWELL, BRIAN L., and WATHEY, ANDREW, 'John Benet's "Lux fulget ex Anglia—O pater pietatis—Salve Thoma"', in Meryl Jancey (ed.), St Thomas Cantilupe, Bishop of Hereford: Essays in his Honour (Hereford, 1982), 159–80.

VAN DIJK, STEPHEN J. P., Sources of the Modern Roman Liturgy (Leiden, 1963).

——and WALKER, JOAN HAZELDEN, The Origins of the Modern Roman Liturgy (London, 1960).

WAGNER, PETER, Einführung in die gregorianischen Melodien, 3 vols. (Leipzig, 1911–21; repr. Hildesheim, 1962). Volume i has been translated into English: Introduction to the Gregorian Melodies, i (2nd edn., 1907), trans. A. Orme and E. G. P. Wyatt, repr. with a new introduction by Richard Crocker (New York, 1985).

——'Zur mittelalterlichen Offiziumskomposition', Kirchenmusikalisches Jahrbuch, 21 (1908), 13–32.

WEAKLAND, REMBERT, OSB, 'The Compositions of Hucbald', Études grégoriennes, 3 (1959), 155–63.

WRIGHT, CRAIG, Music and Ceremony at Notre Dame of Paris, 500–1550 (Cambridge Studies in Music; New York, 1989).

ZIINO, AGOSTINO, see *Francesco d'Assisi.*

ZIJLSTRA, A. MARCEL J., 'The Office of St Adalbert: Carte de Visite of a Late Medieval Dutch Abbey', *Plainsong and Medieval Music*, 3 (1994), 169–83.

CHAPTER III   INSTRUMENTAL MUSIC, *c*.1300–*c*.1520

(i) *Primary Sources, Reference Works, and Editions*
Tinctoris, *De inventione*

AGRICOLA, MARTIN, *Musica instrumentalis deutsch* (Wittenberg, 1529, rev. edn., 1545); facs. of 1529 edn. (Hildesheim, 1985); mod. edn. in quasi-facs. by Robert Eitner (Berlin, 1896); English trans. in William E. Hettrick, *The 'Musica instrumentalis deudsch' of Martin Agricola* (Cambridge, 1994).

ARNAUT DE ZWOLLE, HENRI, [*Treatises on musical instruments*] (Paris, Bibliothèque Nationale de France, MS lat. 7295, fos. 128–32); facs. edn. with transcription and commentary in G. Le Cerf and E. R. Labande, *Les Traités d'Henri-Arnaut de Zwolle et de divers anonymes (Paris: Bibliothèque nationale, ms. Latin 7295)* (Paris, 1932; repr. 1972).

Das Buxheimer Orgelbuch, ed. Bertha A. Wallner, 3 vols. (Das Erbe deutscher Music, 36–8; Kassel, 1958).

The Codex Faenza, Biblioteca Comunale, 117 (Fa), facs. edn., ed. Armen Carapetyan (Rome, 1961).

DURÁN, DOMINGO MARCOS, *Súmula de canto de órgano* (Salamanca, *c*.1504), facs. edn. (Madrid, 1976).

Das Glogauer Liederbuch (Berlin, former Preußische Staatsbibliothek, MS 40098; currently in Kraków, Jagiellonian Library), vols. 1–2, ed. H. Ringmann and J. Klapper; vols. 3–4, ed. C. Väterlein (Das Erbe deutscher Musik, 3, 4, 85, and 86; Kassel, 1936–81); facs., ed. Jessie Ann Owens (Renaissance Manuscripts in Facsimile, 6; New York, 1986).

JONAS, LUISE, *Das Augsburger Liederbuch*, 2 vols. (Berliner musikwissenschaftliche Arbeiten, 21; Munich, 1983).

Keyboard Music of the Fourteenth and Fifteenth Centuries, ed. Willi Apel (Corpus of Early Keyboard Music, 1; Rome: American Institute of Musicology, 1963).

Keyboard Music of the Late Middle Ages in Codex Faenza 117, ed. Dragan Plamenac (Rome, 1973).

The Manuscript London, B. M. Add. 29,987, facs., ed. Gilbert Reaney (Rome, 1965).

Medieval Instrumental Dances, ed. Timothy McGee (Bloomington, Ind., 1989).

TINCTORIS, JOHANNES, *Liber de arte contrapuncti (1477)*, English trans. by A. Seay as *The Art of Counterpoint* (American Institute of Musicology, 1961).

VIRDUNG, SEBASTIAN, *Musica getutscht (Basel, 1511)*, facs. ed. Leo Schrade (Kassel, 1931); also ed. K. W. Niemöller (Kassel, 1970) and Robert Eitner (Berlin, 1894). Eng. trans. by Beth Bullard as *Musica getutscht: A Treatise on Musical Instruments* (Cambridge, 1993).

(ii) *Books and Articles*
Fenlon, *Music*; Strohm, *Rise*

APEL, WILLI, *The History of Keyboard Music to 1700*, trans. and rev. by Hans Tischler (Bloomington, Ind., 1972).

ARLT, WULF, 'Instrumentalmusik im Mittelalter: Fragen der Rekonstruktion einer schriftlosen Praxis', *Basler Jahrbuch für historische Musikpraxis*, 7 (1983), 32–64.

BAINES, ANTHONY, *Brass Instruments: Their History and Development* (New York, 1981).

——'Fifteenth-Century Instruments in Tinctoris's "De Inventione et Usu Musicae"', *Galpin Society Journal*, 3 (1950), 19–27.

——*Woodwind Instruments and their History* (New York, 1957).

BARONCINI, RODOLFO, 'Voci e strumenti tra Quattro e Cinquecento', *Rivista italiana di musicologia*, 32 (1997), 327–65.

BARRY, WILSON, 'Henri Arnaut de Zwolle's Clavicordium and the Origin of the Chekker', *Journal of the American Musical Instrument Society*, 11 (1985), 5–13.

BERNHARD, MADELEINE B., 'Recherches sur l'histoire de la corporation des ménétriers ou joueurs d'instruments de la ville de Paris', *Bibliothèque de l'École des Chartes*, 3 (1841–2), 377–404; 4 (1842–3), 525–48; 5 (1843–4), 254–84, 339–72.

BOORMAN, STANLEY (ed.), *Studies in the Performance of Late Medieval Music* (Cambridge, 1983).

BOWLES, EDMUND A., 'Haut and Bas: The Grouping of Musical Instruments in the Middle Ages', *Musica disciplina*, 8 (1954), 115–40.

BOYDELL, BARA, *The Crumhorn and other Renaissance Windcap Instruments* (Buren, 1982).

BROWN, HOWARD MAYER, *Instrumental Music Printed Before 1600: A Bibliography* (Cambridge, Mass., 1967).

——'Instruments', in *Performance Practice: Music before 1600* (Norton/Grove Handbooks on Music, ed. Howard M. Brown and Stanley Sadie, i; London, 1989), 167–84.

——'Instruments and Voices in the Fifteenth-Century Chanson', in J. W. Grubbs (ed.), *Current Thought in Musicology* (University of Texas, 1976), 89–137.

——'Minstrels and their Repertory in Fifteenth-Century France: Music in an Urban Environment', in Susan Zimmerman and Ronald F. E.

Weissman (eds.), *Urban Life in the Renaissance* (Newark, Del., 1989), 142–64.

BROWN, HOWARD MAYER, 'Notes (and Transposing Notes) on the Viol in the Early Sixteenth Century', in Fenlon, *Music*, 61–78.

——'St. Augustine, Lady Music and the Gittern', *Musica disciplina*, 38 (1984), 25–65.

——and SADIE, STANLEY (eds.), *Performance Practice*, 2 vols. (Norton/New Grove Handbooks in Music; London, 1989–90).

CORBO, ANNA MARIA, *San Ginesio e la tradizione musicale maceratese tra la fine del '300 e l'inizio del '500: giullari, suonatori e strumenti musicali* (Comune di San Ginesio, 1992).

CRANE, FREDERICK, *Extant Medieval Musical Instruments: A Provisional Catalogue by Types* (Iowa City, 1972).

——*Materials for the Study of the Fifteenth-Century Basse Danse* (Brooklyn, 1968).

DAALEN, MARIA VAN, and HARRISON, FRANK LL., 'Two Keyboard Intabulations of the Late Fourteenth Century on a Manuscript Leaf now in the Netherlands', *TVNM* 34 (1984), 97–107.

D'ACCONE, FRANK A., *The Civic Muse: Music and Musicians in Siena during the Middle Ages and the Renaissance* (Chicago, 1997).

DOWNEY, PETER, 'The Renaissance Slide Trumpet: Fact or Fiction', *EM* 12 (1984), 26–33.

DUFFIN, ROSS, 'The Trompette des Menestrels in the 15th-Century Alta Capella', *EM* 17 (1989), 397–402.

EDWARDS, WARWICK, 'Songs without Words by Josquin and his Contemporaries', in Fenlon, *Music*, 79–92.

FALLOWS, DAVID, '15th-Century Tablatures for Plucked Instruments: A Summary, a Revision and a Suggestion', *Lute Society Journal*, 19 (1977), 7–33.

GILLIODTS-VAN SEVEREN, LOUIS, *Les Ménestrels de Bruges* (Bruges, 1912).

GÖLLNER, THEODOR, 'Notationsfragmente aus einer Organistenwerkstatt des 15. Jahrhunderts', *Archiv für Musikwissenschaft*, 24 (1967), 170–7.

GÓMEZ, MARICARMEN, 'Minstrel Schools in the Late Middle Ages', *EM* 18 (1990), 213–15.

GUSHEE, LAWRENCE, 'Minstrel', in *New Grove*.

HAMM, CHARLES, 'Musiche del Quattrocento in S. Petronio', *Rivista italiana di musicologia*, 3 (1968), 215–32.

HEARTZ, DANIEL, 'The Basse Dance, its Evolution circa 1450 to 1550', *Annales musicologiques*, 6 (1958–63), 287–340.

——'Hoftanz and Basse Dance', *JAMS* 19 (1966), 13–36.

HÖFLER, JANEZ, 'Der "Der Trompette de menestrels" und sein Instrument: Zur Revision eines bekannten Themas', *TVNM* 29 (1979), 94–132.

HOWELL, STANDLEY, 'Paulus Paulirinus of Prague on Musical Instruments', *Journal of the American Musical Instrument Society*, 5–6 (1979–80), 9–36.

IVANOFF, VLADIMIR, 'Das Lautenduo im 15. Jahrhundert', *Basler Jahrbuch für Historische Musikpraxis*, 8 (1984), 147–61.

KINKELDEY, OTTO, 'Dance Tunes of the Fifteenth Century', in David Hughes (ed.), *Instrumental Music* (Cambridge, Mass., 1959), 3–30, 89–152.

KRAUTWURST, FRANZ, 'Konrad Paumann in Nördlingen', in E. H. Meyer (ed.), *Festschrift Heinrich Besseler* (Leipzig, 1961), 203–14.

KREITNER, KENNETH, 'Music in the Corpus Christi Procession of Fifteenth-Century Barcelona', *EMH* 15 (1995), 153–204.

LEECH-WILKINSON, DANIEL, 'Un libro di appunti di un suonatore di tromba del quindicesimo secolo', *Rivista italiana di musicologia*, 16 (1981), 16–39.

LITTERICK, LOUISE, 'Performing Franco-Netherlandish Secular Music of the Late 15th Century', *EM* 8 (1980), 474–85.

LOCKWOOD, LEWIS, *Music in Renaissance Ferrara, 1400–1505* (Cambridge, Mass., 1984).

McGEE, TIMOTHY, 'Instruments and the Faenza Codex', *EM* 14 (1986), 480–90.

——*Medieval and Renaissance Music—A Performer's Guide* (Toronto, 1985).

MACMILLAN, DOUGLAS, 'The Mysterious Cornamuse', *EM* 6 (1978), 75–7.

MARIX, JEANNE, *Histoire de la musique et des musiciens de la cour de Bourgogne sous le règne de Philippe le Bon (1420–1467)* (Strasburg, 1939; repr. Baden-Baden, 1974).

MARROCCO, W. THOMAS, 'Fifteenth-Century *ballo* and *bassadanza*: A Survey', *Studi musicali*, 10 (1981), 31–41.

MEYER, KENTON T., *The Crumhorn* (Ann Arbor, 1983).

MOSER, HANS JOACHIM, *Die Musikergenossenschaften im deutschen Mittelalter* (Rostock, 1910).

MUNROW, DAVID, *Instruments of the Middle Ages and Renaissance* (London, 1976).

MYERS, HERBERT, 'Slide Trumpet Madness: Fact or Fiction', *EM* 17 (1989), 383–9.

PAGANUZZI, ENRICO, et al., *La musica a Verona* (Verona, 1976).

PAGE, CHRISTOPHER, 'Court and City in France, 1100–1300', in James McKinnon (ed.), *Antiquity and the Middle Ages* (Man and Music; London, 1990), 197–217.

——'German Musicians and their Instruments, a 14th-Century Account by Konrad of Megenberg', *EM* 10 (1982), 192–200.

——'The Performance of Songs in Late Medieval France', *EM* 10 (1982), 441–50.

——*Voices and Instruments of the Middle Ages: Instrumental Practice and Songs in France 1100–1300* (Berkeley and London, 1987).

POLK, KEITH, 'Civic Patronage and Instrumental Ensembles in Renaissance Florence', *Augsburger Jahrbuch für Musikwissenschaft*, 3 (1986), 51–68.

——'Ensemble Instrumental Music in Flanders—1450–1550', *Journal of Band Research*, 11 (1975), 12–27.

POLK, KEITH, *German Instrumental Music of the Late Middle Ages* (Cambridge, 1992).

—— 'Innovation in Instrumental Music 1450–1510: The Role of German Performers within European Culture', in John Kmetz (ed.), *Music in the German Renaissance* (Cambridge, 1994), 202–14.

—— 'Instrumental Music in the Urban Centres of Renaissance Germany', *EMH* 7 (1987), 159–86.

—— 'Patronage and Innovation in Instrumental Music of the 15th Century', *Historic Brass Society Journal*, 3 (1991), 151–78.

—— 'The Schubingers of Augsburg: Innovation in Renaissance Instrumental Music', in *Quaestiones in musica: Festschrift für Franz Krautwurst* (Tutzing, 1989), 495–503.

—— 'The Trombone, the Slide Trumpet and the Ensemble Tradition of the Early Renaissance', *EM* 17 (1989), 389–97.

—— 'Vedel and Geige—Fiddle and Viol: German String Traditions in the Fifteenth Century', *JAMS* 42 (1989), 484–526.

—— 'Voices and Instruments: Soloists and Ensembles in the 15th Century', *EM* 18 (1990), 179–98.

—— 'Wind Bands of Medieval Flemish Cities', *Brass and Woodwind Quarterly*, 1 (1968), 93–113.

PRIZER, WILLIAM F., 'Bernardino Piffaro e i pifferi e tromboni di Mantova: strumenti a fiato in una corte italiana', *Rivista italiana di musicologia*, 16 (1981), 151–84.

—— 'The Frottola and the Unwritten Tradition', *Studi musicali*, 15 (1986), 3–37.

RAMALINGAM, VIVIAN, 'The *Trumpetum* in Strasbourg M 222 C 22', in *La Musique et le rite—sacré et profane. Actes du XIIIᵉ congrès de la SIM, Strasbourg, 1982* (Strasburg, 1986), ii. 143–60.

REMNANT, MARY, *English Bowed Instruments from Anglo-Saxon to Tudor Times* (Oxford, 1986).

—— *Musical Instruments of the West* (London, 1978).

ROKSETH, YVONNE, 'The Instrumental Music of the Middle Ages and the Early Sixteenth Century', in NOHM iii. 406–65.

SALMEN, WALTER, *Der Spielmann im Mittelalter* (Innsbruck, 1983).

—— (ed.), *Musik und Tanz zur Zeit Kaiser Maximilians I.* (Innsbruck, 1992).

SCHRADE, LEO, *Die handschriftliche Überlieferung der ältesten Instrumentalmusik* (Lahr, 1931).

SCHWAB, HEINRICH W., *Die Anfänge des weltlichen Berufsmusikertums in der mittelalterlichen Stadt* (Kieler Schriften zur Musikwissenschaft, 24; Kassel, 1982).

SMITS VAN WAESBERGHE, JOZEF, 'Een 15de eeuws muziekboek van de stadsminstrelen van Maastricht?', in Jozef Robijns (ed.), *Renaissance Muziek 1400–1600: Donum natalicium René Bernard Lenaerts* (Leuven, 1969), 247–73.

SOUTHERN, EILEEN, *The Buxheim Organ Book* (Brooklyn, 1963).

STAEHELIN, MARTIN, 'Münchner Fragmente mit mehrstimmiger Musik des späten Mittelalters', *Nachrichten der Akademie der Wissenschaften in Göttingen, I. Philologisch-historische Klasse*, 6 (1988), 167–90.

STEVENS, JOHN, *Music and Poetry in the Early Tudor Court* (London, 1961).

STRADNER, GERHARD, 'Zur Ausbildung verschiedener Instrumentengrössen', in Salmen (ed.), *Musik und Tanz*, 177–82.

STROHM, REINHARD, 'The Close of the Middle Ages', in James McKinnon (ed.), *Antiquity and the Middle Ages* (London, 1990), 269–312.

——'Instrumentale Ensemblemusik vor 1500: Das Zeugnis der mitteleuropäischen Quellen', in Salmen (ed.), *Musik und Tanz*, 89–106.

—— *Music in Late Medieval Bruges* (Oxford, 1985; rev. edn., 1990).

SZABOLCSI, BENEDIKT, 'Die ungarischen Spielleute des Mittelalters', in F. Blume (ed.), *Gedenkschrift für Hermann Abert* (Halle, 1928), 154–64.

TIELLA, MARCO, 'The Violeta of S. Caterina de' Vigri', *Galpin Society Journal*, 28 (1975), 60–70.

VACCARO, JEAN-MICHEL (ed.), *Le Concert des voix et des instruments à la Renaissance* (Paris, 1995).

VANDER STRAETEN, EDMOND, *Les Ménestrels au Pays-Bas* (Brussels, 1878).

—— *La Musique aux Pays-Bas avant le XIXe siècle*, 8 vols. (Brussels, 1867–88; repr. New York, 1969).

VOGELEIS, MARTIN, *Quellen und Bausteine zu einer Geschichte der Musik und des Theaters im Elsass 500–1800* (Strasburg, 1911; repr. 1979).

WEISS, SUSAN F., 'Bologna Q18: Some Reflections on Content and Context', *JAMS* 43 (1988), 63–101.

WELKER, LORENZ, ' "Alta Capella": Zur Ensemblepraxis der Blasinstrumente im 15. Jahrhundert', *Basler Jahrbuch für historische Musikpraxis*, 7 (1983), 150–61.

WOLFF, CHRISTOPH, 'Conrad Paumanns Fundamentum organisandi und seine verschiedenen Fassungen', *Archiv für Musikwissenschaft*, 25 (1968), 196–222.

WOODFIELD, IAN, *The Early History of the Viol* (Cambridge, 1984).

WRIGHT, CRAIG, *Music at the Court of Burgundy: A Documentary History* (Brooklyn, 1979).

WRIGHT, LAURENCE, 'The Medieval Gittern and Citole: A Case of Mistaken Identity', *Galpin Society Journal*, 30 (1977), 9–42.

YOUNG, CRAWFORD, 'Zur Klassifikation und ikonographischen Interpretation mittelalterlicher Zupfinstrumente', *Basler Jahrbuch für historische Musikpraxis*, 8 (1984), 67–103.

ŽAK, SABINE, *Musik als 'Ehr und Zier' im mittelalterlichen Reich* (Neuss, 1979).

ZIPPEL, GIUSEPPE, *I suonatori della Signoria di Firenze* (Trento, 1892).

ZÖBELEY, HANS RUDOLF, *Die Musik des Buxheimer Orgelbuchs* (Tutzing, 1964).

CHAPTER IV   DANCES AND DANCE MUSIC 1300–1530

(i) *Primary Sources, Reference Works, and Editions*

GUGLIELMO EBREO OF PESARO, *On the Practice or Art of Dancing*, ed. and trans. Barbara Sparti (Oxford, 1995).

Das Lochamer-Liederbuch, ed. Walter Salmen and Christoph Petzsch (Wiesbaden, 1972).

Medieval Instrumental Dances, ed. Timothy J. McGee (Bloomington and Indianapolis, 1989).

Oswald von Wolkenstein, Handschrift A: Vollständige Faksimile-Ausgabe des Codex Vindobonensis 2777 der Österreichischen Nationalbibliothek (Codices Selecti, 59; Graz, 1977).

(ii) *Books and Articles*

BOWLES, EDMUND A., *Musikleben im 15. Jahrhundert* (Musikgeschichte in Bildern, 3/viii; Leipzig, 1977).

BUSCH, GABRIELE CH., *Ikonographische Studien zum Solotanz im Mittelalter* (Innsbruck, 1982).

CRANE, FREDERICK, *Materials for the Study of the Fifteenth-Century Basse Danse* (Brooklyn, 1968).

GSTREIN, RAINER, 'Tanzmusik-Ensembles zur Zeit und am Hofe Kaiser Maximilians I.', in *Muziek aan het Hof van Margaretha van Oostenrijk = Jaarboek van het Vlaamse Centrum voor oude Muziek*, 3 (1987), 79–96.

HAMMERSTEIN, REINHOLD, *Die Musik der Engel* (Berne, 1952).

OSTHOFF, WOLFGANG, *Theatergesang und darstellende Musik in der italienischen Renaissance*, 2 vols. (Tutzing, 1969).

RIMMER, JOAN, 'Medieval Instrumental Dance Music', *Music and Letters*, 72 (1991), 61–8.

SALMEN, WALTER, 'Das Freiburger "tantzhus oder kornhus"', in Hans Schadek (ed.), *Der Kaiser in seiner Stadt: Maximilian I und der Reichstag zu Freiburg 1498* (Freiburg, 1998), 186–97.

——'L'Iconographie des lieux de la danse et de son accompagnement musical avant 1600', *Imago musicae*, 4 (1987), 99–109.

——'Jüdische Hochzeits- und Tanzhäuser im Mittelalter', *Aschkenas*, 5 (1995), 107–20.

——*Jüdische Musikanten und Tänzer, 13.–20. Jahrhundert* (Innsbruck, 1991).

——*Musikleben im 16. Jahrhundert* (Musikgeschichte in Bildern, 3/ix; Leipzig, 1977; 2nd edn. 1983).

——*Spielfrauen im Mittelalter* (Hildesheim, 2000).

——*Der Spielmann im Mittelalter* (Innsbruck, 1983).

——*Tanz im 17. und 18. Jahrhundert* (Musikgeschichte in Bildern, 4/iv; Leipzig, 1988).

——*Tanz und Tanzen vom Mittelalter bis zur Renaissance* (Hildesheim, 1999).

——'Tanzen in Klöstern während des Mittelalters', in *Die Klöster als Pflegestätten von Musik und Kunst* (Stiftung Kloster Michaelstein, 1999), 67–74.

——*Der Tanzmeister: Geschichte und Profile eines Berufes vom. 14. bis zum 19. Jahrhundert* (Hildesheim, 1997).

——'Zur Choreographie von Solotänzen in mittelalterlichen Spielen', in Katrin Kröll und Hugo Steger (eds.), *Mein ganzer Körper ist Gesicht* (Freiburg, 1994), 343–55.

——'Zur Praxis von Totentänzen im Mittelalter', in Franz Link (ed.), *Tanz und Tod in Kunst und Literatur* (Berlin, 1993), 119–26.

——(ed.), *Musik und Tanz zur Zeit Kaiser Maximilians I.* (Innsbruck, 1992).

SCHWAB, HEINRICH W., *Die Anfänge des weltlichen Berufsmusikertums in der mittelalterlichen Stadt* (Kieler Schriften zur Musikwissenschaft, 24; Kassel, 1982).

SMITH, A. WILLIAM, *Fifteenth-Century Dance and Music*, 2 vols. (New York, 1995).

CHAPTER V   POLYPHONIC MUSIC IN CENTRAL EUROPE, *c*.1300–*c*.1520

(i) *Primary Sources, Reference Works, and Editions*
CS; RISM B/iv.3–5

Engelberg Stiftsbibliothek Codex 314, ed. Wulf Arlt and Manfred Stauffacher (Schweizerische Musikdenkmäler, 11; Winterthur, 1986).

Das Glogauer Liederbuch (Berlin, former Preußische Staatsbibliothek, MS 40098; currently in Kraków, Jagiellonian Library), vols. 1–2, ed. H. Ringmann and J. Klapper; vols. 3–4, ed. C. Väterlein (Das Erbe deutscher Musik, 3, 4, 85, and 86; Kassel, 1936–81); facs. edn. Jessie Ann Owens (Renaissance Manuscripts in Facsimile, 6; New York, 1986).

Die Hohenfurter Liederhandschrift (H 42) von 1410: Facsimileausgabe, ed. Hans Rothe (Cologne, 1984).

Locheimer Liederbuch und Fundamentum organisandi des Conrad Paumann, ed. Konrad Ameln (Berlin, 1925, repr. Kassel, 1972).

Oswald von Wolkenstein, Abbildungen zur Überlieferung, i: *Die Innsbrucker Wolkenstein-Handschrift B*, ed. H. Moser and U. Müller (Litterae, 12; Göppingen, 1972).

Oswald von Wolkenstein, Handschrift A: Vollständige Faksimile-Ausgabe des Codex Vindobonensis 2777 der Österreichischen Nationalbibliothek (Codices Selecti, 59; Graz, 1977).

OSWALD VON WOLKENSTEIN, *Die Lieder Oswalds von Wolkenstein*, ed. Karl Kurt Klein and Walter Salmen (Altdeutsche Textbibliothek, 55; Tübingen, 1962).

PELNAR, IVANA, *Die mehrstimmigen Lieder Oswalds von Wolkenstein*, 2 vols. (Münchner Veröffentlichungen zur Musikgeschichte, 32; Tutzing: Schneider, 1982).

Sources of Polyphony up to c. 1500, ed. Mirosław Perz, 2 vols. (Antiquitates musicae in Polonia, 13 and 14; Graz, 1973–6).

Das Tenorlied, ed. Norbert Böker-Heil, Harald Heckman, and Ilse Kindermann, 3 vols. (Catalogus musices, 9–11; Kassel, 1979–86).

Tractatulus de cantu mensurali seu figurato musice artis (Melk, Stiftsbibliothek, 950), ed. F. Alberto Gallo (CSM 16; Rome, 1971).

WARD, TOM R., *The Polyphonic Office Hymn from 1400–1520: A Descriptive Catalogue* (Neuhausen-Stuttgart, 1980).

(ii) *Books and Articles*

Sachs, *Contrapunctus*; Strohm, *Rise*

ANGERER, JOACHIM, 'Die Begriffe *Discantus*, *Organa* und *Scolares* in reformgeschichtlichen Urkunden des 15. Jahrhunderts', *Anzeiger der Österreichischen Akademie der Wissenschaften, Philosophisch-Historische Klasse*, 109 (Vienna, 1972), 146–70.

——*Die liturgisch-musikalische Erneuerung der Melker Reform* (Vienna, 1973).

BAUCH, GEORG, *Geschichte des Breslauer Schulwesens vor der Reformation* (Codex Diplomaticus Silesiae, 25; Breslau, 1909).

BRAUNSCHWEIG-PAULI, DAGMAR, 'Studien zum sogenannten Codex St. Emmeram: Entstehung, Datierung und Besitzer der Handschrift München, Bayerische Staatsbibliothek, clm 14274 (*olim* Mus.ms.3232a)', *Kirchenmusikalisches Jahrbuch*, 66 (1982), 1–48.

BREWER, CHARLES, 'The Introduction of the *Ars Nova* into East Central Europe: A Study of Late Medieval Polish Sources' (Ph.D. diss., City University of New York, 1984).

BRINER, ANDRES, 'En anonymer unvollständiger Musiktraktat des 15. Jahrhunderts in Philadelphia, USA', *Kirchenmusikalisches Jahrbuch*, 50 (1966), 27–44.

ČERNÝ, JAROMÍR, 'Die Ars nova-Musik in Böhmen', *Miscellanea musicologica*, 21 (1970), 47–106.

——'K nejstarším dějinám moteta v českých zemích', *Miscellanea musicologica*, 24 (1971), 7–90.

——'Petrus Wilhelmi of Grudziądz—an Unknown Composer of the "Age of Dufay"', *Musica antiqua Europae orientalis IV: Bydgoszcz 1975* (Bydgoszcz, 1975), 90–103.

——'Petrus Wilhelmi de Grudencz', *Hudební věda*, 12 (1975), 195–238.

——'Vícehlasé písne konduktového typu c českých pramenech 15.století', *Miscellanea musicologica*, 31 (1984), 39–142.

——'Zur Frage der Entstehungs- und Verwandlungsprozesse der mehrstimmigen Repertoires in Böhmen', in *Trasmissione e recezione delle forme di cultura musicale: Atti del XIV Congresso della Società Internazionale di Musicologia*, ed. Angelo Pompilio *et al.*, 3 vols. (Turin, 1990), i. 168–74.

CHMEL, J., *Regesta chronologico-diplomatica Friderici III. Romanorum Imperatoris (Regis IV)* (Vienna, 1859).

COBIN, MARIAN, 'The Aosta Manuscript' (Ph.D. diss., New York University, 1979).

CUYLER, LOUISE, *The Emperor Maximilian and Music* (London, 1973).

DUNNING, ALBERT, *Die Staatsmotette: 1480–1555* (Utrecht, 1970).

EHMANN, WILHELM, *Adam von Fulda als Vertreter der ersten deutschen Komponistengeneration* (Berlin, 1936).

EWERHART, RUDOLF, *Die Handschrift 322/1944 der Stadtbibliothek Trier als musikalische Quelle* (Regensburg, 1955).

FALLOWS, DAVID, 'Dufay and the Mass Proper Cycles of Trent 88', in Nino Pirrotta and Danilo Curti (eds.), *I codici musicali trentini. Atti del Convegno Laurence Feininger: La musicologia come missione* (Trento, 1986), 46–59.

—— 'Two Equal Voices: A French Song Repertory with Music for Two More Works of Oswald von Wolkenstein', *EMH* 7 (1987), 226–41.

FEDERHOFER, HELLMUT, 'Die Niederländer an den Habsburgerhöfen in Österreich', *Anzeiger der phil.-hist. Klasse der österreichischen Akademie der Wissenschaften*, 7 (1956) (Mitteilungen der Kommission für Musikforschung, 6; Vienna, 1956), 102–20.

FEDERHOFER-KÖNIGS, RENATE, 'Ein anonymer Musiktraktat aus der 2. Hälfte des 14. Jahrhunderts in der Stiftsbibliothek Michaelbeuern/Salzburg', *Kirchenmusikalisches Jahrbuch*, 46 (1962), 43–60.

FISCHER, KURT VON, 'Kontrafakturen und Parodien italienischer Werke des Trecento und frühen Quattrocento', *Annales musicologiques*, 5 (1957), 43–59.

—— 'Neue Quellen zur Musik des 13., 14. und 15. Jahrhunderts', *Acta musicologica*, 36 (1964), 79–87.

FLOTZINGER, RUDOLF, and GRUBER, GERNOT, *Musikgeschichte Österreichs*, 2 vols. (Graz, 1977).

GÖLLNER, THEODOR, *Formen früher Mehrstimmigkeit in deutschen Handschriften des späten Mittelalters* (Münchner Veröffentlichungen zur Musikgeschichte, 6; Tutzing, 1961).

—— (chairman), 'Critical Years in European Musical History: 1400–1450', in *Report of the Tenth Congress of the IMS, Ljubljana, 1967* (Kassel, 1970), 60–6.

GOTTLIEB, LOUIS E., 'The Cyclic Masses of Trent Codex 89' (Ph.D. diss., University of California at Los Angeles, 1958).

GUDEWILL, KURT, 'Beziehungen zwischen Modus und Melodiebildung in deutschen Liedtenores', *Archiv für Musikwissenschaft*, 15 (1958), 60–88.

—— 'Deutsche Liedtenores mit F-dur-Melodik und Oktavambitus', in *Festschrift für Walter Wiora* (Kassel, 1967), 269–77.

HAMM, CHARLES, *A Chronology of the Works of Dufay Based on a Study of Mensural Practice* (Princeton, 1964).

HOFFMANN-ERBRECHT, LOTHAR, *Heinrich Finck—musicus excellentissimus* (Cologne, 1982).

JUST, MARTIN, *Der Mensuralkodex Mus. ms. 40021 der Staatsbibliothek Preußischer Kulturbesitz Berlin*, 2 vols. (Würzburger musikhistorische Beiträge, 1; Tutzing, 1975).

LEVERETT, ADELYN PECK, 'A Paleographical and Repertorial Study of the Manuscript Trento, Castello del Buon Consiglio, 91 (1378)' (Ph.D. diss., Princeton University, 1990).

——'Song Masses in the Trent Codices: The Austrian Connection', *EMH* 14 (1995), 205–56.

MAAS, CHRIS, 'Toward a New Obrecht Edition', *TVNM* 26 (1976), 84–108.

MANTUANI, JOSEF, *Die Musik in Wien: Von der Römerzeit bis zur Zeit des Kaisers Max I.* (Geschichte der Stadt Wien, iii/1; Vienna, 1907; repr. Hildesheim, 1979).

MIXTER, KEITH E., 'Johannes Brassart: A Bibliographical and Biographical Study', *Musica disciplina,* 18 (1964), 37–62; 19 (1965), 99–108.

MUŽÍKOVÁ, RENATA, 'Pauli Paulirini de Praga Musica mensuralis', *Acta universitatis carolinae, Philosophica et historica,* 2 (1965), 57–87.

PERZ, MIROSLAV, 'Il carattere internazionale delle opere di Mikolaj Radomski', *Musica disciplina,* 41 (1987), 153–9.

——'Die Einflüsse der ausgehenden italienischen Ars Nova in Polen', in *L'ars nova italiano del Trecento: secondo convegno internazionale* (Certaldo, 1971), 465–83.

——'The Lvov Fragments', *TVNM* 36 (1986), 26–51.

PIETZSCH, GERHARD, *Fürsten und fürstliche Musiker im mittelalterlichen Köln* (Beiträge zur Rheinischen Musikgeschichte, 66; Cologne, 1968).

——*Zur Pflege der Musik an den deutschen Universitäten bis zur Mitte des 16. Jahrhunderts* (Hildesheim, 1971).

PLANCHART, ALEJANDRO E., 'Guillaume Dufay's Benefices and his Relationship to the Court of Burgundy', *EMH* 7 (1987), 117–71.

REISS, JOSEF, 'Paulus Paulirinus de Praga Tractatus de musica (etwa 1460)', *Zeitschrift für Musikwissenschaft,* 7 (1924–5), 259–64.

ROEDIGER, KARL, *Die geistlichen Musikhandschriften der Universitätsbibliothek Jena*, 2 vols. (Jena, 1935).

RUMBOLD, IAN, 'The Compilation and Ownership of the "St Emmeram Codex" (Munich, Bayerische Staatsbibliothek, Clm 14274)', *EMH* 2 (1982), 164–235.

SCHLAGER, KARL HEINZ: 'Cantionale', in *Geschichte der katholischen Kirchenmusik*, ed. K. G. Fellerer, 2 vols. (Kassel, 1972), 286–93.

SCHMALZ, ROBERT F., 'Selected Fifteenth-Century Polyphonic Mass Ordinaries Based upon Pre-existent German Material' (Ph.D. diss., University of Pittsburgh, 1971).

SNOW, ROBERT J., 'The Manuscript Strahov D.G.IV.47' (Ph.D. diss., University of Illinois, 1967).

——'The Mass-Motet Cycle: A Mid-Fifteenth-Century Experiment', in R. J. Snow (ed.), *Essays in Musicology in Honor of Dragan Plamenac on his 70th Birthday* (Pittsburgh, 1969), 301–20.

STÄBLEIN, BRUNO, *Schriftbild der einstimmigen Musik* (Musikgeschichte in Bildern, 3/iv; Leipzig, 1975).

STAEHELIN, MARTIN, 'Beschreibungen und Beispiele musikalischer Formen in einem unbeachteten Traktat des frühen 15. Jahrhunderts', *Archiv für Musikwissenschaft*, 31 (1974), 237–42.

—— *Die Messen Heinrich Isaacs*, 3 vols. (Publikationen der Schweizerischen Musikforschenden Gesellschaft, ser. 2, vol. 28; Berne, 1977).

—— 'Zur Begründung der Kontrafakturpraxis in deutschen Musikhandschriften des 15. und frühen 16. Jahrhunderts', in *Florilegium musicologicum: Hellmut Federhofer zum 75. Geburtstag* (Mainzer Studien zur Musikwissenschaft, 21; Tutzing, 1988), 389–96.

STROHM, REINHARD, 'Meßzyklen über deutsche Lieder in den Trienter Codices', in *Liedstudien: Wolfgang Osthoff zum 60. Geburtstag* (Tutzing, 1989), 77–106.

—— 'Native and Foreign Polyphony in Late Medieval Austria', *Musica disciplina*, 38 (1984), 205–30.

—— 'Zur Rezeption der frühen Cantus-firmus-Messe im deutschsprachigen Bereich', in W. Konold (ed.), *Deutsch-englische Musikbeziehungen: Referate des wissenschaftlichen Symposions 'Musica Britannica' (1980)* (Munich, 1985), 9–38.

TIMM, ERIKA, *Die Überlieferung der Lieder Oswalds von Wolkenstein* (Germanische Studien, 242; Lübeck, 1972).

WARD, TOM R.: 'A Central European Repertory in Munich, Bayerische Staatsbibliothek, Clm 14274', *EMH* 1 (1981), 324–43.

—— 'Music and Music Theory in the Universities of Central Europe during the Fifteenth Century', in *Trasmissione e recezione delle forme di cultura musicale: Atti del XIV Congresso della Società Internazionale di Musicologia*, ed. Angelo Pompilio *et al.* (Turin, 1990), i. 49–57.

—— 'Music in the Library of Johannes Klein', in John Kmetz (ed.), *Music in the German Renaissance: Sources, Styles and Contexts* (Cambridge, 1994), 54–73.

—— 'Music in the University: Leipzig, Universitätsbibliothek, MS 1084', in Martin Staehelin (ed.), *Gestalt und Entstehung musikalischer Quellen im 15. und 16. Jahrhundert* (Wolfenbüttler Forschungen, 83; Quellenstudien zur Musik der Renaissance III; Wiesbaden, 1998), 21–34.

—— 'The Structure of Manuscript Trent 92-I', *Musica disciplina*, 29 (1975), 127–47.

WELKER, LORENZ, 'Ein anonymer Mensuraltraktat in der Sterzinger Miszellaneen-Handschrift', *Archiv für Musikwissenschaft*, 48 (1991), 255–81.

—— 'New Light on Oswald von Wolkenstein: Central European Traditions and Burgundian Polyphony', *EMH* 7 (1987), 187–226.

WOLF, JOHANNES, 'Ein Breslauer Mensuraltraktat des 15. Jahrhunderts', *Archiv für Musikwissenschaft*, 1 (1918–19), 329–45.

WRIGHT, PETER, 'On the Origins of Trent 87_1 and 92_2', *EMH* 6 (1986), 245–70.

—— 'The Related Parts of the Trent, Museo Provinciale d'Arte, Mss 82(1374) and 92(1379): A Paleographical and Text-Critical Study' (Ph.D. diss., Nottingham University, 1986). (Subsequently published in Outstanding Dissertations in Music from British Universities, New York, 1989.)

CHAPTER VI   THE MUSIC THEORY OF THE FOURTEENTH AND EARLY FIFTEENTH CENTURIES

(i) *Primary Sources, Reference Works, and Editions*
CS; GS; La Fage; Sachs, *Contrapunctus*; RISM B/iii.1–6; Strunk; Strunk², Zaminer

ANONYMOUS II, *Tractatus de discantu (Concerning Discant)*, ed. and trans. Albert Seay (Texts/Translation, 1; Colorado Springs, Colo., 1978). Also in CS i. 303–19.

ANONYMOUS V, *Ars cantus mensurabilis mensurata per modos iuris*, ed. and trans. C. Matthew Balensuela (Greek and Latin Music Theory, 10; Lincoln, Nebr. and London, 1994). Also in CS iii. 379–98.

ANONYMOUS of Vallicelliana C 105, *De musica tractatus*, in La Fage, 422–8.

ANSELMI, *Musica. Georgii Anselmi Parmensis De musica*, ed. Giuseppe Massera ('Historiae Musicae Cultores' Biblioteca, 14; Florence, 1961).

ANTONIUS DE LENO, *Regulae de contrapunto*, in CS iii. 307–29. Also in Antonius de Leno, *Regulae de contrapunto*, ed. Albert Seay (Critical Texts, 1; Colorado Springs, Colo., 1977).

ANTONIUS DE LUCA, *Ars cantus figurati*; Anonymus, *Capitulum de quattuor mensuris*; Anonymus, *Tractatulus mensurationum*; Anonymus, *Compendium breve de proportionibus*; Anonymus, *Tractatulus prolationum cum tabulis*, ed. Heinz Ristory (CSM 38; Neuhausen, 1997).

AURELIAN, *Musica disciplina. Aureliani reomensis Musica disciplina*, ed. Lawrence Gushee (CSM 21; n.p.: American Institute of Musicology, 1975). Translation: *The Discipline of Music*, trans. Joseph Ponte (Translations, 3; Colorado Springs, Colo., 1968).

BERNHARD, MICHAEL (ed.), *Clavis Gerberti: Eine Revision von Martin Gerberts Scriptores Ecclesiastici de Musica Sacra Potissimum (St. Blaise 1784), Teil 1* (Bayerische Akademie der Wissenschaften, Veröffentlichungen der Musikhistorischen Kommission, 7; Munich: Verlag der Bayerischen Akademie der Wissenschaften, 1989).

Berkeley Treatise. *The Berkeley Manuscript: University of California Music Library, MS. 744 (olim Phillipps 4450)*, ed. Oliver B. Ellsworth (Greek and Latin Music Theory, 2; Lincoln, Nebr. and London, 1984).

BERNO, *Musica*, in GS ii. 62–79. Also in Alexander Rausch, *Die Musiktraktate des Abtes Bern von Reichenau: Edition und Interpretation* (Tutzing, 1999).

BOEN, JOHANNES, *Ars (musicae)*. *Ars (musicae) Johannis Boen*, ed. F. Alberto Gallo (CSM 19; n.p.: American Institute of Musicology, 1972).

——*Musica*, in Wolf Frobenius, *Johannes Boens "Musica" und seine Konsonanzenlehre* (Freiburger Schriften zur Musikwissenschaft, 2; Stuttgart, 1971), 32–78.

BOETHIUS, *De musica*. *Anicii Manlii Torquati Severini Boetii De institutione arithmetica libri II, De institutione musica libri V*, ed. Gottfried Friedlein (Leipzig, 1867). Translation: *Fundamentals of Music*, trans. Calvin M. Bower (Music Theory Translation Series; New Haven, 1989). Excerpts translated in Strunk, 79–86, and Strunk², 137–43.

CASSIODORUS, *Institutiones*. *Cassiodori Senatoris Institutiones*, ed. R. A. B. Mynors (Oxford, 1917). Translated by Leslie Webber Jones (New York, 1946). Excerpt translated in Strunk, 87–92, and Strunk², 143–8.

Cum notum sit, in CS iii. 60a–62b, as part of the 'Ars contrapuncti secundum Johannem de Muris'.

De diminutione contrapuncti, in CS iii. 62b–68b, as part of the 'Ars contrapuncti secundum Johannem de Muris'.

Dialogus de musica, in GS i. 252–64. Partially translated in Strunk, 103–16, and Strunk², 198–210.

FRANCO, *Ars cantus mensurabilis*. *Franconis de Colonia Ars cantus mensurabilis*, ed. Gilbert Reaney and André Gilles (CSM 18; n.p.: American Institute of Musicology, 1974). Also in CS iii. 1–16 and CS i. 117–35. Translation in Strunk, 139–59, and Strunk², 226–45.

GROCHEIO, *Musica*. *Die Quellenhandschriften zum Musiktraktat des Johannes de Grocheio*, ed. Ernst Rohloff (Leipzig, n.d.).

GUIDO, *Micrologus*. *Guidonis Aretini Micrologus*, ed. Joseph Smits van Waesberghe (CSM 4; n.p.: American Institute of Musicology, 1955). Also in GS ii. 1–24. Translated in *Hucbald, Guido, and John on Music*, 57–83.

——*Regulae rhythmicae*, in *Guido d'Arezzo's* Regule rithmice, Prologus in antiphonarium, *and* Epistola ad Michahelem: *A Critical Text and Translation*, ed. and trans. Dolores Pesce (Musicological Studies, 73; Ottawa, 1999), 327–403. Also in GS ii. 25–34.

HUCBALD, *De harmonica institutione*, in GS i. 104–22. Translated in *Hucbald, Guido, and John on Music*, 13–44.

Hucbald, Guido, and John on Music, trans. Warren Babb, ed. Claude V. Palisca (Music Theory Translation Series; New Haven and London, 1978).

ISIDORE, *Etymologiae*. *Isidori hispalensis episcopi Etymologiarum sive originum libri XX*, ed. W. M. Lindsay, 2 vols. (Oxford, 1911). Excerpt translated in Strunk, 93–100, and Strunk², 149–55.

JACQUES DE LIÈGE, *Speculum musicae*. *Jacobi Leodiensis Speculum musicae*, ed. Roger Bragard, 7 vols. (CSM 3; Rome, 1955–73). Books 6 and 7 also in CS ii. 193–433 under Johannes de Muris as author. Excerpts translated in Strunk, 180–90, and Strunk², 269–78.

JOHANNES 'Cotto', *Musica. Johannis Affligemensis De musica cum tonario*, ed. Joseph Smits van Waesberghe (CSM 1; Rome, 1950). Also in GS ii. 230–65. Translated in *Hucbald, Guido, and John on Music*, 101–87.

JOHANNES DE GARLANDIA, *De mensurabili musica*, ed. Erich Reimer, 2 vols. (Beihefte zum Archiv für Musikwissenschaft, 10–11; Wiesbaden, 1972).

——(attr.), *Introductio musice*, in Nigel Gwee, '*De plana musica* and *Introductio musice*: A Critical Edition and Translation, with Commentary, of Two Treatises Attributed to Johannes de Garlandia' (Ph.D. diss.; Louisiana State University, 1996).

JOHANNES DE MURIS, *Ars practica mensurabilis cantus secundum Iohannem de Muris*, ed. Christian Berktold (Bayerische Akademie der Wissenschaften, Veröffentlichungen der Musikhistorischen Kommission; Munich, 1999).

——*Compendium musice practice, Notitia artis musice. Johannis de Muris Notitia artis musicae et Compendium musicae practice, Petrus* [sic] *de Sancto Dionysio Tractatus de musica*, ed. Ulrich Michels (CSM 17; n.p.: American Institute of Musicology, 1972). Book II also in GS iii. 292–301; partially translated in Strunk, 172–9, and Strunk[2], 262–9.

——*Musica ⟨speculativa⟩*, ed. Susan Fast (Musicological Studies, 61; Ottawa, 1994). Also in GS iii. 255–83.

JOHANNES DE OLOMONS, *Palma choralis*, ed. Albert Seay (Critical Texts, 6; Colorado Springs, Colo., 1977).

JOHANNES VETULUS DE ANAGNIA, *Musica. Johannis Vetuli de Anagnia Liber de musica*, ed. Frederick Hammond (CSM 27; n.p.: American Institute of Musicology, 1977).

Lexicon musicum Latinum medii aevi, ed. Michael Bernhard, 4 fasc. to date (Munich, 1992–).

Libellus cantus mensurabilis, in CS iii. 46–58.

MACROBIUS, *Somnium Scipionis. Ambrosii Theodosii Macrobii Commentarii in Somnium Scipionis*, ed. Jacob Willis (Leipzig, 1963). Translation: *Commentary on the Dream of Scipio*, trans. William Harris Stahl (New York, 1952).

MARCHETTO, *Lucidarium. The Lucidarium of Marchetto of Padua*, ed. and trans. Jan W. Herlinger (Chicago and London, 1985). Also in CS iii. 64–121.

——*Pomerium. Marcheti de Padua Pomerium*, ed. Giuseppe Vecchi (CSM 6; n.p.: American Institute of Musicology, 1961). Also in CS iii. 121–88. Excerpt translated in Strunk 160–71, and Strunk[2], 251–61.

Mensurabilis musicae tractatuli, ed. F. Alberto Gallo and Piero Paolo Scattolin, 2 vols. to date (Bologna, 1966–).

MEYER, CHRISTIAN (ed.), *Mensura monochordi: la division du monocorde (IXe–XVe siècles)* (Publications de la Société Française de Musicologie, 2nd ser., 5; Paris, 1996).

Musica enchiriadis, in *Musica et Scolica Enchiriadis una cum aliquibus tractatulis adiunctis*, ed. Hans Schmid (Bayerische Akademie der

Wissenschaften, Veröffentlichungen der Musikhistorischen Kommission, 3; Munich, 1981). Also in GS i. 152–72.

NICOLAUS OF CAPUA, *Compendium musicale*, in La Fage, 308–38.

ODINGTON, *Speculatio musicae. Walteri Odington Summa de speculatione musicae*, ed. Frederick F. Hammond (CSM 14; n.p.: American Institute of Musicology, 1970). Also in CS i. 182–250. Part 6 translated by Jay A. Huff (MSD 31; n.p.: American Institute of Musicology, 1973).

PETRUS DICTUS PALMA OCIOSA, *Compendium de discantu mensurabili*, in Johannes Wolf, 'Ein Beitrag zur Diskantlehre des 14. Jahrhunderts', *Sammelbände der Internationalen Musik-Gesellschaft*, 15 (1913–14), 504–34.

PHILIPPE DE VITRY, *Ars nova. Philippi de Vitriaco Ars nova*, ed. Gilbert Reaney, André Gilles, and Jean Maillard (CSM 8; n.p.: American Institute of Musicology, 1964). Also in CS iii. 13–22. Translated by Leon Plantinga: 'Philippe de Vitry's *Ars Nova*: A Translation', *Journal of Music Theory*, 5 (1961), 204–23.

PROSDOCIMO, *Contrapunctus. Prosdocimi de Beldemandis Contrapunctus*, ed. and trans. Jan Herlinger (Greek and Latin Music Theory, 1; Lincoln, Nebr. and London, 1984). Also in CS iii. 193–9.

—— *Expositiones. Expositiones tractatus practice cantus mensurabilis magistri Johannis de Muris*, ed. F. Alberto Gallo (Prosdocimi de Beldemandis opera, 1; Bologna, 1966).

—— *Monacordum*, in Prosdocimo de' Beldomandi, *Brevis summula proportionum quantum ad musicam pertinet* and *Parvus tractatulus de modo monachordum dividendi*, ed. and trans. Jan Herlinger (Greek and Latin Music Theory, 4; Lincoln, Nebr. and London, 1987). Also in CS iii. 248–58.

—— *Tractatus musice speculative*, in D. Raffaelo Baralli and Luigi Torri, 'Il *Trattato* di Prosdocimo de' Beldomandi contro il *Lucidario* di Marchetto da Padova', *Rivista musicale italiana*, 20 (1913), 707–62.

—— *Tractatus practice cantus mensurabilis*, in CS iii. 200–28.

—— *Tractatus practice de musica mensurabilis ad modum italicorum*, in CS iii. 228–48. Prosdocimo's revision: Claudio Sartori, *La notazione italiana in una redazione inedita del "Tractatus practice cantus mensurabilis ad modum ytalicorum" di Prosdocimo de Beldemandis* (Florence, 1938); a translation of the latter: *A Treatise on the Practice of Mensural Music in the Italian Manner*, trans. Jay A. Huff (MSD 29; n.p.: American Institute of Musicology, 1972).

Quatuor principalia musicae secundum Simonem Tunstede, in CS iv. 200–98.

Quilibet affectans, in CS iii. 59a–60a, as part of the 'Ars contrapuncti secundum Johannem de Muris'.

Quot sunt concordationes, in CS iii. 70a–74b, as part of the 'Ars discantus secundum Johannem de Muris'.

REMI, *Martianus Capella. Remigii Autissiodorensis Commentum in Martianum Capellam*, ed. Cora E. Lutz, 2 vols. (Leiden, 1962–5).

RIEMANN, HUGO, *Geschichte der Musiktheorie im. IX.–XIX. Jahrhundert* (Leipzig, 1898; 2nd edn., Berlin, 1920). Partial translation: *History of Music Theory, Books I and II: Polyphonic Theory to the Sixteenth Century*, trans. Raymond H. Haggh (Lincoln, Nebr., 1962).

ROBERTUS DE HANDLO, *Regule*. Robertus de Handlo, *Regule*, and Johannes Hanboys, *Summa*, ed. Peter M. Lefferts (Greek and Latin Music Theory, 7; Lincoln, Nebr. and London, 1991).

Le Roman de Fauvel in the Edition of Mesire Chaillou de Pesstain: A Reproduction in Facsimile of the Complete Manuscript Paris, Bibliothèque Nationale, fonds français 146, ed. Edward Roesner, François Avril, and Nancy Freeman Regalado (New York, 1990).

Sex sunt species principales, in *Philippi de Vitriaco Ars nova*, ed. Gilbert Reaney, André Gilles, and Jean Maillard (CSM 8; n.p.: American Institute of Musicology, 1964), 55–60.

SPECHTSHART VON REUTLINGEN, HUGO, *Flores musicae (1332/42)*, ed. Karl-Werner Gümpel (Akademie der Wissenschaften und der Literatur, Mainz, Abhandlungen der Geistes-und Sozialwissenschaftlichen Klasse, Jahrgang 1958, no. 3; Wiesbaden, 1958).

THEODONUS DE CAPRIO, *Regule contrapuncti*, in Raffaelo Casimiri, 'Theodonus de Caprio non Theodoricus de Campo', *Note d'archivio*, 19 (1942), 94–8.

Tractatus figurarum: Treatise on Noteshapes, ed. and trans. Philip E. Schreur (Greek and Latin Music Theory, 6; Lincoln, Nebr. and London, 1989).

UGOLINO, *Declaratio. Ugolini Urbevetanis Declaratio musicae disciplinae*, ed. Albert Seay, 3 vols. (CSM 7; Rome, 1959–62).

Volentibus introduci. Version AC in CS iii. 23a–27b, as part of the 'Ars contrapuncti secundum Philippum de Vitriaco'; version Pi in Sachs, *Contrapunctus*, 170–3.

(ii) *Books and Articles*

ADKINS, CECIL DALE, 'The Theory and Practice of the Monochord' (Ph.D. diss., State University of Iowa, 1963).

ATKINSON, CHARLES M., 'From *Vitium* to *Tonus acquisitus*: On the Evolution of the Notational Matrix of Medieval Chant', *Studia musicologica Academiae Scientiarum Hungaricae*, 31 (1989), 181–97.

BARBOUR, J. MURRAY, *Tuning and Temperament: A Historical Survey* (East Lansing, Mich., 1953).

BERGER, KAROL, *Musica Ficta: Theories of Accidental Inflections in Vocal Polyphony from Marchetto da Padova to Gioseffo Zarlino* (Cambridge and New York, 1987).

BERNHARD, MICHAEL, 'Das musikalische Fachschrifttum im lateinischen Mittelalter', in Zaminer, iii. 37–103.

——'Überlieferung und Fortleben der antiken lateinischen Musiktheorie im Mittelalter', in Zaminer, iii. 7–35.

ELLSWORTH, OLIVER B., 'A Fourteenth-Century Proposal for Equal Temperament', *Viator*, 5 (1974), 445–53.

FULLER, SARAH, 'A Phantom Treatise of the Fourteenth Century?—The *Ars Nova*', *Journal of Musicology*, 4 (1985–6), 23–50.

GALLO, F. ALBERTO, 'Marchetus in Padua und die "franco-venetische" Musik des frühen Trecento', *Archiv für Musikwissenschaft*, 31 (1974), 42–56.

——'Die Notationslehre im 14. und 15. Jahrhundert', in Zaminer, v. 257–356.

——*La teoria della notazione in Italia dalla fine del XIII all'inizio del XV secolo* (Antiquae Musicae Italicae Subsidia Theorica; Bologna, 1966).

GÜNTHER, URSULA, FINSCHER, LUDWIG, and DEAN, JEFFREY (eds.), *Modality in the Music of the Fourteenth and Fifteenth Centuries* (MSD 49; Neuhausen-Stuttgart, 1996).

GUSHEE, LAWRENCE, 'Jehan des Murs', *New Grove*, ix. 587–90.

——'The *Tabula monochordi* of Magister Nicolaus de Luduno', in Graeme M. Boone (ed.), *Essays on Medieval Music in Honor of David G. Hughes* (Isham Library Papers, 4; Cambridge, Mass., 1995), 117–52.

GWEE, NIGEL, '*De plana musica* and *Introductio musice*: A Critical Edition and Translation, with Commentary, of Two Treatises Attributed to Johannes de Garlandia' (Ph.D. diss.; Louisiana State University, 1996).

HERLINGER, JAN, 'A Fifteenth-Century Italian Compilation of Music Theory', *Acta musicologica*, 53 (1981), 90–105.

——'Fractional Divisions of the Whole Tone', *Music Theory Spectrum*, 3 (1981), 74–83.

——'Marchetto's Division of the Whole Tone', *JAMS* 45 (1981), 193–216.

——'Marchetto's Influence: The Manuscript Evidence', in André Barbera (ed.), *Music Theory and its Sources: Antiquity and the Middle Ages* (Notre Dame Conferences in Medieval Studies, 1; Notre Dame, Ind., 1990), 235–58.

——'Medieval Canonics', ch. 3 of *The Cambridge History of Western Music Theory*, ed. Thomas Christensen (Cambridge and New York, forthcoming).

——'What Trecento Music Theory Tells Us', in Eugene Narmour and Ruth A. Solie (eds.), *Explorations in Music, the Arts, and Ideas: Essays in Honor of Leonard B. Meyer* (Festschrift Series, 7; Stuyvesant, NY, 1988), 177–97.

JACOBSTHAL, GUSTAV, *Die chromatische Alteration im liturgischen Gesang der abendländischen Kirche* (Berlin, 1897).

KARP, THEODORE, 'From the Aural to the Written Tradition: The *Coniunctae* of the Anonymous Berkeley Theory MS', in id., *Aspects of Orality and Formularity in Gregorian Chant* (Evanston, Ill., 1998), 181–223.

KATZ, DANIEL SETH, 'The Earliest Sources for the *Libellus cantus mensurabilis secundum Johannem de Muris*' (Ph.D. diss., Duke University, 1989).

KOLLER, OSWALD, 'Aus dem Archive des Benedictinerstiftes St. Paul im Lavantthal in Kärnten', *Monatshefte für Musikgeschichte*, 22 (1890), 22–9, 35–45, and supplement.

LONG, MICHAEL, 'Musical Tastes in Fourteenth-Century Italy: National Styles, Scholarly Traditions, and Historical Circumstances' (Ph.D. diss., Princeton University, 1981).

MCKINNON, JAMES W., 'Jubal vel Pythagoras: Quis Sit Inventor Musicae?', *MQ* 64 (1978), 1–28.

MEYER, CHRISTIAN, 'Le *De synemmenis* et sa tradition: contribution à l'étude des mesures du monocorde vers la fin du XIIIe siècle', *Revue de musicologie*, 76 (1990), 83–95.

MICHELS, ULRICH, *Die Musiktraktate des Johannes de Muris* (Beihefte zum Archiv für Musikwissenschaft, 8; Wiesbaden, 1970).

MONTEROSSO, RAFFAELLO, 'Un compendio inedito del *Lucidarium* di Marchetto da Padova', *Studi medievali*, 3rd ser., 7 (1966), 914–31.

NIEMÖLLER, KLAUS WOLFGANG, 'Zur Tonus-Lehre der italienischen Musiktheorie des ausgehenden Mittelalters', *Kirchenmusikalisches Jahrbuch*, 40 (1956), 23–32.

PAGE, CHRISTOPHER, *Discarding Images: Reflections on Music and Culture in Medieval France* (Oxford, 1993).

PANTI, CECILIA, 'Una fonte della *Declaratio musicae disciplinae* di Ugolino da Orvieto: quattro anonime *questiones* della tarda scolastica', *Rivista italiana di musicologia*, 24 (1989), 3–47.

PESCE, DOLORES, *The Affinities and Modal Transposition* (Music: Scholarship and Performance; Bloomington and Indianapolis, 1987).

PEVERADA, ENRICO, *Vita musicale nella chiesa ferrarese del Quattrocento* (Ferrara, 1991).

POWERS, HAROLD S., 'Mode', in *New Grove* xii. 376–450.

RAHN, JAY, 'Marchetto's Theory of Commixture and Interruptions', *Music Theory Spectrum*, 9 (1987), 117–35.

REIMER, ERICH, 'Musicus und Cantor: Zur Sozialgeschichte eines musikalischen Lehrstücks', *Archiv für Musikwissenschaft*, 35 (1978), 1–32.

——*Die Musiktraktate des Johannes de Muris* (Beihefte zum Archiv für Musikwissenschaft, 8; Wiesbaden, 1970).

RIETHMÜLLER, ALBRECHT, 'Probleme der spekulativen Musiktheorie im Mittelalter', in Zaminer, iii. 163–201.

RISTORY, HEINZ, 'Ein Kurztraktat mit Binärmensuration und praefranconischem Gepräge', *Studi musicali*, 15 (1986), 151–6.

——*Post-franconische Theorie und Früh-Trecento: Die Petrus de Cruce-Neuerungen und ihre Bedeutung für die italienische Mensuralnotenschrift zu Beginn des 14. Jahrhunderts* (Europäische Hochschulschriften, ser. 36: Musikwissenschaft, 26; Frankfurt and New York, 1988).

SACHS, KLAUS-JÜRGEN, 'Die Contrapunctus-Lehre im 14. und 15. Jahrhundert', in Zaminer, v. 161–256.

——'Counterpoint', sections 1–11, in *New Grove*, iv. 833–43.

—— 'Musikalische Elementarlehre im Mittelalter', in Zaminer, iii. 105–61.

SMITS VAN WAESBERGHE, JOSEPH, *Musikerziehung: Lehre und Theorie der Musik im Mittelalter* (Musikgeschichte in Bildern, 3/iii; Leipzig, 1969).

STRUNK, OLIVER, 'On the Date of Marchetto da Padova', in id., *Essays on Music in the Western World* (New York, 1974), 39–43.

CHAPTER VII MUSIC THEORY AND MUSICAL THINKING AFTER 1450

(i) *Primary Sources, Reference Works, and Editions*
CS; GS; RISM B/iii; Sachs, *Contrapunctus*; Strunk; Strunk²; Tinctoris, *Opera*; Tinctoris, *De inventione*

AARON, PIETRO, *Compendiolo di molti dubbi, segreti et sentenze intorno al canto fermo, et figurato* (Milan, *c*.1545; facs. edn., Bologna, 1970).

—— *Libri tres de institutione harmonica* (Bologna, 1516; facs. edn., New York, 1976).

—— *Lucidario in musica* (Venice, 1545; facs. edn., Bologna, 1969).

—— *Toscanello* (Venice, 1523; rev. edns. 1529, 1539; 1529 edn. repr. Bologna, 1969; trans. Peter Bergquist (Colorado College Music Press Translations, 4; Colorado Springs, Colo., 1970)).

—— *Trattato della natura et cognitione di tutti gli tuoni di canto figurato* (Venice, 1525; facs. edn., Utrecht, 1966).

ANONYMI, *Tractatus de cantu figurativo et de contrapuncto (c. 1430–1520)*, ed. Christian Meyer (CSM 41; Neuhausen-Stuttgart, 1997).

ANONYMOUS, *Arte de canto llano* (n.p., n.d.; facs. edn., Madrid, 1978).

ANONYMOUS, *Tractatulus de cantu mensurali seu figurativo musice artis* (Melk, Stiftsbibliothek, MS 950), ed. F. Alberto Gallo (CSM 16; n.p.: American Institute of Musicology, 1971).

Anonymous (15th-Century), Quatuor tractatuli italici de contrapuncto, ed. Albert Seay (Colorado College Music Press Critical Texts, 3; Colorado Springs, Colo., 1977).

ANONYMUS XI: RICHARD JOSEPH WINGELL, 'Anonymous XI (CS III): An Edition, Translation, and Commentary' (Ph.D. diss., University of Southern California, 1973).

ANONYMUS XII: *Tractatus et compendium cantus figurati*, ed. Jill M. Palmer (CSM 35; Neuhausen-Stuttgart, 1990).

The Berkeley Manuscript: University of California Music Library, MS. 744, ed. Oliver B. Ellsworth (Greek and Latin Music Theory, 2; Lincoln, Nebr. and London, 1984).

BERMUDO, JUAN, *Comiença el libro primero de la declaracion de instrumentos* (Ossuna, 1549).

BURZIO, NICCOLÒ, *Florum libellus*, ed. Giuseppe Massera ('Historiae musicae cultores' Biblioteca; Florence, 1975).

Burzio, Niccolò, *Musices opusculum* (Bologna, 1487), trans. Clement A. Miller (MSD 37; n.p.: American Institute of Musicology, 1983).

Cochlaeus, Johannes, *Tetrachordum musices* (Nuremberg, 1512; facs. edn., Hildesheim, 1971); trans. Clement A. Miller (MSD 23; n.p.: American Institute of Musicology, 1970).

A Correspondence of Renaissance Musicians, ed. Bonnie J. Blackburn, Edward E. Lowinsky, and Clement A. Miller (Oxford, 1991).

Coussemaker, C. E. H. de, *Histoire de l'harmonie au moyen âge* (Paris, 1852).

Del Lago, Giovanni, *Breve introduttione di musica misurata* (Venice, 1540; facs. edn., Bologna, 1969).

Despuig, Guillermo, *Ars musicorum* (Valencia, 1495; facs. edn., Bologna, 1975; Madrid, 1976). Books V and VI also in Guillermus de Podio, *Ars musicorum libri vi et viii*, ed. Albert Seay (Colorado College Music Press, Critical Texts, 8; Colorado Springs, Colo., 1978).

Durán, Domingo Marcos, *Comento sobre Lux bella* (Salamanca, 1498; facs. edn., Madrid, 1976).

——*Lux bella* (Seville, 1492; facs. edn., Madrid, 1976).

——*Sumula de canto de organo contrapunto y composicion vocal practica y especulativa* (Salamanca, c.1504; facs. edn., Madrid, 1976).

Escobar, Cristóbal de, *Esta es una introduction muy breve de canto llano* (Salamanca, c.1498; facs. edn., Madrid, 1978).

Espinosa, Juan de, *Tractato de principios de musica practica y teorica sin dejar ninguna cosa atras* (Toledo, 1520; facs. edn., Madrid, 1978).

Estevan, Fernand, 'Reglas de canto plano è de contrapunto è de canto de órgano'. Primer tratado de música escrito en castellano de Fernand Estevan: Comentario, estudio, transcripción y facsímil, ed. M.a Pilar Escudero García (Madrid, 1984). See also the partial edition in Gümpel, 'Zur Frühgeschichte'.

Fogliano, Lodovico, *Musica theorica* (Venice, 1529; facs. edn., Bologna, 1970).

Gaffurio, Franchino, *De harmonia musicorum instrumentorum opus* (Milan, 1518; facs. edn., New York, 1979); trans. Clement A. Miller (MSD 33; n.p.: American Institute of Musicology, 1977).

——*Practica musice* (Milan, 1496; facs. edn., Farnborough, 1967); trans. Clement A. Miller (MSD 20; n.p: American Institute of Musicology, 1968).

——*Theorica musice* (Milan, 1492; facs. edn., Rome, 1934); trans. Walter Kreyszig (Music Theory Translation Series; New Haven, Conn., and London, 1993).

Guerson, Guillaume, *Utilissime musicales regule* (Paris, c.1495).

Guilielmus Monachus, *De preceptis artis musicae*, ed. Albert Seay (CSM 11; n.p.: American Institute of Musicology, 1965).

Hothby, John, *Calliopea legale*, in Coussemaker, *Histoire de l'harmonie au moyen âge*, 297–349. New edn. and English trans. by Timothy L. McDonald, *La Calliopea legale* (CSM 42; Neuhausen-Stuttgart, 1997).

——*De arte contrapuncti*, ed. Gilbert Reaney (CSM 26; Neuhausen-Stuttgart, 1977).

——*Opera omnia de musica mensurabili*, ed. Gilbert Reaney (CSM 31; Neuhausen-Stuttgart, 1983).

——*Opera omnia de proportionibus*, ed. Gilbert Reaney (CSM 39; Neuhausen-Stuttgart, 1997).

——*Quid est proportio* (London, British Library, Add. 10336, fos. 58^r–62^v, and Lambeth Palace, MS 466, fos. 19^r–22^v).

——*Tractatus quarundam regularum artis musice* (Florence, Biblioteca Nazionale Centrale, MS Pal. 472, fos. 9^r–15^r).

——*Tres tractatuli contra Bartholomeum Ramum*, ed. A. Seay (CSM 10; Rome, 1964). Includes: *Excitatio quaedam musicae artis per refutationem*, 17–57; *Dialogus Johannis Octobi anglici in arte musica*, 61–76; and a letter to an unnamed cleric, 79–92.

Hucbald, Guido, and John on Music, trans. Warren Babb, ed. Claude V. Palisca (Music Theory Translation Series; New Haven and London, 1978).

MARTÍNEZ DE BISCARGUI, GONÇALO, *Arte de canto llano y contrapunto y canto de organo con proportiones y modos* (Zaragoza, 1538; facs. of 1511 edn., Madrid, 1976).

ORNITHOPARCHUS, ANDREAS, *Musice active micrologus* (Leipzig, 1517); repr. in facsimile, together with John Dowland's English translation of 1609, by Gustave Reese and Steven Ledbetter (New York, 1973).

RAMOS DE PAREJA, BARTOLOMÉ, *Musica practica* (Bologna, 1482; facs. edn., Bologna, 1969; Madrid, 1983); ed. Johannes Wolf (Leipzig, 1901); ed. Clemente Terni, trans. Gaetano Chiappini (Madrid, 1983). English trans. by Clement A. Miller (MSD 44; Neuhausen-Stuttgart, 1993).

SCHANPPECHER, MELCHIOR, *Die Musica figurativa des Melchior Schanppecher, Opus aureum, Köln 1501, pars III/IV*, ed. Klaus Wolfgang Niemöller (Beiträge zur Rheinischen Musikgeschichte, 50; Cologne, 1961).

SPATARO, GIOVANNI, *Errori di Franchino Gaffurio . . . in sua deffensione et del suo preceptore Maestro Bartolomeo Ramis hispano subtilemente demon-strati* (Bologna, 1521).

——*Johannis Spadarii . . . ac Bartolomei Rami Pareie eius preceptoris honesta defensio in Nicolai Burtii Parmensis opusculum* (Bologna, 1491) (repr. in Johannis Spatarii Opera omnia, 1; Bologna, 1967).

TINCTORIS, JOHANNES, *The Art of Counterpoint*, trans. Albert Seay (MSD 5; n.p.: American Institute of Musicology, 1961).

——*Complexus effectuum musices*, in *On the Dignity and the Effects of Music: Egidius Carlerius, Johannes Tinctoris, Two Fifteenth-Century Treatises*, trans. J. Donald Cullington, ed. Reinhard Strohm and J. Donald Cullington (Institute of Advanced Musical Studies Study Texts, 2; London, 1996).

——*Concerning the Nature and Propriety of Tones*, trans. Albert Seay (Colorado College Music Press Translations, 2; Colorado Springs, Colo., 1967).

TINCTORIS, JOHANNES, *De inventione et usu musicae*; extant portions ed. in Weinmann, *Johannes Tinctoris und sein unbekannter Traktat*, and Woodley, 'The Printing and Scope'.

——*Dictionary of Musical Terms by Johannes Tinctoris*, trans. Carl Parrish (New York and London, 1963).

——*Expositio manus*, trans. Albert Seay, 'The *Expositio manus* of Johannes Tinctoris', *Journal of Music Theory*, 9 (1965), 194–232.

——*Proportionale musices*, trans. Albert Seay in 'The *Proportionale musices* of Johannes Tinctoris', *Journal of Music Theory*, 1 (1957), 22–75; rev. as *Proportions in music* (Proportionale musices) (Colorado College Music Press Translations, 10; Colorado Springs, Colo., 1979).

WOLLICK, NICOLAUS, *Enchiridion musices* (Paris, 1509 and 1512; facs. of 1512 edn., Geneva, 1972).

(ii) *Books and Articles*

Lowinsky, *Culture*; Palisca, *Humanism*; Reese, *Renaissance*

BARTHA, DÉNES, *Das Musiklehrbuch einer ungarischen Klosterschule in der Handschrift von Fürstprimas Szalkai (1490)* (Musicologica Hungarica, 1; Budapest, 1934).

BENT, MARGARET, 'Accidentals, Counterpoint, and Notation in Aaron's *Aggiunta* to the *Toscanello*', *Journal of Musicology*, 12 (1994), 306–44.

——'Resfacta and *Cantare Super Librum*', *JAMS* 36 (1983), 371–91.

BERGER, KAROL, *Musica Ficta: Theories of Accidental Inflections in Vocal Polyphony from Marchetto da Padova to Gioseffo Zarlino* (Cambridge, 1987).

BERGQUIST, PETER, 'The Theoretical Writings of Pietro Aaron' (Ph.D. diss., Columbia University, 1964).

BLACKBURN, BONNIE J., 'Did Ockeghem Listen to Tinctoris?', in *Johannes Ockeghem: Actes du XLᵉ Colloque international d'études humanistes. Tours, 3–8 février 1997*, ed. Philippe Vendrix (Paris, 1998), 597–640.

——'Leonardo and Gaffurio on Harmony and the Pulse of Music', in Barbara Haggh (ed.), *Essays on Music and Culture* (Paris, 2001), 128–49.

——'A Lost Guide to Tinctoris's Teachings Recovered', *Early Music History*, 1 (1981), 29–116.

——'On Compositional Process in the Fifteenth Century', *JAMS* 40 (1987), 210–84.

BRANCACCI, FIORELLA, 'L'enciclopedia umanistica e la musica: il *Panepistemon* di Angelo Poliziano', in Piero Gargiulo (ed.), *La musica a Firenze al tempo di Lorenzo il Magnifico* (Florence, 1993), 299–316.

BUSSE BERGER, ANNA MARIA, *Mensuration and Proportion Signs: Origins and Evolution* (Oxford, 1993).

CALDWELL, JOHN, 'The Concept of Musical Judgement in Late Antiquity', in Charles Burnett, Michael Fend, and Penelope Gouk (eds.), *The Second Sense: Studies in Hearing and Musical Judgement from Antiquity to the Seventeenth Century* (Warburg Institute Surveys and Texts, 22; London, 1991), 161–8.

CARETTA, ALESSANDRO, CREMASCOLI, LUIGI, and SALAMINA, LUIGI, *Franchino Gaffurio* (Lodi, 1951).

DYER, JOSEPH, 'Singing with Proper Refinement from *De modo bene cantandi* (1474) by Conrad van Zabern', *EM* 6 (1978), 207–27.

FEDERHOFER-KÖNIGS, RENATE, 'Ein Beitrag zur Proportionenlehre in der zweiten Hälfte des 15. Jahrhunderts', *Studia musicologica Academiae Scientiarum Hungaricae*, 11 (1960), 145–57.

FERAND, ERNST T., 'What is *Res Facta*?', *JAMS* 10 (1957), 141–50.

GALLO, F. ALBERTO, 'Le traduzioni dal Greco per Franchino Gaffurio', *Acta musicologica*, 35 (1963), 172–4.

GÜMPEL, KARL-WERNER, 'El canto melódico de Toledo: algunas reflexiones sobre su origen y estilo', *Recerca musicològica*, 8 (1988), 25–45.

——'Gregorianischer Gesang und Musica ficta: Bemerkungen zur spanischen Musiklehre des 15. Jahrhunderts', *Archiv für Musikwissenschaft*, 47 (1990), 120–47.

——*Die Musiktraktate Conrads von Zabern* (Akademie der Wissenschaften und der Literatur, Abhandlungen der Geistes- und Sozialwissenschaftlichen Klasse, Jg. 1956, no. 4; Mainz, 1956).

——'Das Tastenmonochord Conrads von Zabern', *Archiv für Musikwissenschaft*, 12 (1955), 143–66.

——'Zur Frühgeschichte der vulgärsprachlichen spanischen und katalanischen Musiktheorie', *Gesammelte Aufsätze zur Kulturgeschichte Spaniens*, 24 (Münster, 1968), 257–336.

HARRÁN, DON, *In Defense of Music: The Case for Music as Argued by a Singer and Scholar of the Late Fifteenth Century* (Lincoln, Nebr. and London, 1989).

——'In Pursuit of Origins: The Earliest Writing on Text Underlay (*c*.1440)', *Acta musicologica*, 50 (1978), 217–40.

——'Intorno a un codice veneziano Quattrocentesco', *Studi musicali*, 8 (1979), 41–60.

——*Word-Tone Relations in Musical Thought: From Antiquity to the Seventeenth Century* (MSD 40; Neuhausen-Stuttgart, 1986).

JUDD, CRISTLE COLLINS, 'Modal Types and *Ut, Re, Mi* Tonalities: Tonal Coherence in Sacred Vocal Polyphony from about 1500', *JAMS* 45 (1992), 428–67.

——'Reading Aron Reading Petrucci: The Music Examples of the *Trattato della natura et cognitione di tutti gli tuoni* (1525)', *EMH* 14 (1995), 121–52.

KAUFMANN, HENRY W., 'More on the Tuning of the *Archicembalo*', *JAMS* 23 (1970), 84–94.

LOWINSKY, EDWARD E., 'The Concept of Physical and Musical Space in the Renaissance', in *Papers of the American Musicological Society, Annual*

Meeting, 1941, ed. Gustave Reese (n.p., 1946), 57–84; rev. repr. in Lowinsky, *Culture*, i. 6–18.

——'Music of the Renaissance as Viewed by Renaissance Musicians', in Bernard O'Kelly (ed.), *The Renaissance Image of Man and the World* (Columbus, Ohio, 1966), 129–77, repr. in Lowinsky, *Culture*, i. 87–105.

MILLER, CLEMENT A., 'Early Gaffuriana: New Answers to Old Questions', *MQ* 56 (1970), 367–88.

——'Gaffurius's *Practica musicae*: Origins and Contents', *Musica disciplina*, 22 (1968), 105–28.

PALISCA, CLAUDE V., 'Mode Ethos in the Renaissance', in Lewis Lockwood and Edward Roesner (eds.), *Essays in Musicology: A Tribute to Alvin Johnson* (n.p.: American Musicological Society, 1990), 126–39.

POWERS, HAROLD, 'Is Mode Real? Pietro Aaron, the Octenary System, and Polyphony', *Basler Jahrbuch für historische Musikpraxis*, 16 (1992), 9–52.

——'Mode', §§I–III, *New Grove*, xii. 376–418.

REANEY, GILBERT, 'The Manuscript Transmission of Hothby's Theoretical Works', in Michael D. Grace (ed.), *A Festschrift for Albert Seay* (Colorado Springs, Colo., 1982), 21–31.

——'The Musical Theory of John Hothby', *Revue belge de musicologie*, 42 (1988), 119–33.

REESE, GUSTAVE, *Music in the Renaissance* (New York, 1954; rev. edn., 1959).

SACHS, KLAUS-JÜRGEN, 'Arten improvisierter Mehrstimmigkeit nach Lehrtexten des 14. bis 16. Jahrhunderts', *Basler Jahrbuch für historische Musikpraxis*, 7 (1983), 166–83.

——'Boethius and the Judgement of the Ears: A Hidden Challenge in Medieval and Renaissance Music', in Charles Burnett, Michael Fend, and Penelope Gouk (eds.), *The Second Sense: Studies in Hearing and Musical Judgement from Antiquity to the Seventeenth Century* (Warburg Institute Surveys and Texts, 22; London, 1991), 169–98.

——'Die Contrapunctus-Lehre im 14. und 15. Jahrhundert', in Zaminer, v. 161–256.

——'Counterpoint, §§1–11', *New Grove*, iv. 833–43.

SANDERS, ERNEST H., 'Discant, English', *New Grove*, v. 492–5.

SCATTOLIN, PIER PAOLO, 'La regola del "grado" nella teoria medievale del contrappunto', *Rivista italiana di musicologia*, 14 (1979), 11–74.

SCHMIDT, ANTON WILHELM, *Die Calliopea legale des Johannes Hothby: Ein Beitrag zur Musiktheorie des 15. Jahrhunderts* (Leipzig, 1897).

SEAY, ALBERT, 'The *Dialogus Johannis Ottobi Anglici in arte musica*', *JAMS* 8 (1955), 86–100.

——'Florence: The City of Hothby and Ramos', *JAMS* 9 (1956), 193–5.

——'Hothby, John', *New Grove*, viii. 730.

STEVENSON, ROBERT, 'Spanish Musical Impact beyond the Pyrenees (1250–1500)', in Emilio Casares Rodicio *et al.* (eds.), *España en la Música de Occidente: Actas del Congreso Internacional celebrado en Salamanca*, 2 vols. (Madrid, 1987), i. 115–64.

——*Spanish Music in the Age of Columbus* (The Hague, 1960).

TROWELL, BRIAN, 'Faburden', *New Grove*, vi. 350–4.

——'Sight, Sighting', *New Grove*, xvii. 307–8.

WARD, TOM R., 'A Central European Repertory in Munich, Bayerische Staatsbibliothek, Clm 14274', *EMH* 1 (1981), 325–43.

——'Music and Music Theory in the Universities of Central Europe during the Fifteenth Century', in *Atti del XIV Congresso della Società Internazionale di Musicologia: Trasmissione e recezione delle forme di cultura musicale*, ed. Angelo Pompilio, Donatella Restani, Lorenzo Bianconi, and F. Alberto Gallo (Turin, 1990), i. 49–57.

WARREN, CHARLES W., 'Brunelleschi's Dome and Dufay's Motet', *MQ* 59 (1973), 92–105.

WEINMANN, KARL, *Johannes Tinctoris (1445–1511) und sein unbekannter Traktat "De inventione et usu musicae"*, ed. Wilhelm Fischer (Tutzing, 1961).

WINTERNITZ, EMANUEL, *Leonardo da Vinci as a Musician* (New Haven, 1982).

WOODLEY, RONALD, 'Iohannes Tinctoris: A Review of the Documentary Biographical Evidence', *JAMS* 34 (1981), 217–48.

——*John Tucke: A Case Study in Early Tudor Music Theory* (Oxford, 1993).

——'The Printing and Scope of Tinctoris's Fragmentary Treatise *De inventione et usu musice*', *EMH* 5 (1985), 239–68.

——'Renaissance Music Theory as Literature: On Reading the *Proportionale Musices* of Iohannes Tinctoris', *Renaissance Studies*, 1 (1987), 209–20.

——'Tinctoris's Italian Translation of the Golden Fleece Statutes: A Text and a (Possible) Context', *EMH* 8 (1988), 173–244.

WRIGHT, CRAIG, 'Dufay's *Nuper rosarum flores*, King Solomon's Temple, and the Veneration of the Virgin', *JAMS* 47 (1994), 395–441.

CHAPTER VIII   MUSIC, HUMANISM, AND THE IDEA OF A 'REBIRTH' OF THE ARTS

(i) *Primary Sources, Reference Works, and Editions*
Tinctoris, *Opera*; Tinctoris, *De inventione*

ALBERTI, LEON BATTISTA, *On Painting and Sculpture: The Latin Texts of 'De Pictura' and 'De Statua'*, ed., with trans. and notes, Cecil Grayson (London, 1972).

CARLERIUS, EGIDIUS, and TINCTORIS, JOHANNES, *On the Dignity and the Effects of Music: Egidius Carlerius, Johannes Tinctoris, Two Fifteenth-Century Treatises*, trans. J. Donald Cullington, ed. Reinhard Strohm and J. Donald Cullington (Institute of Advanced Musical Studies Study Texts, 2; London, 1996).

PICCOLOMINI, ENEA SILVIO, *Der Briefwechsel des Eneas Silvius Piccolomini*, ed. Rudolf Wolkan, 3 vols. (Vienna, 1909–18).

——*Ausgewählte Texte aus seinen Schriften*, ed. and trans. Berthe Widmer (Basle and Stuttgart, 1960).

Prosatori latini del Quattrocento, ed. Eugenio Garin (Milan and Naples, 1952).

Reden und Briefe italienischer Humanisten, ed. Karl Müllner (Vienna, 1899; new edn., B. Gerl, Munich, 1970).

VALLA, LAURENTIUS, *Elegantiarum linguae latinae libri sex* (Lyons: Seb. Gryphius, 1544).

(ii) *Books and articles*

Lowinsky, *Culture*; Palisca, *Humanism*; Strohm, *Rise*

BENT, MARGARET, 'Humanists and Music, Music and Humanities', in *Tendenze e metodi nella ricerca musicologica: Atti del Convegno Internazionale, 27–29 settembre 1990*, ed. Raffaele Pozzi (Florence, 1995), 29–38.

——'Resfacta and *Cantare super librum*', *JAMS* 36 (1983), 371–91.

BINZ, LOUIS, *Vie religieuse et réforme ecclésiastique dans le diocèse de Genève pendant le Grand Schisme et la crise conciliaire (1378–1450)* (Geneva, 1973).

BLACKBURN, BONNIE J., 'On Compositional Process in the Fifteenth Century', *JAMS* 40 (1987), 210–84.

BOUQUET, MARIE-THÉRÈSE, 'La cappella musicale dei duchi di Savoia dal 1450 al 1500', *Rivista italiana di musicologia*, 3 (1968), 233–85.

BROWN, HOWARD M., 'Emulation, Competition, and Homage: Imitation and Theories of Imitation in the Renaissance', *JAMS* 35 (1982), 217–66.

BUCK, AUGUST, 'Über die Beziehungen zwischen Humanismus und bildenden Künsten in der Renaissance', in id. (ed.), *Die humanistische Tradition in der Romania* (Bad Homburg, Berlin, and Zürich, 1968), 243–52.

——(ed.), *Zu Begriff und Problem der Renaissance* (Darmstadt, 1969).

BURCKHARDT, JACOB, *Die Kultur der Renaissance in Italien* (18th edn., Leipzig, 1928).

CAHN, PETER, 'Zur Vorgeschichte des "Opus perfectum et absolutum" in der Musikauffassung um 1500', in Hortschansky (ed.), *Zeichen und Struktur*, 11–26.

CECCHETTI, DARIO, ' "Florescere—Deflorescere": in margine ad alcuni temi del primo umanesimo francese', in *Mélanges à la mémoire de Franco Simone: France et Italie dans la culture européenne* (Geneva, 1980), 143–55.

EDMUNDS, SHEILA, 'Catalogue', in Agostino Paravicini Bagliani (ed.), *Les Manuscrits enluminés des Comtes et Ducs de Savoie* (Turin, [1992]), 195–218.

ELDERS, WILLEM, 'Guillaume Dufay as Musical Orator', *TVNM* 31 (1981), 1–15.

——'Humanism and Early Renaissance-Music: A Study of the Ceremonial Music by Ciconia and Dufay', *TVNM* 27 (1977), 65–101.

FALLOWS, DAVID, 'The *Contenance angloise*: English Influence on Continental Composers of the Fifteenth Century', *Renaissance Studies*, 1 (1987), 189–208.

——*Dufay* (rev. edn., London, 1987).

FERGUSON, WALLACE K., *The Renaissance in Historical Thought: Five Centuries of Interpretation* (Cambridge, Mass., 1948).

GARIN, EUGENIO, *Italian Humanism: Philosophy and Civic Life in the Renaissance*, trans. P. Munz (Oxford, 1965).

GOMBRICH, ERNST H., 'The Renaissance Conception of Artistic Progress and its Consequences', in id., *Norm and Form* (London, 1966), 1–10 and 137–40 (first publ. in Congress Report, *XVIIe Congrès d'Histoire de l'Art*, Amsterdam, 1952).

HORTSCHANSKY, KLAUS, 'Musikwissenschaft und Bedeutungsforschung: Überlegungen zu einer Heuristik im Bereich der Musik der Renaissance', in id. (ed.), *Zeichen und Struktur*, 65–86.

——(ed.), *Zeichen und Struktur in der Musik der Renaissance. Symposium, Jahrestagung der Gesellschaft für Musikforschung Münster (Westfalen) 1987* (Kassel, 1989).

HUIZINGA, JAN, 'Das Problem der Renaissance', in id., *Parerga*, ed. W. Kaegi (Amsterdam, 1945), 87–146.

JUNG, MARC-RENÉ, 'Rhétorique contre philosophie? Un inédit de Martin Le Franc', in B. Vickers (ed.), *Rhetoric Revalued*, 241–6.

KOSELLECK, REINHART, ' "Neuzeit": Zur Semantik moderner Bewegungsbegriffe', in id., *Vergangene Zukunft: Zur Semantik geschichtlicher Zeiten* (Frankfurt am M., 1992), 300–48.

KRISTELLER, PAUL OSKAR, 'The Modern System of the Arts: A Study in the History of Aesthetics', *Journal in the History of Ideas*, 12 (1951), 496–527; also in id., *Renaissance Thought II: Papers on Humanism and the Arts* (New York, Evanston, and London, 1965), 163–227.

——'Music and Learning in the Early Italian Renaissance', *Journal of Renaissance and Baroque Music*, 1 (1947), 255–74; also in id., *Renaissance Thought II: Papers on Humanism and the Arts* (New York, Evanston, and London, 1965), 142–62.

LOCKWOOD, LEWIS, *Music in Renaissance Ferrara, 1400–1505* (Cambridge, Mass., 1984).

——'Renaissance', *New Grove*, xv. 736–41.

LOWINSKY, EDWARD E., 'Music in the Culture of the Renaissance', in Lowinsky, *Culture*, i. 19–39.

——'Music of the Renaissance as Viewed by Renaissance Musicians', in Lowinsky, *Culture*, i. 87–105.

MARIX, JEANNE, *Histoire de la musique et des musiciens de la cour de Bourgogne sous le règne de Philippe le Bon (1419–1467)* (Collection d'études musicologiques, 28; Strasburg, 1939).

MECONI, HONEY, 'Does *Imitatio* Exist?', *Journal of Musicology*, 12 (1994), 152–78.

MILA, MASSIMO, *Dufay* (Turin, 1972).

NIEMÖLLER, KLAUS WOLFGANG, 'Die musikalische Rhetorik und ihre Genese in Musik und Musikanschauung der Renaissance', in Heinrich Plett (ed.), *Renaissance Rhetorik* (Berlin, 1993), 285–311.

——'Zum Paradigmenwechsel in der Musik der Renaissance: Vom "numerus sonorus" zur "musica poetica"', in *Abhandlungen der Akademie der Wissenschaften in Göttingen, Phil.-Hist. Klasse*, 3. Folge (Göttingen, 1995), 187–215.

OWENS, JESSIE ANN, 'Music Historiography and the Definition of "Renaissance"', *Notes*, 47 (1990), 305–30.

PANOFSKY, ERWIN, *Renaissance and Renascences in Western Art* (Stockholm, 1960).

PARIS, GASTON, 'Un poème inédit de Martin Le Franc', *Romania*, 16 (1887), 383–437.

PIAGET, ARTHUR, *Martin Le Franc, prévôt de Lausanne* (Lausanne, 1888, repr. Caen, 1993).

PIROTTA, NINO, 'Music and Cultural Tendencies in 15th-Century Italy', *JAMS* 19 (1966), 127–61.

RECKOW, FRITZ, 'Zwischen Ontologie und Rhetorik: Die Idee des *movere animos* und der Übergang vom Spätmittelalter zur frühen Neuzeit in der Musikgeschichte', in W. Haug and B. Wachinger (eds.), *Traditionswandel und Traditionsverhalten* (Tübingen, 1991), 145–78.

SCHOECK, RICHARD J., '"Lighting a Candle to the Place": On the Dimensions and Implications of *Imitatio* in the Renaissance', *Italian Culture*, 4 (1983) (Binghamton, 1985), 123–43.

SCHRADE, LEO, 'Renaissance: The Historical Conception of an Epoch', in *International Musicological Society, Report of the Fifth Congress, Utrecht 1952* (Amsterdam, 1953), 19–32.

SIMONE, FRANCO, 'La coscienza della rinascita negli umanisti', *La Rinascita*, 2 (1939), 838–71; 3 (1940), 163–85.

ULLMAN, B. L., 'Renaissance—the Word and the Underlying Concept', *Studies in Philology*, 49 (1952), 105–18.

VASOLI, CESARE, 'Umanesimo e rinascimento', in *Storia della critica*, ed. Giuseppe Petronio, vii (Palumbo, n.d.).

VICKERS, BRIAN, 'Rhetoric and the Sister Arts', in id. (ed.), *In Defence of Rhetoric* (Oxford, 1988), 340–74.

——(ed.), *Rhetoric Revalued: Papers from the International Society for the History of Rhetoric* (Medieval & Renaissance Texts & Studies, 19; Binghamton, NY, 1982).

WEISINGER, HERBERT, 'Renaissance Accounts of the Revival of Learning', *Studies in Philology*, 45 (1948), 105–18; orig. publ. in *Papers of the Michigan Academy*, 30 (1945), 625–38, trans. as 'Die Erneuerung der Bildung in Selbstzeugnissen der Renaissance', in Buck (ed.), *Zu Begriff und Problem*, 228–44.

——'Renaissance Theories of the Revival of the Fine Arts', *Italica*, 20 (1943), 163–72.

WOODLEY, RONALD, 'Iohannes Tinctoris: A Review of the Documentary Biographical Evidence', *JAMS* 34 (1981), 217–48.

——'Renaissance Music Theory as Literature: On Reading the *Proportionale musices* of Iohannes Tinctoris', *Renaissance Studies*, 1 (1987), 209–20.

INDEX

Page numbers in bold type distinguish the more important references.

Printed in the USA/Agawam, MA
February 3, 2020

749420.040